2¹⁵

Ronald E. Ossmann

A COMPANION TO THE BIBLE

A COMPANION TO
THE BIBLE

EDITED BY

T. W. MANSON, D.Litt., D.D.

RYLANDS PROFESSOR OF BIBLICAL CRITICISM AND
EXEGESIS IN THE UNIVERSITY OF MANCHESTER

EDINBURGH : T. & T. CLARK, 38 George Street

1950

PRINTED IN GREAT BRITAIN BY
MORRISON AND GIBB LIMITED
FOR
T. & T. CLARK, EDINBURGH

FIRST IMPRESSION . . . 1939
SECOND IMPRESSION . . . 1943
THIRD IMPRESSION . . . 1945
FOURTH IMPRESSION . . . 1946
FIFTH IMPRESSION . . . 1947
SIXTH IMPRESSION . . . 1950

PREFACE

THE form and contents of this book are determined by the conviction stated in the introductory chapter : that the primary and vital interest of the Bible is that it records the authentic word of God—His gracious revelation of Himself in terms of personality and life in the midst of the life of men. It is a revelation which gives true knowledge of a real God, that is, something more than probable propositions about the Absolute.

Consequently the main interests of the *Companion to the Bible* must be fixed on two matters : the content of the revelation and the historical context within which it is first given. As a matter of historical fact, the revelation is given within the framework of the History of Israel. Hence it is important to have a clear idea of the course of that history, both the outward fate of Israel as a small buffer-state between great empires, and the inward social and economic conditions, which gradually evolved from the simple code of the nomad clans to the elaborate refinements of Mishnah and Talmud. We must also take account of the physical conditions—the geography of Palestine—which had so great an influence on the course of Hebrew history ; and we must not overlook the great mass of archæological evidence. On the religious side, we need to know something of the cult-practices of the Hebrew people : the sacrificial system, the priesthood, and the later developments of synagogue organization and worship ; and the Christian Church with its ministry and sacraments. To complete that side of the picture, the whole must be set on the background of primitive Semitic religion, and later popular superstitions.

A most important part of this reconstruction of the historical environment of the divine revelation is the history of the documents themselves in which it is recorded. Hence we need Introductions to the Old and New Testaments and, as necessary accompaniments of these, a sketch of the extra-canonical literature, and some information about the languages in which the records have been made.

Finally, there is the supremely important business of the content of the revelation itself—that knowledge of God which is eternal life, that fear of God which is the beginning of wisdom. To focus attention on these great matters is the task that is undertaken in the chapters on the " Religion of Israel," the " Life and Teaching of Jesus Christ," and the " History and Doctrine of the Apostolic Age." The bearing of this knowledge and fear of God on the relations of man with his neighbour is the concern of Biblical ethics.

The book as a whole will have achieved its purpose if it helps students of the Bible to a fuller and deeper under-standing of the Biblical revelation in its historical setting. In order to make it as widely useful as possible the contributors have eschewed the luxury of footnotes. Quotations in foreign tongues are, as far as possible, avoided, and Semitic words and phrases are transliterated. The Bibliographies appended to each chapter are the work partly of the individual con-tributors and partly of the Editor. They make no pretence to exhaustiveness ; indeed, they are meant to help the reader who, having begun his studies with this " Companion," wants to know what he should read next.

It is a considerable time since the book was planned, and its course has not been a smooth one. Illness and death have deprived us of four of the original team of contributors. I am specially grateful to those scholars who kindly came in in their places and did the work at short notice. The com-pletion of the book has also been considerably delayed by my own ill-health, and I must acknowledge the patience of the contributors and the publishers during a period when the whole enterprise seemed to be at a permanent standstill. In the later stages I have had valuable assistance, for which I am most grateful. I am particularly indebted to my friend and colleague, Mr. W. Fitzgerald, of the Department of Geography in the University of Manchester, for help in the preparation of the maps ; and to two of my students in the Faculty of Theology : Mr. A. J. B. Higgins, B.A., who checked and indexed the references to the Bible and the Apocrypha and Pseudepigrapha ; and the Rev. J. E. Yates, B.D., who is responsible for the Index of Authors and the General Index.

T. W. MANSON.

THE UNIVERSITY OF MANCHESTER,
April 1939.

CONTENTS

PAGE

PREFACE v

PART I

THE BOOK

I. THE NATURE AND AUTHORITY OF THE CANONICAL SCRIP-
TURES 3
By T. W. MANSON, D.Litt., D.D., Rylands Professor
of Biblical Criticism and Exegesis in the University of Manchester.

II. THE BIBLICAL LANGUAGES 13
A. Old Testament Languages—Hebrew and Aramaic.
By C. J. MULLO-WEIR, B.D., D.Phil., Professor of
Hebrew and Semitic Languages in the University
of Glasgow.
B. The Language of the New Testament.
By W. F. HOWARD, D.D., Professor of New Testament
Language and Literature, Handsworth College,
Birmingham.

III. INTRODUCTION TO THE OLD TESTAMENT . . . 31
By H. H. ROWLEY, D.D., Professor of Semitic Lan-
guages in the University College of North Wales,
Bangor.
1. Lower Criticism.
2. Higher Criticism.
(i) The Law.
(ii) The Former Prophets :
Joshua ; Judges ; Samuel ; Kings.
(iii) The Latter Prophets :
Isaiah ; Jeremiah ; Ezekiel ; Hosea ; Joel ;
Amos ; Obadiah ; Jonah ; Micah ; Nahum ;
Habakkuk ; Zephaniah ; Haggai ; Zech-
ariah ; Malachi.
(iv) The Writings :
Psalms ; Proverbs ; Job ; Song of Songs ;
Ruth ; Lamentations ; Ecclesiastes ; Esther ;
Daniel ; Chronicles-Ezra-Nehemiah.

IV. THE APOCRYPHA AND PSEUDEPIGRAPHA . . . 78
By W. O. E. OESTERLEY, D.D., Litt.D., Emeritus-
Professor of Hebrew and Old Testament Exegesis
at King's College, University of London.

PAGE

IV. The Apocrypha and Pseudepigrapha (*continued*).
Epistle of Jeremy ; 1 Esdras ; Tobit ; Ecclesiasticus ; The Song of the Three Holy Children ; Judith ; Prayer of Manasses ; Additions to Esther ; Susanna ; Bel and the Dragon ; 1 Maccabees ; 2 Maccabees ; The Wisdom of Solomon ; Baruch ; 2 Esdras ; Enoch ; The Sibylline Oracles ; The Testaments of the Twelve Patriarchs ; Jubilees ; 3 Maccabees ; The Psalms of Solomon ; 4 Maccabees ; Assumption of Moses ; Slavonic Enoch ; The Syriac Apocalypse of Baruch ; Testament of Abraham ; Ascension of Isaiah ; Apocalypse of Abraham ; Apocalypse of Moses ; The Greek Apocalypse of Baruch ; The Book of Joseph and Asenath.

V. The New Testament and Other Christian Writings of the New Testament Period . . . 97
By T. W. Manson.

1. The Primitive Tradition and the Earliest Documents.

2. The Pauline Corpus :
The Thessalonian Correspondence ; The Corinthian Correspondence ; The Letter to the Galatians ; The Letter to the Philippians ; The Letter to the Romans ; The Letters to the Colossians and to Philemon ; The Letter to the Ephesians.

3. The Epistle to the Hebrews.

4. The Synoptic Gospels and Acts :
Mark ; Matthew ; Luke–Acts.

5. The "Catholic" and "Pastoral" Epistles :
1 Peter ; James ; Jude ; 2 Peter ; The Pastoral Epistles.

6. The Johannine Literature :
The Gospel ; 1 John ; 2 and 3 John ; The Apocalypse.

7. Non-Canonical Literature of the Period :
1 Clement ; 2 Clement ; The Epistles of Ignatius ; The Epistle of Polycarp to the Philippians ; The Martyrdom of Polycarp ; The Didache ; The Epistle of Barnabas ; The Shepherd of Hermas ; The Epistle to Diognetus ; Miscellaneous.

PART II

THE LAND AND THE PEOPLE

VI. The Geography of Palestine . . 133
By W. J. Phythian-Adams, D.D., Canon of Carlisle.
The Lands and Peoples of Syria and Palestine ;
The Geography of Syria and Palestine : Distinctive Features.

PAGE

VI. THE GEOGRAPHY OF PALESTINE (*continued*).
The Geography of Palestine ; Survey in Detail.
(I) Galilee (including the Plains of Acre and Esdraelon).
(II) The Maritime Plain.
(III) The Hill Country of Ephraim with Gilead.
(IV) The Hill Country of Judah.
(V) The Negeb ("South Country") with the Arabah and Mount Seir.

VII. ASIA MINOR 157
By W. M. CALDER, LL.D., D.Phil., F.B.A., Professor of Greek in the University of Edinburgh.
Geography.
Communications.
Provinces.
Population and Society.
Language.
Religion.

VIII. BIBLICAL ARCHÆOLOGY 172
By J. W. JACK, D.D.
1. Excavations.
The Early Period ; The Patriarchal Period ; The Hebrew Conquest ; Period of the Monarchy ; Antiquity of Civilization and Commerce.
2. Tablets and Inscribed Potsherds.
The Tell el-Amarna Tablets ; Cappadocian Tablets ; Hittite Tablets ; Nuzi Tablets ; Mari Tablets ; Nippur Tablets ; Codes of Laws ; The Ras Shamra Tablets ; The Lachish Letters ; Seals and Seal Impressions ; Antiquity of Writing.
3. Surrounding Nations.
The Sumerians ; The Hittites ; The Hurrians ; The Hyksos ; The Philistines ; Connection of Israel with Surrounding Peoples.
4. Israelite Daily Life and Habits.
Houses ; Water Supply ; Furniture and Utensils ; Clothing ; Agriculture and Crafts ; Weapons ; Recreations.

IX. THE HISTORY OF ISRAEL 204
By T. H. ROBINSON, Litt.D., D.D., Professor of Semitic Languages in University College, Cardiff.
1. The Birth of the Nation.
The Heritage of Israel ; Moses.
2. The Settlement in Palestine.
Biblical Narratives ; The Occupation of Eastern Palestine ; The Conquest of Southern Palestine ;

PAGE

IX. THE HISTORY OF ISRAEL (*continued*).
The Conquest of the Central Hills ; The Conquest
of the North ; Date of the Conquest ; The Rise of
Israel to Pre-eminence in Palestine ; The Philistines ; Saul.

3. The Monarchy : Its Rise and Zenith.
David ; Solomon ; The Prophetic Movement ; The
Disruption ; Omri and Ahab ; Jezebel and Elijah ;
The Prophetic Revolution.

4. The Monarchy : Its Decline and Fall.
The Supremacy of Damascus ; Economic Changes ;
The Assyrian Conquest ; Assyria and Judah ; The
Fall of Assyria and the Eclipse of Egypt ; Judah
and the Chaldeans : the Fall of Jerusalem.

5. The Restored Israel.
The Exile ; Persia and the Return ; Nehemiah ;
Ezra ; The Greek Period : Egyptian Rule in
Palestine ; The Seleucid Empire : Gradual Hellen-
ization ; Antiochus Epiphanes ; The Maccabæan
Revolt ; The Maccabæan Priest-Kings ; The
Roman Period : Herod the Great ; Roman Pro-
curators.

PART III

THE RELIGION OF THE BIBLE

X. THE EARLY BACKGROUND OF HEBREW RELIGION . 271
By S. H. HOOKE, M.A., B.D., Professor of Old Testament Studies in the University of London.

XI. THE RELIGION OF ISRAEL 287
By H. WHEELER ROBINSON, D.D., Principal of Regent's
Park College ; Reader in Old Testament Studies
in the University of Oxford.

1. Nomadic Religion and the Beginnings of Yahwism.
2. The Influence of Canaanite Religion.
3. The Religion of the Pre-Exilic Prophets.
4. The Exilic Developments.
5. The Second Temple.
6. The Religion of the Wisdom Literature.
7. The Religion of Apocalyptic.
8. Religion under the Law.
9. The Unity of the Development.
10. The Forms of Mediation.
11. The Relation to Christianity.

XII. ANGELOLOGY AND DEMONOLOGY IN EARLY JUDAISM 332
By W. O. E. OESTERLEY.
I. Angelology.
II. Demonology.

PAGE

XIII. BIBLICAL ETHICS 348
By W. F. LOFTHOUSE, D.D., Principal of Handsworth .
College, Birmingham.
Introductory.
Old Testament.
New Testament.
Relation of Ethics of Jesus to those of Old Testament.
Paul.

XIV. THE LIFE AND TEACHING OF JESUS CHRIST 367
By C. H. DODD, D.D., Norris-Hulse Professor of
Divinity in the University of Cambridge.
1. Sources of Information.
2. The Course of Events.
3. The Messiah and the Kingdom of God.
4. Ethical Teaching of Jesus.
5. The Life of Jesus in the Light of His Teaching.

XV. THE HISTORY AND DOCTRINE OF THE APOSTOLIC AGE . 390
By C. H. DODD.·
A. The First Century of Church History.
1. The Primitive Church in Jerusalem.
2. The Rise of Hellenistic Christianity.
3. Paul and the Gentile Mission.
4. Persecution and Consolidation.
B. Christian Thought in the First Century.
1. The Primitive Gospel.
2. Paul.
Redemption; Justification; Reconciliation,
or Atonement; Expiation through Sacrifice.
3. The Epistle to the Hebrews.
4. The Fourth Gospel.

XVI. THE PRIESTHOOD AND THE TEMPLE . . . 418
By N. H. SNAITH, M.A., Professor of Old Testament
Studies in Wesley College, Headingley, Leeds.
1. The Priestly Caste.
2. Priesthood and Torah.
3. The Temple and its Ritual.

XVII. THE SCRIBES AND THE LAW 444
By Rabbi L. RABINOWITZ, M.A.

XVIII. THE SYNAGOGUE AND ITS WORSHIP . . . 453
By L. RABINOWITZ.

PAGE

XIX. THE ORGANIZATION AND WORSHIP OF THE PRIMITIVE
CHURCH 462
By J. W. HUNKIN, D.D., Bishop of Truro, Honorary
Fellow of Gonville and Caius College, Cambridge.

1. The Society and its Organisation.
The Church; Organization; Presbyters; Dea-
cons; Apostles; Ordination; Government and
Discipline; Expansion; Enemies without;
Enemies within; Missionary Zeal.

2. Rites and Worship.
Baptism; Worship; The Lord's Supper.

APPENDIX 489
By T. W. MANSON.

Authors Calendar and Chronology; Weights, Measures,
and Money.

INDEX OF SCRIPTURE REFERENCES . . . 501

INDEX OF AUTHORS 504

GENERAL INDEX 507

MAPS . . . . at end

PART I
THE BOOK

I. THE NATURE AND AUTHORITY OF THE CANONICAL SCRIPTURES

THE Bible is first and foremost a religious book—or rather a library of religious books. It is a record of religious experience and of convictions about the real nature of the Universe based upon that experience. The authority of the Bible consequently stands or falls with the reliability of religious experience and the validity of convictions based upon it. If religion is just a widespread illusion, which has for centuries hampered and crippled mankind, filling our minds with superstitious fears and preventing us from achieving our true destiny as free men, then obviously the question of the authority of the Bible need not arise.

Here at the outset we are faced by a fundamental issue from which there is no escape. We have to choose between a thorough-going theism, such as is taught by Christianity, and a thorough-going atheism. We have to think of the Universe either as the working out of a divine purpose or as a more or less regrettable accident. Between these two extremes there does not seem to be any permanently habitable half-way house. The question is too big to be properly discussed within the limits of this chapter ; it must suffice to state what seems to be the main issue.

On the one side it can be held that by the consistent application of scientific methods it is possible to discover the truth, the whole truth, and nothing but the truth about the Universe ; and that the practical use of this truth, as and when it is discovered, will be to make human life as satisfactory as human life can be made in such a world as this. There seems no convincing reason to suppose that either claim can be justified. For scientific methods can only reveal *how* things come to be as they are, and not *why* they are so and not otherwise. That is, science can never give more than a description of the world —a mathematical picture of it. It cannot give, in the full sense of the word, an explanation of the world. If the attempt is made to meet this difficulty by saying that no such explanation is possible, that is merely to beg the question. It amounts to saying that because no explanation is discoverable by the

3

methods which I choose to employ, therefore there cannot be any explanation.

Further, scientific methods will not explain qualitative differences in the world. There is no scientific criterion whereby we may distinguish between, say, two pieces of music, one of which is glorious and inspired, while the other is dull, stale, flat, and unprofitable. Science can say that if we draw the bow across the strings of the violin, certain wave-motions in the air will be set up, will impinge on the drum of the ear and cause other changes to take place in the nervous system and the brain. It cannot say whether the result of the bow-drawing will be worth listening to or not. And, what is more, science as such does not care. As we well know, scientific method produces with equal impartiality the poison and the antidote, the lethal gas and the small box-respirator ; but it is not ready with any scientific reason why we should use the one rather than the other. That is to say, it has no answer to the question *why ?* as applied to human conduct.

This means that there is no very good reason for supposing that the further application of scientific methods alone will make human life more satisfactory. The scientific Utopias in novel form, of which there have been a good many in recent years, are dreams as vague and unsubstantial as anything in the wildest Apocalypses.

It must be contended that while scientific methods can and do give us truth about the world and man, they do not and cannot give us the whole truth. The whole truth is a complex thing containing some elements that are reached by this way, and other elements, not less important, reached in other ways. One of the ways by which truth is reached is, it is claimed, by revelation ; and it is certainly claimed that religious truth, if there is such a thing, is so reached.

But here we must pause to consider what is meant when we speak of revelation as distinguished from discovery by scientific investigation. The way in which we tend to make the distinction is by taking knowledge and dividing it into two sorts : things which men have found out for themselves by observation and experiment : for example, that the combination of glycerine with nitric acid will produce a high explosive ; and things which have been supernaturally communicated to men without any investigation on their part, say that God created the world out of nothing in six days about 4000 B.C. Then, when it is found that the world can hardly have been made so recently, and that it was a good deal longer than six days in the making, it is thought that revelation is discredited and that scientific knowledge is the only reliable sort. But all this is because we have wrong ideas about the nature of revelation, thinking that it is a kind of short-cut to results which can only be reached by the methods of science.

In my view it is not the business of revelation to provide information which can be discovered by chemists or geologists ; but to do something quite different. Consider what we mean when we use the word in ordinary speech. The most characteristic employment of the word is to describe something that happens between persons. We know some one and think that we thoroughly understand him ; and then, one day, he does something which upsets all our previous views. The man we thought to be hard and selfish turns out to be the soul of kindness—or *vice versa*. Some action of his puts him in a new light, and we say, " What a revelation ! " What has happened is that some significant act has permitted us to see what was previously hidden. We know our man in a way we did not know him before, and our new knowledge flows directly from something which *he* has said or done. Now revelation in the religious use of the word is something like that. It is that by what he says or does God reveals, not scientific information about the world, but *Himself*. What is given in revelation is not knowledge of chemistry or geology, but knowledge of God. Not merely knowledge *about* the Divine Nature, a sort of supernatural psychology, but knowledge *of* God.

The Bible contains the testimony of people who claim to have received that kind of knowledge. If the claim is just, it simply does not matter that the first chapter of Genesis may not be sound science or that the history of the Kings of Israel and Judah may have to be corrected in the light of the Assyrian and Babylonian monuments. Those things are of secondary moment. The crude science of Genesis is no more to be worried about than the still cruder views about religion held by some scientists. If the Bible gives true knowledge of a real God, that is a fact of decisive importance beside which other matters are relatively insignificant. If the Bible does not give such knowledge, then it ceases to have any but a literary and antiquarian interest.

But supposing it to be granted that the Bible does contain such knowledge of God, the fact remains that it is not the only religious literature in the world. There is the Koran ; there is the literature belonging to the religions of Zoroaster and the Buddha ; there are books like the *Meditations* of Marcus Aurelius, the *Enchiridion* of Epictetus, or the *Hymn* of Cleanthes among the Stoic writings. Why confine ourselves

to an arbitrarily selected portion of the world's religious
literature ? Or, for that matter, even if we stick to the religion
of Israel and of the Christian Church, why canonize only a
selection from its books, and neglect, say, the *Confessions* of
St. Augustine, the *Fioretti* of St. Francis, Luther's *Freedom of
a Christian Man*, or William Law's *Serious Call*? Why confine
attention to one particular portion of the world's religious
writings ; and, within that narrow sphere, use only the selection
that is technically known as " canonical " ? It can be pointed
out that we do in fact take up a more catholic attitude in other
matters. We regard Japanese colour-prints or Chinese porcelains
as beautiful in the same unrestricted sense that we regard
Greek sculptures or Italian paintings as beautiful. We do not
in the case of a scientific truth ask whether the discoverer of
it was European or Asiatic. Surely we ought to say the same
about religious truth. What reason have we for supposing
that the Hebrew people and, after them, the primitive Christian
Church had a monopoly in this matter ? More than that, is it
not a fact that the religious books of other peoples *do* contain
much that is valuable and worthy of study and acceptance ?
Is it not, in any case, presumptuous to suppose that God, in
revealing Himself, confined His revelation to a small section
of the people of the world and left the rest in darkness ?

To all that, it may be replied in general terms that we do
not need to defend the religion of the Bible by claiming that all
other religions are utterly worthless. It may well be the case
that Buddhism, for example, contains religious teaching which
it would be worth our while to ponder. But when we consider
the possibilities of the case, there are only three religions that
really come into account : the religion of the Bible, the religion
of the Buddha, and the religion of Mohammed. The last of the
three is a degenerate offshoot of Judaism and Christianity
and really has nothing to contribute : the Allah of the Koran is
an inferior copy of the God of the Bible. Classical Buddhism is
an intellectual and moral discipline, which certainly has many
admirable qualities ; but it is not a religion in our sense of
the word. It is not the self-revelation of a God, the announcement of true knowledge of a real God. Indeed, Buddhism can
get along without the idea of God at all. So in the end it is
not a matter of choosing between religions. The practical
issue at the moment is the religion of the Bible or no religion ;
and it is a fact that those who abandon the religion of the
Bible—whether Jews or Christians—do not commonly attach
themselves to Buddhism or Mohammedanism. They just
drop religion altogether. We may therefore consider the

possibility of successful competition by other religious books
for a place in the canon as somewhat remote.

But we are now faced by another question : Why insist on
the whole Bible, when it seems clear that some parts of it are,
let us say, more profitable for study than others ? As early as
the second century A.D. that question was raised by a very
devout but unorthodox Christian named Marcion. He proposed
to do away with the Old Testament entirely and to be content
with a Bible containing the Gospel of Luke and the Epistles of
St. Paul ; and even these he edited to bring out more clearly
what he thought to be the essence of religion. And there are
certainly many devout Christians to-day who would not feel
that they had been deprived of anything specially valuable
if considerable sections of the Bible were eliminated—the books
of Chronicles for example. It is, of course, obvious that the
fifteenth chapter of Luke or the thirteenth of 1 Corinthians is a
good deal more edifying than some of the lists of names in the
historical books of the Old Testament ; and there seems to be
no good reason why we should not skip the parts that have no
real religious interest for us. But it is just as easy to turn over
the dull pages as to cut them out ; and there is one good reason
for leaving them in. They may not mean much to us ; but
they meant a lot in their day : and a Roll of Honour is still
honourable even if the names are the names of strangers.
But, apart from this, there are three reasons for keeping the
Bible as a whole.

(1) It is unique in the world's literature in that it gives the
religious experience of a people over a period of something like
a millennium and a half. If we are to study the history of
religion, the way in which, from the crudest beginnings, religious
truth is more and more clearly perceived until it culminates
in what may be called its final revelation, there is no book or
collection of books that even approaches the Bible both for
quantity of material and quality. Things in the Old Testament
that seem unedifying, sometimes barbarous and revolting, are
nevertheless of the greatest interest and value to the historian of
religion, who sees in them the first gropings of man in his search
for God. It soon becomes apparent to the serious student that
the history of religion as exposed in the Bible is every bit as
interesting and important as the history of scientific progress or
the history of artistic development. We may still not approve all
the actions of all the characters in the Bible. We may still not
find it good that Samuel hewed Agag in pieces before the Lord ;
but we will, I think, see that Samuel is as important a figure
in religion as Copernicus in astronomy ; even though we do

not approve all Samuel's acts any more than we accept all the astronomical views of Copernicus. We see, in fact, the evidences of growth and development that one expects to see in anything that is truly alive ; and this may seem to be a pretty strong indication that religion is one way of dealing with reality, that the historical process is not the purely negative one of gradually getting rid of a mass of primitive superstitions, but the positive one by which, starting from those very primitive superstitions, man comes slowly and painfully, but nevertheless surely, to a knowledge of the truth. For the tracing of that momentous progress there is no book to be compared with the Bible.

(2) The Bible is peculiar in that it is not the book of an individual, and its religion is not the religion of an individual. The Koran is the work of one man and Islam is essentially the religion of Mohammed. Buddhism and Zoroastrianism and Confucianism are one-man religions. The religion of the Bible is made up by the experiences of many men over many centuries. But all of them men of one race. That is a significant fact which invites further consideration. One suggestion may be made about it.

Revelation, if it means anything at all, means primarily an act of God whereby He manifests His real nature to men : It is essentially a personal thing ; and it would seem that to be effective it demands not only a readiness on the part of God to make the revelation, but also some kind of receptiveness on the part of man to whom the revelation is made, some real interest which responds to the revelation. Now when we compare the Bible with the literatures of other nations, it does seem that that quality of interest and responsiveness flourished among the Hebrew people in a way that has no parallel elsewhere. Other nations had other gifts—science as we know it is the legacy of Greece—but Israel had the genius for religion. Here we should remind ourselves that the Bible is, for all practical purposes, the whole surviving literature of the ancient Hebrews and the primitive Church (and the New Testament is a very Hebrew book). Compare it with the literature surviving from ancient Greece and Rome. In the classics we read plays, poems, political speeches, philosophical treatises, and so on ; and we pick out here and there the bits that show a specifically religious interest. The literature of the Hebrews is first of all religious, and the data for the re-construction of the political and social history of the people are contained in the religious documents. We have in the Bible the religious record through the centuries of a people who cared greatly about religion.   From that point of view the Bible is unique.

(3) What follows under this head is linked up with the question, why we do not add to the Bible books of proved religious worth belonging to the Christian centuries.   This question compels us to consider one more claim made for the Bible, namely, that it is not only unique but also final, and that this finality is reached in the New Testament.   Again, it is necessary to go back to the idea of Revelation.   It has been urged above that revelation is essentially the mani-festation of the real nature of God.   The question is how that manifestation can take place.   It can, one would think, take place through a variety of means.   A man may reveal his character by some simple act, for example, the way he shakes hands, or by a spoken word.   In one or other of these ways we may learn something about him.   In the last resort, of course, the only way in which we can really know a person is by living with him.   We may use this, admittedly imperfect, analogy in the sphere of religious revelation.   The Bible claims that God is revealed by His acts—both in the creation of the natural world and in the providential control of history.   " The heavens declare the glory of God and the firmament showeth His handywork."   The Israelites, when they think of their past history, find themselves recalling and retelling " the mighty acts of Jehovah."   Again, the formula of prophecy is " The word of the Lord came to So-and-so " ; and the prophetic word is the revelation of the nature of God.   Through the marvels of Nature, the mighty events of history, the word of the inspired prophet, God discloses Himself—as the writer to the Hebrews says, πολυμερῶς καὶ πολυτρόπως, partially and sporadically.   We get glimpses of the character of God.   But, still pursuing the analogy, to know God fully one must live with Him.   The claim of the New Testament is that the full revelation did come in that way.   " The Word became flesh and dwelt among us."   To put it in another way, the fullest revela-tion could not be made in terms of isolated acts or messages : it could only be made in terms of personality and life : and the personality and life were the personality and life of Jesus of Nazareth.   If that claim is just it means that the Biblical revelation is final, in the sense that all is revealed there that men can possibly take in.   It is a revelation in terms of the highest category we can know—that of personality.   There may be far more than that in the divine Nature.   If so that residue must remain unrevealed, for the simple reason that we cannot take it in any more than an electric-light bulb can take

in the electrical energy of the lightning flash.   The possibilities
of revelation are limited by the capacity of human beings to
receive it.   For us the revelation in terms of human personality that is given in the New Testament is and remains
final.   Hence, any later Christian writing can only be exposition of what is given in the Bible.   It cannot create new
material or produce new truth.   It can only make explicit what
is there implicit.   As St. Paul puts it : " Other foundation can
no man lay than that which is already laid."

To sum up, the claim that the Bible makes is to give a
record of the religious experience of a people who were
peculiarly fitted to be the recipients of divine revelation.   The
revelation received by them and recorded in the Bible claims
to be true knowledge of a real and living God.   It claims to
give to men all that can be given to men.   Those are
staggering claims.   They express what is essential to the idea
of canonicity.   That the claims are just cannot perhaps, in
the strict sense of the word, be proved.   It may be contended
that revelation, in the sense defined, is a miracle, in fact *the*
miracle ; and that to attempt to prove a miracle is to embark
on a self-contradictory enterprise.   On the other hand, we may
find reasons that embolden us to believe that the claims are
just.   For example :

(1) We may note that within Christendom the great
movements of the Spirit in revivals of living religion have
regularly been accompanied by a return to this Biblical
revelation.   There is a kind of *testimonium Spiritus Sancti*
in the course of Christian history.

(2) We may consider that the more closely the word of
God in the Bible is studied in the light of its historical development in Old Testament and New Testament and in the subsequent thought of the Church, the more clearly it appears
that it has a certain spiritual self-consistency, akin to the
logical self-consistency of a body of scientific truth.   This
spiritual self-consistency, which we can see in the same way
that we can see the cogency of a scientific system or the
æsthetic self-consistency of a great symphony, speaks to us
in a way that we cannot reject unless we wilfully shut our eyes
to the truth.   In some such way as this we may understand the
testimonium Spiritus Sancti in the experience of the individual.

The Bible is Holy Scripture because it has these qualities.
The qualities are in it and not in us.   The canonicity of the
Bible does not depend on the arbitrary judgements either of
individuals or of Councils or even of the Church as a whole,
any more than scientific truth depends on the judgement of

individual scientists or of the Royal Society. To canonize
the Scriptures is to recognize something that is there before the
Church says so.

The process by which the Church arrived at a final and
explicit statement of the contents of the Canon is very long
and complicated. In the Roman communion the final decisions
were taken by the Council of Trent and the Vatican Council.
In the Eastern Orthodox Church there is no corresponding
list of canonical writings proclaimed officially as absolutely
binding, and the exact frontiers of the Canon are not fixed
to the last detail. Among Protestant communions there are
still differences as to what may be included in the Canon.
The history of the process, by which these varying conclusions
were reached, is too complex for full treatment in this volume.
Only a few main points can be noted.

The process of canonization of the Old Testament by
the Jewish religious authorities will be found sketched in outline below (p. 33 f.). The primitive Church took over the
Jewish scriptures and made them its own. Alongside the Old
Testament stood the words of Jesus and the account of His
ministry. Then came those documents which emanated or
were believed to emanate from Apostles : the Pauline Corpus,
the documents ascribed to John, the letters of others who
had had a share in the earliest life of the Church. By the
end of the second century the main contents of the New
Testament were widely agreed upon throughout the Christian
world. The uncertainties were on the fringes and affected
some seven books that are now in the Canon, but were not
immediately accepted by all the Churches. These are : Hebrews,
James, Jude, 2 Peter, 2 and 3 John, and Revelation. On the
other hand, a few books not now in the Canon appear to have
enjoyed temporary and local canonicity. The earliest account
of the Canon to agree exactly with the contents of our English
New Testament is that of Athanasius in his thirty-ninth Festal
letter of A.D. 367. For further study of the history of the Canon
the reader may consult Souter's *The Text and Canon of the
New Testament*, where the relevant original documents are
given in a convenient form.

In the actual formation of the Canon in the Church the
chief practical considerations that seem to have weighed are
(a) the fact that a book was regularly used for public reading
in the Church services, and (b) the belief that it was of Apostolic
origin, that is, written either by an Apostle or by a disciple of
an Apostle. These two tests of canonicity are an attempt to
make sure both that the book has something to say to the

Church, and that what it says really originates from the circle to whom the revelation in Jesus Christ was given.

BIBLIOGRAPHY

A. S. Peake, *The Bible : its Origin, Significance and its Abiding Worth.*

C. H. Dodd, *The Authority of the Bible.*

H. E. Ryle, *The Canon of the Old Testament.*

A. Souter, *The Text and Canon of the New Testament.*

Th. Zahn, *Geschichte des neutestamentlichen Kanons.*

W. Zoellner and W. Stählin (editors), *Die Kirche Jesu Christi und das Wort Gottes.*

(Contains valuable information about the doctrines of Inspiration and Canonicity in different communions.)

II. THE BIBLICAL LANGUAGES

(A) Old Testament Languages—Hebrew and Aramaic

The Old Testament is written in Hebrew with the exception of a few Aramaic passages, namely, Dan. 2^4–7^{28} ; Ezra 4^8–6^{18} and 7^{12-26} ; Jer. 10^{11} (a gloss) ; and a few scattered words, including *yĕghar sāhădhûthâ* ("heap of witness") in Gen. 31^{47}. In the Old Testament, Hebrew is called " the lip of Canaan " (*sĕphath kĕna'an*, Isa. 19^{18}), and " Jewish " (*yĕhûdhîth*, 2 Kings $18^{26. 28}$ and Neh. 13^{24}), while the name " Hebrew " (*'ibhrîth*) seems to be a late invention of Palestinian rabbis and occurs first (in its Greek form) in the Prologue to Ecclus. (*c.* 130 B.C.). In the New Testament and Josephus, " Hebrew " is used ambiguously to denote both Hebrew and Aramaic. The Aramaic language (*'ărāmîth*, 2 Kings 18^{26}) was called by the Greeks " Syriac " or " Chaldee," the latter name being due to the erroneous supposition that the language spoken in Chaldæa during the time of Daniel was Biblical Aramaic.

The earliest history of the Hebrew language is obscure, but the Hebrews seem to have migrated out of the peninsula of Arabia, and early tradition associates them with Babylonia, North Mesopotamia, Canaan, and Egypt. This tradition is corroborated by an examination of the language which seems to be a mixture of Accadian, proto-Aramæan (" Amorite "), and Canaanite, with a number of Egyptian loan-words. The Canaanite glosses in the El-Amarna letters (*c.* 1400 B.C.) closely resemble Hebrew as does also the Moabite language on the Moabite stone (*c.* 850 B.C.). A comparison of the early Hebrew Siloam inscription (*c.* 700 B.C.) with the Hebrew of Isaiah shows their language to be identical, and since that time the Hebrew language changed remarkably little in Biblical or even post-Biblical times. It began, however, to be supplanted by Aramaic after the Exile, and although Hebrew apparently continued to be a spoken language for some centuries later, it had become unintelligible to the common people by the beginning of the Christian era, so that an Aramaic translation or " Targum " had to be given in the synagogues after readings of Scripture. Hebrew continued its development as a literary and liturgical language until in the nineteenth century of our era it became again a spoken tongue. Certain dialectal differences seem to have existed within it in Old Testament times (cf. *shibbōleth* and *sibbōleth*, Judg. 12⁶), and some traces of this still survive in the Hebrew text of the Old Testament, but most have been removed by the scribes.

Hebrew and Aramaic belong to the Semitic group of languages, named after Shem, the reputed ancestor of many of them (Gen. 10²¹⁻³¹), and spoken in various parts of South-West Asia and North Africa. These languages, most of which are now dead, may be classified roughly into four main families : (i) Eastern, including Accadian (Assyro-Babylonian) ; (ii) Northern or Central, including the numerous dialects of Aramaic ; (iii) Western, including Canaanite, Hebrew, Moabite, and Phœnician ; and (iv) Southern, including Arabic and Ethiopic. Semitic languages have a much closer affinity to one another than have, *e.g.*, Italian, French, and Spanish within the Indo-European group; cf. Acc. *kalbu* (" dog "), Aram. *kĕlebh*, Heb. *kelebh*, Arab. *kelb*, Eth. *kĕleb*. Several consonants, however, undergo permutation in the various languages according to fixed laws, *e.g.* Arab. *dh* = Aram. *d* = Heb. *z* ; cf. Arab. *dhahab* (" gold "), Aram. *dĕhabh*, Heb. *zāhābh*.

Semitic languages are distinguished from Indo-European by very noticeable characteristics. The most obvious of these is that with the exception of particles almost all the words are based upon roots containing three letters, all of which are consonants. Only a few roots of two or four consonants are found. It is probable, however, that the tri-consonantal roots are differentiations from originally bi-consonantal roots. Vowels occupy a secondary place in Semitic languages and are generally not represented in writing. In pronunciation, however, they are used to form substantives and verbs according to fixed grammatical patterns. The available number of patterns is increased by such devices as adding a preformative letter (generally *aleph, h, m, n,* or *t*) to the root or by strengthening (" doubling ") the middle radical letter. Thus from the root G-D-L we have in Hebrew *GāDaL*, " he was great "; *GōDeL*, *GĕDúLâh*, and *GĕDuLLâh*, " greatness "; *GāDôL*, " great "; *miGDāL*, " a tower "; *hiGDîL*, " he magnified "; and *GiDDēL*, " he eulogized."

Another peculiarity of the Semitic languages is that the verb does not distinguish actions as past, present, or future, but indicates them simply as completed (perfect) or not yet completed (imperfect). In contrast to this defectiveness in the tense-system the verb is prolific in means of designating actions as intensive, causative, reciprocal, active, passive, or reflexive. Cf. Hebrew *QāDaSH*, " he was holy "; *QiDDēSH* and *hiQDïSH*, " he sanctified "; *hithQaDDēSH*, " he sanctified himself "; *niQDaSH*, " he showed himself to be holy "; and *QuDDaSH*, " he was sanctified."

Other important features of Semitic languages are these : (*a*) the noun governing a genitive assumes a contracted form known as the Construct State ; (*b*) the oblique cases (objective and genitive) of the personal pronouns are expressed by suffixing contracted forms of these to the verb and the noun respectively ; (*c*) there are only two genders—masculine and feminine ; (*d*) compound words, whether nominal or verbal, are almost non-existent except in proper names, and prepositions are never used to form derivatives ; (*e*) adverbs are scarce ; (*f*) there are a few additional gutturals and emphatic consonants not found in Indo-European languages ; and (*g*) most of the languages, including Hebrew, are written from right to left.

Biblical Hebrew is distinguished from the other principal Semitic languages by having a much smaller vocabulary and a much less developed syntax. It has been computed that the language contains only about 2050 roots and about 5000 words (excluding proper names) of which only about 500 are in frequent use. Many words occur only once and some are of doubtful meaning. Probably in the spoken language many more words existed. Owing to the Hebrew fondness for the literary device of " parallelism " synonyms are numerous, but instead of being used to express different shades of meaning they all seem to mean exactly the same and to be interchangeable. Thus *ḥāzāḳ* and *ḥāzēḳ* both =" strong " (in its various senses), *ḥōzeḳ, ḥēzeḳ, ḥozḳâh,* and *ḥezḳâh* all =" strength"; similarly, *yēshaʿ, yĕshûʿâh, tĕshûʿâh,* and *môshāʿôth* all =" deliverance " or " victory." On the other hand, a single derivative is used frequently in a variety of different senses, *e.g. bĕrēkh* =" bless," " greet," " congratulate," " curse," " favour," and " praise," while *ḥayil* =" strength," " courage," " worth," " virtue," " riches," and " army." The word for " law " (*tôrâh*) is the same as that for " instruction " while *tôdhâh* means " thanksgiving," " thank-offering," " praise," and " choir." *Massâ* (literally =" what is lifted up ") means " burden " (physical or metaphorical), " transport," " tribute," and " utterance," while *mishpāṭ* denotes " judgement," " place of judgement," " verdict," " penalty," " law-suit," " crime," " justice," " ordinance," " prerogative," " duty," " rightness," "custom," and "manner." Translators have sometimes planned to represent a Hebrew word always by the same English word, but this is manifestly impossible, and there is sometimes considerable disagreement as to the exact shade of meaning of the the Hebrew term. Further ambiguity arises from the fact that some of the Hebrew consonants, *e.g.* *Ḥ* '(*'ayin*) and *SH* represent two different consonants which have coalesced—*S* represents at least three—so that one triliteral root may have two or more unconnected meanings. Thus the roots *Ḥ-P-R* and *Ḥ-L-S* both form three verbs of quite different meaning while *'-N-Y* and *'-R-B* both form four.

Nearly all Hebrew roots express some physical action or denote some natural object. Hence, *gāzar* " to decide " originally meant " to cut "; *'āmēn* " to be true " orig. = " to be firmly fixed "; *yāshar* " to be right " orig. = " to be straight "; and *kābhēdh* " to be honourable " orig. = " to be heavy." " Sin " is expressed by roots meaning " to miss the mark," " to be crooked," and " to break bounds." Hebrew is very poor in abstract terms and has often to express intellectual or religious concepts and emotions by metaphors or symbols, this being one cause of the frequent anthropomorphisms. Thus " intellect " or " mind " is rendered by " heart "; " reins " (*i.e.* " kidneys ") = " emotions " or " volitions " or " motives." " Bowels " represents " compassion," hence the prophet can address God with the words " the sounding of Thy bowels " (Isa. 63[15]). " Hand," " arm," and " right arm " frequently represent " activity," " action," or " intervention "; " horn " = " vigour," " rule," or " dignity "; " wind " = " spirit "; " breath " = " soul," " life," or " self," *e.g.* " my soul " = " my life " or " myself," just as " his name " = " him " or " himself." " Bones " = " being " (*e.g.* Ps. 35[10]), and the word for " descendants " is " seed," while " anger " is often spoken of as " heat." Similarly, " he was angry " is normally translated by " he burned " or " his nostril burned," and " to cover the face of " is " to reconcile " (Gen. 32[20]), while " to think " must often be rendered by " to say." A " patient " man is " long of breath " and the " obstinate " are " hard of neck." Owing to the limited vocabulary circumlocutions are frequently necessary. Thus for " religion " Hebrew has to substitute " fear of the Lord " (Prov. 8[13]), and " a metropolis " is " a city and mother " (2 Sam. 20[19]). Very common are such phrases as " son of possession " = " heir " (Gen. 15[2]), " sons of valour " = " warriors " (Deut. 3[18]), " sons of pledging " = " hostages " (2 Kings 14[14]), " master of

dreams " = " dreamer " (Gen. 37[19]), " masters of a covenant " =
" confederates " (Gen. 14[13]), " man of the soil " = " farmer "
(Gen. 9[20]), and " men of warfare " = " warriors " (Num. 31[28]).
In poetry this usage is still more extended than in prose, but
its principal use is to form adjectival phrases, such as " sons
of wickedness " (2 Sam. 7[10]), " sons of rebellion " (Num. 17[10]),
" sons of tumult " (Jer. 48[45]), " sons of affliction " (Prov. 31[5]),
" master of nostril," *i.e.* " of anger " (Prov. 22[24]), " man of
form," *i.e.* " of beauty " (1 Sam. 16[18]), " man of blood "
(Ps. 5[6]), and " man of courage " (2 Sam. 17[10]).

Hebrew is very deficient in adjectives and often has to
make use of cumbrous expressions. " A double heart " is
" a heart and a heart " (Ps. 12[2]) and " diverse weights " are
" a stone and a stone " (Deut. 25[13]). " The royal family " is
" the seed of the kingdom " (2 Kings 11[1]), " a false report " is
" a report of falsehood " (Ex. 23[1]), and " an everlasting
covenant " is " a covenant of eternity " (Gen. 17[7]). Even
when an adjective is available this last construction is often
preferred, especially in poetry, *e.g.* " ambassador of faithful-
ness " (Prov. 13[17]), " God of my righteousness " = " my
righteous God " (Ps. 4[1]), " throne of His holiness " (Ps. 47[8]),
and " rock of my strength " (Ps. 62[7]). The adjective in
Hebrew has no comparative or superlative and no word for
" than," but must say " bring your small " (= " youngest ")
" brother " (Gen. 42[34]), " the serpent was cunning from every
beast " (Gen. 3[1]), " Israel loved Joseph from all his sons."
(Gen. 37[3]), and " I am not good from " (*i.e* " better than ")
" my fathers " (1 Kings 19[4]). The word " too " is similarly
represented, *e.g.* " hard from the Lord " = " too hard for the
Lord " (Gen. 18[14]). Another method of expressing the superlative is by repetition of a noun, *e.g.* " holy of holies," " song
of songs," " king of kings " " to generation and generation,"
or of an adjective, *e.g.* " talk no more proudly, proudly " =
" so very proudly " (I Sam. 2[3]) or " deep, deep " = " very deep "
(Eccles. 7[24]).

Hebrew has a poorly-developed tense-system, and the
Perfect, Imperfect, and Participle may all indicate past, present,
or future time, although normally the Perfect expresses past
time. A distinctive and colourful usage is the " Prophetic
Perfect," *e.g.* " my people has gone into exile " (Isa. 5[13]), *i.e.*
" will inevitably go," but this occasionally leads to ambiguity,
as in Isa. 9[1ff.]. More commonly the Imperfect is ambiguous
as it not only represents the Indicative Mood (present, past
frequentative, past progressive, and future) but may also
have a potential, conditional, optative, imperative, or final

meaning. Frequently, also, Hebrew does not distinguish a statement from a question.

One of the most characteristic features of Hebrew is its poverty in subordinating conjunctions. Sentences are almost invariably co-ordinated, using the word "and." English translators usually try to show the logical connexion between successive sentences, but this is sometimes uncertain. Hence, in Gen. 1^2–3^1 all except three of the fifty-six verses begin with "and," but the English versions translate this variously as "and" (1^2), "so" (1^{27}), "thus" (2^1), "but" (2^6), and "now" (3^1). Elsewhere we find it rendered "therefore" (Gen. 3^{23}), "as" (Gen. 18^1 R.V.), "then" (Gen. 19^{24}), "although" (Job 2^3), "because" (Ps. 5^{11}) and "(in order) that" (Gen. 19^{32}).

The features above delineated emphasize the desirability of studying the Old Testament with a commentary that suggests alternative interpretations, and preferably of reading it in the original languages. One who has "read himself into" the Semitic mind is often able to "read into" Scripture unnoticed shades of thought which the writer had failed adequately to express, simply because the language possessed no resources for conveying his meaning.

The deficiency in conjunctions coupled with the lack of abstract terms and compound words makes Hebrew an unsuitable language for precise definition or logical reasoning. On the other hand, the co-ordination of clauses adds impressiveness to the denunciations of a prophet and gives to simple narrative a naïve and archaic effect which is heightened by the frequent use of direct speech, the introduction of a new thought or scene by the word "behold" and the device of repeating a phrase superfluously as in Gen. 3^{19}, $6^{6f.,\ 11f.}$, $11^{8f.}$ Vividness and colour are enhanced by the sensuous nature of the vocabulary and the abundant use of metaphor, simile, metonymy, hyperbole, the rhetorical question, and other figures of speech. Very popular is a play on the sound of words which is facilitated by the uniformity of grammatical patterns and inflexions and the vocal resemblance of unrelated roots, but this effect is difficult to reproduce in English.

Two minor features almost peculiar to Hebrew are (a) the lengthening or shortening of vowels according to their relation to the accented syllable ("tone-syllable") of the word, and (b) the usage of "Waw Consecutive" with Perfect and Imperfect, whereby a series of past events is introduced by a verb in the Perfect and continued by a series of Imperfects each introduced by "and," a series of future events being introduced by an Imperfect and continued by Perfects with " and." Similarly, an Imperative is continued by " and " with the Perfect.

Hebrew verse is characterized chiefly by two types of correspondence, namely, of sound and of thought, known respectively as " rhythm " and " parallelism." The former corresponds roughly to " metre," lines being of approximately equal length but without feet and the rhythm being marked simply by the number of accented syllables in the line. Unaccented syllables are not counted, but the lines are divided into two (or sometimes three) by a strong pause. The commonest rhythms are 3+3, 2+2 and 3+2, the last being called "Elegiac" or kinah-rhythm, as it is used by preference for dirges (e.g. in the Book of Lamentations). The rhythms cannot satisfactorily be imitated in a translation. It is otherwise with parallelism which assumes chiefly four forms : (a) " synonymous " or " repeating," where one line is echoed by the next in different language, e.g. " Why art thou cast down, O my soul : and why art thou disquieted within me ? " (Ps. 43⁵) ; (b) " antithetic " or " contrasting," where a contrary thought is expressed, e.g. " For the Lord knoweth the way of the righteous : but the way of the ungodly shall perish " (Ps. 1⁶) ; (c) " constructive " or " complementary," where the thought is completed by the second line, e.g. " My help cometh from the Lord : who made heaven and earth " (Ps. 121²) ; and (d) " climactic " or " ascending " (a much rarer type), where a word or phrase in the first line is taken also into the second and the sentence then completed, e.g. " The floods have lifted up, O Lord : the floods have lifted up their voice " (Ps. 93³). Very often groups of lines are arranged in strophes—usually of unequal length—which are sometimes closed by a refrain (e.g. Ps. 46 or Ps. 80) and other devices are employed such as alphabetical acrostics where each line (e.g. Prov. 31¹⁰⁻³¹), pair of lines (e.g. Ps. 37), or group of lines (e.g. Lam. 1) begins in Hebrew with a successive letter of the alphabet or each line in a strophe begins with the same letter (e.g. Ps. 119). Archaic words and grammatical usages are frequent in poetry and the use of figures of speech is commoner than in prose.

A " golden " and a " silver " age of Biblical Hebrew are generally recognized, the former being the " classical " period which continues to about a century after the Exile and to which belong the JE documents together with Deuteronomy, Judges, Samuel, the older part of Kings, many of the Psalms, and the earlier Prophets. The prose is marked by dignity, lucidity, simplicity, power of dramatic presentation, and life-likeness of portraiture, while the verse is distinguished by terseness and vigour, the vividness and variety of the metaphors, and the smoothness and balance of the rhythm. Among the finest masterpieces in prose are the Joseph-stories in Genesis and the narrative in 2 Sam. 9–20. Some of the best psalms belong to this period as well as Amos, Hosea, and the earlier chapters of Isaiah, but already in Jeremiah the sentences are more laboured and the rhetorical figures lacking in force and originality. Similar signs of decadence appear in Haggai, Zechariah, Malachi, Ezekiel, and the later chapters of Isaiah, while most of the Hagiographa belong definitely to the " silver " age, Chronicles, Esther, Ecclesiastes, and Daniel betraying the most obvious evidences of lateness. The " silver " age in general is characterized not only by the introduction of foreign loan-words from Aramaic and Persian, but also by the use of Hebrew words in new meanings, the abandoning of some classical Hebrew constructions, and the adoption of Aramaic syntactical usages. The verse is artificial and unimaginative and the prose pedestrian, unpolished, and often obscure.

Biblical Aramaic differs from Hebrew chiefly by its preference of dentals to sibilants, its larger vocabulary which includes many loan-words, its greater variety of conjunctions, and its development of an elaborate tense-system through the use of the participle with pronouns or with various parts of the verb " to be." In place of the definite article *ha-* which Hebrew prefixes to nouns, Aramaic suffixes -*â*. The language is less euphonious and poetical than Hebrew but superior as a vehicle of exact expression. Aramaic languages fall into two main groups, an Eastern and a Western, which differ dialectically. Biblical Aramaic belongs to the Western group, that of Ezra having closer affinities with Hebrew than the later Aramaic of Daniel. Closely related to it is the Egyptian Aramaic of the fifth century B.C. The Aramaic of the Targums of Onkelos and Jonathan, dating from the second Christian century, probably closely resembles the language of Jesus. The main dialects of Eastern Aramaic are that of the Babylonian Talmud (A.D. 200–500) and the " Syriac " of Northern Mesopotamia, of which an abundant Christian literature has survived.

The " square " script in which Hebrew is written was borrowed from Aramaic. The " old Hebrew " or " Phœnician " script in which probably the whole of the Old Testament was originally written resembles the " square " script only slightly, although both are apparently modifications of the " Sinaitic " script which seems to have some affinities with ancient Egyptian writing, and which is found in the Sinai peninsula (*c.* 1850 B.C.)

and afterwards in Palestine where it presumably evolved into the " Phœnician " script of the Moabite Stone, the Siloam inscription, and numerous inscriptions on potsherds, seals, and coins. The Aramaic script, which is first found about the eighth century B.C. in North Syria, Asia Minor, and Assyria, gradually developed into the present square character, and although it is not known to have been used for Hebrew until the second century B.C., it is conjectured from Matt. 5^{18} that the Old Testament was written in this character by the beginning of the Christian era. The Accadian language and cuneiform script were used by the Canaanites before 1400 B.C. for official purposes, and may have been used afterwards by the Hebrews, since seventh-century documents in cuneiform have been found at Gezer. Cuneiform was written upon clay tablets with a sharp stylus (cf. perhaps Isa. 8^1, Jer. 17^1), while the alphabetical scripts were written with ink on potsherds or engraved upon stone. Many of the letters mentioned in the Old Testament may have been written on potsherds. The " rolls " or " scrolls " were probably mostly of papyrus (e.g. Jer. 36^{23}), but perhaps sometimes of sheepskin or goatskin. They were written in ink (Jer. 36^{18}) with a pen. The Old Testament text was originally purely consonantal, but at some time after A.D. 200 the letters ' (aleph), h, w, and y were occasionally inserted to represent long vowels, and after A.D. 500 the Jewish grammarians (" Massoretes ") invented and inserted, sometimes inaccurately, a complete system of vowel-signs or " points."

BIBLIOGRAPHY

(a) Driver, G. R., in The People and the Book (ed. A. S. Peake), 1925, pp. 73–120 and 481 f. ; (b) Kautzsch, E., Gesenius' Hebrew Grammar, 2nd English edition, 1910 ; (c) Davidson, A. B., Introductory Hebrew Grammar, 24th edition, 1932 ; (d) Brown, F., Driver, S. R., and Briggs, C. A., A Hebrew and English Lexicon of the Old Testament, 1906 ; (e) Strack, H. L., Grammatik des biblisch-aramäischen, 6th edition, 1921 ; (f) Stevenson, W. B., Grammar of Palestinian Jewish Aramaic, 1924 ; (g) King, E. G., Early Religious Poetry of the Hebrews, 1911 ; (h) König, Ed., article "Style of Scripture" in Hastings' Dictionary of the Bible, vol. v. pp. 156–169; (i) Benzinger, I., Hebräische Archäologie, 3rd edition, 1927, § 37, Die Schrift.

(B) The Language of the New Testament
THE ORIGINAL FORM OF THE WRITINGS

The visitor to the British Museum can now look at two great codices of the Greek Bible, one dating about the middle of the fourth century, the other about a century later. They are handsome volumes written by a professional scribe upon vellum, and show the dignity with which the Christian scriptures were treated when Christianity had become the state religion of the Roman Empire. But the books which form the New Testament had a far humbler origin. The earliest of them were letters dictated by a busy missionary, written on papyrus by some friend of his, and then sent by the hand of a trusty messenger to the leader of a community of converts in some distant city. During the lifetime of the Apostle Paul some unknown preachers or catechists were writing down on sheets of papyrus, first in Aramaic and later in Greek, such sayings and stories of Jesus as were treasured in the memory of His disciples or were handed on by word of mouth wherever Christians met together. Stories also gradually became current regarding incidents in the life of Jesus. In due course the good news of Jesus as a whole, His life, teaching, death, and resurrection came to be written down in Greek by various writers. One of these writers also wrote a narrative of the spread of the good news from Jerusalem to Rome. Another writer, embodying both Jewish and Christian material, gave to the Church an Apocalypse, to do for the Christian Church in a time of persecution what a Jewish Apocalypse known as the Book of Daniel had done for the Chosen People during the persecution under Antiochus Epiphanes two and a half centuries before.

If it were possible to recover the autograph, that is the original document which left the hand of the writer, of any of the New Testament writings, we should certainly find that it was written on papyrus. The letter to Philemon, or the Second Epistle of St. John, would probably be written on a single sheet a little more than five inches in width and about ten inches in height. The writing would be in two columns about two inches in width. A sheet of writing material was made of strips of pith taken from the papyrus reed and laid vertically side by side and then covered with strips laid above these horizontally. These were soaked in water from the Nile, treated with some glutinous matter, dried in the sun, and then polished with ivory rollers. The side on which the strips ran horizontally was called the *recto* and provided an easier surface for the stylus or pen. As a rule this side alone was used. But some-times the *verso* was used as well. Sheets were fastened together side by side to form a roll. It has been calculated that the extreme length of a papyrus roll would be about thirty-two feet, and this represents the size that would be required for each of the writings attributed to St. Luke. In Rev. 5[1] we are told that the Seer was shown " a book written within and on the back, close sealed with seven seals." Some scholars think that this refers to a papyrus roll in which the woes had over-flowed from the *recto* to the *verso*. Others think that a comma should follow the word " within," in which case a papyrus codex, or book, is described, so sealed that only the outside could be seen. Recent discoveries have made it certain that as early as the second century Christian writers used the codex form of book instead of the roll, but we may consider it most probable that all but the shortest books in the New Testament were sent forth originally in the form of rolls.

THE LANGUAGE OF THE NEW TESTAMENT

There can be little doubt that every book in the New Testa-ment was written in Greek, and this Greek was the common dialect (the *Koine*) spoken throughout the Mediterranean world. It is significant that when Paul sent a letter to the Christians in Rome it was written in Greek, not Latin. In the four centuries that had passed since Alexander made his conquests and bequeathed the world of Hellenism as his legacy, the Greek language had undergone a considerable change. The Attic dialect, in which Thucydides wrote his history, Plato composed his *Dialogues*, and Demosthenes delivered his speeches, belonged to a golden age of literature which had passed away never to return, although in the second century A.D. some writers (known as the Atticists) were to strive unsuccessfully to recap-ture the secret of an earlier age. Hellenistic Greek was far simpler in inflexions and in syntax. The reader who passes from the great classical authors to the history of Polybius, written in the later middle of the second century B.C., will be struck by the altered meaning of many words, and by many constructions which depart from earlier standards of style. But the student of New Testament Greek recognizes many of these as characteristic of the vocabulary and syntax of the New Testament. So also if he goes forward into the second century A.D. he will often find in the Discourses of Epictetus, and in Plutarch's Lives and Moral Essays, words and idioms that recall the language of the Acts and the Epistles. The tens of thousands of papyri which have been unearthed in

Egypt in the last half-century furnish innumerable lexical and grammatical parallels to the Greek Testament.

There is, however, one factor that must never be left out of account when we speak of New Testament Greek. Christianity first sprang to life on Jewish soil. The two languages spoken at different times by the Jews of Palestine have left their mark upon the Christian scriptures. (1) Jesus and His first disciples spoke Aramaic. The earliest traditions of His teaching and of His ministry were handed down in that language. Though the four Gospels were all composed in Greek, some of the sources were probably literal translations from the Aramaic. It is generally recognized that the Gospel of Mark bears strong traces of an Aramaic mind in some of the constructions, as well as of Roman residence in a number of Latinisms of vocabulary. The sayings of Jesus in Matthew and Luke often bear the stamp of the Aramaic original, and there is at least one clear case in which Luke has followed a mistaken, or else a literal, translation from the Aramaic where Matthew avoids the pitfall. In Luke 11[41] we read, " Howbeit give for alms those things which are within, and all things are clean to you." Matt. 23[26] gives the saying in a more intelligible form, " Cleanse first the inside of the cup and of the plate, that the outside thereof may become clean also." Whether the translation followed by Luke mistook two letters which in Aramaic are not unlike (*dakki* = " cleanse," *zakki* = " give alms "), or whether the same Aramaic phrase meaning " to make righteous " was given the meaning " to purify " in one rendering, and " to give alms " (as so often) in the other, we need not determine. In either case an Aramaic original supplies the clue. (2) In the synagogues of the Dispersion the Old Testament was read in the Greek translation made in Alexandria. This translation, known as the Septuagint (LXX), was produced by a succession of scholars at different times, and though the quality of the translation varies greatly in different books, the work as a whole bears the impress of the Hebrew idiom which has been rendered into Greek. This Greek translation of the Old Testament has left its mark inevitably upon the Greek of the New Testament. But it is instructive to observe how differently this influence can be traced in various writers. Luke, who could write (as his Preface shows) in the freest Hellenistic, was so steeped in the idiom of the LXX that many passages in his Gospel might almost be literal translations from a Hebrew original. Some Semitic scholars so explain the hymns in the first two chapters. But " nests of Hebraisms " (as they have been called) can be found throughout the Gospel, and to a much smaller degree Aramaic or Hebrew influence can be traced throughout Acts. Prof. C. C. Torrey would even contend that an Aramaic source lies behind chapters 1–15. Whether. this be so or not, from time to time in later chapters phrases recall the language of the LXX.

The Epistle to the Hebrews, on the other hand, although quotations from the LXX abound in every chapter, is written with a rhythm and balance of clauses which is as far as possible removed from the Hebraic structure of these citations. Paul, again, whilst familiar with Aramaic, and steeped in the Old Testament both in its Hebrew and Greek forms, speaks the ordinary Greek of an educated man, though he falls into the use of Biblical phraseology, as might be expected in one who was " a Hebrew sprung from Hebrew parents."

A very different phenomenon meets us in the Revelation of St. John. Ever since R. H. Charles's studies in the language of this book were published it has been impossible to deny the presence of Semitic constructions behind many of the astonishing departures from normal syntax in the Greek of the apocalyptist. We shall perhaps come nearest to a solution of this problem by recognizing three factors : (a) a mind that thought in Aramaic and found in the vernacular Greek many idioms sufficiently close to his mother-tongue for his purpose ; (b) sources in translated Greek and in Hebrew which he worked into his book in Hebraic Greek ; and (c) a knowledge of the LXX and of Apocalypses already current in a Greek form, which supplied him with a vocabulary and often suggested an idiom. The thorough investigation of the language of the New Testament in the light of Hellenistic syntax and also of Semitic constructions has done much to help the exegete. But the most interesting contributions have been made on the lexical side.

VOCABULARY

To understand the meaning of a New Testament word we must not simply assume that a lexicon of classical Greek will supply our need. It is important to know how it is used in the LXX, in writers of the Hellenistic age, and in the inscriptions and the papyri representing the language of everyday life.

" The name that is above every name " (Phil. 2⁹⁻¹¹) was conferred by God upon the Son " that every tongue might confess that Jesus Christ is LORD." This word κύριος is full of meaning. The first Christian creed acknowledged Jesus as Christ. But to the Gentile world that title (the literal translation of the Hebrew word for " Anointed ") was meaningless. However, there was an appropriate word at the disposal of the first missionaries, as κύριος was the designation given to the divinities worshipped in the religious cults of the Græco-Roman world (" My lord Serapis " is found in many papyri). Still, this transposition would have been impossible without the Semitic background of the primitive Church. Κύριος is constantly used in the LXX to translate the sacred tetragrammaton for which the word *Adonai* was substituted when the Hebrew scriptures were read aloud. Moreover, the urgent prayer of the earliest Aramaic-speaking Church, *Marana tha*, " Our Lord, come ! " shows that personal devotion had prepared the way for theological identification. " The highest place that heaven affords is His, is His by right." So " Jesus is Messiah " became " Jesus is Lord," and the two creeds were fused in one title " Our Lord Jesus Christ."

The words δικαιοσύνη (righteousness) and ἐλεημοσύνη (alms) are obviously identical in their use in Matt. 6[1, 2]. This specialized use of the former word is clearly evident in the Book of Tobit, for the two ideas often found expression in the same Hebrew word for " righteousness." Yet in that book the two Greek words are used twice side by side. It is equally significant that the word δικαιοσύνη is often used in the LXX to render the Hebrew word for " mercy " which also carries the conception of " covenant loyalty." Numerous passages can be cited from the LXX to show that the parallelism of the underlying Hebrew brings δικαιοσύνη into very close affinity with ἔλεος (" mercy ") or else with σωτήριον (" salvation "). The bearing of this upon the interpretation of Rom. 3[25] has been brought out effectively by recent commentators (*e.g.* C. Anderson Scott and C. H. Dodd). The same difficult passage in Romans contains the word ἱλαστήριον (A.V. and R.V. " propitiation "). This word and its cognates bear one set of meanings in classical Greek and also in the *Koine*, but have a different significance in the LXX. Whereas in the former the verb ἱλάσκεσθαι (or its compounds) regularly means " to placate," " to propitiate," with a personal object, and only secondarily means " to expiate," with an impersonal object, it is quite otherwise in the LXX. C. H. Dodd (*The Bible and the Greeks*, ch. iv.) has proved from an examination of the LXX uses of the words from this root that " Hellenistic Judaism, as represented by the LXX, does not regard the cultus as a means of pacifying the displeasure of the Deity, but as a means of delivering man from sin, and it looks in the last resort to God Himself to perform that deliverance, thus evolving a meaning of ἱλάσκεσθαι strange to non-Biblical Greek." The application of this linguistic study to the New Testament passages where these words occur (Luke 18¹³, Heb. 2¹⁷, 8¹², 9⁵ ; Rom. 3²⁵ ; 1 John 2², 4¹⁰) leads to the same result. " Propitiation " in the sense of placating an angry God is not in accord with Biblical usage. Christ is sent as the divine means of forgiveness, whereby sin is removed.

These will serve as examples of the theological importance of the LXX as a key to the language of the New Testament. Sometimes, however, the papyri warn us that a word may be used in a wider sense than is usual in the Greek Old Testament. Διαθήκη was preferred to the classical συνθήκη as the regular translation of the Hebrew word for " covenant," because the preposition in the latter compound might suggest a contractual agreement made by equals. The covenant idea which plays so large a part in Hebrew religion is of cardinal importance in the New Covenant of our Lord, and so some expositors have wished to retain this meaning wherever the word occurs in the New Testament. Deissmann, on the other hand, seeing that the word always means " will " in the *Koine*, would give the sense " testament " to it in all its New Testament occurrences. The latter meaning seems to be required in Heb. 9¹⁵ff· and Gal. 3¹⁵. Probably both meanings are covered by διαθήκη, which is equivalent to the legal term " instrument " : in one case an instrument which God draws up and sends to His people to express His will ; in the special sense of " instrument " suggesting a disposition made of property in view of ultimate death.

The papyri have illustrated a number of other legal and financial metaphors in the New Testament. The ordinary technical meaning of ὑπόστασις justifies the definition of faith in Heb. 11¹ as " the *title-deeds* of things hoped for. . . ." Καταντάω is so commonly used of property " descending to " an heir, and τέλος of " toll," that there is some justification for translating 1 Cor. 10¹¹, " who are *heirs* of the *revenues* of the ages," rather than " upon whom the *ends* of the ages are *come.*" Ἀρραβών is often found in agreements, for the " part-payment " as a pledge of what will be fully paid later on. Thus when Paul writes of the " *earnest* of the Spirit in our hearts " (2 Cor. 1²² ; cf. 5⁵, Eph. 1¹⁴) he means that the gift of the Spirit is both a foretaste and a pledge of the inheritance which is not yet fully ours. Paul, again, was probably using a metaphor from accountancy in the famous passage (Phil. 4⁸) : " Reckon (λογίζεσθε) these things among your assets," for a little later (v.¹⁵) he says playfully, " No church communicated with me so as to have a debit and credit account " (εἰς λόγον δόσεως καὶ λήμψεως), and adds (vv.¹⁷⁻¹⁸), " It is not your gift that I am looking for, but the interest that is accumulating to your credit (τὸν κάρπον τὸν πλεονάζοντα εἰς λόγον ὑμῶν). *I give you a receipt* for what you owed me. I have been over-paid ! " This word ἀπέχω is regularly used in the papyri when a receipt is signed. Those who translated our Lord's sayings into Greek were happy in their choice of this word to bring out the nuance in His condemnation of ostentatious piety. " They have their full reward " (ἀπέχουσι). It is all the reward they will have !

Under this heading we note that λογεία ("*collection*," 1 Cor. 16[1]), formerly regarded as peculiar to this New Testament occurrence, is very common in the papyri with this meaning. Another word rescued from oblivion by the papyri is the adjective δοκίμιος. Thus the phrase used in James 1[3] and 1 Pet. 1[7] means " the *approved* element in your faith," *i.e.* " what is genuine in your faith." Another obscure phrase has been made intelligible by a study of the *Koine*. The A.V. translates 1 Pet. 2[2] " the *sincere* milk *of the word*." But ἄδολος which meant " honest," " guileless," in classical prose, was also used by the tragedians of " unadulterated," and in this sense the word is constantly used in the papyri. Λογικός, which often has the meaning " rational," " spiritual," is found in the vernacular with the sense " metaphorical." Peter therefore is speaking of " pure milk " in the figurative sense.

The word ἡλικία can mean either " age " or " stature." The latter is evidently the meaning in Luke 19[3] and Eph. 4[13]. But the overwhelming evidence of the papyri encourages the other interpretation in the remaining passages. This is specially significant in Matt. 6[27], Luke 12[25]. After all, it is worry that shortens life, and the desire to add eighteen inches to one's height is so rare an eccentricity that Jesus is hardly likely to have deprecated it. (Ps. 39[5] answers the objection that a spatial measure could not be used of time.)

In earlier Greek, ἀπάτη meant " deceit," in later usage the idea of " pleasure " predominated. Perhaps " beguilement " best renders the word in the New Testament. When the translators of 1611 described Apollos as an " eloquent " man they were guided by the Vulgate rendering *eloquens* (Acts 18[24]). The Revisers of 1881 followed the classical usage by translating λόγιος " learned." But Jerome was right, as is shown by the protest of Phrynichus—that second-century Atticist who so stubbornly resisted the innovations of the *Koine*.

So also we must abandon the classical meaning " to be ambitious " for φιλοτιμέομαι, given in the R.V. margin for this word in its three occurrences in the New Testament

(Rom. 15²⁰, 2 Cor. 5⁹, 1 Thes. 4¹¹). In later Greek the word simply meant " to be zealous," " to strive eagerly." Philological debate has always been busy with the derivation of συκοφαντέω, and the earlier editions of Liddell and Scott actually informed us that one of the etymological theories was a *fig*ment! The history of the word is interesting. In classical Greek it was used of false accusations, especially for the extortion of money. In the LXX the meaning was rather " to oppress." In the New Testament it occurs in Luke 3¹⁴, 19⁸, where the A.V. gives the meaning " to accuse falsely," and the R.V. " to exact wrongfully." Examples from the papyri favour the former. In the imperial age tax-collectors had no power to collect arrears, but could denounce the defaulter to the proper revenue officials. So that Zacchæus probably said, " If I have falsely accused any defaulter before the government and had him condemned to pay up arrears. . . ."

Allusions to the religious and social background of the epistles have been brought to light by inscriptions and papyri. The rendering " for freedom " (Gal. 5¹·¹³, R.V.) is justified and illustrated by inscriptions showing that ἐπ' ἐλευθερίᾳ was a regular formula used in the legal process for the manumission of a slave. So also Ramsay has settled the much discussed meaning of ἐμβατεύω in Col. 2¹⁸ with the help of inscriptions from Klaros. The verb was a technical term in the mystery religions for " setting foot on " the entrance to the new life of communion with the divinity. Paul is therefore quoting the word from the jargon of those who are causing the trouble in the church at Colossæ. The allusion is to one who is " taking his stand on what he has seen " in the mysteries ; he is parading his degree as an initiate.

BIBLIOGRAPHY

Article " Hellenistic Greek," by Albert Thumb, in *Dict. of Apos. Church*, vol. i. (invaluable for characteristics of the *Koine*).

Grammar of N.T. Greek, by J. Hope Moulton, vol. i. (Prolegomena) ; indispensable for students of the Greek Testament. The Appendix on Semitisms in vol. ii. summarizes and discusses much of the recent work in that field.

The Vocabulary of the Greek Testament, illustrated from the Papyri and other non-literary sources, by J. H. Moulton and G. Milligan, is a veritable storehouse, as also is Deissmann's *Light from the Ancient East.*

A Manual Greek Lexicon of the N.T., by G. Abbott-Smith (3rd ed.), is the best we have in English, though *A Pocket Lexicon to the Greek N.T.*, by A. Souter, is both cheap and valuable.

For those who read German two books are supremely good. Blass-Debrunner, *Grammatik des neutestamentlichen Griechisch* (6 Aufl.), and Bauer, *Griechisch-Deutsches Wörterbuch zu den Schriften des NT und der übrigen urchristlichen Literatur* (3 Aufl.).

Two fascinating books by G. Milligan are out of print, *The N.T. Documents*, and *Here and There among the Papyri*. Those who know no Greek would find great delight in J. H. Moulton's *From Egyptian Rubbish Heaps* and R. Martin Pope's *Studies in the Language of St. Paul*.

For an elementary N.T. Greek Grammar, J. H. Moulton's *Introduction to N.T. Greek* is still the best, though Huddilston's *Essentials of N.T. Greek* is simpler for beginners. Nunn's *Syntax of N.T. Greek* should be mentioned.

A concise grammar which combines examples from the LXX and from the papyri with those from the N.T. is *Grammaire du Grec biblique*, par F.-M. Abel.

III. INTRODUCTION TO THE OLD TESTAMENT

THE study of the composition, collection, and transmission of the books of the Old Testament is rendered difficult by their antiquity, and the consequent long history through which they have passed. On the one hand, their text has suffered corruption in the course of transcription, and on the other, traditions, which both require examination and hamper it, have become attached to them. The restoration of the text is the task of Lower Criticism, and that of examining authorship, date, sources, and purpose the task of Higher Criticism.

1. LOWER CRITICISM

The Old Testament has come down to us in Hebrew, save for Jer. 10^{11}, Ezra 4^{8}–6^{18}, 7$^{12\text{-}26}$, Dan. 2^{4b}–7^{28}, which are in Aramaic. Before the invention of printing, copying was necessarily done by hand, and although this was done with extraordinary care, after the fixation of a standard text, so that manuscript variations are relatively few and unimportant, there is evidence that before the text was fixed corruption had invaded it. This was to some extent recognized by the Massoretes, *i.e.* the rabbinical scholars who standardized the text, and studied it with minutest care. Though they were unwilling to alter a single letter of the standard text, they acknowledged that it was often inexact, and placed in the margin the letters they believed to be original.

Anciently, MSS. did not represent the vowels, save certain long vowels, which could be indicated by consonants. But since the same consonants could often be read in different ways, to yield quite different meanings, the work of fixing the text included attaching vowel signs, on a system probably invented in the sixth and seventh centuries A.D. Moreover, the consonantal script itself had a history. For the current square character was an Aramaic development, into which, at a relatively late date, the Scripture text was transcribed from the old script found in Hebrew and Phœnician inscriptions.

Errors of many kinds could therefore invade the text, including (*a*) confusion of consonants similar in the old script ; (*b*) confusion of consonants similar in the square script ;

31

(c) wrong Massoretic vocalization. To these we may add (d) wrong division of words, since in the oldest manuscripts the letters were continuous; (e) the transposition of consonants to yield different words; and certain forms of transcriptional error, to which the copyist of any language is liable, including (f) dittography, or the accidental repetition of a letter or group of letters; (g) haplography, or the omission to repeat a letter or group of letters; (h) duplication or omission through homoioteleuton, or the accidental jump backwards or forwards, through the recurrence in the text of the same group of letters. Finally, (i) a copyist might incorporate in the text a gloss or comment that a previous hand had entered in the margin.

A careful study of the passages duplicated in the Old Testament, of which there are many, will reveal the possibilities of corruption in the text. For while some of the changes are certainly intentional, others are as certainly accidental. But while the double tradition is of value in these passages, the work of Lower Criticism concerns the entire Old Testament. The student must therefore seek other help, and primarily that of the ancient versions. Of these we may note (a) the *Samaritan Pentateuch*, not strictly a version, but a Samaritan transmission of the Hebrew text in the Samaritan development of the old Hebrew script; (b) the *Samaritan Targum*, or translation of the Pentateuch into the Samaritan dialect of Aramaic; (c) the *Septuagint* (LXX) Greek version, traditionally supposed to have been prepared in Alexandria for Ptolemy Philadelphus (285–246 B.C.), but actually only begun in that age, and not completed until long subsequently; (d) the Greek version of *Aquila*, a literal rendering of the Hebrew, made early in the second century A.D. because of the Christian use of the LXX; (e) *Theodotion's* revision of the LXX, prepared in the second century A.D.; (f) the Greek version of *Symmachus*, also made in the second century A.D.; (g) the *Syriac* (Peshitta) version, dating probably from the second century A.D.; (h) the *Targums*, or Jewish Aramaic renderings of the Old Testament, namely, the Targum of Onkelos (Pentateuch), the first Jerusalem Targum, of pseudo-Jonathan (Pentateuch), the fragmentary second Jerusalem Targum (Pentateuch), the Targum of Jonathan ben Uzziel (Prophets), and various Targums on the remaining books, becoming increasingly free and interlarded with midrashic stories; (i) the Old *Latin* version, resting on a Greek text, and not directly on the Hebrew; (j) the *Vulgate* Latin version, made directly from the Hebrew by St. Jerome, in the fourth century A.D.

A further instrument of textual criticism, resting on the study of Hebrew poetical forms, is much used to-day. A great deal of the Old Testament is in poetry, including much in the prophetical books. While the principles of Hebrew poetry are far from fully understood, it is apparent that it rested on parallelism of idea, and rhythm of accent (cf. Gray, *Forms of Hebrew Poetry*, 1915). This instrument is often much overworked, but it has a legitimate use.

Where none of these means will enable us to recover the text, conjectural emendation must often be resorted to, though here again far too ready recourse is commonly had to it.

2. HIGHER CRITICISM

Before turning to Higher Criticism proper, we may consider the question of the Canon. In the Hebrew Bible we find a threefold division into (*a*) the *Law*, containing the Pentateuch ; (*b*) the *Prophets*, divided again into (i) the Former Prophets or Joshua, Judges, Samuel, Kings, and (ii) the Latter Prophets or Isaiah, Jeremiah, Ezekiel and the Twelve (*i.e.* the Minor Prophets) ; (*c*) the *Writings* including Psalms, Proverbs, Job (commonly called the Poetical Books, though containing by no means all the poetry in the Old Testament), Song of Songs, Ruth, Lamentations, Ecclesiastes, Esther (commonly called the Five Rolls), Daniel, Ezra, Nehemiah, Chronicles. In the Greek Bible, which contained also the books of the Apocrypha, the order was different, and its order has been partly followed in our Bible.

It has been commonly supposed that the three divisions of the Hebrew Canon correspond to three stages in the growth of the Canon, and that the fact that the Samaritans regard only the Pentateuch as canonical means that while its canonicity antedates the Samaritan schism, the Prophetic Canon was not fixed until later, and the Canon of the Writings later still. This view Oesterley and Robinson (*Introduction to the Books of the Old Testament*, 1934) dispute, holding that the canonicity of all the books was first declared *c*. A.D. 100. But behind formal canonization there lay a long process of growth in authority and veneration, and we know that there were discussions in the first century A.D. as to whether certain books, particularly in the Writings, " defiled the hands." The idea of canonization was therefore abroad, and it is significant that the discussions appear to have been as to whether certain books should be excluded from the category of sacred books, rather than whether fresh books should be brought into that category. The Law was doubtless the first part of the Canon to be recognized as sacred, and it is probable that the Prophets secured such esteem that fresh works would not be admitted, before the Writings had reached that point, while it is certain that by New Testament times the Writings had achieved a similar position. But since the recognition was gradually reached, the inviolability of the text was also reached but gradually, and additions were made to it after the general recognition of sacredness. (Cf. Wheeler Robinson, " Canonicity and Inspiration," in *The Expository Times*, xlvii. pp. 119 ff.)

Coming now to the more specific tasks of Higher Criticism, we soon find reason to doubt the traditions of authorship that have become attached to many of the books. That literary processes lie behind some is beyond dispute. The Chronicler cites by name several works he used, and amongst them the Books of Kings certainly figured. Similarly, the author of Kings used older sources, to which he explicitly refers. Occasionally we find mention of earlier works in the Pentateuch (Num. 21^{14}), and in Joshua (10^{13}), and the work cited in Joshua is stated in 2 Sam. 1^{18} to have contained a poem by David. Nor can dependence on older sources be limited to the cases acknowledged. Often, without acknowledgement, the Chronicler quotes from Samuel and Kings, and the sections of Isaiah (36–39) and Jeremiah (52^{1-27}) which are repeated substantially in 2 Kings (18^{13}, 18^{17}–20^{19} and 24^{18}–25^{30}) must have been borrowed on one side or the other, or extracted from some still earlier source or sources. That the prophetical books rest on older works is suggested by the fact that they contain not only oracles and autobiographical matter, but also biographical matter, related in the third person, while the fact that we find oracles ascribed independently to different prophets (cf. Isa. 2^{2-4} and Mic. 4^{1-3}, and Obad. $^{1-4, 5f.}$ and Jer. $49^{14-16, 9, 10a}$) warns us not to assume authorship from the book in which a passage occurs. Further, we can learn much about the literary habits of Hebrew authors from duplicated passages. While their divergencies are sometimes due to the accidents of transmission (see above), they are sometimes deliberately introduced. Thus, when we find Ps. 14 repeated in Ps. 53, with the substitution of *God* for *Yahweh*, we must attribute the change to editorial preference, since Yahweh is found commonly in the first book of Psalms but rarely in the second. Moreover, the Chronicler seems to have been conscious of no impropriety in introducing material changes into the passages he quotes. Thus, he directly reverses (2 Chron. 14^5, 17^6) statements which he found in his

sources (1 Kings 15¹⁴, 22⁴³) concerning Asa and Jehoshaphat ;
he substitutes *Satan* (1 Chron. 21¹) for *Yahweh* (2 Sam. 24¹)
as the instigator of David's census, and *six hundred shekels of
gold* (1 Chron. 21²⁵) for the *fifty shekels of silver* stated in the
earlier source (2 Sam. 24²⁴) to have been paid by David for
Araunah's threshing-floor.

Hence we conclude (a) that the presence of a passage in a
particular book is not in itself a guarantee of its authorship ;
(b) that there was little sense of literary proprietorship amongst
the Hebrews, but that an author felt himself at liberty to use
or alter what he found in earlier works ; (c) that it is necessary
to consider, not merely the date and authorship of the books as
they now stand, but the sources that lie behind them.

(i) THE LAW

The first division of the Canon is accorded by the Jews
greater authority and sanctity than the rest of the Old Testament. Traditionally its authorship is ascribed to Moses, but
in modern times this is generally rejected by Protestant
scholars, though still maintained by Roman Catholic scholars
and a few Protestants. The lines of evidence for its rejection
may be briefly indicated.

(a) *Anachronisms.* So long ago as the twelfth century A.D.
Ibn Ezra observed some indications of non-Mosaic authorship.
Thus Deut. 34 records Moses' death, while Gen. 12⁶, 13⁷ imply
a time after the Israelite conquest of Canaan. Similarly,
Gen. 36³¹ cannot have been written before the time of Saul,
while Gen. 14¹⁴, with its reference to Dan, which did not receive
its name until a later age (Judg. 18²⁹), must be post-Mosaic.
These might, however, be regarded as glosses and additions.

(b) *Doublets.* Of the many ætiological stories in Genesis,
several form pairs. Thus Beersheba receives its name from a
covenant between Abraham and Abimelech (21³¹), and again
from a covenant between Isaac and Abimelech (26³³) ; Luz is
twice renamed Bethel by Jacob (28¹⁹ and 35¹⁵), while his own
name is twice divinely changed to Israel (32²⁸ and 35¹⁰).
Moreover, other narratives of ostensibly different events
contain curious duplications of detail. Thus, Hagar twice
leaves her mistress, once before Ishmael's birth (16⁶ᶠᶠ·) and
once after Isaac's (21¹⁰ᶠᶠ·) ; but on both occasions her mistress's
jealousy was the cause, on both the crisis came near a well in
the wilderness, and ended in an angelic appearance and the
promise of greatness for Ishmael. Again, Abram passes off
Sarai as his sister in Egypt (12¹⁰ᶠᶠ·), and again when he visits
Abimelech (20¹ᶠᶠ·), while Isaac similarly deceives Abimelech

($26^{6ff.}$). It is more probable that we have variant traditions of single incidents than that the incidents were duplicated.

(c) *The Divine Names in Genesis.* In Ex. $6^{2f.}$ we read " I am Yahweh, and I appeared unto Abraham, unto Isaac, and unto Jacob as El Shaddai, but by my name Yahweh was I not known unto them." In agreement with this, we find in Gen. 17^1 and 25^{11} the divine announcement to Abraham and Jacob : " I am El Shaddai," but there are other passages where, in direct contradiction to Ex. $6^{2f.}$, the name Yahweh is put into the mouth of the patriarchs and others (Gen. $15^{2. 8}$, 16^2, 24^{31}), of angels (18^{14}, 19^{13}), or of God Himself in addressing men (15^7, 28^{13}), while in Gen. 4^{26} we are told that men began to call on the name of Yahweh in the days of Seth, and even before this the name is found on Eve's lips (4^1). Such contradictory views would appear to imply at least two authors.

(d) *Discrepant Narratives.* There are several cases of disagreement in Genesis. Some are found in separate narratives and some in what appears to be a single account. In Gen. 1, 2 we have two irreconcilable accounts of Creation. According to the first, God created heaven and earth, then vegetation and animal life, and lastly man. According to the second, Yahweh God formed man out of the dust of the ground, and set him in the Garden of Eden. Then He formed all the animals, and lastly woman. In the one case, therefore, man and woman are said to have been created together, after the animals, and in the other separately, the one before, and the other after, the animals. Again, in the account of the Flood, we read in Gen. $6^{19f.}$, 7^8 that all the animals were taken into the Ark in pairs for their preservation, while in 7^2 Noah is bidden to choose the clean beasts and birds by sevens and the unclean by twos ; and in 7^{12} the waters are said to have lasted forty days, whereas in 7^{24} the period is a hundred and fifty days. In the narrative of Joseph's expulsion, his brothers are said to have sold him to a caravan of Ishmaelites (Gen. $37^{27. 28b}$), who took him to Egypt, and immediately beside this we learn that he was kidnapped by Midianites (^{28a}).

Nor are disagreements limited to Genesis. In Ex. 25–31 Moses is instructed to make the Tabernacle, and in 35–40 he repeats the instructions, and it is made. But in the interval we read of another Tent (33^{7-11}) of an altogether simpler character. That this was not a temporary Tent, to be used till the other was prepared, is clear from the fact that it continues to figure in the subsequent history (Num. 11^{16-30}, 12^4). According to the one account, the Tent was elaborate in construction and furnishing, requiring for its care more than 8000 Levites (Num. 1^{49-53}, 3, 4), while its position was always in the centre of the camp, both in travelling and in resting (Num. 2) ; according to the other, it was simple, requiring for its care a single Ephraimite, while its position was outside the camp and afar off. Again, in Num. 13, 14 we have two accounts of the spying of Canaan combined. In the one, the spies went to Rehob, in the extreme north (13^{21}), and reported that the land was impoverished (13^{22}), while two spies, Joshua and Caleb, calmed the people ($14^{6f.}$) and were excepted from the punishment (14^{30}) ; in the other, the spies only reached Hebron (13^{22}), and reported that the land was fertile ($13^{27.}$ $14^{8f.}$), while only Caleb is mentioned as dissenting from the majority (13^{30}, 14^{24}).

(e) *Discrepant Laws.* Disagreements are also found in the legal sections of the Pentateuch. Thus, Ex. 20^{24} commands an altar to be erected to Yahweh in every place He shall appoint, while Deut. 12^{14} limits the offering of sacrifice to one sanctuary. According to Deut. 18^7, any Levite might offer sacrifice, whereas Ex. 28^1 limits the right to Aaron's descendants. The Feast of Tabernacles is a seven-day feast in Deut. 16^{15}, but an eight-day feast in Lev. 23^{36}. In Ex. 21^{2-7} it is enacted that a Hebrew male slave must be released in the seventh year, but it is stated explicitly that a female slave is not entitled to release, while Deut. 15^{12} declares her equally entitled to release.

(f) *Theological Differences.* Some passages are marked by a naïve anthropomorphism. Thus in Gen. 2, the Deity forms man from the dust and breathes into his nostrils (2^7) ; He plants a garden (2^8), in which He later walks (3^8) ; He builds woman from the man's rib (2^{22}), and subsequently makes coats of skin and clothes them both (3^{21}). In the Flood narrative, He shuts Noah in the Ark (7^{16}), and smells the sweet savour of His sacrifice (8^{21}). All this is alien to the first account of Creation, which avoids anthropomorphism, save for " Let us make man in our image " (1^{26}), representing creation as achieved by the mere fiat of God. There are also many passages, which avoid the cruder anthropomorphism, but represent divine revelation as given through dreams (Gen. 20^3, 28^{12}, $31^{10. 24}$, $38^{5. 9}$, 40^5, 41^1), and angels (Gen. 21^{17}, 22^{11}, 28^{12}, 31^{11}, 32^1).

(g) *Stylistic Differences.* Deuteronomy is marked by an ornate, rhetorical style absent elsewhere from the Pentateuch. In the other four books there are many passages marked by an equally strongly characterized formal and repetitious style, and others by great simplicity. Even the reader of the Old Testament in translation can appreciate these differences, but in Hebrew there are lexical differences which make still more distinct these three main styles. Lesser differences can be found within the simpler narratives, though their general similarity makes separation much harder.

If we confined our view to Genesis, we might suppose that this evidence is not irreconcilable with Mosaic authorship, but that Moses could have extracted his material from older documents. Against this we may note : (*a*) that the same literary styles as are found in Genesis appear in the later books of the Pentateuch ; (*b*) that if Moses found the name *Yahweh* freely used in older sources, he could hardly have stated that it was first revealed to him ; (*c*) that the disagreements concern not only the pre-Mosaic period but the Mosaic, including events in which Moses appears as a leading actor ; (*d*) that contradictions are found in the laws Moses is represented as issuing.

It is often supposed that the case of Pentateuchal criticism can be shattered by the demonstration that we cannot depend on the accuracy of the transmission of the divine names in the Hebrew text. This supposition ignores the considerations (*a*) that whether we have sufficient evidence to *analyse* the sources or not, Ex. 6[2f.] and the texts above cited clearly demonstrate the *use* of at least two sources ; and (*b*) that the clue of the divine names forms but one of many clues, and that it cannot be employed beyond Ex. 6, since all the sources employ *Yahweh* thereafter. It should be added that the general reliability of the transmission has been established by Skinner (*Divine Names in Genesis,* 1914).

Reference has been made to the repetitious formality of style that marks much of the Pentateuch. Using this clue, we can separate a group of passages, containing most of the genealogical sections of Genesis, the first account of Creation, and a large portion of the legal and ritual sections of the Pentateuch. Owing to this last characteristic, it is usually called the Priestly Code, or P. With the exception of one instance at Bethel (Gen. 25[9ff.]), it contains no stories of theophanies, and knows nothing of angels to mediate between God and man. It records no erection of altars by the patriarchs, and contains no evidence of sacrifice having been offered before the consecration of Aaron. Its author apparently regarded sacrifice, not as man's spontaneous offering to God, but as God's ordinance, which could not rightly be offered before the ordinance had been given. It represents Moses as having first received the revelation of the name *Yahweh* (Ex. 6), and hence does not use the name in the earlier narrative.

Having separated this source, we find in the remaining material some of the pairs of stories, above referred to. Separating these by means of the clue of divine names, we find other differences of vocabulary and style marking the two groups of narratives, despite their general similarity. We also find differences of outlook and interest. The source that represents the name *Yahweh* as having been used from primeval time is called the Yahwistic (Jehovistic), or J source, while that which, like P, uses only *Elohim* (God) in Genesis, but that is distinguished from P by its style, is called the Elohistic, or E source.

The J source gives a sketch of human history from the Creation, and represents the patriarchs as sacrificing, without the need of priest, under sacred trees, by wells or stones. Simple anthropomorphism abounds in it, and though occasionally Yahweh is represented by His angel, angels are not characteristic of this source. It betrays a special interest in the south. It is Judah who takes the lead in the Joseph story, and Abraham's residence is at Hebron.

The E source is much shorter, and begins with Abraham. Like P, it dates the beginning of God's worship under the name *Yahweh* in Moses' days (Ex. 3[15]), and thereafter, though there is still a frequent preference for *God*, *Yahweh* is freely used in its narrative. Its anthropomorphism is less strongly marked than J's, and there is a greater fondness for dreams and angels. It delights in scenes of blessing and farewell (Gen. 27, 48, 50), and represents the patriarchs as offering sacrifice, and presents them somewhat more grandly than does J. It appears to be interested chiefly in the north. Reuben takes the lead in the Joseph story, and in the Mosaic age the Ephraimite Joshua is particularly prominent. In the Jacob stories Bethel and Shechem figure largely, and while in the Abraham story the patriarch is associated with the southern Beersheba, we learn from Am. 5[5], 8[14] that in the eighth century B.C. northern Israelites still went thither on pilgrimage. Hebron, on the other hand, is unmentioned. It should, however, be emphasized that it is often very difficult to separate J and E, and the symbol JE is employed when it is impossible, or unnecessary, to effect the separation.

The remaining source to which we have referred is confined to Deuteronomy, which consists almost wholly of material from this source. Hence it is called the Deuteronomic, or D source. Apart from its rhetorical style, concern for the purity of Yahwism marks it. It demands the elimination of all shrines save one, and limits priestly rights to the Levites, though it knows no distinctions within the tribe. It delights in historical retrospect, but only as a basis for moral exhortation. It has deep humanitarian interest, and frequently commends the poor and helpless to the mercy of men.

In determining the order and date of these sources, we begin with D ; 2 Kings 22, 23 records the finding of a Law-book in the Temple in the eighteenth year of Josiah (621 B.C.), and the religious reform that followed. The book apparently contained legal sections, exhortations, and curses on those who disregarded it. The reforms it led to were the centralization of the worship, the destruction of images, sacred pillars (*maṣṣebōth*), and posts (*asherim*), the suppression of sacred prostitution, and the celebration of the Passover in Jerusalem. The Law-book would appear to have been smaller than the Pentateuch, and it was almost certainly Deuteronomy, or a part of it, since here alone do we find sufficient to account for every item of the story. If we examine the history, from the Settlement to Josiah's reign, we find no evidence of acquaintance with the special provisions of Deuteronomy. In the pre-monarchical period sanctuaries were common, and even Samuel was conscious of no impropriety in sacrificing in several places. Nor did the establishment of Solomon's Temple bring any attempt at centralization, while Elijah, so far from advocating such a policy, complained that Yahweh's altars had been broken down, and himself repaired one on Carmel. In Hezekiah's reign, indeed, there was an attempt at centralization, and it has been suggested that Deuteronomy was the basis of that attempt (so formerly Sellin ; cf. *Introduction to the Old Testament*, E.T., 1923). Since there is no mention of any book as the basis of that reform, however, it is more likely that Deuteronomy was written later, during Manasseh's reign, and that it embodied the lessons of the earlier failure, and thought out the implications of centralization. During this 'long reign, which was a period of religious reaction, providing no opportunity for reform, the book was lost and forgotten, until rediscovered in 621 B.C. Some scholars think it was more probably written in Josiah's reign, shortly before its publication (so now Sellin ; cf. *Einleitung in das A.T.* 7th ed., 1935), but it is more likely that the reaction under Manasseh would quicken the defeated reforming school to think through a programme for more enduring reform.

That J and E are earlier than D can hardly be disputed, while P is as certainly later. It was formerly held by Ewald,

Hupfeld, and Knobel that P was the oldest of the sources, but Graf, Wellhausen, and Kuenen so firmly established the view that it is the youngest that it has not been seriously challenged since. As E displays a special interest in northern Israel, it was doubtless composed before the fall of that kingdom, and therefore earlier than D. Moreover, we find by a comparison of the narrative sections of the sources that D shows a knowledge of JE, but ignorance of P. Thus, whereas in Num. 13, 14 P represents the spies as journeying to Rehob, and Joshua and Caleb as exempted from the general punishment, while JE represents the spies as only reaching Eshcol, near Hebron, and Caleb alone as exempted, in D we find Eshcol mentioned as the limit of the spies' journey, and Caleb alone as exempted (Deut. 1[24, 36]).

Even clearer is D's acquaintance with the legal sections of JE, and ignorance of P's. Indeed, D seems to be largely a revision of the laws of JE (often quoted verbatim) in the interests of the centralization of the cultus. It is to be noted that JE allows many altars (Ex. 20[24-26]), and we have seen that this was the unchallenged practice until Josiah's reign, save for the brief duration of Hezekiah's reform. D contends for the principle of centralization, and enjoins the destruction of all rival shrines. On this P has nothing to say, but assumes the centralization for which D contends. On the priesthood JE says nothing, since neither J nor E recognize a priestly tribe. D, however, recognizes only Levites as priests, but places all members of the tribe on an equal footing. In P we find a distinction between ordinary Levites, who occupy a subordinate position in the Temple service, and the family of Aaron, which alone is entitled to specifically priestly privileges, while at their head stands a hereditary high-priest, who nowhere appears in D. We know that the legislation of P was followed in post-exilic times, down to the fall of the Jewish state, and we may therefore say that the known development of practice confirms the conclusion to which the study of the codes leads, that D is intermediate between JE and P.

Further, while Deut. 18[6f.] enacts that the country Levites shall be at liberty to offer sacrifice at the central shrine, 2 Kings 23[9] observes that " nevertheless the priests of the high places came not up to the altar of Yahweh in Jerusalem." Apparently D intended to provide for the displaced country priests, but the power of the Jerusalem priesthood was too strong. Now Ezekiel (or Deutero-Ezekiel : see below) rationalizes this violation of D's law. In his sketch of the ideal state of the future, he allows in the sanctuary, with full priestly rights, only the priests the Levites, *the sons of Zadok*, because they kept the sanctuary of Yahweh when Israel went astray, while the Levites who went astray are punished by being reduced to perform the menial tasks of the Temple. By non-Zadokites Ezekiel plainly means the country priests, who had failed to establish their equality with the Zadokite, or Jerusalem, priesthood, but who were now to be brought in on a lower footing. Equally plainly Ezekiel was unacquainted with the law of P, but provides a stepping-stone between D and P. This means that not only was P's law regulative only of post-exilic practice, but that it was of post-exilic promulgation. This does not mean that everything in it was of post-exilic origin, since in any re-codification of usage much that is ancient will inevitably survive, the older usage being eliminated only where it conflicts with the principles the re-codification is intended to serve.

It is generally believed that the law of P was first promulgated by Ezra (Neh. 8). His law appears to have agreed with P's in requiring an eight-day celebration of the Feast of Tabernacles (Neh. 8$^{14-18}$), instead of D's seven-day celebration (Deut. 16^{13}), while the arrangement of worship set forth in Neh. 10^{34} is that of P, and the Temple tax (Neh. 10^{32}) appears only in P (Ex. 30$^{11ff.}$). The date of Ezra's promulgation of the law has been generally held to be 444 B.C., but in recent years (see below, p. 76) many scholars date it in 397 B.C.

As between J and E, the former seems the more primitive, yet it cannot be earlier than the days of the monarchy. For it was not until the period of the monarchy that Judah and Israel came into the stream of a common life, and while J appears to have been written in Judah, and to display a special interest in the south, it is a corpus of Israelite, and not merely Judahite, traditions. Moreover, Gen. 15^{18} refers to the traditional boundaries of Solomon's kingdom (cf. 1 Kings 4^{21}). Further, the J source seems to be continued in Joshua, and to have contained an excerpt from the Book of Yashar (Josh. 10^{13}). Since the Book of Yashar was not compiled before the days of David (cf. 2 Sam. 1^{18}), the J source was at least as late, while the language of Josh. 6^{26}, which is also assigned to J, would seem to point to the ninth century B.C., when Jericho was rebuilt, in the days of Ahab (1 Kings 16^{34}). Hence most scholars date J c. 850 B.C.

That E is younger is generally agreed, though it is certainly older than the fall of Samaria. Joseph's dreams refleet the sovereignty of his house, while Balaam's oracles imply Israel's prosperity. Moreover, the Gilead covenant (Gen. 31$^{44ff.}$)

between Israel and Aram would suggest that the long struggle between the two peoples was past. On these grounds most scholars assign E to the prosperous reign of Jeroboam II., c. 800–750 B.C.

The process of combination of the sources can only be conjectured. J and E seem to have been first combined, and D added at a later date. The material of this work seems then to have been inserted in a frame-work which P supplied. At each editorial stage, the editor's hand was responsible for some slight additions or modifications.

We must not omit to observe that each of these four sources itself had a history. The many poetical fragments which were incorporated in them were doubtless taken over from other sources, and beyond these J, E, D, and P seem to have embodied other older sections, or to have received later additions. (For a full study of the sources behind our sources, see Eissfeldt, *Einleitung in das A.T.*, 1934, and Hempel, *Die althebräische Literatur*, 1930–34.) It is usual to distinguish in J an older element, J_1, and a younger element, J_2, though Eissfeldt (*Hexateuchsynopse*, 1922) regards an expanded J_1 as a separate source, which he calls the Lay source, or L, and which he regards as the oldest of the sources. To the original D, which probably consisted of Deut. 12–26, 28 only, successive additions were made by other members of the same school, especially 5–11 and 1–4. P, on the other hand, embodied a considerable earlier section, called the Holiness Code, or H. This stands in Lev. 17–26. It is generally held to be slightly later than D, but Oesterley and Robinson regard it as slightly earlier. H and D are quite independent of one another, and H has affinities with Ezekiel. Von Rad (*Die Priesterschrift im Hex.*, 1934) has recently analysed the whole of P into two separate strands, much as Eissfeldt has J.

That a history lies behind the legal sections of the Pentateuch may be particularly readily supposed, since much ancient usage is embodied in any codification. Recent study, analogous to that of the *Formgeschichte* school in New Testament criticism, has attempted to get behind our present codes by studying the forms of the commands (cf. especially Alt, *Die Ursprünge des israelitischen Rechts*, 1934). It is to this question of the history of the sources that the next stage of criticism will more largely address itself.

In recent years there have been several fundamental challenges to the view above presented. Oestreicher and Welch (*The Code of Deuteronomy*, 1924, and *Deuteronomy: the Framework*, 1932) have argued that D is much older than is generally allowed, and Hölscher and Kennett (*The Church of Israel*, 1933) have argued that it is younger, dating from the post-exilic age. Both sides have fastened on the weakness of the generally accepted view, that it fails to account adequately for the links between D and the northern kingdom, but neither has been able to present a more satisfying view. (For an examination of the arguments of both attacks, see a Symposium in *Journal of Biblical Literature*, 1928.) More recently Volz and Rudolph (*Der Elohist als Erzähler*, 1933, and *Der "Elohist" von Exodus bis Josua*, 1938) have argued that there never was such an independent source as E. Few .have been convinced by their arguments, though Sellin (*Einleitung*, 7th ed., 1935) professes to have been influenced by them.

(ii) THE FORMER PROPHETS

1. *Joshua*. The Book of Joshua is manifestly not by the hero, nor could it have been written until long after his time. For (a) in 10[13] the Book of Yashar, which included David's elegy on Saul and Jonathan (2 Sam. 1[18]), is quoted ; (b) in 9[27], 15.[63], the age of the Conquest is looked back upon, over an obviously long interval ; (c) in 19[47] events which did not take place until much later than the age of the Conquest (cf. Judg. 18) are already described ; (d) the dominant view of the book is that the conquest was achieved in a single generation, with the almost complete extermination of the inhabitants, whereas there are fragments of an older view (13[13], 15[13-19. 63], 16[10], 17[11-13. 16-18], 19[47]), also represented in Judg. 1, showing that this is not to be trusted.

That the book is a compilation from different sources is indicated by further duplications and discrepancies. Joshua gives two farewell addresses (23, 24) ; 4[9] says he set up twelve stones in the midst of Jordan, while 4[8. 20] say the Israelites carried twelve stones from Jordan and erected them in Gilgal ; in 3[17] the people cross the river, and again in 4[11] ; the king of Hebron appears to have been killed twice (10[26. 37]), and while Hebron is captured and its inhabitants destroyed in chap. 10, in 14[12] it is still in Canaanite hands, and in 15[14] is taken by Caleb.

The sources of Joshua continue the Pentateuchal sources, and hence many writers speak of the Hexateuch, to include the Pentateuch and Joshua. This, however, is misleading. For while the sources overlap, it must not be supposed that the Hexateuch ever formed a single work. Moreover, the process of compilation was different. Joshua's framework belongs to D, and not P, as in the Pentateuch, and it is generally supposed that into it were fitted extracts from an already combined JE narrative. (Note that Eissfeldt finds his additional source, L, continued in Joshua, in 2–7, 24.) The material from P was incorporated at a later date. In the first half of Joshua there is little from P, but in the second half, which deals with the division of the land, there was ample scope for the geographical and statistical details in which the P school delighted.

The issue of the Deuteronomic Book of Joshua could not have been earlier than the Exile, and in its present form, with the insertion of material from the P school, it must come from a time subsequent to 397 B.C. Of the antiquity of some of its material, however, and especially of the poem from the Book of Yashar, there can be no doubt.

2. *Judges.* The Book of Judges falls into three parts : (*a*) 1^1–2^5, briefly recounting the story of the partial conquest of Canaan ; (*b*) 2^6–16^{31}, relating the stories of the Judges ; (*c*) 17–21, an appendix, telling of the Danite migration and the founding of the sanctuary of Dan (17, 18), and of the Benjamite outrage and the rape of the maidens of Shiloh (19–21).

Turning first to (*b*), we observe that the narratives stand in a schematic framework, resting on a philosophy of history. Disloyalty to Yahweh brings foreign oppression, until the raising up of a Judge, who brings deliverance and peace, until fresh defection from Yahweh starts the circle again.

The religious pragmatism of the editor's philosophy of history reveals him as a member of the Deuteronomic school. But the stories he incorporated in his framework were much older. Most of them prove on examination to be composite, and they are believed to have belonged to two collections of Hero stories, connected, perhaps, with the J and E cycles, in the sense that they issued from writers of the same school, though not, probably, standing in continuous documents with the Pentateuchal sources. Eissfeldt once more finds a third cycle, akin to his source L (*Quellen des Richterbuches*, 1925). More ancient than any of these cycles is the Song of Deborah, which is perhaps the oldest surviving considerable literary composition in Hebrew, and which may reasonably be regarded as contemporary with the events it describes.

The chronological scheme is usually considered in relation to 1 Kings 6^1, which dates the building of the Temple 480 years after the Exodus. Since the figures are too high as they stand, it is sometimes supposed that the years of foreign domination are included in the period of each Judge, while the years of the usurpers, Abimelech and Saul (according to the later view of him) are to be disregarded. Garstang (*Joshua-Judges*, 1931), on the other hand, thinks the Minor Judges and the Abimelech story are later accretions, by ignoring which he can effect the necessary reduction. He then accepts the chronological scheme as historical, but offers for the religious pragmatism of the author the view that the periods of oppression and of peace corresponded to the withdrawal and reassertion of Egyptian authority. Most scholars recognize that the Judges were local heroes, whose periods may have synchronized, or overlapped, and attach no historical weight to the chronology.

Reverting to (*a*), we find an account quite inconsistent with the dominant view of Joshua. For here the division of the land takes place before the conquest, and not after, and instead of the tribes fighting as a single unit, under Joshua, they fight each for themselves; or in local combinations. Moreover, instead of the extermination of the Canaanites, we learn of the failure of the newcomers to dislodge them from many places. Much of this material is found, indeed, scattered in the Book of Joshua (see above), and it is generally regarded as an extract from the J cycle.

As for (*c*), it consists of manifestly old narratives, which became attached to the book subsequently to the compilation of the main portion. They stand outside the chronological and pragmatic scheme, and are not concerned with Judges. Each of these stories appears itself to be composite.

3. *Samuel.* In Hebrew MSS. the Books of Samuel stand as one book, but in the LXX they are divided and called 1 and 2 Kingdoms, our present Books of Kings being called 3 and 4 Kingdoms.

That Samuel cannot have been the author of this work is clear from the fact that he dies in 1 Sam. 25. Equally clearly the work rests on earlier sources, for it contains duplicate and discrepant accounts of several events. There are two accounts of the establishment of the monarchy, marked not alone by disagreement of detail, but by a totally different attitude to the monarchy as an institution. In 1 Sam. 9^1–10^{16}, $11^{1\cdot11}$, Samuel is a local seer who, acting under divine guidance, privately anoints Saul to deliver the people from the Philistines. Saul later brilliantly leads the Israelites against Ammon, and the tribes thereupon acclaim him as king. But according to $7^{2\cdot17}$, 8, $10^{17\cdot24}$, 12, the desire for a king proceeds from the people, and is displeasing to Samuel and to God. It is an act of rebellion against God, and wholly unnecessary, since they have been already completely and permanently delivered from the Philistines (7^{13}). In this account Samuel is a national figure, by whose means the desired king is chosen by lot. Similarly, there are two stories of David's introduction to Saul (16^{14-23} and $17^{55}-18^5$), two of David's sparing Saul's life (24 and 26), two of David's flight to Gath (21^{10-15} and 27^{5-12}), and two of Saul's death (1 Sam. 31^{1-7} and 2 Sam. 1^{1-16}).

At least a double strand, therefore, runs through much of the work, and Cornill and Budde analysed the whole on a two-source theory, connecting the sources with the J and E cycles. The stories of Samuel's infancy they connected with E, and the long, continuous section found in 2 Sam. 9–20 with J. They found a few brief Deuteronomic additions, and a few redactor's insertions. Eissfeldt, however, has analysed the work on the basis of a three-source theory (*Komposition der Samuelisbücher*, 1931), finding here, as in the Pentateuch, an additional source. The evidence for a third source is often very strong, and there is certainly much that does not fit easily into a two-source hypothesis. While his analysis is not always convincing, Eissfeldt's case for a third source is well grounded.

Kennedy finds the analysis even less simple, and traces the material to a number of sources. He assigns the infancy-stories of Samuel to a separate source, which was unconnected with the main body of what Cornill and Budde call E, and the passages dealing with the Ark to a lost *History of the Ark*. Further, he ascribes 2 Sam. 9–20 to a *Court History of David*, and believes it forms the oldest piece of continuous prose narrative in the Old Testament. The later of the two sources that deal with the establishment of the monarchy he connects with D. He believes the earlier of the accounts of the establishment of the monarchy and the *Court History of David* formed the earliest nucleus of the book, but towards the end of the Exile a Deuteronomistic writer prepared a second account of the establishment of the monarchy, marked by an attitude of hostility to the institution. Later a redactor combined these two works, prefixing sections from an old account of Samuel's infancy, and from a *History of the Ark*. This redactor, Kennedy believes, omitted what is now 2 Sam. 9–20, but it was subsequently restored.

In this last particular Kennedy is not alone, for other scholars believe the Chronicler's omission of all material contained in this section, despite his close following of much of the narrative of Samuel, is to be explained by the excision

and subsequent restoration of these chapters.   Sellin further
thinks that what is now an appendix to Samuel (2 Sam. 21–24)
contains material that once stood in the body of the work,
but was later omitted, and still later reinstated.   He holds that
2 Sam. 8 was composed to take the place of these excluded
sections.   On this view the appendix was restored earlier than
2 Sam. 9–20, since the Chronicler makes use of the former.   It
is by no means certain, however, that the Chronicler's non-use
of 2 Sam. 9–20 implies that it did not lie before him.   It is
equally likely that he refrained from recording David's sins and
family misfortunes, because these narratives would not serve
to point the lessons in which he was interested.

The appendix (2 Sam. 21–24) appears to have had a history
of its own.   It contains six sections, of which the first and last
are connected, and similarly the second and the fifth, and the
third and the fourth.   Apparently there were two successive
insertions into the appendix.   The material of the appendix is
certainly old.   However the rest of this material may be
related to the other sources of the work, the two poems (22,
23[1-7]) have a separate origin, and the same may be said of the
other poems that lie in the work.   That David's laments over
Saul (2 Sam. 1[19-27]) and Abner (2 Sam. 3[33f.]) are genuinely
Davidic is agreed by most, though Hannah's Song (1 Sam. 2[1-10])
can hardly be attributed to Hannah.   It may be noted that
some scholars believe the narratives of the infancy of Samuel
belonged originally to the life of Saul (so Lods, *Israël*, 1930, E.T.
1932, and Hylander, *Die literarische Samuel-Saul-Komplex*,
1932).   But despite the fact that the name Saul would suit
the etymology of 1 Sam. 1[20] better than Samuel's, the view
seems improbable.

It is clear that the Books of Samuel have had a complicated history, any assured recovery of which is difficult to
secure.   It certainly contains much early and historically
valual le material, and equally certainly the material that
shows a bias against the monarchy is relatively late.   It
cannot have reached its present form until a late date, though
there is no need to suppose that its history was still incomplete
in the days of the Chronicler.

4. *Kings.*   The Books of Kings, like those of Samuel, form
a single book in Hebrew MSS., and are treated in the LXX
as a continuation of the preceding work, whose story they
certainly carry on.   Oesterley and Robinson adopt this view,
which is supported by the fact that 1 Kings 1 continues
2 Sam. 20 (the appendix, 2 Sam. 21–24, intervening).   The
method of compilation of the two works is quite different,

however, and this would suggest that while the one was written to continue the record of the other, it was compiled by another hand.

Here we find a compiler's framework, into which narratives from various sources have been fitted. The framework consists of the formulæ with which the various kings are introduced and dismissed. Throughout the period of the divided monarchy we find this framework with only minor variations. The opening formula records (*a*) the synchronism of the accession with the regnal year in the sister kingdom, (*b*) the length of the reign, and (*c*) a judgement on the reign. In the case of Judahite kings we have further (*d*) the age of the king at his accession, and (*e*) his mother's name. At the close of the reign the formula indicates where further information may be obtained, and records the king's death and burial, and his successor's name.

The judgements on the kings are significant for the dating of the compiler. For in the case of the Israelite kings, they are usually comparisons with Jeroboam, who is condemned for creating rival sanctuaries to the Jerusalem shrine, while in the case of Judahite kings, they are also always from the standpoint of the centralization of the worship. Uniformly, therefore, we find the Deuteronomic standpoint. Moreover, the religious pragmatism of Deuteronomy is stamped on the compiler. He endeavours to show the connexion between the prosperity or adversity of the kings and their religious attitude. In the case of Solomon, he arranges his material to show a connexion between the troubles Solomon suffered and his love of foreign wives and their cults. His phraseology is also influenced by Deuteronomy, so that we may say with confidence that he was acquainted with the spirit, outlook, and style of Deuteronomy.

Since the last event recorded is the release of Jehoiachin, on the accession of Evil-merodach, in 561 B.C., it might appear to have been written not earlier than this. But possibly it received an appendix after it was first compiled, and many scholars believe that the verses about Jehoiachin's release are such an addition. Indeed, since the regular formula ceases with Jehoiachin's reign (597 B.C.), it may be that the original work ended here. There are some slight indications that the final editing was done in Babylon.

Into the framework extracts from older sources were inserted. Some are named, and others may be detected. (*a*) 1 Kings 1¹–2¹¹ is quite certainly from the same source as 2 Sam. 9–20. (*b*) For Solomon's reign the compiler used an

Acts of Solomon (1 Kings 11⁴¹), which Oesterley and Robinson assign to the early ninth century B.C.   There are references to (*c*) a *Royal History of Judah*, and (*d*) a *Royal History of Israel*.   These are quite unconnected with the Books of Chronicles, nor do they appear to have been court records, since the extracts seem to be of too informal a character. (*e*) Oesterley and Robinson believe there was a separate source dealing with Ahab's reign, which they call *Acts of Ahab*. As this was principally concerned with Ahab's wars with Aram, others think rather of a *History of the Syrian Wars*. (*f*) The compiler seems to have had access to a *Temple History*. Finally (*g*) there are several stories concerning prophets recorded here, and it is probable that the compiler used prophetic biographies.   There are three principal cycles of stories, dealing with Elijah, Elisha, and Isaiah.   Lesser extracts from prophetic sources, such as the story of Micaiah, may have been taken from a collection of prophetic stories.

(iii) THE LATTER PROPHETS

The method of compilation of the prophetic books was wholly different from that of the books so far examined.   Most of the actual oracles spoken by the prophets were short poems. How far the prophets compiled collections of their own oracles we cannot tell, but we know that Jeremiah at one point in his life made a collection of his (but see below), and had them publicly read in the Temple (Jer. 36).   The manuscript was taken to the king and read to him, and as it was read, he cut it off from the roll, section by section, and cast it into the fire. Jeremiah thereafter re-dictated the contents of the roll, and added to them.   Whether other prophets similarly collected their oracles, or whether that was left to their disciples, we have no means of knowing.

The principles on which such collections as have survived were made, by whomsoever they were made, are far from clear.   Sometimes we find a collection of utterances on foreign nations ;   sometimes several oracles with the same initial word stand side by side ;   sometimes the occurrence of a particular word, which was treated as a catchword, appears to have determined the arrangement, and quite unrelated oracles that contained it were set side by side.   Frequently it is difficult to tell when one oracle ends and another begins, and the lack of chronological or other clear arrangement makes it hard to determine at what point in a prophet's life a given oracle was uttered.

Nor is oracular matter the only type contained in these

books.   There is autobiography, usually in prose, recounting the prophet's experiences.   Much material of this type stands in Jeremiah and Ezekiel ; and some in Amos, Hosea, and other prophets.   Most of this almost certainly issued from the prophets themselves.   Beyond this, we find biographical prose written in the third person about the prophet.   In the case of Jeremiah, it is often thought this may have been written by Baruch, and in general it may have come from the disciples of the prophets.

That the prophets did not compile their own books, in the form they now have, is therefore clear, since they contain material of these various kinds woven together.   This is made still clearer by the examples above noted of oracles attributed independently to two different prophets.

1. *Isaiah.*   The Book of Isaiah falls into two main divisions, chaps. 1–39 and 40–66.   The first consists of a number of prophetic oracles, followed by four chapters of biographical matter, substantially repeated in 2 Kings, and contains frequent mention of Isaiah's name.   The second consists of oracles alone, with no biographical matter, and no mention of Isaiah's name.   It is improbable that the second part has any connexion with the Isaiah of the first part, and we can only guess at the reasons which led some editor or copyist to attach it to the first part.

Confining ourselves first to chaps. 1–39, we find in the first five chapters oracles only datable on internal grounds, with a general heading to the book in 1¹, and a fresh heading, either to a particular oracle, or to a small collection of oracles, in 2¹, while the prophet's call is not recorded till we reach chap. 6.   In chaps. 7 and 8 are oracles arising out of a defined and dated historical situation, though we cannot assume that all in the chapters belongs to that date.   The next four chapters contain oracles with only internal indications of date, while chaps. 13–23 form a collection of oracles on foreign nations.   Chaps. 24–27 are an apocalyptic section, and chaps. 28–35 consist of undated oracles, some of which resemble in character those found in the early chapters.   Chaps. 36–39 form the historical appendix to the whole.

From the historical and biographical sections, as well as from 1¹, we learn that Isaiah prophesied in Jerusalem in the latter part of the eighth century B.C., and that he pronounced oracles on the royal policies of Ahaz and Hezekiah, particularly in connexion with the Syro-Ephraimite attack in 735–4 B.C., and the events that led up to Sennacherib's expedition of 701 B.C., while chap. 20 tells us he both acted and uttered oracles referring to the capture of Ashdod in 711 B.C. We therefore have a historical background into which many undated oracles fit, while others yield an insight into the general social conditions of the age. Many oracles, however, not only cannot be related to the conditions of this age, but point definitely to another. Thus, 13[1]–14[23] (unless, as some hold, 14[4b-23] is an independent poem, originally belonging to another context) presupposes that Babylon is an oppressive imperial power, and is doubtless of exilic origin ; 21[1-10] comes from the same age, and looks forward to the fall of Babylon ; 24–27 reflect post-exilic conditions, and apocalyptic hopes of a divine breaking into history and world-judgement, and are generally recognized to be not earlier than the age of Alexander, while some would place them in the second century B.C. ; 34, 35 come from the exilic or post-exilic age, and look forward to the return of the Jews, either from Babylon or from the Dispersion, and to triumph over the Edomites, whose cruelty at the time of the Exile aroused undying hatred. Further, 11[10-16] is probably post-exilic, as are also the Psalm-fragments in 12, while the Messianic passage in 11[1-9] is generally held to be not earlier than the Exile. Some have also, denied 9[2-7] to Isaiah, but on less convincing grounds. Clearly, therefore, much non-Isaianic material has been incorporated in the book ; and to the passages noted others, which are doubtfully or improbably to be attributed to Isaiah, might be added. That the collection is of late compilation would seem certain, since it appears to rest on several earlier collections, which themselves contain post-Isaianic material. Oesterley and Robinson assign the compilation to *circa* 350 B.C., and believe additions were made subsequently, down to 300 B.C.

Turning to the second part of the book, we find that the historical background here presupposed is quite different. The people are in exile (47[6]), and Jerusalem is in ruins (44[26ff.]), but the exiles will shortly return (48[20], 51[11], 52[11f.]), and Jerusalem will be delivered (52[2], 54), while Babylon will be overthrown (48[14], 47[1-5]). Deliverance and destruction are alike to be achieved by the hand of Cyrus, who is twice named (44[28], 45[1]).

The prophets did not transport themselves to a future age, and predict the future that should arise out of that future ; they predicted the future from the standpoint of their own age, which is therefore to be discovered by studying the conditions which they presuppose. By this test we recognize that these chapters do not come from Isaiah of Jerusalem, but from an anonymous prophet who lived in Babylonia in the latter part of the exilic period. He is commonly referred to as Deutero-Isaiah.

It is improbable, however, that his work extends to the whole of chaps. 40–66. Chaps. 56–66 are probably not his work, though Glahn (*Der Prophet der Heimkehr*, 1934) has recently tried to rehabilitate the view of the unity of 40–66, while Torrey (*The Second Isaiah*, 1928) would attach 34, 35 to 40–66, and regard the whole as the work of a single author, who lived, however, not in the exilic period, but *c.* 400 B.C.

Imbedded in 40–55 are four poems, generally known as the Servant Songs (42^{1-4}, 49^{1-6}, 50^{4-9}, 52^{13}–53^{12}), around which endless discussion has centred. It is not agreed whether they are by Deutero-Isaiah, or whether they were taken from some other work, nor is there agreement on their interpretation. The traditional view was that though in other passages in Deutero-Isaiah Israël is called the Servant of Yahweh (41^8, $44^{1f.\ 21}$, 48^{20}), the Servant of these poems, and especially of 53, was the Messiah. This has given place to two schools of interpretation, the one (largely represented in English work) giving a collective interpretation to the Servant of these poems, and the other (largely represented in German work) giving an individual, though non-Messianic, interpretation. But within each school there are great varieties of view, in the former school differing as to whether the Servant is the empirical Israel, the faithful remnant, or the ideal Israel, and in the latter as to whether the Servant is Jeremiah, Zerubbabel, Jehoiachin, Moses, an unknown contemporary, or the poet himself. A final solution of the problems of authorship and interpretation raised by these poems has yet to be found. Probably there was some fluidity in the author's thought, and Wheeler Robinson's view that the Servant is to be understood in the light of the Hebrew concept of corporate personality has much to commend it.

Chaps. 56–66 are commonly referred to as Trito-Isaiah, but whereas Deutero-Isaiah was undoubtedly a single individual, it is improbable that Trito-Isaiah was. The passages here preserved are so miscellaneous that they probably come from more than one hand, though several may come from a single author. They were written under the influence of Deutero-Isaiah's work, and reflect the conditions of the post-exilic age. The background appears to be Palestinian (57^{3-7}), and while the walls of Jerusalem are not yet built (60^{10}), the Temple is already standing (56^{5-7}, 60^7). The period is therefore between the Return and the time of Nehemiah. Oesterley and Robinson, while assigning the greater part of the collection to a single author living in that age, regard 59, 63^7–64^{12}, 66$^{5.\ 17\text{-}24}$ as coming from the latter half of the fourth century B.C.

2. *Jeremiah.* The Book of Jeremiah contains relatively little that is unconnected with Jeremiah, though it cannot have reached its present form until long after his day. It falls into four main divisions: (*a*) chaps. 1–25, consisting largely of poetic oracles dealing with Judah, interspersed with prose, mainly autobiographical; (*b*) chaps. 26–45, consisting largely of prose, biographical and autobiographical, but containing some poetic oracles; (*c*) chaps. 46–51, consisting almost wholly of poetic oracles dealing with foreign nations; and (*d*) chap. 52, consisting of a historical appendix, which is duplicated in 2 Kings. In the LXX the oracles on foreign nations are transferred to follow 25^{13}, and their order is different.

The period of Jeremiah's prophetic activity was from 626 B.C. until shortly after the fall of Jerusalem in 586 B.C., and we have an unusually full account of his life and experiences. While it is not always easy to determine with confidence when the undated oracles were uttered, there are few which cannot be attributed to Jeremiah. It is almost universally agreed, however, that 10$^{1\text{-}16}$ is non-Jeremianic, but later than Deutero-Isaiah, while 17$^{21\text{-}27}$ is un-Jeremianic in its standpoint, and recalls the age of Nehemiah. Some have denied 30, 31 to Jeremiah, but parts of them, including especially 31$^{27\text{-}34}$, on insufficient grounds. On the other hand, 50^1–51^{58}, which looks forward to the imminent fall of Babylon, is almost certainly non-Jeremianic.

It is not to be supposed, however, that with the exception of such passages as these, the book came from Jeremiah's hand. We know that in 605 B.C. Baruch prepared a roll at Jeremiah's dictation, and this was perhaps subsequently added to (36^{32}). Oesterley and Robinson suggest that this roll consisted of the autobiographical prose work, whose extracts are to be found scattered through chaps. 1–35. The oracles, on the other hand, were in their view collected after the age of Jeremiah into collections which were not complete until the end of the fifth century B.C. The biographical prose they attribute to Baruch. From these collections of material, they believe, the Book of Jeremiah was compiled in the fourth century B.C., but subsequently added to, the oracles on foreign nations having been brought in after the divergence of the Palestinian and Egyptian texts. Against this, it is to be noted that chap. 36 would seem to imply that Baruch's roll contained oracles rather than autobiography, and that some of the oracles dealt with foreign nations. Such a collection may well have been added to, both during and after the prophet's life, or have been supplemented by other independent collections, into which some non-Jeremianic material was incorporated.

3. *Ezekiel.* Until recently the Book of Ezekiel has been regarded as unique in its unity and authenticity, and has been wholly attributed to the priest Ezekiel, who was one of the exiles of 597 B.C., and who thereafter prophesied in Babylonia. Its divisions were taken to be: (*a*) chaps. 1–24, a chronologically ordered collection of prophecies delivered before the fall of Jerusalem; (*b*) chaps. 25–32, prophecies on foreign peoples; (*c*) chaps. 33–39, prophecies of the restoration of Jerusalem; (*d*) chaps. 40–48, the ideal picture of the restored community.

The unity of the book was disputed, indeed, by Kraetzschmar (*Ezechiel*, 1900), but with little effect. In 1924 Hölscher renewed the challenge (*Hesekiel, der Dichter und das Buch*), but vitiated his work by the arbitrariness of the Canon with which he started. For he held that Ezekiel could only write poetry, and that all that was not poetry was not his. Since relatively little poetry stands in this book, Ezekiel's share was reduced to diminutive proportions. The rest, including the entire section 33–48, was ascribed to another, who lived in the fifth century B.C. Torrey next attacked the common view, and maintained (*Pseudo-Ezekiel*, 1930) that the book was written *c.* 230 B.C. as a pseudepigraph, purporting to have been written in the reign of Manasseh, and addressed to a Palestinian circle, but that it was later recast by an editor, who transferred it to the age of the Exile. Almost simultaneously and independently, James Smith (*Book of Prophet Ezekiel*, 1931) argued that Ezekiel wrote in Palestine, but in northern Israel in the age of Manasseh, and that chaps. 40–48 presented a sketch, not of the Jerusalem Temple, but of that on Gerizim. None of these views has commanded any notable following, though together they have exercised much influence, and it is now being increasingly believed that the prophecies of the first part of the book were addressed to a Palestinian audience, as Torrey and Smith agree, while there is a growing disposition to distinguish between the earnest prophet of 1–24, and the calm dreamer of 40–48. Herntrich (*Ezechiel-probleme*, 1932) has combined these positions in the view that Ezekiel prophesied in Jerusalem until 586 B.C., but that his prophecies were amplified and edited by an exilic hand, when their Babylonian material was imported, and that the editor is responsible for 40–48. This view is substantially followed by Oesterley and Robinson, and also by Harford (*Studies in Ezekiel*, 1935), but is rejected by Cooke (*Commentary on Ezekiel*, 1936).

4. *Hosea*. Hosea prophesied in the northern kingdom during the last years before the fall of Samaria. His prophetic ministry began *c.* 740 B.C., and appears to have ended before 722 B.C., since there is no reference to the fall of Samaria. The Book of Hosea consists of a number of prophetic oracles, whose text is in a badly preserved state, combined with biographical and autobiographical narratives. The most discussed question connected with the book is the relation between the biographical account of Hosea's marriage in chap. 1, and the autobiographical account in chap. 3, and there is no agreement as to whether we have two accounts of a single event, or whether chap. 3 related Hosea's experience at a later date. It is generally agreed to-day that these chapters are not to be merely allegorically explained, but that Gomer was a real person, who was unfaithful to her husband, and that it was from the bitter experience of his own home that Hosea was led to the deepest element in his teaching of divine love.

Editors have suspected of being later additions all the hopeful passages, and all passages in which Judah is mentioned. It is generally agreed that 1^{10}–2^1 is not Hosea's, and it is possible that in some cases Judah has been substituted for Israel (so 12^2), or that some additions have been made by southern scribes, through whose hands the text has reached us (so, perhaps, 1^7, 4^{15}, 8^{14}, 11^{12b}), but we need deny very little to Hosea.

The date at which the book was compiled from the oracular collection, or collections, and the prose material of the two types, cannot be determined with any certainty. If the Judahite additions already stood in the collection of oracles, before it was used by the compiler of our book, it must have been long subsequent to the age of Hosea. Oesterley and Robinson place it in the Exile, or later.

5. *Joel*. This little book contains no explicit indication of date, and older writers regarded it as coming from the period of the minority of Joash, or from the age of Jeremiah. A pre-exilic date is now generally abandoned for a post-exilic on the grounds that (*a*) there is no reference to the northern kingdom, but Israel is synonymous with Judah (2^{27}, $3^{2. 16}$) ; (*b*) $3^{2. 17}$ clearly imply a date after the fall of Jerusalem and the dispersion of the Jews, while the fact that the Temple is used ($1^{13f.}$) would carry us down beyond 516 B.C. ; (*c*) there is no mention of a king, but the priests and elders are the leaders

of the community ; (d) there is no reference to Assyrians or Babylonians, as in all other pre-exilic prophets, though there are references to other foreign oppressors, and also to Greeks (3^6) ; (e) there is no mention of the sins that prevailed in pre-exilic Israel, while the frequent allusions to priests and offerings, and the assembly of the whole people for fasting, weeping, and mourning (2^{12}) suggests post-exilic Judaism ; (f) the reference to " the meal offering and the drink offering " ($1^{9. 13}$, 2^{14}) points definitely to the post-exilic period.

It remains to be considered whether the work is a unity. Its first two chapters treat of a plague of locusts which devastated the land, but from 2^{28} to the end it treats of an apocalyptic Day of Yahweh, when He will bless the Jews, but will assemble the nations in the valley of Jehoshaphat and punish them for their treatment of His people. Some recent writers have argued that these two parts are of independent origin, the apocalyptic section being from a later hand. Oesterley and Robinson attach 1^{15}, $2^{1-11. 20}$ to the apocalyptic section, and date it in the second century B.C.

6. *Amos.* The Book of Amos contains the oracles of the earliest of the writing prophets, who, though himself a southerner, delivered his prophecies in the northern kingdom in the reign of Jeroboam II., *circa* 760 B.C. It contains a short biographical section in 7^{10-17}, and some autobiographical material in 7-9. The fact that it contains the three types of material suggests that it was compiled after Amos's time, and this conclusion is reinforced by other considerations. The book falls into three divisions : (a) chaps. 1, 2 consisting of seven oracles on the peoples surrounding Israel, followed by one on Israel itself, all introduced by a similar formula ; (b) chaps. 3-6, a collection of oracles denouncing the social abuses that prevailed in Israel ; (c) chaps. 7-9, a series of visions, in which some other oracles have been incorporated. The oracle against Judah in $2^{4f.}$ is generally recognized to be by a later hand, but the fact that it is introduced by the same formula as the surrounding oracles, suggests that it was already written when the book was compiled. The formula introducing the oracles of this group may be due to the compiler of the book, or the compiler of the collection of oracles on which he drew. Doubts have been raised against a few other passages, and especially against the closing verses of the book. Most scholars are agreed that 9^{11-15} date from after the fall of Jerusalem, and many believe 9^{8b-10}, which ill accord with 9^{1-4}, to be also from another hand.

7. *Obadiah.* This is the smallest book in the Old Testa-

ment, and it gives no explicit information as to the prophet's period. From v.[11] it is clear that the fall of Jerusalem is past, but it is disputed whether the book is a unity. About a quarter of it is duplicated in Jeremiah ([1-4]=Jer. 49[14-16], and [5f.]=Jer. 49[9-10a]), and it is agreed that the editor of the oracles in Jeremiah owed the passage to the Book of Obadiah, and not *vice versa*. But in view of our uncertainty as to when Jer. 49 was compiled, this proves nothing for the date of Obadiah. Sellin believes that Obad. [1-10] refer to Edom's revolt against Jehoram (852 B.C.), while [11-14] were added in the Exile, and [15-21] in the age of Malachi. Rudolph, on the other hand, finds (*Zeitschrift f. d. alttest. Wiss.*, 1931, pp. 222 ff.) the whole to be by one hand, shortly after 586 B.C., with the possible exception of verses 19–21.

8. *Jonah.* This book is unique in the prophetic Canon in that it contains no oracular matter, but, with the exception of the psalm in chap. 2, consists wholly of biographical matter. We read in 2 Kings 14[25] of a prophet Jonah, the son of Amittai, who lived in the time of Jeroboam II., shortly before Amos, and the book doubtless purports to tell his story. But it was not written until long after his time. This view rests partly on the fact that in 3[3] the fall of Nineveh (612 B.C.) is looked back on as long past, but more securely on the evidence of the language, which marks it as definitely post-exilic, and probably not earlier than the fourth century B.C.

Though it contains no oracles similar to those found in the other prophets, it rightly stands in the prophetic Canon, for its unknown author delivers a truly prophetic message through the medium of this story. It is probably to be read, not as history, but as allegory. Jonah, swallowed by the fish for his disobedience, and vomited out to fulfil his divinely appointed mission of converting the heathen, symbolizes the Jewish people, swallowed up in the Babylonian Exile for their disloyalty to God, but brought forth again in the Return that they might lead the nations to God.

Apart from the psalm in 2[2-9], the book is a unity. That psalm, however, has no relevance to its context. It is not a prayer for deliverance, but a psalm of thanksgiving for deliverance from some peril in the sea, and is doubtless an interpolation into the text.

9. *Micah.* Micah was a contemporary of Isaiah's, as we learn from the heading of the book, and from Jer. 26[18], but we know little about him, as the book consists only of oracles. It falls into three sections : (*a*) chaps. 1–3, which deal with the social injustices rampant in Judah, and close with the

prophecy of doom upon Jerusalem, cited in Jeremiah ;
(b) chaps. 4, 5, which contain promises of restoration ; (c)
chaps. 6, 7, which contain miscellaneous oracles.

It is agreed that chaps. 1–3 are the work of Micah, but
the rest of the book is commonly denied to him. By some a
genuine core is found in 4, 5, but there are several indications
of a date not earlier than the Exile, which must then be treated
as glosses. In chaps. 6, 7 there are oracles which might be
Micah's, but the whole collection cannot be ascribed to him.
The great passage 6^{1-8} is generally taken to come from the
reign of Manasseh, though some have argued for the time of
Ahaz. The latter is far less likely, indeed, and though there
is no a priori ground for supposing that Micah might not have
lived until Manasseh's reign, the fact that in the heading to
the book Manasseh is unmentioned is against this. To this
should be added the consideration, which weighs equally
against Micah's authorship, whether in the reign of Ahaz, or
in Manasseh's, that in spirit and temper it differs so widely from
chaps. 1–3. Qther fragments in this collection may be even
later. Thus, 7^{7-20} is commonly held to be exilic, or post-exilic.

10. *Nahum.* The Book of Nahum opens with a mutilated
acrostic poem (1^2–2^2), generally held to be of post-exilic
origin, followed by oracles against Assyria (2^3–3^{19}). It is the
latter which constitute the work of Nahum, whose date can
only be determined on the internal evidence of his oracles.
These look forward to the destruction of Nineveh (612 B.C.),
and since in 3^8 there is a reference to the sack of Thebes
(663 B.C.), we can define broadly the period of their origin as
between these dates. Since the fall of Nineveh seems to have
been imminently expected, it is probable that their date is
very close to 612 B.C. Humbert (*Zeitschrift f. d. alttest. Wiss.*,
1926, pp. 226 ff., *Archiv f. Orientforschung*, 1928–9, pp. 14 ff.,
and *Revue d'hist. et de phil. religieuses*, 1932, pp. 1 ff.) has
suggested that the book of Nahum is a liturgy prepared for
the festival in 612 B.C. that celebrated the fall of Nineveh,
and Sellin now favours this view.

11. *Habakkuk.* This little book has raised problems which
have received the most varied solutions. It contains oracles in
chaps. 1, 2, and a psalm in chap. 3. The oracles represent
the Chaldæans as the instrument of justice on the wicked
oppressor, and then seem to go on to pronounce judgement
upon the Chaldæans, who now appear to be identified with
the oppressors. The period is apparently the end of the
seventh century B.C., when the Neo-Babylonian empire was
rapidly rising, but Duhm, by substituting *Kittim* for *Kasdim*

in 1[6], and *hay'wani* (the Greek) for *hayyayin* (wine) in 2[5], very cleverly transferred the oracles to the Greek period of Alexander. While he has had some followers, most scholars feel it is precarious to base a theory on a conjectural emendation. Budde preferred to vary the arrangement of the book, and Marti to assume that the original work of Habakkuk had received many interpolations, but Cannon (*Zeitschrift f. d. alttest. Wiss.*, 1925, pp. 62 ff.) has shown that it is possible to accept the whole of chaps. 1, 2 as the work of Habakkuk, who first hailed the Chaldæans as God's instrument of justice, and at a later period, after experience of Chaldæan ruthlessness, looked for vengeance upon them. The psalm in chap. 3, which Duhm regarded as integral to the book, most others regard as of independent origin, and post-exilic. It should be added that again a liturgical interpretation has been suggested for the work. Sellin, who formerly followed Duhm, now follows Balla (*Relig. in Geschichte u. Gegenwart*[2], ii. cols. 1556 f.) in holding the book to be the liturgy for a day of prayer at a time of crisis, when deliverance from the Chaldæans was sought.

12. *Zephaniah.* The prophet Zephaniah, who was perhaps a descendant of king Hezekiah (cf. 1[1]), appears to have prophesied *c.* 626 B.C., at the time of the Scythian peril, and his emergence would then be contemporary with Jeremiah's. He believed that the inroads of the Scythians heralded a Day of Yahweh, that should bring a general judgement upon all the nations. The anticipation of the destruction of Nineveh in 2[13] has led to the suggestion that the prophecies should be carried down nearer to 612 B.C., but it is not necessary to suppose that all the oracles in the collection, brief as it is, come from a single year. A few verses (*e.g.* 2[15], 3[14-20]) have been held to be later additions.

13. *Haggai.* The Book of Haggai contains brief addresses uttered on various occasions, the exact date of each being recorded in its heading. All the dates fall within a single year, the second year of Darius Hystaspis, 520 B.C. There is no reason to doubt the authenticity of the utterances, and Haggai thus belongs to the immediately post-exilic period. It is probable that he did not compile the book himself, since he is consistently referred to in the third person, but it was doubtless prepared very shortly after 520 B.C.

14. *Zechariah.* That the Book of Zechariah is not a unity is now everywhere agreed. The prophet Zechariah, who was contemporary with Haggai, and whose genuine prophecies are supplied with dates, ranging from 520–518 B.C., is concerned only with chaps. 1–8, while chaps. 9–14 form a wholly

independent collection. The reasons for this view are : (a) whereas in 1–8 the background of the early Persian period is clear, in 9–14 there is nothing whatever of this ; (b) whereas in 1–8 the land is at peace, and the interest is in rebuilding the Temple, in 9–14 we find pictures of war, and Jerusalem is besieged ; (c) whereas in 1–8 the leaders of the community, Zerubbabel and Joshua, are named, in 9–14 we find only references to unnamed shepherds. In addition, the literary style and the theological ideas of the second part are quite different from those of the first.

The work of Zechariah consists of eight Night-visions, related in the first person, to which are attached introductory notes ($1^{1.\ 7}$, 7^1) in the third person. These visions, which are filled with Messianic hopes, centring round Zerubbabel, may without hesitation be ascribed to Zechariah.

The remaining chapters have called forth less agreement. Earlier writers thought they were pre-exilic, but most moderns have recognized them to be post-exilic. A third view has distinguished between 9–11 and 12–14, finding the former to be mainly pre-exilic, and the latter post-exilic. The reference to Greece in 9^{14} points clearly to a late post-exilic period, and this would far better suit the conditions. It is by no means certain, however, that the whole of 9–14 comes from one hand, and Oesterley and Robinson have assigned the different portions of this collection to different dates, as follows : 9^{1-8} and 11^{1-3}, 218 B.C. or 199 B.C. ; 9^{9-12}, 164 B.C. ; 9^{13-17}, 165 B.C. ; 10^{3-12} towards the end of Jonathan's high-priesthood (died 142 B.C.) ; 11^{4-17} and 13^{7-9}, c. 160 B.C. ; 12, 13^{1-6}, after Simon's death (134 B.C.) ; 14, an apocalyptic section, from a strongly nationalistic writer.

15. *Malachi.* It is doubtful if Malachi, which means *my messenger*, is a proper name at all. But it is possible to determine within narrow limits the author's date. The land is ruled by a *pekah*, or governor (1^8), and it is therefore after the fall of Jerusalem ; and since the Temple is standing (1^{10}, $3^{1.\ 10}$) it is after 516 B.C., and probably a long time after. On the other hand, no distinction is drawn between priests and Levites (2^{4-9}, 3^3), and therefore it is before the promulgation of P (397 B.C.). Its agreement with P (cf. 3^{10} with Num. 18^{21-33}) in the matter of the tithe (D's tithe law was quite different) shows that in some respects the usage codified in P is older than the promulgation of P (cf. above, p. 42). As the condemnation of mixed marriages (2^{10-16}) indicated that Nehemiah's work was not yet done (cf. Neh. 13^{23-27}), we should probably assign the oracles to c. 460 B.C.

(iv) THE WRITINGS

1. *Psalms*. The Book of Psalms consists of 150 poems, but 9 and 10 were originally one poem, as also were 42 and 43, while in several cases two poems have been combined in a single psalm. The collection is divided into five books : 1–41, 42–72, 73–89, 90–106, 107–150 ; but probably originally Books ii. and iii. were one, and so also Books iv. and v.

Several psalms are duplicated. Thus $14 = 53$, $40^{14-18} = 70$, $108 = 57^{8-12}$ and 60^{7-14}. By comparing 14 and 53, we find that *Elohim* (God) stands in 53 in four places where 14 had *Yahweh*. Similarly, 70 substitutes *Elohim* for *Yahweh* three times, while retaining the latter twice. This appears to be no accident, for we find *Yahweh* used 272 times in Book i., and *Elohim* used absolutely 15 times, while in Pss. 42–83 *Yahweh* stands 40 times, and *Elohim* 200 times. Book i. is attributed almost exclusively to David, only Pss. 1 and 2 (introductory to the entire book), 10 (the completion of 9), and 33 being without ascription to him. Book i. was therefore a Davidic Yahwistic Psalter, while Books ii. and iii. formed an Elohistic Psalter, attributed to various authors. To this latter an appendix (84–89) was added, but without the editorial change of *Yahweh* to *Elohim*. Books iv. and v. are again Yahwistic, the poems bearing various ascriptions or being without ascription. Altogether 50 Psalms have no ascription, of which 34 are " orphans " (*i.e.* without heading at all).

Book i. is generally recognized to be the oldest of the three collections, though it is improbable that it was made before the Exile. The other collections must have been completed by about 100 B.C., so that the compilation of the Psalter may be placed broadly between the Return and 100 B.C. The recognition of this formerly led to the assignment of an increasing number of individual psalms to the post-exilic period, and especially to the Maccabæan age. This tendency reached its climax in Duhm, who held no psalm to be pre-exilic, perhaps two to come from the Persian period, and the rest to be from the Greek period, the vast majority being Maccabæan. From this there has been a reaction, and to-day it is recognized that while the compilations are post-exilic, the contents may be partly, and especially in the case of Book i., pre-exilic.

It is, however, extremely difficult to date the individual psalms, and recent students have been less concerned to define the date than to discuss the form and use of the psalms. It is many years since Smend argued that many of the psalms which read like individual prayers were really national prayers, and that where the Psalmist uses " I," it should be understood collectively. In this he has been followed by some commentators, who have given a national interpretation to many psalms. This view has been disputed by Balla (*Das Ich der Psalmen*, 1912), and is rejected by Gunkel. Wheeler Robinson (*The Psalmists*, 1926, p. 47) has here again, as in the case of the Servant of Yahweh, applied the concept of corporate personality, to yield a fluidity which can pass from the individual to the collective without difficulty.

There is a growing tendency to-day to think of the Psalter less as a Hymn-book, in our sense of the term, than as a book of ritual poems, to be used in various ritual acts, whether private or public. Mowinckel (*Psalmenstudien*, 1921–4) goes much further, and attempts to define the purpose of the ritual in many cases. He holds that the references to *workers of iniquity* and the like are to sorcerers, whose wiles the worshipper tried to counter by ritual acts. He bases himself largely on Babylonian parallels, where sickness and misfortune were associated with magic, whose spell was to be broken by incantations, and he believes the Psalter had a corresponding use. Other psalms Mowinckel believes to have belonged to an annual Enthronement Festival, similar to the Babylonian New Year Festival. All the psalms which contain such phrases as " Yahweh is king " or " Yahweh reigneth," he ascribes to the ritual of this festival.

Another characteristic modern approach to the Psalter is associated especially with the name of Gunkel, who studied particularly their forms and types, and classified their uses on this basis. He held that many psalms were written, not for use in the Jerusalem Temple, but for the Jews of the Diaspora, and that while some psalms may have originated as cultic poems, most of them no longer presuppose cultic action. In particular, the psalms he classes as individual laments were in his view sung by the suffering in their homes, with no cultic association.

The headings of the psalms have attracted much discussion. The personal ascriptions were doubtless early understood to imply authorship, but it is impossible to accept them as authentic in that sense. Beyond these there are other terms, such as *Miktam*, *Maskil*, and occasionally cryptic phrases (*e.g.* 22, 56), while the term rendered " For the chief musician " stands at the head of fifty-five psalms. Some have supposed that while such phrases as those over Pss. 22, 56 indicate tunes, all the other terms indicate older collections in which the poems stood, so that where a psalm has more than one term, it implies that it stood in more than one of these collections. Kennett (*Old Testament Essays*, 1928), on the other hand, supposed that all of the terms in the headings had musical significance, and indicated the mode of accompaniment, while Mowinckel assigns to them all cultic significance, and finds them to indicate the particular magical use to which the poem is to be put.

A further subject of recent study is the relation between the Psalms and the Babylonian and Egyptian Psalms. As observed above, Mowinckel bases his views on the uses of these poems, but some have made verbal studies, and have suggested literary dependence. In particular, the Egyptian *Hymn of Ikhnaton* has been connected with Ps. 104. That Egypt and Babylon had religious poetry similar in form to the Hebrew Psalms is freely allowed, but actual literary dependence is neither proved nor likely. There is a difference in quality and spirit marking the Hebrew poems, a difference derived from her own spiritual experience.

2. *Proverbs*. The Book of Proverbs is a collection of Wisdom writings of very varied character. The title ascribes the work to Solomon, and again in 10^1 he is named as the author of the collection that follows, while 25^1, though ascribing the following collection to him, states that it was collected by the men of Hezekiah. Clearly, therefore, Solomon cannot have prepared the work in its present form. Moreover, it contains some admittedly non-Solomonic material. Thus 24^{23} attributes the sayings that follow to " the wise men " ; 30^1 the sayings that follow to Agur ; 31^1 the section that follows to Lemuel.

The book is commonly analysed into eight sections, but Oesterley subdivides one of them to yield a total of ten. These are (a) 1^1–9^{18}, of which 1^{1-6} are an introduction to the whole book ; (b) 10^1–22^{16} ; (c) 22^{17}–23^{14} ; (d) 23^{15}–24^{22} ; (e) 24^{23-34} ; (f) 25–29 ; (g) 30^{1-14} ; (h) 30^{15-33} ; (i) 31^{1-9} ; (j) 31^{10-31}.

The characteristic of the first section is the personification of Wisdom which reaches its climax in chap. 8. It presents its material, moreover, not in brief aphorisms, such as we find in most of the book, but in connected sections, developing each a single theme. It is generally agreed that this is the latest part of the book, and Oesterley would date it about the middle of the third century B.C.

Section (b) is probably the oldest in the book. Probably it is of pre-exilic origin (so Gressmann, Sellin, Oesterley). This view rests on the consideration that *the Wise* are already referred to in pre-exilic writers as a separate class, who might therefore be presumed to have left some deposit of their wisdom, and on the undeveloped literary character of the sayings. For each verse is commonly an independent and self-contained thought. Further, there are frequent references to the king, some of which, despite Gray's reminder that Ben Sira could also refer to the king, are thought to point to the time of the Hebrew monarchy.

The section 22^{17}–23^{14} has many points of connexion with the recently published Egyptian text, *The Wisdom of Amen-em-ope*, and it is on this ground that Oesterley separates it from the two short sections that follow, with which it has been common to take it. The fresh heading in 24^{23} accounts for the separation of the verses that follow. These three sections Oesterley regards as of approximately the same date and closely connected with one another. We may here observe that Hebrew Wisdom literature, like Hebrew psalmody, has parallels in other ancient literatures, and especially in Egyptian, whose oldest known fragment of this kind, the *Teaching of Ptah-hotep*, goes back to the third millennium B.C. Here again, we find that the Hebrew literature, though it grew from a common stock, developed a quality of its own. In the case of *The Wisdom of Amen-em-ope*, however, the case for the literary dependence of the author of Prov. 22^{17}–23^{14} would appear to be proved, though there are differences of outlook between the two works. The date of the Egyptian work is probably the eighth or seventh century B.C., and Oesterley assigns these three sections of Proverbs to the seventh century B.C.

The ascription of 25–29 to the age of Hezekiah rests, according to Sellin, on a sound tradition, so far, at any rate, as its kernel is concerned. While he recognizes it to be later than 10^{1}–22^{16}, marked by a spirit of scepticism instead of the confidence of the earlier section, he finds a definitely pre-exilic nucleus in it, and in this Oesterley concurs.

The remaining sections are all short, and impossible to date, though they are probably late. We do not know who Agur or Lemuel were. The final section is an alphabetic acrostic poem in praise of the virtuous woman, and its language marks it as post-exilic. These four sections stand in relatively different positions in the LXX, and are distinguishable in their contents.

3. *Job.* The Book of Job is one of the world's masterpieces, superb as literature, and wrestling with a great and enduring problem. It consists of a prologue and epilogue in prose, between which stands a dialogue in poetry. It has been

held by many that the prologue and epilogue are older than the rest of the book, and come from a different hand. But while it is probable that the work rests on a traditional story of a good man who suffered, both prologue and epilogue are thoroughly integral to it, and a separate literary origin need not be assumed.

The book has gathered some accretions, however, and has probably suffered some loss. The chief accretion is the Elihu speeches. After Job's dialogue with his three friends, Elihu suddenly appears without introduction, delivers his speeches without interruption (32–37), and is thereafter ignored. The fact that his speeches can be dropped from the book without disturbing its structure, indicates that he is in no way integral to its conception, and despite the effort of Cornill and Budde to defend this section, it may be regarded as an attempted solution of the problem of the book by a later writer, who failed to perceive the author's real message.

The second Yahweh speech (40^6–41^{34}) is also commonly regarded as an accretion. Cheyne and Van Hoonacker, indeed, rejected both Yahweh speeches, but this involves injury to the structure and plan of the book. It is asserted that these speeches are inconsistent with the epilogue, since here Job is rebuked, while there he is pronounced in the right. But, as Gray observes, the difference of judgement is not on the same issue. He is vindicated in relation to the Satan's charge, made in the prologue, but he is rebuked for his ignorant criticism of God's ways. The second speech of Yahweh, however, with its lengthy descriptions of Behemoth and Leviathan, contributes nothing material to the work, and falls below the level of brilliance of the first speech. Moreover, as Peake says, after Job has unreservedly thrown up his case ($40^{4f.}$), the second speech of Yahweh comes perilously near nagging.

Chap. 28 is also generally recognized to be an addition, whose affinities are with the first section of the Book of Proverbs. If Job had already reached this insight into the limitations of human achievement, compared with the inscrutable wisdom of God, he had already reached his goal, and the ironical tone of Yahweh's speech would be uncalled for. On the other hand, it is impossible to attribute the chapter to any of Job's friends.

The loss from the book would appear to be in the third round of the dialogue. The scheme of the dialogue is as follows : following an opening soliloquy of Job's, each of the three friends speaks in turn, and after each speech Job replies ; a second cycle follows the first, and a third is begun, but not completed before Job makes his final soliloquy. It is probable that the third cycle was once complete, but that part of it has been lost, and part misplaced, so that $27^{7\text{-}10.\ 13\text{-}23}$, which perhaps once belonged to Zophar's third speech, are now attributed to Job.

The complete integration of the book then left is clear. The dialogue deals with the question of innocent suffering, which the friends, fortified by the current orthodoxy, hold to be unthinkable, since suffering is the proof of divine disfavour. Job, however, maintains his integrity, and insists that there is a problem. But the explanation of his suffering cannot be deduced from the human side. The intellectual problem therefore remains, and the book in no sense claims to solve it. It declares that there is an explanation, though the sufferer cannot discern it. In the case of Job it is given to the reader in the prologue, which is vital to the book. It was essential that the reader should know that Job was genuinely innocent, and equally so that Job should never know the cause of his suffering. Had he been granted a knowledge which is denied to other sufferers, the book could have brought no message to them. What the explanation is in any given case is not ascertainable by the sufferer, but, as in the case of Job, there is a reason hidden in the heart of God, and worthy of God. God had, as it were, staked Himself upon Job, and in his suffering he was not merely vindicating himself, but vindicating God. It is therefore wrong to impugn God's justice on the basis of our ignorance, and it is for this that Job is condemned in Yahweh's speech, which is the climax of the book, and whose burden is that the human mind cannot comprehend God, and therefore humble trust is wiser than the effort to comprehend. Hence, though reason cannot solve the problem, faith can transcend it. This carries the further consequence that, since suffering may be innocent, and not the mark of divine disfavour, communion with God is not necessarily broken by it, and faith can maintain that communion. It is this point that Job reaches, resting in God, even in his suffering. The epilogue then comes, not as the anti-climax so often supposed, but as the inevitable sequel to the prologue. It belongs less to the message of the book than to its artistry. God's confidence in Job is vindicated, and the Satan discomfited. Clearly, then, the trial must end, and the suffering, which is the form of the trial, must terminate. Job's renewed prosperity is not the reward of his righteousness, and the giving away of the case to the friends, but the sign that the test is finished.

We may then accept the work, shorn of the passages noted, as a unity. It is generally recognized to be a product of the post-exilic age, and is probably to be dated *circa* 400 B.C. In recent years a Babylonian text, sometimes called the *Baby-lonian Job*, has come to light, and it has been suggested that it provided the source of the Book of Job. But the Babylonian sufferer, while unconscious of the sin that has caused his suffering, is far from certain that he has not sinned. This is in marked contrast with the rectitude of Job, announced in the prologue, and confirmed by his own conscience.

4. *The Song of Songs.* The Song of Songs is ascribed in its title to Solomon, but on linguistic grounds alone it is certain that the work is post-exilic, though its precise date cannot be fixed. Some would date it *c.* 400 B.C., and others somewhat later. No book in the Bible has given rise to greater varieties of interpretation, and there is no agreement even as to the class of literature to which it belongs.

The traditional rabbinical interpretation regarded it as an allegory, treating under the figures of human love of God's dealings with Israel. This view is still defended by some Christian scholars (Joüon, *Cantique des Cantiques*, 1909, and Ricciotti, *Il Cantico dei Cantici*, 1928). In general, however, Christian exegesis has traced the dealings of Christ with His Church in all the imagery of the work, and the most absurdly fanciful interpretations have been indulged in.

In modern times this view has been widely abandoned, and has been replaced in many works by the view that the book is a dialogue or drama. One school, following Delitzsch, found in it two main characters, Solomon and the Shulamite, who was wooed and won by the king. Another, following Ewald, found three principal characters, Solomon, the Shula-mite maiden, and her rustic lover. According to this view, the maiden resisted the royal advances, and was finally allowed to return to her true love. A further development of this view adds a chorus, and in this form it has been recently presented afresh by Pouget and Guitton (*Cantique des Cantiques*, 1935). The chief difficulty about this view is the absence of rubrics, which the interpreters must liberally supply.

The most popular view for many years has been that the book consists of a collection of love lyrics, or marriage songs. In 1873 Wetzstein published a study of modern marriage customs in Syria, and in the light of these customs, which may well have altered little in two thousand years, Budde inter-preted the Song. It is customary for the wedding to be celebrated for seven days, during which the bride and bridegroom are crowned, and songs are sung in their honour. Hence it has been supposed that in the Song we have a selection from a single cycle of such songs. A few writers have thought that the selection consists not only of marriage songs, but more generally of love poems (cf. *Journal of Theological Studies*, xxxviii, pp. 337 ff.).

The latest view, somewhat along the lines of recent work on other books, finds in it a liturgy, but this time a liturgy of the Adonis-Tammuz cult. This view is associated especially with the name of Meek (*American Journal of Sem. Lang.*, xxxix. 1 ff. and *The Song of Songs : a Symposium*, 1924), and is adopted by Wittekindt (*Das Hohe Lied*, 1925). The Adonis-Tammuz cult is known to have been widely prevalent in Syria, and to have existed within Israel. On Meek's view the Shulamite was a temple prostitute, representing the goddess, while her partner represented the god. The rites culminated in their marriage and union, and were supposed to result in fertility in Nature. Meek holds that the ancient practice has been reinterpreted in the Song, which has been absorbed into the religion of Yahwism. In view of the strong opposition of the prophets to all that belonged to the fertility cult, it would be surprising for the liturgy of that cult to be brought into the corpus of sacred literature in post-exilic days. Moreover, while it is said to have been reinterpreted and absorbed into Yahwism, it singularly lacks any clear trace of the Yahwism it was made to serve. It must be allowed, however, that the Song does contain allusions to the Adonis-Tammuz practices, though this does not mean that it is a cult poem. For since it is agreed that the Adonis-Tammuz rites were deeply imbedded in popular superstition, it might well be that essentially sensuous poems should contain allusions to those rites (cf. *Journal of Royal Asiatic Society*, 1938, pp. 251 ff.).

5. *Ruth.* The Book of Ruth tells a simple story, laid in the age of the Judges, and to that fact it owes its transfer in the Greek Canon to follow Judges. It presents no history of public events, and instead of revealing the turmoil and strife that fill the Book of Judges, gives a picture of humble village life. While the author has doubtless worked with old traditions, the book is of post-exilic origin. For the opening verse suggests that the author was familiar with the deuteronomistic editor's Book of Judges, and the way in which old customs are explained implies that they were now obsolete. In Deut. 25[9] it is laid down that the brother-in-law who declines the duty of levirate marriage, has his shoe publicly drawn off by the wronged woman, who spits in his face. While in Ruth 4[9]

it is not the brother-in-law, but a more distant next-of-kin, who declines the duty, the drawing off of the shoe figures in the ceremony. But here he draws off his own shoe, and there is no spitting, nor is the woman present. Either we have a later modification of the custom, or, as is more probable, the modification is due to the more distant relationship of the *Goel*. In either case, since the custom was clearly already obsolete, we are carried down beyond the age of Deuteronomy.

Many scholars believe the book was written in the period of Nehemiah and Ezra, to protest against their attitude to mixed marriages by its quiet reminder that even David had a Moabite ancestress. Seilin, who formerly dated the book in the age of Zerubbabel, now accepts this view. While this date may well be correct, it is doubtful if a polemic purpose inspired the book. The closing genealogy appears to be a later addition.

6. *Lamentations.* In the Book of Lamentations are five separate poems, of which the first four are acrostic. While the fifth consists of the same number of verses as the letters of the alphabet, it is not acrostic. Moreover, its rhythm differs from that of the others.

Traditionally the book has been assigned to Jeremiah, but the reasons against this view are decisive. For (*a*) the statement in 2[9] suggests that the author was not one of the prophets ; (*b*) 4[7] suggests that the writer had vainly looked for help from Egypt, whereas Jeremiah had consistently declared that hope to be vain ; (*c*) 5[7] presents a view against which Jeremiah had explicitly protested (Jer. 31[29f.]) ; (*d*) the expectation of trouble as about to fall on the Chaldæans (3[64-66]) is in disagreement with Jeremiah's point of view ; (*e*) the linguistic évidence is against it.

It is unlikely, indeed, that all the poems are from one hand, for (*a*) the order of the letters of the alphabet differs in chap. 1 from that of chaps. 2-4 ; (*b*) from a literary standpoint there are differences in the quality of the chapters, chaps. 2 and 4 being superior to the others, and chap. 3, which appears to have been written with Jeremiah in mind, being the poorest.

There is no reason to doubt that the poems date from the period of the Exile, save perhaps chap. 3, which may be somewhat later, and chaps. 2 and 4, which may be from a single author, would seem to have been written by an eye-witness of the fall of Jerusalem.

7. *Ecclesiastes.* Traditionally the Book of Ecclesiastes, like the Song of Songs, has been attributed to Solomon, since it purports to have been written by a king who is the son of

David. Luther rejected the tradition, which is now completely abandoned. For (a) the author frequently writes from the standpoint of the subject, condemning the iniquities of the regime under which he lives (3^{16}, 4^1) ; (b) he appears to be living in a province of a great empire, and warns against the activity of the common spy (10^{20}) ; (c) the anarchy that appears to prevail in the land (4^{13-16}, 10^{16-20}) suggests either the last century of Persian rule or the period of the later Seleucids and Ptolemies ; (d) the linguistic evidence is so strong that Delitzsch could say : " If the book of Koheleth be as old as Solomon, then there can be no history of the Hebrew language." It was probably written in the Greek period, in the third century B.C. Oesterley and Robinson place it c. 250 B.C., while some editors, following Friedländer's suggestion that the reference in 9^{13-18} is to the Roman siege of Syracuse, would place it at the end of the century.

Concerning the integrity of the book, widely differing views have been held. Its inner contradictions led Herder to see in it a dialogue between two persons, while Cornill thought it reflected the varying moods of a single person. Others have assigned the book to more than one author, Siegfried finding no less than eight hands. M'Neile argued that the original work had been interpolated by two hands, the one, whom he called the Hasid interpolator, introducing the glosses breathing orthodox religious conviction, and the other, whom he called the Hokmah interpolator, adding the maxims of worldly wisdom. Recently Galling (Zeitschrift f. d. alttest. Wiss., 1932, pp. 276 ff.) has argued on fresh lines for the unity of the work, suggesting that it contains the casual jottings of the author, who sometimes quoted a current maxim to add his own mordant observation as a corrective.

A question much discussed in recent years is the relation of Ecclesiastes to foreign thought. Langdon has argued for Babylonian influence, but more commonly Greek influence is discerned. Sellin finds the influence of Epicurean, Stoic, and Heracleitean philosophy confusedly mixed, while Ranston (Eccles. and the Early Gk. Wisdom Lit., 1925) argues for the influence of the early Gnomic writers, Hesiod and Theognis. Others, including M'Neile, have denied the alleged Greek influence, while Galling explains much in the book from Egyptian influence.

8. *Esther*. The Book of Esther enjoyed extraordinary popularity amongst the Jews, but its origin is very obscure. In the ὕμνος πατέρων in Ecclus. 44–49, there is no reference to Esther or Mordecai, though most of the greater heroes of

Old Testament story figure in it.   From this it is generally
regarded as probable that the book is later than Ecclesiasticus
(c. 180 B.C.). On the other hand, it is earlier than 2 Maccabees
(dated by Oesterley and Eissfeldt about the beginning of the
Christian era), where there is a reference (15³⁶) to " Mordecai's
day." We may perhaps date Esther c. 150 B.C.

It is impossible to maintain the historicity of the story.
Ahasuerus is generally identified with Xerxes (485–465 B.C.),
and since Mordecai is represented as having been carried into
captivity in 597 B.C., he would be somewhat elderly nearly
120 years later. Moreover, Xerxes did not have a queen named
Esther.   Hoschander (*Esther in the Light of History*, 1923)
has recently transferred the story to the reign of Artaxerxes II.
(404–359 B.C.), and maintained that a basis of history underlies it.   The book shows acquaintance with Persian customs,
and its author had access to good sources of information.

Cornill finds in it a reflection back into history of the
Maccabæan struggle.   This seems unlikely, though the fact
of that struggle may have influenced the author to present
in a Jewish dress older legends gathering round the feast of
Purim, and to give a nationalistic significance to the feast.

Most scholars explain the book from eastern mythology.
The Feast of Purim has a non-Jewish name, and was probably
of foreign origin.   Zimmern finds its source in the Babylonian
New Year's Festival, in honour of Marduk (=Mordecai),
when the gods gathered in an assembly, or *puḥru* (whence
Purim).   Jensen, on the other hand, connects Esther with
the Babylonian goddess Ishtar, Haman with the Elamite god
Humman, Vashti with an Elamite goddess Mashti, and
resolves the story into the presentation in the dress of history
of a mythological conflict between the Babylonian and the
Elamite gods.   Lagarde, again, looked to the Persian festival
of Farwardigan for the origin of Purim, and Meissner modified
this by pointing to the Persian festival of Sakaia, in which
elements of Farwardigan were combined with elements from
the Babylonian New Year Festival.   It is clear that no final
answer to the question of the sources of the book can yet be
given.

9. *Daniel*.   The Book of Daniel is partly in Hebrew and
partly in Aramaic.   The first six chapters contain narratives
about Daniel, and the last six Daniel's visions.   But the
change of language does not coincide with the change in
character, the Aramaic section being 2⁴ᵇ–7²⁸.

That the book is not the work of one who lived in the
sixth century B.C. is certain.   For (*a*) there was no siege and

capture of Jerusalem in the third year of Jehoiakim (1^1) ; (*b*) Belshazzar was neither the son of Nebuchadrezzar, nor the king of Babylon, but the son of Nabonidus, the last king of the neo-Babylonian Empire ; he was, however, charged for many years with the administration of Babylon, while his father dwelt in Têma ; (*c*) Darius the Mede is an unhistorical figure, for whom history allows no room, since Cyrus annexed the empire of Nabonidus after having previously annexed the Median kingdom ; (*d*) the use of the word " Chaldæans " in a non-ethnic sense, to denote a learned, priestly class, though amply paralleled in later classical authors, is unknown in the sixth century, while it is inconsistent with all that we know of the exclusiveness of the Babylonian priesthood that a Hebrew should have been admitted to its membership, and inconsistent with the rigid loyalty of character ascribed to Daniel that he should have consented to become such a heathen priest.

To these decisive considerations others might be added, such as the position of the book in the final division of the Canon ; the non-mention of Daniel in the ὕμνος πατέρων in Ecclus. 44–49 ; and the character of the language. For the Aramaic sections are not in Babylonian Aramaic of the sixth century B.C., but in Aramaic which is later than that of Ezra, which is itself later than that of the fifth century Aramaic papyri from Elephantine, while the Hebrew, which is inferior to the Aramaic in style, is late. In both parts there are Persian loan-words, suggesting by their number a long period of Persian influence, and in the Aramaic there are a few Greek loan-words.

The interest of the book culminates in the reign of Antiochus Epiphanes, and in his persecution of the Jews, which became acute in 168 B.C. In chaps. 2 and 7 the interest is centred in the fourth kingdom, which is clearly the same in both cases, while the *little horn* of $7^{8.\ 25}$ is the same as the *little horn* of $8^{9ff.}$, to which is attached an interpretation that definitely locates it in the Greek period that followed Alexander. So also chap. 9 culminates in a similar attack upon the Jews, while the vision of the last three chapters enters with such detail into the history of the Seleucids and the Ptolemies as to be an important historical source for the period, and it, too, culminates in the reign of Antiochus Epiphanes, whose death, however, did not take place in Palestine (11^{45}), but in Persia. The phrase " abomination of desolation," or the like, is found in 8^{13}, 9^{27}, 11^{31}, 12^{11}, where the reference is doubtless the same, binding the chapters together once more in their point of climax. In 1 Macc. 1[54] the heathen altar which Antiochus set up in Jerusalem is called " the abomination of desolation." The Temple was desecrated, and so lay for three years, after which it was cleansed and reconsecrated. It is probably to this period that the half week (9[27]), and the time and times and half a time (7[25] ; cf. 12[7]) refer.

In view of the inaccuracy of the knowledge of the sixth century and the remarkable accuracy of the knowledge of the third and early part of the second centuries, it has been generally held that the book was a pseudepigraph, written in the time of Antiochus Epiphanes. That the accuracy of its knowledge falls short of the death of Antiochus, which took place in 164 B.C., has led scholars to date it with precision just before that date. The purpose of the book was then to hearten the persecuted people, and to promise them deliverance. All the other considerations noted are consistent with this date, as also is the theology of the book, where we find the resurrection of the just and unjust expected (12[2]), and a developed angelology revealed.

While all of these positions are still challenged by upholders of traditional views (cf. my *Darius the Mede*, 1935, and *Journal of Theol. Stud.* xxxii. pp. 12 ff.), in recent years they are being modified by an increasing number of scholars, who hold that the book is composite. Many years ago Meinhold held the Aramaic part to be extracted by the author of the visions from an older work, while Dalman held the stories and the visions to come from two different hands, a redactor combining the two works by translating the beginning of one into Hebrew, and the beginning of the other into Aramaic. Torrey advanced a similar view, save that he believed chaps. 7–12 were written definitely to be attached to 1–6, and the author of 7–12 translated 1[1]–2[4a] into Hebrew and wrote 7 in Aramaic. Kent and Montgomery follow Torrey, who dated the stories in the middle of the third century B.C. Baumgartner goes further, and assigns the stories to the Persian period, while Welch holds that chaps. 1–6 and probably 7 had a Babylonian origin, and had already taken literary shape before they were taken over by the writer of our present work. Hölscher, in an important article which has greatly influenced all subsequent discussion (*Theologische Stud. u. Krit.*, xcii. pp. 113 ff.) holds 1–6 to belong to the third century B.C., with 7 as a later appendix. This work was glossed in the Maccabæan age, and 8–12 were then added to it. Sellin similarly holds 1–7 to be an older work, with Maccabæan interpolations, and 8–12 to be Maccabæan, while Haller is in substantial agreement with Hölscher, save that he holds 7 to be the oldest chapter in the book. There is thus no agreement amongst those who divide the book as to where chap. 7 belongs, and it is held to be glossed or not according as it is connected with the first or second part. I believe all of these views to be mistaken, and still adhere to the unity of authorship (cf. *The Expository Times*, xlvii. pp. 216 ff.).

10. *Chronicles-Ezra-Nehemiah.* In the Hebrew MSS. the two books of Chronicles are combined, as also are Ezra and Nehemiah, but the latter work stands after the former, which closes the Canon. Originally all seem to have formed a single work, whose second part was probably added to the sacred collection before the first, which covered the ground of Samuel and Kings, and was therefore less essential. The reasons for the view that we have a single work are : (*a*) the concluding verses of Chronicles are identical with the opening verses of Ezra, but the passage is mutilated in Chronicles ; (*b*) the style of those parts of the two works which come from the editor, as distinct from his sources, is the same ; (*c*) the outlook and interests of the editor are identical in the two works, and include a love of genealogies and statistics, and veneration for the Temple and all that pertains to its service.

The date of the work cannot therefore be earlier than the period of Ezra and Nehemiah. This conclusion is reinforced by other considerations : Thus (*a*) the work is written under the influence of P, and the history is frequently rewritten in its light, *e.g.* the Carites of 2 Kings 11 are changed into Levites in 2 Chron. 23, and similarly in 1 Chron. 15 Levites are supplied to carry the Ark into Jerusalem, and the first failure explained by their absence then, whereas 2 Sam. 6 does not mention them on either occasion ; (*b*) not only is the account of Chronicles carried down to the reign of Cyrus (537 B.C.), but the genealogy of 1 Chron. 3 carries the Davidic line down to the sixth (LXX eleventh) generation after Zerubbabel (*c.* 520 B.C.) ; (*c*) in Neh. 12[11, 22], the high-priestly line is carried down to Jaddua, who was high-priest in the time of Alexander ; (*d*) in 1 Chron. 29[7] is mentioned the *daric*, a coin which was perhaps (but cf. my *Darius the Mede*, pp. 45 f.) first coined in the reign of Darius Hystaspis, and which was certainly not circulated in Palestine until post-exilic times ; (*e*) the references to " the king of Persia " (Ezra 1[1], 3[7], 4[3], 7[1]) imply that the Persian empire no longer exists (in Haggai, Zechariah, the *sources* of Ezra-Nehemiah, and the fifth-century Aramaic papyri, we find simply " the king "). We are therefore carried down to a date not earlier than 300 B.C. for the work.

The reader of the work would suppose that Ezra and
Nehemiah were contemporaries, but the view is rapidly gaining
ground that whereas Nehemiah belongs to the reign of
Artaxerxes I., Ezra belongs to that of Artaxerxes II., and first
came to Jerusalem in 397 B.C. The reasons for this are :
(a) the absence of reference to either in the other's memoirs,
and the fact that on the rare occasions when both names stand
in a single context, there is independent reason to suspect the
text ; (b) the fact that Ezra finds the wall already built (Ezra
9⁹) ; (c) the fact that whereas Nehemiah was contemporary
with the high-priest Eliashib (Neh. 3¹), Ezra was contemporary with Johanan (Ezra 10⁶), the grandson of Eliashib
(Neh. 12¹¹· ²²) ; (d) the evidence of the Elephantine papyri that
Johanan was high-priest in 408 B.C. ; (e) the evidence of
the Elephantine papyri that whereas the Elephantine Jews
sent to Jerusalem to àsk the high-priest's aid, they simultaneously sent to Samaria to ask the help of the sons of
Sanballat, the governor—probably because Sanballat, the
adversary of Nehemiah, was now aged, and administration
was actually in his sons' hands.

For the period of the divided monarchy, the Chronicler
ignores the northern kingdom, and he also deals scantily with
Saul. For him the Davidic dynasty is alone legitimate. Nor
does he mention David's sin or family misfortunes, or the
succession trouble on Solomon's accession. The history is
treated with great freedom to suit his interests, and little
historical value can be attached to statements on his unsup-
ported authority when they appear to accord with his favourite
ideas. He may well, however, have had access to good sources
of information now lost to us, and there is a tendency to-day
to credit his narratives, where they do not appear to be dictated
by his theories.

Of his sources, in addition to our books of (a) Samuel and
(b) Kings, and probably (c) Isaiah, he names several in
Chronicles, but it is probable that the same work is separately
named for the several sections, from the prophets who appear
in it, and for most of Chronicles his extra-Biblical sources
did not exceed two, (d) the " Midrash of the Book of Kings,"
and (e) the " Midrash of Iddo the Seer " (so Oesterley and
Robinson, though some would identify these two). For Ezra-
Nehemiah he used (f) Memoirs of Nehemiah and (g) Memoirs
of Ezra, sometimes quoting verbatim, most probably, but
sometimes working over his extracts. In the Aramaic sections
in Ezra he quotes documents which purport to be official
documents sent to, or from, the Persian monarchs. These

doubtless rest on (*h*) an older Aramaic source. Further, he had access to (*i*) Temple records, and trustworthy genealogical lists.

It should be noted that Welch has recently (*Post-Exilic Judaism*, 1935) denied the unity of Chronicles-Ezra-Nehemiah, assigning Chronicles, save 1 Chron. 1–9, to *c.* 520 B.C., and holding that it was written under the influence of D, and accusing the author of Ezra-Nehemiah of perverting valuable historical sources by his wrong arrangement of them. He assigns Neh. 10 to shortly after 586 B.C., and denies any Return under Cyrus, but maintains a Return under Darius 1. Ezra he reduces to a man without originality, incapable of introducing a new law, and Nehemiah becomes a mere wall-builder. An even more radical criticism is associated with Torrey (*Comp. of Ezra-Nehem.*, 1896, and *Ezra Studies*, 1910), who maintains that Ezra is a purely fictitious creation of the Chronicler, and that there was no Return of the Exiles. A less violent challenge to the usual view is presented by von Rad (*Das Geschichtsbild des chronistischen Werkes*, 1930), who would modify it by finding evidence of two hands, the one under the influence of D, and the other under that of P. Oesterley and Robinson accept this view, as also does Sellin.

BIBLIOGRAPHY

J. A. Bewer, *The Literature of the Old Testament in its Historical Development*, 2nd ed., 1933.

S. A. Cook, *The Old Testament : a Reinterpretation*, 1936.

S. R. Driver, *Introduction to the Literature of the Old Testament*, 9th ed., 1913.

G. B. Gray, *A Critical Introduction to the Old Testament*, 1913.

W. O. E. Oesterley and T. H. Robinson, *An Introduction to the Books of the Old Testament*, 1934.

H. Ranston, *The Old Testament Wisdom Books*, 1930.

H. Wheeler Robinson, *The Old Testament : its Making and Meaning*, 1937.

H. Wheeler Robinson, ed. by, *Record and Revelation*, 1938.

D. C. Simpson, *Pentateuchal Criticism*, 2nd ed., 1924.

IV. THE APOCRYPHA AND PSEUDEPIGRAPHA

I

BEFORE dealing with the individual books belonging, respectively, to these two bodies of literature, there are some technical terms which demand some notice.

The Hebrew word *ganaz*, in its primary sense, means " to store up " ; it then came to have the meaning " to store up in secret," and thus " to hide," especially in reference to the withholding of secret wisdom from all but the initiated. Ultimately, though not until after the fixing of the Hebrew Canon, it was used in reference to books, in the sense of " to withdraw from use." The term *ganaz* was applied to un- canonical books only. There was one exception when it was used in reference to canonical books, but in this case it was not to the books as such, but to damaged copies, or to those on which the text had been rubbed out through use ; these were " hidden " in the sense that they were stored up in the *Genizah* (from the same root), a small chamber attached to the ancient synagogues for this purpose. It is probable that *ganaz* was not applied to the books of the Apocrypha, with the exception of 2(4) *Esdras*, for the Rabbis regarded these as containing edifying, orthodox teaching ; the reading of these books was permitted.

In the next place, we have the Greek term *apokryphos* (" hidden "). This was applied originally to books in a good sense, books which were held to contain esoteric truths to be communicated only to the initiated ; and kept hidden from the outside world. Thus *apokryphos* corresponds with the Hebrew *ganaz*.

It is a question of some importance to consider why and when the term " apocryphal " came to be applied to books not belonging to the Hebrew Canon. In the Christian Church Origen used the term in reference to the pseudepigraphic books, but not in reference to those of the Apocrypha. It was not until the fourth century, and in the Greek Church, that a distinction was first made between the books of the Hebrew

Canon and the books of the Apocrypha, which were, however, regarded as edifying and worthy to be read. They were not called apocryphal, this term being still used in reference to the pseudepigraphic books. In due course the Latin Church followed the example of the Greek Church ; Jerome (d. A.D. 420) took the lead here ; he made a distinction between *libri canonici* and *libri ecclesiastici*, the latter applying to the books of the Apocrypha ; but to these he applied the term " apocryphal," and he was the first to do so. But as hitherto this term had been applied only to the pseudepigraphic books, Jerome's new use of " apocryphal " did not meet with general approval. Augustine (d. A.D. 430), for example, uses " apocryphal " in the old sense (*De Civ. Dei*, xv. 23). By degrees, however, Jerome's use of the term became general, and has continued ever since. Thus it has come about that the sacred books not included in the Hebrew Canon are known as the " Apocrypha " ; though there is not, nor has there ever been, anything " hidden " about them or their teaching.

One or two other technical terms remain to be considered. Uncanonical books of a sacred character came, in course of time, to be divided by the Jewish religious authorities into two categories, though the dividing line varied at first according to the opinions of different teachers. These two categories consisted, on the one hand, of books which contained orthodox teaching, but which, for reasons into which we cannot go now, were not admitted into the Canon. Roughly speaking, these consisted of the books of the Apocrypha. The other category included books which for one reason or another were looked upon as heretical. They were designated *Sepharim hachizonim*, " Outside books," the latter word being equivalent to the Greek οἱ ἔξω, an expression which in the New Testament is used of " those that are without," *i.e.* outside the community of the faithful (cf. Mark 4[11] ; 1 Cor. 5[12, 13] ; Col. 4[5] ; 1 Thess. 4[12]). In Jewish writings *Sepharim hachizonim* are synonymous with *Siphre haminim*, " the books of the heretics." Among the large number of books included in this category were those known by the term *Ha-Gilyonim*, from the root meaning to " uncover " or " reveal " ; this refers to the " Apocalypses," *i.e.* the Apocalyptic literature, of which the Pseudepigrapha consist, in the main. The term Pseudepigrapha (" False titles "), though expressing a truth, is very unsatisfactory, as it gives no indication of the contents of the books included under it. At the same time, it must be added that the term Apocrypha is even worse, as that contains a positive untruth.

II

There is no shadow of doubt that the books of the Apocrypha, both from the religious and literary point of view, stand on a much higher plane than those entitled Pseudepigrapha. We shall, therefore, devote more attention to the former than to the latter.

In giving what must inevitably be a very brief account of these books, we shall attempt to take them in their chronological order, realizing, however, that, in some cases, there are differences of opinion. Exact dates are, in most cases, out of the question, especially as in most of the writings there is but little that gives indications of date ; but, as a rule, it is possible to state the period to which a book, or its component parts, belongs.

Epistle of Jeremy. There are reasons for the contention that the earliest piece in the Apocrypha is the Epistle of Jeremy. This purports to have been written by the prophet Jeremiah to those of his people who should be carried away captive to Babylon. Its central theme is the futility of idols, the worship of which, the prophet fears, his people may be guilty of when they are in the land of exile ; against this they are warned (v.[5]). It is possible that a date may be inferred from the words of v.[3] : " So when ye be come into Babylon, ye shall remain there many years, and for a long season, even for seven generations ; and after that I will bring you out peaceably from thence." The writer must have had some purpose in making this statement, and it may well be that he intended it as an indication of the time at which he was writing. A generation, according to the Old Testament, was forty years ; seven generations would be 280 years ; so the end of the Exile took place, according to the writer, in 317 B.C. or 306 B.C., the dates of the two occasions of leading into exile being 597 B.C. and 586 B.C. Either of these dates for the end of the Exile is, of course, absurd ; the writer knew that well enough ; hence the probability that he made his statement with a view to indicating the time at which he wrote. Towards the end of the fourth century B.C. would be appropriate for the Epistle, since during this period the Jews of the Dispersion were attracted, as throughout the Greek period, by alien cults.

There is nothing to show the country of the writer, but there is no reason to doubt that it was actually intended for the Jews in the Babylonian Dispersion.

Most authorities hold that the Epistle was written in Greek ;

Ball has, however, given convincing reasons for the view that it was originally written in Hebrew.

1 Esdras. Next in date, probably about a century later, is 1 Esdras (in the Vulgate 3 Esdras), known also as the " Greek Ezra," in order to distinguish it from the more literal Greek translation of the canonical Ezra-Nehemiah, designated Esdras β' in the Septuagint. It is evident that this book, as we now have it, is not in its original form ; this is suggested by the fact that both its beginning and end are very abrupt ; it is also possible that the section 3^1-5^6, which gives the narrative of an intellectual competition between three members of Darius's bodyguard, did not originally form part of the book ; this section is peculiar to it, and seems to have been inserted in order to explain how Zerubbabel, one of the three and the winner of the competition, obtained permission to go to Jerusalem for the purpose of rebuilding the Temple. The book, for the most part, corresponds with that of Ezra and partly with Nehemiah. But in one respect it is manifestly superior to these, namely, between the books of Ezra and Nehemiah there is a gap in the history of twelve years ; but the " Greek Ezra " makes what is said in Neh. 8 follow immediately after the end of Ezra ; in this way the Ezra narrative is continued without the break occasioned by the insertion of Neh. 1^1-7^{72a} ; this makes the historical sequence logical. Less important, but noteworthy, is the fact that in the " Greek Ezra " there is no mention of Nehemiah in the section on the reading of the Law (9^{37-55}), as is the case in Neh. 8^9. Thus, according to the " Greek Ezra," Nehemiah does not co-operate with Ezra on this important occasion. This is one of the many arguments which can be adduced to show that Ezra and Nehemiah were not contemporaries.

In other respects the historical sequence of events as recorded in this book leaves much to be desired ; the writer's main object seems to have been to explain how it was that the Temple came to be rebuilt ; and its cult re-inaugurated.

A close comparison between 1(3) Esdras and the corresponding portions in Ezra and Nehemiah shows that the former was not dependent on the latter. There are good grounds for the view that our book is an older translation of a Hebrew-Aramaic original ; excluding, however, the section on the competition between the members of Darius's bodyguard, which is Greek in origin.

In its present Greek form 1(3) Esdras was, in all probability, written in Egypt.

Tobit. A book of a very different character, but belonging

approximately to the same period (*c.* 200 B.C.), is Tobit. A
point of particular interest about this book is that it offers
a good illustration of borrowing from alien sources, which can
be paralleled in the case of some other Jewish writings belonging to the Greek period. The borrowed material will be seen
to correspond with some of the main themes of the book.
These themes consist partly of thoroughly Jewish, and partly
of quite non-Jewish, elements. Thus, the strict observance
of the Law is often enjoined, which in practice consists, among
other things, of deeds of kindness ; the giving of alms is
especially pointed to. The observance of the feasts, the
offering of first-fruits and tithes, the rendering of the priestly
dues, are all insisted on. The support of widows, orphans,
and proselytes, is also enjoined. These are all good deeds,
the fulfilling of the Law ; and their inculcation plays a marked
part in the book. But in addition to these strongly Jewish
traits, there are three outstanding themes which have been
borrowed from alien sources ; these are : the faithful travelling
companion ($5^{3ff.}$, etc.) ;   the burial of corpses left derelict
($1^{17. 18}$, $2^{3. 4}$, $12^{12. 14}$) ; and the overcoming of the demon
($3^{8. 17}$, $6^{7. 14. 17}$, 8^3). There are, further, the references to
Achiacharus ($1^{21. 22}$, 2^{10}, 11^{17}, 14^{10}), which show that the
writer was acquainted with the story and Wisdom of Ahikar ;
his references to it take for granted that his readers were
well acquainted with this story. The themes mentioned were
taken from current popular literature ; they have been transmitted through the ages, though it is not possible to trace
the steps in the transmission ; but in the ancient Egyptian
Tractate of Khons some traces of them are to be discerned.
The stories containing them must have enjoyed world-wide
popularity, for they have come down to us in a combined
form in the German folk-tale called, "Der gute Gerhard and
die dankbaren Toten," a folk-tale which exists in many
countries, though the forms vary.

Among the various versions of Tobit the Armenian ap-
proximates most closely to these three themes. Two of
them, those of the activity of the demon Asmodæus, and the
faithful travelling companion, who in the Tobit form appears
ultimately as an angel, Raphael, mark the influence of Persian
demonology and angelology.

The Book of Tobit was almost certainly originally written
in Hebrew. There are no sufficient reasons for doubting
unity of authorship. Egypt is most likely to have been the
country of its origin.

Ecclesiasticus. The Book of Ecclesiasticus must be pronounced the gem of the Apocrypha. Written by " Ben Sira," living in Jerusalem, soon after 200 B.C., in Hebrew, it was translated into Greek by his grandson, in Egypt, in 132 B.C. The book has had many titles assigned to it in early days. Taking all the evidence into consideration it may be asserted that the original title ran : " The Instruction," or " The Wisdom of Jesus the son of Sira." The title " Ecclesiasticus " is usually supposed to be due to its having been regarded by the Early Church as the " Church Book " *par excellence* among the *Libri Ecclesiastici, i.e.* among those books which, though not admitted into the Canon, were of an edifying character, and meet to be read in Church. This implies, however, that the book was not reckoned as canonical by the Early Church, which is not the case, for it has been regarded as Scripture from the earliest days. There is a good deal to be said in favour of the view that the title " Ecclesiasticus " was originally formed on the model of the title " Ecclesiastes," given to the Hebrew book *Qoheleth* (" Preacher "). It will be granted that Ben Sira was essentially a preacher. It should also be pointed out that Ecclesiasticus did not occupy the position of importance that the Book of Wisdom did in the Early Church (see below).

A large portion, about two-thirds, of the Hebrew of Ecclesiasticus has been discovered since 1896, when the first fragment was found in the " Genizah " of an ancient synagogue in Cairo ; since then further fragments have come to light, the most recent having been discovered in 1931. One important outcome of the discovery of these MSS. is that they witness to the existence of two Hebrew recensions of the book. A similar phenomenon had previously been found to be the case with the Greek Version ; here a secondary recension exists, which owed its origin to the desire to make the book more acceptable to later orthodox, *i.e.* Pharisaic, circles. This secondary Greek version is now seen to depend upon the secondary Hebrew recension. The special interest of the existence of this latter lies in the fact that it witnesses to its popularity among the Jews in spite of its not having been included in the Hebrew Canon.

The Song of the Three Holy Children, which we have next to consider, is an addition, inserted after Dan. 3^{23}, in the Septuagint. It consists of three quite independent pieces : " The Prayer of Azarias," " The Hymn of the Three Children," and a narrative portion. These are the titles given in the ecclesiastical canticles added as an appendix to the Psalter in MSS. of the Septuagint—the narrative portion does not, of course, figure there ; but these titles do not occur in the text of the Book of Daniel either in the Septuagint or in any of the versions ; in all of these the additions are treated as a unity. It is possible that, of these three additions, the narrative portion may at one time have formed part of the text of the canonical Daniel. But this cannot be postulated of the two other additions ; they have no bearing on the narrative itself, and come in quite inappropriately ; and there is no point of contact between them and the context in which they stand in the Septuagint. It is not difficult, however, to see why the additions (apart from the narrative portion, which may be original) were made ; the Prayer was added in order to show that one of the faithful, Azarias, rather than the pagan king, Nebuchadrezzar, was the first to recognize and bless the God of Israel (see Dan. $3^{28.\ 29}$) ; it was, further, intended to show that the deliverance from the fire was in answer to prayer. The Hymn, doubtless belonging to some collection of hymns, was added as an expression of praise and gratitude to the Creator of all. The similarity in various details between the Hymn and Ps. 148 may be noted.

That all three additions were originally written in Hebrew hardly admits of doubt ; Kuhl's retranslation of the Greek into Hebrew is very convincing (*Die Drei Männer im Feuer*, 1930). He holds also, not without good grounds, that all three additions were inserted in the text of the canonical Daniel before it was translated into Greek. In this case the dates of the additions are not difficult to determine. Since the Hymn certainly, and the Prayer probably, belonged to traditional material, they are earlier than the Book of Daniel (*c*. 166 B.C.) ; the Prayer, from internal evidence, may be dated after the persecution of Antiochus Epiphanes, approximately 168 B.C.

Judith. In the Book of Judith we have a composition of high literary quality ; the story is skilfully told, the scenes dramatically presented ; while unnecessary details are avoided, they are full when needed ; interest is kept up throughout. In one passage, the poetical piece, containing the thanksgiving of Judith (16^{17}), we have a literary composition as fine as the best passages in the Old Testament, worthy, it has been truly said, to be placed side by side with the Song of Deborah. On the other hand, the book is at times marred by a low ethical standard, and here and there one comes across some rather indecently suggestive passages.

The main object of the book is a religious one, namely, to impress upon the people that as long as they are faithful to God by observing His precepts and refraining from idolatry, they will be secure under His protection, even in the face of their strongest enemies. The divine power is illustrated by the way in which the mightiest foe is brought to a downfall, though God's instrument in bringing this about is but a solitary woman.

The religious standpoint of the book is Pharisaic, which is evident in many passages ; but it is not the strict form of this which is characteristic of later days.

The book is not history, though the use of well-known historical names might lead one to suppose so ; but it is impossible to reconcile the historical setting of the book with actual history. The names are used for convenience. But historical conditions are discernible which point to the period at which the book was written. These suggest some time during the Maccabæan struggle, and probably during the years of Jonathan's leadership (160/159–142/1 B.C.) ; at this time the Temple was again in possession of the orthodox Jewish party ; but the Syrians still menaced the country. There are other indications which point to this period.

That the book was originally written in Hebrew is certain ; as Cowley remarks : " The translation is so literal that it can be put back into Hebrew with ease, and in some cases becomes fully intelligible only when so retranslated."

Prayer of Manasses. Belonging approximately to the same time, *i.e.* about the middle of the second century B.C., is the Prayer of Manasses. Although this prayer is mentioned in 2 Chron. 33[18], it has never formed part of the Septuagint text. There is little doubt but that the Chronicles passage was inserted by a later scribe who was acquainted with the current legendary details about the life of Manasseh. The text of the Prayer occurs for the first time in literature in the *Didascalia*, lib. ii. 21 (*c.* A.D. 200–250) ; but the date of its composition is much older ; its deeply devotional spirit suggests a *Hasid*, one of the " pious," often mentioned in some of the later psalms, as the writer ; in this case, Hebrew will have been the language in which it was originally written. Like some other apocryphal literary pieces it may well have been written during the Maccabæan period.

Additions to Esther. Of the rest of the chapters of the Book of Esther little need be said, as they are of small importance. Six in number, they were clearly added to the Greek text of Esther with the purpose of imparting to it a religious tone, which in the book itself is conspicuously absent. That

7

they were originally written in Greek is evident.   They may be dated about 130–125 B.C.

Susanna. Approximately of the same date, or a little later, is the history of Susanna, added as chap. 13 to the Book of Daniel. This is a folk-tale, no doubt, circulated orally before it was reduced to writing. It assumed its present form some time during the former half of the last century B.C. It was at this period that the Pharisees, with their strict ideas regarding legal observances, became the dominant party. For reasons into which we cannot go now, the son of the Pharisaic leader at this time, Simeon ben Shetach, was executed through a miscarriage of justice, due to the witnesses not having been properly examined. It was this episode, according to Ball's highly probable theory, which prompted a scribe to utilize Susanna, making the conception of Daniel as judge the kernel of the whole narrative. It is, as he says, " a contrast between two kinds of criminal procedure, which are represented, not by a dry general description, but by a concrete instance of the actual working. The author's aim is to portray certain deplorable effects inherent in the administration of justice in his own time, and to suggest a radical cure." To see the force of Ball's convincing argument one must, of course, study carefully the text of the story.

Bel and the Dragon. Another addition to the Book of Daniel occurs in the Septuagint after 12^{13}, Bel and the Dragon, though this title does not occur in the Septuagint ; indeed, there is no authority for this title, and, in any case, it is misleading, as the addition consists not of one, but of two separate stories : The Story of Bel (vv.$^{1-22}$), and the Story of the Dragon (vv.$^{23-42}$) ; and these two stories have nothing to do with one another. Both stories are variations of episodes narrated in the Book of Daniel itself. The first is based upon Dan. 3, the narrative about the golden image ; the second on Dan. 6, the story of Daniel in the lions' den. Each story has the object of illustrating the folly of idolatry, and especially of identifying the god with his image.

There is considerable difference of opinion as to the language in which these stories were originally written ; whether Greek, Aramaic, or Hebrew ; the subject has been fully treated by Witton Davies, and his contention that they were originally written in Hebrew is entirely convincing.

I Maccabees. We come next to I Maccabees. The first matter to which attention must be drawn is the question of the sources used by the compiler. While data are wanting for indicating all of these, some are clearly referred to in the text.

Thus, in 9^{22} mention is made of " the rest of the acts of Judas . . ." implying that the compiler has recorded *some* of these acts. In 16^{24} the " Chronicles of John Hyrcanus's high-priesthood " are mentioned ; the compiler does not, it is true, make any use of this book, but the fact that he mentions it shows that the utilization of sources was in his mind. Definite references to other sources occur in 11^{37}, $14^{18ff.\ 27}$. A number of poetical pieces are quoted which seem to be taken from collections of lyrics or religious poems ($1^{25-28.\ 36-40}$, $2^{8-12.\ 44}$, $3^{3-9.\ 45}$, 7^{17}, 9^{41}, 14^{6-15}) ; that these are not the compositions of the compiler is to be gathered from the fact of their very different character and style of writing from the rest of the book. In one instance the source of the quotation is known, 7^{17} being quoted from Ps. $79^{2.\ 3}$. There are, in addition, a large number of documents, official and otherwise, which are quoted, thirteen in all ; in most cases there is no reason to doubt the authenticity of these. To go into details would be out of place here.

As to the reliability of the history recorded—it covers a period of about seventy years, roughly 175–104 B.C.—there is no sort of doubt ; here and there are few questionable state-ments are made ; but taken as a whole, the history is entirely trustworthy, and its reliability is confirmed by the numerous dates which are given.

The book must have been written before the capture of Jerusalem by Pompey in 63 B.C., since there is no mention of Roman suzerainty. As the history is brought down to the death of John Hyrcanus in 104–103 B.C., it was after this date that the compilation was made ; and as mention is made of the existence of a written account of this high-priest, the prob-ability is that some time elapsed before our history was compiled. There are, moreover, indications in the book itself that it was written some time after the events recorded. The approximate period may thus be 90–70 B.C.

Jerome definitely states that the book was written in Hebrew ; and this is borne out by the Greek text constantly betraying translation from a Hebrew original.

2 Maccabees. Of a very different character is 2 Maccabees. This book is largely an abbreviation of the history of Jason of Cyrene (2^{23}). The narrative is put together in a haphazard fashion without proper historical sequence ; its historicity is inferior to that of 1 Maccabees. It is strongly Pharisaic in character. The leadership of Judas alone is dealt with ; this exception to the otherwise anti-Hasmonæan attitude may to some extent be accounted for by his connexion with the institution of the Feasts of Ḥanukkah and of Nicanor, a connexion which would have been looked upon with favour by the Pharisaic compiler.

A striking characteristic of the book is the compiler's love of the miraculous, and of supernatural apparitions. The date, both of Jason's work and of the epitome of it in 2 Maccabees, is most difficult to decide ; authorities differ widely on the subject. Perhaps it is safest to say that the former was written about 130 B.C., the latter during the first half of the first century B.C.

The Wisdom of Solomon was probably held in higher estimation by the Early Church than any other book in this collection. This can be readily understood ; it prophesies the sufferings of Christ—so the Early Church interpreted 2^{12-20} ; it describes the happiness of the righteous departed ; it tells of the distress of spirit of the wicked (5^{1-9}) ; and it has a strongly expressed discourse against the heathen (13^{1-5}) ; the book is that of the Apocrypha which is most quoted by the Early Fathers. The title comes from the Greek MSS. ; the Old Latin Version has : " The Book of Wisdom " ; the Syriac version expresses a doubt as to Solomonic authorship.

The question of unity of authorship, or otherwise, is difficult to decide, the arguments in favour of either view being very strong. There are striking differences between the two parts of the book, 1^1-11^1 and 11^2-19 ; but the possibility must be recognized of the same writer having assumed different attitudes of mind at different periods of his life. Upon the whole, we are inclined to agree with the upholders of unity of authorship. There is a good deal to show that in chap. 2 the author combats what he believes to be the erroneous teaching of Ecclesiastes. He was a Hellenistic Jew with some knowledge of Greek philosophy, whose home was in all probability Alexandria ; that he wrote his book in Greek is generally recognized.

The date of the book is also difficult to decide ; either the latter half of the last century B.C., or, according to others, about A.D. 40 ; there is much to be said in favour of each.

Baruch. The Book of Baruch consists of three independent pieces, written by different authors : 1^1-3^8, 3^9-4^4, 4^5-5^9 ; the last two are in poetry. The first, judging from internal evidence, was written soon after the destruction of Jerusalem in A.D. 70 ; the other two may be dated at the end of the first century A.D. All three pieces were originally written in Hebrew, as has been conclusively shown by Kneucker ; this is further supported by the fact that the book was used for liturgical purposes. That it was written in Palestine is generally acknowledged.

2 Esdras. 2(4) Esdras is a composite work. Chaps. 1, 2, containing both Jewish and Christian elements, belongs in its present form to the middle of the second century A.D., but the Jewish parts are older. Chaps. 3–10 constituting the main part of the book, is an apocalyptic work, the "Ezra Apocalypse," written about A.D. 100 (see below under the *Syriac Apocalypse of Baruch*). Chaps. 11, 12, the "Eagle Vision," are also apocalyptic ; indications in the vision point to some time during the reign of Domitian as the date, *circa* A.D..90, though some scholars hold to a somewhat earlier date, A.D. 69–79. Chap. 13, the vision of the "Man from the Sea," also apocalyptic, was written before the destruction of Jerusalem, about A.D. 66. Chap. 14, "Ezra and the Holy Writings," is of a very different character ; it deals with the inspiration both of the canonical scriptures and of the apocalyptic books ; its contents would, therefore, point to A.D. 100–A.D. 120 as the time of its composition, since it was during this period that the question of the Canon was being discussed. Chaps. 15, 16 are the least important part of the book, to which they form an appendix ; they consist of denunciations against Egypt, Asia, and Babylon, ending with a prophecy of terrors and tribulations which are to come upon the world ; only the Lord's elect will ultimately be saved. Internal evidence points to some time between A.D. 240 and A.D. 270 as their date.

III

Coming now to the Pseudepigrapha, we shall again attempt to enumerate the books in their chronological order, though it will be realized that here, too, the opinions of scholars differ.

Enoch. The Ethiopic Book of Enoch, 1 Enoch, the most important book in this body of literature, is an apocalyptic work of composite character, and of very different dates. According to Charles, the oldest portions are chaps. 12–36, and the "Apocalypse of Weeks" ($91^{12\text{-}17}$, 93). These belong to about 200 B.C. or a little later ; they are, at any rate, pre-Maccabæan. Some fragments of the "Book of Noah" have also been incorporated (6–11, 54^7–55^2, 60, 65^1–69^{25}, 106, 107) ; these are likewise pre-Maccabæan. Chaps. 83–90, the "Dream Visions," can be dated 165–161 B.C. ; about half a century later are chaps. 72–82, the "Book of the Heavenly Luminaries," or the "Book of Astronomy." Chaps. 37–71, $91^{1\text{-}11.\ 18.\ 19}$–104, the "Parables" or "Similitudes," belong to the former half of the first century B.C. The latest portion is 1-5, some half-century later ; in any case, pre-Christian.

The writers of the pre-Maccabæan portions were *Hasidim*, "pious ones," or "saints"; Leszynsky holds, however, that they emanated from Sadducæan circles ; this is disputed ; but that the "Book of Astronomy" portion is Sadducæan seems certain. Some of the later portions were written by Pharisees ; but not all. There were many apocalyptists who were neither Sadducees nor Pharisees. All the portions of the book were originally written either in Hebrew or Aramaic ; but it is difficult to decide which. The book is of importance for the study of Christian origins.

The *Sibylline Oracles* consisted originally of fourteen books, of which twelve have survived. These all belong to a late date, with the exception of the Procemium and books iii.-v. ; these, too, are of different dates ; the Procemium and book iii. belong, in the main, to the middle of the second century B.C., while books iv. and v. are of later date, the latter half of the first century A.D. The whole was written by Jews, though Christian elements have been added. They were written in Greek, in Egypt, and were put forth in the interests of Jewish propaganda. The apocalyptic element is almost wholly absent.

The Testaments of the Twelve Patriarchs. The ground-work of this book is Sadducæan, but it has been much worked over later by a Pharisee. There are grounds for believing that it may, in its original form, have been written by a Sadducee with the purpose of effecting a better feeling between the Sadducæan and Pharisaic parties ; the peaceable tone of the book is very striking, even allowing for Christian interpolations, and the virtue of unity among the descendants of the patriarchs is often urged. A further notable trait in the book is its universalism ; all the Gentiles will be saved through Israel, and Israel will, in the last Judgement, be judged according to the norm of the best heathen. But the apocalyptic element is otherwise scanty. The book was originally written in Hebrew ; its date is about 100 B.C.

Jubilees. The date of the Book of Jubilees is uncertain, some scholars holding that it was written at the end of the second century B.C., others putting it some half-century later. The title is derived from that of the Hebrew (*Sepher ha-yobeloth*), in which the book was originally written. It is known by other titles ; among them "The Apocalypse of Moses," though but for one or two passages, it is not an apocalyptic work. It is also called "The little Genesis," as being inferior to the canonical Genesis ; and it purports to be a revelation given to

Moses, and gives a history, divided up into jubilee periods of forty-nine years, from the Creation to the coming of Moses. Most scholars hold that it was written by a Palestinian Pharisee ; but, with the exception of its strongly marked spirit of exclusiveness, there is nothing that forbids us to agree with Leszynsky's contention that the author was a Sadducee, who ascribed Mosaic authorship to the book for the purpose of obtaining the needful authority for Sadducæan views concerning the Law. Box believes the author to have been one of the *Ḥasidim*, not a Pharisee. The book exists in its entirety only in an Ethiopic translation, made from the Greek version of the Hebrew. Of the Greek version only fragments are extant, they occur in the writings of early Church writers. The book has much that is of importance to students of the New Testament.

3 Maccabees. The apologetic work which goes under the name of 3 Maccabees belongs, according to some scholars, to approximately the same date as the preceding ; but according to others it should be dated during the earlier half of the first century A.D. The lines taken by the apologist are : firstly, that although the Jews were despised on account of their religion, they were good and loyal citizens, and useful to the State (see especially 3^{3-9}). More stress is, however, secondly, laid on the argument that, in spite of their apparent defencelessness, there was a danger in interfering with or injuring them because they had a supernatural ally in their national God, who would punish their oppressors : " the God of heaven surely protects the Jews, fighting on their side continually as a father for his children " (7^6). The book is, further, directed against heretics and Jewish renegades. It is written in Greek, but in the worst possible style ; Emmet well describes this in saying that " the style is rhetorical and bombastic to a degree ; the sentences are full of repetitions and awkwardly constructed, with a marked absence of connecting particles. The vocabulary shows a fondness for rare or unique compounds and poetical words, and the result is very artificial, the numerous purple passages quite failing to convince. In a word, the book is a specimen of the worst kind of pseudo-classicalism, a sort of Baboo Greek, such as was not uncommon in the Hellenistic period."

The Psalms of Solomon. That this title is original is very doubtful ; there is nothing in the Psalms themselves which would remotely suggest Solomonic authorship. It was added later by one who perhaps thought that as David had written so many psalms, his example may have been followed by his son, and so imputed these to him. The collection consists of eighteen psalms, and graphically presents a picture of the Pharisaic standpoint. The general point of view of the Psalms has been well summed up by Buchanan Gray : " It is the Pharisaic piety that breathes through the Psalms ; it is their opposition to the worldly, non-Davidic monarchy, and to the illegitimate high-priesthood of the ruling Hasmonæan king, Aristobulus, that finds expression here ; the Messianic hope (especially 17²³ᶠᶠ·), the firm belief in the future life which characterizes them later, and renders them naturally political quietists, and indifferent to political schemes, are already conspicuous here."   The present Greek text is a translation from a Hebrew original, made for the benefit of Greek-speaking Jews ; from the superscription to the Psalms, and the occurrences of the term διάψαλμα, it is clear that these psalms were sung in the synagogal service.   There is no reason to doubt that Palestine was their place of origin.   Whether they are all the work of one author, or not, is open to question.

   4 Maccabees.   Written at the beginning of the Christian era, we have in 4 Maccabees a book the main object of which is to inculcate " inspired reason " (εὐσεβὴς λογισμός).   In illustration of this the writer elaborates the story, taken from 2 Maccabees, of the martyrdom of Eleazar, an aged priest, and of an unnamed mother with her seven sons, who suffered death after heroically-borne tortures at the command of Antiochus Epiphanes.   The author writes, further, with the object of commending the accepted Greek philosophy of his day, which, as a Jew, he regards as fully embodied in the Mosaic Law.   He seeks to combine Greek philosophy with Jewish religious beliefs ; but his representation of the former is very moderate as compared with the forceful utterances of religious truths.

   Professor Bacon (*Hibbert Journal*, xv. 1917) has argued convincingly that the book contained a " Memorial Day address," delivered on the Feast of Dedication, in memory of Eleazar and the seven martyrs, who prepared the way for the recovery of the Temple from the tyrant, and proved themselves worthy of the resurrection to eternal life.   There is much in the book pointing to its having been composed in the nature of a sermon, perhaps originally delivered orally (see especially 1¹⁰· ¹², and the use of the second person).   That Greek was the language in which the book was originally written is generally recognized ; the writer was probably a native of Alexandria.

   Assumption of Moses.   Belonging similarly to the early

years of the first century A.D. we have next to consider a
writing—or rather part of one, for in its present form it ends
in the middle of a sentence—which bears the title : The
Assumption of Moses. Among the apocryphal lists occur the
titles of two writings : the one just mentioned, and The
Testament of Moses. Now the writing under consideration
makes no mention of the assumption of Moses ; but it is a
Testament, similar to the Testaments of the Twelve Patriarchs,
a prophecy rather than a historical account of what happened
to Moses. The problem with which we are faced, therefore, is
as to whether there were originally two distinct writings, the
" Testament " and the " Assumption " ; or whether these
formed two parts of one writing. The titles in the apocryphal
lists would suggest the former ; the breaking-off of our book in
the middle of a sentence would suggest the latter, especially as it
has the title " Assumption." Scholars differ in their views on
the subject ; but the want of decisive *data* makes it impossible
to decide the question with certainty. The author, as Charles
has rightly pointed out, was a Pharisee but " a Pharisee who
was the antithesis of the Zealot exactly in those respects in
which Pharisaism differed from Zealotism. His book was
designed as a protection against the growing secularization of
the Pharisaic party through its adoption of political ideals
and popular Messianic beliefs." Leszynsky holds that the
author was a Sadducee ; but in this case his arguments are not
convincing. There is one pronouncedly apocalyptic passage,
10^{1-10}, written in poetry, between which and certain elements
in the Synoptic Gospels there is almost verbal identity. This
poetical piece looks as though it were a quotation from some
popular apocalpytic writing. Our book exists in only one
extant MS. in Latin ; the text is imperfect and corrupt ; all
authorities are agreed that it is translated from a Greek text ;
but there are strong grounds for believing that the Greek was a
translation from a Hebrew or Aramaic original, more probably
the former.

Slavonic Enoch. An Apocalypse in the strict sense of the
word is the Book of the Secrets of Enoch, known also as the
Slavonic Enoch (2 Enoch), as it has survived only in this
language. This is an entirely different book from that of
1 Enoch, excepting that it sometimes reproduces the
phraseology and conceptions of this latter. The book is not
a unity, for some sections evidently go back to a Hebrew
original, and are, at the latest, pre-Christian. The main part
of the book, however, was certainly written in Greek, and
belongs to the middle of the first century A.D., or thereabouts.

at any rate before the destruction of the Temple, for the sacrificial system is referred to as still in vogue in 59[2]. The author was a Jew, but of the hellenistic type, for in questions affecting the origin of the earth, sin, death, etc., he adopts Platonic, Egyptian, and Zend elements in a way which would have been impossible for a Palestinian Jew (Charles) ; on the other hand, he was an upholder of the Law. A point of interest about the book is that it presents us for the first time with the Jewish conception of the millennium. Interesting also is the fact that the teaching regarding the seven heavens, which appears in the Rabbinical literature, is here treated with a fullness not found elsewhere.

The Syriac Apocalypse of Baruch, so called from the best form in which it has come down to us (a Latin translation of this is also extant), is to be distinguished from the Greek Apocalypse of Baruch (see below). The writer claims to have received from the Almighty revelations concerning the future, and writes with the object of heartening his people who are suffering under the tyranny of the Roman yoke. The book is, however, composite in character ; but all its component parts may be assigned to the period A.D. 50–100. There is a striking similarity both in thought and diction between this book and the Ezra Apocalypse (see above, under 2 Esdras) ; so numerous are the points of contact that it was thought at one time that both were the work of one author. That this, however, is not the case is now generally recognized. The question arose which was indebted to the other, *i.e.* which of the two was the earlier in date. It is very difficult to answer with certainty ; but whereas an earlier generation of scholars held that the Ezra Apocalypse was the earlier, more modern scholars incline to the belief that this Apocalypse presents a more developed form, and that it was written subsequently to the other ; this may be taken as the more likely. The authors of our book were all Pharisees ; some clearly lived before, others after, the destruction of the Temple in A.D. 70. According to Charles, the portions written before this date included an Apocalypse (27–30[1]) and the two visions (36–40 and 53–74) ; these chapters are important for the Messianic teaching contained in them. The portions written after A.D. 70 include the rest of the book ; a few chapters added by a final editor are but slightly later.

This Apocalypse, like the Ezra Apocalypse, is one of the most important for the study of Judaism at the beginning of the Christian era. All the vital doctrines come in for consideration—the doctrine of God, of the Law, of the Messiah, original sin, and free-will, works and justification, forgiveness, and the resurrection. The present Syriac is translated from the Greek version of a Hebrew original.

Testament of Abraham. Of somewhat uncertain date is the Testament of Abraham, a work quite distinct from the Apocalypse of Abraham (see below) ; James believes it to have been written in its original form in Greek in the second century A.D. by a Christian writer, and that it embodies earlier material. Others, Kohler and Ginzberg, with more probability, maintain its Jewish character, apart from Christian interpolations ; and regard is as originally written in Hebrew, and later translated into Greek ; its date they put during the first century A.D. However this may be, the Greek exists in two recensions, represented by distinct MSS. The eschatology of the book is peculiar, and in some respects unique, pointing to Alexandria rather than Palestine as the place of origin of the book.

Ascension of Isaiah. In the writing known as The Ascension of Isaiah we have a composite work made up of three originally distinct writings : The Martyrdom of Isaiah (1^1–3^{12} and $5^{1b\text{-}14}$), The Testament of Hezekiah (3^{13}–5^{1a}), and The Vision of Isaiah (=The Ascension of Isaiah, 6^1–11^{40}). The first of these is Jewish, the other two are Christian. As we now have it the book belongs to the second century A.D., but the Jewish part is certainly older. In its complete form the book exists only in Ethiopic, but there are fragments in Greek, Latin, and Slavonic. The original language of the Christian parts was Greek, that of the Jewish part probably Hebrew or Aramaic. The Christian parts alone are apocalpytic, the Jewish part is legendary. The book is not without importance from a doctrinal point of view ; and the Testament of Hezekiah gives an interesting picture of the conditions in the Christian church at the close of the first century.

Apocalypse of Abraham. The Apocalypse of Abraham belongs to the end of the first, or beginning of the second century A.D. It consists of two distinct parts (1–8 and 9–32), the second of which alone is apocalyptic, containing a revelation to Abraham concerning the future of the Jewish race. The book is extant in Slavonic, translated from the Greek, which was probably itself a version of a Semitic original. Its interest lies mainly in the picture it gives of the apocalyptic ideas of later Judaism.

Apocalypse of Moses. In the book called the Apocalypse of Moses we have a writing the title of which is difficult to account for. Of the forty-three chapters of which it consists, almost the whole have their parallel in the fifty-three chapters of the book called the Life of Adam and Eve. The name of Moses is not mentioned in our book in spite of its title ; it is strictly a legendary life of Adam and Eve. The original language of both books was Hebrew. They belong, in all probability, in their present form to the end of the first century A.D. For the study of the Jewish doctrine of sin our book is of value. There is but little of an apocalyptic character in it ; the life hereafter and the resurrection are, however, referred to. It appears to have enjoyed considerable popularity in the Early Church.

The Greek Apocalypse of Baruch has affinities with the Syriac apocalypse here and there ; it is also interesting to note that in the latter, the Almighty promises to grant Baruch cosmic revelations (76^3), but these are not further mentioned in that book, while in the Greek Apocalypse, we find the promise fulfilled. But otherwise the two are quite independent writings. The date of our book, which contains some Christian elements, is the latter part of the second century A.D.

The Book of Joseph and Asenath, known also as the Confession and Prayer of Asenath, belongs, in all probability, to the second century A.D. It is a romance elaborated from the scanty references to Asenath occurring in Gen. $41^{45.\ 50}$, 46^{20}, where it is said that Pharoah gave her (she was the daughter of Potipherah, priest of On), to Joseph, to wife, and that she bore him Manasseh and Ephraim. The book is essentially Jewish in character, but has been subjected to some Christian revision. It belongs, according to Kohler, " to the hellenistic propaganda literature by which Jewish writers endeavoured to win the non-Jewish world for the Jewish faith."

BIBLIOGRAPHY

Fritzsche, *Kurzgefasstes exegetisches Handbuch zu den Apokryphen des Alten Testamentes* (1851).
Volkmar, *Handbuch der Einleitung in die Apokryphen* (1860).
Wace, *The Holy Bible according to the Authorized Version with an Explanatory and Critical Commentary . . . Apocrypha* (1888).
Ball, *The Variorum Apocrypha* (1892).
Kautzsch, *Die Apokryphen und Pseudepigraphen des Alten Testamentes* (1900).
André, *Les Apocryphes de l'ancien testament* (1903).
Charles, *The Apocrypha and Pseudepigrapha of the Old Testament* (1913).

The works on the individual books of these two bodies of literature are many in number, and would take up too much space to enumerate.

V. THE NEW TESTAMENT AND OTHER CHRISTIAN WRITINGS OF THE NEW TESTAMENT PERIOD

1. THE PRIMITIVE TRADITION AND THE EARLIEST DOCUMENTS

OUR earliest records of the Primitive Church show us a body engaged not in book-production but in preaching. The subject of the preaching is stated by St. Paul (1 Cor. 1²³)—a crucified Messiah. To the Jews this topic is offensive, almost blasphemous, for " a crucified Messiah " is a contradiction in terms : to the Gentiles it is nonsense, for " a crucified Messiah" means no more than a Jewish agitator very·properly condemned and executed by the lawfully appointed guardians of the *pax Romana*. When the time comes for a Christian apologetic, the line of defence against Jewish criticism is that the crucified Messiah was part and parcel of the eternal purpose of God as shown in the Old Testament ; against Gentile criticism that the condemnation was undeserved and the crucifixion a miscarriage of justice. But Paul and the earliest preachers are not on the defensive. They are proclaiming the glorious fact that a crucified Messiah is for them the power of God and the wisdom of God.

The content of this earliest preaching can be gathered partly from the speeches in the first half of the Acts (2¹⁴⁻³⁹, 3¹³⁻²⁶, 4¹⁰⁻¹², 5³⁰⁻³², 10³⁶⁻⁴³, 13¹⁷⁻⁴¹) and partly from passages in the Pauline Epistles, where the Apostle appears to be handling traditional material (notably 1 Cor. 15¹⁻⁷ ; Rom. 1¹⁻⁴, 8³⁴, 10⁸⁻⁹) ; possibly also from certain passages in the Pastoral Epistles (Windisch, *ZNW*, xxxiv. (1935), 213–238). In bare outline the message is as follows :

The promises made in the Old Testament are fulfilled.
The Messiah ben David has come.
He is Jesus of Nazareth, who
    Went about doing good and executing mighty works
      by the power of God,
    Was crucified according to the purpose of God,

Was raised by God from the dead,
Is exalted by God and given the name Κύριος,
Will come again for the judgement and restoration of
    all things.
Therefore all you who hear the message repent and be
    baptized.

(For a fuller discussion of these matters see C. H. Dodd, *The
Apostolic Preaching and its Developments*.)

If we now set beside these results the conclusions reached
by recent criticism of the Synoptic Gospels, they confirm and
illuminate one another in a striking way. For it is increasingly
evident that the kernel of the Gospels is the Passion Narrative,
and it is precisely the Passion Narrative that resists form-
critical analysis. But the content of the earliest preaching is just
the Passion Narrative stated in the form " Jesus of Nazareth
is the Messiah ben David crucified, raised from the dead, and
exalted as Lord." It is the story of the Cross put into theological form. Thus we are led to the conclusion that the earliest
composition of the Primitive Church, the germ of our New
Testament is the Passion Narrative told as a piece of history
and preached as a gospel. This is not a written document ;
but it may be conjectured that its form and content were
fairly firmly fixed.

But while the Passion Narrative is the kernel of the earliest
Gospel, it is not the whole of it. The apostolic preaching sees
the Passion as the culmination of the Ministry (Acts 2²², 10³⁸).
It is therefore reasonable to suppose that the early oral tradition prefixed to the Passion story an outline of the Ministry
with stories illustrating its purpose and method.

Further, a large part of the activity of Jesus had been
teaching addressed to all kinds of audiences. It was inevitable
that this too should be treasured up in the memories of those
who heard it, and repeated when believers met together.
When new members were added to the community they must
be instructed about the kind of life that Jesus had prescribed
for those who entered the Kingdom of God as His disciples.
Thus alongside of the oral tradition about the crucified Messiah
ben David there would grow up the oral tradition of the teaching of Jesus. This latter probably first took written form in
the document known as Q, which was used by the authors of
Matthew and Luke. By comparison of these two Gospels
we can reconstruct Q with a fair amount of probability, though
we cannot be certain that all of it has been incorporated
in Matthew and Luke, or that the exact wording has been

preserved. Yet there is a large measure of agreement among scholars as to the scope and content of the document, and differences of opinion concern the minor details and the fringes of the subject. I should assign to Q the matter contained in Luke $3^{7-9.\ 16.\ 17}$, 4^{1-13}, 6^{20-49}, $7^{1-6a(?).\ 6b-9.\ 10(?).\ 18-35}$, 9^{57-62}, $10^{2.\ 3.\ 8-16.\ 21-24}$, $11^{9-26.\ 27-28(?).\ 29-36.\ 37-41(?).\ 42-52}$, $12^{1(?).\ 2-12.\ 22-34.\ 35-38(?).\ 39-46.\ 47-50(?).\ 51-59}$, $13^{18-30.\ 34.\ 35}$, $14^{15-24.\ 26.\ 27.\ 34-35(?)}$, $16^{13.\ 16-18}$, $17^{1-6.\ 22-37}$. Study of the document thus, reconstructed leads to the conclusion that it was compiled primarily as a manual of instruction in the meaning of discipleship for the use of those who were converted by the preaching of the Gospel. It may be conjectured that the need for such a treatise would be felt most acutely as soon as the Church began to make converts in large numbers, and especially when converts began to be drawn from non-Jewish circles. This happened at Antioch (Acts 11^{19-26}), where there arose a mixed community of Jewish and Gentile Christians ; and it is permissible to suppose that it was there that Q was written down in Aramaic and first translated into Greek, probably before the middle of the first century.

The question whether the statement of Papias preserved by Eusebius (*Eccl. Hist.* iii. 39. 16) refers to Q is still in debate. In my opinion the question ought to be answered in the affirmative (see the discussion in *The Mission and Message of Jesus*, pp. 308–312), in which case the possibility emerges that Q was put together by the Matthew whose name appears in the list of the Twelve (Matt. 10^3).

It is probable that other collections of material concerning the Ministry were put together at an early date. There is, for example, the so-called " Little Apocalypse " embedded in Mark 13 : there is the collection of conflict-stories (Mark 2^1-3^6, $11^{27}-12^{34}$) : there is the mass of teaching peculiar to Matthew, which may be derived from a Jerusalem compilation made up on similar lines to Q perhaps about a decade later than that document. And more besides. In fact, it becomes increasingly likely that the process by which the oral tradition was reduced to writing and finally presented in the Gospels was a good deal more complicated than we usually think ; and that much of the material, which was later incorporated in the Gospels, was in written form at an earlier date than is commonly allowed. If we ask what literature the Church possessed at the time when Paul and Barnabas set out on the first Missionary Journey, the answer will be : the Old Testament ; an outline of the Ministry of Jesus and a detailed account of the Passion, the latter in a fixed form if not written down ; a collection of

the teachings of Jesus (Q) probably in writing ; possibly other
collections of material—parables, conflict-stories, proof-texts
from the Old Testament, either written down or on the way
to being written down.

2. THE PAULINE CORPUS

The oldest written documents of the New Testament that
have come down to us direct are the letters of St. Paul. (The
Synoptic Gospels, though they incorporate material which is
of earlier date than the earliest Pauline Epistle, are themselves
later than the latest of Paul's letters.)   These letters are all
addressed to people who are already Christians.   They presuppose a Gospel which has already been preached and
accepted ; and their primary purpose is to give further explanation and direction where problems and difficulties of belief or
practice have arisen.

The main critical problem in connexion with the Pauline
Corpus is that of arranging the letters in chronological order
and fitting them into their proper places in the missionary
career of the Apostle.   A fixed point is provided by the
Corinthian correspondence, which can be confidently placed
in the period covered by Acts 19, and the Epistle to the Romans,
which was most probably written during the three months' stay
in Greece (Corinth) mentioned in Acts 20$^{2f.}$.   It is generally
agreed that 1 Thessalonians and, if genuine, 2 Thessalonians
are earlier than the Corinthian Epistles ; but there is no sign of
unanimity about the placing of the remaining letters.   There
are two questions in debate :   (a) whether Galatians was
written about the same time as the letters to Corinth and Rome
or at a date anterior to the Thessalonian correspondence ;
(b) whether any or all of the so-called " Captivity Epistles "
were written during Paul's stay in Ephesus.   The former
problem is further complicated by the question whether the
Galatians to whom the letter is addressed were the Celtic
peoples who had their homes in the districts about Pessinus,
Ancyra, and Tavium or the South-Galatian communities
founded by Paul and Barnabas on their first expedition into
Asia Minor.   The treatment of the Epistles which follows is
based on the view that there is a slight balance of probability
in favour of placing Galatians and Philippians in the Ephesian
period.

(a) *The Thessalonian Correspondence.*   Two letters addressed from " Paul, Silvanus, and Timothy to the Church
of the Thessalonians."   Thessalonica (modern Salonica), an

important commercial city at the head of the Thermaic Gulf
and on the main road linking Rome with the East (the *Via
Egnatia*), capital of the Roman province of Macedonia, had
been evangelized by Paul on his second missionary journey
(Acts 17$^{1-9}$).   His stay in the city was probably longer than
the brief notice in Acts would suggest (cf. 1 Thess. 2$^{1f.\ 9}$,
Phil. 4^{16}).   After leaving Thessalonica Paul went on to Berœa
and Athens, and later to Corinth.   The correspondence falls
within the period covered by these movements.

The genuineness of 1 Thessalonians is now generally
recognized ; but 2 Thessalonians is rejected by some scholars.
The main objection to it is that there does not seem to be
any point in writing it to a community which already has
1 Thessalonians.   But this argument tells just as much against
the view that it is a forgery ; for there would be just as little
point in fabricating 2 Thessalonians if 1 Thessalonians was
already in existence.   The fact that 2 Thessalonians looks
like a "pale ghost" of 1 Thessalonians must be otherwise
explained.   Two solutions of the problem are offered.

(i) Harnack suggested that the two letters were sent to
different sections of the community—2 Thessalonians to the
Jewish Christians and 1 Thessalonians to the Gentile Christians.
Against this view is the fact that both are addressed to "the
Church of the Thessalonians" without any hint of the exist-
ence of two sections.   Moreover, it is scarcely credible that
Paul would have countenanced such a division in the Church,
had it existed.

(ii) Grotius, and others since, maintained that 2 Thessalonians is the earlier of the two letters.   In favour of this
view it is argued that the troubles and persecutions, which
in 1 Thessalonians are treated largely as things of the past,
are at their height in 2 Thessalonians.   Further, the disorders
in the community are described in 2 Thess. 3^{11} as something new, of which the writers have just heard ; whereas in
1 Thess. 4$^{10.\ 12}$ and 5^{14} they are spoken of in a way that would
be unintelligible if we did not already know the fuller description in 2 Thess. 3.   It is also argued that the emphasis
on the signature (2 Thess. 3^{17}) is pointless except in a first
letter.   It is evident from the letters that the community is
obsessed by the idea of the imminent return of Christ ; and
in both letters this matter is dealt with at some length.   The
statements made are more easily intelligible if 2 Thessalonians
is prior to 1 Thessalonians.   For 2 Thess. 2$^{1-12}$ is an explanation why the Parousia is not to be expected immediately—
there is to be a Satanic Parousia first, a final effort of the

Kingdom of Evil. Then the question arises in Thessalonica: what of those who die in the meantime before the return of Christ? To that question the answer is given in 1 Thess. 4^{13}–5^{11}.

If we assume the priority of 2 Thessalonians, the order of events may be reconstructed somewhat as follows: Pau arrives at Athens and sends word to Silvanus and Timothy to follow from Berœa as quickly as possible (Acts $17^{14f.}$). Silvanus and Timothy come to Athens and report the latest news from Thessalonica. Paul writes 2 Thessalonians, and sends it to Thessalonica by the hand of Timothy (cf. 1 Thess. 2^{17}–3^5). Later, Paul moves on to Corinth and is there joined by Silvanus and Timothy (Acts 18^5), who have been in Macedonia. Paul then writes 1 Thessalonians as a reply to questions unresolved by 2 Thessalonians. On this hypothesis 2 Thessalonians would be dated in the latter part of 49 and 1 Thessalonians early in 50.

(b) *The Corinthian Correspondence.* The two letters preserved in the New Testament supply evidence that Paul wrote two others to the Corinthian community. The first of these (A) preceded 1 Corinthians (B) and is referred to in that epistle (1 Cor. 5^9). The other (C) was written after 1 Corinthians and is referred to in 2 Cor. (D) $2^{3f. 9}$, 7^{8-12}. A, B, and C were written from Ephesus, D from Macedonia.

Corinth was an important and wealthy city on the Isthmus of Corinth, capital of the senatorial province of Achæa and seat of the Proconsul. Here Paul carried on a mission which may be dated with great probability as beginning in the winter of 49–50 and ending in the summer of 51. It is described in Acts 18^{1-18}. After his departure further propaganda was carried on by Apollos (Acts 18^{27}–19^1). In the meantime Paul went, by way of Ephesus, to Cæsarea, Jerusalem, and Antioch whence, after staying some time, he began a new journey through Asia Minor (Acts 18^{19-23}). This journey terminated at Ephesus (Acts 19^1) where a ministry extending over some three years began. It is not possible to determine with certainty the length of time between the departure from Corinth and the arrival at Ephesus. The indications given in Acts are too slight to allow of reckoning forward from 51. A definite result could be reached by reckoning back from the Procuratorship of Festus (Acts 24^{27}), but unfortunately that date is not fixed with certainty (estimates vary from 55 to 61). On the whole a date about 60 seems the more likely, and in that case the Ephesian ministry would be dated about 54–57, and the Corinthian correspondence would belong to a time when the Church at Corinth had been in existence for over five years.

From the explanation given by Paul in 1 Cor. 5^{9-13} it appears that letter A dealt with the maintenance of moral standards within the Church—Corinth was a byword for sexual vice—and that the admonitions had been misunderstood. It has been thought that a fragment of this letter is preserved in 2 Cor. 6^{14}–7^1, a passage which seems to be out of place in its present context. This is possible, though it cannot, of course, be proved.

Letter B in the series (our 1 Corinthians) is a long communication containing Paul's comments on reports that had been brought to him about the affairs of the community (1–6) as well as a detailed reply to a letter sent to him from the Church (7–16). It reveals a society torn by internal dissensions of all kinds. There are party divisions (1^{20}–4^{21}), social cliques (11^{17-22}), even law-suits between members (6^{1-11}). There are rival interpretations of the nature of Christian morality and Christian worship. The life of the community would seem to be the negation of the principles laid down in chap. 13. The most serious trouble was the division of the Church into sections with party names, the factions whose rallying cries were " I am of Paul " or " Apollos " or " Cephas " or " Christ." The most probable interpretation of these party labels explains the first two in terms of personal attachment of members to the two men who had worked in the Corinthian mission-field. 1 Cor. 3^{4-9} makes it clear that there was no rivalry between the two men and that the Paul and Apollos parties were not on the same footing as the other two. The Cephas party and the Christ party both represented a challenge to the authority of Paul, the former wishing to subordinate him to the Jerusalem apostolate represented by Peter, the latter wishing to throw off all human authority whatsoever. It is Paul's right to the title of Apostle that is at stake ; and in 1 Corinthians we have the first indications of a controversy which becomes violent in 2 Corinthians and Galatians, and is probably referred to in Philippians.

It is inferred from 2 Cor. $13^{1f.}$ that, after sending 1 Corinthians, Paul paid a personal visit to Corinth (the so-called " painful visit ") in the hope of dealing with the situation effectively. This visit was a complete fiasco, and Paul returned to Ephesus humiliated.

As a result letter C was written (the " severe letter "). From the references to it in 2 Corinthians it is clear that it was written in great grief and indignation and that it probably presented

some kind of ultimatum to the Corinthian community.   It was
dispatched by the hand of Titus, and Paul, after a period of
anxious waiting, first at Troas and then in Macedonia, received
a satisfactory report from Titus.   It has been argued that a
part of letter C is preserved in 2 Cor. 10–13, the main reason
being the abrupt change of temper in these chapters.   It can,
however, be said on the other side that there was a recalcitrant
minority who had remained unmoved by the severe letter and
the visit of Titus, and that the conclusion of 2 Corinthians is
directed to these persons.   However that may be, it would
seem that these chapters have in mind the " Christ party "
(10^7) and the " Cephas party " ;   and it is probable that it
was with the more violent members of these parties that
Paul's chief difficulties lay.   It is clear that the majority of
the church members were brought over to the side of Paul by
the combined effect of the " severe letter " and the representations of Titus.   Paul's response to this change is given
in the last letter of the series.

Letter D (2 Cor. or 2 Cor. 1–9) shows clearly the relief
which Paul feels at the termination of the dispute.   It reaffirms
(1–7) his claim to the title of Apostle and the claim of his
preaching to be the authentic Gospel of Christ ;   and it is
significant that stress is laid on the apostolic office as a ministry
of reconciliation.   Perhaps it is significant, too, that chaps. 8
and 9 are devoted to the arrangements for the offering to the
Jerusalem Church, especially if Paul had successfully resisted
an attempt to bring the Gentile communities under Palestinian
control.   If chaps. 10–13 are part of 2 Corinthians and not part
of the " severe letter," they must be taken as an indication
that there were still a few in Corinth who had not come over
to Paul's side in the struggle.

The dates of the four letters can be fixed approximately.
Letter D is written from Macedonia when the Ephesian ministry
is ended.   If we place the Ephesian ministry in A.D. 54–57, we
may take the late autumn of A.D. 57 as the date of this letter.
Events moved swiftly in the latter part of this controversy, and
we should probably place the " severe letter " as near as
possible to letter D, sometime during the summer of A.D. 57.
The " painful visit " must have taken place shortly before the dis-
patch of the " severe letter," and should also be dated in A.D. 57.
The interval between 1 Corinthians and the " painful visit "
cannot be determined with certainty ;   but it may have been
considerable, and there may have been a fairly long period
between letter A and 1 Corinthians.   Possibly 1 Corinthians
should be dated about the middle of the Ephesian period.

(c) *The Letter to the Galatians*. There are two great problems here : the date and the destination. Who are the Galatians to whom the letter is addressed ? Two answers are possible : they are the inhabitants of the old kingdom of Galatia, with its main centres at Ancyra, Pessinus, and Tavium (North-Galatian theory) ; or they are the inhabitants of the Roman province of Galatia, primarily the churches founded by Paul and Barnabas on the first missionary journey (South-Galatian theory). The former is the traditional view and still has the support of some scholars. If it is correct, a very early date for the Epistle is automatically excluded. But on the whole it seems that a better case can be made out for the South-Galatian theory, in which case the question of date is open ; any date after the first missionary journey is possible. The choice lies between two : a date before the Council of Jerusalem (Acts 15) or a date during the Ephesian ministry.

The problem partly turns on the relation of the visits of Paul to Jerusalem described in Galatians and those described in Acts. It is generally agreed that the first visit in Galatians (1^{18-24}) corresponds to the first in Acts (9^{26-30}). The traditional view equates the second visit described in Galatians (2^{1-10}) with the visit for the Jerusalem Council (Acts 15), which is the *third* visit recorded in Acts. If this identification is correct, the Epistle must be later than the Council. It is, however, held by many good scholars that this identification is wrong and that the second visit of Galatians corresponds to the second visit in Acts, the famine visit (Acts 11). If this is right, it is possible to date Galatians before the Council. There are two other possibilities : (*a*) that the narrative of Acts is confused and that Acts 11 and Acts 15 are two accounts of one and the same visit which is also described in Gal. 2 ; or (*b*) that the visit described in Gal. 2 is not to be equated with either of the visits in Acts 11 and 15. It is not possible to solve the problem with certainty ; but the issues may be clarified. The proceedings in Gal. 2 cannot be identified with the Jerusalem Council, for the one records a private interview, the other, a large meeting. The most that can be said is that the interview in Gal. 2 may have taken place during the Council visit. The case for identifying the visit of Gal. 2 with the famine visit looks stronger than it really is. Paul says (Gal. 2^2) that he went up κατὰ ἀποκάλυψιν, which the upholders of the theory explain by reference to the prophecy of the famine by Agabus (Acts 11^{28}). But this is rather far-fetched. Paul went up as an official representative of the

Antioch Church conveying the funds raised for the famine relief ; and the narrative in Acts leaves it an open question whether that fund was raised when Agabus prophesied the famine or when the famine actually took place. Further, the business transacted by Paul during the visit described in Gal. 2 has no relation at all to the " revelation " given through Agabus. The real business of the visit concerned the spheres of activity of Paul and Barnabas on the one hand and of the older Apostles on the other ; and that business was amicably settled (Gal. 2⁹). Even the question of the circumcision of Titus was a side-issue, which Paul dismisses in a parenthesis (and his account of the episode is obscure largely because it is a parenthesis). The difficulties are great in identifying Gal. 2 with either Acts 11 or Acts 15 ; and they are not removed, but aggravated, by recent attempts to present Acts 11 and Acts 15 as duplicate accounts of one and the same visit.

There remains the possibility that Gal. 2 describes a visit not recorded in Acts, which means that we are reduced to guessing its place in the framework supplied by Acts. The main purpose of the visit, the purpose which it achieved, was the recognition by Jerusalem of the call of Paul and Barnabas to the Gentile mission. In that case the question is whether it was approval of a project or recognition of a *fait accompli* ; does it fall before or after the first missionary journey ? In favour of the former alternative is the fact that it offers a satisfactory explanation of κατὰ ἀποκάλυψιν in Gal. 2² : the revelation in question is that described in Acts 13². In that case the visit falls between the revelation of Acts 13² and the departure of Paul and Barnabas (Acts 13⁴). This allows us to place the visit of Peter to Antioch in its most natural place, between the return of Paul and Barnabas from Galatia and the Jerusalem Council. If we reject this hypothesis the next best view is that in Gal. 2 we have the description of a private interview with the Jerusalem leaders after the first missionary journey, and perhaps at the time of the Jerusalem Council, in which the older Apostles gave approval to what had been already done by Paul and Barnabas. This would automatically exclude the pre-Council date for the Epistle ; the former alternative leaves it an open question.

The question of date can now be considered from another point of view. If the issue in Galatians is the issue of circumcision of Gentile converts and if that was the main issue before the Jerusalem Council, it is possible to suppose that Galatians was written before the Council. But if, as I think, the Council was occupied primarily, not with the question of circumcision, but with the matters raised by the events narrated by Paul in Gal. 2^{11-13}; and if the occasion of Galatians is, as I think, an attempt to question Paul's status as an Apostle, then the pre-Council date for the Epistle becomes extremely unlikely, and we ought rather to place it in the period when we know that Paul's status was seriously challenged, the period of the Corinthian correspondence. It is not possible to fix the date more precisely, but it may be conjectured that it is not far from the time when the " severe letter " was written.

(d) *The Letter to the Philippians.* The traditional view places the writing of the four letters, Philippians, Colossians, Philemon, and Ephesians (if a genuine letter of Paul) in the period when Paul was under arrest in Rome (Acts 28). This view has lately been challenged by the theory that either Philippians alone or all four should be assigned to the period of the Ephesian ministry, or alternatively, to the time when Paul was in custody at Cæsarea (Acts $23^{31}-26^{32}$). The case for a non-Roman origin is strongest for Philippians, and here the Ephesian hypothesis has definite advantages over the Cæsarean. If Philippians was written from Rome or Cæsarea, Paul was under arrest when he wrote the letter, and the references to his " bonds " must be interpreted in that sense. But if we entertain the Ephesian theory, what was taken as a matter of course becomes a question, and we have to ask whether there is anything in the letter to compel the conclusion that Paul was a prisoner when he wrote it. If, and only if, that question is answered in the affirmative, is it necessary to postulate an Ephesian imprisonment of Paul, an imprisonment for which there is no other evidence of any weight.

A second question, which can be examined separately, may be put thus : if Philippians was written from Ephesus, where in the Ephesian period is its most likely place ? To this question there is only one answer that is at all probable. All the evidence points to a date before 1 Corinthians, that is, probably within the first half of the Ephesian ministry. A comparison of Phil. 2^{19-24} with 1 Cor. 16^{5-11} suggests that Philippians is a good deal earlier than 1 Corinthians ; and this is supported by the absence in Philippians of any reference to the Jerusalem relief fund, for which arrangements were well advanced when 1 Corinthians was written. The statement (Phil. 4^{10}) that the Philippian help for Paul himself had been delayed by " lack of opportunity " is understandable in the light of Acts $18^{22f.}$; and Epaphroditus may have arrived at Ephesus soon after Paul's return from the East. Phil. 2^{25-30} suggests that Epaphroditus had spent a considerable time with Paul, probably engaged in missionary work under the Apostle (cf. Lightfoot, *Philippians*, 61 f.). How long this lasted we do not know. All that can be said is that the indications favour a relatively early date in the Ephesian period for the writing of Philippians.

If that be so, we have to return to the question of an Ephesian imprisonment, and ask whether it is probable. It is not mentioned in Acts, which is strange, since it must have ended in the acquittal of Paul, and an acquittal would have been a good point for Luke, with his strong apologetic interests, to record. Further, in other places (Philippi and Corinth) a clash with the authorities involves the termination of Paul's active work in these places for the time being. Similarly, in Acts 19, the uproar at Ephesus is followed at once by the account of Paul's departure from the city (Acts 20¹). Moreover, in the letter itself there is nothing to compel the belief that it was written in confinement. The references to " bonds " and " the Prætorium " can all be understood of something that is past ; and the plans outlined in 2¹⁹⁻²⁴ suggest that Paul is free to arrange his future movements. The confident preaching of the majority of the brethren (1¹⁴) is easily understandable if the proceedings against the Apostle had ended in an acquittal. Further, if Paul was in prison for preaching Christ, it is difficult to see how others by preaching Christ would increase his affliction (1¹⁷). One would have thought that the first result of such activity would be that those who indulged in it would join him in gaol. The conclusion would seem to be that Paul was a free man when the letter was written early in the Ephesian period. It is still a possibility that he had been under arrest at an earlier stage in that period, and that he is referring to this in the letter. But there is another possibility that is at least worth consideration : that the reference is to the events at Corinth described in Acts 18¹²⁻¹⁷. In support of this it may be urged that Paul's statement of the case in Phil. 1¹³ is consistent with the finding of Gallio in Acts 18¹⁴ᶠ·, and that the subsequent developments as described in Phil. 1¹⁵⁻¹⁸ tally with the situation disclosed in 1 Corinthians.

If this is the case, we may conjecturally restore the sequence of events thus : The Philippian Church, whose foundation is described in Acts 16¹²⁻⁴⁰, had maintained close and friendly relations with Paul, sending contributions to help his work at Thessalonica and at Corinth. They had no opportunity to continue this good work while he was away in the East, but on his return to Ephesus they sent not only money but a volunteer, Epaphroditus, to assist in the work. Epaphroditus

broke down in health and had to be sent back to Philippi
(2^{25-30}), and Paul wrote this letter explaining why Epaphroditus
could not continue and acknowledging the gift of money. At
the same time he gives the Philippians an account of developments since his departure from Corinth and his own attitude
to them (1^{12-30}), and warns them against the divisive influences
of Jewish Christian propaganda, exhorting them to maintain
unity among themselves and loyalty to their own Apostle
($2^{1-4. \ 12-18}$, $3^{1-3. \ 17-19}$). This emphasis on unity and loyalty is
very relevant in view of the situation which was developing
in Corinth and in the Galatian Churches ; and we have no
reason to suppose that the Philippian community failed to
respond to the call.

(e) *The Letter to the Romans.* The movements of Paul
after leaving Ephesus are described in Acts 20^{1-3}. From this
passage we learn that he spent three months in Hellas, presumably with his headquarters at Corinth. During this period—
probably December A.D. 57–February A.D. 58—the letter to the
Romans was written. It differs from the previous letters in
that it is addressed to a Church which Paul had not founded,
or even visited. Its object is to prepare the way for a visit
which he hopes to make, and to enlist the support of the
Roman Church for his missionary plans in the West. Further,
it is not written to meet a particular emergency, but is rather
an exposition, as nearly systematic as anything written by
Paul could be, of the essentials of the Gospel which he preaches.
It is a document that would be valued by any Church where
Paul was known, and there are indications in the text that
Rome was not the only Church to receive a copy.

The principal, though not the only, clue to the early history
of the letter is the doxology (R.V. 16^{25-27}). This piece is an
interpolation, and it appears in three different places in the
MSS. : after 14^{23}, 15^{33}, and 16^{24}. Since an interpolated doxology
would naturally be put at the end of the document, the inference is that Romans, at a very early date, was extant in three
forms. Further, there are what appear to be three full closes in
the letter itself : at 15^{13}, 15^{33}, and 16^{20} or 16^{24}. The didactic
part of the letter ends at 15^{13} ; the rest of chap. 15 is concerned with Paul's own plans and is obviously meant for the
information of the Roman Church ; chap. 16 is widely held
to be a letter to the Church at Ephesus. The most probable
explanation of the data would seem to be that the letter was
written in the first instance to be sent to Rome, and that
this document ended at 15^{33} ; a copy of this letter with a
covering note or postscript (chap. 16) was sent to Ephesus ;

and, possibly, another copy of the didactic portion (ending at 15¹³ and without the Roman and Ephesian *personalia*) was retained at Corinth. At a later date the letter was " edited " by Marcion, who made it end at 14²³. Whether the text on which he operated contained chaps. 15 and 16 we do not know ; but as his work was probably done in Rome, we may suppose that it contained chap. 15 at least.

The letter as it stands seems clearly to be a single composition put together for a definite purpose—to make clear to the Church at large the position of the writer. The first three verses make that obvious. It does not, however, follow that the whole Epistle was specially composed for the purpose : indeed, there is some probability in the view that St. Paul made use of already existing manuscript material (*e.g.* chaps. 9–11) in writing the letter.

At the end of the three months' stay in Corinth, Paul set out for Syria (Acts 20³). The journey, as is clear from Acts 20, 21 and Rom. 15³⁰⁻³², was begun with forebodings of disaster which became more definite as time went on, till they culminated in the prophecy of Agabus (Acts 21¹⁰⁻¹⁴). This prophecy was quickly fulfilled when Paul arrived in Jerusalem : he had only been there a few days when a riot was raised against him (21²⁷ᶠᶠ·), and for his own safety he had to be arrested by the Romans. He was in custody at Jerusalem or Cæsarea some two years (Acts 24²⁷), from early summer of A.D. 58 to summer of A.D. 60 (Acts 21³³–26³²), when on his appeal to the Emperor he was sent under escort to Rome, arriving there after many hardships in the spring of A.D. 61 (Acts 27, 28). He was under open arrest in Rome for "two whole years" (Acts 28³⁰), that is, spring A.D. 61 to spring A.D. 63. There the narrative of Acts ends.

(f) *The Letters to the Colossians and to Philemon.* Colossæ was one of three towns in the Lycus valley about 100 miles east of Ephesus. The other two were Laodicea and Hierapolis, and it appears from Col. 4¹³ that there were Christian communities in all three places. It is generally inferred from Col. 1⁴· ⁸, 2¹ that Paul was not personally acquainted with these churches, which had been founded by others (Colossæ by Epaphras, 1⁷ᶠ·). They may be regarded as daughter-communities of the Church at Ephesus.

It is clear from Col. 4¹⁶ that two letters were sent, one to Colossæ and the other to Laodicea ; but there is no letter to Laodicea in the Canon. On the other hand, it is clear that the letter to Philemon was sent along with Colossians, and it has consequently been suggested that Philemon is really the missing letter to Laodicea. Another suggestion (which goes back to Marcion) is that the letter to the Ephesians is really the letter to the Laodiceans.

Though arguments can be brought forward for placing Colossians and Philemon in the Ephesian ministry, the balance of probability seems to favour Rome as the place of writing, and the composition will accordingly fall in the two-year period mentioned at the end of Acts (c. A.D. 61–63).

Colossians was written to meet certain false doctrines which had obtained a foothold in the community. The essential point at issue was whether Christianity is the final religion. The Colossian heresy—so far as we can infer its nature from Paul's criticism of it in the Epistle—professed to supplement the Pauline Gospel on both the theological and the ethical sides, with elements from pagan mythology and philosophy and Jewish ritual practice. Christianity was in process of being transformed into an ascetic theosophy. Paul's reply to all this is a strong assertion of the uniqueness of the Gospel and the absolute pre-eminence of Christ.

The accompanying letter is actually addressed not to Philemon alone, but to Philemon, Apphia, Archippus, and the Church that meets in Philemon's house. The purpose of the letter is to intercede for Philemon's runaway slave, Onesimus, who had found his way to Paul, been befriended and converted by him, and was now sent back to his master. It is quite possible, even probable, that what Paul really wanted was to have Onesimus sent back again to him as his assistant. More hazardous is the further suggestion (J. Knox, *Philemon among the Letters of Paul*) that Onesimus was so released, and later became the head of the Ephesian community (Ignatius, *Eph.* i.), though it is not impossible. In any case, it may be inferred, from the fact that the letter was preserved, that Philemon did not turn down Paul's request.

(g) *The Letter to the Ephesians* presents a greater variety of problems and solutions than any other in the Pauline collection. Both the Pauline authorship and the Ephesian destination are strongly denied by many scholars. It is argued that the letter cannot be by Paul because its teaching differs in essential points from that of the unquestioned epistles ; particularly that it takes over the wording of Colossians and uses it in new senses. Further, that the style is different from that of the real Paul ; the difference may be crudely stated thus : the difficulty of, say, Romans is that the writer goes off at tangents ; that of Ephesians is that the writer ties himself in knots. Against the Ephesian destination it is urged (a) that in three very old and valuable MSS.

(B S P[46]) the vital words "in Ephesus" are absent from I[1];
(b) that in Marcion's Canon the Epistle was superscribed "To
the Laodiceans"; (c) that it is inconceivable that so abstract
and impersonal a document should have been sent by Paul to
a Church with which his relations had been so prolonged and
intimate; (d) that there is no indication in the letter of any
concrete Church situation to which it is addressed, that it is, in
fact, not a letter at all but a theological tract in epistolary
form.

Solutions of the problem, which maintain the authenticity of
the letter, explain it either (with Marcion) as the letter to the
Laodiceans referred to in Col. 4[16], or as a circular letter,
similar to that in Rev. 1–3, intended to be read in a number of
Asian churches.

Scholars who regard the letter as pseudonymous have
larger scope. It is suggested, for example, that the letter to
the Laodiceans was lost, and that Ephesians is an attempt
by an admirer of Paul to fill the gap. Another hypothesis
makes Ephesians the introductory chapter to the Asian
collection of the letters of Paul. A further development of
this theory suggests that the Onesimus of Philemon became
Bishop of Ephesus, collected the genuine letters of Paul, and
wrote Ephesians as a preface to the whole.

There is no completely satisfactory solution of the problem.
Before the problem can be solved we must have more light on
the formation of the earliest collections of Paul's letters, and
on the early history of the Churches in the province of Asia. In
the present state of knowledge all that can be said is that if
the letter is, in any real sense, Pauline, it must be dated about
the same time as Colossians, and probably after Colossians.
Also in view of the difficulties connected with the style, it may
be necessary to allow a larger part than usual to the amanuensis.
Further if Colossians is rightly placed in the Roman imprisonment, Ephesians might be regarded as Paul's theological
testament, written for all the Gentile Christian Churches.
(Ephesus would certainly receive a copy of such an open
letter; and it may be that Eph. 6[21f.] is to be regarded as a
special note for the Ephesian Church.) The letter would then
be a statement on broad and general lines of what Paul holds as
the essence of the Gospel (1–2), what he has tried to achieve
in the Gentile mission (3) and what he hopes for in his churches
and their members (4–6). (On this view the absence of the
words "in Ephesus" from P[46], which is certainly of Egyptian
origin, and BS which probably present an Alexandrian type
of text, will be explained on the supposition that these

authorities for the text are descended from the copy of the
letter which stayed in Rome, and consequently had no address ;
and this will be a further piece of evidence for the connexion
of the earliest Egyptian New Testament text with Rome.)

With that we come to the end of the Pauline collection.
The other letters attributed to Paul—Hebrews and the Pastoral
Epistles—are not his work, though it is probable that genuine
Pauline material is embedded in the Pastorals.   In particular,
it seems likely that 2 Timothy contains the last letter of Paul
that has survived, a private note to Timothy written when
the Apostle was very near to his end.

3. THE EPISTLE TO THE HEBREWS

There is no good reason for thinking either that this work
was written by Paul or that it was addressed to " the Hebrews."
The superscription in A.V. represents ancient guess-work.   Any
attempt to improve on it must also be guess-work.   Various
conjectures have been made, as, for example, that the book
was written by Barnabas (so Tertullian and, in modern times,
Zahn) or by Priscilla (Harnack).   Other names suggested
have been Silvanus, Apollos (first suggested by Luther), Luke,
and Clement of Rome.   The tendency in recent times is to
regard the problem of authorship as insoluble.   The most
generally accepted view of the destination of the document
is that it was written to a group of Christians in Rome.   The
composition is dated in the period A.D. 75–90.

Any attempt to obtain more definite conclusions must
begin from the contents of the Epistle.   There is good evidence
for thinking that the writer was acquainted with Paul's letter
to the Romans.   (This fixes the upper limit for the composition
about A.D. 58.   The lower limit is fixed by the fact that Hebrews
is quoted in 1 Clement, c. A.D. 96).   Further, the central
argument of Hebrews (chaps. 5–10) is simply Paul's argument
in Gal. 3 lifted bodily and worked out in a new context.
Paul starts with the promise to Abraham, treats the Law as an
interim dispensation, which could not do more than be a
stop-gap until the promise was fulfilled in Christ.   The author
of Hebrews applies this scheme to the ritual of the Tabernacle
and Temple conceived as a means of bringing men into communion with God.   He goes back to the patriarchal history
and there lights on the mysterious contemporary of Abraham,
Melchizedek, in whom he sees foreshadowed the ideal priest.
Then the Aaronic priesthood and cultus are seen as an interim
dispensation like the Mosaic Law, until the perfect high-priest
after the order of Melchizedek, appears in the person of

Jesus Christ.   The argument is worked out in great detail and with a great display of Old Testament scholarship. Negatively its object is to show that the Jerusalem Temple worship is obsolete and ineffective.   That being so, it would have been a telling point, if the writer had been able to point to the Temple in ruins as an indication that God had no further use for it.   That he does not make use of this argument is a clear indication that he is writing before A.D. 70.   The composition of Hebrews may thus be placed in the period A.D. 58–70, perhaps even A.D. 58–66.

If we ask who in this period is the most likely author for the book, the answer is Apollos, who, from the description of him in Acts, would appear to have had the kind of Alexandrian culture which is characteristic of the Epistle, as well as close acquaintance with Paul and Paulinism.   The destination of the letter is more difficult.   If it was written by Apollos between A.D. 58 and 66, the most natural thing will be to suppose that it was written to a Church in one of the districts where Apollos had worked—either Achæa or Asia.   In favour of Asia is the fact that Hebrews appears to be directed against false notions akin to those which Paul attacks in Colossians. The " Colossian heresy " as defined by Lightfoot (*Colossians and Philemon*, p. 71) has two outstanding characteristics: a hankering after Jewish religious observances and a doctrine of intermediaries between God and man.   It is significant that Heb. 5–10 is devoted to proving that the Jewish ritual system is superseded by the high-priestly work of Christ, and that Heb. 1–4 is concerned with proving the uniqueness and supremacy of Christ as against all other intermediaries.

If that is so, the letter may have been written about the same time as Colossians, and to meet the same kind of trouble in the Churches of Asia.

4. The Synoptic Gospels and Acts

(a) *Mark.*   It is generally and increasingly recognized that the relation between the first three Gospels is best explained by the hypothesis that Mark has been used in the composition of Matthew and Luke.   Mark is thus the oldest surviving example of Gospel-writing, if we understand by that the attempt to combine in a single narrative (*diēgēsis*, Luke 1[1]) the story of the Passion and reminiscences of the ministry which led up to it.

The earliest tradition connects our second Gospel with Rome, with St. Peter, and with John Mark, the companion and assistant first of Paul and afterwards of Peter ; and there does not seem to be any good reason for rejecting it. The most probable date for its composition is about A.D. 65 ; for we may follow Irenæus in placing it after the deaths of Peter and Paul, and there is nothing in the Gospel itself to suggest that it was written after the fall of Jerusalem (A.D. 70). Internal evidence tends to confirm the Church tradition that Mark embodies recollections of the oral teaching of Peter ; but it is probable that the author incorporates other matter along with Petrine reminiscences, and some of this matter may already have been written down (*e.g.* chap. 13 or the series of conflict-stories 2^1-3^6). Style and language suggest that we are still very close to the primitive Palestinian tradition, only one remove from the Aramaic-speaking narrators of stories about Jesus. The contents likewise seem to be " the outcome of genuine historical tradition." Time and again " insignificant " details of the Marcan narrative turn out on closer examination to be highly significant ; and this is a fair indication that we are dealing with the products of memory rather than of imagination.

The Gospel comes down to us in what is probably a mutilated form. On the best MS. evidence it ends abruptly at 16^8 with the words " for they were afraid." It has been held (*a*) that Mark really does end here ; (*b*) that a portion has been lost in which the Resurrection appearances were described ; (*c*) that the lost ending was very much longer, and described the early history of the Jerusalem Church as given in Acts 1-12. Of these theories perhaps (*b*) is the most likely.

(*b*) *Matthew.* Comparative study of Matthew, Mark, and Luke leads to the conclusion that Matthew is a revised and enlarged edition of Mark. The revision takes the form of improving the Greek style of Mark, of abbreviating his narratives, and, in a few cases, rearranging the order. The enlargement consists mainly in the addition of narrative matter at the beginning and end of the story (Birth and Infancy stories and extra incidents in the Passion narrative) ; the incorporation of five great discourses (Matt. 5-7, 10, 13, 18, (23) 24-25) ; and the introduction from time to time of proof-texts from the Old Testament. The additional matter in Matthew is derived partly from a source or sources peculiar to this Gospel (M) and partly from the document Q. There are indications which suggest that the writer of Matthew used Q in a Greek version similar to that used by Luke, but revised by reference to the Semitic (Aramaic) original. The outstanding characteristic of the author's methods is his practice of arranging the teaching of Jesus under heads so that matter from his different sources will be brought together, sometimes in juxtaposition, sometimes fused together, in a single paragraph. Matthew is a Greek document making use of Greek sources.

These results contradict the Church tradition, according to which the Gospel was composed by Matthew in the " Hebrew dialect " (Aramaic) and only afterwards translated into Greek. It is, however, probable that this tradition in its original form referred not to Matthew, but to the document Q, and that by a misunderstanding, which is as old as Papias, it was transferred to the (anonymous) Gospel.

The date and place of composition can only be conjectured. The temper and attitude of the book suggest that it originated among Jewish Christians in Palestine or Syria, and it is a plausible conjecture that connects it with the Church of Antioch. As Matthew makes use of Mark, it cannot be earlier than about A.D. 65, and Matt. 22⁷ suggests a date after the fall of Jerusalem, and probably in the last quarter of the first century. The author is unknown ; from the internal evidence it may be guessed that he was a Greek-speaking Jewish Christian of Palestine.

(c) *Luke-Acts* is a single work in two parts, both dedicated to the same person, the otherwise unknown Theophilus. It differs from Matthew and Mark (and John also) in that it is not definitely connected with any great Church. Tradition says that it was composed in the province of Achæa. The truth seems to be that here we have the first piece of Christian apologetic : Luke-Acts was not written in the first instance for ecclesiastical use, but for publication, to commend the new religion to the Empire. It had to do for Christianity what the *Antiquities* of Josephus was to do for Judaism.

The work depends on previously existing sources for its material. The Gospel contains matter from Mark, Q, and from a special source peculiar to Luke (L). It is probable that the first stage in the composition was the bringing together of Q and L to form a document about the size of Mark. This may have taken place at Cæsarea during Paul's detention there. Later, material from Mark was added and the Birth and Infancy narratives were prefixed to produce the Gospel as we know it. Similarly, in Acts it is probable that we have, in the first half, a composition based on the local traditions of the Churches of Jerusalem and Antioch, perhaps also of Cæsarea. The latter part certainly incorporates a travel diary, marked by the use of the first person plural in narrative ([11²⁸], 16¹⁰⁻¹⁷, 20⁵⁻¹⁶, 21¹⁻¹⁸, 27¹–28¹⁶).

Tradition is unanimous in attributing the whole work to Luke, the companion of St. Paul. The fact that it is Luke and not one of the more distinguished characters of the Apostolic Age is itself a strong reason in favour of the tradition. Internal evidence, on the whole, favours the tradition, and the discrepancies between Acts and the Pauline Epistles may fairly readily be explained on the view—probable in itself —that Luke is writing after the death of Paul and before the formation of the Pauline Corpus, and is consequently dependent, where he was not himself an eye-witness, on information supplied by others.

For the dating of the complete work the upper limit is fixed by the end of Acts, which brings us down to about A.D. 63. Acts *may* have been completed any time after that. If we date it soon after A.D. 63, we must put Luke earlier ; and, since Luke includes extracts from Mark, we must place Mark earlier still. This view has been maintained by Harnack ; but it has not commended itself. At the other extreme it is argued that at three points (Luke 3¹ ; Acts 5³⁶ᶠ·, 21³⁸) Luke is dependent on the *Antiquities* of Josephus which was first published in A.D. 93–94. (See Lake and Jackson, *Beginnings of Christianity*, ii. 355–9.) If this dependence were proved, which it is not, it would be necessary to date Luke-Acts about A.D. 95–100 at the earliest. The most probable date may be taken as A.D. 75–85. On the one hand, we must allow time for Mark to get into circulation ; on the other, if the work is by Luke ,the companion of Paul, dates after A.D. 80–85 become increasingly improbable.

5. THE " CATHOLIC " AND " PASTORAL " EPISTLES
(Except the Epistles of John, for which see § 6)

(a) *1 Peter.* The date, character, genuineness, even the unity of this document have all been strenuously disputed, and there is no sign of unanimity in critical opinion. It is held by many that the greater part of the book (1³–4¹¹ or even 1³–5¹¹) is a baptismal address, or a sermon, or a baptismal address (1³–4¹¹) with a pastoral letter (4¹²–5¹¹) attached. Among other conjectures it is suggested that the document is the work of Silvanus or of the Presbyter Aristion. While the various solutions put forward lack nothing in ingenuity, they are not by any means convincing. At the same time, the Petrine authorship is not free from difficulty. The Greek is deemed too good for a Galilean fisherman. The writer seems to be dependent on the letters of Paul, especially Romans and Ephesians. The Old Testament is quoted from the LXX. These difficulties can be met on the assumption, which is not difficult to make, that Silvanus had a very large share in the composition of the letter.

The date can only be guessed at. References to persecution do not seem to imply any organized official attempt to suppress the Church, but rather widespread popular suspicion and hostility. It is still possible to counsel loyalty and respect towards the government (2^{13-17}). Such an attitude is most natural before Nero's outburst. Now the Church tradition is that Peter perished in the Neronian persecution (A.D. 64 or 65), so that a date shortly before the outbreak of the persecution, about A.D. 63, would be consistent with a Petrine origin for the letter. The reference to Babylon in 5^{13} may be taken to mean that the author is writing from Rome, and the greeting from Mark tends to confirm that inference. The letter is addressed to the Christians in five provinces of Asia Minor ; and it tallies with this that the earliest external evidence comes from Polycarp of Smyrna and Papias of Hierapolis.

(b) *James.* This document begins as if it were a letter : "James the servant of God and of the Lord Jesus Christ to the twelve tribes in the Dispersion, greeting." There the resemblance to a letter ends. All the rest is a series of short hortatory passages on various points of belief and practice, strung together without any obvious logical connexion, frequently by means of catchwords. There is no early evidence for the authorship or even the existence of the Epistle, and it did not have an easy entry into the New Testament Canon. Discussions of date and authorship, therefore, move almost entirely in the field of conjecture.

It is probable that the James who appears in 1^1 as the author of the document is James the Lord's brother. There is nobody else who could be referred to in this way except James the son of Zebedee, and he was martyred in A.D. 44. The document claims to be by James the Lord's brother. This may mean that the letter as it stands actually is the composition of James, with the help perhaps of a literary secretary. In that case the composition would have to be dated before A.D. 66 (62 if the dating in Josephus is right), in the lifetime of James. Or, at the other extreme, it may be that the statement is false, and the document a forgery. In that case further inquiry about authorship and date is probably useless labour. Or finally it may mean that the document is a compilation based on genuine Jacobean material. The contents favour some such view as this. The short paragraphs of exhortation suggest the pulpit rather than the desk. The arrangement by catchwords is a common Jewish mnemonic device for the preservation of material in oral tradition. There are details in the utterances that remind us of Palestine and Palestinian

conditions. It is possible that the Jerusalem Christians preserved the memory of the sayings of James the Just and after
his death published them to the Church at large. How long
after we cannot tell ; but it may be conjectured that the
interval was fairly long. A date late in the first or early in
the second century would account for the absence of early
information about the Epistle, and for the shyness of the
Church about taking it into the Canon.

(c) *Jude.* The writer describes himself as " a servant of
Jesus Christ, and brother of James." The natural interpretation of that would be that the Jude meant was the brother
of Jesus mentioned in Mark 6³. But there are indications in
the letter itself which suggest that the author did not belong
to the first generation of Christians (*vv.*³· ¹⁷). On the other
hand, it was known to the author of the Muratorian Canon
and used by the writer of 2 Peter. This makes a date later than
about A.D. 120 unlikely. It has been conjectured by Streeter
that the author may have been Bishop of Jerusalem early in
Trajan's reign (*Primitive Church*, 178 ff.). The letter has the
appearance of being written by a person in authority. It is
not addressed to any community but to the whole body of
Christian people ; and it is directed against a combination of
lax morals and fantastic theology which threatens to under-
mine Church doctrine and discipline. The offending party
are described in very general terms, and the whole thing reads
like a manifesto or open letter condemning certain tendencies
but not accusing any one in particular. The total effect is
rather vague, and by itself the letter seems in the air. If
Burkitt was right about James, and Streeter about Jude, it
might conceivably be that Jude was written as a kind of
covering letter to the collection of James's homilies. But all
these " ifs " only serve to show that we know little or nothing
about the Epistle except that the author is probably not Jude
the Lord's brother.

(d) *2 Peter* is almost certainly pseudonymous. It is a
tract for the times masquerading as a letter. It, like Jude, is
addressed to the Church at large, a fact which the author
overlooks in 3¹. Large parts of the text are taken over from
Jude and, in part, rewritten. They are not improved in the
process. This means that 2 Peter is later than Jude : its
composition probably falls about the middle of the second
century. The author is fighting against much the same kind
of error as Jude. He brings out the additional feature that
the errorists do not believe in a Final Judgement ; and, against
them, he insists on its necessity and certainty.

(e) *The Pastoral Epistles.* The problem of the Pastorals arises out of two facts : first, that they cannot be fitted in anywhere in the life of Paul as described in Acts and the undoubted Pauline Epistles; second, that they show distinct differences in language, style, and ideas from the acknowledged Paulines. The first point could be met if it were shown that the proceedings described in the last chapters of Acts ended in an acquittal and that Paul then resumed his missionary work. The Pastorals might then be assigned to this period. But the evidence for an acquittal and subsequent missionary work is very scanty and falls far short of demonstration. And even if it were convincing, it would only establish that Paul *might* have written the Pastorals. There would still remain the second and more serious difficulty. A detailed examination of the question is given by P. N. Harrison in *The Problem of the Pastoral Epistles.* His conclusion is that the three letters are not the work of Paul but belong to a later time. Some genuine short personal letters of Paul's have, however, been incorporated into 2 Tim. (1^{16-18}, 3^{10-11}, 4^{1-22}) and Titus (3^{12-15}). The hypothesis that these pieces are genuine is not free from difficulty : it is not very easy to visualize their incorporation into a pseudonymous work. However that may be, the letters as a whole do not fit the Paul whom we know from the genuine epistles, nor do they fit the general Church situation in which Paul lived and worked. Rather they reflect the language, ideas, and general situation of a later generation and they should probably be dated about the end of the first century. The emphasis is on Church organization, correct doctrine, good behaviour. Christianity is already being standardized, and the Pastoral Epistles encourage and assist the process. It is easy to believe that the process was inevitable, but difficult to imagine the writer of Galatians helping it on.

6. THE JOHANNINE LITERATURE

This group includes the Fourth Gospel, three Epistles, and the Book of Revelation : the traditional view ascribes all five to John the son of Zebedee. This view was challenged as early as the third century by Dionysius, Bishop of Alexandria, who argued that internal evidence proved the Apocalypse to be by another John than the Apostle. In modern times the apostolic authorship of all five books has been denied (for a survey of the debate, see W. F. Howard, *The Fourth Gospel in Recent Criticism and Interpretation*, pp. 33–105).

It is more and more generally accepted that the Apocalypse and the other four books are not by one writer (for the detailed evidence on which this conclusion rests, see R. H. Charles, *The Revelation of St. John* (I.C.C.), Introduction, pp. xxix–xxxvii, cxvii–cxlii). On the other hand there is still great diversity of opinion with regard to the Gospel and Epistles. There are two main questions : (*a*) whether 2 and 3 John are by the writer of 1 John ; (*b*) whether the Gospel and 1 John are by the same author. Both are still in debate. The issues are stated by A. E. Brooke (*The Johannine Epistles*, I.C.C.), R. H. Charles (*Revelation*, I.C.C.), and C. H. Dodd (*Rylands Bulletin*, xxi. 129–156). The five books may be assigned to any number of authors from one to four ; and here it may be noted that the Gospel and First Epistle have no author's name ; 2 and 3 John are the work of one who describes himself as " the Elder " ; only the Apocalypse gives its writer's name as John.

It has been argued that the authorship of any of the books by John the Apostle is excluded by the early martyrdom of John. The evidence for this early death is not of the best : the *Chronicle* of Georgius Hamartolus (ninth century) and a seventh- to eighth-century epitome of the *Christian History* by Philip of Side (fifth century), both claiming to quote from Papias (second century); the Syriac Martyrology (MS. dated A.D. 411, but depending on an earlier source) and the Carthaginian (in its present form sixth century) ; the prophecy of Jesus preserved in Mark 10³⁹ and Matt. 20²³. No weight can be given to this last ; it can only be used to prove the deaths of James and John if it is a prophecy after the event ; and it can only be argued that it is a prophecy after the event if we otherwise know of the deaths of James and John. It is thus either a circular argument or a superfluous one. The other pieces of evidence, though slight in themselves, have an added weight from the fact that they run counter to what was, from the time of Irenæus onwards, the accepted view in the Church. For Irenæus (*c.* 180) claimed to have heard Polycarp's reminiscences of his " intercourse with John and with the others who had seen the Lord." Now there is little doubt that Polycarp knew the First Epistle (though not apparently the Gospel), and he may have known the author of it. It is possible that the John mentioned by Irenæus was the author of 1 John (perhaps also of 2 and 3 John and the Gospel) : there is no reason why he should have been singled out from the other eye-witnesses unless he had made a name for himself. But there is nothing to show that Polycarp identified this John with the Apostle, though doubtless Irenæus years later—a quarter of a century after Polycarp's death—on the strength of his youthful memories, makes the identification. Clement of **Alexandria**, Tertullian, and Origen also take John the Apostle as the author of the Gospel. The external evidence thus does not lead to any conclusive result : it casts a doubt on the tradition that John the Apostle survived to an advanced age in Ephesus, and it establishes a strong possibility that there was another John (the Elder) in Ephesus who wrote the Epistles and perhaps the Gospel. We turn to the documents themselves.

(a) *The Gospel.* 1 John claims to be the work of an eye-witness (1^{1-4}) and so does the Gospel (1^{14}, 19^{35}). This witness is not given a name, but is referred to in the Gospel as " the disciple whom Jesus loved " (13^{23}, 19^{26}, $20^{2ff.}$, $21^{7.20}$). It is argued that this phrase should indicate one of the three intimate disciples—Peter, James, and John. But it is clear in the Gospel that the beloved disciple is distinguished from Peter ; and James, who was slain by Herod in the forties of the first century, cannot be the writer of the Gospel. There remains only John. Then it is pointed out that an unnamed disciple appears at 1^{40} along with Andrew, and again the suggestion is that that disciple is the author of the Gospel and that his name was John. In 21^{24} the unnamed disciple is mentioned again as the author of the Gospel and a witness whose testimony is true. All this is the more striking in that John the son of Zebedee is never mentioned by name in the Gospel. To these considerations we must add that the Gospel shows traces of first-hand acquaintance with the Palestinian scene : the writer appears to be at home with the geography of the country ; he knows about the customs and ordinances of the Jewish religion in Palestine ; it can even be argued that on the whole his modes of thought are more Jewish than Greek ; and there is undoubtedly Aramaic colouring in the language, however the phenomena are to be explained (transla-tion from an Aramaic Gospel ? use of Aramaic sources ? com-position by one whose mother-tongue was Aramaic ?). These points all suggest that the author of the Gospel is a Palestinian Jewish Christian disciple who was in closest contact with the Master.

But there are other considerations which are not so favour-able to this view. (*a*) The Jesus of the Synoptic Gospels has an unmistakable manner of speech—concise, vivid, searching, and challenging. He disposes of a question or an adversary in a sentence. The Jesus of the Fourth Gospel speaks in a way that does not resemble this and does, all too closely, resemble the style of the author of 1 John. (*b*) The writer of the Fourth Gospel seems to be dependent for some of his information on Mark and Luke. At the same time he contradicts them at several important points (*e.g.* the occasion of the cleansing of the Temple, and the date of the Last Supper). It is difficult to see why an eye-witness should need to use Mark and Luke ; and where he differs from them, it is difficult to believe that he is an eye-witness unless we can be convinced that he is always right and they always wrong, a conclusion which is neither proved nor probable. (*c*) There seem to be indications that, while one mind has shaped the Gospel in its present form, the materials used in its composition were not derived from one source.

It seems possible to begin to reconcile all these divergent pieces of evidence by supposing that the Gospel is the work of John the Elder, and that he used material which included the Gospels of Mark and Luke and an independent tradition of Palestinian Jewish-Christian origin. This last may go back to John the son of Zebedee. We must further suppose that the author of the Gospel had pondered over his materials during many years, and that what he set out to produce was an account of the Ministry of Jesus which would bring out its deepest meaning as the perfect revelation of God in terms of human life.

If, as seems likely, the Fourth Gospel is dependent on Luke, the earliest date for its composition will be after the publication of Luke (*c.* A.D. 80). The lower limit would be approximately fixed about A.D. 110 if it were certain that Ignatius quotes from the Gospel ; but expert opinion is divided on the point. The most that can be said with certainty is that Ignatius was familiar with ideas that are characteristic of the Gospel. The earliest clear use of John is probably in an apocryphal Gospel, of which a fragment on papyrus is preserved in the British Museum (Egerton Pap. 2). The papyrus is dated in the first half of the second century, and the apocryphal Gospel may well have been composed about A.D. 130. This would put the composition of John earlier still, and would make a date later than A.D. 120 improbable. We shall probably not be far wrong if we fix the limits between A.D. 90 and 120. The tradition links it quite firmly with Ephesus, though there are indications which might support the theory of a connexion with Antioch either of the author or of the Gospel at an earlier stage in its composition.

The Gospel in its present form does not appear to be in order ; and it is not possible to make it read consecutively without some rearrangement of sections. (See Bernard, *op. cit.*, pp. xvi–xxx, and W. F. Howard, *op. cit.*, p. 264.)

Whether the dislocations in the text are to be taken as accidents that have happened after the work was completed and put into circulation, or as evidence that it was left unfinished by the author and put together from his papers by an editor or editors is a problem as yet unsolved, as are most of the problems connected with this Gospel.

(b) *1 John.* This document, though grouped with the so-called Catholic Epistles, has none of the formulæ at beginning and end which we expect in a letter : no sender's name, no address, no greetings, and no indications in the letter itself that would fix it to a definite time and place. It *may* be a letter, but it may equally be a tract or (like the so-called second Epistle of Clement) a sermon. It is written to warn the faithful against false teaching which would introduce a docetic Christology and loosen the bond between faith and morals.

The earliest evidence of its use is in quotation by Polycarp, who evidently knew it. It was therefore in existence in Asia Minor in the early part of the second century.

The writer claims to be an eye-witness of the events which constitute the Gospel, and it is widely held that he is identical with the author of the Fourth Gospel. The identification is not free from difficulty (the case against it is best stated by C. H. Dodd in *Rylands Bulletin*, xxi. 129–156) ; but there is real difficulty in imagining two men living apparently at the same time, in the same place and circumstances, and producing works that have so much in common. On the whole it seems easier to account for the differences between the Gospel and the Epistle by supposing that they belong to different periods in the life of one writer. The question of priority remains open.

(c) *2 and 3 John.* These are real letters, and they appear to be by the same hand as the Gospel and 1 John. The writer does not give his name, but describes himself as " the Elder." Presumably he was a person sufficiently well known to do this, and no doubt the two letters were accepted beside the Gospel and 1 John because they were believed to be by the same author.

2 John is addressed to " the elect lady and her children," and this is now generally understood to mean " the Church and its members," but what particular community it was is unknown and likely to remain so. 3 John is sent to one Gaius, a member of the Church and apparently of a community other than that to which 2 John was written. Nothing is known about him or about the other persons mentioned in the letter.

2 John has this in common with 1 John that it is opposed
to those who teach a docetic Christology. Both letters are concerned with the organization of the Churches and particularly
with the question of hospitality and a hearing for travelling
preachers ; and it is perhaps possible to discern in the letters
a stage in the process by which ecclesiastical authority came
to be in the hands of the monarchical bishop. (Cf. Streeter,
The Primitive Church, 83–89.) There is no means of dating
the letters exactly. If they are by the same person as the
Gospel and 1 John, they may be placed in the same period,
about A.D. 90–120.

(d) *The Apocalypse.* This book has two main parts : in chaps.
1–3 we have a letter containing messages to seven Churches in
Western Asia Minor, and in chaps. 4–22 revelations concerning
the future. The first chapter is introductory and describes
how the author received the revelations and was commissioned
to write to the Churches. It differs from the Jewish Apocalypses in that " it is a new message, given to the contemporary
seer " (Burkitt, *Jewish and Christian Apocalypses*, p. 6—one
of the most illuminating books on the subject). The seer
gives his name as John (1¹· ⁴· ⁹, 22⁸) ; he adds no official
designation to the name, and his authority to write as he does
to the Churches is based not on any official position but on
direct revelation. He addresses them not *qua* " Apostle " or
" Elder " but as a prophet repeating a message given and
reporting things seen in his vision. The main purport of the
book is that " the end is not yet," with explanations why
it is so, and exhortation to Christians to live in constant
preparedness for it when it comes.

If the book is a unity, it cannot be earlier than about
A.D. 60, for the Churches in question were not founded before
the middle fifties. It is, of course, possible that the writer has
incorporated earlier material in the book ; but the view is
gaining ground that it is a single piece of work, the product of
one mind. The writer can hardly be the author of the Gospel
and Epistles ; the language and ideas differ too widely. He
could conceivably be John the son of Zebedee ; certainly the
little that we know about the Apostle accords better with the
sentiments of the Apocalypse than with those of the Gospel
and Epistles. The question of authorship is bound up with
that of date.

Three dates have been suggested. (*a*) In the period
between Nero's persecution and the fall of Jerusalem (A.D. 64–
70). Chronologically this would allow authorship by John the
Apostle, even if we suppose (with Charles) that he was martyred

at some time in this period. (*b*) In the reign of Vespasian (A.D. 69–79). But the reason for this view does not exclude a later date. (*c*) In the reign of Domitian (A.D. 81–96), and probably towards the end of it. This view best fits the internal evidence of the book and has in its favour the preponderant weight of patristic testimony beginning with Irenæus. The most generally accepted view places the composition in the period A.D. 90–96.

If it is possible to believe that John the Apostle lived on in Asia Minor to this date, it is possible to believe that he was the author of the book. If Charles is right, then John the Seer is a distinct figure whom we know only from this one work of his.

7. NON-CANONICAL LITERATURE OF THE PERIOD

Besides the books which found a place in the New Testament, there remain other works produced during the first century or so of the Church's existence, which either never were seriously considered or lingered for a time on the fringe of the Canon before being finally excluded. Among these the most important is the group collected together under the name Apostolic Fathers. (There is a handy edition of the texts with translations by K. Lake in the Loeb Library, 2 vols.) The writings comprised in this group are :

(a) *1 Clement*. This is a letter from the Roman Church to the Corinthian, occasioned by disorder and faction in the latter community. The Roman Church intervenes on the side of the properly constituted authorities of the Corinthian Church. The name of Clement is most probably attached to the document because it was the name of the official in the Roman Church who wrote the letter on behalf of the community. The name does not appear in the letter itself, but the letter is called Clement's by Dionysius of Corinth in the second century. Much has been conjectured but little is known about Clement. He appears in the Roman tradition as the second or third Bishop of Rome. The letter looks back on the age of the Apostles, but speaks of presbyters appointed by the Apostles as still alive ; and there is no trace of the controversies and troubles of the second century. The probable date is in the last decade of the first century about A.D. 96.

(b) *2 Clement*. This document, attached to the preceding and labelled " The Second Epistle of Clement to the Corinthians " is neither an Epistle nor by Clement. It is a homily of uncertain date, probably about the middle of the second century. It has been conjectured that it was a letter from

Soter, Bishop of Rome (*c.* A.D. 166–174), to Corinth, or that it was a sermon preached in the Church of Corinth, or that it was an Alexandrian homily ; but nothing is certainly known save that it is one of the oldest Christian sermons in existence.

(c) *The Epistles of Ignatius.* Ignatius was Bishop of Antioch and wrote these letters while on his way to Rome for martyrdom. The date of his martyrdom (and of the journey) is uncertain but may be placed with confidence in the first twenty years of the second century. The collection of letters has come down to us in three forms. The first (the Long Recension) contains thirteen letters, some of which are clearly not genuine ; the second (Short Recension) has seven ; the third (the Syriac) has only three. It is generally held that the second form must be the basis of the edition of the genuine letters, and even that has to be freed from interpolations. On this basis the collection contains letters to the Churches of Ephesus, Magnesia, Tralles, Rome, Philadelphia, Smyrna, and one to the Bishop of Smyrna, Polycarp. All these letters show the burning zeal of the writer, and in particular his concern for his own Church of Antioch, his strong advocacy of episcopacy, and his hostility to the docetic heresy.

(d) *The Epistle of Polycarp to the Philippians.* This letter is connected with the last letter in the Ignatian corpus. Polycarp was Bishop of Smyrna in the second century and was martyred, probably on 22nd February 156, at the age of at least eighty-six. His letter is concerned (*a*) with the request of the Philippian Church for copies of the letters of Ignatius, and (*b*) with disorders in that Church. P. N. Harrison has shown good reasons for thinking that we have in fact two letters of Polycarp ; the earlier (chaps. 13 and 14 of the present epistle) being a covering note sent with a collection of Ignatian epistles ; the later (chaps. 1–12) a letter dealing with the disorders. There is still, however, difference of opinion as to the interval that separates the two letters, and those who accept the division are not all convinced that the second letter should be dated as late as *circa* A.D. 135. (The theory is fully set out in P. N. Harrison's *Polycarp's Two Epistles to the Philippians.*)

(e) *The Martyrdom of Polycarp* is recorded in a letter from the Church of Smyrna to the Church of Philomelium. It is written very soon after the events it describes, and is the earliest document of its kind.

(f) *The Didache.* The sub-title of this book is " The Lord's teaching to the Gentiles by the Twelve Apostles." It falls into two parts. The first (chaps. 1–6), commonly called " The

Two Ways," is a manual of instruction for prospective church members. It has close affinities with chaps. 18–20 of the Epistle of Barnabas. These are perhaps best explained by the theory that both the Didache and Epistle of Barnabas have made use of an earlier Jewish-Christian (perhaps originally Jewish) document. The remainder of the Didache (chaps. 7–16) consists of directions for the worship and organization of the community. The book as a whole presents many still unsolved problems, both of textual and literary criticism, of date and provenance. The date may probably be put in the first half of the second century ; and the place of origin in the East, with some balance of probability in favour of Syria.

(g) *The Epistle of Barnabas* lays no claim to be by the companion of Paul, and the title which makes the attribution is almost certainly wrong. Its affinities are with the school of thought that flourished in Alexandria for centuries ; its main object is to promote the allegorical interpretation of the Old Testament. The date is quite uncertain ; and there is nothing in the document to fix it definitely. Probably the period between A.D. 80 and 130 would cover it.

(h) *The Shepherd of Hermas.* This book, much the largest in the collection, is an Apocalypse recording revelations granted to its author. It is divided into three parts : the Visions, the Mandates, and the Similitudes ; and the main concern of the whole is with the problem of sin *in the Church,* the failure of church members to fulfil the requirements of the Christian way of life. Here we may see the tension, always present in the Church, between the rigorism that would reject the unworthy member and the milder view that regards the church as a school for saints and uses church discipline as an educative force. Hermas allows the second chance to church members (but only one second chance), and with it he develops the beginnings of a penitential system. Tradition places the composition of the book in Rome ; but there is some uncertainty as to the date. According to the Muratorian fragment the work was composed during the episcopate of Pius (c. A.D. 140–155), who was the brother of the author. On the other hand, the book itself (Vis. ii. iv. 3) implies that the writer is a contemporary of Clement (about the end of the first century). The discrepancy may be overcome by supposing that the composition of the book was spread over a long period and that its completion fell within the episcopate of Pius.

(i) *The Epistle to Diognetus* should probably be regarded as an early apologetic work. The author is unknown, as is the recipient, and the date is uncertain. (The " most excellent

Diognetus " of chap 1. reminds us of the " most excellent Theophilus " of Luke 1⁴.) This apologetic writing ends with chap. 10 ; the remaining chapters (11–12) have nothing to do with it, and are probably part of a sermon. (The name of Hippolytus has been suggested as the probable preacher.) The first ten chapters should probably be assigned to the third century or late second century. It is mentioned here for the sake of completeness, though it hardly falls within the period.

(j) A certain number of apocryphal writings fall near the end of our period. Such are the heretical Gospel of Pseudo-Peter, the Acts of John, the Apocalypse of Peter. For fuller information about these and similar documents reference may be made to M. R. James, *The Apocryphal New Testament*.

BIBLIOGRAPHY

The Introductions (the more elementary are given first) by F. B. Clogg, E. F. Scott, A. H. M‘Neile, and James Moffatt.
Vincent Taylor, *The Gospels ; a Short Introduction*.
B. H. Streeter, *The Four Gospels*.
A. D. Nock, *St. Paul*.
K. Lake, *The Earlier Epistles of St. Paul*.
G. S. Duncan, *St. Paul's Ephesian Ministry*.
P. N. Harrison, *The Problem of the Pastoral Epistles*.
B. H. Streeter, *The Primitive Church*.

PART II
THE LAND AND THE PEOPLE

VI. THE GEOGRAPHY OF PALESTINE

(This chapter should be studied with Adam Smith's "Atlas of the Historical Geography of the Holy Land")

The Lands and Peoples of Syria and Palestine. The four hundred and fifty miles of habitable land which link Asia to Africa between the waters of the Eastern Mediterranean and the deserts of Arabia have been from all time, as they must always remain, a notable meeting-place for the peoples of the two continents ; and Palestine, which is a third part of this expanse, small as it is, has had no small *rôle* to play in the drama of their conflict. This *rôle* has been twofold, for we have to distinguish the features which Palestine shares with its much larger neighbour, Syria, to the north, and those which it possesses of its own right and which have made it uniquely a Holy Land. Of the first it is enough to say that in physical structure the whole stretch of country from the Lebanon Mountains to the verge of Egypt may be strictly called continuous. There is first, starting from the west, a strip of coastal plain, then a range of mountains, then a deep declivity or Rift Valley, then another range, and finally another strip of cultivable land which fades out, with its life-giving waters, into the sands of the desert. These are the salient features which both Syria and Palestine possess in common, and it is to these that they owe what is common in their histories. From the west they are open to the maritime enterprise of other peoples, though Palestine falls far behind in this respect as it possesses no good natural harbour south of Carmel. From the east they are exposed to invasion from the desert, a peril from which no empire or civilization has yet been able to protect them for long. Finally, to the north and south they offer a continuous highway, not indeed, as we shall see, a direct or easy one, but sufficiently practicable for the advance of a determined army or the irresistible passage of migrating hordes.

A brief glance at the ethnology of these regions and particularly of Palestine will show how these facts have influenced their history. The earliest inhabitants of these countries date back to the oldest (Palæolithic) Age of Stone, and their

133

development can now be traced, thanks to the continuous stratifications recently discovered at Jericho (Tell es Sultan), from the " Chellean " open-air life of the plateaux east and west of Jordan through the Mousterian (Neanderthal) cave dwellings (Galilee, Carmel, the Judean mountains, etc.) to the first beginnings of village and even city civilization and the dawn of what is called the Early Bronze Age (from 3000 B.C.). But these first settlers (their origin is unknown) cannot have been left very long in peaceful possession of their solitude. From the mountain-plateaux of Armenia a people of " Alpine " or " Armenoid " stock descended (before the fourth millennium B.C.) into the rich lands of Upper Mesopotamia and spread thence southwards through Syria to the borders of Egypt. In the first of their new homes, the " Great Bend " of the Euphrates in which lay the city of Harran and Aram Naharaim the land of Abraham's nativity (Gen. 24⁴⁻⁷, 27⁴³, etc.), these immigrants were known to the inhabitants of ancient Babylonia (Akkad) as the " widespreading Subareans," but in the far south a branch of them retained what was perhaps their own proper name—the " Hurrians," being known to the Egyptians as " Haru " and to the people of Israel as " Horites." Remnants of this non-" Semitic " northern race were absorbed later by the Hebrew Edomites in Mount Seir (Deut 2¹²), but their presence at one period throughout the whole of Palestine is now widely accepted by scholars. The mysterious Perizzites (Gen. 13⁷ ; Josh. 17¹⁵), a nation often contrasted with the " Semitic " Canaanites, would seem to have been of this stock and to have occupied or been driven up into the highlands of Palestine and perhaps Gilead ; and it is probable that the name " Hivite " in some places where it occurs should be read " Horite " by the change of a single letter, as, for example, in the case of Shechem (Gen. 34²).

At the same early period, but possibly after the arrival of these northerners, an even more important migration of peoples invaded this area from the opposite point of the compass. The original homeland of the " Semites " (the name, it must be remembered, refers to the language not to the race of these people) may have been in southern Arabia, but is to be sought more probably in Africa. The first wave of them, the Amorites, were well known to the early Babylonians by the beginning of the third millennium B.C. as the inhabitants of all north Syria between the Amanus mountains and the middle Euphrates : in Palestine, apart from the many Biblical references to them, their presence can be traced by the various places named after or connected with their great god Dagan from the maritime plain where the Philistines adopted the cult to the hill country of Ephraim (cf. Beit Dejan, east of Nablus). Following hard upon them in the first half of the third millennium B.C. (about 2700 (?)) came a second wave of " Semites " who gave the country its familiar name of Canaan. The Canaanites themselves held that they arrived as fugitives by way of the Red Sea, *i.e.* the Gulf of Akabah, and this tradition appears to find some corroboration from the epic poems recently discovered at Ras Shamra (the site of the ancient Ugarit, ten miles north of the modern Latakia) : it may explain also the disasters which at this period befell the Old Kingdom in Egypt from the intrusion of " foreigners," and it may in turn be explained by the first appearance soon after this time of the negro as opposed to the " Hamite " upon the southern borders of that country. It seems clear at any rate that on their arrival in the Arabah Rift south of the Dead Sea, the Canaanites pushed up northwards into the Jordan Valley (Num. 13[29]) and north-westwards to the coast of the Mediterranean, spreading ever northwards up the maritime plain till by sea and land they had occupied what was later to be called Phœnicia.

It was now once more the turn of the north to play its part in this intermingling of racial stocks, and it was once more from the Hurrian area of Harran and Arrapha (modern Kirkuk, the Biblical Arpachshad, Gen. 10[22], etc.) that the newcomers derived their origin. The Habiru or Hebrews were in all probability not a " Semitic " but an " Armenoid " people who claimed kinship with such non-" Semitic " nations as the Elamites (Gen. 10[22]), but they had long adopted the " Semitic " speech which had been brought to these regions from the far south, and little remained but certain indelible physical characteristics to proclaim the secret of their birth. The migration of Abram the Hebrew from the land of his nativity (Aram Naharaim) to Canaan must have taken place in the middle of the second millennium B.C., and it appears to have been followed not long afterwards by the irruption of a mixed horde of northerners and Syrian " Semites " who swept through the country with their new and irresistible weapon, the horse and chariot, and set up in Egypt (about 1750 B.C.) the foreign dynasty of the Hyksos. That many non-Abrahamic Hebrews accompanied this invasion and settled afterwards in Palestine is extremely probable : others came perhaps later in the train of the Hittite monarch, Subbililiuma, who invaded Syria in the fourteenth century B.C., and stayed on to harass the unlucky vassal-princes who administered Canaan for the

Pharaoh, as the famous letters found at El Amarna testify : still later these non-Israelite Hebrews suffered heavily with Israel from the Philistines (1 Sam. 13[7]) and ultimately threw in their lot with their old kinsmen (1 Sam 14[21]).

The Philistines themselves were the last wave of migrants to enter Palestine (which owes that name to them) till many centuries later the Mohammedan conquest peopled a large part of it from the desert. That they arrived both by land and by sea in the company of a confederacy of Sea Peoples who attacked Egypt at the beginning of the eleventh century B.C. is unquestionable, for they are clearly so described (as Peleset) on the Egyptian monuments of this date. What their origin was is, however, not so clear, though it seems certain that their immediate point of departure upon this expedition must have been the south coast of Asia Minor (from Caria to Cilicia (?)). Whether before this they had roved the Ægean or the Adriatic as pirates or whether their old homeland is to be sought, as some suggest, in the region of the Caucasus, must remain for the moment undetermined. All that we really know about them is that they had absorbed much of the Ægean and Achæan civilizations, as both their pottery and their armour (1 Sam. 17[5-7]) bear witness, and that they appear to have been settled as garrisons in Palestine after their conquest by the Pharaoh Rameses III., only to assert their independence when the power of Egypt declined.

This rapid review of the ethnology of Palestine will have sufficed to show how in the main physical features it shares with Syria the fate and function of serving as a meeting-place for the peoples of Asia and Africa : it has indeed received its population literally from all points of the compass, as it is still receiving them though in much smaller measure to-day. Nor is this all, for while Syria and Palestine have given a new home to so many and to such various intruders they have been a highroad and a prey for less permanent, but not more welcome, visitors. Egyptian and Hittite, Assyrian and Babylonian, Persian, Greek, and Roman conquerors have marched and counter-marched through them in turn, have harried their coasts, despoiled their cities, devastated their lands, deported whole sections of their population, while at no moment in their long history have they been free from the raids of marauding Bedouin from the desert. Twice only have they known the blessings of a secure and prosperous peace, but Great Britain has yet to show that she can succeed in making truly permanent what Rome after six centuries was forced under Heraclius to abandon. No words can speak louder than these

harsh and brutal facts, which link the two sections of this
" land-bridge " as companions in misfortune and reveal the
nakedness of their frontiers on every side. From sea and desert,
from the valleys of the Nile and the Euphrates, they lie equally
open to attack as they are equally helpless in resisting it. All
the more remarkable is it that in one small corner of this
territory there could be sown and fostered a seed which should
overshadow the world ; and this, in fact, was due to certain
physical features in which Palestine differed markedly from its
neighbour.

The Geography of Syria and Palestine : Distinctive Features.
It has been said above that, generally speaking, the whole
stretch of country which we have been considering is continuous in the fivefold division of its physical structure. This
is true, but it is very far from correct to assume that this
continuity can be sketched as is sometimes done in a simple
diagrammatic form, in which straight lines or rectangular
blocks drawn vertically and parallel to one another represent
the coast line, the two mountain ranges with the Rift between
them and the cultivable strip which separates them from the
desert. Such a " simplification " of the problem is of no value
to the student of historical geography, for whom the differences
which exist between these two countries are more important
than their general similarity.

We may consider, for example, the strip of coast-land
which is the first of these five divisions, and here we notice
at once a feature which has always distinguished the history of
Phœnicia from that of Palestine. From the great recess of the
Gulf of Alexandretta which links Asia Minor to Syria we can
observe as we move southwards no coastal plain of any notable
extent till we have passed the Ladder of Tyre (Ras en Nakura)
fourteen miles south of that city, and entered the plain of
Acre. From this point southwards, however, the whole aspect
of the country changes. The lofty mountain-range which
hitherto as Amanus Bargylus or Lebanon has overshadowed
the narrow littoral strip, throwing forward great shoulders
at intervals to the edge of the sea, drops more or less abruptly
at the gorge of the Litani River (Nahr el Kasimiyeh) to the
highlands of Upper Galilee, and when it is resumed south of
the Plain of Esdraelon in the hill country of Ephraim and
Judah it is separated from the Mediterranean by a broad belt
of cultivable land which runs in a wide and continuous curve
to the frontier of Egypt at the Wadi el Arish. This division
has been a critical one for the history of the two countries.
To the north of the Ladder of Tyre we find in ancient times a

coast-line dotted with more or less isolated and independent maritime city-states, Tyre, Sidon, Biruta (Beirout), Gebal (Gubla, Byblos), Irkata ("the Arkite"), Simyra ("the Zemarite"), Arvad, Ugarit (Ras Shamra), and so forth : as the Biblical writer put it, "the families of the Canaanites were spread abroad" (Gen. 10[18]). Here communications were easiest by sea and not by land, and the combination of these scattered principalities into one homogeneous state was rarely attempted and still more rarely achieved. At their zenith the maritime Canaanites could command the coast-line of Palestine even as far south as Ascalon, but a hold so tenuous could not be maintained by sea alone, nor could such a confederacy resist for long the compact and organized Empires of the Near East. Hence it was that the eyes of the Phœnicians turned more and more westwards across the Mediterranean, and that their ambitions were satisfied not in conquests but in trade. (For a more detailed description of the maritime plains of Palestine, see below, pp. 141, 145 f.)

Another marked dissimilarity between the physical structure of Syria and Palestine is to be found in their " Rift Valley " sections. Between the lofty ranges of Lebanon and Anti-Lebanon this Rift takes the form of a broad and fertile plain called el Bukaa. Northwards out of this flows the River Orontes, the valley of which is studded with important ancient sites, such as Kadesh (Tell Nebi Mindu), Homs (Abzu ?), and Hamath, and has wide and easy access to the rolling plains around Aleppo and the highroads from Asia Minor and the Euphrates. To the south, on the other hand, the communications become much more difficult. The valley of the Litani, in which Baalbek is the only notable site, drops into a deep gorge as the river carves its way first southwards and then abruptly westwards to the Mediterranean ; and a tumbled mass of hills blocks the neck by which the traveller from this recess of Syria must pass over into Palestine, since the bed of the Hasbani, the northern tributary of the Jordan, provides no facilities for a highroad. How isolated, in fact, are the two countries at this point may be learned from two very dissimilar events in their history. When the Pharaoh, Thutmose III., advancing from Egypt in 1479 B.C., had defeated a confederacy of Amorites at Megiddo in the Plain of Esdraelon, he determined to crush their resistance finally by invading Syria itself, his special objective being the city of their overlord, that Kadesh which has just been mentioned. To accomplish this plan, however, he made no effort to force his way over the pass between Lebanon and anti-Lebanon, which

would have been his shortest route, but transferred his army
to shipboard, landed it on the coast a hundred miles and
more to the north and attacked the enemy through the gap
which opens towards Homs and Hama between the Lebanon
and the Bargylus (Ansarieh) Mountains (the " Entering in
of Hamath," Judg. 3³, etc. ?). So, too, when centuries later
the Danites attacked and captured Laish (near Banias at the
sources of the Jordan) they effected their object with the
greatest ease because the Sidonians dwelling there were completely cut off from their mother city (Judg. 18⁷).

To sum up, we may say that while it may be difficult, as
our modern statesmen have found it, to mark out a completely satisfactory frontier line between Syria and Palestine,
a very real physical barrier does nevertheless exist which
spreads over a wide belt of hilly country from the Ladder of
Tyre to the eastern flanks of Mount Hermon. The approaches,
in a word, from the one to the other, must always normally
be from either flank and not from the direct North ; and as
Palestine possessed in ancient times no natural harbours but
Acre and Tanturah (Dor) and only the one somewhat perilous
roadstead at Jaffa, it follows that the main avenue of access
to it from the valleys of the Orontes and Euphrates lay in
those days to the north-east, where the highroads from
Damascus and the plateau of the Hauran descend upon the
Jordan Valley. That they do not pursue the course of that
valley, but as we shall see below climb immediately up its
western slopes, is a final demonstration of the essential difference between the main physical features of Syria and Palestine.
The Jordan Valley or Ghor is not like the valley of the Orontes,
an important thoroughfare lined with great cities and well-
trodden by armies and caravans : it is for the greater part of
its length a torrid and unhealthy *cul-de-sac* which finds its
end over 1200 feet below the level of the Mediterranean in
the desolate and forbidding waters of the Dead Sea. This
section of the Rift Valley, in short, though in the physical
sense it is one of the most pronounced and remarkable features
of Palestine, has had little historical importance save as providing at one time an inconvenient but practicable link between
the western and eastern ranges and at another an intimidating
but by no means impenetrable barrier to incursions from the
Desert into the Sown. At this point, however, we are already
touching our main subject, to the detailed study of which we
may now turn.

The Geography of Palestine : *Survey in Detail*. Palestine
may be divided into five more or less easily distinguishable

sections. These are : (1) Galilee, including the plains of
Acre and Esdraelon ; (2) The Maritime Plains of Sharon and
Philistia; (3) The Hill Country of Ephraim ("Mount Ephraim")
or of " Israel " (Josh. 11¹⁶) ; (4) The Hill Country of Judah ;
(5) The South Country or Negeb. To each of these (except
the second), in view of what has just been said, we shall relate
those parts of the Jordan Valley and the eastern range with
which they have been most closely connected in the past.

I. *Galilee* (*including the Plains of Acre and Esdraelon*). The
traveller desirous of obtaining the best view of the greater
part of Galilee should, after landing at Haifa, have himself
driven round the Bay of Acre to the town of that name (the
Israelite Accho, the Græco-Roman Ptolemais) and thence by
the road which mounts the highlands of Galilee to the modern
Safed ; if when he has gained a sufficient altitude he will halt
and face southwards, he will find a remarkable panorama
spread at his feet. Behind him rises the rugged plateau of
Upper Galilee, stretching northwards in a tangle of hills and
dry water-courses till it is brought suddenly to an end at the
deep gorge of the Litani, but in front of him and to right and
left extends what is perhaps the most beautiful countryside
in Palestine. Immediately below the road the hillside drops
away to a green valley, the Wadi Shaib, which with the Wadi
et Tuffah marks a clean line of division from west to east
between the highlands of Upper and the milder contours of
Lower Galilee. Beyond this a ridge of hills can be seen which
separates this system of valleys from the long inland plain of
Asochis (the Sahel el Buttauf), and beyond this again two
further ridges with yet another fertile hollow between them.
This latter is the Wadi Rummaneh which is linked by a low
watershed with the wide Sahel el Ahma to the east of it and
thence through the Wadi Fejjas with the Jordan Valley : it
has been from time immemorial the " Way of the Sea " from
beyond Jordan (Is. 9¹) and carries to this day the " Hauran "
road (Darb el Hawarneh). Here as the eye follows its course
towards Damascus, it is caught and held by the blue waters of
the Sea of Galilee which with the Upper Jordan Valley and
snow-capped Hermon marks out on this side a well-defined
frontier. Finally, on the horizon to the south, and at an interval
which betrays the presence of yet another but broader plain
in front of them, a semicircle of hills closes the landscape. Far
to the right by the sea can be discerned the long, high ridge of
Mount Carmel with modern Haifa spreading around its foot
and clambering up its flanks, and this ridge, though it drops
somewhat abruptly at its southern extremity, can be seen

continuing in a range which sweeps round to the spectator's
left till it rises once more in a bluff upstanding bulwark above
the Jordan Valley, the ill-omened mountain of Gilboa (2 Sam.
1[21]) : the historical and strategic importance of this line of
hills will be considered in a moment. This, then, is Galilee,
the Gelil or Circle of the "Nations" (Isa. 9[1]). Actually it is
more easily pictured not as a circle but as an immense U,
the mouth of which is closed by the northern frontier of
Palestine. The outer rim of the U is formed (to begin at its
left or west arm) by the Plain of Acre, the Plain of Esdraelon,
the broad Valley of Jezreel descending between Gilboa and
Little Hermon (Jebel Duby) and the Jordan Rift (including
the Sea of Galilee and Lake Huleh) from the Valley of Jezreel
northwards to the sources of the river under Hermon. Within
this great curve of low-lying plains and lakes are, first, to the
north the highlands of Upper Galilee and then beneath this
the system of alternating transverse valleys and ridges to
which we have already alluded.

The Plain of Acre is about twenty-eight miles in length,
with a width varying from four to six miles. In shape it is a
B of which the larger loop is formed by its southern portion,
and the cross-bar by a ridge of Upper Galilee thrown forward
into the plain opposite the town of Acre. Acre itself is the
centre of this region both literally and historically, for whoever possessed it could control effectively both sections of the
plain, and its importance as the only good-sized natural
harbour south of Tyre and as the great maritime emporium
of the Hauran made it one of the most valuable sites in Palestine
before the rise of modern Haifa on the other side of its bay.
It is for this reason that the town has been so often contested
throughout its history, by Asher in the early days of the
Israelite Settlement (Jud. 1[31]), by Richard Cœur de Lion, by
Napoleon ; and even when in Roman times the great harbour
of Cæsarea might have been expected to oust its older and
smaller rival, Ptolemais still kept its position as a trading
centre (Acts 21[7]), and is standing to-day while Cæsarea is in
ruins.

Of the other ancient sites in its plain five only need be
mentioned. The first of these is the little coastal town of Zib
(Achzib, Josh. 19[29], etc.), nine miles to the north of Acre, which
seems to have watched the entrance of the plain from the
Ladder of Tyre. The remaining four are now no longer inhabited ; they exist to-day simply as rounded heaps (" tells ")
under which lie hidden the ruined walls and houses of towns or
small cities long ago destroyed and forgotten. Their position,

however, is important, for they all lie on or near some pass
into the hills from which the plain might be invaded or
the Arabian caravans might emerge. Opposite Acre itself lies
Tell Berweh, controlling the road from the Jordan Valley
through the Wadi Shaib, while a mile or two south of it rises
the mighty Tell Keisan (possibly Achshaph, Josh. 11¹, etc.),
which must have been at one time the foremost stronghold
in these parts. Then, across the Bay, at the point where
Carmel allows a strip of level land to intervene as a narrow
passage between its steep sides and the sea, lies the old site
which may be Sycamonium (Tell es Semak), but which, whatever its ancient name, was placed here obviously as a sentinel.
Finally, on a tributary of the Kishon (Nahr el Mukutta) at
the south-east angle of the plain stands the mound of El
Harbaj, an abandoned city of the Late Bronze Age (c. 1600–
1200 B.C.), which may once have been " Harosheth of the
Nations " (Jud. 4¹).

Immediately south of this point the narrow Kishon defile,
where Sisera's horses and chariots met their fate, gives access
to the Plain of Esdraelon, which stretches eastward to the
strange bare dome of Tabor (Jebel et Tor) and southwards to
the village of Jenin, an expanse of some twenty miles with a
width varying from six to twelve miles. Here the outer defences of the " Ring of the Nations " appear in their most
remarkable form, showing how this part of Palestine could be
formed into a single kingdom, well able for all its smallness
to offer a fierce resistance to invasion. On its extreme right
flank the frontier of this kingdom was sufficiently guarded by
the formidable sheer mass of Carmel, which rises at its highest
above 1800 feet and for eight miles does not fall below the
1800 contour. But the lower hills which continue the barrier
south-eastwards (perhaps the Naphath Dor of 1 Kings 4¹¹, etc.,
since Dor lies on the coast immediately west of them) are
pierced by a number of easy passes from the maritime plain,
and at the inner mouth of each of these was planted in ancient
times a strongly walled fortress. At the first, which follows
the course of the Wadi el Milh under the shadow of Carmel,
stood Jokneam, now the impressive mound of Keimun. (It
may be noted in passing that it was by this route that Napoleon
led his army to the siege of Acre.) Next, on a rougher road
(which was one of the two passes used by the British in their
great advance in the Palestine campaign) there was a fortress
now called Tell Abu Shusheh, the ancient name of which is
still unknown. Three miles or more to the south-east Megiddo
(Tell el Mutassellim) watched the Musmus Pass (the Wadi

Arah) by which most of the great conquerors of this country, including Lord Allenby, have directed the main body of their invading armies. For this is Har Megiddon—Armageddon— one of the great battlefields and strategic positions of the world, where the Amorite confederacy was met and crushed by Thutmose, where Solomon established his chariots and horsemen (1 Kings 9[19]), where Josiah fought and died (2 Kings 23[29]), and where, as the name El Lejjun still testifies, the Roman legions had a permanent encampment. Yet another four miles to the south-east lies Taanach (Tell Taanuk), near which the levies of Barak overthrew the kings of Canaan (Judg. 5[19]) : here too is a pass, which, crossing the hills in a south-westerly direction, emerges on to the plain of Sharon through the " Gate of Gates " (Bab el Ibweib). Beyond Taanach, six miles once more to the south-east, the gardens and palm trees of Jenin (En Gannim, the " Garden House " of 2 Kings 9[27]) reveal the presence of a defile whose stream gives this little town a welcome touch of verdure. This valley is the " Ascent of Gur " (2 Kings 9[27]), and its sentinel fortress was planted in this case not at its mouth but about a mile and a quarter up it, at a point where the old road to Shechem and Jerusalem branched off to the left, while the main highway to Egypt led through the Plain of Dothan to the " Gate of Gates " (Gen. 37[17, 25]). Here stood Ibleam (now Tell Belameh) where Ahaziah was overtaken by Jehu's chariots and forced to flee wounded on horseback across the hills to Megiddo (2 Kings 9[27]). It is an important position which in Crusader times was crowned with a small castle, and the remains of the rock-hewn tunnel which, as at Megiddo, Jerusalem, Lachish, and other old Canaanite strongholds, led down from the city to its precious water-supply, can be seen to this day inside a later archway at the foot of the mound by the roadside.

From Jenin the ring of hills sweeps north-westwards to Gilboa (Jebel Fukua), and we find no more ancient sites till we stand on the high shelf of the plain where the modern village of Zerin conceals the ruined splendour of Ahab's Jezreel. From this vantage point the wide valley of Jezreel (Nahr Jalud) can be seen stretching in all its length into the haze which rises from the Jordan Valley. It is a scene intimately connected with the history of Israel. Immediately below Jezreel the pools of the Spring of Harod (Ain Jalud) recall the triumph of Gideon and his three hundred (Judg. 7). On the right the slopes of Mount Gilboa bring back the memory of Saul's last gallant stand against the Philistines ; while on the left, leading over a saddle of the hills, can be seen the track to Endor which lies just behind and below this ridge of Little Hermon. Finally, to the east twelve miles away rises the truncated mound of Bethshan (Beisan), where the Philistine garrison fastened Saul's body to the wall, and leading up from it can be traced that road from Gilead which once brought destruction to the House of Ahab (2 Kings 9). It was Bethshan (later Scythopolis) which performed here the function of frontier-fortress to Galilee, and there was a special need for such a place at this point. All through the early period of the Judges, as the excavations on the site have shown, the Egyptian Pharaohs preserved the peace of Esdraelon by the establishment of a garrison of mercenaries in this town, and it must have been at a period when their empire fell into decay that the " Children of the East " took the opportunity of swarming like locusts into the fertile plains of Palestine (Judg. 6³ᶠ·). In the first years of the present British administration the descendants of these Bedouin attempted to repeat the exploit, and it was under the fire of the Beisan garrison that they were induced to withdraw without having divided the spoil.

Other Canaanite fortresses such as Rehob and Pella (Khurbet Fahil, east of the Jordan) are named on the Egyptian monuments as being located in the same neighbourhood, and it is clear that the whole Jordan Valley between this point and the Sea of Galilee was strongly held to protect the approaches from the east. At the south end of the sea itself lie the once important sites of Tell es Semakh and Kerak (Taricheæ), while two miles to the south of it Yenoam (Abeidiyeh) guarded the Darb el Hawarneh at the outgoings of the Wadi Fejjas. The town of Tiberias betrays by its name its comparatively recent origin (it was founded by Herod Antipas about A.D. 26 in honour of the emperor), but in Tell Oreimeh, at Tabgha, eight miles to the north of it, we may perhaps find the ancient Chinnereth after which the lake and district were once called. Between this point and the Jordan the tumbled ruins of Kerazeh and the partly restored synagogue of Tell Hum are all that remain of the glories of Chorazin and Capernaum. Following still northwards up the river we reach in about seven miles the " Bridge of the Daughters of Jacob " (Jisr Benat Jakub), which carries the main road from Damascus. This road runs westward from the bridge to join the ancient highway from Sidon and the Bukaa, and at the meeting-place of these two routes stood the once mighty Hazor (Tell el Kedah). This immense fortress, enclosing within its 60-feet-high ramparts of beaten earth enough space to accommodate

thirty thousand men with their horses and chariots, and guarded
by a citadel which may have maintained a population of
four thousand people, dates back to the days of the Hyksos
invaders (*c.* 1750 B.C.), who perhaps introduced this type of
encampment from the plains of Central Europe and Turkestan.
Nor was it size only which fitted it to succeed Kadesh on the
Orontes as "the head of all the kingdoms" of Galilee (Josh. 11[10]),
for in spite of its apparent remoteness from the centre of that
region its strategic position could hardly have been bettered.
With Abel-beth-Maacah (Abl) to assist it in guarding the
road to the north, and Dan (Tell el Kadi) the descent of the
Wadi el Hoshaba from the north-east, it held in its own grasp
the routes which led from Damascus through Geshur, Golan,
and Bashan and which penetrated Galilee either westwards
by the Wadi el Tuffah or southwards by the Horns of Hattin
(Kurn Hattin). At Hattin itself the remains of a huge fortress
(Madon ?) survive, through which the King of Hazor could
control both the Esdraelon road past Tabor and the Hauran
road through the Wadis Rummaneh and Abellin and was
thus able to support or mobilize his vassal-princes from Acre
to the fords of Jordan (Josh. 11[1-2]). It was no doubt a small
kingdom over which he ruled and which the four northern
tribes—Asher, Zebulun, Naphtali, and Issachar—succeeded
at long last in dividing amongst themselves, but it was perhaps
then as now the goodliest part of Palestine, a land of oak-
forests and olive orchards and rich in corn and wine and oil,
rich too in another sense from the constant passing of caravans
from Syria and Arabia to Egypt and the Mediterranean.
Only one place indeed in Galilee seems to dwell in natural
aloofness from its busy thoroughfares, though for quite a
different reason it has itself become a focus of many roads :
in ancient days a few rough tracks must have been the only
approaches to that high hill above Esdrælon where in its quiet
hollow Nazareth lay waiting.

II. *The Maritime Plain* upon which all the main passes
southwards from Esdraelon converge in the neighbourhood of
Jett and Baka (the Aphek of 1 Sam. 4[1] and 29[1] ?) collects the
tracks issuing from them into a single highroad which it carries
by Lydda, Yebnah (Jamnia), Esdud (Ashdod), Gaza, and
Rafah (Raphia) to the Egyptian frontier at El Arish. So far
as concerns the northern position of this plain, the Plain of
Sharon, this has been its most important if not its sole historical
function, for the greater part of it was thickly forested until
comparatively recent times, and it was only its gradual de-
nudation which made possible the Roman capital and harbour

at Cæsarea and the opening of that approach to Haifa round the north shoulder of Carmel which the Crusaders watched and guarded from their castle of Athlit. Dor, which is six miles south of this, seems to have been connected, as we have seen, not with Sharon but with Esdraelon.

South of a line drawn between Jaffa and Lydda, on the other hand, the maritime plain takes on a new and independent importance, for it was from here that the Philistines extended their dominion over the whole of Palestine or at least as far as Bethshan. Of their Pentapolis or league of five cities, the sites of two, Gath and Ekron are yet unknown, though Gath may possibly be the mound of Arak el Menshiyeh fourteen miles south-east of Ascalon, and Ekron may be sought at Katrah eight miles south-west of Lydda. Ascalon on the coast with its great semi-circle of Hyksos ramparts crowned with Crusader ruins and its Græco-Roman cloisters, the gift of Herod the Great to his birthplace, survives to-day only as an enclave of shady groves and well-watered gardens, an epitome of Palestine's past history both in glory and in decay. Only Gaza, set squarely on its great mound between the hills that so stoutly resisted the British advance in the Great War, stands erect where it has stood since the earliest Pharaohs threw their armies at this gate of Canaan, and flourishes with undiminished vigour as the chief mart of all the Bedouin tribes of the Negeb and the Arabah.

The success achieved by the Philistines in establishing their rule over Israel must appear remarkable in view of the small extent of their territory (about fifty miles long by twelve miles wide) and the paucity of their strongholds. Actually, however, they were in both respects better endowed than is at first sight evident, for they rapidly made themselves masters of the low hills of the Shephelah (Josh. 9¹, 10⁴⁰, etc.), which separate the mountains from the maritime plain. This " Lowland " which is one of the most curious features of Palestine, is also one of its most beautiful, for the Shephelah is a down-country, both fertile and breezy, which runs as a kind of temperate zone between the cold of the highlands and the torrid heat of the plain. In it, as a consequence, were to be found some of the strongest Amorite cities in Palestine, planted for the most part (as usual) near the mouth of some important defile. In the south of this area, for example, where the road from Hebron descends the Wadi Afranj (Wadi of the Franks) on its way to Gaza,'the modern village of Beit Jibrin, though not itself one of these ancient fortresses, is surrounded by three of them, of which the most important was Lachish (Tell el Duweir) : Tell el Hesy (Eglon ?) on the Wadi of the same name lies on this same route as it emerges upon the plain. Northwards from Beit Jibrin a track leads by the Wadi el Judeiyideh into the Wadi es Sunt (the Vale of Elah, 1 Sam. 17², etc.), the sentinel of which was an unknown city in an extremely strong position (possibly Libnah or even Gath), represented to-day by the large mound of Tell es Safi. Yet once more northwards past Jarmuth (Khurbet el Yarmuk) we reach the Wadi Surar (the Vale of Sorek, Judg. 16⁴) where Beth-shemesh (Ain Shems) watches the entrance into the mountains (the route of the Jaffa-Lydda-Jerusalem railway) over against the Danite villages of Zorah (Surah) and Eshtaol (Eshua). Here it was that the Philistine kine brought back the Ark to its own land (1 Sam. 6¹²), for the border of Israel must have run at that time to the west of Beth-shemesh ; and from here at an earlier day the Danite migration set out for its new home under Hermon, having given up the hopeless struggle to contest the Shephelah with the chariots of Canaan (Judg. 18¹¹).

The last valley to the North is also the most important, for not only does the main road from Jerusalem descend past Kirjath Jearim (Kuriyat el Enab) by this Wadi (Wadi Ali), but it is joined at Latron, where the track from Beth-shemesh also strikes it, by the ancient highway through the Beth-horon passes and the plain of Ajalon. It was fitting therefore that over such a route such a guard should be set as the powerful fortress of Gezer (Tell Jezar), a city so strong that it had not fallen to Israel even in the days of Solomon but must be captured and presented to him by his father-in-law, the Pharaoh (1 Kings 9¹⁶). North of the plain of Ajalon, the scene of Joshua's final victory over the Amorites (Josh. 10¹²), the Shephelah comes to an end, for the foothills beyond are integral parts of the range from which they descend. Only one town upon them needs to be mentioned here, Modin (Midieh) the home of the Maccabees (1 Macc. 2¹).

Such was the territory which the Philistines commanded and out of which they were able to fasten a strangle-hold upon their neighbours. With the rolling red corn-land of their own plain and the figs and olives and vines of the Shephelah at their disposal, with their control of the great high-road from Egypt and Babylonia, with their seaport for trade with Phœnicia and their " land-port " for trade with the Bedouin, they possessed advantages which, added to their superior civilization and military equipment, made them for long irresistible. Even when Israel had driven them back within their own borders, they succumbed in the end not to

a Hebrew but to an Assyrian conqueror, if indeed they had
not already succumbed more disastrously to the immemorial
and alien influences of Canaan.

III. *The Hill Country of Ephraim with Gilead.* From the
plain we ascend into the Central Range and it may be convenient if for this purpose we approach it by what has been
always the most obvious and easy road, from Tul Keram on
the plain of Sharon through the broad Wadi Shair to Nablus.
For here between Ebal (Jebel Eslamiyeh) and Gerizim (Jebel et
Tor), not indeed at the modern city itself but on the site of the
ancient Shechem (Balata) which lies a short distance to the
east of it, we are at the true heart of the hill country of
Ephraim. In front to east, north, and south stretches the
Makhneh Plain, probably the first " Camp " of Israel (Heb.
Mahaneh) after Jericho ; and one of the low hills directly
opposite is crowned with the circular ruin of their second
Gilgal (Deut. 11^{30}). From this " navel of the earth " (Judg. 9^{37}),
so intimately connected with the patriarchs Abraham (Gen. 12^{6}),
Jacob (Gen. 33$^{18f.}$), and Joseph (Josh. 24^{32}) important highroads diverged in all directions. That to the west, already
mentioned, united these highlands both with the wealth and
with the politics of the maritime plain, and Samaria (Sebustieh)
perched almost impregnably at the head of a northern
tributary of the Wadi Shair was founded by Omri to serve this
double purpose. This road, however, was of dubious advantage
to Israel, for as Jeroboam was driven from Shechem to build a
temporary capital, Penuel, in Gilead (1 Kings 12^{25}), so even
Samaria itself was to discover too late the penalties of easy
access (2 Kings 17^{5}). To the north of Shechem past the village
of Sychar (John 4^{5} : mod. Askar) lay the routes to Esdraelon
by Bethulia (Judith 4$^{6f.}$; mod. Meselieh) to Bethshan and
Damascus, and by the Wadi Farah to Gilead : near the parting
of these roads stood Tirzah (Tell Farah), which Jeroboam chose
as his capital after Penuel and Omri abandoned after the
burning of its palace by Zimri (1 Kings 16^{18}). To the south
lay the road to Jerusalem, first along the long level Makhneh
Plain, then by a succession of high ridges and deep valleys, two
of which, the Wadi Deir Ballut and its tributary the Wadi Jib,
strike deeply into the heart of this hill country of Ephraim
and thence to the bare and lofty plateau of Benjamin where
the villages of Bireh (perhaps the Beerothite Gittaim, cf.
2 Sam. 4^{3}) and Ramallah watch from their eminence the
distant domes of the Holy City. East of this road at long
intervals along it lie two sites of first importance in the
religious history of Israel : Shiloh (Seilun) hidden away in

the recesses of a small plain five miles south-east of the village of El Lubban (Judg. 21[19]) and betraying by its remoteness the fear or the effect of foreign invasion, and Bethel (Beitin) a little to the north-east of Bireh which marked for long the frontier between Israel and Judah. South of this royal sanctuary (Amos 7[13]) of the northern kingdom the " bare heights " of Benjamin (Jer. 4[11]) though properly part of " Mount Ephraim " came normally under the power of Jerusalem, just as in physical structure they belong rather to the mountainous plateau of Judah than to the land of broad and well-covered valleys which brought the House of Joseph a greater blessing (Deut. 33[13-17]) but an earlier doom.

We have to consider lastly the roads leading eastwards from Shechem. On this side there are two main routes which, diverging near Jacob's Well to the east of the city, run the one to the south, the other to the north, of Gilgal (Juleijil). The former of these strikes off to the south-east past el Ormeh (Abimelech's capital Arumah, Judg. 9[41]) and descending into the Ghor near Herod's agricultural colony of Phasaelis (mod. Khurbet Fusail) leads thence due south to Jericho (Tell-es-Sultan, mod. Eriha) and the earlier Gilgal (Jiljulieh). This was the route most probably taken by the Israelites under Joshua in securing a foothold amongst the mountains, and it is significant that in later days, even after the division of the kingdom, Jericho, as reached more easily from Shechem than from Jerusalem, remained in the possession of the House of Joseph (Josh. 16[7]), so real have been at all times the perils and discomforts of the desolate descent from the west.

The second route strikes across the eastern branch of the Makhneh Plain and leads by alternate tracks to the bridge and ford of Damieh (Adam, Josh. 3[16]) upon which the road through the Wadi Farah also converges. This was, in fact, the chief line of communication between the mountains of Israel and the land of Gilead, and the fellowship which bound these two was always so strong that they cannot be considered apart. It was at Mahanaim in Gilead that Saul and his family found a home under the pressure of the Philistine invasion (2 Sam. 2[8]) and David in a later day took refuge from Absalom (2 Sam. 17[24]) : and it was to Penuel in Gilead that Jeroboam retreated in some unrecorded crisis of his reign. It was from Gilead that the men of Jabesh appealed not in vain for the help of Saul (1 Sam. 11[4]) and it was the city of Ramoth of Gilead that was most hotly contested between the kings of Israel and Damascus. Gilead was, in fact, for Israel something much more than a mere apanage : it was an integral

part of the kingdom into which the tribes both of Manasseh
and of Ephraim overflowed in early days in compensation for
the decadence of Reuben (Josh. 17[17f.] ; Judg. 12[4] ; 2 Sam. 18[6],
" the forest of Ephraim " ; cf. Ps. 60[7], 108[8]), and which with
its famous balm, its oak forests and its splendid grazing
grounds (Num. 32[1]) was a possession as well worth retaining
as it was continually in need of protection. From the north
where it faced the rolling corn lands of the Hauran across
the gorge of the Yarmuk it courted invasion from the Aramæan
kingdoms of Syria : to the east it was open to such incursions
from the desert as that which Gideon pursued " by the way of
the tent dwellers " to the oasis-depression of Sirhan (Karkor,
mod. Keraker ; Judg. 8[10f.]) ; in the south, where its border
was now north now south of the Jabbok (ez-Zerka) it lived in
perpetual fear of Ammonite or Moabite hostility (Judg. 11[12f.]).
Yet, on the other hand, when Israel was in the ascendant the
possession of these central uplands across the Jordan gave it
an opportunity of empire which it was not slow to seize. By
this wedge driven across the cultivable land to the desert
Omri was able to isolate and absorb the treeless plateau of
the Mishor south of the Arnon (Wadi Mojib) where the " sheep-
master " kings of Moab tended their wealth (2 Kings 3[4])
just as it was by his control of Gilead that David at the zenith
of his glory found the means of bringing even Damascus to his
feet (2 Sam. 8[6]). In later days this link between east and
west was not altogether lost, for the Greek cities of the Decapolis always counted Bethshan-Scythopolis as one of their
number ; but the glory of Gilead had by then long since
departed from it. To-day, after centuries of oppression and
misrule, a bare shadow only remains of what was one of the
fairest portions of the heritage of Israel. Of its once famous
sites not one has yet been certainly identified : only at Jerash
(Gerasa) the mournful ruins of temples, theatres, and churches
recall the old security of the Roman Peace and the old zeal
in these regions for Christianity.

NOTE.—It may be useful at this point to enumerate the
divisions of these eastern districts as they existed in our Lord's
day. Peræa, the district between the Arnon and the Jabbok,
the modern Belka, was allotted with Galilee to Herod Antipas
presumably because in both regions, otherwise dissimilar
the bulk of the population consisted of Jews (cf. Mark 10[1])
North of the Jabbok except for Philadelphia (Amman) was
the somewhat vague territory of the Decapolis of which
Gerasa, Gadara (Umm Keis) and Pella lay south of the Yarmuk,
and Damascus north of it. To Philip's Tetrarchy fell the

Jaulan (Gaulanitis) between the Yarmuk and Hermon, the Hauran east of this, the great lava-stretch of El Leja south of Damascus (Trachonitis), and an uncertain fringe of the Arabian desert which St. Luke calls Ituraea : Abilene which he assigns to Lysanias lay on the Upper Abana (2 Kings 5[12]), the modern Barada.

IV. *The Hill Country of Judah.* The extent of the Southern Kingdom which remains to be considered astonishes us by its smallness. It is not much more than eighteen miles as the crow flies from Jerusalem to Hebron, and about twenty-eight from Hebron to Beersheba. Nor is this all the story, for between the Shephelah on the one hand and the grim wilderness of Judæa on the other, the inhabited spine of this mountain plateau is confined to a strip not more than four or five miles broad, while its highland character may be said to leave it at El Dhahariye, only twelve miles south of Hebron. Within this restricted area there are, however, two focal points, Jerusalem and Hebron, and each in turn was the capital of a kingdom (2 Sam. 5[5]).

Jerusalem on its ancient site of Ophel south of the later Temple precincts seems strangely small to have commanded the help of such cities as Lachish and Eglon (Josh. 10[3]) : yet its strategic position on the central ridge was so commanding that the Amorites of the Shephelah could not for their own safety expose it to destruction. Jerusalem barred the door for them to an enemy advancing from the north, and the defection of the Hivite (or Horite ?) cities of Gibeon (El Jib) and Beeroth (Tell el Nasbeh) between five and eight miles distant from it stirred them to instant action. It is remarkable indeed how often in this small stretch of Benjamite territory between the passes of Bethoron (Beit Ur) on the west and that of Michmash (Mukhmas) on the east we have an echo of this menace of invasion. It was at Michmash that Jonathan won his great fight against the Philistines (1 Sam. 14) as it was at Michmash that a more formidable enemy was expected in later years (Isa. 10[28]). It was down the Bethoron Pass that Judas Maccabæus twice drove the Syrian armies in rout (1 Macc. 3[13f.], 7[39f.]) as Joshua had driven the Amorites centuries before (Josh. 10[11]). Nor was the intervening plateau empty of incident, for it was here that Baasha fortified Ramah (Er Ram), only five miles north of Jerusalem (1 Kings 15[17]), and that Asa having outmanœuvred his enemy set up in his turn Geba (Gibeah of Saul, Tell el Ful ?) and the ancient Beeroth now renamed Mizpah (Tell el Nasbeh) : it was at this Mizpah too that the murder of Gedaliah the

Persian governor filled to the brim the cup of Judah's affliction (Jer. 41). Only one figure of peace seems indeed to haunt this stony waste : it was to Ramah that Samuel used to return from judging Israel (1 Sam. 7¹⁶).

The eastern road from Jerusalem has already been mentioned, and its route over the Mount of Olives and through Bethany needs no description. To the west the modern highway to Jaffa follows probably for the most part the course of the ancient road, past Lifta (Netophah), Kulonieh (believed by some to be Emmaus, though this is more probably Amwas in the plain of Ajalon) and Kuryet el Enab (Kiriath Jearim) and thence down the winding Wadi Ali to the Bab el Wad (Gate of the Wadi) and Latron (see above, p. 147). Here at once as with the next Wadi to the north above which is perched the old Hivite stronghold of Chephirah (Kefirah), the loftiness of this western mountain edge of Judah and the depth and narrowness of its gorges are revealed in strong contrast to the easier approaches of Mount Ephraim. The Vale of Sorek to the south confirms this impression ; yet this ravine where the railway now makes its arduous ascent was the route by which the Philistines had perforce to attack Jerusalem, deploying as they reached the summit on to the little plain of Rephaim to the south-east of the city (2 Sam. 5¹⁸, ²²).

Southwards from Jerusalem the highroad to Hebron, Beersheba, and Cairo follows the backbone of the plateau past Bethlehem (four miles) and the ancient reservoirs and aqueducts of El Burak (" Solomon's Pools ") and the Wadi Arrub, having to its east the wilderness of Tekoa where Amos heard and obeyed the call of his God (Amos 1¹, 7¹⁴ᶠ·). At Beth Zur (Beit Sur, four miles north of Hebron), where a track branches off to Adullam (Aid el Ma), the famous cave refuge of David and his warriors above the Shephelah (1 Sam. 22¹, etc.), a great fortress, described even in Roman times as " the strongest place in all Judæa," guarded the approaches from the south throughout the history of the nation (2 Chron. 11⁷; Neh. 3¹⁶; 1 Macc. 4²⁹, 6³¹ᶠ·, etc.). The presence of this stronghold so close to Hebron is to be explained by the comparatively defenceless position of that city. Hebron, or Kiriath Arba, now called El Khalil after Abraham, the " Friend of God," is the only important site in Palestine which lacks both natural and artificial means of protection : it lies, in fact, in a hollow overlooked by hills on all sides, and while like Jerusalem it is an important road-centre, unlike Jerusalem it enjoys this privilege without having the power to enforce it. Whether this peculiarity is due to its great antiquity—it is said to have been founded seven years before the Hyksos capital of Zoan (or Avaris) in the Delta (Num. 13²²)—must remain a mystery : to-day no traces survive of the old city of the Anakim which Caleb captured and in which David was first made king ; only the nobler memories of the place live on in its venerable and closely guarded sanctuary where the bones of the patriarchs are believed to rest in peace.

The importance of Hebron as the southern focal point of Judæa has already been stressed. To the west one of the few good descents to the Shephelah runs through the Wadi el Afranj and by Beit Jibrin to Mareshah, the birthplace of Micah (Mic. 1¹), and the circle of ancient cities which surround it. To the east the only practicable track to the exuberant oasis of Engedi or Hazezon Tamar (1 Sam. 23²⁹ ; 2 Chron. 20², etc.) passes from Hebron through the wilderness of Ziph to Juttah and thence by steep and often precipitous stages to the shores of the Dead Sea. Finally, to the south the main road pursues its course to the village of El Dhahariyeh not far from which the ancient Debir (Tell Beit Mirsim) watched the approaches from the Negeb (Judg. 1¹¹). At this point the hill country of Judah begins to fall away rapidly, its windswept heights and small but fertile hollows giving place to the wide and almost waterless lowland which forms the southern frontier of Palestine. Only sixteen miles onward lies Beersheba, yet at Beersheba one finds oneself in a different world.

V. The Negeb (" South Country ") with the Arabah and Mount Seir. " Amalek dwelleth in the land of the South " was the report brought back by the spies to Moses at Kadesh Barnea (Num. 13²⁹), and this is a true description of the greater part of the Negeb, where wandering or half-settled Bedouin now hold an undisputed domain. That it was not completely true of ancient times is nevertheless established by the presence of a long line of ruined sites which stretches from Tell Arad (Num. 21¹, 33⁴⁰), twenty miles east of Beersheba, through the old site of Beersheba itself (Tell es Seba) to Tell Jemmeh, the Gerar of the patriarchs Abraham and Isaac (Gen. 20¹, 26¹), and Tell el Ajjul (thought by some to be the early site of Gaza) upon the Mediterranean. North again of these forgotten cities which lie disposed along the course of the Wadi Seba and acting as halting-places for caravans from Egypt, Sinai, and Arabia, lay Sharuhen (Tell el Sheria) where the Hyksos made their last stand after their expulsion from Egypt by the Pharaohs of the XVIIIth Dynasty. In the Old Testament these city dwellers of the Negeb are called Canaanites, and since, as we have seen, this people appeared in Palestine from the Gulf of Akabah it is very probable that this description of them is correct. In that case it is they whom we must hold responsible for the " Cities of the Plain " which lie submerged now, according to the latest theory, under the waters of the south end of the Dead Sea. The volcanoes which may have caused their downfall lie close at hand on the summit of Mount Seir, and the remains of a very large open-air sanctuary on the slopes of the Moabite hills at Bab el Dra certainly suggests that some great city or cities must have existed at one time in these parts.

In two widely different contexts of Israelite history the Negeb played an important part, and in both of them it was intimately connected with the Arabah (the prolongation of the Rift Valley which runs from Syria into the Red Sea) and with the mountain range of Seir (Jebel el Shera) beyond it. The former of these concerns the advance of Israel from Horeb, the Mountain of God in the land of Midian (Ex. 3[1]), *i.e.* in the lava plateau of the Northern Hejaz east of the Gulf of Akabah, to its first halting-place at Kadesh Barnea. The site of Kadesh has been long and hotly disputed, but it must suffice to say here that its identification with Ain Kdeis in the centre of the southern Negeb is devoid of material evidence and rests upon a false association of Kdeis (" a water-paddle ") with Kadesh " Holy." Actually this city " in the uttermost part of the border of Edom " (Num. 20[16]) must be sought at or near the amazing rock-hewn fastness and sanctuaries of Petra, the Edomite Sela (2 Kings 14[7], etc.). We must then picture the Israelites as making their first and abortive invasion (Num. 14[45]) of Palestine from this point across the Arabah and up its steep western lip, and being driven back again by the combined forces of Amalek and Canaan down the well-worn caravan route through Kornub (Hormah ?). As a result of this defeat and of the hostility of Edom which, from its capital Bozrah (el Buseira), would command the north-eastern route by the Wadi el Hasa to Kir of Moab (Kerak), Israel was forced to make the long detour which, ascending the Wadi Ithm, near the head of the Gulf of Akabah, leads round the southern slopes of Mount Seir and then northwards up the edge of the desert to Amman.

The other episode arose out of two features of the Arabah which brought Israel for centuries into conflict with Edom, the first the presence of valuable deposits of copper ore at Fenan (Punon) and El Nahas in the foothills of the eastern range, the second the opportunity which the Gulf of Akabah presented for trading ventures down the Red Sea. It is the first of these which most probably explains the Amalekite and Edomite wars of Saul (1 Sam. 14[47f.]) and the subsequent decimation of the Edomites by David (1 Kings 11[15f.]) : the second was actively and successfully prosecuted by Solomon from Ezion-geber (el Meniyyeh, now fifteen miles from the head of the Gulf?), and when this port was blocked in the reign of Jehoshaphat was carried on by Uzziah from the new harbour of Elath (1 Kings 9[26], 22[48] ; 2 Kings 14[22]). The victory which David won and Amaziah repeated in the Valley of Salt (probably the present el Sebha flats at the south end of the Dead Sea) and the conquest by the latter of Sela itself (2 Sam. 8[13] ; 2 Kings 14[7]) mark in this long struggle the ebb and flow of Edomite resistance, but there can be no doubt that for some considerable time the Israelites could claim that their eastern border in the Negeb lay along the foothills of Mount Seir. From the Ascent of Akrabbim (Umm el Akareb near the south-east end of the Lisan promontory in the Dead Sea) and from Sela upwards the mountains might belong to the Edomites (Judg. 1[36], where Edomites should be read for Amorites), but the Rift with its precious mines and its access to the wealth of Ophir must be an integral part of the heritage of the Chosen People (cf. Deut. 8[9] ; Num. 34[3f.]). It is small wonder that an abiding hatred of Israel smouldered amongst the Edomites and finally burst into flame (cf. Ezek. 25[12]), or that when after the Exile the Jews found them in possession of the Negeb and the southern Shephelah it needed the strength of Judas Maccabæus to conquer them. Under John Hyrcanus (125 B.C.) they were brought under the Law and circumcised, and it is of interest to notice that of those who followed our Lord at the beginning of His ministry many came from this new region of " Idumæa " (Mark 3[8]). Meanwhile in their old home in Mount Seir the Nabatæan Arabs had taken possession both of Petra and of Elath, and in due course Nabatæan and Roman townships grew up side by side in the Negeb and flourished there with unexpected success. Elusa (Khalasa), Abda, and Esbeita, Auja and Kurnub were all still prosperous in Byzantine times, till the end came to them, as it came to Gilead, out of the desert, and that peace which is the silence of solitude.

BIBLIOGRAPHY

G. A. Smith, *Historical Geography of the Holy Land and Historical Atlas of the Holy Land.*

John Garstang, *The Heritage of Solomon.*

John Garstang, *Joshua, Judges.*

Le P. F.-M. Abel, *Géographie de la Palestine.*

W. J. Phythian-Adams, *The Call of Israel.*

W J. Phythian-Adams, *The Fulness of Israel.*

W. F. Albright, *The Archæology of Palestine and the Bible.*

G. Dalman, *Sacred Sites and Ways.*

R. A. S. Macalister, *The Topography of Jerusalem* in *Cambridge Ancient History,* vol. iii. pp. 333–353.

P. Thomsen, *Loca Sancta* (I), 1907.

VII. ASIA MINOR

Geography. It is customary to liken the peninsula of Asia Minor to a bridge connecting south-western Asia with the south-eastern corner of Europe. The parapets of this bridge are formed by lofty mountain-ranges running along the northern and southern edges of the peninsula, and on their outward flanks (except where they are fringed by the Cilician and Pamphylian plains on the south) falling steeply down to the sea. Between these ranges lies an elevated central plateau, of a mean height in its western portion of some 3000 feet, increasing in height towards the east. The mountain ranges of the north and south draw near to each other on the western rim of the plateau, but maintain their general westerly direction as they disintegrate and slope gradually down to the coast, opening out at first into plains and terraces, and farther down sinking on their flanks into river valleys with wide and fertile bottoms. The thrusting together of the ranges at the western edge of the plateau raises the level of the terrain, and this western rim is a geographical dividing line. East of it lies an area of level plains, here and there folded into ridges or pierced by volcanic cones, much of it an inland catchment area where rivers extend a belt of fertility along the lower slopes of the southern mountain-range before losing themselves in lakes or marshes on the border of the arid, treeless steppe, an area with a continental climate of restricted moisture and extremes of heat and cold, mainly adapted to pastoral life, but including strips of cornfields along the mountain slopes or hugging the beds of the few small streams that rise out in the plain. West of the rim lies a region of rolling uplands, with hill-locked plains and open terraces breaking down into the upper reaches of the western river valleys, to be succeeded lower down by a landscape and economy of the Mediterranean type and a coast-land which is the eastern counterpart of the coast of Greece. On one side of the western rim lies the high continent of Asia, on the other side a land of transition from Asia to the Mediterrenean.

Communications. Over this great land bridge between Asia and Europe there has passed throughout history a great

avenue of communication. It is first heard of as the Persian
Royal Road, described as one of the wonders of the East by
Herodotus ; it next appears as the route of Cyrus and the
10,000 Greeks, of Alexander the Great, of the Apostle Paul,
of Kaiser Barbarossa ; it was most recently heard of in the
years preceding and following 1914 as the route of the Baghdad
railway. I call it an avenue of communication, not a road ;
actually it consists of several roads, now running parallel to
each other, now interlacing or coalescing, at need throwing
off branches to the north or south coast. Coming from Mesopotamia or Syria (and Palestine) the traveller to Europe may
enter the central plateau either by way of Cæsarea in Cappadocia or by Tarsus and the Cilician Gates ; in either case he
may find himself in due course at Derbe in Lycaonia, at Lystra
in Lycaonia, or at Iconium or Laodicea Combusta in Galatic
Phrygia. From this area a choice of two roads lies open ; he
can proceed westwards by Pisidian Antioch and Apamea to
the Maeander basin, and follow it past Colossæ, Laodicea,
and Hierapolis to Ephesus. Or he can go north-westward along
Phrygia Paroreios to the valley of the Phrygian Cayster (the
Caystroupedion of Xenophon's *Anabasis*) in which lies the
junction of the ancient roads, and of the modern railways,
to the west coast and to Constantinople. His route from this
point will depend on his ultimate destination. Under the
early Roman Empire this will probably be Rome, and for the
journey to Rome the traveller has now a choice of routes.
He can still conveniently diverge on to the Maeander route
past Laodicea to Ephesus and there take ship round Malea
to Puteoli. Or he can skirt Mysia and follow the Hermus
route past Philadelphia and Sardis to the port of Smyrna, or
go by Thyatira and Pergamum to Troas, whence it is a short
crossing to Neapolis, at the eastern terminus of the Via Egnatia.
At the other end of the Via Egnatia lies Dyrrachium and
opposite it Brundisium, whence the Via Appia led to Rome.
In the later Empire and again in Byzantine and modern times
our traveller's destination will probably be Constantinople ; in
this case he will turn northwards from the Cayster valley and
travel by Dorylæum and through Bithynia to the Bosporus.
    There were other roads in Roman Asia Minor, leading
from the central trunk route to the coast, or serving the needs
of outlying districts. A road went northwards from the Cilician
Gates through Cappadocia and Pontus to Amisus on the Black
Sea, and it crossed a northern trunk route leading from Armenia
through Pontus and Bithynia to the Bosporus. There is no
direct mention in the New Testament of missionary activity

along these routes ; but such early activity is implied in the salutation addressed in 1 Peter 1 to Christian communities in Pontus, Cappadocia, and Bithynia, and in the situation described in Pliny's 96th Letter to Trajan. Another noteworthy route is that followed by Paul between Attalia and Perge in Pamphylia and Pisidian Antioch (Acts 13¹⁴, 15²⁴·²⁵) ; this important route has recently been developed as a motor road leading from Attalia to the Upper Maeander.

It will have been observed that in describing the road-system of Asia Minor I have at the same time referred to all the cities or districts in which early Christian missionary activity is described or implied in the New Testament narrative. This is due to no effort at simplification, nor is it an attempt to warp the map of the eastern provinces to serve the needs of exegesis. The great trunk routes over the provinces were the arteries of the Roman Empire, and Christianity claimed from the first to enter into the full current of Imperial life. " These things were not done in a corner."

Provinces. At the date of the missionary activity described in the New Testament (second half of the first century A.D.), Roman rule and organization had been established, mostly for a considerable period, over the whole of the peninsula (the only exception in Paul's lifetime was the district lying between the Cilician Gates and Derbe, which was under the rule of a vassal king, Antiochus of Commagene). The dates of the incorporation into the Empire of the various provinces are a rough index of the progress, in the period with which we are concerned, of Græco-Roman culture among the inhabitants of the several areas. During our period the following were the Roman provinces of Asia Minor, in the order of their annexation :

1. Asia was acquired in 133 B.C. It included the western seaboard with its islands and the regions of Mysia, Lydia, Caria, and large part of Phrygia. On its eastern side it stopped short at the western rim of the plateau beside Apamea, but farther north it extended far on to the plateau in the direction of Paroreios. When Paul entered it, it had been under Greek and then Græco-Roman domination for 400 years, and it remained throughout the most thoroughly hellenized of the Eastern provinces. In the New Testament (probably including the list in Acts 2⁹) " Asia " always refers to the Roman province. It includes the cities of Ephesus (the capital), Pergamum, Troas, Thyatira, Smyrna, Sardis, Philadelphia, Laodicea, Hierapolis, and Colossæ, the cities visited or addressed by Paul, or mentioned as the recipients of Letters in Revela-

tion. All those cities, as we have seen, lay on busy roads, and all were in close touch with the west coast with its long established Greek civilization. But it must not be concluded that Christianity, in its earliest phase, neglected the great cities of Eastern Asia. In the middle of the second century, as we learn from the Smyrnæan letter describing the martyrdom of Polycarp, there was a church in Philomelium. This church had undoubtedly been founded at an early period, possibly by missionaries from "Pisidian" Antioch, and it is only because surviving evidence is scanty and haphazard that we do not hear of first-century churches in important cities like Apamea and Synnada.

2. Cilicia was made a Roman province in 103 B.C. Augustus combined it for administrative purposes with Syria, and it is associated with Syria in Acts 15²³·⁴¹. In the New Testament, "Cilicia" means Cilicia Campestris, the Cilician plain, as contrasted with the mountains of Rough Cilicia on the west (except in Acts 27⁵, where the reference is to the entire Cilician coast). From A.D. 37–74 Rough Cilicia was under the rule of the vassal king referred to above. The cities of Cilicia had been organized on the Greek model early in the second century B.C., and this Greek culture was fostered and developed under the Roman occupation. Tarsus, the birthplace of Paul, was the seat of a great University.

3. Bithynia became a Roman province in 75 B.C., and Pontus was added to it in 65 B.C. The combined province was styled *Bithynia et Pontus*, implying that the two parts retained a certain individuality. This explains the separation of the two in the salutation in 1 Pet. 1. Bithynia was in close touch with Asia, and under their independent kings both Bithynia and Pontus had come under the influence of Greek culture before they were incorporated in the Roman Empire.

4. Galatia was the large central territory, extending from sea to sea, and including Paphlagonia, part of Pontus, ethnic Galatia, Lycaonia, Eastern Phrygia, Isauria, Pisidia, and probably Pamphylia, which had been comprised in the kingdom of the Galatian Amyntas at his death in 25 B.C. or were soon afterwards added to the province formed of the territories under Amyntas's rule. According to the "South Galatian hypothesis" (the truth of which is here assumed) "Galatia" in the New Testament always refers to the province and "Galatians" to its inhabitants of Lycaonian, Phrygian, Greek, Jewish, or Roman race who had been visited by Paul on his three journeys. Paul's Galatian journeys were confined to the Lycaonian and Phrygian portions ("regions")

of the province Galatia. In this area the principal cities were
Iconium, an outpost of Greek culture on the edge of the still
pastoral Lycaonian plain, and Antioch (in Phrygia) and
Lystra (in Lycaonia), which had been refounded as Roman
colonies soon after the incorporation of the province.

5. Cappadocia was the mountainous area lying east of
Galatia and north of Cilicia ; it was made a Roman province
in A.D. 17. Little attention was paid to it (in comparison
with Galatia) till A.D. 70, when Vespasian combined it with
Galatia so as to form a consular province with a garrison
of two legions. Greek institutions and education had made
little progress in Cappadocia ; in the time of Strabo much
of its territory was still temple property, whose cultivators
" were in a general way subject to the king but mostly
took their orders from the priest." During the period covered
by Paul's journeys Cappadocia was separated in the south-
west from Galatia by the vassal-kingdom of Antiochus.
Ramsay has pointed out that in this non-Roman area, twice
crossed by Paul, no missionary activity is recorded.

6. Lycia, two of whose harbours were Patara (Acts 21[1])
and Myra (Acts 27[5]), was independent till A.D. 43, when it
became a Roman province. Claudius combined it with
Pamphylia, which till then had probably been under the
governor of Galatia. Lycia, locked among lofty ranges and
looking towards the sea, had become hellenized early and
thoroughly. The two notices in Acts are incidental to voyages ;
Lycia was passed over by the earliest missions and plays little
part in the early history of Anatolian Christianity.

Population and Society. These provinces, as appears from
the ethnical names applied to the districts of which they were
composed, contained a very mixed population. Names like
Lydia, Pisidia, and Lycaonia remind us that the population
of Asia Minor still contained native elements which can be
traced back to the dawn of history ; and in general the old
Anatolian stock entered largely into the population of areas
which were subsequently settled by mass invasion (such as
Phrygia or Galatia) or occupied by colonists or by immigrants
engaged in trade or administration (Greeks, Jews, and Italians).
The presence of this old Anatolian element imparted a certain
uniformity to the religious and social outlook of the whole
peninsula ; on the central and eastern plateau, where the proportion of aboriginal inhabitants to immigrants of higher
culture was larger than in the west, the native social system
maintained itself for long in conscious opposition to Greek and
Roman institutions.

The mass invasions which made the deepest impress on the country were those of the Phrygians, late in the second millennium B.C., and the Galatians, who entered Asia Minor in 278–7 B.C., and about 232 B.C. were forcibly settled in the area (the north-eastern part of Phrygia and part of Cappadocia) which afterwards bore their name. The Phrygians crossed from Europe and overran the entire north-western part of the peninsula, from Troy on the west to the Halys on the east. On the south-east they penetrated as far as Iconium (Iconium was " the furthest city in Phrygia " for Xenophon, and still in Acts 14[6] the Lycaonian border lies between Iconium and Lystra), and on the south they were held up along the flank of the Pisidian and Carian mountains. A later invasion of Bithynians and Mysians drove the Phrygians away from the coasts of the north-west, and the rise of the kingdom of Lydia deprived them of their conquests on the western flank of the peninsula. The Phrygians, after the fashion of invading hordes in antiquity, intermarried with the conquered Anatolian stocks and took over much of their religion and social structure. In similar fashion the later Galatian invaders settled as over-lords among a mixed population of Phrygians and old Anatolians. They maintained their national character and tribal institutions into the Roman period, but they, too, like the Phrygians, fell under the spell of the native religion and worshipped the gods of the land.

Meantime, since the conquest of Alexander in 334 B.C., Greeks (both from the cities of the west coast and from Greece), and græcized Macedonians had been pouring into inner Asia Minor in large numbers. The self-governing cities of classical Greece were the models of the self-administering cities which the Seleucid and Attalid successors of Alexander planted thickly throughout their territories. These cities are usually described as colonies of Greeks, and Greeks and hellenized Macedonian veterans everywhere formed the dominating element in their population. But it should not be forgotten that they were in most cases refoundations of existing cities, and that their citizen bodies from the first included large numbers of native Anatolians. Thus, Pisidian Antioch claimed descent from colonists who had come from the Greek city Magnesia on the Maeander, and the neighbouring Apollonia proclaimed that it was a " colony of Lycians and Thracians " (Lycian Greeks and Macedonian veterans). There is no reference in the records of either city to a native element in its population ; but it happens that at Hierapolis (another " Greek colony ") two of the city tribes bear old Anatolian names, and were clearly the tribes in which the citizens of the older population were enrolled. The same practice must be assumed everywhere. The Greek cities were founded not as " compounds " among a native population but as mission-stations of hellenism, and the aim of their founders was to educate the native Phrygians, Pisidians, Lycaonians, etc., in Greek ways. Many of these cities bore names which connected them with the dynasty of their founders ; cities like Laodicea, Philadelphia, Antiochia proclaim their status and their mission in their names. It follows that from the first the hellenism of the Greek cities of Asia Minor was Græco-Anatolian rather than Greek ; and as Greek culture filtered through to wider and wider circles it surrendered more and more of its purity. This dilution was, however, held in check by continued immigration from Greece ; from the conquest of Alexander till the mass deportation of 1924, Asia Minor has always acted as a magnet on the Greek trader.

The narrative in Acts introduces us to another important constituent of the population of Anatolia, the Jews. Josephus' statement that Antiochus the Great on one occasion settled 2000 Jewish families in Lydia and Phrygia is not likely to refer to an isolated act, and we may expect to find the descendants of Jewish colonists planted by the Seleucids, and of other Jews who followed them for purposes of trade, in all the Seleucid and other important cities of Asia Minor. Cicero refers to the confiscation of Jewish contributions destined for Jerusalem at Laodicea and Apamea, and Paul preached in the Jewish synagogues of Antioch and Iconium. Among those cities archæology has supplied direct evidence for the presence of Jews only at Apamea ; but this is accidental, for the presence of Jews is attested by inscriptions in several other Anatolian cities—Smyrna, Hierapolis, Acmonia, Apollonia, and others. And the monumental evidence, both in the haphazard manner of its appearance and in its far-reaching implications, warns us that we must allow for the presence of large bodies of Jews in all the principal cities of Asia Minor. The inscriptions, being for the most part epitaphs, introduce us to individual Jews, but in several cases they make it clear that these Jews are members of influential Jewish communities.

In the cemeteries of Hierapolis there are about 300 epitaphs of the Imperial period, three of which can be identified as Jewish. Those three epitaphs are in Greek, and use the formulæ employed by the Greek inhabitants of the city, including the usual provision that a fine is to be paid for violation of the grave. One of them commemorates a certain

" M. Aurelius Alexander, also called Asaph, of the people of the Jews," and directs that the fine for violation of the grave shall be paid " to the people of the Jews." " Paul, also called Saul " was a citizen of Tarsus and also a Roman citizen (Paul is the third name in the full Roman designation ; the first and second are not recorded). The owner of this grave is a citizen of Hierapolis (not stated, but implied in the situation). He is also a Roman citizen, with the full triple name. He too, like Paul, has a Jewish name, Asaph. His Roman name implies that he had acquired the Roman citizenship during the second century, when it was still a signal honour, given to provincials of merit and standing. The other two Jewish epitaphs are on the tombstones of two families of Roman citizens, all the members of which bear Greek or Roman names. One of them betrays itself as Jewish by making the fine for violation payable " to the colony of the Jews resident in Hierapolis," the other by arranging for the decoration of the grave at the Feast of Unleavened Bread and the Feast of Pentecost. The avoidance of Jewish names on these tombstones is characteristic ; in all Asia Minor not more than half a dozen Hebrew names are recorded on inscriptions of the Imperial period. It happens that we can identify these two epitaphs as Jewish by the other details referred to, but it should be noted that the fashion followed by the Jews of the Dispersion of using only Gentile names disguises their identity, and makes it impossible for us to recognize large numbers of monuments which are undoubtedly Jewish. All the more valuable are our three Jewish inscriptions from Hierapolis. The " people (or colony) of the Jews," which they mention as a " juristic person," capable of receiving fines recoverable by civil process in the courts, was the organized Jewish community of Hierapolis, which had a recognized legal status and the right (under Roman Law) to worship in its synagogue. By means of these three gravestones we can recognize the presence in Hierapolis of a Jewish community, including members who belonged to the social aristocracy of the city, burying their dead alongside of their Gentile neighbours in the public graveyards of the city, placing their graves under the protection of the common law, and writing very good Greek. The Jewish inscriptions of Acmonia tell an identical story and introduce us to Jews who held high office in the city. No one who studies these monuments will find anything strange in the influence attributed to the Jews of Antioch and Iconium in Acts 13, 14.

Among the Galatian cities visited by Paul two, Antioch

and Lystra, had been refounded as Roman colonies soon after the establishment of Galatia as a province. This meant that the Seleucid Phrygian city of Antioch (called " the Pisidian " in Acts to distinguish it from Antioch on the Maeander—Strabo describes it more correctly as " Antioch over against Pisidia "), and the Lycaonian township of Lystra each received into its population a body of Roman veterans, who organized the administration of the city on the Italian model, formed its aristocracy, and gave it high status among the cities of the empire. The colonies were the living embodiment of the Imperial connexion, and acted as forcing houses of Roman culture. In this effort they were seconded by the bodies of Roman or Italian immigrants (landowners, traders, administrators, time-expired soldiers) who settled in every considerable city in Asia Minor. These settlers were Roman citizens, and with or without (the point is disputed) the prominent local Greeks, Jews, and Anatolians who had been elevated to the Roman citizenship, they formed themselves into corporations (*conuentus ciuium Romanorum*) with officials of their own, and they individually and collectively held a position of great influence in the eastern cities. They everywhere formed the municipal aristocracy and were the social foci around which gathered all the prominent residents who favoured the Imperial connexion, were anxious to adopt Roman manners, and aspired to or had attained the citizenship. As more and more of the local citizens attained the Roman citizenship, the character of the *conuentus* as an exclusive aristocracy gradually weakened ; it was finally extinguished early in the third century, when the Roman citizenship was awarded to all the citizens of the Greek cities. But in the time of Paul, in the Greek cities as well as in the Roman colonies, the Italian settlers were still the leaders of society.

Roman as well as Greek ideas of civilization—as the very word is there to remind us—were centred in civic institutions, and the Romans continued the Seleucid and Attalid policy of fostering city life throughout the peninsula. But civic institutions had been a Greek import into Anatolia, and the old Anatolian way of life maintained itself side by side with the Graeco-Roman cities for many centuries. " In the Antitaurus," says Strabo, " are deep and narrow canyons in which are situated Comana and the temple of Enyo, whom the people there call Ma. Comana is a considerable city ; its population, however, consists mostly of the inspired devotees and the temple slaves who live in it. Its inhabitants . . . are in a general way subject to the king, but mostly take their orders from the priest. The priest is lord of the temple and of the temple slaves who, when I stayed there, numbered more than six thousand of both sexes. A large territory, too, is attached to the temple, the revenue of which is enjoyed by the priest, who ranks second in honour in Cappadocia after the king ; and in general the priests belonged to the same family as the kings." This eye-witness account refers to Comana in Cappadocia as matters stood there about the beginning of the Christian era ; but elsewhere Strabo implies that a similar theocratic organization had existed before his time at Pessinus and Pisidian Antioch, and monumental evidence proving survival to a much later period proves that in Paul's day large areas on the plateau were still under a form of theocratic control, sometimes exercised by independent priesthoods, more often by the freedmen and slaves of the emperor who had succeeded the Hellenistic king in the ownership of the temple estates. The conditions existing at Pisidian Antioch when it was visited by Paul are instructive and probably typical. Close to Antioch there were three powerful pagan temples (two of which are mentioned by Strabo) owning large estates. Inscriptions of later date show that the cultivators of those estates lived a prosperous life under the direct control of the emperor, and had no contact with the life of the cities. At another temple on the middle Maeander above Hierapolis inscriptions show that the peasants on the temple lands, and even citizens of the neighbouring cities, gave unquestioned obedience to the will of the god of the temple as declared through his priests. In general, it may be said that while the bulk of the western flank of the peninsula formed the territories of Greek cities, the cities of the plateau, in the time of Paul and for much later, remained islands of hellenism in an Anatolian sea. The Christian mission at first confined itself to the Græco-Roman cities. As early as the reign of Trajan, Pliny observed that the Christian " superstition " was making its way into the villages and the open country. This process was completed in the fourth century ; by that time Christian hellenism succeeded (where pagan hellenism had failed) in penetrating to every nook and corner of the peninsula.

Language. In strict Roman theory the language of law and government was Latin. Throughout the earlier Empire the principle was upheld that all government business was conducted in Latin, and a Greek secretariat was maintained in Rome to furnish official Greek translations to accompany all government documents destined for the eastern provinces. The East adapted itself to this principle ; the eastern legal schools conducted their teaching in Latin, and there were Latin teachers in all the eastern cities for the convenience of Greeks and Orientals who wished to qualify for posts in the service of the Roman government. Such was the theory, and such were the limits of its reception. In practice, when administration passed from the centre of the circumference, strict insistence on Latin was found to be unworkable. In the East, Greek had long been the language of municipal government, which was to become an essential element in Roman Imperial administration. And all the educated population—Jews and Anatolians as well as Greeks—spoke Greek. To make the administration of law and government possible, the empire had to meet the eastern provincials at first half-way, and finally (but this came later than our period) on their own ground.

In the few Roman colonies, Latin was the official language of public business; it was the native speech of the highest class of the colonial society ; and a knowledge of Latin was perforce acquired by the local residents. And apart from the colonies, as we have seen, there was in every important city an influential body of Latin-speaking immigrants from the West. Roman insistence on Latin as the language of Imperial government might seem to have provided those Latin-speaking groups with a backing and an excuse for imposing their language, in the spirit of modern Imperialists, on the subject population. That such linguistic imperialism formed no part of the Roman plan, and never entered the heads of the Italian settlers, is abundantly proved by the inscriptions. A statistical analysis has shown that in the cities of Phrygia (omitting the colony of Antioch) the average proportion of Greek to Latin inscriptions of all sorts, public and private, was about thirty to one. And the great majority of the Latin inscriptions are, as might be expected, public or official documents, such as dedications to the emperors and the formularies of milestones. Private inscriptions in Latin are exceedingly rare. Even in the early empire, when pride in the Roman connexion was strong, Latin made no attempt to displace Greek as the language of business and education in Asia Minor. The Christian mission to the eastern Gentiles inevitably used the Greek language. We have seen that the Jews of the Eastern Dispersion spoke and wrote Greek, just as the western Jews learnt Latin.

Greek, then, as the language of culture and of ordinary intercourse, had no rival to fear in the educated society of the Anatolian cities. It remains to consider the linguistic position at the lower end of the social scale. To what extent,

during the New Testament period, had a knowledge of the
Greek language and Greek education spread among the lower
orders in the cities, or again among the villagers on city territories or on temple and imperial estates ?

Strabo provides a certain amount of material for the
construction of a linguistic map of Asia Minor during the
reigns of Augustus and Tiberius, and evidence for the survival
of native idioms till a later period applies *a fortiori* to the first
century. Strabo states explicitly that not a trace of the
Lydian language survived in the highly hellenized region of
Lydia, although Lydian was still spoken by the descendants
of Lydian colonists in the Cibyratis, south of Central Phrygia.
In discussing Homer's Carians, he uses language which *may*
imply that Carian was still spoken in his day. In Cappadocia,
which he knew well, he states definitely that the Cappadocian
language was still spoken. We may fill out his outline of the
linguistic map of the first century with the information casually
recorded in Acts that Lycaonian was spoken by the " multitudes "—the lower orders—in Lystra, and with the evidence
in Lucian and in Jerome that Celtic was spoken in Galatia
in the second century and again as late as the fourth. From
these sources we should conclude that in the parts of Asia
Minor which had been hellenized for centuries the native
languages had died out ; that in the mountains to the south
idioms like Lydian and Carian were still in use ; that on the
central plateau Lycaonian and Galatian, and therefore probably also Phrygian, were still the languages of the common
people ; and that in the east, in Cappadocia, Greek had made
little progress. So far as Phrygia is concerned—and the case
of Phrygia may be taken as typical—the inscriptions exactly
confirm this conclusion.

In Eastern Phrygia—the part of Phrygia which lay to the
east of the western mountain rim—and here alone in Asia
Minor the native idiom began to be used on tombstones in
the latter half of the third century A.D. About 100 of those
tombstones have so far been discovered, most of them in
recent years. The occasion for this unique revival of the
use of a native language is not far to seek ; at this period
paganism was organizing itself for the final struggle with the
Christian Church, and the restoration to epigraphical use of
the Phrygian language, the speech of the Mother Goddess,
and according to old tradition the original speech of mankind
had an obvious place in the pagan revival. These late Phrygian
inscriptions show clearly by the variety of their construction
and vocabulary that Phrygian was still a living language at

the date at which they were composed. The limits of their
distribution coincide exactly with our literary evidence, so
far as it exists, for the limits of Galatic Phrygia (the " Phrygian
and Galatian region " of Acts 16[6]), in other words they mark
the limits of a Phrygian-speaking population. And their
distribution within this area is significant. For the most part
they have been found on the sites of ancient villages which
lay on Imperial estates, but a number of them are from the
sites of Greek cities, showing that Phrygian was spoken by
the lower orders of the cities, just as Lycaonian was spoken
by the " multitudes " of Lystra. At the late date to which
these inscriptions belong it is natural to find that the users
of Phrygian also used Greek ; on most of the tombstones
Phrygian was used only for the formula against violation
while the epitaph proper was in Greek. It cannot be assumed
that in the time of Paul a knowledge of Greek was universal
among the lower orders on the plateau, even. on the city
territories. We learn from the historian Socrates that sermons
were preached in Phrygian as late as the fifth century ; like all
the other native languages of Asia Minor it was extinguished
not long afterwards by the Greek of the Christian Church.

Religion. " To the Jew first, and also to the Greek."
Alongside of the Jewish Synagogues which, as we have seen,
existed in all the principal cities of Asia Minor, the early
missions were confronted with a wide variety of pagan cults, as
well as philosophical systems which (in the words of an
Epicurean gospel displayed on the walls of a colonnade in the
Lycian Oenoanda) offered " the medicine of salvation " to all
their adherents. The eastern cities had accorded divine
honours to their Hellenistic kings, and they continued to
worship the Roman emperors as " gods " and " saviours."
In addition to sharing in the provincial cult of the emperor,
every city had its temple of Augustus with a municipal high-
priest in charge of the ritual, and many surviving inscriptions
record vows paid to the god-emperor by public bodies or guilds
or private citizens. But this cult, after the enthusiasm
called forth by the establishment of the empire had died
down, had become a formality, and the devotion of the people
was directed to the motley company of gods and goddesses,
aboriginal and immigrant, whose temples adorned the cities
and the countryside. The oldest religion of Asia Minor
centred in a goddess, the source of all life on earth, with a
male companion who appeared now as her lover and now as
her son, the Cybele and Attis of the Phrygian form of the
cult. The central and abiding figure was the Mother (the Ma

of the Cappadocians of Comana) ; her male companion was secondary and indeterminate, father and son in different aspects of his being. This stage in the cult is reflected in the primitive name Agdistis, properly a title of the goddess (and still so used in the Roman period), but also used in the plural, and sometimes masculine and sometimes feminine, reflecting an early stage of thought in which the reproductive and creative powers of Nature were merged in one androgynous figure. At a later stage the Phrygians introduced the distinction between a father-god and a son-god, called Papas and Attis. The father-god and the goddess were now the joint givers of increase. These primitive figures, generally under Greek names but with old Anatolian titles and attributes, continued to be worshipped throughout Asia Minor until the extinction of paganism.

With the immigrant Greeks came the Greek pantheon. When the old Phrygian town of Hierapolis was " colonized " by Greeks, the Greeks were " led " thither by the Pythian Apollo, and he now became the tutelary god of the city. Elsewhere bodies of Greeks who settled in Anatolian cities established cults of this or that Greek god, and as the hellenisation of the country proceeded these gods came to represent art, literature, culture as against the gods of the native population. So it was that in the old Apamean myth Apollo contended with Marsyas. This consciousness of a civilizing mission tended for a time to maintain the Greek character of the Greek gods in contradistinction to the Anatolian spirit. But the pressure of the interests vested in the old gods of the land, and the beneficent power, proved by long experience, which they exercised, kept their influence intact. As more and more of the native population came under the influence of Greek education the old cults began to invade the Greek forms of worship, and produce a conception of the gods in which Greek and Anatolian elements are combined. The gods of Asia Minor henceforth appeared as a motley company, in which Greek and Anatolian characters are merged. But in one respect the family relationship of the Greek pantheon fitted into the old Phrygian conception of the godhead. The father-hood of Zeus made him the natural counterpart and equivalent of the Phrygian father-god, and thus Greek influence tended to emphasize the conception of a father-god and mother-goddess, with a son who in Greek might be called by the name of any son of Zeus, Apollo, or Hermes, or what not. This idea of a triune relationship of father, mother, and son is reflected in many of the pagan religious monuments of the Early-

Christian period. The Zeus and Hermes (" Jupiter and Mercury ") of the episode at Lystra reappear as the recipients of a joint dedication in a recently discovered inscription of Lystra ; but in the inscription the father-god is not " Zeus," but " the god who hearkens to prayer." Zeus and Hermes in the remote Lycaonian township of Lystra were Greek only in name. Zeus was the old Anatolian peasant-god " who gave you from heaven rains and fruitful seasons, filling your hearts with food and gladness " ; and Hermes was his son.

On this confusion of race, social structure, language, and cult, Roman organization and Greek education had begun to impose order when Paul, the Greek-speaking Jewish citizen of Tarsus and Roman citizen, came to Pisidian Antioch.

BIBLIOGRAPHY

The numerous books and articles of Ramsay (enumerated in the Bibliography in *Anatolian Studies presented to . . . Ramsay*, edited by Buckler and Calder), and especially *The Historical Geography of Asia Minor*, *The Cities and Bishoprics of Phrygia*, *The Cities of St. Paul*, *The Letters to the Seven Churches*, and the many articles in Hastings's *Dictionary of the Bible*. Add *Monumenta Asiae Minoris Antiqua* (various editors) and *Anatoliun Studies presented to . . . Buckler*, edited by Calder and Keil.

VIII. BIBLICAL ARCHÆOLOGY

WITHIN the last few years, owing to the remarkable discoveries made in the Near East, the Biblical narratives have had unexpected light thrown on them, not only from Palestine but from all the neighbouring regions—Egypt, Asia Minor, Arabia, Mesopotamia, Babylonia, Assyria, and other parts. Exploration and excavation have been undertaken by numerous societies (British, American, French, German, Danish, Hebrew, and others), working on careful scientific lines, and have revealed languages, literatures, arts, customs, domestic habits, political institutions, religious rites, chronologies, and various other matters, all of which were quite unknown even a generation ago. The entire civilization, indeed, of the Near East, as far back as 4000 B.C. or earlier, has been largely uncovered. All these discoveries have greatly transformed our knowledge of Biblical history, showing the background within which the Hebrew people with their unique revelation must be set, if we are to understand the history and determine the revelation. They place the historical events in their correct chronological position, show the various external influences acting on ancient Palestine, determine the age and character of sites, reveal the daily life of the inhabitants, and help to confirm or correct the views of expositors and critics. It may be stated here, without exaggeration, that the results do not in any way lessen the uniqueness of the Bible as a religious document, but rather tend to establish its accuracy in innumerable details.

1. EXCAVATIONS

The number of these is so great that any attempt to describe them all would require many volumes. In this chapter we can only refer to a few of the more recent and important, bearing specially on the Bible :

1. *The Early Period.* We may pass over the various Sumerian and Babylonian versions of the Creation, discovered at Nineveh by Rassam (in 1848), George Smith (in 1873), and others, as well as the famous tablets on the same subject found at Sippar, Nippur, and other places in the Euphrates region, one of which (a six-column text known as the Sumerian

Epic of the Creation and Paradise) is believed to date from as early as 3000 B.C., and is evidently based on an antecedent original older still. All these have numerous points in common with the Creation story so familiar to us in Genesis, though they fall far short of the moral and spiritual level of the latter.

The Flood, however, deserves special reference, as clear evidence of such inundations has recently been obtained at two of the most ancient sites of Mesopotamia. One of these is Abraham's native place, Ur of the Chaldees, now known as al-Mugayyar (" Mound of Bitumen "), about eleven miles west of the Euphrates ; the other is Kish, a few miles to the east of Babylon. At the former city the excavators under Sir Leonard Woolley, in 1929, after digging down thirty feet or more (over an area of thirty by twenty yards) through several old civilizations, came upon a seam of perfectly clean silted clay, water-laid, uniform throughout, and over eight feet in thickness. According to Woolley, this clay deposit could only have been due to some great Flood, " of a magnitude unparalleled in local history." Below the clay, in the previous stratum, they discovered mud floors, pottery sherds, clay bricks, household rubbish, and other signs of occupation, as well as graves with clay figures and coloured earthenware. Here, five thousand or more years ago, the inhabitants dwelt till the waters overwhelmed them (sometime probably about 3000 B.C.) and deposited a deep layer of clay above everything. At Kish, which lay over one hundred miles north, and was probably the oldest city in the world, Mr. L. Ch. Watelin and others, with the collaboration of Professor Langdon, came on a similar deep layer of fine sand, eighteen inches thick, with rows of fresh-water fish and mussels embedded evenly and horizontally at various places. Langdon has described this as " the precipitated sediment of the waters which lay over the city." Beneath this the excavators found well-planned structures, baked brick pavements, flint implements (such as borers, scrapers, and sickle blades), bitumen figurines, and other remains of the mighty men of Kish in earlier ages. However much the Biblical account of the Flood may have been coloured and magnified, it is evident that it bears an historical character. The huge inundations referred to, it is true, belong to different levels and epochs. So far from having taken place at one and the same time, there may possibly have been a thousand years between the two. But they show that floods arising from various causes were not uncommon in lower Mesopotamia. They were apparently local, and confined to certain districts.

They may have been due to the river changing its course, or to some immense overflow, and it only required such a cause, or a combination of such, for an inundation to take the depth and dimensions attributed to the Deluge. The Flood is found mentioned in the Sumerian king-lists (on the Blundell Prism and other tablets), and a description of it is preserved in Babylonian Epics.

2. *The Patriarchal Period.* Here we meet with the Hebrews for the first time in Biblical history. Like the other Semites (Babylonians, Assyrians, Phœnicians, Canaanites, etc.), they came originally from the Arabian peninsula, the recognized homeland of the Semitic race. Other theories of their origin have been advanced, but these have been particularly weak, and have raised more difficulties than they have solved. They are known to have come north in successive waves, extending over many centuries. There is abundant evidence that, before the end of the third millennium B.C., large sections of them (known in Babylonian as Habiru), allured by the attractions of civilization in the Euphrates regions, had made settlements for themselves at various places there, such as Ur of the Chaldees. From here Terah, a Hebrew leader, along with his son Abraham (" the Hebrew," Gen. 14¹³) and a large company of followers, joining together in a great tribal movement, migrated shortly before the second millennium to Haran, farther north in Mesopotamia (Biblical Aram-Naharaim). From this centre of Aramæan life, Abraham and a number of Hebrew clans moved afterwards (*c.* 2090 B.C.) into Canaan, known at that epoch in cuneiform records as Amurru, the land of the Amorites (a Semitic people who had entered it from Arabia about a thousand years earlier). Abraham and some of his followers ventured as far as Egypt, and remained there for some time under friendly Pharaohs. A sculpture on Khnum-heten's Tomb at Beni Hassan, dating from the sixth year of Senusert II. of the XIIth Dynasty and representing a visit of Semites (thirty-seven in number), gives a good idea of what the arrival of the Hebrews would look like.

Though archæology as yet has found no trace of Abraham in Canaan, it has shown that the patriarchal circumstances, as depicted in the Book of Genesis, are not an artificial construction of priestly historians at a much later date (as was once believed by some scholars), but are a remarkably accurate representation of nomadic life in Abrahamic and pre-Mosaic times. The primitive nature of the religious ideas and worship, the particular conception of God, the distinctive ethical colouring, and the other characteristics are in accord with the

established practices of the Hebrew and Hurrian civilizations
of the period. The parallels, indeed, on such matters are
enough to fill a volume, and it is known now that the Biblical
narratives relating to this time contain a greater measure of
real historical material than some scholars had supposed, and
must have been based to some extent on contemporary documents. It has been found that practically every town
mentioned in the patriarchal narratives (Beersheba, Shechem,
Bethel, Jerusalem, Gerar, Dothan, and others) was in existence
at this epoch (c. 2000 B.C.), and that there was also an extensive
and prosperous civilization in the Jordan Valley, as early
Biblical tradition implies. At the Teleilat (Tells of) Ghassûl, in
the eastern valley of the Jordan, some four miles north of the
Dead Sea, Père A. Mallon has laid bare a large city, dating
from Chalcolithic times (c. 3700–3300 B.C.), which appears to
have been destroyed by an immense conflagration. His
discoveries point to a developed and luxurious civilization
even at that early age, with a remarkable knowledge of agriculture and ceramics. It has been thought by some scholars
that the remains may be those of Sodom or one of the Cities
of the Plain, but evidence seems to show that the site was
destroyed at least a thousand years before Abraham, and the
majority of scholars hold that the Pentapolis was situated to
the south of the Dead Sea.

Archæology so far has produced nothing either in support
of or in contradiction to the early date and historical value of
Gen. 14, with its account of the Battle of the Kings. The
names of three of the eastern kings, and perhaps also that of
the fourth (Amraphel) occur together on some late Babylonian
tablets (the Spartoli ones) belonging to the Persian period.
The tablets appear to commemorate some ancient time of
anarchy under foreign conquerors, but their fragmentary
condition and obscure style baffle any proper interpretation of
them. It can be said with certainty, however, that archæology
goes at least to support the underlying statements of the
campaign. Whatever interpretation we may give to the names
of the eastern kings—the writer has no difficulty in equating
Amraphel with Hammurabi (c. 2067–2024 B.C.), the sixth king
of the First or Amorite Dynasty of Babylon—discoveries have
shown that the narrative is in accord with the circumstances
of the time. It is now known from excavations that, from the
days of Lugal-zaggisi of Erech (c. 2777 B.C.), and Sargon of
Akkad (c. 2752 B.C.), the land of Amurru (which included the
Jordan regions) had been more or less subject to raids from the
east, and was at this very time under the suzerainty of Elam

(" twelve years they served Chedorlaomer," Gen. 14⁴). There seems nothing unhistorical, therefore, in the probability of a punitive invasion from the east in the case of revolt. Exploration, moreover, has shown that the route taken in Trans-Jordan by the eastern armies was a well-known one at that early epoch, marked now by several Early Bronze Age mounds (some of great size). If the writer might attempt a precise date for the events referred to, he would be inclined to put them somewhere between 2067 B.C., when Hammurabi ascended the throne, and 2061 B.C. when he rebelled against the supremacy of Elam.

We have external evidence that the city of Jerusalem was in existence as far back as Abraham's day (cf. Gen. 14¹⁸), for it is mentioned as early as *c.* 2000 B.C., under the name Ursalimmu (as Kurt Sethe transliterates it), in some Egyptian texts found at Luxor, in 1925, and the names of two of its ruling chiefs are given. It is also referred to frequently, under the name Ursalim, in the Amarna Letters (*c.* 1400–1370 B.C.), where its King Abdi-Hiba complains of attacks by the Habiru (Hebrews). The name Abdi-Hiba is known to be of Hittite-Mitannian character, and the prophet Ezekiel's allusion to the city, " Thy father was an Amorite and thy mother a Hittite." (Ezek. 16³· ⁴⁵), really discloses the original stock of the population. Excavations have shown that, in those early days, it was a small place, occupying the rather limited plateau of Mount Ophel (*i.e.* the south-eastern ridge). It thus lay between the old Tyropoean Valley (now filled up with débris) on the west and the valley of the Kidron on the east, while its northern limit was marked by the Zedek Valley. It was somewhat narrow in shape, following the ridge, and even as late as David's reign it could not have covered more than eleven or twelve acres, with an average width of about forty yards. By his time, however, it had become a Jebusite stronghold, and had massive walls on both sides, with a rock-hewn shaft on the east communicating with the water supply at the foot of the scarp. With strong defences, one can understand how it withstood the Hebrew invasion under Joshua, remaining for nearly four centuries in Jebusite hands, and how it made a two years' vigorous resistance to the armies of Nebuchadrezzar in 588–586 B.C. Perhaps the most interesting discovery of all has been that of the tortuous underground passage, ending in a vertical shaft fifty feet high, up which Joab is believed to have climbed into the city, and so taken the garrison by surprise (2 Sam. 5⁸ ; 1 Chron. 11⁶). The Millo (" Filling " or " Mound ") which David threw up to protect the breach he had made has also been identified, as well as his " tower that lieth out."

3. *The Hebrew Conquest.* The Conquest under Joshua is associated at its beginning with the capture of Jericho, now Kôm es-Sultân, near El Riha (modern Jericho). Professor Garstang, by careful and thorough investigation, extending over several years, has produced satisfactory evidences that the destruction of the city took place some time between 1407 and 1400 B.C. This conclusion is of great interest and importance, as the date happens to be that of the powerful invasion of Palestine by the Habiru (Hebrews) described in the Tell el-Amarna Letters, and it fixes the Exodus about 1445 B.C., during the reign of Pharaoh Amenophis II., and just after the long and powerful reign of Tuthmosis III. (who was thus the Oppressor). It also accords with the fact that a stele (discovered in 1896), erected by the Pharaoh Merenptah about 1225 B.C., to describe his victories over the neighbouring peoples, records that " Ysirael is desolated, its seed is not," which implies that the Israelites were already in Canaan by this time as a settled people. (See further Appendix, Chronology.—Ed.)

The date of the destruction of Jericho has been reached partly from the fact that the latest pottery and painted fabrics have been found to coincide with the age of Tuthmosis III. and his immediate successors, *i.e.* the fifteenth century B.C., and partly from the important fact that not a single fragment of Mycenæan ware was discovered among the ten thousand potsherds associated with the ruins of the walls or among the fifty thousand or more unearthed in the city. As it is known that this type of pottery entered Palestine about 1350 B.C. and a specimen of it was found outside the walls, it is clear that the destruction took place some years before this. The stratigraphic evidence, too, is corroborated by that of the tombs, about 2000 in number. These were found to contain a vast amount of material, of unparalleled profusion and variety, and an examination of it all has shown clearly that the occupation of the city ended about the time of Amenophis III. (1419–1383 B.C.). The destruction of the place was found to have been due to fire, as stated in the Biblical record: (" They burned Jericho with fire and all therein," Josh. 6²⁴). In some of the chambers explored were found grain, dates, bread, and other stores, charred and blackened by the flames, and the mass of burnt timber here and there was enormous, showing thick deposits of charcoal (in some places two feet deep) and pockets of white ash. The traces of terrific conflagration, indeed, are so impressive that, according to Professor Garstang, " such an effect could only have been obtained by studied preparation."

At the time of Joshua's attack, the main defences comprised two parallel walls of brick (round the summit of the mound), rising probably to thirty or forty feet, the outer one being six feet thick and the inner one twelve feet, with a space of about five yards between. The excavators found that both walls had suffered considerably, and it is not improbable that their fall was due to undermining here and there. The remains of the outer one had fallen down the slope, while the inner one, together with the buildings on it, had largely collapsed into the space between the two, which was filled with the débris. " There remains no doubt," says Professor Garstang, " that the walls fell out so completely that the attackers would be able to clamber up and over the ruins into the city." The excavations have shown, moreover, that the site, after being destroyed, remained desolate, with no appreciable population, for several centuries. The first part of the Early Iron Age (1200–900 B.C.) is not represented at all, and it is apparent that the city was not rebuilt nor its fortifications restored until the time of Hiel the Bethelite, about 860 B.C. (1 Kings 16³⁴).

The capture of Aï by Joshua is dramatically described in Josh. 7, 8, but Madame Krause-Marquet and her assistant excavators found that it was a ruin and uninhabited at the time of Joshua's entry into Canaan (being deserted from about 2000 B.C. till about 1200 B.C.). In this case, it is possible that the sacred historian may have confused Aï with Bethel ; or what is more likely, the Canaanite clans round about, thoroughly alarmed at the fate of Jericho and thrown on the alert, may have leagued themselves together to bar Joshua's advance and concentrated their forces on the summit of " The Ruin " (Aï = " ruin "), which was still a formidable place of defence. Hence Joshua's attack on it, and it was only by a ruse or stratagem on his part that the stronghold was captured. This agrees with the fact that there is no mention of children, as we find in the case of Jericho (6²¹), seeing that the site was only occupied temporarily. If this aspect of the matter be correct, the narrative in Joshua, though no doubt adorned with certain adventitious elements, takes on a new meaning.

The city of Jericho which Joshua attacked was not more than 650 yards in circumference. The ancient Canaanite towns, though regarded by the inhabitants as great and strong, were generally no more than villages within fortified walls. As a rule, they began as citadels or fortresses, around which a number of dwellings, built closely and irregularly, generally developed in course of time. Much labour was spent on raising massive walls, for every inhabited centre was liable to attack. At Tell en-Nasbeh (believed to be Mizpah), the stone ramparts, built of rough blocks (of great size towards the bottom), were more than forty feet high and sixteen to twenty feet thick, and to prevent scaling they were coated with hard yellow plaster to a height of fifteen or eighteen feet. At Shechem (Balâtah, a little south of Nâblus), the gigantic walls, discovered to be double like those of Jericho, with an earth slope of thirty-five feet between them, appear to have been about sixty-five feet high, with an average thickness of seventeen feet, and were strenghtened here and there by huge towers, the bases of which were protected by sloping stone revetments. One can understand how the Hebrews, on hearing the report of the spies ("The cities are great and walled up to heaven"), felt in their own sight as " grasshoppers " (Deut. 1^{28}).

4. *Period of the Monarchy.* Archæology has thrown much light on Solomon's activities. We have now fairly accurate information as to his buildings, the topography of his capital, and his political and commercial administration. At Megiddo (Tell el-Mutesellim) the excavators in 1928–29 unearthed commodious stables erected by him. They stand in units which accommodate twenty-four horses each, with the necessary hitching-posts or pillars. One building, some sixty yards long by twenty-four wide, comprises five such units, giving room for 120 horses under one roof, while another larger one contains the same number of units along with a parade ground (floored with white lime as hard as cement) and quarters for the charioteers and grooms. There seems to be evidence that stables of the same kind with stone pillars existed at Gezer, Taanach, Hazor (Tell el-Qedah), and other places, which like Megiddo lay close to the great trade routes. In this connexion, the claim of the Hebrew historian (2 Chron. 9^{25}) that the great king of Israel had several such centres for his horses, and no less than 4000 stalls may receive corroboration. It seems probable that Solomon engaged in the business of horse-dealing on a large and profitable scale. On the one hand, he purchased chariots in Egypt and exported them to the Hittites or North Syrians, and to the people of Damascus and the Euphrates regions ; while, on the other hand, he bought horses in Cilicia, which, as Herodotus tells us, was famed for its horse-breeding (cf. Ezek. 27^{14}), and he sold these to Egypt, where, owing to lack of extensive pastures, there

could be no export trade of this kind. In his efforts at foreign trading he seems also to have worked the Edomite copper mines in company with the Phœnicians (c. 960 B.C.). The ore was smelted at Ezion-geber (believed to be modern Tell el-Kheleifi), his naval base at the head of the Gulf of Akabah, and his ships, built and manned by Phœnicians, sailed with the copper down the Red Sea to Put and Ophir, and probably to India. He appears also to have had works at Ezion-geber for the manufacture of copper implements, especially spear-heads, fish-hooks, nails, etc., and for the building of ships, the production of ropes, baskets, mats, and pottery, and the manufacture of beads. Excavations by Nelson Glueck have revealed the place as a great industrial centre in Solomon's time, and no doubt under his control.

Considerable information in regard to the northern monarchy of Israel was obtained in 1908–1910, when excavations were made at Samaria under Dr. Reisner. The palace walls, fortress, and store-chambers of King Omri (or Humri, as the Assyrians spelt his name) were uncovered, and a large number of potsherds with Hebrew writing on them, dating, it is thought, from Jeroboam's reign (788-747 B.C.,) found. In 1931 the work was renewed under Mr. J. W. Crowfoot, when further Israelite traces appeared, both in the city and in the tombs. In particular, among other valuable objects (which included four more ostraca), some important carved ivories were discovered, closely related in characteristics and date to those found in 1928 at Arslan Tash, near Carchemish. They seem to have formed part of the decorated furniture in Ahab's palace and the other large houses, being used for the framework of cabinets, couches, tables, stools, or toilet boxes, and perhaps also for the wainscotting of rooms. It is known that during Ahab's reign there was a great display of pomp and luxury, with many " ivory houses," i.e. houses panelled or decorated with this substance (Ps. 45[8] ; Amos 3[15], 6[4]). A noteworthy characteristic is that, with the exception of a few purely Egyptian, the decorations correspond largely with those in Solomon's Temple (1 Kings 6[29]). At Megiddo, too, there has also been found an invaluable collection of carved and incised ivories, over 200 pieces altogether—the most comprehensive group yet known of such art, dating from the thirteenth century B.C. A few of them bear hieroglyphic inscriptions, many of them have Bes figures, sphinxes, and lotus designs, while others had served as inlay in furniture in wealthy houses. One is a beautiful oval gaming board, inlaid with gold. It is evident that there must have been skilled workers in ivory, probably Phœnician craftsmen, who moved about with their patterns from one court to another.

The Assyrian records tell us of an invasion of Israel by Shalmaneser III. which is not referred to in the Biblical history. According to the Monolith inscription of this monarch, he advanced against an alliance of Hittite and Armæan kings, among whom was Ahab (Ahabbu Sir'ilai), and fought them at the Battle of Karkar (on the Orontes probably) claiming to have defeated them there (853 B.C.). We learn that the allied forces totalled in round numbers 63,000 infantry, 2000 light cavalry, 4000 chariots, and 1000 camels, and that Ahab's contribution to these was 10,000 infantry, with 2000 chariots. Twelve years later, as we read on the Black Obelisk (marble), found at Calah by Layard in 1845, the Assyrian monarch launched another great campaign, which resulted in Jehu, king of Israel, having to pay tribute to him. Other Assyrian inscriptions refer to the invasions later on (in 783 B.C.) of the western regions by Tiglath-pileser III.(called Pul in 2 Kings 15[19]) when King Menahem of Israel was forced to pay a tribute of a thousand talents of silver. There are contemporary inscriptions, too, which corroborate other important historical events in the Old Testament, including the capture of Samaria by Sargon II. in 722 B.C. (inscribed on the walls of his palace at Dur Sharrukin or Khorsabad), and the invasion of Judah by Sennacherib in 701 B.C. (recorded on the Bulls of Nineveh and on the Taylor Prism). The excavations at Lachish (Tell ed-Duweir) have revealed the breach made in the limestone walls by Sennacherib, as well as evidence of huge bonfires which Nebuchadrezzar heaped against them when he besieged the city in 587 B.C.

Thanks to archæology, scholars are better able now to trace the activities of the Egyptian rulers during this period. In regard to Shishak, for instance, the first king of the XXIInd Egyptian Dynasty, though his invasion of Judah is recorded on the walls of Karnak, little was known of it till recently, when Sir Flinders Petrie excavated Gerar (Tell Jemmeh), Bethpelet (Tell el-Fara), Old Gaza (Tell el-Ajjûl), and other sites. Shishak appears to have been an Asiatic, probably Persian or Caspian, and he brought with him from Asia the traditions of massive building. He set up a great stele of triumph at Megiddo, and built immense walls at the places just mentioned—at Beth-pelet his wall was twenty-two feet thick—with millions of hard bricks nearly double the usual size, and made out of clay brought from a distance. His invasion of Palestine (1 King 14[25 ff.]) could not have been a mere raid, as some scholars have supposed, but must have been a powerful revival of Egyptian rule, and he continued to hold south Palestine for several years. Solomon had married the daughter of the previous king of Egypt, Pasebkhanu (c. 976–947 B.C.), and it was only after Solomon's death and the consequent weakening of Judah that Shishak was able to venture on his looting conquest.

5. *Antiquity of Civilization and Commerce.* One outstanding result of Biblical archæology has been the extension backward of the origin of civilization in the Near East. Increasing proof has been forthcoming that a highly developed culture, hitherto unsuspected, existed in these regions, Palestine included, at a period much earlier than the date which the Biblical chronology suggests for the creation of the world. Human remains have been found at Moun: Carmel (by Miss Garrod in 1934), dating many thousand years B.C., though we have no evidence of any civilization at such a remote period. We have innumerable inscribed tablets, however, beautiful painted pottery, and exquisite objects of art dating as early as the fifth or sixth millennium B.C. It has been found that such cities as Kish (which existed before 5000 B.C.), Ur (whose royal tombs are not later than 3500 B.C.), Lagash, Tepé Gawra (north-east of Nineveh), Mari (on the Middle Euphrates), and others were prosperous centres of civilization long before the Flood. Even Jericho at the beginning of the fourth millennium was a place of considerable agricultural activity (as Garstang has found from the numerous grain wells of that period), and its inhabitants could make fancy basket-work, pottery and other objects of refinement. There were here and there, no doubt, aboriginal elements of a lower type, with primitive tools and weapons, who had not yet emerged from neolithic influences. But, generally speaking, we find the early dwellers in Palestine, Mesopotamia, and neighbouring regions constructing superb temples and large well-adorned palaces, cultivating the soil, producing fine jewellery and other artistic objects, observing excellent moral and religious laws, and living on the whole much the same as those in later ages. As far back as the time of Abraham (2000 B.C.) education was conducted by competent teachers. Two well-constructed schoolrooms, made to accommodate nearly 150 scholars and dating from the third millennium B.C., have been discovered at Mari, on the Middle Euphrates, and in all the large cities there seems to have been excellent instruction in reading, writing, arithmetic, history, geography, astronomy, and other subjects (cf. the incident in Gideon's experience, Judg.

8[14] R.V. margin). Along with this ancient civilization there went a widespread, well-organized system of commerce, with connexions by wagon or caravan routes for a thousand miles and more from east to west. Sumerian traders, for instance, long before the time of Sargon of Akkad (2752 B.C.), had established a commercial settlement as far west as Cappadocia, and kept up correspondence with it, doing business by means of letters of credit. All this has led Biblical scholars to revise their chronological views on human development in the Near East, and to put the beginnings of civilization much farther back, even into prehistoric times. It follows that, when Joshua entered Canaan, there was already an ancient culture there, and that the Israelites and even the patriarchs were comparatively late-comers on the scene; and consequently we must suppose for early Old Testament history a greater cultural and civilized activity than the Biblical record indicates.

2. TABLETS AND INSCRIBED POTSHERDS

Literary and inscriptional remains are not so numerous in Palestine as one would expect, owing no doubt to the fact that writers largely used papyrus, skins, and similar materials liable to perish in the damp climate. Excavations have not produced, for example, any records of the Jewish monarchy, though many such must have been in existence as late as the post-exilic age. At the same time, a vast amount of written or inscribed material bearing on Palestine and its inhabitants has been disinterred in neighbouring lands, particularly in Egypt, Babylonia, and Assyria, and even a large number of written potsherds (which seem to withstand destruction well) have been dug up in Palestine, giving evidence of considerable literary activity there as far back as the days of the Judges. It used to be thought that writing was practically unknown in those early ages, and that written historical records could not have been in existence then, but this idea has been abundantly disproved by recent excavations. Repeated proof has come to light that writing was habitually used even a thousand years and more before the Hebrews entered Canaan.

Most of the writing in early times was cuneiform, *i.e.* each character or sign consisted of one or more wedges arranged in a variety of ways. This form had originally been pictorial, but as the pictures frequently required to be impressed on clay or carved in stone, modifications became necessary, and hence the cuneiform style developed in course of time (as the hieroglyphic did in Egypt). It is believed to have been introduced at a very remote period (probably as early as the third millennium) by the Sumerians, a non-Semitic race, who ruled on the lower Euphrates.   It was ultimately adopted by the Semitic inhabitants also, and was employed in Canaan in the fourteenth century B.C. for diplomatic purposes.   It was of a syllabic nature (each sign representing a syllable, as in hiero-glyphic and Chinese), but was complicated by being also polyphonic and ideographic.   The second method of writing was alphabetic, and was introduced much later than the cuneiform.   It was used throughout Phœnicia, Palestine, and the southern regions.   The alphabet employed is known as the Phœnician or Canaanite, and is believed to have been derived from Egyptian hieroglyphics.   It has been found in its earliest form in some inscriptions at Serâbit el-Khâdim, in the Sinai peninsula, dating probably from about 1900 B.C.   Specimens dating only a few centuries later have been discovered recently on bowls or potsherds at various places in Palestine.   From Gezer, for instance, we have a sherd with three letters, dating from about 1600 B.C. or earlier ; Beth-shemesh has given us a large fragment, with two lines of lettering on the concave side and five on the other, belonging to about the same date ; at Lachish the excavators have unearthed the broken pieces of a bowl containing seven letters in clear white paint (c. 1300 B.C. or a little later), as well as the fragments of a tall red ewer (about two feet in height), containing an inscription of date somewhere between 1295 and 1262 B.C.   The script has also been found complete and well developed on Ahiram's tomb at Byblos, as far back as 1250 B.C.   There is good evidence that this mode of writing was the usual one in Palestine and must have been widely used by the Israelites.   A third method, consisting in a combination of these two others, has been brought to light by Schaeffer and Chenet at Ras Shamra, on the Syrian coast.   It takes the form of a new cuneiform, of an alphabetic nature, and appears on hundreds of tablets (see 8. below) disinterred at this ancient centre of culture and commerce, as well as on one discovered at Beth-shemesh.

In our further description here of tablets, inscribed pot-sherds (known as ostraca), engraved seals, and similar objects, we can only refer to the more important, especially those recently discovered.   We pass over the great Assyrian Libraries of Sennacherib (705 B.C.), Esarhaddon (681 B.C.), and Ashur-banipal (669 B.C.) discovered at Kouyunjik (the largest mound at Nineveh) by Mr. (afterwards Sir) Henry Layard in 1845-50, and which contain specimens of almost every kind of literature, scientific, historical, religious, and commercial.   We need not refer, moreover, to the official correspondence of the Assyrian kings during the Sargonic period (722–625 B.C.), consisting of 1471 tablets in cuneiform preserved in the British Museum and now translated and published by Professor Leroy Watermann.

1. *The Tell el-Amarna Tablets.* These important tablets, some 350 in number, written in cuneiform, were discovered in 1887 at Tell el-Amarna in Egypt, among the ruins of Pharaoh Akhenaten's palace. They consist of diplomatic correspondence from various rulers in Asia, and particularly from the Egyptian governors of Palestinian towns, to the two Egyptian kings, Amenophis III. (1419–1383 B.C.) and his son Akhenaten (1383–1366 B.C.). Needless to say, they are of immense value for the history of Palestine at this epoch. They show that Egyptian control of the land became so weakened and relaxed from 1400 B.C. onwards that any well-disciplined organized forces could take possession. They describe how invaders were seizing the towns and causing widespread and immanent danger. These attacking forces are described in the letters from the northern towns by the ideogram Sa-Gaz ("fighting men "), and in those (a few years later) from King Abdi-Hiba of Jerusalem as Habiru ; and the view is held by many scholars that the former were people of Hebrew race who entered from the north-east (c. 1400 B.C.), while the latter were the Hebrews from Kadesh Barnea, who entered about the same time as their kinsmen, perhaps in concert with them, and were now (c. 1385 B.C.), after Joshua's death (cf. Judg. 1¹⁻⁸), threatening Jerusalem. There is evidence that the weakness continued for about three-quarters of a century, giving ample time to the invaders.

2. *Cappadocian Tablets.* These amount to over two thousand, written in cuneiform in an Assyrian dialect, and dating from about 1980 B.C. They were discovered at Kara Eyuk, ancient Kanes, in Cappadocia (Asia Minor), where they were found lying in special brick-built chambers, and for the most part properly arranged in rows. They comprise not only contract notes, statements of sales, and legal documents, but business letters of correspondence with the city of Ashur (modern Qal'ah Sharqât), 500 miles eastward, in Assyria. We know that at Kanes there was a trading colony of Sumerians, from the Euphrates delta, as early as the third millennium, before the reign of Sargon the Great (c. 2752 B.C.), and from this time onward there must have been constant business communication between there and the Euphrates-Tigris regions. The merchants at Kanes exported metals and other things across Mesopotamia to the east, and imported wool,

lead, and other commodities from there. The tablets throw an interesting light on this traffic, organized with such remarkable ability at that early epoch.

3. *Hittite Tablets.* These national archives, written in cuneiform (some in Babylonian and others in Hittite languages) amount to many thousands, and were unearthed in 1907–12 by Professor Winckler among the palace ruins at Hattushash (now Boghaz-keui, in the bend of the river Halys), the ancient capital of the Hittite empire in Asia Minor. We know now that the Hittites (Egyptian Kheta) held the key to the Near East from about 1600 to 1200 B.C., especially during the reign of their powerful leader Shuppiluliu (*c.* 1400–1365 B.C.), who bound the Hittite clans into a great confederation and extended his rule beyond the Taurus Mountains into Syria and Mesopotamia. These valuable documents, some of which are copies of older records going back to the beginnings of Hittite history, give us many long-lost pages in the story of the ancient empires of the Near East. Among them are some remarkable treaties made with the rulers of Mitanni, Amurru, Egypt, and other states. These treaties refer to the Sa-Gaz in such a way as to show that these people belonged to the Habiru (Hebrew) stock, as did other Aramæan nomads of the Syrian desert. By the name Hebrew we have to understand not Israel alone, but all the Hebraic peoples whom the traditions of Israel claimed as kindred, and who were found scattered in the vast extent of territory between the Tigris and the Mediterranean.

4. *Nuzi Tablets.* In 1925 Professor Chiera began excavations at Yalghan Tepé (ancient Nuzi), ten miles south-west of Kirkûk in Assyria. Among other important discoveries were over a thousand cuneiform tablets from the latter part of the fifteenth century B.C. Their value for Biblical study lies in the fact that they are written by a non-Semitic people, the Hurrians (believed by many scholars to be the Biblical " Horites," see below), who were widespread at the time from the Tigris to the Mediterranean, and who seem to have left their impress on the Hebrew race with whom they mixed. The tablets consist mostly of legal documents, personal and family records, and commercial communications, and refer frequently to the Habiru as a slave population in the district. They throw considerable light on the legislation and social customs of the Old Testament, showing these to be based to some extent on Hurrian regulations. We discover an explanation of the relationship between Abraham and Hagar, Jacob's deal with Esau as to the birthright, the story of Jacob and Laban, Rachel's removal of the household gods or teraphim, and other

matters which have puzzled scholars. Apart from such illustrations of the patriarchal period, the tablets reveal the existence of many customs found later among the Israelites (such as the gleaning of the cornfields by the poor and destitute, as in the Pentateuchal codes).

5. *Mari Tablets.* These, amounting to many thousands in cuneiform, were unearthed at Mari (modern Tell Hariri, in North Mesopotamia), and include numerous letters to Zimrilim, the last king of this remarkable city-state, who was a contemporary of Hammurabi of Babylon (*c.* 2067–2024 B.C.). As these concern events in the days of Abraham, and refer to the Habiru as present in this region, they are of supreme importance in Bible study. They give us most interesting information regarding the many cities round about (they contain the names of 150 unknown before). A Biblical town which frequently figures in them is Nahur (the " city of Nahor," Gen. 24[10]), to which Abraham sent his servant to find a wife for Isaac. We learn that the king of Haran, where Abraham had been living before he migrated to Canaan, was Ashditakum, and they describe the commercial life, social customs, military equipment, and other matters connected with this region.

6. *Nippur Tablets.* These, about 700 in number, are mostly commercial texts discovered at Nuffar (ancient Nippur) in Babylonia. They form the records of an important Banking Company (" Murashu and Sons "), and date from the reign of Artaxerxes I. (464–424 B.C.) and Darius II. (423–405 B.C.). As they include the names of a large number of Jewish clients —descendants of those exiled—they throw considerable light on the Jewish population that continued to remain in Babylonia. It is a remarkable fact that the vocalization of many of the names is much the same in the Old Testament as on the tablets, thus confirming the Hebrew pronunciation fixed twelve centuries later by the Massoretes.

7. *Codes of Laws.* One great monument of early Babylonian civilization is the stele containing Hammurabi's Code of Laws (282 in number), discovered at Susa (ancient Shushan, Neh. 1[1] ; Esth. 2[8], 3[15]) by M. de Morgan in 1901, and now preserved in the Louvre. As Hammurabi ascended the throne *c.* 2067 B.C., his Code of Laws goes back to the third millennium. Earlier rulers, such as those of Sumeria, had drawn up legal codes, and every city had its inheritance of laws, but while Hammurabi followed these to a great extent, his own were new in many details. They were largely in force in Canaan from the days of the patriarchs, and show many analogies with the Laws of Moses, especially with the " Book of the

Covenant " (Ex. 20²²-23). In addition to Hammurabi's
we have now the Assyrian Code (published in 1920), inscribed
on tablets from the city of Ashur, and dating from about the
twelfth century B.C., as well as the Hittite Code (published in
1921), discovered on tablets unearthed at Boghaz-keui, the
Hittite capital. Both these are similar in many respects to
Hammurabi's, but differ in some particulars from his owing
to different national and social arrangements.

8. *The Ras Shamra Tablets.* These tablets, which are the
most important discovered since the Tell el-Amarna ones,
amount to several hundreds. They were dug up in 1929 and
succeeding years at the mound known as Ras Shamra (the
Ugarit of the Egyptian and Hittite documents), some ten
miles north of Latakia on the Syrian coast. In their present
form they date from about 1470–1366 B.C., though some of
them were undoubtedly composed much earlier. Not many
of them—only those in the Babylonian and Hurrian languages
—are written in the ordinary syllabic cuneiform. The great
majority are in a script hitherto unknown, consisting of
cuneiform of an alphabetic nature, the key to which was
discovered through the Semitic skill of Charles Virolleaud,
Hans Bauer, Père Dhorme, and others. The language on these
latter (which are the most important) is regarded as Proto-
Phœnician, and its similarity to the Hebrew of the Old Testament is so striking that some of the tablets can be readily
transliterated into this. The texts in general consist not only
of commercial accounts, public documents, letters, exercises
in grammar, but mostly of a number of religious poems, rich
in ancestral traditions and myths, and dealing with dramatic
episodes in the realm of the gods, and with the problems of
life and death. They had evidently formed part of a well-
furnished library in a college for the training of priests and
scribes, and afford us valuable evidence as to the nature of
religion in Syria and Palestine several centuries before the
Israelite monarchy. The principal God is El, reminding us of
the frequent occurrence of this name in the Old Testament,
both in appellations and otherwise (cf. El Shaddai, El Elyon,
El Qannā (Ex. 20⁵), etc., as well as " I am El the God of thy
fathers," Gen. 46³). The name Elohim (" God ") also occurs
as a plural of majesty in two of the tablets, but its use may
have been confined to the Sa-Gaz, or Hebrew people, who are
known to have formed a large part of the population of Ugarit.
In one of the tablets we read of a primordial hero or demi-god
named Dan-el, who was the representative of justice, and
this " Daniel," not the Biblical one, is probably the legendary

individual mentioned three times by Ezekiel ($14^{14, 20}$, 28^3). Considerable light is thrown on the ritual customs of the Old Testament, showing that these embody cultural elements common to the Canaanites. Altogether these ancient archives bear in a most significant way on the religion and history of the Old Testament.

9. *The Lachish Letters.* These are ostraca, eighteen in number, and contain ancient Hebrew writing in black ink, in the Phœnician alphabet, dating from 587 B.C., the close of Zedekiah's reign. They were found at Lachish (Tell ed-Duweir) in 1935, in a layer of charcoal and ash, having been preserved there since the city was burned by Nebuchadrezzar that year. They consist mostly of letters sent to the governor of Lachish from some observation post several miles away during the troubled times when Jerusalem was being besieged by Nebuchadrezzar's forces, and when Lachish, Azekah, and other towns were in danger. From references, indeed, in one letter, they seem to have been written at the very time when renewed help was expected or already on its way from Egypt under King Hophra, to relieve the situation. The ostraca are of great importance, as they contain the only Hebrew writings of any length which have survived from pre-exilic times, and help to paint the background of Judæan history during the last years of the monarchy. They make reference to Jeremiah (who is referred to as " the prophet ") and his pro-Babylonian utterances. They also contain many personal names which are found in the Books of Jeremiah and Kings. One of them gives a list of nine, of which no less than seven are compounded with Yahweh ; and as a similar large proportion of Yahweh names appears on the other potsherds we have evidence that the reformation carried out by Josiah had borne fruit.

10. *Seals and Seal Impressions.* A large number of these, bearing Hebrew inscriptions in Phœnician characters, have been discovered in recent years. It will be sufficient here to refer to two or three. Excavations at Tell Beit Mirsim (believed to be Kiriath-sepher or Debir) have brought to light two clear impressions on jar-handles reading " For Eliakim, steward of Yôkîn," the latter individual being evidently Jehoiachin, the king who reigned over Judah for only three months, at the age of eighteen, and was then carried into captivity by Nebuchadrezzar (597 B.C.). In a tomb at Tell en-Naṣbeh (Mizpah) has been found a beautifully worked agate seal, with the words " Jaazaniah, servant of the king," which must have belonged to the royal officer who went to Mizpah (2 Kings 25^{23} ; Jer. 40^8) along with other leaders to

give in his allegiance to Gedaliah, the governor appointed by
Nebuchadrezzar to manage the affairs of the kingdom after
the dethronement of its last king, Zedekiah. In this connexion,
it is interesting to note that from Lachish comes a seal which
reads, " For Gedaliah, who is over the house," and there is
every reason to believe that this was the governor just referred
to, who was treacherously murdered after two months' rule
(Jer. 40, 41). The seal shows the marks of the papyrus on
which it had been used and the vertical lines of the string,
thus giving us proof of the use of papyrus as writing material
in Palestine. A seal of date about 950 B.C., discovered at Gerar,
reads " Shemya, son of Meqyla," and it is clear that this is
" Shimeah, son of Mikloth," mentioned in 1 Chron. 8³², and
belonging to the Benjamite tribe. It will be seen that in many
of the seals we have remarkable confirmation of the Biblical
record, even in names and circumstantial details. In addition
to seals, large numbers of inscribed jar-handles of a national
kind have been found, especially in Judæan territory, dating
from the time of the monarchy.

11. *Antiquity of Writing.* The existence of writing as far
back as the third millennium or even earlier is one of the outstanding contributions of archæology within recent years.
Discoveries such as those mentioned above show that cuneiform writing was in general use long before the time of Abraham
(*c.* 2090 B.C.), and that the alphabetic script was widespread
in Palestine before the days of Moses. That many of the
Hebrews themselves, during their sojourn in Egypt, were
acquainted with writing, probably in the alphabetic form,
seems to be proved from certain of their number being appointed
shôterîm, " officers " (Ex. 5¹⁴), a word which literally means
" scribes " (cf. Assyrian *shaṭâru,* " write " ; Aramaic *sheṭârâ,*
" document "). This implies that the Hebrews kept the usual
account work and registering which the Egyptian taskmasters
required. The mention in the Pentateuch of writing on stone,
or in a book with ink, as early as the Hebrew Conquest, is
far from being an anachronism. Scholars have no difficulty
now in concluding that there were recorders in Israel when
Joshua entered Canaan, moral codes in well-inscribed form
long before the Hebrew one, large numbers of written psalms
ages before David, and numerous written proverbs and aphorisms a whole millennium before Solomon. All this goes to
show that the Israelite historians and prophets could have
had, and probably did have, written sources at their disposal
dating from many centuries before the monarchy. Some of
this ancient material may have been at first in the form of

poetical sagas or stories told in the sanctuaries and round the fire at night, and in the course of time these may have developed into written narratives ; but at the same time there must have been much written material contemporary or almost so with the events themselves, and although this was no doubt revised by redactors in later ages and thus suffered from editorial additions and modifications, there must have been much of it, including laws and actual historical narratives, that had undergone little or no change. There is nothing unreasonable in the view that many of the Pentateuchal laws, including the Decalogue, may have been written down in the first period of Israel's history. Even the Biblical story of the Conquest, in its original form at least, may be derived from early records of almost contemporary date, and much of the Hexateuch undoubtedly contains some very ancient material.

3. SURROUNDING NATIONS

Archæology has shown that the Israelites had close connexions and affinities with neighbouring peoples. A generation ago, it was not unusual to regard them as occupying a detached position in Canaan, separated largely from all others. Archæological research, however, has established their essential similarity to surrounding peoples in language, custom, civil and moral law, social habits, and even in ritual, sacrifice, and other religious usages. Discoveries have shown, for example, how greatly they were influenced by the ancient and imposing civilization of Babylonia, of which country Palestine was for many centuries a province until Egypt, under Tuthmosis III., took possession of it by force of arms shortly after 1500 B.C. They derived from the Babylonians many of their ideals of social life and justice, several of their Old Testament legends, and a number of their religious institutions. Archæology has revealed likewise their dependence on the remarkable culture and peculiar institutions of Egypt as shown by an extensive vein of Egyptianisms (as some scholars believe) within the language of the Pentateuch, and by scarabs, pottery, and other objects of Egyptian manufacture found in Palestinian tells. They came, too, in early times at least, under the influence of the Semitic culture of Arabia, especially of the land of Midian, where Moses learned to call upon the name of Yahweh. In the same way also they were affected to some extent by the civilization and customs of the Hittites, the Hurrians, the Phœnicians, and the other adjacent nations. We know now that, so far from differing from all these peoples, they were more or less closely tied to them, and had numerous correspondencies with them. This, of course, does not detract from their distinct religious character or affect their witness to a direct revelation from God, or lessen the paramount and Divine truth of which they became exponents to the world. In such matters, at least, there was a gulf between them and their neighbours, for their culture and civilization possessed numerous elements not found beside the Nile or the Euphrates, or anywhere else. But at the same time, their unity with surrounding peoples in innumerable ways does take them out of the isolated sphere which they were formerly supposed to occupy. It may be helpful here if we describe the origin and characteristics of some of these adjacent races as revealed to us by recent archæology, particularly those about which there has hitherto been much uncertainty :

1. *The Sumerians.* Some time before the beginning of the second millennium B.C. the great alluvial plain of lower Mesopotamia, watered by the Euphrates and Tigris, was inhabited by two races, quite different in origin and language. The northern part, just about where the two rivers approach nearest to each other, was occupied by a Semitic race, known as Akkadians (from Sargon of Akkad, *c.* 2752 B.C., their greatest ruler) ; the south, at the head of the Persian Gulf, was ruled by a non-Semitic element, the Sumerians. The Akkadians had come from the Arabian desert : not directly *via* the southern *wādis*, but from the north, down the course of the Euphrates. Like the Hebrews and other Semites, they spoke an inflected language, with tri-consonantal roots, but they have left no writing behind them. The Sumerians were a dark-haired people, speaking an agglutinative language something like ancient Turkish (Turanian) in its formation, and writing in a system of conventionalized pictures, which developed later, as we have stated, into cuneiform signs. What their original home was, we do not know. They appear to have come from the mountains to the east, bringing with them a polytheistic religion and innumerable gods, and seem to be referred to in Genesis (11^2), where we read of a people who " journeyed from the east and came into the land of Shinar and dwelt there." The view that they belonged to the neighbouring Elamite country does not seem to be conclusive, and the probability is that they came from somewhere further east, perhaps not far from the Indus Valley. They have left numerous written sources behind them, including legends, omen-texts, king-lists, royal inscriptions, and others. They must have had at their disposal a mass of documentary evidence, from which they compiled political and religious histories, which unfortunately

only survive in excerpts embodied in Babylonian literature of much later date. After about 1700 B.C. their language gave way to the Semitic, and became a purely archaic and literary one.

2. *The Hittites.* We now have authentic information as to the origin of this race. According to a long inscription from Boghaz-keui (ancient Hattushash), they were an Indo-European people who entered Asia Minor (*via* the Bosporus or perhaps the Caucasus) under Pitkanas, their king, shortly before 2000 B.C. They made their capital at Kussara (probably in the Taurus region), and in course of time subjugated Nêsas (Nyssa, modern Bazirgyan Eyuk), Zalpuvas (or Zalpas), Hattushash, and other independent kingdoms, thus making themselves rulers over the whole of that part of Asia Minor. From Kussara they transferred their administration to Nêsas, where they built temples and palatial dwellings, and their language, which is written in cuneiform, has thus become known as Nasian (Nasili). They ultimately moved their centre to Hattushash, which had been the capital of the Hatti, a powerful people who appear in history as far back as about 4000 B.C. From this time (rather uncertain) onward, these invaders naturally became known as " Hittites," taking this name from the defeated race of Hatti (known in letters and treaties mainly as Luvians and other tribes) to whom it primarily belonged, and who may now be distinguished as " Proto-Hittites." They organized themselves into a great political confederacy and gradually extended their empire, until under Shuppiluliu (*c.* 1400 B.C.) they ruled practically from the Ægean Sea to beyond the Euphrates. About 200 years later, however, their supremacy was brought to an end, and their empire ended, through the inrush of the " Sea-Peoples " and kindred races (1190 B.C.). They are mentioned frequently in the Old Testament, having made their way into Palestine about 2000 B.C., probably from Kussara, where there must have been a strong dynasty. We read of them as far south as Hebron (Gen. 23[3], 25[10]) in the time of Abraham, and as dwelling in the mountains of Canaan (Num. 13[29]) along with the Amorites and Jebusites. The term " Syro-Hittites " (or " Neo-Hittites " or Tabalians, as the Assyrians called them) designates the later confederacy of small states, about thirty in number, mostly under the control of Carchemish, which combined together principally to oppose the march of Assyria towards the west. These were states which had long been used to Hittite administration, if not largely peopled by Hittite stock, and they continued to maintain the

Hittite military, political, and social traditions. They lay more to the east, extending from Syria northward in a narrow stretch, and were ultimately crushed out of existence about the eighth century B.C., but have left a number of sculptures and hieroglyphic inscriptions (still mostly undeciphered) at Carchemish, Zendjirli, Arslan Tepé (Malatia), and other places in northern Syria. These were the "Hittites" with whom the Hebrew monarchs had dealings (cf. 1 Kings 10[29] (2 Chron. 1[17]), 11[1] ; 2 Kings 7[6]).

3. *The Hurrians.* Researches have been made into the question of this race (Egyptian Huru, Biblical Horites, perhaps), or "Subareans" as they have been called by some scholars. It is now known from the Boghaz-keui and Nuzi tablets, as well as from the Ras Shamra ones, that they were a non-Semitic (though not Indo-European) people, speaking a language believed by some scholars to be allied to Caucasian. They had their original settlement around ancient Arrapha (modern Kirkûk in south-eastern Assyria), and seem to have migrated westward into Mesopotamia and Palestine about 1900 B.C., or earlier. They appear in course of time to have been scattered over the wide region from Elam to Egypt, either settled in colonies of their own or mixed with other races, such as the Hebrews. Several of the Ras Shamra Tablets are in the Hurrian language, while others of them are a mixture of Hurrian and Semitic, and there are also vocabularies of cuneiform ideograms with their syllabic equivalents in Hurrian. This race from the Tigris regions must not be equated with the Mitannian nation (*c.* 1400 B.C.) in Aram-Naharaim (Egyptian Naharina), the region between the Tigris and the Euphrates, for though this nation had a dialect of Hurrian as its official language (as we know from the Amarna Tablets), and was really part of the Hurrian empire, it was quite short-lived, and owed its organization rather to an Indo-Iranian element which permeated and ruled it.

The Hurrians are believed by many scholars to be the same as the Biblical "Horites." Judging from the Bible, the conclusion might be drawn that the latter were confined to Edom, but there is good ground for believing that there were large groups of them in Palestine also,, for in several passages where "Hivite" is mentioned, the proper reading should be "Horite." This seems to be the case in Gen. 34[2], 36[2] (cf. 36[20]), Josh. 9[7], 11[19], and elsewhere, and indeed the Septuagint has "Horite" in the first and third of these passages. There seems evidence, therefore, that the "Horites" were scattered over Palestine, and there is some uncertainty as to whether such a people as the Hivites ever had a tangible existence. It is clear that the Horites, if they are to be identified with the Hurrians, can no longer be regarded as legendary Edomites or "cave-dwellers," located merely in southern Palestine, but were one of the most important cultural races in western Asia from 1900 onward. Like the Mitannian nation, the Hurrian race succumbed about 1400 B.C. to the powerful Hittite forces, and ended by being absorbed in the Hittite empire.

Recent archæology seems to show that the Hebrews must have been considerably influenced by the Hurrians. That the former continued, after settling in Canaan, to maintain their contact with the latter in Mesopotamia, is evident from the marriages of Isaac and Jacob. They would naturally also take over many Hurrian customs, and there must have been considerable racial intermixture. This is corroborated by the numerous parallels in social conditions as reflected in the Pentateuch and in the Hurrian tablets. The theory is gaining ground, indeed, that the Hebrews came in the course of time to have a large infiltration of Hurrian blood, and that this gave them their characteristic facial expression, so like the Hurri-Hittite type, and so markedly different from the Arabic.

4. *The Hyksos* (" *Princes of the Desert* "). These were foreign invaders, sometimes called " Shepherd Kings " after the historian Manetho, who poured into Palestine and Egypt from the north-east, and ruled over both these lands for a considerable period. They were ultimately driven out by Ahmosis I. in 1580 B.C., but how long their rule extended is still undetermined. According to the longer scheme, in the form adopted recently by Sir Flinders Petrie, it lasted 788 years in both countries, *i.e.* from *c.* 2368–1580 B.C., while Professor Albright and others would give it no more than 150 years (*c.* 1730–1580 B.C.). That they were largely of Semitic origin (probably Phœnicians or Amorites) is evident from several facts. Many of their names, such as 'Anath-Har and Yacqob-Har, preserved in Egyptian inscriptions and scarabs, are thought to be Semitic. The excavations by Montet at Tanis (the Biblical Zoan), now generally believed to be ancient Avaris (the Egyptian capital of the Hyksos), show that their principal gods were El, Baal (Seth), and 'Anath (Anta), and these are well known to have been Semitic. At the same time, they must have included some other racial type, for a number of their names, landmarks, and objects unearthed are clearly non-Semitic. This other group has been sought among the Hittites, Cassites, Indo-Iranians, Hurrians, and others, but

it is now believed by most scholars to have come from Central
Asia, probabiy the Caucasus regions, passing through Syria on
its way to the riches of Egypt.   Their peculiar toggle-pins,
often gold, their daggers with raised veins, and their chariot
models seem to corroborate this.   Their weapon was a composite
bow of long range, and they brought with them horses and fast
chariots.   Among other characteristics they used a peculiar
type of fortification, consisting of huge rectangular ramparts
of *terre pisée*, as found in Palestine at Bethpelet (Tell el-Fara),
Lachish (Tell ed-Duweir), Hazor (Tell el-Qedah), Shechem
(Balâtah), Old Gaza (Tell el-Ajjûl), and several other places.
Excavations show that during the height of the Hyksos rule
Palestine reached a high level in artistic development, due
probably to the wide extent of the Hyksos empire, the large
amount of wealth in their hands, and the encouragement they
gave to commerce.   Among the Hyksos objects unearthed
have been exquisitely formed vases, beautiful woodwork and
carvings, fine jewellery, neat scarabs, and artistic seal cylinders.

5. *The Philistines.*   These powerful fighters, who were of
non-Semitic race, entered Canaan from Asia Minor *c.* 1190
B.C. or earlier.   Their invasion was part of a great movement
of the " Sea-Peoples " (Shardina, Danaua, Zakkal, and others),
which started as far west as the Ægean Islands.   This huge
horde of mixed peoples, some of them fresh from the siege of
Troy, marched in successive waves through Asia Minor, where
they overwhelmed the Hittites, dismembering their empire,
and then turned southward through the Cilician gates towards
Egypt.   They were defeated, however, both on land and sea,
by the Egyptian forces of Ramesses III. (*c.* 1200–1170 B.C.),
and some of them settled in Syria, while the Philistines (called
by the Egyptians " Pulesati ") were allowed by the Pharaoh
to establish themselves in the Shephelah of Canaan, probably
as garrison troops sworn to his service, and ultimately gave
their name to the whole land.   Within the last few years their
origin and history have had much light thrown on them by
archæological research.   For one thing, it is known from
Hebrew tradition that they came from Caphtor (Amos 9[7];
Deut. 2[23]; Jer. 47[4]), and hitherto this has generally been
identified with Crete, but further investigation seems to show
that it may have been located in Cilicia and Cappadocia.   Their
physical features, dress, weapons, and other characteristics are
identical with those found in these regions, and it is not
improbable that there is some identity between the names
Caphtor and Cappadocia.   Again, we now know that, although
the main body entered Canaan about 1190 B.C., there was

probably an earlier settlement of them along the coast in the thirteenth and fourteenth centuries, just as there was of the Danaua in Syria. Several imposing Philistine tombs, recently excavated in the vicinity of Tell el-Fara in south Palestine, indicate a date according to Petrie of about 1320 B.C. for the oldest of them ; and this earlier invasion is corroborated by the sculptures of Medinet Habu at Thebes, which show that there were already many Philistine soldiers in the Egyptian army by the time of Ramesses III., these having no doubt joined it as mercenaries or been taken prisoners. Another conclusion of recent archæology is that, though the Philistines brought with them many arts and crafts not previously practised in Palestine, their pottery was largely eclectic, *i.e.* it was probably not that of their homeland, but was made by potters who had been familiar with Levantine Mycenæan, especially the Cypriote and Rhodian varieties, but had not the originals before their eyes (such models had probably passed out of currency in the catastrophe of 1190 B.C.), and were relying on their memories. It is of a composite character, for it borrows from all kinds of Mycenæan, but is wholly dependent on none, and is combined with native Canaanite elements.

6. *Connection of Israel with Surrounding Peoples.* As we have stated, the Israelites were closely associated in many ways with neighbouring races. Situated as Palestine was between the great empires of the east and west, the country was the meeting-place of civilization and a highroad of commerce. Along its trade routes were carried not only material merchandise, but social, religious, and intellectual products. For this reason, among others, it was impossible for the Israelites to keep their national movements from being influenced by events outside. But apart from this aspect, many of the Israelite laws, customs, and religious institutions were essentially similar to those of adjoining nations. A comparison of the Mosaic Laws, especially the " Book of the Covenant " (Ex. 20²² ff.), with the codes in use among the Babylonians, Assyrians, and Hittites shows remarkable identity in many of the regulations. It is not that the framers of the Israelite Code " copied " the Code of Hammurabi, as is sometimes imagined. They may have been dependent upon it to some extent, as Hammurabi was upon that of Dungi (King of Ur, *c.* 2260 B.C.), but there were principles of legislation which had probably emanated from Arabia, and which were common throughout all the regions of the Near East centuries before Hammurabi's time, indeed long before the Semitic occupation of Babylonia, and it was this body of common law that Israel

14

took as archetype and codified in affinity with her neighbours, at the same time giving it the special golden threads which mark it so highly. Similarly, the religious rites of Israel, though distinctive in their own way, bear a remarkable resemblance to those of other lands. It cannot be replied that Israel's influence led to the adoption of her rites by these countries. The fact is that the rites go back many centuries earlier than Israel's existence, back indeed to the dawn of Semitic religion, and the similarity can only be due to affinity of worship. The Ras Shamra Tablets, for example, dating from about the time of Joshua's Conquest, show that a number of sacrificial practices in the Old Testament are identical with the Phœnician, and in nearly all cases the technical terms used are the same. It is clear from the tablets that the Jewish ritual customs embodied cultural elements which were common to both races, and were widespread also among all Semitic peoples. The Israelites, it is true, cleansed and purified the ritual, as far as they thought necessary for their own use, but this does not affect its resemblance, in a large number of particulars, to that of neighbouring nations. Indeed, excavation has shown that many Biblical references to rites, customs, and institutions, supposed to belong mainly or only to the Israelites, are better explained and illustrated by those of neighbouring lands—such as the idea of a Divine kingship, the " Holy of Holies," the ephod and teraphim, the enemy as one's footstool, the introduction of worshippers into God's presence, and much else. Even some of the characteristics attributed to Yahweh in the Old Testament seem to contain foreign or exotic elements, due to the intimate relationship between Israel and surrounding nations.

4. ISRAELITE DAILY LIFE AND HABITS

The ordinary life and social habits of the Israelites can be surmised and partly read from the innumerable household and other objects discovered. As a rule, the houses in the walled cities were crowded closely together, frequently in a confused mass, with only narrow tortuous passages between them, and with small open areas at the doorways. Jericho, for instance, at the time of Joshua's attack, occupied less than six acres, with most of the houses small in size and clustered together irregularly, some of them leaning against the inner face of the wall and some being on the wall itself. At Beit Mirsim (thought to be Debir) the whole area within the walls was not more than about eight acres, though the population must have numbered between 2500 and 5000 (probably some of it overflowed the walled area). Houses had openings for light and air in each room, and some of the better-class ones had upper chambers ('aliyôth) for seclusion. The house-doors opened outward, and were provided with bolts or bars (cf. 2 Sam. 13¹⁷), perhaps in some cases with locks. The roofs were flat, and sometimes fairly solid. As a rule, they consisted of beams resting upon the walls and supported, if necessary, by brick or wooden pillars. The beams were simply covered in many cases with netted branches, in which clay, chaff, straw, twigs, and other things were mingled, and the whole surface was kept hardened by rubbing-stones, and later on (in Hellenistic times at least) by means of a limestone roller (several of which have been found), otherwise it developed cracks through which the rain percolated. Many houses had no other place where the inmates could take the air, dry their clothes, and do numberless other things essential to their health and comfort. We read of Rahab hiding the spies on the roof, and of David walking there (2 Sam. 11²). A frequent place of meeting for the inhabitants, as a rule, was at the city gate, where there was a " broad place " devoted to traffic, popular assemblies, and gossip (cf. 2 Kings 7¹, Job 29⁷, Neh. 8¹·¹⁶). The principal gate of Tell en-Naṣbeh (Mizpah), one of the finest discovered, was found to be thirteen feet in width, and remarkably well preserved, with the stone door-sockets still in place and a number of stone benches inside.

The water supply for domestic purposes was often a difficulty. In villages and smaller centres of population the only source was generally a spring outside. The women had to make a long and tiresome journey to this, and in time of war, when the enemy were watching, the inhabitants ran the danger of dying of thirst. In the cities, wells were usually sunk either within the walls or immediately outside where they could be protected. Many of these have been discovered. The one at Beth-shemesh, which is within the enclosure, goes back to about 2000 B.C., while the large one at Lachish, sunk on the northern slopes of the city and guarded by advanced ramparts, is believed to date from an earlier period. At Jericho there was an excellent spring (" Elisha's Fountain ") which was included in the site and specially fortified. Other cities preferred tunnel staircases leading down to a spring just outside the walls, or to a subterranean collection of water. Interesting passages of this nature have been excavated at Gezer, Megiddo, and Jerusalem. In later times, however, nearly all cities and other large centres of population had cisterns, both inside and among the rocks outside, for accumulating and storing the rain-water. Many of these have been discovered. At Beth-shemesh one was found to be over forty feet wide at one part, and about seven feet high, with a rock-cut shaft, three feet six inches wide, leading down to it. Beneath the shaft-mouth is the usual depression to catch the last remaining water at the bottom, and help in cleaning the cistern before the good rains came. At the time of their best use, such cisterns were probably cleaned fairly often ; but in times of poverty and neglect the accumulation of mud and lost objects became considerable. In the cistern at Beth-shemesh many objects were discovered at the bottom, including cooking-pots, bowls, figurines, and other things.

Very little of the furniture of Palestinian houses has been discovered so far. This is due to the fact that it was of a scanty and perishable nature, consisting mainly of the necessary utensils for the preparation of food. Beds and bedsteads, for instance, were not in general use. Many people, such as shepherds sleeping in the open, wrapped themselves up in their *simlah* or rug (Ex. 22^{26}), and even indoors this simple method was adopted. Only the better-class people could boast of beds and bed-chambers (cf. 2 Sam. 4^7). At Gezer a limestone model of a wooden bed has been found, which still shows the matting on it, and it is clear that such beds, probably movable (cf. 1 Sam. 19^{15}), were in use as far back as the Early Bronze Age. Everywhere, both in cities and villages, domestic pots, bowls, jars, and other receptacles must have been numerous, for they have been dug up in thousands on many sites. Cooking pots were round-bottomed, with a prominent out-turning rim, and were probably supported over the fire on stones or bricks between which the fuel was laid, or may have been suspended by means of hooks from a tripod. Many of the ovens, as shown by excavations, were similar to the *tannûrs* which are to be found at the present day in Palestine and Syria, consisting of pits in the ground, about a yard wide and the same in depth, somewhat in the form of a huge jar. The walls were generally plastered with cement, and the fire was placed at the bottom, the fuel being grass, thorns, or dried twigs (cf. Matt. 6^{30}). When the oven was sufficiently heated, the inner walls were cleaned of the smoke and soot. The dough, moulded into thin, broad leaves, was then placed on them and retained there by means of a large cushion or spreader. In this rough and ready way the baking was over in a few seconds. The usual diet was practically vegetarian, meat being eaten only on special or ceremonial occasions. The cereals actually found at Jericho by Professor Garstang include wheat and barley, and probably also oats, lentils, and millet.

Clothing among the poorer people consisted in many cases of a simple sheepskin or a mantle of homespun goat-hair. But fine linen garments, though at first used only on ceremonial occasions, were also common, especially among the upper classes. These were usually dyed, trimmed with braid and tassels, sometimes beautifully embroidered, and reached from the shoulders to the knees, as we find in the picture of one of Jehu's ambassadors on the Black Obelisk. Woollen garments must have been in wide use, too, for signs of a woollen textile industry have been found at Beit Mirsim, including spinning, weaving, and dyeing, and evidence shows that nearly every house there had a loom. As a rule, jewellery and valuable ornaments were worn by the better-class people, sometimes to a very large extent. There is hardly a site of any import- ance in Palestine but has yielded gold, silver, and bronze ornaments in profusion, including bracelets, ear-rings, neck- laces, pendants, armlets, beads, and other kinds, and it is certain that there must have been skilful goldsmiths and metal workers who could braze, solder, and make delicate repoussé and filigree work. Oriental dress lent itself to ornamental display, and jewellery was often worn to such an extent that it became a temptation to the covetous, though some of the objects worn were no doubt meant as amulets for protection against evil influences. Face-painting was not uncommon, for numerous cosmetic palettes have been discovered, which were evidently used to prepare the mineral substances, such as powdered *pûk* or *kuhl* (manganese or antimony ; cf. Jezebel, 2 Kings 9[30]), malachite, and hæmatite clay (red ochre). Pro- fessor Albright points out that Isaiah was truly not without justification when he denounced the frivolity of the daughters of Zion (Isa. 3[18-23]).

Agriculture (or " husbandry," as the Old Testament calls it) was the principal occupation of the people. Apart from the crown lands and the estates of the wealthy, every free husbandman had his allotted portion of the common lands. Large numbers of men went out to till their fields by day, returning to their cities or villages at night. The old nomadic life no doubt continued to have its admirers (cf. Jer. 35) down to the end of the monarchy, but the settled tillers of the soil were numerous. Excavations have shown that some places, such as Gezer, were grain-growing centres. Some years ago there was discovered at this site a primitive agricultural tablet, dating probably about 900 B.C., which groups the months according to their agricultural importance ; and within recent years numerous ploughshares, sickles, forks, axes, and other farming implements, as well as granaries and grain-pits (some with the cereals still in them) have been found at many sites. At the same time, a large number of men earned their living as " artificers " (1 Chron. 29⁵) or " craftsmen " (2 Kings 24¹⁴, Jer. 24¹, R.V.), *i.e.* as workers in wood, metal, stone, clay, leather, and other materials. Numerous products of most of these trades have been dug up. The Hebrew pottery, unfortunately, is inferior and uninteresting. It has no beauty of design or colour, and is badly baked and clumsy. It is not even original, being largely borrowed from the Canaanite. Even in the post-exilic period the deterioration is marked. The words of Jeremiah (18³· ⁴) seem applicable, " Then went I down to the potter's house, and behold . . . the vessel that he made of clay was marred in the hand of the potter."

Whenever the country was invaded, or when internal conflicts took place, the men had to arm themselves. Throughout the period of Samuel and Saul, the weapons remained primitive—indeed, the making of swords and spears was prevented by the Philistines. But the sling was adopted as a defensive arm, and some Israelites attained such proficiency in its use that they could boast of 700 chosen men, all left-handed, who " could sling a stone at a hairbreadth, and not miss " (Judg. 20¹⁶). Other fighting men had shields, and were armed with clubs, javelins, daggers, darts, or knives. Numerous specimens of all these have been discovered at various sites. Towards the end of David's reign, chariots were introduced into Israelite warfare, and were adopted largely by Solomon, whose extensive stables have been uncovered at Megiddo. They were manned after the Hittite manner by parties of three—a driver, a warrior, and an armour-bearer, such a group being known as *shalish* or " three-men." It is evident that, in warfare of such a nature, the personal valour of the fighters counted for much and was indispensable for success.

But life in Israel was not all fighting or working. There were long periods of rest, when the people could give free expression to their social customs and institutions. At such times, festivities, dancing, revelry, music, and games were frequent. At Beit Mirsim, in the ruins of the palace, was found a complete set of gaming pieces, consisting of five little three-cornered pyramids and five little cones, all of faience, together with the ivory die which was used to determine

moves.   Games of chance or skill seem to have been widespread throughout the east, having their origin probably in
Egypt.   Religious practices, too, it must be remembered,
occupied much of the people's time.   Ceremonies, sacrifices,
and ritual of various kinds were of constant occurrence, and
were associated with moral precepts.   Hence it was that the
Hebrew race in Palestine was enabled to rise above the culture
of all its neighbours.   By its capacity for serious thought,
and its grasp of Divine revelation, it gained a vision of
imperishable Truth, and made it known to the world.

BIBLIOGRAPHY

S. L. Caiger, *Bible and Spade*, 1935.
W. F. Albright, *The Archæology of Palestine and the Bible*, 1935.
G. A. Barton, *Archæology and the Bible*, 1933.
R. A. S. Macalister, *A Century of Excavation in Palestine*, 1926.
J. Garstang, *Foundations of Bible History: Joshua–Judges*, 1931.
J. G. Duncan, *Digging up Biblical History*, 2 vols., 1931.
I. Benzinger, *Hebräische Archäologie*, 1927.
J. W. Jack, *Samaria in Ahab's Time*, 1929.
J. W. Jack, *The Ras Shamra Tablets*, 1935.

IX. THE HISTORY OF ISRAEL

1. The Birth of the Nation

THE primary interest and importance of the history of Israel lies on the side of religion. That is a truism which it is unnecessary to elaborate, for the influence of Judaism goes out far beyond the Jewish people itself. There is no essential break in the process of revelation as between the Old and New Testaments, though there is a gap which we can fill from other sources. Islam, too, owes all that is most characteristic in its creed and practice to its Jewish heritage, and if the three great monotheistic faiths be eliminated, there is little left of religion in the modern world until we reach the confines of India and China.

The story of Israel has, nevertheless, a profound interest for the student of history in general. Here we have a small people, enclosed within a narrow compass of space and of time, which runs through the whole range of birth, growth, decay, and political destruction. We can look carefully at the various forces which were constantly at work upon the people, we can see how conflicting tendencies in the social theory and in the economic order reacted one on another, we can weigh the possibilities of ultimate political success and the causes which led to failure. Still further, we can trace the record of great ideas in the realm of human organization. Some of these are of value to-day, and we fail entirely to appreciate the history of Israel unless we realize that it does, in one way or another, express and illustrate certain fundamental principles, which are of permanent validity, and can be neglected by no form of the social order. Every attempt men make to live together in an organized community is of the nature of an experiment, and can achieve success only by the full recognition and use of definite laws of personal reaction. Our sketch of the history of Israel must be, primarily, an attempt to understand these laws, and to see how the political ruin of the nation was due to a failure to apply them.

The Heritage of Israel. In the period within which Israel's history falls, the localities in eastern Palestine where the land

204

can be cultivated were few and far between, and it was only
in a few centres that cities could be maintained. It was not
however, an absolutely desert country, and the scanty rainfall
did suffice to provide sufficient pasturage for nomad and semi-
nomad tribes. Men could, and did, live on much the same
plane as the Arab tribes whom Doughty has made so familiar
to us in northern Arabia. The chief areas of population were
in Moab, to the east of the Dead Sea, and in the north-east,
where the Jebel Hauran (the ancient Bashan) was famous for
its breed of large cattle. There were a few centres of civic
life in the intervening country, Gilead, and certain of its
products were famous in Israel's history, but, for the most part
it was a " place for cattle " (Num. 32[1, 4]), *i.e.* for sheep and
goats—more especially the latter. Similar conditions prevailed in the south of western Palestine, but on this side of the
Jordan better watered and arable spots increase in frequency
as the traveller passes northwards, and from Jerusalem onwards the greater part of the land is fit for cultivation. Further,
variations in the levels are not often sudden, and movement is
fairly easy along the line of the central range. But by far the
richest parts of the country are to be found in the coastal
plain and in the plain of Esdraelon. It was here that the great
centres of population were to be found, and the land teemed
with cornfields and with cities.

Additional importance is given to these last-named districts
by the general position which Palestine occupies. Standing, as
it does, at the south-western end of the Fertile Crescent, with
the sea on one side and an impassable desert on the other, the
country formed the only land bridge between Africa and the
northern land-mass of the old world, while the presence of
the great ports of Phœnicia brought no small part of the trade
of the East across its northern extremity. The greatest road
of antiquity was that which, reaching Damascus from the
east, ran down to the south of the Sea of Galilee, crossed the
Jordan by easy fords near the modern Beisan, passed through
the plain of Esdraelon and the gap across the Carmel range
known as the plain of Dothan, and then followed the coast
till it reached Egypt. Another famous route, now known as
the " pilgrim way," and followed to-day by a railway, ran
from Damascus to the northern end of the Gulf of Akabah.
Here it was joined by a route which crossed the north of the
Arabian peninsula, a line which could have been followed only
by specially prepared and equipped caravans. Other roads
led from the north to Damascus and the Phœnician ports.
In a real sense, Palestine was the commercial and political

centre of the ancient world, and the control of the country
was of the first importance to any nation which aspired to
sole empire.

It is, perhaps, partly because of this central position that,
as far as we know, Palestine has been inhabited from the
earliest times. Some of the oldest of human relics, dating
back into the Palæolithic Age, come to us from this country,
especially from Galilee and Carmel. This type of man seems
to have died out, but there are abundant evidences of occupation from the later Stone Age onwards. In a number of places
the spade has revealed the presence of a Neolithic people who
lived in caves and burnt their dead. Such pottery as they
had was primitive in construction, but they were capable of
building structures of some magnitude, a fact which may
have given rise to the tradition of the ancient giants. In
stature they were small, and they belonged to that Armenoid
type which is so well known to us from the Hittites of Asia
Minor and elsewhere. It has been suggested that they contributed to the extraordinary mixture of blood which is found
in Palestine, but Egyptian representations of people from
Palestine are of an entirely different type until a much later
period, and the characteristic Jewish physiognomy (which is
Armenoid rather than Semitic) is more probably due to
immigration at a later period.

It is in the Bronze Age (which in Palestine for centuries
overlaps the later Stone Age) that we meet with a true Semitic
race. They seem to have made their way into the country not
long after 3000 B.C., and, between this date and 2000 B.C.,
spread the whole way round the Fertile Crescent. They came
from Arabia, and were probably at first pastoral nomads, living
on the edge of the cultivated land, till they gradually entered
and settled there. They attained to a high level of culture,
building great cities and producing numerous works of art.
Their language—in Palestine—was an early form of Hebrew,
and they are generally known as the Amorites.

A third wave of emigration from Arabia (the earliest
known to us, the Akkadian, made its way only into Mesopotamia, and does not seem to have affected Palestine directly)
was that known as the Aramæan. Like the Amorite, it
spread round the Fertile Crescent, and, in places, entered the
settled lands, though it tended much more than its predecessor
to remain on the shepherd plane. The last great immigration
was that of the Philistines, a people in whom we may recognize
the remains of the races to whom we owe the Ægean culture,
driven by northern pressure to find homes for themselves in

the south. We know that at the beginning of the twelfth century B.C. they made a desperate attempt to invade Egypt, but were met with an equally vigorous resistance, and were compelled to settle on the maritime plain, in the strip of country that lies between Carmel and the Egyptian frontier. It is to the southern settlements that the name Philistine properly belongs, those to the north, in the district of Dor, being known as Zakaray or Zakkal.

There can be little doubt, then, that many races contributed to the blood of the later Israel. Their culture was of almost equally mixed ancestry. From Mesopotamia, probably during some early period of eastern domination, they derived the basis of their legal system, much of their mythology, and probably some of their ritual practices also. Their architecture, especially in such instances as the great temple at Jerusalem, owed much to Phœnician influence, which, in its turn, was profoundly affected by Egypt. Direct Egyptian influence is surprisingly small, when we remember that for six centuries the country was nominally an Egyptian province. Pottery, in the Israelite period itself, was naturally affected by Philistine models, though it seems to have exhibited characteristic forms of its own.

But what made Israel a people, and gave to the country the sense of a common nationality, was the ancestral tradition introduced by the Aramæan invaders of the middle of the second millennium B.C., towards the close of the later Bronze Age. It is a noteworthy fact that, with the exception of a few stories such as that of Judah's marriage in Gen. 38, the stories of Israel's patriarchs represent them as being Aramæan nomads, living on the shepherd plane, and wandering from place to place as occasion might require. There is no reason to doubt the substantial historicity of the patriarchal narratives, though details have doubtless been modified in the centuries of oral tradition which preceded any writing of Israelite story, and many of the incidents described may, perhaps, be interpreted as tribal rather than as individual history. But we may accept the main outlines of the narrative which traces the ancestry of Israel back to a pastoral group whose home lay in the district of Ur in southern Mesopotamia. Political disturbances connected with the rise to power of the Amorites in the land may have been responsible for the migration of certain tribes. They pursued their way northwards, up the great river valley, and made for themselves a home in the district of Haran. There a portion of them settled, while others, under the leadership of Abraham, took their way westwards, through the land which was later to form the territory of Damascus, and then, turning south, actually entered Egypt for a time. They did not, however, abandon their nomad life, even when they were passing through the settled land, and, receiving reinforcements from northern Mesopotamia, they continued to wander in and around Palestine. At length, somewhere between 1800 and 1600 B.C. some of them made their home on the grazing lands to the north-east of Egypt, where they were caught in the imperial net and subjected to forced labour.

The influence of this tradition on the later history of Israel was of profound importance. The Semitic nomad organizes his life on the basis of the family or clan ; even if new elements are introduced, there must be a fictitious blood-relationship, maintained by some form of adoption. He has little that he can call his own ; the flocks which constitute his wealth belong to the group rather than to the individual, and the conception of private property, while not entirely absent, falls very much into the background. He has a strongly developed sense of corporate personality, and can speak of the whole community as an individual. Yet, within the group, the greatest stress is laid on the value of human personality ; men are worth immeasurably more than things. Any form of external restraint is irksome, and may easily become intolerable. The tribe necessarily has its leaders, and there are families within the group which hold a sheikhly pre-eminence. But their position is a social distinction, and gives them no inherent right over their fellows. The policy of the clan is decided, not by an individual, but by the common feeling of the whole, in which every individual has an equal right to express his mind. It is inevitable that one or other should take the lead through his wisdom, his skill, or his prowess in war, but his position is determined solely by his personal qualities, and may be merely temporary, passing away with the crisis which conferred it. It is not going too far to describe the feeling as being intensely democratic.

Life is very simple in such conditions. The absence of an extensive system of private property means freedom from a mass of complications to which a more highly organized society is exposed. The primary needs of the tribe are concerned with its own maintenance, and the most powerful customs are those which are concerned with the preservation of its man-power and the purity of its blood. The hardships of the nomad life also assist in establishing a high standard of sexual morality, and this, together with a rigid law of blood revenge, form the outstanding features of the nomad ethic, for laxity in these respects would endanger the very existence of the community.

For the general character of Israel before the Exodus we are dependent on such indications as are handed down to us by tradition. No doubt the tradition itself has been considerably modified in the course of centuries by theories as to the nature of the people which sprang up gradually. But it is generally agreed that the organization into twelve tribes, which is so familiar to us all, does not accurately represent the facts of a primitive age. It may, indeed, be regarded as highly probable that only a portion of the group which later became Israel was to be found in Egypt and was delivered from bondage there. The names Israel and Asher both occur in Egyptian inscriptions of the latter half of the thirteenth century B.C., and there is a school of thought which holds that the Exodus belongs to this age, and that, therefore, tribes bearing these names must have been in Palestine before the historical conquest of the land. Others, however, would place the Exodus and the conquest some two centuries earlier, thus giving ample time for the settlement before the end of the XIXth Egyptian Dynasty. In this connexion it may be remarked that Hebrew tradition closely associated Asher with Gad, which was always an eastern tribe, and never settled in western Palestine. It seems more likely, therefore, that there was a time when these two tribes lived in close proximity with one another, and that Asher also was once a nomad people.

On the assumption, then, that all the historical tribes were once members of an association of pastoral nomads (Judah, in its later form, is a possible exception) we may consider the evidence supplied by the patriarchal narratives of Genesis, especially those which tell us of the family of Jacob. It is commonly, though not universally, held that the accounts we have of Jacob's marriages and children are to be interpreted as tribal rather than as individual history. On this view each of the " wives " of Jacob indicates a federation of clans, two major and two subordinate. Of the two more important groups, that of Rachel includes especially Joseph, which clearly played a leading part in the early history of the settlement, and later divided into two, Ephraim and Manasseh, and was augmented by the younger tribes of Benjamin. The group was completed by the adhesion of the two subordinate " Bilhah " tribes of Dan and Naphtali. The other main group included four senior tribes, Reuben, Simeon,

Levi, and Judah (or an element in the later Judah), with two younger additions, Issachar and Zebulon, and two subordinate " Zilpah " tribes, Gad and Asher.

Officially, Moses was assigned to the tribe of Levi. But there seems to have been some confusion as to the proper application of the word, since it, or a closely allied cognate, appears in some forms of Semitic speech simply in the sense of " priest," and it may be the fact that the Hebrew priestly families of later times derived their descent from the brother of Moses which was responsible for the inclusion of Moses in the tribe that bore this name (incidentally, it may be remarked that the tribe of Levi proper seems to have disappeared at a comparatively early date). It has, then, been suggested that Moses properly belonged to the Joseph group ; certainly his chief lieutenant and successor, Joshua, was an Ephraimite. It may, then, have been only the Rachel group which was affected by Egyptian bondage, and the union with the Leah tribes may have taken place after the Exodus, but before the conquest of Palestine.

Let us now glance at another line of thought. Tradition (and there is no reason to doubt its substantial accuracy) describes Moses as a Hebrew belonging to one of the oppressed tribes, bearing an Egyptian name and brought up at the Egyptian court, escaping from Egypt and making his home with a pastoral clan coming under the general head of Midianite. The actual family with which he was allied was that of a priest, and one form of the tradition makes this priest a Kenite, or nomad smith. While in the wilderness, Moses comes into contact with a God who reveals His name as Yahweh, and bids Moses deliver the oppressed Israelites through His authority and power.

Now Kenites are among the early clans which were later welded into the tribe of Judah—others are Kenizzites, Calebites, Jerahmeelites, and possibly Amalekites, though, in so far as these last were connected with Israel, they seem to have belonged to the Joseph rather than to the Leah side. Kenites appear in the later story as enthusiastic Yahweh-worshippers, and it is not difficult to suppose that the work of Moses, on its political side, involved an amalgamation of the two groups with which he was connected—the Rachel group into which he was born, and the Leah group into which he was adopted. The theory is admittedly largely conjectural, but any attempt to reconstruct the pre-Mosaic history of the Israelite clans must necessarily depend on greater or less probability, and no other account of their origin seems to present us with so reasonable or likely an explanation of the facts as this does.

Moses. It is with Moses that the history of Israel proper begins. It may well be, as we have already hinted, that the group he knew did not include all those to whom the name later belonged, but the essential fact remains that it was he who brought into being the confederacy to which others may afterwards have attached themselves. There is room for considerable disagreement as to the details of his work, but the main facts are beyond dispute. Later, Israel looked back on the deliverance from Egypt and the Covenant at Sinai as the basic events of the national history. It is a curious fact that the name of Moses hardly occurs in the prophetic literature, and never in any passage which we can certainly assign to the pre-exilic age. But the narratives in which the story has come down to us (or at least some of them) are far older than the canonical prophets, and they leave us in no doubt as to the prevalence of the tradition which mentioned Moses' name. The escape from Egypt is a familiar theme from Amos onwards, and the whole story demands the presence of an outstanding personality. As has been said elsewhere, if we had no account of Moses, it would have been necessary to invent him.

The Biblical outline of the story is familiar to us all. Moses, having received the divine revelation and commission, returned to Egypt and demanded the liberation of the oppressed Hebrews that they might go and offer sacrifice at some spot three days' journey away in the " wilderness." The reigning Pharaoh refused repeatedly, and each refusal was followed by a national disaster. The first nine of the so-called ten plagues are natural calamities to which Egypt was always more or less subject ; the miraculous element consists in the coincidence of these troubles at the appropriate time. Finally, since the people could not go to the sacred mountain, Yahweh came to Egypt, and arrangements were made to hold the festival as best it could be held in the conditions. The centre of the celebrations was a sacred meal, presumably held originally at the sanctuary, but, in the circumstances, transformed into the domestic rite which became traditional in Israel. But the presence of a powerful God, who came in anger at the wrong done to the people whom He had chosen, introduced a prophylactic element into the ritual, and the houses must be daubed with sacrificial blood—a proceeding for which many parallels can be found elsewhere. Houses not so protected might be and were entered by the destroyer, with disastrous results to the Egyptians. In the confusion the people, already prepared, hurried away from the scene of their forced labours, and endeavoured to escape into the wilderness. They were pursued, and their way was barred by the sea. But an exceptionally low tide, reinforced by a strong drying wind, enabled them to cross the sandy sea-bed in safety, while their pursuers were caught by the tide returning under the sand, and drowned. By the double event, the slaughter of the Egyptians and the deliverance at the sea, Yahweh had attested His own power and His favour to the escaping tribesmen. The latter made their way to the sacred mountain, and there the union of the God and the people was achieved.

So far there will be general agreement as to the historicity of the facts, but we cannot be certain of the details. We do not know where the sea was crossed ; the Gulf of Suez, the Gulf of Akaba (both on the Red Sea) and the Sirbonian Lake (separated from the Mediterranean only by a narrow belt of sand) have all found their advocates. Preference for one site or the other is usually determined by the location of Sinai, and here again there are diversities of opinion. The traditional spot in the Sinai peninsula, recognized only since the second century A.D., is now generally abandoned, but some would place the sacred mountain near Kadesh, others near Petra, others, again, to the east of the Gulf of Akaba. The descriptions of the scene at Sinai suggest a volcano, but we have to go two hundred miles from the Egyptian border before we reach any signs of volcanic activity within recent geological time, and it seems safer to explain the details by reference to severe thunderstorms, coloured, perhaps, by reminiscences of volcanic action seen elsewhere. Nevertheless, one theory which has aroused a great deal of attention is based on the supposition that the sacred mountain was actually a volcano, and that the crossing of the Red Sea was made possible by an earthquake. The matter is complicated by the presence of two different names in the Hebrew tradition itself ; forms of the story which were current in the north appear to have called the place Horeb, those which took shape in the south speak of Sinai.

While, then, we may prefer one explanation to the rest, we must admit that geographical details remain quite uncertain. This, however, is a point of minor importance. What matters is, not where the sacred mountain was, but what happened there, and here we can reach conclusions which are attested, not only by the available narratives, but by the whole course of Israel's political and religious history. For it was here that, for the first time, the various tribes were combined into a single whole, and the idea of the nationality of Israel began. The means by which this result was secured, also, are attested by a tradition so strong and so inherently probable that we need have little uncertainty as to their general character. For the classical statement of the tradition we turn to Ex. 24. The narrative has, no doubt, suffered from later accretions, but its main outlines are not difficult to disentangle. The new order is inaugurated and made valid by a great covenant, made between Yahweh on the one hand and the people on the other. They are treated as a single whole, and, for the first time, we have emerging the conception of Israel as a national entity. An altar is set up, representing the deity, and on the other side stand those who take the part of the people. Victims are slain, and their blood is drained off into bowls. Half the blood is then dashed upon the altar, and Moses proceeds to read the terms on which Yahweh is prepared to enter into relations with the new people. They signify their acceptance of the conditions, and the remainder of the blood is then thrown over their heads.

The symbolism of this ritual is not far to seek. The problem is to unite the two parties into a single whole so closely that they cease to be independent one of another, but form parts of the same entity. It will no longer be possible to think of Israel apart from Yahweh, or of Yahweh apart from Israel. The method is based on the ancient Semitic conception of blood as the seat of the *nephesh*, a term to which, in this con- nexion, the word " personality " corresponds more nearly than any other that we have. It is the vital essence of the man or animal in whom it dwells, and makes him what he is. The casting of the blood of the victim over the altar means that, henceforward, He whom the altar represents is to be regarded as one with the slaughtered beast. In the same way, the flinging of the remainder over the people implies that they too are one with the being from whose veins it has been taken. There is, therefore, a real identity, not only between each of the two parties and the victim, but also between the two parties themselves. In the given and dis- tributed soul-substance of the third they are no longer two but one ; it includes and embraces them both. It is true that the maintenance of the union depends on the observance of the conditions laid down and accepted, but, with this proviso, it is absolute, and, until one party or the other breaks the terms, the bond is indissoluble. A common life runs through the God and the people ; they are, once more, no longer two but one.

It is no longer possible for us to reconstruct the conditions laid down at the sacred mountain. It is worth observing that they are not reached by negotiation, as might have been the case if the two parties had been in any sense equals. Israel has no authority to discuss or to modify the conditions; the nation can only accept or reject them. As the narrative stands, it appears as if the terms were to be found in Ex. 21–23, a section which forms the oldest of the various codes of laws in the Old Testament. But even a superficial examination of this code shows that it is adapted to a community resident in an agricultural land, for many of its provisions are applicable only to growers of crops, while there is nothing which is relevant only to the pastoral life. It is, then, highly improbable that this code formed the basis of the covenant, and it becomes still more unlikely when we find, on comparison with other ancient codes, that the laws of Ex. 21–23 resemble those current elsewhere in the ancient east. The similarities, for instance, with the famous Code of Hammurabi, with the Sumerian, Assyrian, and Hittite codes, are so great as to make independence practically impossible. At the same time, there are striking differences which preclude the hypothesis of direct borrowing, and it has been plausibly argued that the Hebrew code is one of the most primitive, and represents an earlier stage of development than, for example, that of Hammurabi. Since Hammurabi belongs to the same general era as Abraham, we are forced to the conclusion that Israel derived the code in Ex. 21–23 (commonly known as " The Book of the Covenant ") from an agricultural people who had been influenced by eastern culture at some point during the third millennium B.C. The most probable suggestion, then, is that Israel derived this code —no doubt making modifications in detail—from their predecessors in Palestine, who, in turn, had adopted it under Mesopotamian influence in the distant past.

A more plausible suggestion is that the terms of the covenant were comprised in the familiar Ten Commandments, which we find in Ex. 20$^{1-17}$. Here we are not faced with the same objection, and there is no inherent impossibility in the idea that Moses laid down these principles of conduct—though in a simpler form than that in which we now have them—as being the basis on which union between Israel and Yahweh was possible. There is a growing tendency among modern scholars to regard the Decalogue as being actually the work of Moses, especially since the general standard of life which the little code demands corresponds fairly well with that normally recognizable in nomad communities. But we can hardly dogmatize on the point, for there is no more direct evidence for the actual

Mosaic authorship of the Decalogue than of any other part of
the Pentateuch; all we can say is that we know nothing
against the theory.

But, whatever the terms may have been—and we may
assume that they were in one way or another absorbed in
the later religious laws of Israel—the fact of the covenant
remains beyond doubt. Henceforward Israel was the people
of Yahweh, and Yahweh was the God of Israel. By this
great deed of mutual adoption He became an actual member
of the group, sharing in its interests, its fortunes, and its
future. A further elaboration of this thought would carry us
expressly into the sphere of religion, and is adequately discussed elsewhere. For our present purpose it is important to
insist that Yahweh now became the God of the whole group.
He may have been the Deity proper to one of the tribes or to
one association of tribes, but now all had an equal claim on
Him; He was the God of Israel. The connexion between
the tribes may still have been loose, and it may have been that
of what the Greeks called an Amphictyony rather than that
of an organized state, but it was real and fundamental. A new
thing had come into the world—the people of Israel, and,
henceforward, the story of the race was to be governed by that
central idea.

2. THE SETTLEMENT IN PALESTINE

Biblical Narratives. Two pictures of the conquest of
Palestine are preserved for us in the Old Testament. According
to the one, found only in the Book of Joshua, though we have
references elsewhere which suggest the same point of view
(cf. *e.g.* Amos 2⁹), the Israelite armies, under the leadership
of Joshua, overran the land in the course of a few swift and
successful campaigns, exterminating the previous inhabitants.
It is true that the Gibeonites were merely reduced to servitude,
but their escape was due to the trick by which they induced
Israel to enter into alliance with them. The land was then
divided among the tribes, and each went to that portion
assigned to it by the sacred lot.

The other presentation, most familiar from Judg. 2,
though it occurs also in the Book of Joshua, regards the
conquest as having been neither sudden nor complete. It is
only after the death of Joshua that the land is effectively
occupied, and then, though the tribes spread over the whole
land, it is only in the hill country that they succeed in
completely overthrowing their predecessors. Elsewhere, the
newcomers live side by side with the older inhabitants, and

the utmost that they can do is to reduce them to servitude. The tribes appear to act independently, or at most in small groups ; the national sense is still in its infancy. It has long been felt that this presentation of the facts has the greater probability, and archæology has now lent it the weight of its authority, for it seems clear that a fairly long interval separated the destruction of Jericho from that, *e.g.*, of Bethel. We are, thus, once more compelled to fall back on a large measure of conjecture in attempting to reconstruct the progress of the conquest.

The Occupation of Eastern Palestine. We may divide the period between Moses and David into three main sections, the occupation of the land, the consolidation of Israel, and the foundation of the monarchy. The first, again, has four distinct phases, the occupation of trans-Jordanian territory, the conquests in the south, the seizure of the central hills, and the invasion of the north. Tradition assigned the first to the age of Moses himself, and, in a sense, it was a preliminary to the conquest proper. An account of the event is given in Num. 21[21-35], which records the complete overthrow of Sihon, an Amorite king whose home was at Heshbon. Snatches of ancient song, possibly as old as the events themselves, are found in Num. 21[14f. 27-30]. They are clearly incomplete, especially the former, and, therefore, somewhat obscure, but they suggest that Sihon had previously taken possession of territory which had formerly belonged to Moab. A similar tradition may lie behind Jephthah's argument in Judg. 11, and, in any case, it is consistently claimed that the frontier between Moab and Israel was the line of the Arnon—a position which was emphatically denied by the Moabites. But it is clear that Israel has some claim to the whole of the territory to the east of Jordan, at least from the northern end of the Dead Sea, and it is also stated that the district of Bashan, south of Damascus, fell into the hands of Moses. This tradition, however, is commonly regarded as being rather later than that of the conquest of Gilead, and may be associated with a movement back from western Palestine. We hear in the later history of a few towns in this region, but it is important to observe that the whole district was mainly pastoral, and the reason for the settlement of Gad and Reuben on this side of the Jordan is said to have been their wealth in cattle (Num. 32[1-4]). Here we have a section of Israel which, while remaining within the nation, and sometimes playing an important part in its life, never wholly adopted the life of agriculture characteristic of the main body of the people.

The Conquest of Southern Palestine. The conquest of the
south, too, is a subject of much uncertainty. In Num. 14⁴⁵
we read of an abortive attack on Hormah, which, however,
according to Num. 21³, was captured and put to the ban later,
in consequence of an attack made on Israel by the king of
Arad, apparently to the north. In the account of the exploits
of Judah in Judg. 1³⁻²¹, Hormah is the most southerly of the
conquests, and the order is Bezek, Jerusalem, Hebron, Debir,
Arad, Hormah (formerly called Zephath). But we know that
Jerusalem came into Israelite hands only in the time of David,
and the note in Num. 21³ suggests that the original order was
from south to north, not from north to south. It would
naturally have been inverted under the influence of the theory
that the whole land was invaded by all the tribes after the
crossing of the Jordan near Jericho. The reference to Moses's
kindred by marriage, the Kenites, in Judg. 1¹⁶ points in the
same direction, and we are justified in suggesting that the
southern conquests were made gradually by a number of
Yahweh-worshipping clans—Kenites, Kenizzites, Calebites,
and possibly others, who formed the Israelite nucleus of the
tribe of Judah. Like the Transjordanian tribes, they lived
in a country unsuited to agriculture, except in a few spots,
but as they moved northwards they found more and more
arable land, till, in the district round Hebron, they merged
into the general life of the country. Here, too, as in the east,
lay a section of the people of Yahweh whose interests and
instincts were still those mainly of the nomad.

The Conquest of the Central Hills. The greater part of our
information as to the conquest of the land deals with the
occupation of the central highlands. It is generally agreed
that, in the principal narratives of the Book of Joshua, we
have an account, reliable in outline, of the invasions of the
Rachel tribes under the leadership of Joshua the Ephraimite.
The first event to which our attention is called was the crossing of the Jordan in the early spring, when the river level was
at its highest. The narrative is simple and consistent. The
waters " stood still," and were piled into a heap some distance
above the point of passage. The locality indicated is Adam,
some twenty miles away, near the junction of the Jabbok and
the Jordan. More than once in later times there has been a
fall of cliff in this region which has for a time completely
choked the flow of the river. It is generally agreed that the
narrative in Josh. 3 is based on such a landslide, caused,
perhaps, by an earthquake, and that a body of Israelites took
advantage of the unusual circumstance to cross the river and

attack the chief cities on the western bank at a time when they would be least expected. No doubt the story in its present form has received accretions, but the main fact is generally accepted.

The next step was the capture of Jericho, the chief fortress in the plain at the northern end of the Dead Sea. The site has been extensively, though not, it seems, completely, excavated, and the opinion of the excavators is that the walls, which were very strong, were thrown down by an earthquake. The account of the Book of Joshua thus receives striking confirmation ; Jericho was taken because its walls fell, and there was no attempt made at a regular siege. The whole of this plain was now at the disposal of the invaders, and they made their main camp at Gilgal, where there was probably a stone circle of a type which often marks a sacred site. According to Judg. 2¹ this remained the religious centre of Israel till after the death of Joshua, and the accounts of his further exploits assume that he made it his base.

From Gilgal an advance was made into the hill country. The road is steep, whatever route be adopted, for the mountains rise to a height of 3000 feet above the level of the Dead Sea surface. To judge from the reference in Hos. 2¹⁵ there was a tradition current in northern Israel to the effect that the route followed was up the valley of Achor, which leads into the heart of the mountains. The first objective was the city of Ai, where an Israelite force suffered a severe repulse, explained as being due to the violation of the *ḥerem* placed on Jericho. The story of Achan is one of the most interesting and important for the study of Israel's early theology, but it has little bearing on the progress of events, since the city was taken shortly afterwards by stratagem. It is to be noted that, here as in the case of Jericho, we have no suggestion of a siege ; apparently it was difficult, if not impossible, for these raiders from the wilderness to capture a well-fortified place by direct assault. (It should be remarked here that there is a tendency among archæologists to date the fall of Ai some two centuries after that of Jericho.)

The fall of Ai was followed by the submission of Gibeon, to the south-west of Ai. By a trick, the inhabitants succeeded in persuading the Israelites to make a treaty with them. Israel now had a real footing in the hills, and, if they had chosen to make their headquarters there, they would have occupied a central position from which they could have spread in any direction. Our external evidence, derived mainly from the Tell el-Amarna letters, shows how the cities and principalities of Palestine were divided against one another, and how, in spite of their common allegiance to Egypt, they were often ready to make common cause with invaders from the wilderness in order to secure their own position. But the situation was one of danger for others, and it is not surprising to hear that a group of the petty kings to the immediate south-west united to try to recover Gibeon. The attempt brought the Israelites up from Gilgal, probably by a night march, and they fell on the assembled army unexpectedly, with the aid of some unusual celestial phenomenon which has never been satisfactorily explained. In the battles of ancient Israel we notice, for the most part, an absence of serious tactics. The two armies might be drawn up facing one another, but they seldom came to hand-to-hand fighting. As they approached one another, panic would seize one or the other, and they would flee ; the slaughter took place in the flight and the pursuit. At Gibeon the Canaanites were taken by surprise, and tried at once to make their escape, fleeing down the valley which leads past Beth-horon, towards Ajalon. The victory was complete, and five kings are said to have been captured and put to death ; the narrative, perhaps idealized, states that, as a result of this battle, a number of places were destroyed by Israel. Still, there was, as yet, no attempt to settle in the country, and Gilgal remained the headquarters of the people.

Further conquests in the centre of the country are recorded in Judges, and are ascribed to the period after the death of Joshua. The most important of these is Bethel, which was handed over to Israel by treachery. We have no more detailed accounts of the way in which the land was conquered, but the summary given to us in Judg. I is very suggestive. We hear, for instance, that Manasseh failed to conquer the cities and fortresses of the plain of Esdraelon. Later, also, we find that Shechem is still not strictly an Israelite city. But these very failures imply a considerable success, and it is clear that there was, possibly for two or three centuries, a steady movement northwards. The process of extermination may have been fairly complete, and it was probably in the hill country of Ephraim that the purest Israelite blood in western Palestine was to be found. Certainly this district seems to have been the most important centre of Israelite life in pre-monarchic days, and with the transfer of the national sanctuary from Gilgal to Shiloh, where an elaborate and solid temple was built, it became a religious as well as a political nucleus for the nation. The nature of the country made it possible for the new settlers to undertake agriculture in many places, but the comparatively small admixture of Canaanite or Amorite blood meant that the old Israelite, Aramæan tradition, dating from nomad days, was probably stronger here than in any other part of the country, saving only those which had remained on the shepherd plane.

The Conquest of the North. The third area of invasion was in the far north. The conquest of this district also is ascribed to Joshua, but the accuracy of this form of the tradition is open to question. The chief enemy to be overthrown is said to have been a certain Jabin, king of Hazor. Now a king of that name occurs in Judg. 4, in connexion with the story of Sisera, and, though here, too, the link is very doubtful, it seems probable that one form of tradition assigned the conquest of Hazor to the period of the Judges. We may note, further, the inherent improbability of such an undertaking by Joshua. It must be remembered that this country, roughly to the west of Lake Huleh, cannot be reached, as the central highlands can, by a single forced march from Gilgal, and that an attacking force must cross the plain of Esdraelon, firmly held and dominated by strong fortresses, which did not fall into Israelite hands till the time of David. On the whole, it seems much more probable that the subjugation of the north was due to an entirely different wave of invasion, which crossed the Jordan between the Sea of Galilee and the Lake of Huleh, possibly at a time much later than Joshua. We know that one of the tribes settled there, that of Dan, did not enter this part of the country until the twelfth century, and others may not have been there for many generations earlier. It is significant that the tribes to whom this region is assigned all belong to the younger or subordinate groups in the national organization.

We thus reach a position in which the incoming Aramæans occupy three main districts, almost entirely cut off from one another. In the south we have them spreading up gradually as far north as Hebron, and even Bethlehem, but never occupying the great fortress-town of Jerusalem. The Ephraimite hills are strongly held, but are cut off from the northern group by the plain of Esdraelon with its rich soil and its populous cities. Generally speaking, the invaders occupy the high ground, and the land which they hold is often fit for no more than pasture, but they are beginning to take to agriculture, especially in the central hills. The plains are still held by the older inhabitants ; their superior culture and equipment enable them to resist any attacks that may be made upon them, and where the Israelites can effect any kind of settlement among them, they are probably reduced to a condition resembling that of serfdom. And, all the time, the whole country is nominally subject to Egypt.

Date of the Conquest. A word should be said at this point about the date of the conquest. For the Exodus, apart from the conquest, we may assume that it took place not earlier than the expulsion of the Hyksos at the beginning of the sixteenth century, but, apart from that, we have only the very slender evidence supplied by the mention of Pithom and Rameses in Ex. I[11]—names which need not have formed part of the original text. On the surface they would seem to imply that Rameses II. was the Pharaoh of the oppression, and that his son Merneptah was the Pharaoh of the Exodus. But there are strong reasons for placing the Israelite invasion of Palestine 150 to 200 years earlier. Mention has already been made of the presence of the names Asher and Israel on Egyptian monuments of the XIXth Dynasty. One of the common themes of the Tell el-Amarna letters (first half of the fourteenth century) is the invasion of tribes from the wilderness, who, in letters emanating from Jerusalem are called Hebrews. They cannot be certainly identified with Israel, but at least the land was exposed just then to invasions of this kind, and the entire absence of any hint of Egyptian dominion in Joshua and Judges suggests that the sovereign power was very weak. Archæologists date the fall of Jericho with confidence near the beginning of the fourteenth century, and though the date of the destruction of Bethel is put at some century and a half later, this may easily be explained on the ground of the slow advance of the central body through the land. Jerusalem, though equally surrounded by Israelite settlements, held out till the time of David. The references to Dan and Asher in the Song of Deborah strongly suggest that both tribes are established on the coast, a location practically impossible, at least for the former, after the advent of the Philistines about 1200 B.C. The evidence is admittedly not decisive, and we may some day be forced to the conclusion that the events described are to be referred to more than one period, but, as matters stand at present, the balance of probability seems to be heavily on the side of a date somewhere in the first half of the fourteenth century for the Israelite conquest of Palestine.

The Rise of Israel to Pre-eminence in Palestine. We now turn to the second stage, that of consolidation. Our only evidence for this is what we can derive from the Bible itself, and that is mainly confined to the Book of Judges, together with the first few chapters of 1 Samuel. The story that is told for us here is one of repeated periods of oppression, due to apostasy, followed by deliverance through some inspired military leader—a " Judge." In one instance, that of Deborah and Barak, whose exploits are described in Judg. 4 f., the enemy is a Canaanite prince, Sisera by name. As the text of chap. 4 stands, he is associated with the northern Jabin, king of Hazor, but, as we have already noted, it seems not improbable that this prince does not belong to this narrative at all, but has been accidentally introduced from another which described the northern conquests. The poem in Judg. 5 is one of the most important documents we have for our reconstruction of Israel at this early date. We see clearly here the independence of the clans, who are united only by their common allegiance to Yahweh, and, even so, may stand aloof from the general body. We get a picture of the comparatively low cultural level of the Israelites, as compared with the plain-dwelling Canaanites, and, at the same time, of their wild battle fury, which, in favourable circumstances, such as the violent thunderstorm which raged during the battle against Sisera, might win them the victory over a force otherwise too strong for them. It is worth noting, also, that the poem culminates only in the death of Sisera ; there is no city captured, no fresh territory acquired, and the *status quo* remains practically unaltered, save that there may be greater freedom of communication between the sundered portions of the Israelite confederacy. The battle had little effect on the progress of events.

The story of Abimelech (Judg. 9) gives us a picture of the standing of Israel at a later period. Here there is a fairly close connexion between Israelite and Canaanite. They can enter into relations with one another on equal terms, and can, to a large extent, make common cause with one another. There is still, however, a division between the two, and Abimelech, born of a type of marriage which assigned the children to the mother's kin, was able to achieve local sovereignty by playing one race off against the other. We have here a stage in which the two peoples, old and new, are no longer definitely and permanently at war with one another, though the process of mutual assimilation is still not complete.

The other narratives of the book are all of a different type, and help us to understand the ultimate emergence of a single united people. Palestine has always been exposed to raids and invasions from outside its borders, and most of the Judges had to deal with enemies who were as foreign and as dangerous to the Canaanites as they were to the Israelites. We hear of Moabites, Ammonites, Amalekites, Bedouin, entering the land and either imposing a temporary sovereignty on some portion of it, or sweeping the country and retreating with their plunder to some desert fastness. The example of Israel itself shows how unfit were the Canaanites to repel such assaults. Enervated by generations of the settled life, and divided into little principalities and independent townships, they lacked a unifying force which would enable a large group to combine against an enemy, and the military vigour which would enable them to overcome an adversary. They could but suffer and hope that the invaders would at length be exhausted. But Israel had just what the Canaanites lacked. In place of the local Baals, whose cults were necessarily a disintegrating force, they had the sense of oneness in a tradition of common ancestry, and, still more, in their adherence to a single God. It is true that they succumbed with monotonous regularity to the seductions of the local Baals with whom they came into contact, and on whom they relied for agricultural success, but they were always liable to be called back to their unifying allegiance to Yahweh by an inspired Judge, whose Berserk leadership also gave to the combined force exactly the impulse needed to repel and overthrow the invader. The result was that, though their contribution to the physical constitution of the people may have been comparatively small, they did form a kind of military aristocracy, and, as the process of assimilation advanced, they were able more and more to impose on the joint community the ideals and traditions associated with their tribal God and with their Aramæan ancestry. The two elements in the population were slowly welded into a single whole by the hammer-strokes of foreign invasion.

The Philistines. As long as the enemies to be faced were desert raiders or small neighbouring peoples, the local Judges were competent to meet the national need. But the advent of the Philistines at the beginning of the twelfth century B.C. introduced a fresh element into the situation. The newcomers were the representatives of the Ægean civilization, broken before great racial movements from the north. They had attained the highest culture that the world had yet seen, and were skilled in the arts of peace and of war. They were the survivors of terrible struggles, and, though first driven south and then repulsed from the frontiers of Egypt, they were more than a match for the lower tribes of Palestine. Their constitution as a confederacy of five cities left to each a high degree of autonomy, but they were capable of acting together, and often did so act ; it is but seldom that we hear of individual kings in the story of the wars with Israel. Gath alone of the five cities appears to stand somewhat apart from the rest, and it was the smallest and least important of all. It would not have been surprising if the Philistines, in this central spot, had carved out for themselves a new empire, which should have rivalled the glories of Troy or of Crete.

At first they were successful. Such resistance as was offered to them came from the Israelites. The tribe immediately in contact with them was that of Dan, and the Samson stories come to us from a time when the struggle was drawing to a close. The Philistine dominion was already widely recognized, and the tribe of Dan had been pressed back from the coast into a small compass, near the western end of the valley through which the railway to Jerusalem now runs. The two villages mentioned in the Samson story, Zorah and Eshtaol, were only a few miles apart, and the tribe was clearly reduced to very small compass. The Philistine rule does not seem to have been oppressive ; Samson's exploits were due to personal rather than national wrongs, but the sense of foreign domination was there, and the free spirit of the Israelite naturally chafed under it. The pressure, however, increased, and at length the last remnants of the tribe decided to emigrate, and found a new home in the far north of the country.

The way was now open for the Philistines to advance into the central range, and one of the most dramatic stories in the Old Testament (1 Sam. 4) describes the decisive battle which won the land for them. The sites mentioned—Aphek and Ebenezer—have not been satisfactorily identified ; the latter is quite unknown, and for the former two locations have been proposed, one at the entrance to the Vale of Sorek, the other to the north in the plain not far from the western end of the Plain of Dothan. Both sites, however, are a considerable distance from Shiloh, and the narrative of 1 Sam. 4 suggests a spot in that general neighbourhood. Since at least one other Aphek is known, the name may have been applied to a number of places. But, wherever the battle took place, it was for the time decisive, and probably for a generation the Philistines remained in undisturbed authority. They made no attempt to cross the Jordan, and contented themselves with establishing military posts in various parts of the hill country, while it seems that the actual administration was in the hands of special officers. We hear, also, of " Hebrews " who attached themselves to the Philistines, and some scholars hold that these were not Israelites, but represented another wave of invasion from the wilderness. The distinction, however, made in I Sam. 14²¹ (the passage on which this view is based) is hardly certain enough to justify us in coming to a definite conclusion, and it is quite possible that numbers of Israelites had entered Philistine service, and had attached themselves to their masters either as mercenaries or as camp-followers.

Saul. It is with the coming of the Philistines that the Iron Age really begins in Palestine, and the ruling race was careful to keep the control of the metal in its own hands (I Sam. 13¹⁹). Apart from this their government does not seem to have been oppressive, and the story of Saul's early days shows that the people were allowed a good deal of freedom. They could even embark on military expeditions, and they seem to have raised no objection to Saul's kingship as long as he refrained from any act hostile to themselves.

It was, nevertheless, with Saul that effective opposition once more arose. He belonged to that class of Yahweh-inspired enthusiasts who were represented by the prophets and the judges. Both classes stood for the old Aramæan ways and the traditions of the wilderness, and both were intolerant of any foreign control. The story of Saul's meeting with Samuel, his anointing, and his subjection to the prophetic ecstasy, is among the best-known narratives in the Old Testament. (It may be remarked in passing that the account of a formal election, given in I Sam. 10¹⁷⁻²⁷ is rightly regarded by most scholars as a later interpretation of the facts, emanating from a school which regarded the monarchy itself as a violation of true Israelite principles.) The new power conferred on him was first effectively manifested when messengers came and reported the desperate situation of the city of Jabesh Gilead, to the east of the Jordan, threatened by the Ammonite king. Saul delivered the city in the manner of the traditional Judge, and, up to this point, there was nothing to distinguish him from earlier saviours of the people. But the dominance of the Philistines drove him to go further, and when his son, Jonathan, assassinated a Philistine local officer, a speedy attempt was made at vengeance. A punitive expedition made its way up into the hills, and established a temporary base in a hill fort at Michmash, looking eastwards towards the Jordan Valley. Saul's real base was to the east of the Jordan, and he made his camp at Gilgal, where his line of retreat across the Jordan was secured. But his forces, which were organized under himself and Jonathan, melted away, till at last with 600

men only he moved up into the hills to a point where he
could observe the Philistine camp. During the absence of
the greater number of the enemy troops on their errand of
destruction, Jonathan and his squire climbed up into the
Philistine fort, and, filled with wild berserk fury, cut down
many of the garrison left in occupation. The returning raiders
met the fugitives, and were themselves thrown into panic,
and the whole of the hill country was speedily cleared of
Philistine troops, the Israelites picking up and using the
weapons dropped in flight.

The victory of Michmash was the beginning of a period of
comparative independence. It is true that the Philistines
never relaxed their effort to recover what they had there lost,
but it is clear that Israel, under Saul, grew steadily stronger,
and the Philistine attacks for the most part were little more
than raids. At times there were more formal expeditions,
and it was in one of these that David performed his first
exploit in the slaughter of Goliath—if it was indeed David
who killed him. But the Philistine efforts to penetrate the
hill country from the west were wholly unsuccessful, and Saul
had sufficient respite from fighting to be able to consolidate
his kingdom and achieve some kind of organization.

We must not expect to find in Saul's reign the kind of
elaborate system of government which appears under his
successors. He still, apparently, lived in his ancestral home of
Gibeah when he was not on active service against the Philistines.
He had no palace, and his court might be in a tent or in the
open. We hear little or nothing of Saul's judicial work, though
the settlement of disputes was always one of the chief functions
of government, and he must have spent much time in it.
As is natural in the circumstances, we know most of the military
aspect of his reign. The Philistines were not like the earlier
enemies of Israel, threatening only occasional raids. In such
conditions the whole man-power of the nation (or, more
probably, the tribe or district) could be summoned for the
short period during which the crisis lasted. But the Philistines
were a perpetual menace, and Saul was liable to be called on
to meet them at a moment's notice. Hence arose the pressing
need for a permanent force of professional soldiers. The first
move in this direction is noted in 1 Sam. 13², where three
thousand men are definitely enlisted, the remainder being dismissed to their homes. The force is divided into two, the larger
being under Saul and the smaller under Jonathan. We find,
further, in 1 Sam. 14⁵² the statement that the king continued
to recruit throughout his reign, and it is clear that this standing

army was a permanent feature of his organization. At the same time, when the Philistines or other enemies assembled in full force, this body of men was insufficient, and the whole national levies were liable to be called up. In this connexion we find a new post, that of the " Captain of the Host," who is contrasted with the officer set " over the men of war." The former position was held by Abner (1 Sam. 17⁵⁵); the latter by David (1 Sam. 18⁵), until the king's jealousy grew so strong that he removed him and made him " captain of a thousand " (1 Sam. 18¹³). The latter phrase probably means that David was transferred from the royal bodyguard to the popular levies, and indicates that there also some kind of organization had been introduced. We hear of a similar officer in 1 Sam. 17¹⁸, where Jesse is giving David instructions as he sends the lad to inquire after his brothers. Further details are lacking, but these references suffice to show that Saul had attained to some kind of military organization. We have no information as to the methods of civil government, though the remark in 1 Sam. 10²⁷, to the effect that certain ill-disposed persons refused to recognize Saul and brought him no " gift," suggests taxation of some kind.

Saul thus succeeded, under Philistine pressure, in securing the real unity of the country. His dominions, however, were limited; he never, as it seems, exercised any effective control over the country north of the Ephraimite hills, and his frontier was Mt. Gilboa, overlooking the valley of Jezreel. The plain of Esdraelon, with its fortresses, had fallen by this time into Philistine hands, a fact which is attested not only by the mention of Bethshan in 1 Sam. 31¹⁰, but by the archæological evidence. His strongest base, however, was probably to the east of Jordan, where his early exploit in the relief of Jabesh Gilead gave him a secure hold on the loyal affections of the people. The extent of his authority in the south is uncertain; his conquest of Amalek may have given him a nominal control over the land, but Jerusalem remained in other hands, and David seems to have found some sympathy and help in Judah. It is noteworthy that whenever we hear of Saul in the south, he has an army with him, as if he were not sure of the friendliness of the people.

Saul's reign, begun with triumph and continued in successful struggle, closed in gloom. For this his own temperament was partly responsible. In some way or other he failed to maintain his religious enthusiasm; tradition assigned the cause to a rupture with Samuel. The very ecstatic spirit which had made him what he was in his early days became in later life his bane, and developed into a form of melancholia. The rise of David aroused his jealousy, and the younger man was driven into direct opposition, even taking service under a Philistine. While the historian, writing from a pro-Davidic point of view, does his best to relieve his hero from blame, it is impossible not to suspect that there is another side to the story. And at length the Philistines developed a new strategy, and, instead of trying to force a way through the western passes, where their chariots were comparatively useless, made a great assault from the north, with their main bases at Bethshan and Jezreel. Here they won an overwhelming victory ; Saul and the strongest of his sons were killed, and the Israelites were utterly routed. To the east of the Jordan, in the district where Saul had made his best friends, a son of Saul's, Ishbaal by name, still managed to retain some independent authority and to keep alive the semblance of a kingdom, but to the west the whole of the central hill country was once more completely in the hands of the Philistines, and the situation was practically what it had been when Saul first became king. To all outward appearance he had effected nothing.

3. The Monarchy : Its Rise and Zenith

David. The defeat and death of Saul left Israel, to all outward appearance, where she had been at his accession. But a new element had been introduced into the thinking and outlook of the people. They had been, for a time, bound together in a single political unity, and the conception of Israel as a single whole had gained in strength. There had been some kind of national organization, and, though it was still at an elementary stage, the mind of the tribes had been prepared for a more extensive system. Given a real leader, who could combine the two ideals of the Aramæan nomad and of the settled community, there was still hope that Israel might once more rise into independence.

The conditions were fulfilled in David, the most striking personality that Israel produced after Moses. Though his home was in the north of the territory occupied by Judah, and was, indeed, only a few miles from Jerusalem, his occupation and upbringing were those of the shepherd, and his natural sympathies were with the traditions of that order. He was probably of very mixed ancestry ; there seems to have been a smaller proportion of Aramæan blood in Judah than elsewhere, and it naturally decreased the farther north the group spread. He had connexions with Moab (cf. 1 Sam. 22[3f.]) and with Gath : tradition gave him a Moabite ancestress, and he retained the loyal friendship of Gittites long after he had reached the height of his power. He was a man of high physical courage, outstanding military skill, and almost unique statesmanship—unique, at least, in Israelite history. Above all, he had an extraordinary personal charm, and, in spite of the strong passions inevitable in a man of his temperament, he made and kept friends in every class of the community. He could be as cruel and vindictive as any man of his time, but there were occasions when he had a magnanimity and a tenderness exceedingly rare in that rough age. The outstanding blot on his personal life is the seduction of Bathsheba and the murder of Uriah, but it must not be forgotten that, on the normal view of oriental kingship, he did nothing unusual, and that his repentance and submission are without parallel in the records of eastern monarchy. We may contrast the attitude of Jezebel to Elijah with that of David to Nathan.

The story of David's early years is too familiar to need more than a passing reference. We cannot here attempt to decide as between the conflicting accounts of his first introduction to Saul. There is, however, no doubt that he rose swiftly to high military command, and that he made for himself a great reputation. When he fell into disfavour, a group of stern and desperate men gathered round him, and till near the end of Saul's reign he led the life of a brigand chief. His connexion with Gath enabled him to establish a small principality at Ziklag, and, when freed from the danger of royal interference, he was able to move northwards and make his headquarters at Hebron, where, in defiance, as it seems, of his Philistine masters, he assumed royal state. The house of Saul, under the weak Ishbaal, still maintained itself nominally to the east of the Jordan, and we hear of occasional clashes between the forces of the two Israelite kings. But the murders of Abner and of Ishbaal put an end to the rivalry within Israel, and David had taken care to secure the goodwill of the people by his courteous and friendly treatment of the men of Jabesh Gilead. He stood alone as the champion of Israel against the foreign oppressor.

It seems clear that the Philistines, however ready to tolerate David as a subordinate prince, were not prepared to see him exert any extensive authority. Their attacks on him had a certain amount of success, for they seem to have controlled Jerusalem, and were thus able to march into the heart of the hill country and threaten David from the north. Once at least he was compelled to take refuge in his old haunt at Adullam, but the decisive victory of the valley of Rephaim, to the south of Jerusalem, cut the city off from the plains. It was captured through the ingenuity and daring of Joab, who, with a small body of men, climbed up the shaft by which the city procured water from the Virgin's spring, while David made a demonstration outside the walls. With the possession of this fortress, one of the strongest in the ancient east in spite of its small size, David was in a position to occupy the whole of the hill country without serious difficulty. His choice of it as his capital shows, too, his political insight. It was newly won territory, and could be claimed by neither of the two portions into which the land had hitherto been divided. It is, indeed, held in some quarters, that it remained technically an independent principality, and that David held three separate crowns, those of Judah, of Jerusalem, and of Israel. While interesting and suggestive, however, the theory lacks sufficient evidence to justify us in adopting it with any certainty.

It is a curious fact that we have no record of David's later wars against the Philistines, beyond a few possible references in the list of heroic exploits recorded in 2 Sam. 23$^{8-23}$. But the main facts are beyond dispute. Not only was the territory ruled by Saul completely recovered, but the fortresses in the plain of Esdraelon were taken for the first time. Either the Philistines were exhausted by their unsuccessful efforts during the campaigns which ended with the fall of Jerusalem, or David's influence produced a division among themselves. Much of the coastal plain still remained in their hands, and we hear in later times of more than one siege of Gibbethon, still a Philistine city, but the back of their power was broken, and they never again succeeded in re-establishing their authority over the centre of the land.

The conquest of the plain of Esdraelon was succeeded by the occupation—again unrecorded—of the far north, and a natural frontier was found between the kingdoms of Israel and Hamath in the watershed which separates the basin of the Litany from that of the Orontes. David then turned his attention to his other borders. Edom was harried and desolated, so that the control of the northern arms of the Red Sea and the ports there passed into the hands of the Israelite king. Moab, despite its early friendliness to David, was savagely treated, and was reduced to the status of a tributary monarchy. The same fate befell Ammon, though it seems that a portion of its territory was included in the dominions under direct Israelite government. The Aramæan tribes to the north-east, ranging over the country between the Jordan Valley and the Euphrates, were subdued, and, like the Edomites, were kept in subjection

by governors appointed from the court of Jerusalem. With
Phœnicia David entered into a close alliance ; the interests
of the two kingdoms in no way clashed with one another, and
it was to the advantage of both that friendly relations should
exist between them, especially since Israel now controlled the
most important roads along which passed the commerce on
which the life of Phœnicia depended.

David's position was thus as strong as it could possibly
be. Egypt had fallen into one of her periodic states of depression under the last kings of the XXIst Dynasty, and, in any
case, had her hands too full with the Libyans on her western
frontier to pay much serious attention to Palestine. The
Philistines were reduced to practical impotence, and round the
rest of his frontiers David had established a ring of states,
either subject or friendly to him. An Israelite kingdom was
now well founded, and, with wise government, might have long
held a high position among the nations.

David did not neglect the internal organization of his
kingdom. The military arrangements, already apparent
under Saul, were maintained and even extended ; special
orders of honour were introduced, and the royal bodyguard
was strengthened by the accession of foreign mercenaries.
At the same time the national levy was not neglected, and
the popular and autocratic elements were thus still combined
one with another. For domestic administration David seems
to have relied on the old tribal divisions ; a system which
in some ways cut across these was introduced by Solomon.
Justice was in the hands of the old local courts, though an
appeal now lay to the king himself, and the number of litigants
who availed themselves of this privilege grew to be very
large indeed. The court had certain officers appointed for it,
and we hear of a kind of secretariat. The cultus received
special attention from the king. He probably acted himself
as the supreme priest, but he appointed sons of his own to
sacerdotal offices, and had, besides, two superior priests. One
of these was Abiathar, a representative of the old house of Eli
and the priesthood of Nob, who had followed David's fortunes
from his early days. The other was Zadok, whose origin is
uncertain, and who comes into prominence only with the
establishment of the main sanctuary at Jerusalem. It is
possible that he represented the old priesthood long established
at the city's chief shrine. David gave clear pre-eminence to
Jerusalem as a holy place, and revived the old nomad tradition
by transporting thither the Ark, which was held to have been
the principal, perhaps the only, cult-object surviving from the

wilderness days (a rival may have been found in the famous bronze snake). The nomad tradition was still further maintained by the fact that the Ark was housed in a tent, not in a solid building, though David is credited with the intention of building the temple actually erected by his son. He certainly seems responsible for the selection of the ancient rock-altar to the north of the Jebusite city as the spot where the sanctuary was to be finally located.

Little is said about David's finances, or the means he used to secure what he needed for his building works. The latter were by no means so extensive as those of his son, but they were yet considerable, and some means must have been found for the provision of labour and material. We hear nothing in his reign of taxation or of forced labour ; the revolts which took place seem to have had other causes. We may, then, conclude that David's government was oppressive in neither direction, and that he relied on other sources than his immediate subjects. His workmen appear to have been derived from Tyre, and it is probable that such of his material as could not be supplied locally was drawn from the same source. We may fairly assume that his main source of revenue was to be found in his control of the trade-routes. Since there is no mention of any payment made by him to Tyre (as there is in the case of his son), we may suppose that what the latter supplied was given in consideration for the protection afforded to Tyrian commerce on the roads. In addition, it may be taken for granted that tolls in money or in kind would be levied on every caravan that passed through his dominions, and there can have been few routes that he could not touch. We can best understand the enormous treasure which is said to have accumulated in his reign on this hypothesis.

The domestic life of David's court is brought vividly before us in an important section of 2 Samuel, comprising chaps. 9–20. Among other features it serves to show how the king, in his later years, seems gradually to have allowed the normal conceptions of eastern monarchy to overweigh the genuine Israelite tradition. It is true that the ideals of the latter always remained prominent ; his court had room for the prophet, representing all through Israel's history those nomad ideals, and standing for the rights of man against all superimposed authority. The classical illustration of the conflict between the two tendencies is to be seen in the story of David's sin with Bathsheba, and it is clear that he himself maintained at heart the genuine Israelite point of view. The abuse on which Absalom was able to play was the delay in the administration

of justice in the royal courts, not oppressive treatment of the
people in general, and a considerable section of the people
adhered to the old king, for his army was drawn from the
national levies under Joab as well as from his mercenary
bodyguard. The other rebellion, that of Sheba, seems to have
had a tribal origin, and this, too, was put down with the help
of representatives of the people as a whole.

Solomon. The reign of Solomon proved fatal to any
chances Israel may have had of reaching a commanding
position among the nations. Born in the latter part of his
father's life, when the early struggles were but memories of
older men, he had little or no sympathy with the true Israelite
conceptions of society. His very accession was a triumph of
the principles of autocracy over those of democracy, for it was
achieved solely through the royal bodyguard under Benaiah,
and the popular leaders, Adonijah, Abiathar, and Joab, were
the chief sufferers. His court was magnificent but extra-
vagant and wasteful, and even the treasure accoumulated by
David could not stand the drain made upon it. His buildings,
including the Temple, were also beyond the normal resources
of the land, and he resorted to the hateful practice of forced
labour. For the supply of the royal court and, presumably,
also for the maintenance of labour drafts, the country was
divided into twelve districts. From these Judah was excluded, and thus received preferential treatment which could
not fail to aggravate the general discontent felt over all the
rest of the land. The financial difficulties were enhanced by
Solomon's failure to maintain the dominions acquired by his
father. Revolts took place both in Edom and among the
Aramæan tribes to the north-east, and the independence of
these districts must have meant a very serious loss of revenue.
It became necessary to pay the king of Tyre for his goods and
services, and the kingdom had no longer the resources needed.
A little could be done with the export of grain, but the supply
cannot have been large. In the end, Solomon was forced
actually to cede territory to escape bankruptcy. We have
also a darker suspicion. Solomon was the first Israelite king
to establish a force of chariotry—some of his stables have been
recovered at Megiddo. He does not seem to have been able
to breed his own horses, and had to import them from the
north or from Egypt. In Deut. 17[16], among the rules laid
down for the monarchy, we have the sinister requirement that
the king shall not increase the number of his horses, nor cause
the people to return to Egypt that he may have many horses.
Clearly this is a denunciation of an old grievance, and it is

not difficult to suppose that the man-power of Israel was the best exportable commodity at the king's disposal. Nor is it absurd to suggest that the practice goes back to the days of Solomon, and that here, too, he violated the fundamental principles and outraged the deepest sentiment of the genuine Israel.

The Prophetic Movement. Solomon's methods of government did not pass unchallenged. It is true that we hear of no extensive revolt in Israel itself, but a strong protest was made. As ever through the history of the monarchy. the prophetic party was the repository of the old Aramæan ideals. Again and again members of this order rose to assert the rights of the individual Israelite and the democratic principles on which the national life was founded. The discontent found a spokesman in Ahijah, who selected as his instrument a certain Jeroboam. The actual course of events is uncertain, partly owing to the fact that the LXX gives us a very different account of the events from that recorded in the traditional Hebrew text. But it is clear that Jeroboam had been himself an overseer in the district of Ephraim, a part of the country where the true Israelite element was probably stronger than in any other. It is not clear whether he actually raised the standard of revolt in the reign of Solomon himself, but his treasonable designs were known, and he was compelled to take refuge in Egypt. That country was no longer ruled by the XXIst Dynasty, whose later kings were, on the whole, favourable to Solomon, and had entered into an alliance with him, cemented by his marriage to an Egyptian princess. But the policy was reversed by Sheshonk, the first king of the XXIInd Dynasty, and he gave willing harbourage to Jeroboam. During the old king's lifetime there was no prospect of a successful movement, but with his death a new situation arose, and Jeroboam was not slow to take advantage of it.

It must be recognized that kingship in Israel had a unique quality. Saul had been of the type of the old judge, and had received a divine appointment, attested by his liability to the prophetic ecstasy. David's authority was based on a covenant, a mutual agreement in which three parties were concerned— the king, the people, and Yahweh. It must have included terms and conditions on two sides, that of the monarch and that of the nation, while Yahweh's share was to see that the bargain was duly kept. We have, thus, something in the nature of a charter and a coronation oath, imposing limitations on the royal prerogative, and ensuring certain rights and liberties to the subject. The passage already cited from Deut. 17,

though in its present form it may date from the latter part of
the seventh century, almost certainly implies a traditional
restraint on the absolute will of the sovereign, and there are
several instances—even in the reign of David—where this
becomes apparent. It must be recognized that this formed a
unique phenomenon in the ancient world. Everywhere else
the king was an absolute autocrat, against whom none of his
subjects had any rights whatsoever ; even in the court language of Israel the ordinary citizen is the " slave " of the king.
Under the genuine Israelite conception of social organization,
on the contrary, the subject was the " brother " (Deut. 17²⁰)
or the " neighbour " (Jer. 22¹³) of the king, and in the very
terms used we have a totally new theory of the relation between
the government and the governed.

The Disruption. Solomon, raised to the throne by a
palace revolution, seems to have been bound by no restrictions
whatever, and his reign was that of the typical eastern despot.
His death, however, gave a new opportunity for the revival
of the national claims, already emphasized from the prophetic
point of view. His son, Rehoboam, was asked to grant a
new charter and to enter into a new covenant, whereby the
freedom of the subject from the oppressive forced labour should
be assured. This, with his father's example before him, he
refused to do ; the tribes at Shechem repudiated him and
elected Jeroboam, who returned opportunely from Egypt.
Judah, which had less ground for dissatisfaction, and was
probably more easily overawed by the royal bodyguard,
remained faithful to the house of David, and henceforth the
nation was cut politically in two.

According to 1 Kings 12²²ᶠᶠ· Rehoboam was restrained from
making any immediate attack on Jeroboam by a message from
the prophet Shemaiah, but in 14³⁰ we hear of continual war
between the two kingdoms. There is ground for supposing
that Rehoboam met with a considerable measure of success, and,
left to himself, he might have recovered the whole kingdom.
But we gather that Jeroboam appealed to his former protector,
Sheshonk, and that the latter was only too glad of an opportunity to assert once more the ancient claim of the Pharaohs
to empire in Palestine. Certainly the Egyptian king invaded
the country in or about 928 B.C., and he has left us a record of
his triumphs. The places he mentions include cities as far
north as the plain of Esdraelon, which leads us to suspect that
they had by this time fallen into the hands of Rehoboam.
Neither the Israelite nor the Egyptian records state that
Sheshonk actually captured Jerusalem, though both mention

an enormous spoil taken from the city. We must suppose that Rehoboam, finding his situation hopeless, consented to hand over his treasures, and that Sheshonk accepted his submission rather than undertake the very difficult task of reducing Jerusalem by force.

The political separation of the two kingdoms was thus complete, and was emphasized by Jeroboam's religious policy. The ancient bull-cult of Palestine was transferred to Yahweh, and two of the old sanctuaries, those of Bethel and Dan, were raised to special eminence. The former was still the royal sanctuary *par excellence* in the middle of the eighth century. But the conception of an ideal Israel, unified in and through its common relation to Yahweh, still held its place. The shepherd of the east or south, the merchant of the Esdraelon cities, and the farmer of the Ephraimite hills or of the Judæan Shephelah all felt themselves to be within the community of the covenant. As late as the eighth century, while Samaria still stood, the message of at least one southern prophet, Amos, was practically confined to the north, while both Micah and Isaiah felt that Samaria was as much within their purview as Jerusalem or Gath. The old Aramæan tradition was still maintained, and its strength was constantly reinforced by the prophets and the conceptions in Church and State of which they were the outstanding champions. It is true that the two kingdoms might stand apart from one another, though for a considerable period they were in close alliance, with the North as the dominant partner, but conflict between them was always a kind of civil war, and they never failed to think of themselves as being one. There were times when the hostility between them grew to such a pitch that Judah, ever the weaker, appealed for help outside the community, but even foreign interference failed to break the bond that united all who claimed a common descent and a common faith.

Dynastically there is a striking difference between the two communities. Except for a short period in the latter half of the ninth century, the South maintained its unbroken fidelity to the house of David. The North, however, had no such continuity, and the first fifty years after the disruption saw no less than three families on the throne. The first two, those of Jeroboam and of Baasha, are barren of outstanding incidents. They were a period of petty local struggles and of border warfare, which seldom achieved anything more effective than desultory plundering raids. We hear of attacks on the Philistines and of spasmodic attempts by Judah to recover her dominion over Edom, but the outstanding feature of the time is the steady rise of Damascus to a position of supremacy in her little world. The kingdom had been founded before the death of Solomon, and its position at the junction of several of the great trade-routes gave it an opportunity of achieving wealth and importance. Its authority seems to have embraced the greater part of eastern Israelite territory, though the inhabitants of trans-Jordan remained individual members of the community of Yahweh, and contributed not a little to the thought of the whole body. We may suspect too (though here direct evidence is lacking) that the Syrians held the northern part of the country, and thus secured the whole of the route which led from Damascus to the Phœnician ports. Civil war and minor armed excursions with no real policy behind them reduced Israel to a low ebb, and if either Egypt or a Mesopotamian power had been in a position to make a serious attack on the land, it could hardly have maintained its independence.

Omri and Ahab. With the rise of the house of Omri, however, almost exactly half a century after the division of the kingdom, there came a change. The founder of the dynasty was a man of keen political insight, and with something of David's statesmanship. One of his most important acts was the building of a new capital which may have helped to allay the local rivalries that had played so large a part in the dynastic struggles of the preceding fifty years. The new city, Samaria, has been excavated, and gives us an idea of the splendour to which Omri and his son attained. The Israelite empire was once more extended beyond the bounds of western Palestine ; Moab was subdued, and some, at least, of the territory east of the Jordan was re-occupied. Judah entered into a close alliance with the North, probably not wholly of her own free will. Like David, Omri sought and obtained the friendship of Phœnicia, which suggests recovery of the main trade routes, or of a substantial portion of them. The league between the two peoples was cemented by the marriage of Ahab, son of Omri, to Jezebel, daughter of Ethbaal, king of Sidon, and Israel entered once more into the arena of international politics. The part played by Omri may be gauged from the fact that Assyrian inscriptions of the ninth century B.C. allude to Israel under the name of " the house of Omri," though Omri himself had been succeeded by his son before the two peoples came into close contact with one another.

Ahab appears to have been as great a man as his father. His buildings in Samaria (if they have been rightly identified) surpassed the older structures in size and magnificence. The border rivalry with Damascus still continued, but Ahab's military skill secured him, not only freedom from the pressure of the enemy, but also some degree of superiority. He was wise enough not to press his advantage, for a new and far more terrible enemy was now on the horizon, and he was prepared rather to unite with Benhadad of Damascus in the common defence of the west against Assyrian aggression.

Assyria, under Shalmaneser III, had at last recovered from a period of depression, and was once more making a bid for western empire. The immediate objective seems to have been the kingdom of Hamath, in northern Syria, whose conquest would leave an uninterrupted path to the ports whence Cyprus and the Mediterranean in general could be easily reached. But both Ahab and Benhadad saw that their own interests were involved, and made common cause with Hamath. Not only so, but they succeeded in building up a coalition which embraced practically all the tribes and principalities of the west. The only important omission we have from the list supplied by Assyrian records is that of Judah, which suggests that the South was so far subject to the North that it needed no special mention. The first great battle was fought in 853 B.C. at Karkar, on the Orontes. The Israelite contribution to the combined forces of the allies was 10,000 infantry and 2000 chariots, by far the largest contingent in the latter arm, and second only to Damascus itself in the former. The struggle seems to have been fierce and deadly ; Shalmaneser claims the victory, having slain countless numbers of the enemy. But it is significant that his expedition went no farther, and that he had to fight again and again in the same spot, with equally little result. It is curious that we have no mention whatever of these campaigns (Ahab himself took part only in the first) in the Bible ; had we the story told from the Palestinian point of view, we should probably have heard of great victories.

It would seem that the combination of forces against the great eastern enemy did not put an end to the local jealousies between the Palestinian states. Hardly had the Assyrians been repulsed at Karkar, when Ahab undertook an expedition for the recovery of Ramoth Gilead, one of the cities beyond the Jordan still in the hands of Damascus. The story of his death is one of the most familiar in the Old Testament, and it serves to illustrate, among other interesting points, the subordination of Jehoshaphat, king of Judah. The latter would hardly have allowed himself to be made an obvious target for the enemy's archers if he had been a free agent.

Ahab's successor, Ahaziah, had only a short reign, but he was clearly not the man his father had been, and his brother, Jehoram, who succeeded him, was not much stronger. The alliance against Assyria was, however, maintained, and Shalmaneser's repeated efforts to break through to the Mediterranean were fruitless.

Jezebel and Elijah. To all outward appearance, the policy of the house of Omri was thus crowned with success. But it had another aspect, which affected the domestic history of Israel. The alliance with Phœnicia brought Jezebel into the kingdom, and with her came conceptions in religion and social life which were diametrically opposed to those of the genuine Aramæan tradition. This is not the place to describe or discuss her attempt to instal the Tyrian Baal, Melkart, in Yahweh's place as the supreme god of Israel, but her attitude towards her husband's subjects is of almost equal importance. She held that normal oriental view, to which reference has already been made, according to which the life and property of every subject were at the absolute disposal of the sovereign. To her, as to most of the people of her age, the phrase " limited monarchy " would have seemed a contradiction in terms, for the central fact about monarchy was that its powers and rights were unlimited. Her point of view is illustrated by the familiar story of Naboth and his vineyard. The three main figures in the tragedy are clearly drawn. First we have the free peasant, stubborn, short-sighted and uncompromising, who insists on his right to keep his land, however much the king may want it, or however attractive may be the offers that are made to him. Next the king, bitterly exasperated by the peasant's refusal, but compelled by national custom and instinct to accept the verdict against him. Finally, the foreign queen, who is unable to understand where the difficulty lies, and (though even she must respect the forms of justice) is determined to get what she wants at any cost. It is significant that Ahab himself seems to be unaware of what his wife is doing until Naboth is actually dead and his property liable to confiscation. Nowhere is the contrast between the various conflicting ideals more clearly, even sharply, drawn, and we may suspect that there were other instances in which the royal prerogative was thus strained owing to Jezebel's influence.

Conduct of this type could not fail to arouse the bitter hostility of the party that held to national tradition, headed by the prophets. A spokesman was found in Elijah, who bitterly denounced the royal tyranny, and laid on Ahab and his house the guilt of blood with which the vineyard of Naboth

itself was tainted. Jezebel was too strong for him, and he was
unable to effect any improvement in person (the slaughter
of the prophets of Baal belongs to the religious side of history
rather than to that of social politics). But he left behind him a
sentence, to be carried out with appalling ferocity a few years
later under the influence of Elisha.

The Prophetic Revolution. It is worth while noting especially
that Elijah came from the country to the east of the Jordan,
and thus sprang from a community which, uncontaminated
by the agricultural life, and by close intermixture with the
predecessors of Israel, maintained in all its strength and fresh-
ness the doctrine of the rights of the individual. But his
attitude was shared by many in western Palestine. Elisha
himself was a native of Abel-Meholah, which lay in the Jordan
Valley, to the west of the river. The prophets in general
could be relied on to take the same point of view, which may
explain Jezebel's attempts to exterminate them. We find also
the Rechabites, a new family group, which, eschewing alike
the solid homes of the settled land and the products of the vine,
sought to maintain, even in an agricultural land, the habits
and customs of the nomad life. We hear also of Nazirites, an
obscure group, of whom little is known save that they, also,
tended in the same direction, and would make no use of wine
or grapes, and that they refused to allow their hair to be cut.

The combination of these various elements, all emphasizing
the traditional, Aramæan, aspect of Israelite life, led to an
explosion in the year 842 or 841 B.C. The revolutionary
parties found a leader in Jehu, whose swift action forestalled
resistance, and uprooted the whole house of Ahab. Jezebel
herself was one of the first victims, and their number included
also Jehoram, king of Israel and Ahaziah, king of Judah, whose
father had married Athaliah, daughter of Ahab. The slaughter
of all Ahab's family followed, and Jehu completed his work
with a general massacre of all the worshippers of Baal, probably
the whole of the ecclesiastical establishment introduced by
Jezebel. Whatever else may or may not have been achieved
by the prophetic party, they did succeed in eliminating, once
and for all, the cult of the Tyrian Baal.

Politically, however, the revolution was disastrous. A
similar event had taken place in Damascus, where, again, the
revolution is traced to the Israelite prophetic party. Here
Benhadad was assassinated by Hazael, one of his chief officers.
But the new Syrian king had to maintain, perforce, the old
hostility to Assyria, while Jehu, still feeling insecure, abandoned
the alliance and appealed to Assyria for support. The defec-

tion of Israel, which meant the loss of the greater part of the chariotry of the united army, proved fatal to the coalition, and from that point onwards Damascus and the rest were fighting a losing battle. But, fortunately for them, Shalmaneser's main objective had always been farther north, and he was content with the general submission of the Palestinian states. Though Hazael was defeated in 841 and 839 B.C., the city was not so severely handled as to make recovery impossible. The revolution of Jehu had produced the contrary result in Judah, where Athaliah had seized the crown, nearly exterminating the house of David, and, for six years the family of Ahab could still claim a representative on the southern throne. Northern Israel was thus still further weakened, and, with Damascus still strong on her frontier, she entered on the lowest period in her history.

4. The Monarchy: Its Decline and Fall

The Supremacy of Damascus. The prophetic revolution in northern Israel thus reduced the country to the level of a vassal state of Assyria. Six years later a similar movement in Judah brought an end to the reign of Athaliah, but it is significant that the motive force here was that of the priest-hood, not that of the prophets. A single son of Ahaziah, Joash by name, had survived Athaliah's massacre of the royal family, while still an infant, and when he was seven years of age the priest, Jehoiada, organized a revolt which placed the child on the throne. Naturally, Judah had been independent of the North during the reign of Athaliah, and neither Jehu nor his immediate successors seems to have made a serious attempt to reassert the authority of Israel over the South. For the remainder of the ninth century, the dominant power was still Damascus, and it is clear that Israel suffered severely in the conflict between the two. Slave raids and plundering expeditions were frequent, and, once at least, Samaria itself was besieged and in imminent peril. But in 802 B.C. Damascus was subdued by Assyria, and, though the city was not destroyed, it is clear that the whole country was greatly weakened, and the kingdom of Israel began to recover. The nadir of Israel's political fortunes was reached under Jehoahaz, the son of Jehu; but before the end of his reign the land began to revive, and more than one defeat was inflicted on the Aramæans by his successor, Jehoash. From 782 to 745 B.C. Assyria herself was passing through a period of weakness and even distress; she had many frontiers to defend, and only the strongest of her kings proved equal to all the demands made on them. The relaxing of pressure from the east, however, did not avail Damascus in her local struggles, and we hear of Zakir, king of Hamath, as one of her most dangerous adversaries. Jeroboam II, the great-grandson of Jehu, proved himself the most successful king Israel had had since the days of Omri and Ahab. Taking advantage of the weakness of Damascus, he recovered much of the territory to the east of the Jordan, lost during the preceding half-century, and restored northern Galilee, which seems to have fallen under the sway of Damascus. Israel found herself once more in control of portions of the great trade routes, and, though the country never rose to the height it had reached in the last years of David, it was once more in a position to play an important part in international politics. We hear, it is true, of no foreign marriage, such as those of Solomon or of Ahab, but later generations looked back on the age of Jeroboam II. as one of prosperity and wealth.

Judah, too, recovered some of her old strength. The normal indication of southern revival was the extension of territory to the south, and the Gulf of Akaba once more fell into Judæan hands. At the same time, there was bitter hostility between north and south, which came to a head with war between Jehoash of Israel and Amaziah of Judah. The latter suffered a disastrous defeat, and the wall of Jerusalem itself was partially destroyed. We may assume that, for a time, Judah was once more subordinate to Israel. We hear also of expeditions carried into Philistine territory, and it certainly seems as if in the eighth and seventh centuries Judah exercised control over a fairly large area in the Shephelah and the coastal plain. The general impression that we gain is that the first half of the eighth century witnessed a great revival of the power and wealth of both kingdoms.

Corroborative evidence is offered from the works of the great prophets, especially Amos and Isaiah. In their burning denunciations we can see clear pictures of the luxury in which the upper classes of Israel lived. Solid and elaborate houses, with special rooms for different seasons of the year, and with costly decoration of ivory and ebony, were to be found in Samaria. The furniture matched the buildings; whereas the common oriental sits on the ground or squats on his heels, the Ephraimite magnates were not content with the ordinary stool of honour, but must have soft couches on which they could sprawl at length. The best of food and drink was at their disposal; they seem to have had cattle farms for the express purpose of supplying their tables, as if that which was

ordinarily to be had in the city bazaars was not good enough
for them. Wine was to be had in any quantity, and, if it
failed, it was always possible to institute some kind of suit
against a poor man and take what he had. Unguents and
perfumes of the richest were used freely (see especially Am. 6$^{1\text{-}6}$).
The standard of luxury and extravagance was set, as so often,
by the women, who, though they took little or no active part
in the business life of the community, yet exercised great
influence through the pressure they could bring to bear on
their husbands. We are reminded of the condition of the
French aristocracy in the days which preceded the Revolution.

Economic Changes. But, underneath this fair and prosperous surface there lay a seething mass of corruption. During
the century which followed the death of Ahab a complete change
passed over the economic character of the country. The
strength of the nation had lain in the free and independent
peasant landowner, the man typified by Naboth, who had,
no doubt, many weaknesses and faults, but yet presented to
the world, at home and abroad, a sturdy front. The class
which, under the inspiration of the old Israelite ideals of the
worth of the individual, had held its own in the face of royal
aggression, and had wrung from an oriental monarchy a
formal recognition of its rights, was also that which had faced
the armies of Assyria on the field of Karkar, and, refusing
to admit defeat in spite of fearful carnage, had held the eastern
empire in check. History tends to show that it is an organization of this kind which assures the greatest political and social
stability, maintaining its own self-respect and fighting to the
last for its land and home.

But by the middle of the eighth century all was changed,
and the peasant farmer had all but disappeared. The land
was now parcelled out in large estates (cf., *e.g.* Is. 5$^{8ff.}$), worked
by the labour of serfs, if not of actual slaves. The owners
seem to have lived for the most part in the big cities, where
they passed their time in luxurious idleness, supported by
the labours of their dependents on the soil itself. The old
small proprietors had either become tenant farmers or actual
slaves, and the conditions of the two classes did not differ
greatly in practice. The wealthy pursued their selfish way
in utter disregard of the sufferings of their poorer neighbours,
caring only for what they could extract from them, and Micah
can speak of the rich as crushing the bones of the poor and
flaying the very skin from their flesh (Mic. 3^2).

It is possible to trace with some accuracy the process by
which this result had been achieved. One of the most oppressive

of all the customs of the east is the law of debt. The small
farmer, tempted to spend more than he had, perhaps, by the
luxury of the city which he occasionally visited, or with his
crops and cattle destroyed or carried off in some savage border
raid, was compelled to resort to the money-lender. As security
for his loan he could but mortgage his land, for his personal
property was too small to be of any value except against the
smallest sums. If another bad season followed and the debt
could not be paid, the money-lender would foreclose, and the
old owner was homeless. He might be retained by the new
owner as a tenant-farmer, paying as rent a large proportion
of his crop. The conditions seem to have been usually onerous,
and the rent exorbitant, with the result that a further loan
would be needed to keep body and soul together. This time
the man had nothing to pawn except the persons of his family
and of himself, and, when once more the loan was called in,
they passed into actual slavery. The scene depicted for us
in 2 Kings 4¹ᶠ· cannot have been exceptional ; the story is
told as if it were a normal event, and the money-lender is
mentioned with the definite article, showing that he was one
of the regular characters of Palestinian life. Nor is there any
resentment against him, for he is simply carrying out the usual
practice of his class. But the effect is certain, and the wide
spread of the practice could end only in the virtual disappearance of the free landholder from the economic life of Israel.

A just application of the laws of debt would have been
bad enough, but there are not wanting signs of a yet worse
practice. It would seem that the example set by Jezebel in
manipulating the course of justice was only too faithfully
copied in other spheres. We may be sure that some kind of
legal authority must be obtained by the money-lender before
he could seize either land or person, and the easy corruption
of justice, one of the permanent evils of eastern life, gave
ample opportunity for dishonest practices. It was not necessary
even that a loan should have been made ; a wealthy man who
coveted the person of a poor man simply had to go before the
authorities and state that such a loan had been made, claiming
forfeit from his victim. There might be no truth at all in the
charge, but a small bribe to the judge would suffice to procure
a verdict, and hand the poor man over to the rich as his slave.
It was literally possible to " buy the poor for a pair of shoes."

The type of social problem, then, had undergone a change.
It was no longer a question of conflict between the prerogative
of the crown and the privilege of the subject. That had been
settled once and for all, and Jeroboam and Jehu, each in his

own age, had shown that such infringement of the rights of the individual could not be and would not be tolerated. So far the old Aramæan traditions of Israel had won their way, and the prophetic party had triumphed. Monarchy in Israel was something unique, in that it had room for a democratic element, and Jehoiakim alone of the later kings ever dared to swerve from the right path in this direction. But there had grown up a new class in the country, that of the wealthy capitalist, and it was here that the danger lay. During the early history of the monarchy it is probable that foreign trade was at least controlled by the king, and it may have been almost entirely in his hands. The new plutocrats, as we have seen, apparently owed their position to their exactions from their poorer brethren rather than to successful adventures abroad or to the tolls which might be taken from passing caravans. They were thus the greater peril to the community as a whole. For while Solomon had demanded and received the unpaid services of his subjects for one-third of every year, leaving the peasant free for the remaining eight months to till his own fields, the new order reduced the lower classes to a complete subjection, giving them nothing whatever that they could call their own, either in property or in time.

As always, there were members of the prophetic party who, as the champions and representatives of the ancient Aramæan tradition, protested against the situation. It is true that the facts were not noticed, even by the majority of the prophets of the time ; those attached to the court and to the cultus failed to appreciate the danger which threatened the nation. But a small group of others saw through the fair surface to the real state of the people ; the names of four of these men of the eighth century are known to us—Amos, Hosea, Isaiah and Micah. The first of these was a shepherd of the south, and so came from that stratum in the social order which had never lost the old tradition and had never been implicated in the complex life of agricultural and civic Palestine. He was thus free alike from the blinding influence of familiarity and from the numbing sense of complicity in the evils which were sapping the life of the nation. Hosea and Isaiah were men of the cities, and it is the more remarkable that they appreciated so clearly the situation. Micah was himself a peasant, and knew from bitter experience what the poor farmer had to bear. Hosea and Isaiah were more occupied with the religious situation than with social and political oppression, but neither of them was blind to the facts, and all realized the doom that threatened the country. For, as universal experience has shown, such a condition as that which prevailed in Israel in the eighth century B.C. must be fatal in the long run. A society may be wrecked by an internal explosion, as were those of France at the end of the eighteenth century and Russia in recent years, or the utter depression of the lower classes may leave the country without that free man power which alone can defend it against foreign aggression. The ancient classical world fell for sheer lack of free men, and, in the last resort, it was the same cause which led to the downfall of the Hebrew kingdoms.

The Assyrian Conquest. The brilliance of Jeroboam's reign was but the last leap of an expiring flame and, after his death, the end was not long delayed. The old habit of assassination was resumed, and of the six kings who followed him, one only handed on the crown to his son. That was the usurper, Menahem, who avenged on Shallum the murder of Zechariah, the son of Jeroboam. We gather that the nation was once more divided by local jealousies ; Menahem is especially described as coming from Tirzah, the original seat of Omri's government. Menahem seems to have felt the need of external support, and made his submission to Assyria. The great eastern empire, under Tiglath-pileser III, was just entering on the last of her periods of success. The new king, who did not belong to the old royal house, was one of the greatest who ever sat upon the throne of Nineveh, and the early years of his reign were spent in strengthening his nearer frontiers. Here his most powerful adversary was the kingdom of Urartu, which lay to the north of Mesopotamia, among the hills and the great lakes of southeastern Anatolia. Urartu had the help of small principalities in northern Syria, and it was necessary to reduce them also. A great campaign in 738 B.C. effected this object, and it seems that detachments were sent south to secure the submission of Samaria and Damascus. Tiglath-pileser introduced new methods of imperial government, deporting numbers of the people from the lands he conquered and planting in their stead colonies from distant parts of his dominions. At the same time he thoroughly organized his new provinces, appointing officials directly from the court of Nineveh, and not relying, as his predecessors had done, on the casual fidelity of local princes, who might (and did) refuse to pay tribute whenever they thought it was safe. These measures secured a permanence to the empire, and when Assyria fell, her ruin was brought about, not so much by the defection of the outlying provinces, as by direct attack on the heart of the empire.

Egypt seems to have grown nervous, and to have used all her influence with the Palestinian states to organize western resistance against Assyria. In northern Israel her efforts seem to have been seconded by the prophetic party, which could not endure the sense of dependence on a foreign power ; we may suspect also that Assyria imposed certain religious and cultic forms in token of her supremacy. Menahem's son, Pekahiah, was murdered by Pekah, whose home was in Gilead (so the obscure phrases in 2 Kings 15^{25} seem to imply), and the usurper tried, with the help of Rezon of Damascus, to re-organize the old western alliance which had successfully resisted Shalmaneser III a century before his time. But a change had come over Israel, and she no longer had the vigour which she had shown in earlier days. Judah, too, manifested an unexpected independence, and refused to be coerced into the alliance. Ahaz, the reigning king, was, indeed, seriously alarmed by the allies' threat to depose him and place a Syrian on his throne, and appealed to Tiglath-pileser, against the advice of Isaiah. It is possible that Jerusalem was actually besieged, and that it was in this extremity that Ahaz offered his own son in sacrifice. But a reference in Hosea (Hos. 5$^{8f.}$) suggests that the danger was not all on one side ; possibly Judahite bands operated from the south while the Assyrians were attacking the country in other directions. In 734 B.C. Tig-lath-pileser set about the reduction of Damascus in earnest. His method, however, was not that of direct assault ; he aimed first at outflanking the enemy, and the initial campaign was aimed at Philistia, Gaza being the actual point of attack. The king's strategy was abundantly justified ; Israel was reduced in the following year and Damascus itself was besieged. In place of Pekah, a certain Hoshea was placed on the throne of Samaria, and when Damascus fell in 732 B.C. the country was re-organized in the Assyrian fashion. A province of Damascus was formed, and the greater part of northern Israel was similarly treated ; the territory left to Hoshea comprised only the hill country to the south of the plain of Esdraelon. Megiddo seems to have been the capital of the new province. Ahaz was confirmed in his kingdom, and accepted some form of Assyrian cult.

The death of Tiglath-pileser in 727 B.C. seemed to give opportunity for movement in the west, though his successor, Shalmaneser V, had little trouble elsewhere. Once more Egypt showed herself to be the evil genius of Palestine, and, under her influence, Hoshea revolted. Shalmaneser appeared with an army in 724 B.C., and Hoshea was captured and imprisoned. But his disappearance did not end the resist-ance, and Samaria held out for another three years (the account in 2 Kings 17$^{4-6}$ is confused, but this seems to have been the order of events). At length the city fell, in 721 B.C., and the territory assigned to Hoshea was organized as an Assyrian province. It is possible that Judah also received some accession of land, as a reward for fidelity to the suzerain power. Shalmaneser had died during the siege of Samaria, and the actual arrangements were carried out by his successor, Sargon, who continued the policy of extensive deportation inaugurated by Tiglath-pileser. The northern kingdom had reached its end.

Assyria and Judah. The survival of Judah was in part due to the policy of submission pursued by Ahaz and his son Hezekiah, and partly to the geographical position of the country. Northern Israel had lain across the greatest of all the routes, and could interfere directly alike in war and in peace. Jerusalem was in the hills, and, though her authority throughout the eighth and seventh centuries stretched down to the Philistine plain, and indeed nearly to the coast, her situation did not make her so great an obstacle as northern Israel had been. She might be troublesome to an army moving down towards Egypt along the coast road, but her activities would be limited to occasional raids, and the occupation of the city itself was not necessary to the would-be conqueror unless she chose to make herself particularly dangerous. Further, Jerusalem was an exceedingly strong fortress, and if her submission or neutrality could be secured in other ways, it was not worth while to pay the price of a successful siege, especially since the end desired could be attained by curtailing her territory to the west.

These facts became obvious before the end of the reign of Hezekiah. A rebellion broke out in Philistia in 711 B.C., and Judah seems to have been in some way implicated, but escaped without serious penalty ; the chief sufferer was Ashdod. But on the death of Sargon, in 705 B.C., practically the whole of the empire rose against his successor, Sennacherib. The leading spirit was Marduk-apal-iddina of Babylon, who all his life was to Assyria what Hannibal was to Rome, save that he proved himself utterly incompetent in military affairs. He had been a thorn in the side of Sargon, and succeeded in combining practically all the outlying portions of the empire ; his embassy to Hezekiah is recorded in 2 Kings 20$^{12-21}$. One Palestinian prince alone, Padi of Ekron, remained faithful to his allegiance, and he was deposed by his own subjects, a Greek adventurer being placed on the throne, while Padi was imprisoned in Jerusalem. The religious reform ascribed to Hezekiah was, probably, a feature of independence, since it must have included the elimination of any forms of cult imposed by Assyria on her subject states.

For three years Sennacherib was occupied nearer home, where he completely defeated Marduk-apal-iddina, and restored his general position. But in 701 B.C. he was ready to deal with his western rebels. His account of the expedition is one of the best known of all Assyrian records, and may be supplemented from the Biblical narrative (2 Kings 18^{13}–19^{37}). The Assyrian armies swiftly reduced the rebel cities, a detachment was sent to Jerusalem, and closely besieged the place. The Judæan king made a complete submission, and surrendered Padi, thus saving his people from the horrors of an Assyrian sack and securing a comparatively mild penalty for himself. An Egyptian army did make some attempt to help the allies, but suffered a crushing defeat at Eltekeh, and Sennacherib was able to complete his work. It seems that a detachment of his army suffered from a sudden and terrible attack of bubonic plague, which had been endemic in the marshes on the Egyptian frontier for many centuries, and this disaster, coupled with news of a renewed rising by Marduk-apal-iddina in Babylon, may have determined Sennacherib to settle Palestine as quickly as possible. The work, however, was done as thoroughly as it needed to be ; the rebels were all punished, and Padi was restored to his throne. Hezekiah escaped with an enormous tribute, and was allowed to retain his crown, but was shorn of the greater part of his territory, that of Padi being similarly increased. Judah never again revolted against Assyria, and even when, in 690 B.C., Sennacherib made a further expedition to the west, organizing Ammon, Moab, and Edom as provinces of the empire, Judah and Jerusalem remained untouched.

The long reign of Manasseh, Hezekiah's son and successor, was a time of external peace. Judah remained faithful to Assyria, and though both Esarhaddon and Ashur-bani-pal made several expeditions against Egypt, the armies passed down the coast road without leaving any mark on the history of the little hill state. Once, indeed, Manasseh was summoned, along with twenty-one other subject kings, to do homage to Esarhaddon at the foundation of a new suburb of Nineveh, and this journey may have given rise to the story of his captivity in Babylon, mentioned in 2 Chron. $33^{11\text{-}16}$. For the latter there seems to be no historical basis, for there is no mention of any expedition in the Assyrian annals, and the reign of Esarhaddon and that of Ashur-bani-pal down to 639 B.C. are very completely documented.

Nevertheless, the reign of Manasseh ranks as the blackest period in the whole history of Israel. We have no reason to suppose that the social abuses of the eighth century were aggravated; the seventh century prophets make little complaint on that score. But the age was one of grave religious defection from Israel's high standards, and countless heathen practices are said to have been introduced, including human sacrifice on an extensive scale. It is supposed that an especial attack was made on the prophetic party, but the only actual statement of oppressive government is that he filled Jerusalem with innocent blood (2 Kings 21[16]). It was certainly his religious policy and not his domestic government which earned him the condemnation he received from the prophetic elements in the nation.

The Fall of Assyria and the Eclipse of Egypt. Manasseh died in 641 B.C., and his son Amon was murdered two years later. The year of the accession of the child Josiah was significant in the history of the ancient world. From it come our last dated inscriptions of Ashur-bani-pal, though the king lived on until 626 B.C., and it marks the beginning of the decline of Assyria. The next forty years saw a complete change pass over the political face of western Asia. The northern defences were weak, and hordes of wild barbarians from the north—those whom the Greeks called Scythians and Cimmerians—broke into the Fertile Crescent, carrying their raids as far as the borders of Egypt, and playing some part in the great events which took place in Mesopotamia. In 626 B.C., on the death of Ashur-bani-pal, Babylon finally asserted its independence under a king belonging to the new Chaldean dynasty, Nabopolassar by name. At the same time the Medes, a people of the mountains to the east of Mesopotamia, became aggressive, and Nabopolassar made common cause with them against Nineveh. In Egypt, too, there was a revival of activity, and the young King Necho sought to play a part in world affairs, in the hope of renewing the ancient supremacy of the Pharaohs. He, however, came to the help of Assyria, and during the decisive war made annual expeditions into Mesopotamia.

It was in 616 B.C. that the campaigns of Nabopolassar and his allies began in earnest. For a time he made but slow progress, and the Egyptian army, though it was in the field only for a short time—never more than three months in any one year—proved effective in driving back the Chaldeans. But in 614 B.C. the Medes took and sacked Ashur, the ancient capital of the empire, and two years later Nineveh itself fell before the combined assault of the Medes and Chaldeans. Resistance continued farther west, and Haran was captured by the allies in 610 B.C. Even this did not end the war, though our most reliable record, that of the " Babylonian Chronicle," breaks off here. Necho, at least, continued his Mesopotamian expeditions, and in the course of that of 608 B.C. put Josiah of Judah to death. The account in Chronicles (2 Chron. 35$^{20-24}$) gives a circumstantial description of a battle ; that of 2 Kings (2 Kings 23^{29}) rather suggests a judicial execution. On his return, three months later, Necho deposed Jehoahaz, the second son of Josiah, whom the people had placed on the throne, and installed his elder brother, Eliakim, whom he named Jehoiakim. He thus asserted at once his own authority and his desire not to interfere with the official religion of Judah ; otherwise he would not have insisted on his nominee taking a name which contained the element Yahweh.

Necho continued his expeditions for three years, and, it would seem, there was still some kind of Assyrian government which he could claim to support, though it had moved west-wards after the fall of Haran. We have no certain information as to the detailed course of events after 610 B.C., but we do know that in 605 B.C. Necho suffered a crushing defeat at Carchemish on the Euphrates. This was one of the decisive battles in history. If any semblance of Assyrian independence survived up to that point, it now ceased to be, and this was also the last attempt ever made by an Egyptian monarch at securing world dominion. Henceforward Egypt never rose above the level of a second-class power, and though, under the early Ptolemies, she did once again play an important part in international affairs, she never attained a position of authority among the Greek kingdoms which followed Alexander the Great.

It was inevitable that the fortunes of Judah should be affected by these great events. Josiah was, after David, nearer to the Hebrew ideal of kingship than any other who had sat on the throne of Judah. His place in history is primarily due to the reforms which he carried through in 621 B.C., on the basis of a law-book found in the Temple. It is usual to identify this document with Deuteronomy, or with a substantial portion of it, mainly on the ground that the book demands that centralization of sacrifice which was the outstanding feature of Josiah's reforms, and makes modifications in existing practice which suggest that the principle was new. It is essentially a compromise between the natural human demand for some kind of cultus and the moral requirements of the

prophetic party, and includes a revision of the old law of
agricultural Israel, emphasizing repeatedly the humanitarian
and democratic spirit inherited from the genuine Israelite,
Aramæan tradition of the nomad age.

It is a striking fact that Josiah earned the commendation
of the greatest of Israel's prophets, not because he carried out
a complete reform of the cultus, but because he lived and
ruled in accordance with the democratic theories of prophetic
tradition. He " ate and drank and did justice and righteousness " (Jer. 22[15]). He was at one with his people, displaying
no aloofness or pride in his dealings with them and carrying
out his duties with a full sense of his responsibility to the
nation. In the administration of justice, the first of the tasks
of oriental monarchy, he had shown himself to be absolutely
fair, and had never taken advantage of his position to oppress
his subjects.

Jehoiakim was a complete contrast to his father, resembling
him only in his strength of character. He had been placed on
the throne by a foreign power, and could doubtless call on that
power for help in case of need. He had clearly not been
compelled to take the usual covenant or grant the normal
charters ; he was in Judah's declining years what Solomon
had been in the early days of the monarchy. He embarked on
extensive building schemes, for which, like Solomon, he employed forced labour, and he was indifferent to the claims of
justice. He had no respect for the traditions of his people,
either in secular or in religious life. His attitude towards the
prophets is well illustrated by the burning of Jeremiah's roll,
and he is the only king, whether of the north or of the south,
charged by the historian with the execution of a duly accredited
prophet of Yahweh. In him the autocratic principle had one
of its outstanding exponents.

Judah and the Chaldeans : the Fall of Jerusalem. Jehoiakim's foreign policy proved as dangerous as his domestic
government. Deserting the traditional isolation of Judah, he
threw in his lot with Egypt, and deserves credit for his loyalty
to his overlord. While he seems to have submitted nominally
to the Chaldeans after 605 B.C., he returned to his old allegiance
in 598 B.C., and tried to throw off the Babylonian yoke.
Nebuchadrezzar, the victor of Carchemish, had succeeded his
father, Nabopolassar, a few months after that battle, and he
was soon in Palestine. Jehoiakim died, either before Jerusalem
was besieged or shortly after the siege began, and his young
son, Jehoiachin, surrendered to the Chaldeans after a resistance of three months. The king was carried away to Babylon,

together with members of the better classes of the people to
the number of 3023 (the figures are derived from the note in
Jer. 52$^{28-30}$, which seems to be copied from an authentic
record) ; doubtless Nebuchadrezzar hoped thus to remove all
possible leadership. A third son of Josiah, named Mattaniah,
was placed on the throne, and his name was changed to
Zedekiah.

The new king resembled neither his father nor his eldest
brother. He was a man of comparatively mild nature, and
of good instincts and impulses, but he was fatally weak, and
quite unfit to deal with the difficult situation which confronted him. Egypt, close at hand, was constantly trying to
stir up revolt against Babylon, and there had arisen in Jerusalem itself a new aristocracy which entirely lacked the steady-
ing influence of tradition. Jeremiah sharply contrasts the
new nobility with the old, comparing the latter to a basket
of very good figs, and the former to a mass of fruit so rotten
as to be positively sickening to look at (Jer. 24). There were
better elements—we hear, in particular, of the family of
Shaphan—but they were overruled alike in domestic and in
foreign matters. Under these conflicting influences Zedekiah
vacillated between Egypt and Babylon. Once, it seems, he was
summoned to Babylon, and his loyalty was quickened by a
personal interview with Nebuchadrezzar. But in 588 B.C. he
took the fatal step of definite revolt against his overlord, apparently in conjunction with other peoples of Palestine, especially
the Ammonites. Egypt, as usual, promised help, but, as usual,
her help was futile. Jerusalem was besieged, and, though an
Egyptian army brought temporary relief with a demonstration
to the south, it either withdrew without fighting or was repulsed by the Chaldeans. Nebuchadrezzar himself was engaged
in military operations in the far north, at Riblah on the Orontes,
but his generals surrounded Jerusalem. The city, though
weakened by internal division and by famine bravely endured
horrors which are depicted for us in Lam. 2 and 4, until at
last, in 586 B.C. a breach was made in the walls and the king
fled. He was overtaken, carried to Riblah and blinded, the
last sight on which his eyes rested being the execution of his
sons. He was then taken to Babylon, to end his days as a
wretched prisoner.

Judah was now organized as a Babylonian province. The
walls of Jerusalem were broken down, and the temple destroyed
though the great altar remained and men offered sacrifice amid
the ruins of the main building. Gedaliah, a member of the
house of Shaphan, was appointed as the Babylonian official

in charge of the country, and Mizpah was made the seat of his Government. Under his wise and generous rule the country seemed likely to recover, but the jealousy of Ammon stirred up Ishmael, a scion of the house of David, treacherously to attack and murder him. Ishmael was unable to make any use of his deed, and was compelled to take refuge in Ammon, but Johannan, the officer in charge of the troops left in Judah, so dreaded the possibility of Chaldean vengeance that he insisted on taking the last remnants of the people down to Egypt, against the protests of Jeremiah. As a separate people and an individual state, Judah, like Samaria, had ceased to be.

5. THE RESTORED ISRAEL

The Exile. Politically, the capture of Jerusalem by Nebuchadrezzar was the end of the Jewish state, and from the day that the city fell, the nation has never had an independent native government in a land of its own. There was a short period from the middle of the second century B.C. to the middle of the first, when a practical independence was secured, but even then the country was still nominally a part of the Syrian kingdom. Yet the sense of nationality, indeed of peculiar separateness, has endured through the centuries, and to-day there is no people more conscious of its own identity than that of the Jews.

It is to its religion that Jewry owes this permanence, and, while the subject is of far more importance than the facts we have to trace, it lies strictly outside the scope of our present study. Our immediate task is rather to follow the course of events and see how the spiritual life of Israel worked in secular affairs, maintaining and strengthening the sense of unity and uniqueness which alone have made the endurance of the nation possible. The ancient Aramæan—we may fairly say, Mosaic—tradition could no longer directly affect the political constitution of Israel, but it could and did concentrate with the more force on the religious life, and so control in a real sense the national fortunes.

Archæological evidence goes to show that southern Palestine was left in a state of comparative desolation throughout the greater part of the sixth century B.C. Most of the larger towns were destroyed by Nebuchadrezzar, and, though peasant life may have continued, its work was carried on under remarkable difficulties. Unfortunately, hardly any historical inscriptions of the later Babylonian Empire have been recovered; Nebuchadrezzar, for instance, seems to have been much more interested

in the performance of his religious duties and in his building
operations than in his conquests and provincial administration.
We are thus left with little direct evidence as to the state of
Judæa during the period, and are compelled to fall back on
other indications. The condition of the country is, perhaps,
reflected in Lam. 1 and 3, and there are occasional references
which suggest that the country was particularly exposed to
raids from the wilderness, especially from the south. Semi-
pastoral tribes, such as the Edomites, easily made their way
into the country, and many of them gradually settled down
on the land, as the Israelites themselves had done centuries
earlier, though they do not seem to have occupied or rebuilt
any of the old cities. Nor did they form any conscious national
life of their own ; there was no community covering the whole
country. The great altar at Jerusalem still remained, and
was used for sacrifice, but the buildings which had surrounded
it lay in ruins, and any priesthood which survived there must
have been poor and scanty. There was much to be said for
Ezekiel's view that Yahweh had left the land.

The true Israelite tradition was carried on outside the
borders of Palestine. We may neglect the Egyptian communities ; neither that whose remains have recently been
recovered near Assouan, nor the descendants of those who
fled with Johannan after the murder of Gedaliah, played any
real part in the continuation of the national life. But in
Mesopotamia the Jews, even in the midst of their foreign
neighbours, maintained their own identity. The conditions
under which they lived were not oppressive ; they were given
freedom to live their own life, and later we hear of at least one
very big Jewish commercial establishment, the firm of Murashu
and Sons, in Babylon. The reform of Josiah had shown how
religious life could be carried on without sacrifice, for it is
clear that it was only seldom in the year that the majority of
Judahites could come up to Jerusalem. It is, at the same
time, inconceivable that men should have tried to live without
some external expression of their religion, and we may safely
assume that it was in the exile, or even earlier, that the first
beginnings of synagogue worship appeared.

There is reason to believe, also, that the Exile was a time
of literary activity. Two great prophets are commonly
assigned to this age, and, though there is a growing tendency
to locate the work of Ezekiel mainly or wholly in pre-exilic
Jerusalem, we can safely assign " Deutero-Isaiah " (Isa. 40–55)
to the years which preceded the Return. Further, it is
commonly held that much of our historical literature took

shape in Babylon. What documents exiled scribes could take with them, we do not know, but it is obvious that the Books of Kings could not have reached their present form till after the fall of Jerusalem, and their repeated appeal to extant annals suggests that, in some way or other, the royal records, and perhaps other " state papers," found their way into Babylonia. On the whole, we have a picture of a people who can be fairly contented and prosperous, and are in a position to maintain what they regard as the essentials of their national life, and even to reinforce, in some aspects, their sense of unity and of uniqueness.

For reasons which are still obscure, the situation of the exiles changed for the worse towards the end of the Babylonian Empire. There is in Deutero-Isaiah a note of hostility to Babylon which has hitherto been wanting. Perhaps the monotheistic tendencies of Nabuna'id led him to attack the peculiar faith of his Jewish subjects, as well as the cults of various Mesopotamian deities. But, whatever be the reason, there can be no doubt as to the feeling, which is manifested, not only in Deutero-Isaiah, but also in other prophetic utterances of the period, e.g. in Jer. 50, 51. In some way or other, Babylon had become another Egypt, the oppressor of the Jewish people.

Persia and the Return. Deliverance came, in a certain sense, with the conquest of Babylon by Cyrus. The Persian king completely reversed the religious policy of Nabuna'id (to which it seems he was to some extent indebted for his success), and not merely tolerated, but actively supported, the religions of many of the subject peoples including the Jews. The latter claimed him as the author of a decree which enjoined the rebuilding of the ruined temple at Jerusalem, and Jews were given permission to return to their own land. The first governor appointed under the new régime was Sheshbazzar, and it seems that for eighteen years little or no progress was made. With the arrival of Zerubbabel, however, a member of the old royal house of Judah, at the beginning of the reign of Darius, the work was undertaken in earnest and vigorously prosecuted. There are hints, too, which point to an attempt on Zerubbabel's part to carve out an independent principality for himself ; he seems to have been hailed in some quarters as the coming Messianic king (cf. Zech. 6⁹⁻¹⁵) and we know nothing of his last days. In fact a curtain falls over Judah and her people, not to be raised for three-quarters of a century.

But if we have no history of Judah during the first hundred years of Persian dominion, we can form some kind of picture of the conditions of life. Those who returned from Mesopotamia seem to have been comparatively few in number, and the land was in a state which might well have discouraged them. As we have seen, its civic population had been destroyed or dispersed and strangers from the south had settled in many places. The districts available were not particularly fertile, and we get a general impression of a discouraged, almost of a hopeless community. The religious interest was still fairly keen and the race of prophets was not yet extinct ; it is to this age that we normally attribute Malachi and the greater part of Isa. 56–66. But, again, it seems that we have here something of the old troubles, people falling into heathen worship, setting ritual above morality, ignoring the rights of personality.

Nehemiah. From this lifeless and dull process of deterioration the people was rescued by the energy and idealism of Nehemiah. He himself illustrates several points of interest in the general situation of Israel in the Persian Empire. He had attained to high position at court, without in any way sacrificing his racial or religious principles, and there was little or nothing to attract him in the situation of Palestine. But he was possessed by a fervour for his people and for his faith which was almost entirely lacking in Judah. It may have been the very isolation of the Jew in the empire which strengthened men's sense of uniqueness ; in their own land they had quite readily admitted elements which Nehemiah regarded as foreign, particularly from Samaria. With all this the new Governor would have nothing to do, for his conception of Judah was that of a " peculiar people," who must stand apart in every way from the rest of the world, and tolerate no admixture of blood or cult. His work, then, had a double aspect. On his arrival at Jerusalem in 444 B.C., he found the walls in ruins ; there is no direct evidence to show that they had ever been rebuilt since 586 B.C., though some scholars are inclined to suspect that there had been an attempt at revolt, perhaps under Zerubbabel, which had resulted in another siege and overthrow of the city. Many of the people were heavily in debt, and felt severely the incidence of taxation. The forces which we have already observed in the ninth and eighth centuries were once more at work, and the peasants were losing both their land and their freedom.

Nehemiah's first care was to rebuild the walls of the city itself. He had to overcome both the lethargy of his own people and the hostility of neighbouring officials and chieftains, led by Sanballat, governor of Samaria, Tobiah an Ammonite, and Geshem, an Arab. They used every artifice to try to interfere with his work, and went so far as to plot his assassination, and to threaten a charge of treason against him. But his energy and enthusiasm were infectious ; the wall was built in spite of opposition and mockery, while he was quite as clever as his adversaries, seeing through their plots and disregarding their threats. Probably he was secure in his position at the Persian court, and knew that his loyalty would not seriously be called in question by Artaxerxes.

Nehemiah then turned his attention to the amelioration of the economic and social condition of the people. He persuaded the wealthier Jews to surrender the lands and persons whom they had taken in pledge for debt—incidentally he tells us that men were in the habit of redeeming their fellow-countrymen who had fallen into slavery abroad—and relieved the burden of taxation to some extent by supplying the needs of his own court from his private resources. He then took steps to repopulate Jerusalem. It is clear that most of the people were anxious to live on their country estates and lands, but he found a certain number of volunteers, and filled in the gaps still left by a form of conscription. This done, he returned to Susa.

We do not know how long this first governorship of Nehemiah lasted, but we are told that he returned to Jerusalem again in 432 B.C. Once more he found conditions very far from what they should have been. The Temple was suffering from neglect, for the Levitical dues had not been paid, and the Levites themselves had been compelled to betake them to their ancestral homes in order to secure a living. Foreigners had been allowed to take a prominent place in Jewish life ; a grandson of Eliashib, the high-priest, had married a daughter of Sanballat, and Tobiah the Ammonite had been granted a residence within the Temple itself. The Sabbath was not being observed, and numbers of the people had married foreign wives, with the result that many of their children could not speak the language of their fathers. With characteristic energy, Nehemiah set himself to correct all these evils with a strong hand, and succeeded in laying down the principle of isolation, though there is no reason to doubt his loyalty to the Persian court.

Ezra. The reforms carried out by Nehemiah during his second period of office do not seem to have been permanent, and when next we hear of the little community, many of the evils have reappeared. But his principles had been accepted in certain quarters, and were reinforced by a fresh migration

from Mesopotamia, led by Ezra in 398 B.C.   He found to some
extent the same evils as those with which Nehemiah had dealt
on his second governorship.   He, however, was in no sense a
secular official, and his main concern was with the religious life
of the nation.   He is credited with the formal promulgation
of the law, read and expounded at a great assembly.   It is
usual to identify this law with those sections of the Pentateuch
classed as priestly, though it is probable that even these have
received additions since his time.   Ezra is the real founder
of Judaism as distinct from the earlier stages of the religion of
Israel.

   We know little of the fortunes of the Jews during the last
century of Persian dominion.   Josephus tells us that Bagoas,
the general of Artaxerxes III, who came to the throne in
358 B.C., " defiled the Temple and imposed tribute on the
Jews," and speaks of the people being " enslaved," but
ascribes their troubles to the sacrilegious murder of the high-
priest John by his brother Joshua in the Temple itself.   We
know, however, that there was widespread revolt against
Artaxerxes, especially in the west, and that he put it down
with ruthless cruelty.   We may, then, assume that Joshua's
action had a political aspect, and that the Jews were implicated
in the great revolt.

   The Greek Period : Egyptian Rule in Palestine.   Once again
the curtain falls, to be lifted only with the conquests of Alexander.   To the Jews it was immaterial who was the supreme
ruler, provided that he treated them fairly and gave them a
certain measure of freedom, especially in religious matters.
Persian dominion was now as unpopular with them as that of
Babylon had been, and the relations between the Jews and the
conqueror seem to have been friendly.   In particular, he transferred large numbers of them to his new city of Alexandria,
which was, for centuries, one of the most important Jewish
cities of the world, and developed its own characteristic type
of thought.   In the general mixture of nations who were to be
found there, Greek philosophy made a stronghold for itself, and
the combination of Jewish and Greek ideas had a profound
influence on the moulding of early Christian thinking.

   With the division of Alexander's empire, Palestine became
once more the meeting-place between the two great empires,
the Syrian and the Egyptian.   The centre of importance was, it
is true, shifting steadily westwards, and within a century of
Alexander's death the hand of Rome could be felt in the
eastern Mediterranean, but, for a time, the two great powers
could maintain their rivalry without serious interference from

the outside. The history of the third century B.C. is complicated, with varying movements and combinations of parties,
but Palestine was little affected thereby. The land remained
under the control of the Ptolemies, to whom Egypt had fallen,
though the Seleucids, the kings of Syria, cast jealous eyes on
it, and would not be satisfied till it had passed into their hands.
This conquest, however, was not achieved till the beginning of
the second century, and the third, which practically covers the
Egyptian rule of Palestine, was a time of comparative peace
and security for the Jews. The Ptolemies were mild rulers,
and, in particular, they made no attempt to interfere with
Jewish religious thought and practice. Judah had now entirely
abandoned the hope and ambition of independence and
conquest, and was satisfied with a foreign master, provided
that national characteristics and prejudices were respected.

The Seleucid Empire: Gradual Hellenization. From
198 B.C., however, when Palestine passed into the hands of
Antiochus III, the situation was very different. The Ptolemies
were content to be Egyptians; the Seleucids insisted on being
Greeks. They felt themselves called to be apostles of Greek
culture throughout their dominions, and, though in most cases
they succeeded only in imposing a thin veneer, they did at
least set an ideal for all the diverse nations under their sway.
Judæa was no exception, and, from the beginning of the second
century there grew up a party in the nation which aimed at
the adoption of Greek thought and customs. But, unlike other
peoples, the Jews contained a conservative element. There
were those among them who clung passionately to the ancestral
tradition, to the sacred language (by this time Hebrew had
given way to Aramaic as the popular speech), and to the God-
given law. The former class included many of the wealthier
and more prominent members of the community, and it is a
striking fact that the priests themselves seem to have taken a
leading part in the hellenizing process. In the absence of any
native secular head to the Jewish community, the high-priests
were the officials with whom the governing authority naturally
had to deal, and they were thus the first to come under the
influence of the new thought.

In a very real sense, the history of post-exilic Judaism is
the story of a conflict between the spirit and the world. It was
a genuinely religious enthusiasm, backed by the prophetic
message, which had restored the Temple and its full cultus.
Yet, by the end of the third century, the high-priesthood had
degenerated into an office which was almost entirely secular
and political. Certain duties had to be performed in connexion

with the worship of the people, but the only function reserved
to the high-priest was the task of purifying the nation on the
Day of Atonement, and we have Rabbinic evidence which
shows that even for this a high-priest might need the most
careful instruction and guidance from learned scribes. The
story of Israel during the second and first centuries B.C. does
not suggest that the majority of the high-priests were interested in religious matters, and their moral standard fell far
below that normally demanded of civilized man. They appear
to have absorbed the externals of Hellenistic culture, and to
have accepted its superficial agnosticism, without entering into
the true Greek respect for moral principle. In this, it is true,
they did not differ greatly from the great mass of their contemporaries, but they had behind them a long tradition of
ethical monotheism, which should have preserved them from
the more flagrant and shameful forms of iniquity. It seemed,
however, impossible for a Jew to take half measures in the
matter ; either he must belong whole-heartedly to the Hellenistic party, headed by the high-priests, or he must range
himself with the strict conservatives, or Hasidim, as they
began to be called, who clung with passionate intensity to the
religion of their fathers, and held national custom, even in
small matters, to be a part of that religion.

Antiochus Epiphanes. With the accession of Antiochus IV
(Epiphanes) in 175 B.C. the rivalry between the two parties
developed into open hostility. The Hellenists had now an
active patron in the king, and were not slow to use their
advantage. The high-priest Onias—one of the few in the line
who clung to the old tradition—was deposed by the court, at
the instance of his brother Jason, who paid an enormous price
for the honour. He in turn, however, fell before the intrigues
of a certain Menelaus, who could not claim even to belong to a
priestly family. This flaw in his title, naturally, passed unnoticed by Antiochus, who accepted from him a yet greater
bribe than Jason had given. But in 169 B.C., while the king
was engaged in an attempt to conquer Egypt, a rumour of
his death reached Palestine. Jason returned, drove Menelaus
into the citadel, and massacred a number of his supporters,
believing that he was now safe. But Antiochus was not
dead ; on the contrary, he was victorious, and was prevented
from adding Egypt to his dominions only by the threat of
Roman intervention. Thus baulked of the prize he had
coveted and almost won, he came back to Jerusalem in a
spirit of wild vindictiveness. The city was treated as though it
had been conquered in war, and the Temple was defiled and

18

despoiled of its rich treasures. Further, Antiochus determined that there could be no peace in Judæa unless the Jewish barbarian superstition were stamped out. The Temple, for all practical purposes, was turned into a sanctuary of Zeus, heathen sacrifices were offered on the altar of Yahweh, and were demanded elsewhere of every loyal subject ; circumcision, Sabbath observance, and the possession of a copy of the Law were made capital offences. The royal edicts were enforced with the utmost cruelty, and, for the first time in history, we have reliable and detailed records of a bitter religious persecution.

The Maccabæan Revolt. For nearly a year, as it seems, the faithful Jews suffered without retaliation, even submitting to massacre on the Sabbath rather than defile the holy day by resistance. But a new spirit arose. The attempt to enforce the royal edict of heathen sacrifice at Modin led to an out-break, in which the king's commissioner and his guards lost their lives. The leaders on the Jewish side were a certain Mattathias and his five sons, who fled to the hills and embarked on a guerilla warfare. Antiochus was too deeply concerned with events on his eastern frontier to take effective measures, and the Jewish bands, led by Judas, the third son of Mattathias, won victory after victory. The first really large army led against them was commanded by a prominent Syrian general named Lysias, who might have put down the revolt. But in 165 B.C. he heard of the death of Antiochus in the course of his campaign against the Parthians, and agreed to a compromise with Judas and his party. The Temple was to be purified and restored to its original purpose, and the Jews were to be accorded religious freedom, while Menelaus was allowed to retain the high-priestly office. The purification and rededication of the Temple are still celebrated in the Jewish winter festival of the Hanukkah.

The Maccabæan Priest-Kings. Judas had now won for the Hasidim all that they most earnestly desired. But he and his family seem to have been dissatisfied with what had been achieved and were bent on a career of actual conquest, leading to complete independence. Judas himself, after at least one more great victory, fell in battle at Elasa, and the leadership of the Jewish political patriots passed to his brother Jonathan. We cannot here follow in detail the whole course of events ; they are too closely bound up with the intricate history of the Seleucid kingdom, which itself was normally torn asunder by rival factions. Jonathan was an astute politician, just as Judas had been an inspiring military leader, and well

knew how to use the situation to the best advantage of himself
and of his people. In 158 B.C. he was allowed to return to
Palestine from the wilderness, and established himself at
Michmash. In 152 B.C. Jerusalem, except for the citadel,
was placed in his hands, and he was allowed to assume the high-
priesthood. By adroitly taking first one side and then the
other in the frequent civil wars, Jonathan secured possession
of the greater part of the Philistine plain, especially of Ashdod
and Ekron. In 145 B.C. he succeeded in taking a further step,
and commuted all future tribute to the Syrian court for a sum
of 300 talents. In 143 B.C., however, he fell into a trap laid
for him by Tryphon, the leader of one of the Syrian factions,
and was put to death.

Simon, the last surviving son of Mattathias, at once assumed
the leadership of the Jewish people. A later generation looked
back on him as the ideal Jewish ruler, and we have in
1 Macc. 14⁴⁻¹⁵ a Greek translation of a Hebrew panegyric on
him. The poet first lists his conquests, Joppa, Gazara,
Bethsur, and the citadel of Jerusalem itself, whose garrison
was at length starved out. But more important were the
peacefulness and security of his government, and the spirit of
justice which marked his rule. Under him the Jews achieved
practical independence and even issued their own coinage.
They were, however, still nominally subject to the Syrian
crown, and were liable to be reduced again to a position of
subordination. In 135 B.C. Simon was treacherously murdered by his own son-in-law, but his son, John Hyrcanus, at
once seized his authority. His reign opened inauspiciously,
for the Syrian king, Antiochus Sidetes, once more asserted his
sovereignty, and in 134 B.C. the Jews were compelled to dis-
mantle Jerusalem, submit to a general disarmament, and pay
both a lump sum as indemnity and a regular tribute. But
on the death of Antiochus Sidetes in 129 B.C. Syrian affairs
once more fell into confusion, and for sixty-five years the Jews
enjoyed complete political freedom.

The events of this short period of independence—the only
one the Jews have known since 586 B.C.—illustrate the lack
of real political genius on the part of the rulers of the people.
The nation was still divided into two great sections. On the
one hand, there were the supporters of the Maccabæan priest-
princes, aiming first of all at political power, and known to
history as the Sadducees. Over against them, and regarding
them with a prejudice which at times amounted to bitter
hatred, were the descendants of those who had, down to
the cleansing of the Temple in 165 B.C., supported Judas

Maccabæus, but had then withdrawn their aid, on the ground that religious freedom was all they needed. Hence arose the party known as Pharisees. Political power naturally remained almost continually with the Sadducees, and John Hyrcanus embarked on a career of genuine conquest. Territory to the east of the Jordan was occupied, and the Edomites were not merely conquered but forcibly compelled to adopt Judaism as their faith, a step which was to have momentous consequences for the Jews a century later. In the north, too, fresh land was acquired, and John overran Samaria, captured Shechem, and destroyed the Samaritan temple on Mt. Gerizim. In spite of the efforts of the Syrian king, Samaria too was destroyed and the ancient fortress of Bethshan taken.

John Hyrcanus died in 104 B.C. and was succeeded by his son Aristobulus, whose short reign of one year saw the conquest and the forcible conversion of the people of Galilee. Aristobulus is also remarkable for having been the first of the Maccabæans to assume the title of king, and his brother, Alexander Jannæus, ruled territories almost as extensive as those ascribed to David—perhaps even more extensive, since he could claim a considerable stretch of the coast, including the district of Ashdod and other Philistine cities.

On the death of Alexander Jannæus, in 76 B.C., his widow Alexandra became queen, and, for the only time in Jewish history, the Pharisees, her favourites, achieved political power. But they were no better than their predecessors, and on the death of the queen the Sadducees came back to power under her son, Aristobulus II. But two new factors now appeared. The one was Antipater, an Idumæan official who had a genius for intrigue, and the other was Rome, now taking an active part in the affairs of the East. Antipater attached himself to Hyrcanus, the brother of Aristobulus, and the conflict between the two was ended only in 63 B.C., when Pompey abolished Jewish kingship and incorporated Judæa in the province of Syria.

The Roman Period: Herod the Great. During the next thirty years, Rome herself was passing through a period of turmoil, revolution, and civil war. Through it all Antipater, and his greater son Herod, managed to retain their power, save for a brief spell when a Parthian invasion of Syria placed Aristobulus once more on the throne. But Herod secured from Rome the title of king and, with a Roman army at his back, made himself master of Jerusalem in 37 B.C. In spite of the domestic tragedies and private crimes which have stained his memory, Herod proved himself to be an able ruler and made some attempt to consider Jewish sentiment. His Edomite blood, however, was never forgotten, and to the end of his days he remained unpopular with his subjects in spite of the magnificent Temple which he built.

Roman Procurators. On the death of Herod in 4 B.C. his kingdom was divided ; Judæa was directly administered by a Roman procurator, whose seat was at Cæsarea, though he necessarily had to appear in Jerusalem from time to time, and a garrison was maintained in the castle overlooking the Temple. For the most part Roman Imperial Governors aimed at honest and impartial treatment of the provincials entrusted to them ; the corruption which stained so much of the administration of the later Republic was much less in evidence under the Cæsars. But Romans were apt to be rigid, unimaginative, and unsympathetic with people whose tradition they did not share and whose outlook they did not understand. It was particularly difficult for them to accept the point of view held by the Jews, a nation not only differing from Rome as east and west always differed, but unique among Orientals. In no other case had the government to deal with a people whose instincts, indeed whose very existence, was bound up with their religion. They were accustomed to despise the eastern cults, and better-class Romans held it a sign of decadence that these faiths penetrated the western Mediterranean. But they usually found the Oriental sufficiently catholic to admit almost any form of worship and to revere almost any deity ; the emperor-cult, for instance, officially imposed as the token of loyalty to the supreme power, seldom met with any opposition outside Palestine. Nor did they commonly find racial pride and a strong national tradition so strikingly in evidence as they were among the Jews ; in them they were faced with a problem which they entirely failed to solve.

To some extent the Roman government tried to meet the situation by special concessions. Officially the demand for sacrifice to the genius of the emperor was waived in their case, and the sanctity of Jerusalem was generally respected, though individual procurators sometimes erred in this matter. But it was the misfortune of Judæa that the land was small and, so it seemed to the imperial power, politically insignificant. The best type of Roman naturally wanted a wider sphere for his activities, and the procurators were commonly drawn from a lower social order and men of a baser character. In the whole list of governors there is not one who bears an ancient Roman name, and Felix, brother of Nero's freedman-favourite

Pallas, is a fair representative of the kind of man who was appointed to rule the most difficult district in the whole of the empire. It is not surprising that revolts were frequent, and, indeed, there was constant discontent which broke out into disturbance on the slightest pretext. The great majority of the movements were small and local, but once or twice the imperial government received warning from the spirit of the people, and was compelled to make concessions. Foreign taxation was always a grievance, and on at least one occasion the census which was connected with it led to a very serious outbreak.

The Emperor Claudius tried the experiment of placing the country under the rule of a native prince, and appointed Herod Agrippa king of Judæa. But he lived only three years after his ascension of the throne (A.D. 41–44), and even in that short time showed that he was too Jewish for Rome ; the experiment was not repeated, and the line of procurators was continued. Even the Roman historian, Tacitus, admitted that the methods of these men were too much for the patience of the Jews, and in A.D. 66 the great revolt began.

As in Maccabæan days, the Jews were able to carry on guerilla warfare with some success against such forces as could be spared to act immediately. Doubtless the leaders of the nation were inspired by minor victories to believe that the triumphs of the sons of Mattathias would be repeated in their own day. But Judas and his brothers had won the freedom and independence of Judah, less through their own courage and ability than through the weakness and division of the dominant power. Now the situation was reversed ; Rome was united (the disturbances of the years A.D. 68–70 were an incident which did not affect the main issue), and it was the Jews who were torn by factions. To the older parties of the Pharisees and Sadducees was now added a third, that of the Zealots. They formed the extreme wing of the Jewish nationalists, and would hear of no compromise, either with Rome or with their fellow-countrymen. They had been in existence as a party for at least forty years before the final war, and their main stronghold was in Galilee. To the natural Jewish characteristics they added a fervid and passionate Messianic belief which made them ready to stake everything on the chances of success. Like other Jews, they failed to appreciate the true strength of Rome, and did not realize that, if the empire chose to take the matter seriously and put forth its strength, the Jewish national forces could not hope to hold out against the enemy. The best prospect for the Jews was a resistance which should lead to some kind of arrangement by which better government could be secured. But the rift which the Zealots created not only destroyed any opportunity the people might have had of making resistance : it led to excesses which made any kind of compromise impossible.

The story of the last days may be read in Josephus ; here we must be content with a bare outline of the main events. Vespasian took the field in A.D. 67 with adequate forces—those of the province of Syria were hardly sufficient. He spent a year in slow but sure reduction of the country, from north to south, and was about to attack Jerusalem in earnest when the news of Nero's death reached him. On the instigation of his immediate superior, Mucianus, he entered the lists as a candidate for the imperial crown, and the Jews were allowed another year in which to strengthen their material defences and to weaken their strength by inner conflicts. At length Titus, son of Vespasian, appeared with an army ; and, after a desperate resistance, involving frightful suffering to the besieged, Jerusalem was taken, its walls broken down, and its Temple burnt. The last of all Jewish attempts to win political independence had ended in disaster.

But the Jewish people did not die. Their national spirit was still maintained by their tradition and by their faith. Even the triumph of the daughter faith of Christianity did not affect the Jewish sense of unity and uniqueness. For nearly two thousand years the nation has retained its identity largely owing to the ceaseless persecution to which it has been subjected. Whether it will ever again reach the position of a political entity, none can say. But it has left to the world lessons of political life, especially in its insistence on the supreme value of human personality, and the primary demand for a recognition of a spiritual factor in organized society, which the world at large can neglect only at its peril.

BIBLIOGRAPHY

H. W. Robinson, *The History of Israel : its Facts and Factors.*
N. H. Baynes, *Israel among the Nations.*
A. Lods, *Israel from its Beginnings to the Middle of the Eighth Century.*
A. Lods, *The Prophets and the Rise of Judaism.*
W. O. E. Oesterley and T. H. Robinson, *A History of Israel.*
E. R. Bevan, *Jerusalem under the High Priests.*
A. H. M. Jones, *The Herods of Judæa.*

There are many relevant and valuable chapters in the *Cambridge Ancient History.*

PART III

THE RELIGION OF THE BIBLE

X. THE EARLY BACKGROUND OF HEBREW RELIGION

THE words of Jahweh to Moses in Ex. 33[23], " I will take away mine hand, and thou shalt see my back : but my face shall not be seen," might be taken as symbolic of the aspect in which Hebrew religion presents itself to our inquiries. The face which it presented to the ancient world is veiled in a darkness only feebly illuminated by the sources at our disposal. With the coming of the great prophets the later stages of its development stand out in a light so bright that it only emphasizes the darkness in which the origin and the early stages of the pre-prophetic religion of Israel are still shrouded.

This is due partly to the relative unimportance of the Hebrew people among the numerous small peoples of the ancient East. They were not sufficiently interesting to their more important neighbours to cause a reflection of their religious beliefs and habits in contemporary records. It is, however, much more due to the fact that the development of the prophetic religion produced on the one hand an obliteration of many characteristics of the early religion which seemed to the prophets unworthy of the new conception of Israel's God put forward so passionately by them : on the other hand, the ultimate effect of the prophetic protest was a drastic recasting of the traditions of the people in such a way as to throw the colouring of later religious conceptions over the early history of the nation.

A further difficulty lies in the fact, pointed out a quarter of a century ago by Professor Driver in his Schweich Lectures, *Modern Research as Illustrating the Bible*, that excavation, from which we might have hoped for some light on the characteristic forms of early Hebrew religion, shows no sharp break between the Canaanite and Hebrew occupation of the sites hitherto excavated, a fact which subsequent excavation has in the main amply confirmed.

These preliminary considerations must accordingly be our apology for the tentative and provisional nature of the positions here advanced. Our inquiry will fall into three main divisions. We shall first attempt a brief survey of the general character of the religion of the ancient East about the time when the Hebrew people first emerge into the light of history, that is, about the beginning of the second millennium B.C. We shall then go on to describe, as far as our sources allow, the character of the religion of Canaan, the immediate environment in which the Hebrews found themselves on entering the land which later writers regarded and described as the land of promise. Lastly, we shall touch on the very difficult and obscure problem of the nature of the religion which the Hebrews brought with them when they entered Canaan.

In the traditions of the Hebrew people concerning their own origins two great ancient civilizations play an important part, those of Mesopotamia and Egypt. The sagas of Genesis represent the ancestor of the Hebrews as coming into Canaan from Mesopotamia, while the Moses sagas reflect the tradition referred to by Hosea in the words, " Out of Egypt have I called my son." Both these countries exercised a profound cultural and political influence on Canaan during the second millennium B.C., an influence which is abundantly attested by recent archæological evidence. A third important source of cultural influence is to be found in the relations between Canaan and the successive Hittite kingdoms. In the Hebrew traditions of the settlement in Canaan we find Hittites mentioned as occupying the hill country of Judah, and there is good ground for believing that before the arrival of the Jebusites Jerusalem was a Hittite city.

A fourth source of influence revealed by excavational evidence comes from the Mediterranean. The results of excavations at Byblos and Ras Shamra show ancient and well-established trade connexions between the coastal cities of Palestine and various centres of Mediterranean civilization, and the settlement of an Ægean people, known to us by their Egyptian name of Pelestiu, or Philistines, on the southern coast of Palestine, had a decisive effect on the course of Hebrew history. Mr. Starkey's excavations at Tell Duweir, the site of ancient Lachish, have shown the presence of Ægean influence in an inland city.

Then we have the recently discovered evidence of the Nuzi and Kirkuk tablets, showing that the Horites, formerly regarded as the negligible remnants of a troglodyte race of aboriginal inhabitants of Palestine, dispossessed by the incoming Hebrews, are in reality the Hurrians, an important group of mixed racial elements, who were forced to move southward from their home around Harran into Palestine about the

seventeenth century B.C.   Professor Speiser has shown that
their laws and social and religious customs throw interesting
light on incidents of the patriarchal narratives in Genesis.

Hence it is clear that in order to understand the cultural
background of the Hebrew people we must know something
of the general religious and cultural pattern presented by these
intermingled elements.   Modern research has shifted the
emphasis formerly laid on the importance of the study of
pre-Islamic Arab religion and social organization as the main
source of light on the early religion of the Hebrews.   While
it is probably true that the various waves of Semitic invasion
of what is not quite accurately called " the Fertile Crescent,"
producing in turn the Semitic conquerors of Mesopotamia,
the Amorite kingdom, the Aramæan settlements, and ultimately the Hebrew settlement in Canaan, flowed out from
Arabia and originally possessed a nomad type of culture, it is
probably equally true that when the first wave of Hebrew
settlement, represented by the Abraham saga, entered Canaan,
the original nomad element had already been largely transformed by the influence of Mesopotamian culture.

We shall return to the question of the nomad element in
Hebrew traditions later when we come to deal with the
third part of our subject, namely, the nature of the religion
which the Hebrews brought with them when they entered
Canaan.

Our first task is somewhat simplified by the fact that, in
spite of many important differences, the various civilizations
of which we have spoken as contributing to the Canaanite
culture pattern possessed certain broad characteristics in
common.   In the first place, we find from the evidence at our
disposal that all these civilizations had arrived at a type of
social organization in which the institution of the kingship
was central.   In Egypt the Pharaoh was divine, both in life
and in death.   In Mesopotamia, from very early times, the
association between the king and the god was so close that in
the central acts of the great seasonal rituals the king took the
place of the god, suffering, dying, and triumphant.   When we
remember that in the development of Hebrew religion the
kingship of Jahweh found abundant and emphatic expression
in the ritual psalms and in many other ways, the significance
of the place of the king in the religious life of the ancient
East becomes apparent.

But significant as the kingship may be in itself, its importance is still more evident when the function of the king is seen
in relation to the general religious pattern of the ancient East.

The predominant trend of life was agricultural, although war and commerce were assuming an increasing importance. Those aspects of human behaviour which may be characterized as religious were mainly concerned with the control of the powers upon which the fertility of crops, herds, and the human species seemed to depend. Hence the activities directed to this end assumed a seasonal character which followed the cycle of the agricultural year. Such fundamental myths as those of Tammuz in Mesopotamia, or of Osiris in Egypt, are in origin agricultural, and represent the vital drama of dying and reviving vegetation. Other elements, such as solar and astral cults, mummification rituals, and other subsidiary ritual activities, entered into and complicated the central fertility aspect of the cult. But the general pattern stands out clearly from our sources. We find in all excavations a great complex of sacred buildings, ziqqurats, pyramids, temples, and tombs, which constitute the focus of the religious activities of the community. At the turning points of the year, especially in the spring and the autumn, rituals took place of which the king was the centre, and which enacted the drama of the dying and rising vegetation symbolized by a divine figure, Osiris, Tammuz, or Marduk, as the case might be.

Hence, at the period with which we are dealing, the beginning of the second millennium B.C., we find that the king, representing both the god and the people, is the centre of great emotional religious activities whose object is to secure for the community those material benefits upon whose continuance the well-being of the community depends. These activities had assumed what we might almost call a stereotyped form, and involved the existence of an organized body of people possessing the knowledge of the right way in which the ritual must be performed and of the myth which embodied the situation enacted in the ritual. It is possible that in the beginning a single individual possessed the knowledge and the magical powers in virtue of which he became the focus of the religious activities of the community, and that with the increasing complexity of urban life a devolution took place. The god became the embodiment of the mysterious powers whose control had been the original purpose of the ritual ; the priest became the depository of the sacred knowledge necessary for the right performance of the ritual ; while the king, still representing the god in the great annual rituals, came to be the centre of the secular activities of the communities, the head of the state for the purposes of war, politics, and justice, and, as representing the god, the owner of the land.

Early Mesopotamian sources point to the existence of " priest-kings," of whom the mysterious figure of Melchizedek may have been a representative surviving in Canaan in the time of Abraham.

The general pattern of the annual ritual as seen, for example, in the Babylonian New Year Festival, consisted of the preparation of the sacred buildings by purificatory rites, some of them symbolic of elements in the myth. Then the king went through a ceremony in which he divested himself of his regalia at the door of the shrine, made a confession to the priest, who struck him on both cheeks and then restored to him the emblems of his kingship. This part of the ritual probably represents an earlier ritual killing of the king when his strength showed signs of waning. Then came the central and probably secret part of the ritual, the dramatic representation of the death of the god, followed by his resurrection. A ritual combat was an essential part of the ritual, representing the triumph of the god over an adversary, Horus over Set, Marduk over Tiamat, and, doubtless, other gods over other foes in the many centres of the ritual. A memory of this element of the ritual survives in Hebrew poetry in the myth of the fight between Jahweh and the dragon.

A very early and essential element in the ritual was a sacred marriage, in which we know from early evidence that the king played the part of the god. Many excavated sites show the existence of the sacred processional road, the *via sacra*, and literary evidence shows that a sacred procession of the king, representing the god, with his consort, and a retinue of lesser divinities and visiting gods, was another important and probably popular feature of the annual festival.

A final element which may be mentioned was a ceremony called " the fixing of destinies " which took place at some point during the New Year Festival at Babylon. It probably consisted in the performance of certain magic rites by which the gods in council determined the fortunes of the state and the individual for the coming year.

Thus the general setting of religious life in the ancient East presents us with the picture of a complex of sacred buildings, sacred persons, and sacred acts, all existing for the purpose of securing by ritual, *i.e.*, by magical, means the prosperity and material well-being of the state and of the individuals composing it. Not only the great matters, the movements of the heavenly bodies and the changes of the seasons, eclipses, pestilences, wars, and affairs of state were capable of being influenced and controlled by ritual, but the small daily matters of the individual's life, business ventures, private quarrels, sickness, headache, toothache, birth, marriage, and death, all had their appropriate rituals whose pattern reflected the pattern of the great central rituals.

Against such a background the multiplicity of gods with their many names is seen to be of less significance than the powers and functions which they represent, Hence we can understand the ease with which such a symbol of virility and fertility as the bull could be transferred from one god to another. We find him in Mesopotamia, Anatolia, Crete, and Egypt. He stands for Hadad as for Jahweh. In such a background we have to do, not with personalities, but with forces.

Another point of great importance for the understanding of the religious background of the period with which we are occupied is that the meaning of sin is very different from that which emerges as a consequence of the prophetic discovery of a God with a moral character. Enmeshed in the mysterious machinery of such a system as that which we have been describing, the individual never knew when some inadvertent omission or breach of ritual might not expose him to the attack of hostile powers. Hence a vast mass of early and late Babylonian texts deal with ritual means of averting the consequences of such "sins of ignorance," and in this light we can understand the survival in early Hebrew ritual legislation of provision for such sins.

One more point may be dealt with before we turn to the second part of our task. Under such conditions as we have described religion was almost entirely concerned with the present life and its material considerations. Any preoccupation of religion with the life after death was largely in the way of ritual protection for the living from the unpleasant attentions of the spirits or ghosts of those who had died under unfortunate circumstances or whose funeral ritual had been neglected. The state of the dead in the " land of no return " as described by the spirit of Enkidu to his friend Gilgamesh is an utterly miserable and hateful existence, dark and hopeless. This at least holds good for Mesopotamia. Egypt, with its extraordinary preoccupation with death, had developed in connexion with the elaborate ritual of mummification a somewhat different picture of the life after death. Nevertheless, the life lived by the devout Egyptian in the fields of the blessed was one of purely material enjoyments, and although in theory the judgement of Osiris which determined the fate of the soul of the deceased was a moral one, yet in practice every one who could afford the cost of even the cheapest form of mummification could thereby secure union with Osiris, apotheosis, and the happy immortality which it involved. But, unless perhaps in rare cases, mummification was not practised either in Mesopotamia or in Palestine, and it is doubtful whether the Egyptian conception of the after-life really enters into the background of Hebrew religion. In Canaan, Mesopotamian influence was probably, in this respect at least, stronger than Egyptian.

It is possible that fuller knowledge of Hittite and Hurrian sources will in the future add further details to this general picture of the religious background of the ancient East and may explain certain points in which Hebrew forms of myths differ from the related Mesopotamian forms, but it is not likely that the main outlines of the picture here drawn will undergo any material alteration.

Until quite recently our knowledge of religious conditions in Canaan at the time of Hebrew settlement there was almost entirely dependent upon the testimony of the Old Testament writers, supplemented by the material results of excavation in Palestine, and by the late and scanty information preserved in the fragments of Philo of Byblos. But a very valuable source of early documentary evidence has been found during the last six years in the French excavations at Ras Shamra, the site of a city anciently known as Ugarit, an important sea-port in the second millennium B.C. on the northern coast of Syria, near the modern Latakia. The material consists of a large number of tablets containing a series of poems of ritual and religious significance. The contents of these tablets have enormously enlarged the boundaries of our knowledge of the religion of Palestine and Syria at the time when the Hebrews were beginning to settle in the country. We have in them, in spite of much that is still uncertain, a remarkably detailed picture of the Canaanite pantheon, the priesthood, the seasonal rituals, the sacrificial system and its nomenclature, together with a number of important myths whose close relation to the ritual is immediately apparent. The fact that the language of these documents is a Semitic dialect closely related to Hebrew, Aramaic, and the language of the various inscribed monuments already known to us from Palestine and Syria, suggests that we may legitimately use the evidence of these tablets to form a picture of the general religious and social black-ground of Canaan in the middle of the second millennium B.C.

Hence we shall now consider in turn the three lines of evidence which contribute to such a picture.

First there is the evidence of the Old Testament writers.

19

As far as the social and religious conditions of Canaan are concerned, the picture presented by the sagas of Genesis is remarkably devoid of detail and local colour. We should not know from Genesis that Canaan in our period was a region of many small city states with a relatively high culture, as the evidence of the Tell el-Amarna Letters and of excavation shows. References to sacred places, trees, wells, and stones are isolated from any cultural context. The sacred standing stone at Bethel was, as the analogy from Gezer and other sites suggests, in all probability part of an elaborate Canaanite sanctuary where Jacob sought favourable omens for his journey. The mention of Philistines in Canaan at this period is clearly an anachronism, and, like other traits in the book, shows that the compiler of the stories of the patriarchs was not in a position to give us an accurate historical picture of Canaan in the early part of the second millennium B.C., but was wholly concerned with the religious value of the stories for his own times. But the body of myths preserved in the first section of the book, and such incidents as the sacrifice of Isaac, the covenant ritual in chap. 15, and the allusion to the practice of sacred prostitution in the story of Judah and Tamar give hints of the conditions of belief and practice in Canaan at the time when the Hebrews entered the land.

Further light on the state of religion in Canaan at the time of the Hebrew settlement there is afforded by the large number of prohibitions contained in the various layers of Pentateuchal legislation. These prohibitions imply that the forbidden practices existed among the Hebrews, and although only some of these practices are characterized as Canaanite by the legislators, it seems reasonable to infer that most of them belong to the general pattern of the fertility cult which, as we know from the evidence of excavation and from the Ras Shamra texts, existed in Palestine before the entry of the Hebrews. It is only possible here to refer briefly to some of these prohibited practices to illustrate their general significance

First of all we find the prohibition of sacred prostitution both male and female, and the reference to the " hire " of the temple prostitutes shows that it was the usual custom for such gains to go into the temple revenues. Moreover, various passages, some showing signs of editing to remove what the later religious point of view felt to be discreditable elements in the history of the religion of the nation, prove the existence of this institution at an early stage in Hebrew religion and of its survival to a comparatively late date.

We also have the prohibition of ritual tattooing and of

ritual disfigurement and mutilation as a funerary custom, both probably elements in Canaanite religious practice. One of the most frequent objects of denunciation is the cult of the *masseboth* and the *asheroth*, the standing stones and the sacred poles, generally referred to in connexion with the cult of the Canaanite *bamoth*, or high places. These cult objects should not be thought of as isolated elements, but rather as integral parts of an elaborate religious system, connected with a temple, as at Gezer and other excavated sites, and implying the existence of the general ritual pattern in which they were important symbols. Indeed, the main significance of these prohibitions which we are discussing is that they imply a condemnation, not of ritual practices in general, but of certain particular implications of the type of ritual which they represented. This is borne out by the prohibition of customs which in themselves appear perfectly harmless. There is, for instance, the prohibition in the Book of the Covenant of the practice of seething a kid in its mother's milk. The evidence of the Ras Shamra texts shows that this practice formed part of a fertility ritual, and suggests that the prohibition was not due to humanitarian motives but to the knowledge of its original ritual meaning.

Not only prohibitions, however, bear witness to the nature of the early religious environment of the Hebrew immigrants into Canaan, but there are survivals in Hebrew ritual itself which point in the same direction. We have already spoken of the survival of a ritual provision for " sins of ignorance " and its implication. Certain very striking elements in the ritual of the Day of Atonement suggest the survival of ancient sanctities, of dim fears of hostile spiritual powers. The ritual by which the sins of the community are transferred to the " scape-goat " which is then driven out into the desert for Azazel, bear the closest resemblance to the common Babylonian *puhu*, or substitution ritual, which is found in so many ritual texts, early and late. Another similar survival is the grim water-ordeal for the wife suspected of unfaithfulness, a ritual which has its counterpart both in the early Assyrian laws and in later codes.

Finally, at the very heart of early Hebrew religion, in its great seasonal feasts, we find important evidence of the presence of elements which cannot but suggest the influence of a culture pattern which the Hebrews were either familiar with before their entry into Canaan or, more probably, which they came into contact with when they settled in the land. Here the first part of our discussion to some extent coalesces

with the second because of the long-continued presence of
Mesopotamian influence in Canaan.   But a careful study of the
ritual prescriptions for the Hebrew seasonal festivals, together
with the evidence of the ritual psalms, affords a strong pre-
sumption that a central feature of early Hebrew religion was
a great New Year Festival whose outline in many ways resembled the general pattern of the corresponding Canaanite and
Babylonian pattern.   As we are dealing at present with the
question of the Canaanite background, and as the Hebrew
evidence does not necessarily prove that the forms referred to
are due to the influence of the Canaanite background, we shall
leave the discussion of the point until we come to deal with the
evidence from the Ras Shamra texts.

Turning now to the excavational evidence, we find first
of all that in all the important city sites excavated the existence is attested, by the middle Bronze Age, of a developed
cult of the local god with temple, priesthood, and all the
necessary cult-vessels and other sacred objects connected with
the cult.   The temple arrangements show the existence of a
sacrificial system the elaborate nature of which is further
attested by the evidence of the Ras Shamra texts.   Although,
according to Hebrew tradition, the institution of the kingship
whose religious significance in the ancient East we have already
referred to, was adopted by the Hebrews comparatively late,
yet it is probable that earlier local attempts, such as those of
Abimelech at Shechem, of Gideon, and possibly others of which
no record has been preserved, point to the influence of Canaanite
kingship upon the Hebrews at an early date in their history.
The existence of the institution in Canaan is abundantly proved,
both by documentary evidence such as that of the Tell el-
Amarna Letters and the Ras Shamra texts, and by such excavational evidence as the sarcophagus of Ahiram at Byblos,
or the seal of Atanahili at Taanach.   The latter affords such
an interesting example of the nature of the Canaanite religious
background in the middle of the second millennium B.C. that
in spite of its familiarity it may be briefly referred to here.
The seal, a cylinder seal of the common Mesopotamian type,
contains a cuneiform inscription giving the name of the king
and his father, and stating that he is the servant of Nergal, a
Mesopotamian deity.   The pictorial part of the seal represents the king clothed in a Mesopotamian *kaunakés* doing
homage to the god, who has the horned cap characteristic of
gods on Mesopotamian seals and is dressed in an Egyptian
tunic, while Egyptian hieroglyphic signs, such as the familiar
ankh symbol, occupy the space round the figures.   No better

example could be adduced of the way in which Babylonian and Egyptian cultural influence mingled in the Canaanite background.

Although the well-known Samaria ivories belong to the early period of the Israelite monarchy, yet their close resemblance to the Nimrud ivories and those from Arslan Tash, together with the predominantly Egyptian character of their art motives, bears further witness to the presence and influence of the mixed Canaanite religious background upon Hebrew culture.

The chief importance of the excavational evidence from Canaan during the middle and late Bronze periods lies in the great mass of cult objects, figurines, amulets, seals, vessels of every kind, censers, all bearing witness to the existence of an elaborate ritual involving the existence of sacred buildings and sacred persons as the focus of a cult through which the desires and needs of the community were expressed. Baudissin describes the general nature of Canaanite religion in the second millennium B.C. in the following words : " It is not possible to speak of a religion of the West Semites as an independent and homogeneous thing, since the Aramæan peoples who are comprised under this designation show in their religion as far back as we can trace them not only the influence of the Babylonians, which is also true in the case of the Phœnicians, but also the possession of conceptions of the gods almost completely identical with those of the Babylonians, a fact which goes to prove how much the Aramæans borrowed from the Babylonians, and how much the latter borrowed from the former " (*Adonis und Eshmun*, p. 2).

This statement may be supplemented by a quotation from a recent important book by Professors Graham and May entitled *Culture and Conscience* : " The labours of the excavator have brought to light in Palestine several interesting examples of late Bronze Age temples. A study of the remains of these buildings and of the surviving objects associated with them cannot fail to leave the impression that in this age the influence of the great neighbouring cultures, especially those of Mesopotamia and of the Nile Valley, was brought to bear more directly on this area. The world's way of life was being more firmly than ever imposed on Canaan ; nor is it difficult to see why this is so. While the Hyksos power remained of imperial status, their wide political connections made for such an interpenetration of cultures ; and Palestine, by reason of its location, became a natural focal point of diverse cultural influences. After the collapse of their authority this clashing of influence was intensified, because the Hyksos adventure had made the entire Near Eastern world, and especially Egypt, conscious of the strategic importance of the Syro-Palestinian corridor, which, from this time on, became a bone of contention between the great powers. It is, perhaps, a sound generalization that it was the audacious success of the Hyksos which stimulated the rise in the Near Eastern world of genuine, conscious, political imperialism ; and in such an age any strategic and debateable area is bound to experience diverse cultural influences." And again—" On the whole, the evidence points to the conclusion that, while Mesopotamia stimulated most the faith of this area, Egypt was more influential in the ordering of it." (op. cit. pp. 102–5).

This general view of the nature of the Canaanite religious background in the second millennium B.C. is reinforced and amplified in detail by the new evidence of the Ras Shamra texts. What can only be inferred from the excavational evidence and the witness of the Old Testament writers is set out clearly and decisively in these documents. They give us a picture of the prosperous life of an important coastal city whose cultural history has already been traced back beyond the beginning of the second millennium, a city where many streams of culture mingled, Babylonian, Egyptian, Mycenæan Hittite, Hurrian, together with native Canaanite elements In the texts we have in poetic form a group of myths, clearly of a ritual nature, which show a close relation to the general myth and ritual pattern prevalent in the ancient East at this period. The material is far too extensive to be described in detail, but an excellent summary of the nature of the texts and of their bearing on Hebrew religion may be found in Dr. J. W. Jack's monograph, *The Ras Shamra Texts and their Bearing on the Old Testament* (T. & T. Clark).

The general character of the myths and the rituals is agricultural, and directed to the securing of the seasonal rains and of the fertility of crops and herds. The principal cycle of myths takes the form of the story of a conflict between Aleyan-Baal, who represents the principle of fertility, and Mot who represents the opposing forces of sterility and death We have the myth of the death and resurrection of the god in various forms, and similarly of the ritual combat. There is a reference to a conflict between Baal and a seven-headed dragon which presents close resemblances with the reference in Hebrew poetry to the conflict between Jahweh and the dragon. The ritual of the sacred marriage recurs repeatedly and the connexion between the institution of temple pros titutes and that ritual is fully established. The evidence shows the existence of an elaborate sacrificial ritual, and the names of the various types of offering present surprising parallels with the Levitical nomenclature in the Old Testament, proving that many of these technical terms which Old Testament criticism has hitherto regarded as the product of the post-exilic period belong in fact to the early background of Hebrew religion. Indeed, parallels with the language of the Old Testament are so numerous as to prove beyond the possibility of doubt that the religious situation portrayed by these texts must be regarded as an essential element in the early background of Hebrew religion.

A brief quotation from Professor S. A. Cook's indispensable book *The Religion of Ancient Palestine in the Light of Archæology*, in which he refers to recent excavational work at Beth-Shan, may serve to bring this part of our discussion to a close : " Of Beth-Shan it must suffice to say that the cultural history points to Egypt, Crete (linear signs), and Cyprus, to the Anatolian Hatti, and to Babylonia. It supplements the discoveries at Byblos, and gives us a vivid picture of the religious and other conditions in this part, at least, of Palestine, and of the indebtedness to surrounding lands " (*op cit.* p. 98).

Thus the broad conclusions which may be drawn from these three lines of evidence are that the religious background of Canaan in the second millennium B.C. was characterized by the intermingling of many streams of influence, and in particular by the influence of Mesopotamia and Egypt. The type of religion thus produced was adapted to the nature of the country and was predominantly agricultural. The king had the same central place in the cult, and the main lines of the cult followed the pattern of a seasonal ritual in which the death and resurrection of the god, represented by the king, a ritual combat, a sacred marriage, and a procession were the main features. Round these central elements were grouped the institutions of the temple and its cultus, the priesthood, the sacrificial system, and all the lesser details of daily religious life by which the desires, needs, and emotions of the community were expressed.

It is in such a picture as this, rather than in the assumption of a primitive animism displaying itself in a cult of sacred trees, wells, and pillars, however true the assumption may be, that the actual early background of Hebrew religion as it developed itself in Canaan is to be envisaged. It is possible that such an animism or animatism underlies the beginnings of culture in the Nile Valley, in Mesopotamia, and in Canaan ; but such antecedents lie so far back in the mists of remote time that it is difficult to assign any definite place to them in the shaping of the general religious background of the Hebrews. Religion in Canaan had for so long been exposed to many streams of external cultural influence that it is almost impossible to determine whether any particular feature considered in isolation, such as the presence in various parts of Canaan of sacred trees, wells, and eminences, represents a genuine survival of primitive animistic beliefs, or a simplification and degradation of elements belonging to a more developed stage of religion.

There is one more point to be dealt with before we conclude this survey, namely, the nature of the religion which the Hebrews brought with them when they came into Canaan. Two separate problems meet us here : first, the question of the nature of the religion of those Hebrew settlers whose movements are represented by the sagas of Genesis; and secondly, the nature of the Jahweh-cult which, according to the tradition of Exodus, was promulgated by Moses among the Hebrew tribes who had escaped from Egypt, during their sojourn in the wilderness of Sinai. With regard to the first question it can only be said that there is not enough evidence in Genesis to warrant any conclusions. The point of view of the compiler of the stories is that of a much later stage in the history of Hebrew religion. For instance, we find Abraham, in the story of the destruction of the cities of the plain, occupied with the problem of the moral government of the world, and Jahweh is " the Judge of all the earth." We hear of altars being built in various places, but nothing concerning a priesthood, a cult, or sacrifices, except in the case of Noah. There are elements in the Jacob-saga which point to a very early stage in religious development, for instance, the story of Jacob's conflict with a supernatural adversary. We also have details such as the account of the institution of circumcision which clearly reflect the desire of a later age to refer the origin of what had come to be regarded as a distinctive Jewish rite to the ancestor of the race. Hence, while it is probable that the religion of the first Hebrew settlers in Canaan did not differ greatly from that of the inhabitants of the country, we have not the necessary material to construct even a conjectural picture of the nature of their gods and of their religious practices.

With regard to the second point, the Hebrew tradition represents Jahweh as being the god of the Midianites, apparently a pastoral desert tribe, and associates him with Sinai as a god of thunder, lightning, and storm. But for the nature of his cult we are dependent upon the early ritual legislation in the Book of the Covenant, and there the Hebrews are already treated as an agricultural people, settled in Canaan. The Passover has been treated by Robertson Smith and others after him as containing elements of a nomadic or pastoral type of ritual, combined later with an agricultural seasonal festival. This is possible, but the details are capable of another interpretation. With regard, then, to the original nature of Jahwism it can only be said that in the form in which the records have reached us, it is impossible to differentiate the hypothetical nomadic element in the religion from the later agricultural form of the cult. While it is undeniable that the tradition of a sterner, simpler form of religion connected with the desert underlies the prophetic protest against the Canaanite type of cult, it must be remembered that there are at least three possible sources of such a nomadic tradition. It is generally admitted that all the successive waves of Semitic settlement in the Fertile Crescent, as it is somewhat erroneously called, came originally from Arabia. Hence the nomadic tradition may just as well have existed among the Semitic inhabitants of Mesopotamia, the Aramæans, the Amorites, or the Canaanites themselves, as among the ancestors of the Hebrew people. Secondly, the tradition of a wilderness sojourn is too deeply imbedded in the records of the Hebrews to be devoid of historical foundation, but it is complicated by the fact, now generally accepted, that not all the component elements of what was later the Hebrew nation were in Egypt and passed through the experiences of the bondage and the wilderness sojourn. Hence this possible source of nomadic tradition with its contribution to the picture of the background of Hebrew religion must be interpreted in the light of the history of the growth of the historical tradition. Thirdly, there is little doubt that an infiltration of elements from Arabia and its fringes into Palestine continued to take place at intervals during the history of the Hebrew people up to and possibly even after the end of the monarchy. Hence it is almost impossible to determine the source of the nomadic element in the Hebrew religious tradition. It is, however, quite possible that the Hebrew tendency towards monotheism may have been due in part to the presence of the nomadic element in its religious background.

Hence it may be said in conclusion that the picture of the early background of Hebrew religion derived from the various sources at our disposal, new and old, is one which could hardly have been put together from the accounts of the Old Testament writers. We are forced to recognize the necessity of using external sources in order to understand the rock from which the Hebrews were hewn, the hole of the pit from which they were digged. Coming into Canaan at intervals during the second millennium B.C., the separate groups which ultimately made up the nation found an ancient civilization, with an agricultural type of cultus, organized into small city states. The general pattern of that civilization was determined by the convergence of many streams of culture, Mesopotamia and Egypt being the predominant influences. The religion which the ancestors of the Hebrews brought with them probably did not differ very widely from that of the environment into which they entered, and after their settlement such differences as did exist would tend to disappear. Nevertheless, nomadic ideals survived in those districts of Hebrew occupation where agricultural elements were weaker, and possibly were reinforced by fresh accessions from the desert. In contrast with the official prophets, who were attached to the temple and the court and formed part of the general fertility type of religion prevalent in the early period of the monarchy, the new prophets with whom the protest originated seem to have come from those parts of the country where such nomadic ideals survived, in the hill country where pastoral pursuits were the main occupation of the people.

We find that the protest gradually comes to embrace the whole pattern of the religion which had its source in the mixed background which we have attempted to describe. Indeed, the new conception of God, and the rejection of all the traditional ritual forms, temple, ark, and sacrificial system, can only be rightly understood against the background of a religion where the god was the incarnation of the desires and material needs of the community, a god who annually died and rose again, a cult whose roots were in the earth and of the earth.

BIBLIOGRAPHY

S. A. Cook, *The Religion of Ancient Palestine in the Light of Archæology.*
S. H. Hooke, *The Origins of Early Semitic Ritual.*
E. O. James, *The Origins of Sacrifice.*
W. R. Smith, *The Religion of the Semites* (3rd edition, with additional notes by S. A. Cook).
W. C. Graham and H. G. May, *Culture and Conscience.*

XI. THE RELIGION OF ISRAEL

1. NOMADIC RELIGION AND THE BEGINNINGS OF YAHWISM.

WE have no direct and contemporary evidence as to the religion of Israel prior to its settlement in Canaan. The earliest relevant documents belong as literature to a period subsequent to that settlement by several centuries, and are coloured by the later experience to an extent which it is difficult to estimate in detail. They contain, however, earlier records, such as songs, sayings, and oracles, which have doubtless come by oral transmission from a remote past. The evidence is so far conclusive that the Hebrew people passed through a longer or shorter nomadic period which greatly influenced its subsequent history in Canaan, and that those tribes which were to become the nucleus of the future nation drew their inspiration from a striking deliverance from Egyptian control, which was ascribed by their prophet-leader, Moses, to the power and purpose of Yahweh.

From the retrospective evidence of the Old Testament, supplemented by what is known of the ways of Bedouin Arabs in ancient and modern times, we can form a picture of this nomadic background, and against it we can throw into contrast the new religion of the Israelites based on the redemption from Egypt. The unit of the nomadic life was the clan (*mishpachah*), the group of families with a real or artificial (covenanted) blood-tie, loosely controlled by the sheikhs, or heads of families. The size of the clan was dictated by practical considerations (W. R. Smith, *Kinship and Marriage in Early Arabia*, pp. 36 ff.). It could not be so small as to be defenceless against the perils of the desert, and it could not be so large as to exceed the grazing and watering facilities of its own range of wanderings. Naturally, it was a religious as well as a social unit, as were all such groups in ancient times. This corporate consciousness continued in Canaan, notwithstanding the disintegrating effects of local settlement. Thus we hear of David being summoned from the court of Saul to attend a clan sacrifice at Bethlehem (1 Sam. 20²⁹).

The general character of this nomadic religion prior to

Yahwism has been well defined as " a polydemonism tinged with polytheism " (Lods), such as could centre in the cult of a holy mountain (like Sinai), or a holy oasis (like Kadesh). This type of religion is specially linked with natural objects concerning the life and welfare of the clan or tribe, namely, springs, trees, rocks, sun, moon and stars, together with flocks, herds, and the wild creatures of the desert. As an illustration from this nomadic period we have the " Song of the Well " (Num. 21$^{17.18}$). There would be primitive forms of sacrifice of a simple kind (not including the burnt-offering), and chiefly concerned with the disposal of the mysterious blood. Further, there would be magical rites to work good or ill, fear of the dead, expressed in " mourning " customs, and the general atmosphere of animism. Many of these things survived into the later religion of Israel, such as the ordeal of jealousy (Num. 5$^{11-31}$), the goat for Azazel on the Day of Atonement (Lev. 16$^{8ff.}$), purification from pollution through contact with a corpse by the use of the ashes from burning a red cow (Num. 19). In particular, we may note the custom of blood revenge, at first indiscriminate and as unlimited as that of Lamech's desert-song (Gen. 4$^{23.24}$), afterwards controlled by the relatively merciful limitation of the *lex talionis* (Ex. 21$^{23-25}$). The primitive justice still administered in the desert by the sheikhs of the clan (cf. Doughty, *Arabia Deserta*, i. 248, 249) is illustrated by the account of the day-to-day administration of Moses (Ex. 18).

Against this nomadic background the redemptive act of Yahweh in delivering these semi-nomadic Israelites on the borders of Egypt from the wrath of Pharaoh stands out clearly as something new, something that never ceased to be a " well of salvation " from which inspiration and new hope could be drawn through all the generations to come. The essence of the redemptive act is described in the story of the crossing of the Red Sea, " which the Egyptians essaying to do were swallowed up " (Heb. 11^{29}). The act is glorified in the " Song of Moses " (Ex. 15$^{1-18}$) of much later date, but its nucleus is the couplet of Miriam's song (v.^{21}), which may well go back to the event :

> "Sing ye to Yahweh, for he is highly exalted.
> Horse and rider hath he thrown into the sea."

Who was this Yahweh, who henceforth became the God of Israel ? Etymology yields no clear light, and the words of Ex. 3^{14}, " I am that I am " should rather be translated " I will be that I will be " (R.V. 3rd mar.), a play upon the name that makes it purposely enigmatic, and suggestive of the future revelation through events. Alleged pre-Mosaic occurrences of a related divine name $Ya(u)$ in Babylonian inscriptions are doubted by competent authorities, and the earliest attested instance of the name outside Israel does not carry us back beyond the eighth century B.C. (Hamath and N. Syria). At Horeb, Yahweh declares to Moses that He is " the God of thy father, the God of Abraham, the God of Isaac and the God of Jacob " (E in Ex. 3[6]), whilst a later document (P in Ex. 6[3]) declares that He was known to them as *El Shaddai*. On the other hand, Gen. 4[26] (J) implies that the name " Yahweh " had been used from the beginning. The most plausible conjecture as to the immediate introduction of the name Yahweh to Moses and the Israelites traces it to the Kenites. Moses, during his enforced exile from Egypt, is said to have married the daughter of Jethro, the priest of Midian (Ex. 3[1]) belonging to its Kenite branch (Judg. 1[16], 4[11]), who takes the initiative in offering sacrifice when Israel is at the holy mountain (Ex. 18[12]). The Kenites may be connected with Cain (same word in Hebrew) who bore the Yahweh-sign (Gen. 4[15]) ; to them belonged the later Jonadab, the Rechabite Yahwist (1 Chron. 2[55]).

However this may be, our concern is with the attributes ascribed to Yahweh by the Israelites rather than with the prior history and meaning of the name. We find Him localized at the mountain of Sinai (Horeb) where He is associated with seismic, volcanic or storm phenomena ; these features persist into the later history (Judg. 5[4, 5] ; Hab. 3[3ff.] ; Ps. 18[7ff.]). He is also connected with Kadesh, the " holy " place, which was also known as " Spring of judgement " (Gen. 14[7]), implying some form of water-oracle (Num. 20[1-13], cf. Ex. 17[1-7]). He became Israel's war-god from the beginning, as in the ancient fragment of song " Rise up, O Yahweh, and let thine enemies be scattered " (Num. 10[35]). But none of these associations or attributes are sufficient to distinguish Yahweh from the gods of other Semitic peoples, such as the Moabites who speak of their god, Kemosh, much as the early Israelites did of Yahweh. What was it that made the essential and vital difference, a difference that must go back, in some degree, to Moses ? At least two distinctive features emerge, which go far to explain the subsequent developments. The first is that Yahweh is represented as taking the initiative in freely choosing Israel as His people (Ex. 3[7] ; cf. Deut. 7[6-8]). This is an ethical act, involving that freedom which is the fundamental principle of morality. In the Semitic nature-

Ronald E. Osmann

religion, especially as we shall see it in the Baalism of Canaan, the god is fundamentally linked with his people by quasi-physical ties. He depends on them as they on him. If they are defeated in battle, he is defeated, as we see from the ideas represented on the Moabite Stone concerning both Kemosh and Yahweh. Doubtless, the lower religion of Israel itself, the popular and even the official religion of the mass of the people continued on this level, as we can see from the rebuke of Amos. In this, as in other respects, he recalls the old nomadic tradition by insisting on the moral character of the relation between Yahweh and Israel (3^2). This makes the " Day of Yahweh " no inevitable victory of Israel, but (for a sinful people) a day of defeat and punishment (5^{18}). In this free choice of Israel (cf. Deut. 4^{37}), there is the germ of the whole moral conception of Yahweh which distinguished the eighth-century prophets, and forms a unique element in the religion of Israel.

The second feature is that Yahwism begins and is founded on a redemptive act of *history*. The only definition of Yahweh is " the out-of-Egypt-bringing God," as a German might say (Ex. 20^2; I Kings 12^{28}; Hosea 12^9). He is known by what he does, not simply by what he says through the sacred oracle, (Urim and Thummim), or through the tribal custom. In that self-disclosure in act lies the beginning and the prophecy of the subsequent revelation through history. This meant that God was for ever inspiring His people to sing a new song of thanksgiving, that (until the much later days of written revelation) the religion was always able to keep abreast of the times, and to adjust itself to new needs, that there was always the hope of some great thing yet to be, out of which was to develop the prophetic faith in a divine purpose controlling all history and bringing it to its final goal. (We owe to Israel's prophets and apocalyptists the conception of the unity of history.)

Thus, along two great lines of development the work of the prophets was initiated. It was fitting, therefore, that Israel's leader and Yahweh's interpreter at this epoch should be regarded as the first of the great prophets, to be followed by Samuel, Nathan, Ahijah, Elijah, Elisha, and Micaiah, and so to the culmination of prophecy in the period between the eighth and sixth centuries. Moses is represented by later ages as unique in his relation to Yahweh (Ex. 33^{11}; Num. 12^{6-8}; Deut. 34^{10}). That representation is so far justified that the uniqueness of Israel's religion begins in the " covenant " enacted through him between Yahweh and Israel (Ex. 24^{4-8}).

2. The Influence of Canaanite Religion

We are to think, then, of a semi-nomadic group of Hebrew tribes which had escaped from Egyptian control under the leadership of Moses, and were united by faith in Yahweh as the delivering God of Israel. This group may have been joined by other nomads, as it turned its eyes towards the settled land of Canaan, into which other Hebrews had made their way since, at least, the Amarna period (c. 1400). What did this group of Yahweh-worshippers bring with them in the way of religious institutions? What were the new influences to which they were exposed in Canaan? What effect had these on the faith that Yahweh was the one and only national God of Israel?

They were already familiar with the conception of holy places (Kadesh and Sinai) at which their God could be specially worshipped with due rites, and would be thus prepared to find and use similar holy places in Canaan. They had relatively simple forms of sacrifice to Him, of which the most common was probably that disposal of the animal's blood at a stone representing the Deity which is illustrated by Saul's injunction on the battlefield (1 Sam. 14$^{33-35}$). The two chief types of pre-exilic sacrifice, namely, burnt-offerings and "peace-offerings," are mentioned in connexion with the covenant at Sinai (Ex. 24^5) and the latter at least—the communion meal—goes back to these early days. Offerings of firstlings seem to have been connected with the important full moon festival of the spring-time, known as the " Passover," which was subsequently to be united with the Canaanite agricultural festival of " Unleavened Bread." The very ancient verses about the ark of the covenant (Num. 10$^{35.\ 36}$) suggest that this portable shrine or throne, with which Yahweh's presence was in some way identified, goes back to the nomadic period. We do not know whether it was empty or whether, for example, it contained sacred stones. But it is very unlikely that these stones had the Decalogue inscribed upon them, since this seems to be a much later codification of Hebrew religion and morality, influenced by the teaching of the great prophets. Circumcision seems to have been a pre-Yahwistic rite, though the new faith was eventually to give it a new meaning.

The faith of the Israelites in Yahweh as their war-god was confirmed by their successful, though very partial and incomplete, invasion of Canaan. As they settled down there, they were exposed to religious influences of a kind very different from those of the desert. True, these Canaanites were predominantly a Semitic people, and in some respects doubtless shared the beliefs and practices of their nomadic kinsfolk, *e.g.* as to the power of blessings and curses, magic and divination, and customs relating to death. But the economic differences in the agricultural life of a settled people had led to important religious developments amongst them. Chief of these was the worship of the local Baalim, to whom was ascribed the fertility of the soil and of the flocks and herds. The result was a type of nature worship, with the " sympathetic magic " of sexual acts (sacred prostitution) at its centre. With the " Baal " or " lord " of the local sanctuary, represented by the stone pillar (Mazzebah), was linked the goddess Asherah, symbolized by the wooden post bearing that name, a conventionalized form of the sacred tree (Judg. 6^{26}, where it is " cut down "). At early periods, the stone pillar was regarded as the actual dwelling of the god (cf. Beth-el, " house of God," Gen. $28^{18. 19}$). The Canaanites had also many idols, chiefly however of the statuette type, used for amulets. From them was probably derived the bull-worship of Israel (1 Kings $12^{28ff.}$). The story of the making of the golden calf by Aaron (Ex. 32) is usually regarded as an indirect condemnation of this northern cult, similar to the direct condemnation by Hosea (Hosea $8^{5. 6}$, 10^5, 13^2).

Excavations of Canaanite sanctuaries have brought to light altars on which victims were sacrificed by the knife, and there is some evidence also that victims were burnt. This appears to be confirmed by the Ras Shamra tablets. Scholars have hesitated to accept Dussaud's theory (based on much later evidence) that the Hebrew sacrificial system was in large part derived from the Canaanite ritual, though there can be little doubt that it was deeply influenced by it, *e.g.* by the custom of the burnt-offering. The Canaanites sometimes offered human sacrifices, especially at the foundation of a new building (cf. 1 Kings 16^{34}). They had their festivals, as at the vintage season (Judg. 9^{27}), and it is probable that the three great festivals of the settled Hebrews followed Canaanite usage, since they are agricultural (except for the Passover elements linked with the first). We may also suppose that much of the Hebrew mythology, ultimately going back to Egyptian and Babylonian beliefs, reached Israel by way of the Canaanites, whose land had long been under the influence of Egypt and Babylon. On these and other matters the recent discovery of the Ras Shamra tablets may be expected to throw considerable light, when the texts have been more fully studied.

A point of particular interest in connexion with Canaanite influence is the origin of the Nebi'im, or ecstatic prophets. The earliest reference to such prophecy in Palestine is to be found in an incident at Byblos, about 1100 B.C., where the prince has refused to receive a certain Wenamon (Unamun) who is in charge of an image of the god Amun. It is recorded that whilst the prince was engaged in sacrificing to his own gods, the god took possession of one of his pages, who cried in a " prophetic " frenzy : " Bring the god hither ! Bring the messenger that hath him. It is Amun that sent him, it is he that caused him to come " (Erman, *The Literature of the Ancient Egyptians*, p. 177, E.T.). Later on, we find four hundred and fifty " prophets " of Baal at Carmel, dancing round his altar and mutilating themselves to attract his attention (1 Kings 18[22. 28]). To such bands of " prophets " there is a close Hebrew parallel in the story of the band met by Saul (1 Sam. 10[5. 6. 10ff.], 19[20ff.]). Whatever the ultimate origin of the Nebi'im of this type—whether they derive from the early Semites or from Aryans of Asia Minor—whatever their relation to the great prophets of Israel, there seems little doubt that the introduction of ecstatic prophecy into the religion of Israel was due to Canaanite influence (cf. Jepsen, *Nabi*, pp. 246, 247).

It is not, however, in this or that detail that the chief significance of the Canaanite influences consists. It is rather in the general character of the Canaanite Baalism as a type of nature-worship and its strong entrenchment in the agricultural life of Canaan, a life in which the Israelites necessarily shared. The challenge was twofold, first through the temptation to add Baalism to Yahwism as a supplementary cult, with an important and essential department of its own (since Yahweh had nothing to do with agriculture) ; and second, to keep Yahweh as the one and only God of Israel, but to conceive Him as the apotheosis of a Baal, in fact to " Baalize " Yahweh. Instead of the stern and jealous Deity of the desert, the God of the storm and the earthquake and the battle, requiring from His people a moral obedience, of however crude a type, He tended to become the God of luxurious plenty, sexual in nature and in worship. Elijah won the battle against the first danger in the ninth century, Baalism being represented by Melkart of Tyre ; Amos and Hosea contested the second in the eighth century.

The struggle between Baalism and Yahwism was of the greatest importance for the development of the idea of Yahweh. Only as a religion has to meet the challenge of its opposite does it discover its own nature and potential strength. The old naturalistic elements in the conception of Yahweh were sublimated into features of His occasional theophany, and His power over Nature was more and more developed in idea, until there arose the conception of Him as the Creator of the heavens and the earth. The ethical conceptions which were latent in Yahweh's free choice of Israel were equally developed and emphasized. The old nomadic morality, crude and stern as it might be, was felt by the nobler minds to be infinitely better than the sensuality of the Canaanites.

The Yahwism which entered Canaan with the Israelites was itself of great social and political influence. It became the centre and basis of nationality, as we can see from the Song of Deborah. Here the tribes are rallied in the name of Yahweh ; that is their one common bond. Yahweh comes from His ancient abode in Sinai (Judg. 5$^{4.\ 5}$) to the help of His people against Canaanite pressure, and those who do not come to the help of Yahweh against the mighty are bitterly cursed (v.^{23}). The people who were to lose their political existence and become primarily a religious community, in the far-off post-exilic days, were here constituted into a people by their original faith. They were able to absorb many elements in Canaan without losing their own identity, because of their faith in Yahweh. This applies both to other Hebrews already settled there who were brought to join them (e.g. " Asher," and other " concubine " tribes), and also to the Canaanites themselves who were gradually absorbed. No more striking example could be found of the political power of an intense religious faith, operating like a magnet amongst the scattered and varied inhabitants of what has been called " a land of tribes," a land of which the topography makes for disunion rather than union.

3. THE RELIGION OF THE PRE-EXILIC PROPHETS

The moral element in the conception of Yahweh, which has been emphasized as present from the beginning, found its clearest and fullest expression in the religion of the greater prophets, from the eighth to the sixth century. Elijah is their true forerunner, not only in the matter of Naboth's vineyard, but also in his return to Horeb to recover his inspiration and strength. The Rechabites (Jer. 35$^{6ff.}$; cf. 2 Kings 10$^{15.\ 23}$) not only abjured viniculture and agriculture in general, but carried their nomadism to the point of continuing to dwell in tents. We can see the nomadic tradition very clearly in Amos, the first of the great series. He denounces in Puritan fashion the luxury and " culture " of the northern

kingdom ($3^{10.\ 12.\ 15}$, 4^1, 5^{11}, 6^{4-6}), and its elaborate and excessive religiosity ($4^{4.\ 5}$, 5^{21-23}). He contrasts his own times
with the days of the desert, when there were no such sacrifices and offerings in the worship of Yahweh (5^{25} ; the words
can be taken as expressing a *relative* truth, in view of what
was said about nomadic religion). One of the most significant
features of this prophetic movement is illustrated in the
opening chapter of Amos, where nationality is transcended,
and moral standards are applied to man as man, of whatever
nation. Hosea brings out the deeper thought of the importance of the *inner* attitude as the source of conduct (4^{12}, 5^4, 14).
Out of his personal experience of sorrowful love, he enters
into the very heart of God's grace (11^8). He also hopes for
a new beginning as from the wilderness ($2^{14.\ 15}$), and bitterly
denounces the influences of Canaan. Micah shares the more
democratic outlook of the desert in his attitude towards the
oppressed poor (3^{1-3}). Though Isaiah belongs to a different
social level,.he is not less indignant at the treatment of the
helpless ($1^{17.\ 23}$, $5^{7.\ 8}$, $10^{1.\ 2}$). His scorn for Canaanite idolatry
(2^8) is matched by his condemnation of ceremonial worship
without morality (1^{11-17}). His own sense of the true attitude
of man before the Holy One of Israel is shown in the account
of his call (6). But this attitude towards the externals of
worship is most explicit and pronounced in Jeremiah ($7^{1\text{ff}}$).
In the spirit of Amos, he thinks of the nomadic period as
one in which God gave no commandments concerning burnt
offerings or sacrifices (7^{22}), which at least implies that the
elaborate ritual ascribed to Moses in the Pentateuch was
unknown to both these prophets. The wilderness days were
the time of Israel's golden youth ($2^{2.\ 3}$). In the spirit of Amos,
also, Jeremiah contrasts the luxurious dwelling of Jehoiakim
with the simpler life of his father Josiah, whose glory was
not in cedar panelling and vermilion paint, but in judging
the cause of the poor (22^{13-17}). In relation to man, as in
relation to God, the essentials of life are moral. This is the
cardinal message of the great prophets, and their perennial
monument is that they have made it a commonplace of our
religious theory, whatever may hold of our practice.

What is the relation of these prophets, with their highly
developed moral and religious teaching, to such " prophecy "
as we have ascribed to Canaanite influence, *e.g.* that of the
ecstatics encountered by Saul ? By some scholars, the view
has been, and is, taken that the canonical prophets are the
direct descendants of these early *Nebi'im*, and continue in
greater or less degree their ecstatic and abnormal behaviour

(so *e.g.* Gunkel, Hölscher, and T. H. Robinson). Others (*e.g.* Davidson, Volz, Jepsen) clearly distinguish and indeed contrast the two classes ; Davidson, for example, says of the canonical prophets, "the violent excitation usual in early prophecy had almost disappeared . . . (the prophet) was conscious of being an independent individual person . . . his communion with God was a communion of two moral persons " (*HDB*, iv. 115*a*). There is, however, far too much evidence of psychological abnormality for it to be explained away, even in Jeremiah, whose prophetic consciousness comes nearest to this moral definition. He was controlled from without, and as it seemed to him irrationally (20[7. 9]) ; he saw strange visions (4[23-26]) ; he had to wait ten days on one occasion for the desired word of Yahweh (42[7]). There seems to have been no difference between the *forms* of " false " prophecy and the true ; the difference was in the moral and religious quality of the message (Jer. 23[21. 22]), and Jeremiah was unable *at the time* to denounce as false the prophecy of Hananiah, contradicting his own (28[6]). The element of important truth in those views which minimize or deny the " ecstatic " element is that in the canonical prophets this element was thrust from the centre to the circumference of their teaching. Something of the old forms remained theirs, and without it they would not have recognized themselves or have been recognized by others as divinely commissioned prophets. But they had risen far above the former levels ; they were individuals emboldened to challenge the nation or its kings, not bands of professional dervishes echoing the royal policy. This is well brought out in the contrast of one of their forerunners, Micaiah, with the four hundred court prophets of Ahab (1 Kings 22[6ff.]).

Another aspect of the spirituality of the greater prophets is seen in their attitude towards idols, from Hosea onwards. We may regard this as the negative side of their positive emphasis on morality. Implicitly at least, they substituted their own moral consciousness for the material image as the means of approach to God, and of the realization of His presence. This may be regarded as the most important Old Testament preparation for the Christian doctrine of the Incarnation. No material image is worthy to represent God ; the truest representation of Him is found in the highest and most spiritual characteristics of human personality.

The " ethical theism " of the prophets found its necessary sanctions through the interpretation of current events and of the background of political history. The fact that Israel lay in the corridor between the great empires of the Nearer East, those of Egypt and Mesopotamia, had consequences as important for religion as for politics. The chequered history of Israel brought great opportunities for religion to develop through the very demands made by it. How different was the lot of Moab, lying off the main route ! " Moab hath been at ease from his youth, and he hath settled on his lees, and hath not been emptied from vessel to vessel, neither hath he gone into captivity " (Jer. 48[11]). The prophets of Israel had to face a challenge as severe as any people could be called to meet. On the one hand, there was the confidence in a divine election of Israel, as true for the prophet who moralized it as for the people who materialized it. On the other, there was the repeated disappointment of political hopes, after the transient successes under David and Solomon, and finally, the two captivities, and the cessation of political independence. The faith of the prophets, both in quantity and in quality, is seen in their refusal to accept such events as implying any failure of the divine purpose. They persistently reinterpreted that purpose to meet the new denials of it. They regarded political overthrow or social disaster as the penalty for social immorality, so that what had seemed to hide God really revealed Him. It is important to see how this prophetic faith works out in practice. Isaiah is the clearest example of it. History, he says, is under the control of God (22[11] ; cf. 5[12], 10[12]). Since His purpose cannot fail, there will be a " righteous remnant " (8[16-18]), even though the nation as a whole be condemned. But that righteous remnant will need a local habitation, and so Zion will stand, whatever the Assyrians may do (28[16] ; cf. 7[9]). Isaiah is pre-eminently the prophet of faith and his faith makes its fact by a resolute reinterpretation of the bare event, as well as by unbroken confidence about the true Israel's future. It is significant of the variety of such interpretation of history that Isaiah's contemporary, Micah, proclaimed the downfall of Jerusalem at that very crisis (3[12] ; cf. Jer. 26[18]). The overthrow of Israel constantly asserted by the pre-exilic prophets was not, indeed, a merely political inference, but neither was it a merely moral inference. It was a unity intuitively perceived, yet one that can be analysed by us into these two lines of approach, since the prophets never taught without reference to, and often prompting from, contemporary events, though their teaching can never be resolved into shrewd political calculation.

The religion of the eighth-century prophets was driven underground during the pagan reaction of Manasseh's long reign (692–639 B.C.) but reappeared in the Book of Deuteronomy, of which the central portion (12–26, 28) was the programme of Josiah's reformation in 621 B.C. (2 Kings 22, 23). There are, of course, many ancient elements in this book, as in all codes of law, but its characteristic quality is not in these, but in their manner of presentation and their general setting, and especially in the present introductions (1–11). We see the influence of the prophets, especially of Hosea, in both the humanitarian morality and in the centralization of worship and festivals at Jerusalem in order to secure their purification and adequate control. We note in particular the command to *love* God, because He can be seen to be lovable in His redemptive work (6[4.5]; cf. [21ff]).

The most interesting figure in Old Testament prophecy, Jeremiah, was a contemporary of this reformation and seems at first to have supported it (11). If so, the resultant emphasis on the temple, as though this guaranteed security, subsequently alienated him (7[2ff.]; cf. 26); and he may even have had Deuteronomy in view when he spoke of the false pen of the scribes having wrought falsely (8[8]). It was inevitable that the Deuteronomic reform, however necessary a compromise between prophetic and priestly interests, should work out in favour of those who represented the institutional side of religion. But Jeremiah, besides his anti-sacrificial attitude, was also a pronounced individualist. Through his own experience of the revelation of God to the inner man, he was led to the conviction that the only cure for social and religious ills must be found in a " new covenant " (31[31ff.]), in strong and explicit contrast with such an externally expressed covenant as Deuteronomy had set forth. His personal experience of God (*e.g.* 15[15-19]) opened out a new epoch of religion, and is reflected in many subsequent psalms. He had discovered that the true Israelite, as well as his God, could do without a temple, and therefore he could contemplate the overthrow of the state without fear, though with profound sympathy with those who would suffer through it. In many other aspects also—his personal communion with God, the spirituality of his religious emphasis, his shrinking from, and yet acceptance of, a divine mission to be fulfilled in isolation and suffering—Jeremiah is in himself the truest prophecy of that other Prophet with whom some of His contemporaries identified him (Matt. 16[14]).

4. THE EXILIC DEVELOPMENTS

The capture of Samaria by the Assyrians in 722 B.C., and the deportation of 27,290 of its inhabitants, had relatively little

consequence for religion. The former religion of the northern
kingdom seems to have been continued without marked change,
except for the introduction of foreign cults brought by the
colonists with whom Assyria resettled the land. On the other
hand, those who were deported, like their fellow-sufferers
twelve years before (2 Kings 15^{29}) cease to figure in the history
of Israel.

Very different were the results of the overthrow of the
southern kingdom by the Babylonians. The Judæans deported in 597, 586, and 581 B.C. (Jer. 52$^{28-30}$, but cf. 2 Kings
24$^{14-16}$) were to hold the future in their hands. They were
allowed to maintain their social contacts and to develop their
religious thought, literature, and institutions, with the result
that when there was an opportunity to return to Judæa
(from 538 B.C. onwards) those who availed themselves of it
were able to carry back a strong faith and a literary expression
of it. The survivors in Judæa had indeed maintained their
faith and worship in some sort (cf. Jer. 41^5, describing a
pilgrimage of northern Yahwists to " the house of Yahweh ").
But all the evidence suggests that the initiative of the real
revival came from Babylonian exiles rather than from " the
people of the land." As for those who carried Jeremiah
against his will into Egypt (Jer. 43$^{4ff.}$), nothing was to be
expected from men turning back to the worship of " the
queen of heaven " in their disillusionment with Yahwism
(44$^{18ff.}$). At the most, they were likely to continue a worship of Yahweh like that of the military Jewish colony at
Elephantine, of which we hear in the next century.

It is not difficult to state, from the direct evidence of
Ezekiel and Deutero-Isaiah and other literature of the Exile,
and from reasonable inference based on the subsequent course
of the history, what were the chief effects of the Exile. In the
first place, we may set the general influence upon the religious
outlook of the ordinary people. As they followed the advice
of Jeremiah (29$^{5-7}$) and settled down to their new life, they
were compelled to realize in the most forcible manner that the
prophetic words of warning had been fulfilled ; certainly
Ezekiel left no loophole of escape from this conviction. However slow they might be to learn the higher and more spiritual
lessons of those prophets, the negative side of their teaching, e.g. the denunciation of idolatry and foreign cults, had
been confirmed. Though there were survivals of it, even in
Babylon (Ezek. 14$^{2-6}$), the change of surroundings wrought
in time a change of outlook ; removal from temptation gave
time for a new conception to develop. Those who returned

to Judæa were immune from the fascination of the former high places and their ways of worship.

A further result of the new surroundings was the growth of a worship of Yahweh deprived of its familiar external expression in the Temple. The spiritual offerings of prayer (1 Kings 8⁴⁶⁻⁴⁹) and fasting (Zech. 8¹⁹) replaced the animal sacrifices of the visible altar. Existent institutions were re-interpreted and given a new importance, e.g. the Sabbath and circumcision. In such gatherings as those which Ezekiel was wont to address (33³⁰), we may see the far-off beginnings of the synagogue—first mentioned apparently in the Macca-bæan days (Ps. 74⁸). The growth of a new individualism, with its sense of moral responsibility, which is seen in the teaching of Ezekiel, became the basis of that new type of personal piety which underlies so many of the psalms.

Another feature, destined to be of the greatest importance for the future of religion, was the growth of a religious literature and the new emphasis that was eventually placed on the written, as distinct from the spoken, word. There will be a long period, it is true, before we can begin to speak of " Religion under the Law " ; it is not probable that the Pentateuch attained even literary completion before the fourth century. But the materials for the Torah were now being gathered, whether previously written, like the early stories of the patriarchs and of Israel's wanderings, or now first zealously recorded, lest they should be forgotten. An example of the latter is the " Law of Holiness " (Lev. 17–26), in which old ritual is given new meaning. Much of the earlier material of the Priestly Code may also have been now first recorded. But it was not only the legalistic material for the Pentateuch that engaged the attention of the scribes ; they were also concerned with the history of Israel, as it is set forth in the sequence of the books, Joshua–2 Kings. They incorporated and rearranged the older material, editing it from the " Deuteronomic " standpoint, i.e. from that of the doctrine of strict retribution such as the prophets had taught and Deuter-onomy had enforced. This religious emphasis is specially seen in the framework of Judges and 1 and 2 Kings (see above, pp. 45 f., 49).

One of the great results of the Exile is seen in the general character and new outlook of exilic prophecy, i.e. the work of Ezekiel and Deutero-Isaiah. Both are prophets of a restora-tion of Israel (Ezekiel only after 586 B.C.), though in very different ways. Ezekiel may be described as a sacramentalist and an individualist. He is concerned with the holiness of

God in the ancient sense, *i.e.* of His awe-inspiring unapproach-
ableness. Therefore, since His honour is involved, every pre-
caution must be taken to prevent dishonour to Him, when He
has restored Israel to its land. The elaborate arrangements
which he plans for the temple and its worship (40–48) are the
expression of this " sacramentalism." The nation will be
restored by the supernatural act of God, as is dramatically
portrayed in the vision of the valley of dry bones (37). When
we look for further detail of the process, the answer is in
Ezekiel's individualism. God deals with men in the coming
judgement one by one (18) and though this is on the basis
of strict retribution, yet it is combined, though hardly reconciled, with the declaration of a supernatural regeneration
of those who shall be restored to the land of Israel (36^{24-28}).
It should not be overlooked, however, that the change is confirmed by the revulsion of these same individuals from their
former deeds, as they see the new grace of God towards them
(36^{31} ; cf. 16^{60-63}).

But it is Deutero-Isaiah who is above all others the prophet
of grace. God is for him pre-eminently the Redeemer, able
to redeem because He is the creator of the world and the
controller of history. He conceives the deliverance to come
through that history and idealizes Cyrus as God's " Messiah,"
unlike Ezekiel, whose deliverance is by a " supernatural "
overthrow of Israel's enemies. Two great conceptions emerge
in Deutero-Isaiah as never before, namely, his monotheism
and his universalism (combined with " evangelism "). He
makes explicit, in contrast with the idolatrous religion on which
he pours such scorn, that Yahweh is the only God (44^6, 45^{22}).
He represents the religion of Israel as the universal religion,
to be propagated by faithful Israelites, and sanctioned by the
overwhelming miracle of the restoration. His expectations,
at least in the later phase of his prophecies, culminate in the
conception of the Servant of Yahweh (42^{1-4}, 49^{1-6}, 50^{4-9},
$52^{13}-53^{12}$). Scholars have differed widely as to the exact
interpretation of this figure, perhaps because the ancient
categories of thought are not ours. Ancient thought was
largely influenced by the doctrine of corporate personality,
enabling it to pass from the representative individual to the
many conceived as one, much more easily than our modern
thought and its expression allow. Consequently, there are
elements of truth in the view that the Servant portrays
Jeremiah or the prophet himself, conscious of representing the
divine purpose for Israel and of knowing the right interpretation of its sufferings. But it is Israel that is the inclusive idea,

and the hope can be fulfilled only as Israel as a people shares in the prophet's consciousness and becomes the willing sacrifice (by its own interpretation of past suffering) and the future revealer (vindicated by the divine restoration to Jerusalem) through whom the nations of the world are moved to come and are sacrificially enabled to come into the presence of the God of the whole world.

Thus in Ezekiel and Deutero-Isaiah we have two contrasted national ideals, both of the greatest importance for the future of religion. Here we might legitimately begin to trace the differences which were to emerge at last in Judaism and Christianity. Ezekiel offers the ideal of a purified ritual combined with the moral allegiance of divinely changed hearts. He is rightly said to initiate the religion of the second temple, which was so much more than " mere " ritual, since it was the centre of inspiration and devotion for so many of the psalmists. Ezekiel's influence counted for far more than that of Deutero-Isaiah in the post-exilic period. On the other hand, Deutero-Isaiah, though not without his disciples (cf. the Book of Jonah), became the most important Scripture for the new Israel that gathered round Jesus of Nazareth and for Jesus Himself in the interpretation of His own life and death.

5. THE SECOND TEMPLE

In the post-exilic period of the religion of the Old Testament, the temple built at the initiative of Haggai and Zechariah (520–516 B.C.) is the centre of interest and influence. To maintain its cult was a foremost religious duty (Mal. $1^{7. \ 8. \ 13. \ 14}$, 3^{8-10}) and the enforced cessation of the daily offerings in time of scarcity was the greatest of calamities (Joel $1^{9. \ 13}$). In fact, Haggai argued that it was the failure to restore the temple which had been the cause of scarcity and economic distress (1^{4-10}). Most of what we know about the history and religion of this period (prior to the Maccabæan rebellion) is related to the temple, directly or indirectly. For we must not forget that the post-exilic community settled around Jerusalem was relatively small and had lost all political significance. Its interest was religion, real or conventional, and its religion was the temple, spiritualized or materialized.

However few the number of those who returned from Babylon in or after 538 B.C., the religious initiative and ideal seems to have sprung from them, and we know that the work was supported from Babylon (Zech. $6^{9ff.}$). This does not mean that " the people of the land," those who had remained in Judæa, counted for nothing. It is clear that worship of some sort was carried on at Jerusalem after the fall of the city in 586 B.C. (Jer. 41⁵). Part of the trouble in the next century was due to the " vested interest " in Jerusalem of the remaining inhabitants of Judæa and the difference of their religious ideas from those of the reformers from Babylon. But the relations of parties in this early post-exilic period are obscure and our data are scanty, with the result that there is much controversy as to detail and even as to the general course of events. After the short period of the rebuilding of the temple (520–516 B.C.), for which the prophecies of Haggai and Zechariah give us reliable information, we know practically nothing till we come to the middle of the fifth century. From a misplaced Aramaic document (Ezra 4$^{11-22}$) we infer ($v.$^{12}) that there had been an attempt to build the walls, and that the frustration of this ($v.$^{23}) led to the intervention of Nehemiah (Neh. 1^3).

The work of Nehemiah, as the governor of the province, is well known. All that concerns us here is his reforms of such abuses as the appropriation of temple buildings for the use of " foreigners," the abandonment of temple duty by Levites and singers, since their allowances were stopped, the disregard of the Sabbath through commercial interests, and especially the marriage of Jews to women of the surrounding peoples, with the result that a generation was growing up which could not even speak Hebrew (Neh. 13$^{4ff.}$). Nehemiah was an ardent nationalist, and he forbade any such marriages in future. This was in 432 B.C., and a generation afterwards we find that this measure had not been effective, for Ezra has to proceed to the much stronger action of compelling the divorce of all such " foreign " wives (Ezra 10). In saying this, it has been assumed that Ezra followed, instead of preceding, Nehemiah (as Ezra 7^7 suggests) ; probably Ezra came in the seventh year of the *second* Artaxerxes, *i.e.* 397 B.C.). The religious conditions about the middle of the fifth century are illustrated by Malachi, especially as regards the neglect of the cult (1$^{6ff.}$), and (the contrary action to that later enforced by Ezra) the divorce of native wives in order to marry foreign women (2$^{10-16}$). It is clear from the action of Nehemiah and Ezra that nationalism was becoming a strong feature of the " reformed " religion and that it had strong opposition to encounter from the general body of those who had remained in Palestine.

It is in connexion with Ezra that these reform movements, promoted by Jews returned from Babylon, find their most systematic expression. This reformation is linked to the law-

book which Ezra brought back with him (Ezra 7⁶·¹⁴; Neh. 8¹).
Different views are still held as to its contents; it is difficult
to believe that it can have been the whole Pentateuch, and it
is much more likely to have been only the earlier part of the
Priestly Law. Whatever its scope, it became the basis of a
" covenant " after being solemnly read to and accepted by the
whole people (Neh. 8–10, of which 8 and 9 belong to the memoirs
of Ezra, and have been editorially inserted here, when the
work of Nehemiah and Ezra was co-ordinated). This new
law-book seems temporarily to have replaced, though it was
subsequently combined with, the Deuteronomic law-book.

Henceforth Israel was to be the people of a cult (2 Chron.
13¹⁰·¹¹), till by the rise of synagogues and the shifting of
emphasis, it became the people of a book. The central feature
of the cult was the morning and evening burnt-offering (Ex.
29³⁸⁻⁴²) of a lamb together with flour, oil, and wine. The
form of this sacrifice is evidently dictated by the original
idea of a " meal " offered to the deity, but long before this time
such primitive ideas were probably submerged, and the thought
of them now provokes only scorn (Ps. 50¹³). There were also
sin offerings (Num. 15²²ᶠᶠ·) amongst the public sacrifices.
Private offerings were of greater variety and included (besides
sin-offerings, Lev. 4²⁷–5¹³) the guilt or trespass-offering (5¹⁴⁻¹⁹)
and the ancient peace-offerings (3), the feature of these being
that a large part of the flesh was eaten by the worshippers.
This goes back to early ideas of sacramental communion with
the deity, but again we may suppose that such ideas were now
largely lost or assimilated to the general idea of a gift to God
which the Law commanded. More and more would this idea
of doing what was commanded dominate the thought of the
worshipper in the regular sacrifices. On the other hand, there
were large numbers of private offerings in fulfilment of vows
or in gratitude for some deliverance from sickness, etc., which
would be simply eucharistic, whilst the elaborate ceremonial
of the Day of Atonement (Lev. 16), which became more and
more important, emphasized the expiatory features of sacrifice. Our safest guide to the general attitude of the worshippers is found in the Book of Psalms, which should always
be associated with the Book of Leviticus, as though they were
written in parallel columns. The Book of Psalms is very
varied in attitude and contains some elements critical of the
sacrificial system (e.g., 50⁷ᶠᶠ·, 51¹⁷), but on the whole it presupposes the cult, and expresses the inner and spiritual side
of the outer and visible worship offered at the Temple.

The Book of Psalms affords valuable evidence, also, as

to the general religious ideas of the post-exilic period. To that
period it belongs in its present form, whatever earlier elements
have been incorporated in it. The wide range of the religious
feeling exhibited, combined with the relative simplicity of the
underlying ideas, enables us to use the collection as an epitome
of Jewish theology in the post-exilic period of the Old Testament. The fundamental ideas of God are three : That He is
holy, retaining the majesty of the numinous, and not completely to be comprehended by man (Ps. 90) ; that He is
" righteous," *i.e.* conforming to the norm of forensic justice
at the highest moral level (illustrated most simply by the
description of the acceptable worshippers of such a God
(Ps. 15, 24) cf. 11⁷, " Yahweh is righteous, He loveth righteous
deeds " ; and thirdly, that He is loving or merciful, having the
quality of *chesed*, or covenant-love, which comes near to the
New Testament conception of " grace " (86⁵, etc.).   These
ideas of God are applied to every aspect of personal life, as
well as to nature, history, and social relations.   If Nature
specially reveals God's majesty (29, 104), history reveals His
righteousness and His grace (105, 106).

In strong contrast with the high level of this monotheistic
worship at Jerusalem, we have the phenomenon of a Jewish
temple at Elephantine in Egypt, existing from the sixth
century, and worshipping Yahweh as one of a pantheon of
five, of whom 'Anath appears to be the consort of Yahweh,
as the queen of heaven (cf. Jer. 44¹⁷).   In all probability,
the worship of this military colony, concerning which we have
the direct evidence of fifth-century Aramaic papyri, represents
a survival from earlier and pre-Deuteronomic religion.   It use-
fully reminds us how much the later Judaism owed to its great
prophets, and how necessary was the discipline of the Exile
to enforce their teaching.   The religion of Israel which the
Old Testament shows us was the religion of a minority ; behind
it was a religion of the majority, which is perhaps best illustrated by the papyri of Elephantine.   In post-exilic Judah
itself there were probably more varieties of religion than the
edited records allow us to see, though fortunately some of
them can be traced in the abundant literature of the Wisdom
writers and the apocalyptists.

6. THE RELIGION OF THE WISDOM LITERATURE

The Wisdom literature of Israel (more especially Proverbs,
Job, Ecclesiastes, and the extra-canonical Ecclesiasticus and
" Wisdom of Solomon") is by no means wholly a native product ;
it belongs in part to an international stock of sayings and

speculations, traceable in Babylon, Egypt, and Greece, though the monotheism and morality of the Jews have given a specific quality even to the borrowed material. The conception of " Wisdom " as sagacity and efficiency, together with the forms of gnomic sayings in which it found expression, go back to very early days. But the Wisdom literature, though, like the Psalms, incorporating earlier Israelite as well as extra-Israelite material, belongs, like the Psalms, to the post-exilic period in its present form. In four ways it is significant for the religion of Israel.

(1) The prophetic morality is here transferred from national to individual application, together with the doctrine of divine retribution. " Wisdom " also supplies us with the nearest approach to a systematization of Hebrew ethics. They are characterized by the very close interrelation of morality and religion, the conception of morality as revealed law, the emphasis on the will of the individual and on the social righteousness of the community (this last is a development of the corporate personality of the nomadic clan, clarified in the moral consciousness of the prophets). Hebrew ethics are often accused of being utilitarian, as indeed to some extent they are, since they largely appeal to the motive of the reward of well-doing by prosperity and long life. But Hebrew Wisdom always presupposes Hebrew religion, to which it is intended to be a practical introduction, especially for the young ; higher levels of motive are, of course, also supplied by that religion (e.g. Deut. 6).

(2) Just as Wisdom writers are responsible for the individualized application of prophetic morality, so from them comes the challenge to the doctrine of divine retribution. So long as men were treated in the mass, whether as nations or as families, it was possible to assert with plausibility that complete divine retribution would come, sooner or later, within this unit. But after Jeremiah and Ezekiel had thrown a new emphasis on the individual, which the wise men had continued and developed, it became apparent to some thinkers at least that the doctrine of retribution (and so of divine providence) broke down when applied simply within the span of the individual life. The authors of Proverbs and Ecclesiasticus remain content with the orthodox doctrine ; Job and Ecclesiastes challenge it—the former with belief in some hidden divine purpose which would explain and justify the experience of life ; the latter as a pessimist and agnostic, though not an atheist. The prologue to Job is especially notable, as it suggests witness-bearing to the reality of disinterested religion,

i.e. martyrdom for truth, as a new answer to the problem of innocent suffering.

(3) In the background of all the Wisdom books, except the Wisdom of Solomon, there is the belief in Sheol as the abode of " shades " or " weak ones " (*rephaim*), the ghostly replicas of men, and not to be identified with their " souls " or " spirits." Proverbs and Ecclesiasticus still take this for granted, so that for them there is no " life " (as distinct from ghostly " existence ") after death. Job dares to hope that he will be vindicated after his death and restored (at least temporarily) to witness his vindication ($19^{25.\ 26}$). Ecclesiastes explicitly rejects the new belief (3^{21}). The only book to accept it—though in the form of Greek immortality, and not of Hebrew resurrection— is the Wisdom of Solomon, in which book it takes a prominent place.

(4) Finally, the Wisdom literature makes a very important contribution to the conception of " mediation " between God and man. In Prov. 8, Ecclus. 24, and Wisdom $7^{22\text{-}8^1}$ we can trace the development of the personalized figure of Wisdom, which is more than a personification, if less than a person. Wisdom is conceived as the companion and helper of God in the creation of the world, which exhibits His wisdom, and she continues to inspire men with the qualities that make for right and successful life, in the individual and the society. In the Wisdom of Solomon we see again the Greek (Stoic) influences, so that we meet there with a conception of divine immanence, very different from anything we find in the Old Testament. The hypostasized conception of Wisdom, together with the parallel conception of the Spirit of God, are the Hebrew contributions to the ultimate conception of the Logos, which was destined to be so important an idea for the Christology of the New Testament and of the Patristic writers.

7. The Religion of Apocalyptic

The apocalyptic literature belongs approximately to the last two centuries B.C. and the first century A.D. It is well exemplified in the Canon by Isaiah (24–27), Daniel, and the New Testament Book of Revelation ; its chief extra-canonical representatives are the various writings ascribed to Enoch and Baruch, the Testaments of the Twelve Patriarchs, and 4 Ezra. Apocalyptic is the most direct continuation of prophecy, and indeed began in the later prophetic books (Ezek. 38, 39 ; Joel, Zech. 12–14). It differs, however, from prophecy generally and chiefly in the following points : (1) it is deliberately pseudonymous and not simply anonymous ; some notable figure of the past is represented as receiving a vision of things to come which he has recorded ; (2) its view of history is deterministic, following the divine appointment (*e.g.* 4(2) Esdras 4[37]) and culminating in some crisis which is that of the writer's own age (Dan. 11[31ff.]) ; (3) its emphasis is thus on the future and tends more and more to become extramundane, in contrast with the prophetic conception of a Kingdom of God in this world (though this may be included) ; (4) apocalyptic is literary, not oral, and is marked by the excessive use of symbolism, the use of animal figures being especially noticeable. In general, apocalyptic builds on earlier prophecy (*e.g.* Dan. 9[2]), which it adapts to present needs by various artifices, arithmetical, allegorical or dogmatic ; it also draws copiously on ancient cosmic mythology and on foreign ideas (*e.g.* Iranian). Whilst it represents a genuine and very important development of Judaism for the period indicated, it became unpopular with Rabbinical Judaism after A.D. 70, partly, no doubt, because of the Christian interest in, and use of, these books. But the failure of Bar Cocheba as "Messiah" (supported by R. Akiba) in A.D. 135 must also have fostered this Rabbinical withdrawal from apocalyptic.

Much of this literature repels the modern reader because of its obvious artificiality ; yet its ancient popularity should remind us that it served an important purpose for religion in times of political and social distress. It met the scepticism as to ancient promises by their renewal in new and appropriate form, and by their reinterpretation in relation to (1) a vast and impressive scheme of history ; (2) it brought to the front the new belief in life after death ; (3) it was frequently associated with the conception of a transcendent Messiah, in contrast with the political or Davidic Messiah of prophecy.

(1) In regard to the first of these points—the new conception of history—we ought to remember that the modern conception of history as the unity of rational purpose (immanent or transcendent) really goes back through the Christian idea (cf. Augustine's *City of God*) to Jewish apocalyptic and its forerunner, Hebrew prophecy. (The only partial parallel in the ancient world is Iranian, *i.e.* Persian, which may have influenced, but did not originate, the contribution of Israel.) The prophets had interpreted contemporary history as the working out of a divine purpose ; the apocalyptists systematized and universalized this conception, as we may see, *e.g.* from the Book of Daniel ; the belief of Christendom in a future Kingdom of God made belief in the

natural unity of history part of our modern outlook. Apocalyptic, therefore, served as an important link between Hebrew prophecy and the Christian faith, since the religious faith of both the Old Testament and the New rests on the actuality of history and its full inclusion in the purpose of God.

(2) The rise of belief in a real life after death is the most important feature of the doctrinal development of Judaism in this period ; it naturally affected most other lines of doctrine. To the process of this change the apocalyptic literature is our chief witness. The old Sheol belief was the background rather than the stage of this development, which was partly due to the sufferings and death of " martyrs." It is significant that the only two clear references in the Old Testament to resurrection are found in Apocalypses. It was felt that those who had been deprived by death of their share in the victory and glory of the coming age must be restored to life on earth (Isa. 26^{19}) : it came to be felt that great sinners must also be brought back to life for their full punishment (Dan. 12^2). From such simple beginnings came that copious growth of eschatological speculation in all its bewildering variety which meets us in the apocalyptic books. It cannot be summarized, since it varies from writer to writer. But it transforms Sheol into either a waiting-room for the suspended judgement, or a place of punishment for the wicked, modelled on the " Gehenna " conception, in contrast with " Paradise " as the final abode of the blessed (cf. 4 Ezra 7^{36}). The older prophetic belief in a Kingdom of God on earth is often included as a preliminary stage leading up to the final judgement ; hence the " millennial " ideas of the Book of Revelation (20). The resultant realm of apocalyptic forms the background of the New Testament, which selects from and often transforms its details. The Book of Revelation shows the closest approximation to Jewish apocalyptic and contrasts with the more sober and restrained use of it in the Synoptic Gospels. The Book of Revelation illustrates the typical (though not universal) sequence of (1) Woes ; (2) The First Overthrow of Evil Powers ; (3) Millennium ; (4) Final Overthrow of Evil, General Resurrection and Judgement ; (5) The Age to Come (see The Beginnings of Christianity, Jackson and Lake, i. p. 134).

(3) In regard to the " Messianic " hope, which in the larger or narrower sense is so prominent in apocalyptic, this is the most convenient place to summarize the Old Testament preparation for it. In the larger sense, the term is loosely used to denote the hope of national restoration which inspires so many prophetic utterances and finds its noblest expression

in Deutero-Isaiah (40–55) ; it will be the sequel to that " Day of Yahweh " when evil will be judged and good vindicated (Isa. 1²⁶ ; Zeph. 3⁸ᶠᶠ· ; Zech. 8, etc.). Its setting is often conceived as a rejuvenated world of increased fertility, etc. (Isa. 32¹⁵⁻¹⁸, 35¹·², ; Ezek. 47⁷ᶠᶠ· ; Joel 3¹⁸, etc.) ; for this golden age to come God will create new heavens and a new earth, on which men shall live long and happy lives (Isa. 65¹⁷⁻²⁵). This divine re-creation does not necessarily involve a "Messiah," *i.e.* an " anointed " prince to rule this happy people. But this figure is found in certain passages, which describe such a ruler (Isa. 9⁶·⁷, 11¹⁻⁹ ; Jer. 23⁵, 33¹⁵ ; Ezek. 34²³, 37²⁴) of the lineage of David. This goes back to the promise made to David through Nathan (2 Sam. 7¹²ᶠᶠ· ; cf. Ps. 89). We can see the historical character of the hope in the recognition of Zerubbabel, the grandson of the last Davidic king, Jeconiah, as the Messiah (Haggai 2²³ ; cf. Jer. 22²⁴ ; Zech. 3⁸, 6¹²) and a later variant of this belief occurs as far down the generations as Simon the Maccabee, if Ps. 110 refers to him as priest-king (cf. 1 Macc. 14⁴¹). The Testament of Reuben (6⁷ᶠᶠ·) looks for a Messiah from the stock of Levi, and the " Zadokite " fragments for one from Aaron (9¹⁰). The prayer for a restored Davidic prince appears in the (Pharisaic) Psalms of Solomon (17²¹ᶠᶠ·) of the time of Pompey ; he is to overthrow the Romans.

The distinctive " Messianic " contribution of apocalyptic (in the narrower sense) is to offer as an alternative to this quasi-historical Davidic or Levitical prince a transcendent figure, coming from heaven. This figure is seen in the " Similitudes " of Enoch (37–71), and is there called Anointed, Righteous, Elect, and Son of Man. The last-named title is apparently derived from Dan. 7¹³, where, however, it designates the " corporate personality " of the saints of the Most High (v.²⁷) ; in Enoch, as in the New Testament, the connotation is individualized. In 4 Ezra, belonging to the latter part of the first century A.D., we have a similar figure (13) coming up from the mysterious depths of the sea, the " Man " whom God calls " My Son." The importance of these conceptions for the Christology of the New Testament is obvious. Jesus is represented as turning from the Davidic to the transcendent conception of the Messiah, which however He transformed by assimilating it to Isa. 53.

The " Messianic " hope of Israel was both her glory and her ruin. In its various forms it inspired some of the great prophetic and apocalyptic utterances and repeatedly brought consolation to Israel in its darkest days. On the other hand the very revival of such hopes in the first Christian century to which the New Testament witnesses, led eventually to the catastrophe of A.D. 70 and the destruction of such political existence as remained to Israel. The continued existence of the Jewish faith after that event was due to a previous religious development running parallel with both the apocalyptic literature and the ritual of the Temple, a development which proved able to continue without both, namely, the religion of the Law, which remains to be described.

8. Religion under the Law

Our two previous topics, namely, Wisdom and Apocalyptic, have shown us special developments of post-exilic religion, with the religion of the Temple as their background. We have now to notice a further development of religion to be seen in the attitude taken to the Torah, the Jewish " Law." This new attitude was destined to become the fundamental characteristic of the Judaism contemporary with early Christianity, and of all subsequent orthodox Judaism. The chief features of this development may be indicated under five heads, namely, the growth of the " Canon " of the Old Testament, the rise and significance of the Synagogue, the (new) emphasis on oral tradition as interpretative of the Torah, the codification of this tradition in the Mishnah (c. A.D. 200), and the fundamental conceptions of God and man.

(1) When we try to trace the growth of the " Canon " (as distinct from that of the literature which eventually obtained ' canonical " authority), we are at once impressed by the paucity of evidence as to the formal recognition of the literature as authoritative and inspired. It is true that the Deuteronomic Law was accepted as the basis of Josiah's reformation in 621 B.C., and that the introduction of a law-book (probably the earlier parts of the Priestly Code) to the post-exilic community was connected with the return of Ezra from Babylon to Jerusalem, probably in 397 B.C. But we do not know when this law-book was joined with the earlier one and with other elements to make our Pentateuch. The process must have been completed before the Samaritan " schism," since the Samaritan Pentateuch is identical ; but we can only conjecture that the date of this definite breach between Jews and Samaritans was late in the fourth century, i.e early in the Greek period, beginning with Alexander c. 330 B.C. Our collection of the " prophetical" books (including Joshua, Judges, 1 and 2 Samuel, 1 and 2 Kings on the Jewish reckoning) must have been complete by about 200 B.C., since ben Sira

evidently had it before him in 180 B.C. The third part of the
Old Testament, known as "The Writings," had not been
precisely defined even in the New Testament times, when
Palestinian Jewish scholars were still debating whether certain
of the writings (Ecclesiastes, Canticles, Esther) ought to be
regarded as "sacred" Scripture. There is no evidence of any
inclination to accept the "Apocrypha," *i.e.* the "plus" of the
Greek Scriptures of Hellenistic Judaism and the early Christian
Church.

For our present purpose, it is the Torah (*i.e.* the Pentateuch)
that alone concerns us, since the "Prophets" and the
"Writings" were always regarded as of subordinate authority
and assigned to levels of inspiration lower than the unique
revelation supposed to have been given on Sinai to Moses. At
first, as we have seen, the Deuteronomic and Priestly Codes of
Law were of importance primarily as prescribing the right way
of worshipping the God of Israel, and the emphasis fell on the
ritual of the Temple. But in the course of centuries there was
a remarkable though subtle change of emphasis. The Torah
came to be reverenced for its own sake. We see the beginnings
of this new regard in the Book of Psalms, when Pss. 1, 19$^{7-14}$,
and especially 119, are devoted to the praise of the Torah
as a divine revelation. When the Maccabæan revolt occurs
(167 B.C.) it is clear that the desecration of the Torah rolls
(1 Macc. 1^{56}, 3^{48}) is felt as keenly as that of the Temple (1^{54}).
But the most convincing proof of the change of emphasis is in
the fact that after A.D. 70, when the temple had been destroyed,
Judaism was able to continue on the basis of the Torah only,
though now deprived of that ritual which it was the chief
original purpose of the Torah to enforce.

(2) This independence of the temple had been made possible
by the rise and universal extension of the synagogues which
had functioned for centuries before as the supplement of temple
religion. We do not know when they began to be, though the
needs of the exiles in Babylon would doubtless give rise to local
gatherings for worship. The earliest dated evidence for the
existence of synagogues comes from Egypt in the middle of
the third century B.C. (Elbogen, *Der Jüdische Gottesdienst*,[3]
p. 446); there is an apparent reference to them in Ps. 74^8.
Their primary function was the reading and interpretation of
the Torah, and they became the effective centres of the religion
of ordinary folk in each place, at home or abroad, where there
were Jewish settlements. (The details of this religion and of
the synagogue worship are described in Chap. XVIII.) They did
not replace the temple, with which they were linked by lay

representation, frequent pilgrimages at the festivals, and the
occasional presentation of private offerings at the temple altar.
But they inevitably moulded the religious life of Jews in
Palestine and in the Dispersion, so that it became natural to
think of the prayers of the synagogue as the spiritual equivalent of sacrificial offerings. Thus they prepared for the
time when those sacrificial offerings were no longer possible.
These had temporarily ceased in 586 B.C. and in 168 B.C.; when
they finally ceased in A.D. 70, they were no longer essential.
So was it that the triumphal arch of Titus in Rome, which still
yields our last glimpse of the seven-branched lampstand, the
golden table and the silver trumpets, celebrates the defeat of
a people, but not of a religion.

(3) We must not, however, think of the Jewish Torah
simply as a written document. Every religion that builds
on a book is compelled to devise means to reinterpret that book
so as to adapt its original meaning to the changing needs of
successive generations. Thus it came to pass that alongside
of the written Torah there grew up a mass of interpretation,
natural or artificial, which formed the unwritten Torah, " the
tradition of the elders " (Mark 7[3]). In course of time this
body of tradition claimed not only equal authority with the
written law, but even a like origin, for it was traced back to
Sinai and ascribed to Moses, by whom it was handed down
through a long chain of witnesses (Pirke Aboth, I. 1 f.). Of this
oral tradition the scribes of the Pharisees (Mark 2[16]) were the
exponents, whilst their antagonists, " the priests and the
Sadducees " (Acts 4[1]) rejected it. This conflict, which is
partly that of religious progressives and class conservatives,
first emerges in the latter part of the second century B.C. under
John Hyrcanus ; it continued into the first century A.D. until
the war of A.D. 66–70 put an end to the Sanhedrin, the stronghold of the Sadducees. Since the political Zealots had been
discredited by the same series of events, the Pharisees remained the leaders of future Judaism (see below, Chap. XVII)
and their Rabbis devoted themselves to making explicit the
divine revelation contained in the written Law. Their exegesis
(midrash) has the two main divisions of " Halakhah " and
" Haggadah," the former being juristic and the latter (of
great variety) containing all the non-juristic elements. The
Halakhah forms the unwritten Law of Judaism.

(4) The Mishnah, consisting mostly of this Halakhah, has
six divisions, each containing a number of tractates, sixty-
three in all, and (from a Jewish standpoint) a systematic
(topical) classification of the discussions and decisions of

Rabbis during the previous centuries as to the right interpretation and expansion of the Torah. Before A.D. 70 at any
rate, the remembrance of these seems to have been purely
dependent on oral tradition. After the destruction of Jerusalem
the importance of some permanent record must have been
apparent, though nothing written has survived except so far
as it may have been incorporated in the Mishnah (c. A.D. 200) ;
indeed it is alleged that this was the first written record. The
first leading figure in the process of its creation is that of
Jochanan ben Zakkai who gathered disciples at Jamnia (near
the coast, between Joppa and Ascalon) without objection from
Rome, since his object was religious and not political. The
Beth-din or " tribunal " thus virtually established for Judaism
was very different from the Sanhedrin, now no longer existent,
but eventually came to exercise great authority over Judaism,
an authority recognized by the Romans. The non-political
attitude of these Rabbis was, however, abandoned by Akiba
the outstanding supporter of Bar Cocheba, whose Messianic
claims led to the disastrous outbreak of A.D. 132–5. Akiba
did much towards the systematization of the oral tradition
into the Mishnah, and his work was continued by his disciple
Rabbi Meir, but the final contribution was that by Judah
the Patriarch (Nasi), who arranged the Mishnah in its present
form. This indicates the definite transition to Judaism.

(5) It is not possible within a few lines to give any comprehensive and adequate account of the doctrines of Judaism
as formulated by the Rabbis of the Tannaite period (extending
from Jochanan ben Zakkai to the Patriarch Judah—five
generations). This has been done elaborately in the classical
work of G. F. Moore (*Judaism*, 1927). A brief characterization
of Judaism as built up on this basis will be found at the
beginning of the article on " Judaism " in the *ERE*, vol. vii.
p. 581, by Mr. Herbert Loewe. He remarks that " the foundation of Judaism rests on two principles : the unity of God and
the choice of Israel." Judaism opposes all polytheism and
idolatry, but is not exclusive ; it regards Christianity and Islam
as teaching its own truths in less pure form, and holds that
every righteous man has a share in the world to come. Man is
free and responsible for his use of freedom, and Judaism " lays
more stress on works than on faith." The cardinal doctrine
of God is thus admirably summarized by Moore (*op. cit.* vol. i
p. 423) :

> " The idea of God was eminently personal. He was supra-
> mundane but not extramundane ; exalted but not remote
> He was the sole ruler of the world he had created, and he ordered

all things in it in accordance with his character, in which justice and mercy were complementary, not conflicting, attributes. His will for man was righteousness and goodness ; and that they might know what He required, He had defined his will in two-fold law. His far-reaching and all-embracing plan had for its end the universality of the true religion in an age of universal uprightness, peace, and prosperity—the goal to which all history tended—' the reign of God.' "

As for the doctrine of man, the most notable feature in the Old Testament ideas had been the identification of human personality with the *body* rather than with the soul or spirit which merely animates it (cf. Gen. 2⁷). Consciousness is supposed to be diffused through the different members of the body, including its peripheral (eye, ear, mouth) as well as its central (heart, liver, kidneys, bowels) organs, so that the flesh can long for God (Ps. 63¹) and the bones can acknowledge Him (Ps. 35¹⁰). Man is essentially " flesh " as God is essentially " spirit " (Isa. 31³). Because man is thus made up of many distinct psycho-physical parts, he is the more accessible to external influences, for good or for evil. His " soul " has no independent existence, and simply goes out at death ; " spirit," later its synonym, is not assigned to man's normal nature before the Exile (see further, *The Christian Doctrine of Man*, by H. Wheeler Robinson, pp. 11 ff.).

These beliefs continued in Jewish religion under the Law, though the new belief in a life after death changed the emphasis from the body to the soul or spirit (*e.g.* Enoch 9¹⁰, 22⁵, 103⁴), but not to the point of dualism (ct. the Hellenistic Wisdom of Solomon). For Palestinian Judaism that life still depended on a resurrection of the body. The deepened consciousness of man's sin is best seen in 4 Ezra ; the initial sin of Adam brought the sentence of death on the whole race, according to the conception of corporate personality (3⁷ ; cf. 2 Baruch 54¹⁵). The Jewish doctrine of the Yetzer Hara (evil impulse) is not to be identified with the (Augustinian) doctrine of original sin. Man remains morally free and is therefore responsible : " Each of us has been the Adam of his own soul " (2 Baruch 54¹⁹).

9. THE UNITY OF THE DEVELOPMENT

For our present purpose " religion under the Law " must be taken as but one phase (although the final one) of the religion of Israel. Its finality for Judaism has led to the editorial adaptation and arrangement of the Old Testament from this particular standpoint, so that many of the original data for earlier phases of the religion must have been omitted or altered so as to make them inoffensive to the ultimate Jewish beliefs. In particular, the Torah has been placed before the prophets, which is largely a reversal of the true order, as Biblical criticism has reconstructed it.

If, however, we are unable to find, like the orthodox Jew, the unity of the historical process in a complete and primal revelation of God's will to Moses, that does not mean that we must abandon the idea of unity altogether. In some sense, the religion of Israel, however critically interpreted, must be a unity, since it is a process of living growth, with constant assimilation of new elements, within the continuity of life. The seed and root, the stalk and foliage, may all appear different from the flower which the plant bears, yet there is a unity embracing them all. What, then, is the unity which runs through all those eight phases of Israel's religion which we have reviewed ?

We have seen that (1) Yahweh first reveals Himself by redemptive *activity*, involving the free choice of Israel, an activity which makes essential use of a " prophetic " personality to interpret His acts in Nature and history. In strong contrast stood (2) the nature-cults of Canaan, and reaction from them eventually led to the clearer conception of, and stronger faith in, the desert-God of Sinai. This found classical expression in (3) the pre-exilic prophets, and more particularly in those of the eighth century, through whom the majesty and moral righteousness of Yahweh is seen to be extra-national, as well as national. They interpreted history as the activity of God and found its unity in His purpose. In Jeremiah the individual relation to Him had its most spiritual expression. In (4) the Exile, deprivation of the accustomed means of worship led to new conceptions of religion, and a more spiritual-ized approach to God, whilst distance robbed the Nature-cults forever of their enchantment, at least for that minority which was to direct the future of Israel. The monotheism of Deutero-Isaiah, if not his universalism, was to become the permanent possession of Israel, whilst Ezekiel combined the hope of regeneration with the demand for a purified ritual. (5) The second temple became the centre of an intense, if narrow, nationalistic religion, and made Israel the people of a cult which could nurture the fine devotion of the Psalms. Parallel with this cult and this devotion there ran (6) the moral teaching and religious thought of the Wisdom literature, and eventually (7) the passionate panorama of apocalyptic. Strong as was the popularity of this for centuries, it was eventually abandoned by the sober rationalism of the Rabbis in whose work (8) the religion of the Law found its formulation, and future Judaism its foundation.

Such a review brings out at least three primary conceptions, so inter-related that they may be regarded as a unity, namely, (1) the conception of one living God, revealed in history, (2) the consciousness of His covenanted "election" of Israel to be His people, and (3) the inseparability of morality and religion in regard to both the activity of God and His requirements from man. These are the essential and characteristic ideas of the religion of Israel, and all else is subordinate to them. If they seem commonplaces to us, it is because the Old Testament has made commonplace something that was unique in the ancient world.

(1) The explicit description of Yahweh as "the living God" is not the most frequent or the earliest of the various terms applied to Him, but it is perhaps the one best qualified to bring out the impression made upon us by the successive phases of Israel's religion, the impression of a God of boundless energy and vitality, never at a loss to meet the demands of changing circumstances and apparent defeat, a God who is not so much venerable with age (Dan. 7^{13}), as possessed of the vitality of perennial youth—"for ever He is young" says a late Midrash. It was the voice of the living God which Israel heard speaking from the midst of the fire of Horeb (Deut. 5^{26}) ; it is the living God whom Jeremiah describes as God in truth and everlasting royalty, at whose wrath the earth and its inhabitants tremble (Jer. 10^{10}). The youthful David is indignant that a Philistine should have reproached the armies of the living God (1 Sam. 17$^{26.\ 36}$), as is Hezekiah at the blasphemy of Sennacherib (2 Kings 19$^{4.\ 16}$), or Jeremiah at that of his own contemporaries (Jer. 23^{36}). To be reckoned as "the sons of the living God" is the opposite of being "not my people" (Hosea 1^{10}). The temple courts afford approach to the living God and so satisfy the keenest desire of the religious Israelite (Pss. 42^2, 84^2). Yahweh is the fountain of living water (Jer. 2^{13}, 17^{13} ; cf. Ps. 36^9) ; He is the life, the long life of Israel (Deut. 30^{20}). So it is that Abigail can wish nothing better for David encompassed by dangers than that he should be bound up in the bundle of life with Yahweh his God (1 Sam. 25^{29}). There can be no stronger oath than that by the life of the god (Amos 8^{14}) and men swear "by the life of Yahweh" (Judges 8^{19}, etc.), even as Yahweh Himself swears by His own life (Deut. 32^{40}). In fullest contrast with the living God are the no-gods of the nations, identified with their idols, which have the detailed semblance of life (*i.e.* the

bodily members) without its animating principle (so *e.g.* Ps. 115[4ff.]). The same contrast is felt between the Baal of whom Elijah on Carmel scornfully says, " peradventure he sleepeth " (1 Kings 18[27]) and the God of Israel, "who slumbers not nor sleeps " (Ps. 121[4]). The sheer energy of the living God issues in countless forms of activity, of which His *ruach* (wind-spirit) is best known (*e.g.* Judg. 15[14], Ezek. 37, Joel 2[28]). It is the activity of Yahweh, not His metaphysical essence nor His self-enjoyment that is His *life*, and He stands out as this living personality over against the conception of " fate " amongst other peoples (cf. P. Kleinert, " Zur Idee des Lebens im Alten Testament," in *Theologische Studien und Kritiken*, 1895, pp. 700 ff.).

Given, then, this fundamental idea of God, it is plain that the revelation of His will is not confined to Sinai, though it began there for Israel. He advances from Nature into history, and history becomes more and more clearly the unfolding of His purpose. Thus, such a review of the phases of religion as we have made becomes an essential part of the constructive idea of God ; He is known only as He is seen in dynamic movement. This quality of the Old Testament religion is of primary importance, especially as it is continued in that of the New Testament (cf. the conception of the Holy Spirit) and the amazing vitality of the Christian faith through many generations shows Jesus Christ to be the same yesterday, to-day, and for ever, just because He can similarly meet the changing needs of successive generations.

Bound up with this conception of the living God under the historic name of Yahweh, there is the complementary idea of the time-series as *real*, intensely real. It is the form through which Yahweh chiefly manifests Himself, the form which makes Him so much more than a God of Nature. He is creator of Nature and its constant ruler, not a non-normal dispenser of its gifts, like the Baalim. Nature consequently becomes the arena of history, and the changing sequence of natural phenomena is taken up into the purpose which runs through history, and gives it its unity. The key to that unity is seen in His relation to a particular people, Israel. Here, worked into shape through the actuality of the time-series, we may see the true character of God, displayed in the great companion attributes of " righteousness " and " loving-kindness." They are not antithetical, but complementary ; indeed they are but different aspects of the unity of His character and purpose. They are not conceived as abstract qualities, metaphysical attributes of deity, but as the source of the concrete and historic acts through which He is known. Thus His " righteousness " is displayed in His " righteousnesses " (righteous acts, cf. Judg. 5[11], 1 Sam. 12[7], Micah 6[5], Ps. 103[6]) and His " loving-kindness " (*chesed*) is the kernel of which " covenant " (*berith*) is the shell.

(2) The covenant with Israel is the second great integrating principle in the unity of the religion of Israel. It is so central and important a conception that the most recent full-scale treatment of the theology of the Old Testament (Eichrodt) has made it dominant and brought everything else within its ægis, so reverting (from a more historical standpoint) to earlier theological method, which has its permanent record in the very contrast of the " Old " and " New " Testaments (dispensations or " covenants," cf. Gal. 4[24-26], 2 Cor. 3[4-11]).

The term " covenant " (*berith*) can be used in a non-theological sense of such an agreement as that between Abraham and Abimelech (Gen. 21[27]) which, as was usual, involved an oath and religious sanctions. As applied to the relation between God and man, it is always God who takes the initiative, so that the terms of the *berith* virtually become God's ordinance. The history of religion in Israel is marked by a series of such covenants, the specific contents of the ordinance being differently conceived at different periods. Thus at Sinai, Yahweh promises that if Israel will obediently keep His covenant, she shall hold a unique relation to Him among all the peoples of the earth (Ex. 19[5], JE), whilst the earliest code of Israel's laws (Ex. 20[22]–23[19]) is called " the Book of the Covenant " (24[7]). In Deut. 4[13] the contents of the Horeb covenant are defined as the Decalogue ; in Deut. 29, however, they are (editorially) regarded as the Deuteronomic Code itself. This code was the basis of Josiah's reformation, and is described in 2 Kings 23[2ff.] as " the Book of the Covenant." In the (later) Priestly writings, the different phases of the religion and the growth of its institutions are linked with a series of covenants established through representative persons, such as Noah (Gen. 9[9-17]), the patriarchs (Lev. 26[42]), Phinehas (Num. 25[12]), and the word denotes more distinctly a divine and authoritative promise. Indeed, the very terminology of covenant-making reflects this change ; the earlier phrase was " to cut a covenant ' (Gen. 15[18], JE), with reference to the sacrifice and mutual oath of the participators who passed between the pieces of the divided victim, invoking a like fate on themselves if they violated the agreement, and the later phrase was " to set up a covenant," used of the action of a superior (Gen. 6[18]).

The initiative, then, is Yahweh's, and the human choice

involved in its acceptance by Israel (Josh. 24[14ff.] ; Deut. 11[26ff.], 30[15ff.]) is always conceived as being exercised within a previous choice of Israel by Yahweh (*e.g.* Josh. 24[2, 3]). Thus the " election " of Israel, as involved in the covenant-idea, is a fundamental doctrine of the Old Testament : it is the special application to Israel of the whole conception of divine providence. It becomes explicit in terminology chiefly in Deuteronomy and Deutero-Isaiah (*e.g.* Deut. 7[7] ; Isaiah 44[1]). The doctrine of election primarily appeals to the deliverance from Egypt for its proof ; the promises given to the patriarchs appear to be a secondary and derived form. In the older tradition, represented by the prophets, the Sinai covenant falls into the background and becomes a mere episode between the Exodus and the entrance into Canaan. For Jeremiah, who makes most frequent reference to the covenant, the election *is* the covenant (so Kurt Galling, *Die Erwählungstraditionen Israels*).

It might reasonably be claimed that some form of the doctrine of election (here underlying the covenant idea) is necessary to any religion with belief in a divine purpose and in the relation of men to that purpose. The strength and importance of the doctrine in Israel may be seen when we think of the great " tensions " to which her religion was exposed in the course of its development, tensions which in one form or other have a permanent place in all religious life. One of them is the clash between outward events and inward faith ; how could Judah, for example, reconcile the overthrow of Jerusalem in 586 B.C. with Yahweh's election of His people ? The answer is found in Deutero-Isaiah's reinterpretation of Israel's sufferings in exile as destined to become a sacrificial offering, which would move the nations of the earth to penitence when they saw the people of Yahweh at last restored, and would enable them to approach Him themselves (Isa. 53). This constitution of a new fact by the religious reinterpretation of the mere event is a principle of great importance in Biblical religion and culminates in the doctrine of the Cross. But it is mentioned here in order to bring out the survival-value of the doctrine of election which could inspire it. Another tension is seen in the growing sense of difference between God and man, God who is " spirit," and man who is " flesh " (Is. 31[3]). How holy is God, how sinful is man ! (Isa. 6). Yet by the grace of God He is the Holy One *of Israel* (Isa. 12[6]). The glory of God is such that no man could see Him, yet the grace of God can grant partial vision to His chosen servant (Ex. 33[22, 23]), and Israel, " the fewest of

all peoples " (Deut. 7⁷) can take refuge in the thought that
Yahweh's love, not Israel's merit, was the motive of His choice.
Yet another tension is that between nationalism and universalism, where again Deutero-Isaiah's conception of an
election to service is the noblest corrective to the mere sense
of national privilege rebuked by Amos (3²). The broader
universalistic teaching of Deutero-Isaiah continues to be
represented in the Old Testament (cf. Jonah ; Isa. 19²⁴. ²⁵,
25⁶⁻⁸ ; Mal. 1¹¹) in spite of the " nationalism " emphasized by
Nehemiah and Ezra.

(3) The third great characteristic of the religion of Israel
is the close interrelation of morality and religion (Deut. 4⁷⁻ ⁸).
There is no parallel to such closeness of interrelation amongst
other ancient religions. It is seen both in the prophetic
emphasis on morality as God's chief requirement from man and
also in the moralization of the idea of God. In both respects,
the conception of " corporate personality " has exercised a
great influence. Thus, when we ask what is the distinctive
feature of the contents of Hebrew ethics, our answer will be
" social righteousness," *i.e.* the right relation of the individual
members of the unitary society to one another. But the
primary qualities of such rightness—justice to all and mercy
to the weak—are applications of the group idea, in a way very
different from that of the much more individualized and
limited Greek ethics, which sprang from the idea of an artificial
state, and emphasized a harmonious development of faculty
rather than a group-consciousness. This consciousness with
its strongly democratic features goes back to the constitution
of the desert clan, from which the Hebrew ideas of justice
(*mishpat*) and mercy (*chesed*) are ultimately derived. What
the great prophets did was not to invent new virtues, but
to give old virtues a new place in religion—always the surest
way of fostering them. Hebrew morality at its best (*i.e.* in
Job 31) was what it was because it developed from the customs
of a people strong in the sense of corporate personality. But
may we not say that the same corporate conception also
operates, *mutatis mutandis*, in regard to Yahweh ? As we
have seen, He enters (by a blood-rite) into the covenant
relation (an ancient way of creating " kinship " where it did
not exist by nature, as we see in the story of David and
Jonathan, 1 Sam. 18³) on his own initiative, and the relation
thus voluntarily assumed stands in strongest contrast with the
quasi-physical ties which are supposed to bind nature-gods
to their people. Yet once He has entered into that relation
He becomes, we might almost say, the supreme representative

of the group, *morally* bound to it so long as His people are faithful to His ordinances. We have here, though at a higher and moralized level, a conception similar to that of "the bundle of life" in which David is to be bound up with Yahweh (1 Sam. 25²⁹). We really need to apply this corporate conception so as—in the sense defined—to include Yahweh in the group, if we are to give full force to some of the most intense expressions of His relation to Israel. He is the father of His people, and they are His sons (Hosea 11¹; Isa. 1²; Jer. 31¹· ⁹; Mal. 1⁶). He is the husband of Israel, and we could hardly have greater realism than in the description of this in Ezekiel 16⁸, or stronger expression of the inviolability of the new betrothal than in Hosea 2¹⁹ᶠᶠ·. So, in the repeated appeal to Yahweh "for His name's sake" (Jer. 14⁷; Ps. 23³ etc.), we mark the consciousness that the covenanted God is one with His people and that His honour is involved in covenant-fidelity to their interests.

Only when we take all this into account does the full significance of the prophetic "moralization" of Yahweh's personality emerge. The prophets were not arbitrarily referring moral excellences which they admired to the character of their God; they were confident of His full moral fulfilment of the relation in which He stood to Israel, whether for weal or woe, and even before that relation had found expression in the idea of a formal covenant. Consequently they can speak with the greater intensity of His passionate reaction to Israel's infidelities—the Bible knows nothing of an impassible God —as in the deeply emotional words which Hosea (11⁸) puts into Yahweh's mouth : "How shall I give thee up, Ephraim? how shall I deliver thee up, Israel (*i.e.* to vengeance)? . . . mine heart is turned within me, my compassions are kindled together." Such a prophet is virtually asserting that the wrong done to a fellow Israelite is also a wrong done to Yahweh as the highest and representative member of the society; and we have an anticipation of the thought of Matt. 25⁴⁰· ⁴⁵ : "Inasmuch as ye did it . . . as ye did it not . . . unto one of the least of these my brethren, ye did it . . . ye did it not . . . unto me."

It should be always remembered that the relation of Yahweh to His people never ceases to be a relation to Israel as a corporate unity, even though from the time of Jeremiah onwards there is an increasing recognition of the place and importance of the individual Israelite, to which Jeremiah so greatly contributed through his own personal experience of fellowship with God. The individual throughout remains one of the nation which Yahweh has chosen, and that fact conditions all his thought and experience. Thus, when Jeremiah conceives a new covenant in contrast with the national and external covenant which has failed, a covenant marked by moral inwardness, direct dependence on God and fellowship with Him (like the prophetic consciousness of Jeremiah himself), it still remains " a new covenant with the house of Israel and with the house of Judah" ($31^{31ff.}$), *i.e.* the new individualism operates within the old corporate relation.

It was Jeremiah also who seems to have been the first to raise Israel's greatest religious problem, the suffering of the innocent and the prosperity of the wicked (12^1). This fact is significant, since it was not until the new individualism arose that the doctrine of a complete moral retribution within the present life was seen to break down. So long as the religious units were nations, or even families, there was more scope in which to find the judgements of God, since it was sufficient that *any* member of the unitary group should be seen to receive the due reward or penalty (as in the ancient Semitic custom of blood-revenge). But once the instinctive claims of the individual were recognized, it became likely that some one would arise to state the problem in the terms of the Book of Job and to argue against the righteousness of God because of the innocence of some sufferers. Jewish thinkers felt this problem so much because prosperity or adversity without moral reasons for it cut at the roots of their faith in a righteous God righteously governing this world, a God ever morally faithful to those who stood in a covenant relation to Himself.

10. THE FORMS OF MEDIATION

To complete this statement of the theological significance of the religion of Israel, we must take into account the varied means by which the relation between God and man was maintained, the working system of the religion as distinct from its cardinal ideas of God and man.

Six types of mediation may be indicated, though some of them will include a host of subvarieties. There are (*a*) the divine control of physical events, (*b*) and of history, which was interpreted through (*c*) the moral consciousness, especially that of the prophets. These three are of wide range and general character ; to them must be added three more specialized types, namely, (*d*) different kinds of personal agency, whether angels, patriarchs, kings, priests, prophets, righteous men, (e) the cultus and its sacrificial features, (f) the written Torah.

(1) In earlier parts of this article enough has been said to illustrate the nature of the first three. In the classical period of Israel's religion (eighth to sixth centuries) Yahweh is conceived as the creator of the world, which therefore manifests His majesty and power, whilst the course of events within the world shows His providential control of history and thus manifests His moral purpose. This revelation through history has the wealth of the orchestral symphony as compared with the unaccompanied solo of a Muhammad, and it is a revelation without full parallel in method, as it is unique in the contents afforded by the moral consciousness. History, in manner and content, is indeed the ultimate sacrament of Israel. Prophecy morally interpreting this history killed idolatry not so much by scorn and denunciation as by offering a far higher means of contact with God. The moral consciousness of the prophets was a spiritual and dynamic fact and factor ; the worship of God through a material idol emphasized the physical and the static, and the chains that bound the idol to its wall (Isa. 40^{19}, 41^7) are symbolic of the way in which an idol imprisons religion.

(2) It is sometimes said that the priest represented man to God, whilst the prophet represented God to man. That is broadly true, though the oracular answers of God came through the priests, and the prophets are often intercessors (e.g. Ex. 32^{31-32} ; Jer. 14^{21}, 15^1. The high-priest represents the people before Yahweh by bearing the names of the tribes on his shoulders and on his breast (Ex. $28^{12.\ 29}$), " when he goes in unto the holy place, for a memorial before Yahweh continually," whilst he bears on his forehead the inscription " holy to Yahweh " (vv.$^{36-38}$). It is probable that to-day we underestimate the importance of the priest in both the history and the religion of Israel. In his representation of Israel, he is said to " bear the iniquity of the holy things " (ibid.), i.e. take upon himself the guilt of any ritual error ; so the priest-prophet Ezekiel symbolically bears the iniquity of the house of Israel (4^4). If the Israel of the future is to share in the prophetic consciousness (Jer. $31^{31ff.}$), so also she is to be named " priests of Yahweh " (Isa. 61^6), " a kingdom of priests " (Ex. 19^6). There is a priestly element, as well as a prophetic, in the portrayal of the suffering Servant of Yahweh (Isa. 53^{4-6}, cf. Ex. 28^{38}, and note the asham, or guilt-offering of Isa. 53^{10}, an interesting parallel to the interchange of sacrificer and sacrifice in the Epistle to the Hebrews).

(3) Sacrifice and the related features of the cultus offer means of mediation so full of detail (see below, Chap. XVI) that it would here be impossible even to give a mere list of holy objects, holy places, holy seasons, and holy acts which are conceived to bring God and man into relation. The common feature seems to be the setting apart of a representative of the whole. By being brought into this special relation to God, these representative objects share in their own degree His holiness and become media of His relation to men. How far such a procedure constitutes a " sacrament " depends on the definition of a term we use very loosely. One mark of the sacrament proper does belong to these media, since they are all ultimately conceived to rest on the ordinance of God, whatever their particular origin in pre-historic practice (see, *e.g.*, §2 for the probably extensive influence of the Canaanite religion on Hebrew sacrifice). The demand for obedience is the *ultimate* emphasis of the cult, and this implies a moral response. In the classical description of the worship given by ben Sira (50[14ff.]) the culminating moment is reached when the sacrifice has been offered, and the libation poured out " as a sweet-smelling savour to the Most High." Then the priestly trumpets are blown to call the attention of God to the service that has been rendered, and all prostrate themselves in worship and cry out in prayer, whilst the chant of the Levites rings out above their heads, until the priest has finished the service of the altar of God " and has brought nigh its *ordinances* unto it " (see Hebrew text).

Whatever view we may take of the origins of Hebrew sacrifice or of sacrifice in general, there does not seem to be anything in the Hebrew ritual itself that offers a principle of mediation different from that found elsewhere. Israel, it has been rightly said, is distinguished not by the institution, but by the ultimate abandonment of sacrifice. There are primitive beliefs underlying the blood-rites and the communion feast, and doubtless the common conception was that of a gift to God, a gift which on occasion might have propitiatory or expiatory value (so Buchanan Gray, *Sacrifice in the Old Testament*, p. 32). Ultimately, however, the ritual came to be regarded supremely as that act of obedience to Yahweh's declared commands which gave to His people the opportunity of closest communion with Him. What that meant we know from some of the most impressive of the psalms. The obedient " guest " in Yahweh's temple found there the mighty protection of His hospitality. There stood the Israelite at the centre of those other realms of Nature, history and contemporary

social life, in each of which the presence of the living God had
been manifested to him.   There, in a new and spiritualized
sense, he found his Jacob's ladder linking earth and heaven.
To elect souls, the concrete expression of religion in the ritual
could become the framework of such a vision as Isaiah's.
In the temple, as the penitential psalms show, the worshipper
could wrestle in prophetic spirit for forgiveness and restoration
and begin to cherish the intimations of a life beyond death
which should defeat the last enemy.   None who has rightly
interpreted the many psalms of the cult will ever make light
of the value of religious ritual as a medium of access to God,
even for those whom it trained to a " prophetic " super-
session of it.   Of the Psalms at their highest levels we can
say :

> " The tumult and the shouting dies—
>   The captains and the kings depart—
> Still stands Thine ancient sacrifice,
>   An humble and a contrite heart."

(4) From about 300 B.C., the completion of the written
Torah provided a new kind of " mediation " (in the sense in
which the word is used throughout this section of the article).
It is not sufficient to say that writing simply added the quality
of permanence to the spoken word (cf. Sanday, of prophecy, in
ERE, ii. p. 570).   There was added also a certain fixity
and limitation to revelation, with the result that, as already
seen, all future inevitable expansion and adaptation to changing
circumstances must henceforth disguise themselves as exegesis.
Hence the development of the unwritten Torah of tradition—
a development paralleled in both Islam and Catholic Christianity.   Further, there is the tendency for every written
revelation to be conceived as equally authoritative in all its
parts, so that minor details of ritual, or even the " fossil "
remains of superseded ideas and practices, are ranked alongside of the major principles of morality and religion.   This
is a defect from which none of the " religions of a book " have
wholly escaped.

II. The Relation to Christianity

(1) The great debt of Christianity to Israel was, as Burkitt
points out (*The Legacy of Israel*, p. 71), not the hierarchy, the
creeds and the sacraments, but Jesus and the Bible.   Of the
latter debt, it is sufficient here to recall that the Old Testament was taken over by the Christian Church in its larger
Greek form (*i.e.* with the Apocrypha), but without the oral
tradition of Judaism (save, *e.g.*, in the occasional appearance

of " Rabbinism " in the Pauline Epistles). On the other hand, Jesus is represented as speaking with a new and direct authority and not as the scribes, who appealed to " the tradition of the elders." The appeal to Scripture made by Him and His disciples is to the prophetic rather than to the legalistic elements, or to the Law as interpreted in the light of prophetic teaching (*e.g.* Matt. 5$^{17ff.}$). The " argument from prophecy " based on a Christian reading of the Old Testament figured largely in Early Christian apologetic, and it is difficult to see how the Early Church could have found spiritual nourishment without the Old Testament. The most obvious proof of this is that the Christian writings were themselves a gradual accretion to the existent body of Jewish Scriptures already accepted by the Church.

(2) It is the new fact of Jesus, accepted by His disciples as the hoped-for Messiah, that gives the centre for orientation in the new landscape of the Christian faith. True, He Himself radically altered the Messianic idea by adding His Cross to it, in the light of Isa. 53. But this Jewish Messianic conception, however transformed, served the needs of the first generation of Jewish Christians, until in course of time and of the Gentile mission, the first creed, " Jesus is the Christ " (Acts 17^3), was replaced by the form of expression more natural to Gentiles, " Jesus is Lord " (1 Cor. 12^3). Jesus, in the days of His flesh, had been regarded as both prophet and rabbi— the prophet of the coming " Kingdom of God " and the rabbi whose teaching agreed with much current Jewish doctrine. Yet there was from the beginning a vital difference, made by His own personality and attitude, which gave new force and meaning to familiar truths. Because of that difference, He gathered round Him the beginnings of a new society, like that which we see emerging first in the group of Isaiah's disciples (Isa. 8^{16}) and continued in such other groups as those of Mal. 3^{16} and the " pious " of the Psalms. So came into being that " Israel of God " (Gal. 6^{16}; cf. Ro. 2^{29}, Phil. 3^3) which was to be the nucleus of the Church. Its members are spiritually sons of God, and if we seek for a principle of unity in the New Testament Scriptures, we shall hardly find a better one than " sonship," which continues the Old Testament unity of an " elect " nation and carries it forward to the election of individuals into a society with the spiritual inheritance of the ancient Israel.

(3) This is the proper place to notice the great service rendered to the new faith and its development by Hellenistic Judaism. From the standpoint of Palestinian Judaism this

was a transient phase, which seems to have left little mark on
the main development which led to the Mishnah and the
Talmud (see R. Travers Herford, *Talmud and Apocrypha*).
Just as the Palestinian teachers moved away from the apocalyptic, discredited for them by its Jewish revolutionaries and
by its Christian interpreters, so they drew the lines of a
Hebrew Canon of Scripture narrower, as we have seen, than
that of the Greek Bible. Indeed, the new Greek rendering
made by Aquila (*c.* A.D. 130) is evidence that the Septuagint
itself was no longer regarded as satisfactory, probably owing
to its Christian use and associations. Hellenistic Judaism
(see Bevan's characterization of it in *The Legacy of Israel*)
seems to have faded out, but not before it had profoundly
influenced early Christianity. We saw that the Wisdom
literature of Israel culminated in the Greek "Wisdom of
Solomon," one of the chief products of Hellenistic Judaism,
and ranking with the works of Philo and Josephus as representative of it at its best (*op. cit.* p. 62). As Dr. Bevan has
said: "The Christian Church inherited the great problem of
Hellenistic Judaism, how to find the right relation between
Hebrew religion and Greek philosophy and culture" (*op. cit.*
p. 65).

(4) The category of mediation, of which use was made
in characterizing the religion of Israel in its historical form,
serves equally well to bring out the *differentia* of the new faith
as compared with the old. For the Christian, there is one
Mediator between God and men (1 Tim. 2[5]) through whose
Person and Work mediation itself acquires a new and specialized connotation. To develop this idea is, of course, beyond
the scope of the present article. Here we confine ourselves
to noticing the difference made by His mediation (in the
larger sense previously employed) in regard to (*a*) sin, (*b*) suffering, (*c*) death, always the three great tests of a religion, which
challenge its power to redeem.

(*a*) In the Old Testament there are four classes of terms
used to describe sin, according as they denote deviation from
the right way, guilt before a tribunal, rebellion against a lawful superior, and something intrinsically evil. The common
element is opposition to the will of God, and man's full moral
responsibility is implied. The idea of sin is at first unmoralized;
it denotes the breach of a social custom or taboo. The
Old Testament has no doctrine of "original" sin. The
prophetic moralization of sin included an implied or explicit
appeal for repentance, of which man is conceived as fully
capable. The "grace" of God consists essentially in forgive-

ness, following upon this repentance, the forgiveness (even in
Ps. 51) being largely identified with the remission of the penalty,
such as the sickness or adversity which first brought the
conviction of sin. But notwithstanding this simple " prophetic " scheme of sin and grace, the ritual of sacrifice in
post-exilic times was usually regarded as a necessary accompaniment of repentance. It was a gift to God, according
to His command, which served to restore the broken communion with Him. There is nothing penal, however, even in
the sin-offering ; it is the sinner's offering, with which he is
identified by " the laying on of hands," not a substitute for him.
The teaching of Jesus, according to the Synoptics, continues
this prophetic conception of sin, repentance and forgiveness,
though with a much increased emphasis on the inwardness of
sin, and a deliverance of the conception from entanglement
with traditional taboos, which had passed into the Torah,
written or unwritten. The revolutionary factor is, however,
rather in the personal attitude of Jesus to the sinner, which
creates a new doctrine of grace. Jesus does not wait for a
righteousness which shall qualify for grace ; He takes the
initiative in seeking the sinner and welcoming him into forgiveness, so giving the basis for a new estimate of human
personality. Apart altogether from sacrifice, Judaism is a
religion of righteousness by works. Christianity as taught
and exemplified by Jesus, and elaborated in the Pauline
soteriology, is essentially a religion of redemptive grace (to
which, however, Hosea and Deutero-Isaiah had already made
important contributions, whilst the *principle* was already
implicit in the emphasis on the divine initiative). This
divine initiative of redemptive grace is indeed the *differentia*
of Christianity over against all other religions, and not
Judaism only ; cf. Karl Holl's forcible words : " Jesus reverses, as we may say, the usual relation of religion and
morality. Every other religion, at least of the higher kind,
makes the personal relation to God depend on the right conduct
of man. The more moral any one is—in the widest sense of
morality, including observance of the cult—the nearer he
stands to God. But Jesus begins with God ; it is He who
creates something new by forgiveness, from which, however,
a real, close, and warm relation to God arises, and with it a
morality that may even dare to take God Himself as its
model " (*Urchristentum und Religionsgeschichte*, p. 22).

(*b*) We have seen how constantly the Old Testament
makes suffering the penalty for sin, and leaves no room for
suffering that may have other explanations. It was against

this, as we saw, that Job's protest was made. Another still more important contribution was that of the Suffering Servant (Isa. 53), who being innocent made a vicarious offering of his sufferings (*i.e.* those of Israel in exile) as a sin-offering for the nations of the world, through which they might draw near in penitence and self-rebuke to the God of Israel.

The influence of this interpretation of suffering on both Jesus and His followers can hardly be overrated ; it is visible throughout the New Testament. What Jesus did was to take the interpretation of Israel's sufferings offered by the prophet and to actualize it as a fact of history in Himself. Thus Jesus, making use of the inevitable suffering brought on Him by His holy purpose, at once proved the disinterestedness of genuine piety (creating a new ethical emphasis on " cross-bearing ") and also wrought a revolutionary change in religion, by showing that holy suffering accepted by grace can transform evil into good, the sin of the crucifixion into the glory of the Cross. If this actualized grace of history wrought out in the time-series according to Hebrew realism be also true of the eternal God, then there is no room for the Greek doctrine of impassibility, and a really Biblical doctrine of Atonement is suggested.

(c) In regard to death, we must remember that belief in the resurrection was held by most Jews of the time of Christ. The new feature was not His teaching that there is a life beyond death, but the fact of His own resurrection, without which there would have been no Christian Church at all. Thereby the quality of the resurrection life was profoundly altered for all who belonged to Him. In this latter connexion, the Pauline doctrine of the Holy Spirit should be noted ; he who is a member of the Body of Christ finds " the Lord the Spirit " already imparting to him the " gifts " and " fruits " of the Spirit of life, a life that needs only to grow until it escapes from this body of death, and finds another spiritual body more adequate to its needs. (There are parallels to this line of thought in Jewish apocalyptic.) It was the resurrection of Jesus Christ from the dead that begat Christians unto a living hope (1 Pet. 1[3]) ; it was through Him that they could thank God for the victory over death (1 Cor. 15[57]).

BIBLIOGRAPHY

H. W. Robinson, *The Religious Ideas of the Old Testament.*
C. F. Burney, *Outlines of Old Testament Theology.*

W. O. E. Oesterley and T. H. Robinson, *The Religion of Israel.*
T. H. Robinson, *Prophecy and the Prophets in Ancient Israel.*
J. Skinner, *Prophecy and Religion.*
G. F. Moore, *Judaism in the First Centuries of the Christian Era.*
G. B. Gray, *Sacrifice in the Old Testament.*
   Also the following essays in *Record and Revelation* (ed. by H. W. Robinson, 1938) :
   " The Religion of Israel : Origins," by A. Lods.
   "   ,,   ,,   ,,   Prophecy," by N. W. Porteous.
   "   ,,   ,,   ,,   Worship," by N. H. Snaith.
   "   ,,   ,,   ,,   Ethics," by W. A. L. Elmslie.
   The Theology of the Old Testament, by H. W. Robinson :
      " The Philosophy of Revelation."
      " The Characteristic Doctrines."
(On pp. 486–489 of the same book there will be found a more detailed bibliography, including foreign literature.)

XII. ANGELOLOGY AND DEMONOLOGY IN EARLY JUDAISM

THE remnants of animistic and polytheistic conceptions, signs of which are clearly discernible in the earlier Old Testament writings, were combated and, to a large extent, eradicated by the eighth-century prophets. The superhuman beings, belief in the activity of whom had been handed down from time immemorial, were transformed into supernatural agents of Yahweh. Originally non-moral, the spirits believed in during the earliest ages were either harmful or beneficent in their behaviour towards human beings, and it depended upon their whims and on the measure in which they were placated by men as to which attitude they took up; but there was no class-division as between the harmful and the beneficent. It was only with the growth of moral ideas, owing, in the first instance, to the Mosaic inculcation of belief in an ethical God, that ultimately a differentiation arose between these supernatural beings as evil and good. Both were, however, conceived of as the agents of Yahweh; hence we read, on the one hand, for example, of an evil spirit from Yahweh troubling Saul (1 Sam. 16^{14}); while, on the other, an angel (properly " messenger ") from Yahweh comes to Elijah to comfort and encourage him. Though the distinction between a spirit (*ruach*) who is evil, and an angel (*mal'ak*) who is good, is not carried out consistently (*e.g.* evil angels are referred to in Ps. 78^{49}, Job 4^{18}, and good spirits are mentioned in Judg. 3^{19}, 11^{29}, and elsewhere), yet, generally speaking, when evil is imputed to one of these supernatural beings it is a spirit (*ruach*), not an angel (*mal'ak*), who is spoken of. Thus, it may be asserted that, so far as the Israelites were concerned, the beginnings of a distinction between supernatural beings were due to Yahwehism.

I

Illustrative of the fact that among the Israelites, as among all the Semites, gods developed from the originally non-moral spirits, is the mention of " the angel (*mal'ak*) of Yahweh," who is at one time represented as distinct from Yahweh (*e.g.*

Num. 20³¹, Judg. 13⁸⸱ ⁹); and at another identified with Him (*e.g.* Gen. 16¹³, Ex. 3², Num. 22³²⸱ ³⁵).

In the former case, however, the functions of " the angel of Yahweh " are very different from those of the superhuman beings characteristic of earlier ages, of whom we have echoes, *e.g.* in Gen. 3²⁴, 6²⸱ ⁴ ; 1 Kings 22¹⁹.

In pre-exilic times the mention of angels, whether under the name of *mal'akim*, or otherwise designated (as, *e.g.*, in Isa. 6²ᶠᶠ⸱), is rare ; and they are mostly theophanic (Gen. 28¹²⸱ ¹³, 32¹⸱ ², and elsewhere). In exilic and post-exilic times, on the other hand, when the monotheistic belief was firmly established, and there was not the danger of a reversion to polytheistic tendencies, the activity of angels as the means of communicating God's will to men was fully recognized (see, *e.g.*, Ezek. 3¹², 8²⸱ ³, 9²⸱ ³, 11²⁴) ; if we regard Ezek. 40–48 as belonging to this prophet—though there is a strong tendency among some modern scholars to deny this—then Ezekiel may be said to mark a transition from the *direct* communication of Yahweh (Ezek. 44²) to that conveyed by an intermediate agent (Ezek. 40³⸱ ⁴) ; the latter is not called an angel, simply " a man," but he is clearly superhuman. In any case, after the Exile there is never any direct communication to men from God, it is always an angel who delivers the divine message ; most notable here is Zech. 1–8 ; in some of the later psalms, also, angelic intermediaries are mentioned (*e.g.* Ps. 91¹¹).

In the later Greek period the belief in angelic activity among men became greatly developed ; and it is during this period that an angelology in the strict sense is first to be discerned. The cause of this striking development is to be sought in the conception of the divine transcendence. " The Jew became loath to *describe* God as mixing too freely and frequently with men—and in describing anything the name must inevitably be used—but it does not follow, as a conse-quence, that he did not continue to *harbour the idea and cherish the belief* of God's close contact with men. But as he thought it sacrilege to put the belief into words, he was forced to fall back upon a substitute. This substitute was the angel " (Abelson, *The Immanence of God in Rabbinical Literature*, pp. 13 f. [1912]). These words are true as far as they go, but they do not sufficiently take into account the fact that the transcendental conception of God resulted in putting Him far from the world, and in effacing, to some extent, the reality of the divine Personality ; the Almighty recedes, as it were, into the highest heavens (see, *e.g.*, Weber, *Jüdische Theologie auf Grund des Talmud und verwandter Schriften*, pp. 163 ff.

[1897]), and deputes the carrying out of His will to angels ; in
1 Enoch 39¹², e.g., it is said : " Those who sleep not bless thee :
they stand before thy glory, and bless, praise, and extol,
saying, Holy, holy, holy is the Lord of Spirits ; He filleth
the earth with spirits." A developed angelology became,
therefore, a necessity, and so exaggerated, in some respects,
was the position assigned to angels that had it not been for
Judaism's deeply rooted monotheism, this fundamental tenet
would itself have been in danger. Indeed, though official
Judaism always repudiated the worship of angels, it is evident
that this was prevalent in many quarters, notably among
the Jews of the Dispersion. Something closely akin to their
worship appears in Tob. 11¹⁴, where, in gratitude for having
received his sight again, Tobit cries : " Blessed art Thou, O God,
and blessed is thy name for ever, and blessed are all thy holy
angels " ; that the latter should be coupled with the name of
the Almighty in this way comes dangerously near to worship ;
and that it developed into direct worship is shown by the
prohibitions of this occurring in somewhat later literature ;
in the *Ascension of Isaiah*, vii. 21, e.g., it is said : " And I fell
on my face to worship him, but the angel who conducted me
did not permit me, but said unto me, Worship neither throne
nor angel . . . " ; similarly in Rev. 19¹⁰, 22⁸⁻⁹ ; and the
worshipping of angels is directly alluded to in Col. 2¹⁸.

As to the *origin of the angels*, indications occur in the
Old Testament of their identification with the stars, and
as existing before the creation of the world ; thus, in Job 38⁷ :
" When the morning stars sang together and all the sons of
God shouted for joy," in reference to the beginning of the
Creation ; in Ps. 89⁵⁻⁷ the thought of this identification comes
out clearly ; see also Isa. 24²¹. Of special interest is the
Septuagint of Ps. 148¹⁻³, where " all his host," rendered πᾶσαι
αἱ δυνάμεις αὐτοῦ, is parallel to " all his angels " ; that both
" angels " and " hosts " are conceived of as luminaries is
evident from the succeeding couplet in which the mention
of " sun and moon " and " stars and light " completes the
list of the heavenly bodies who are called on to praise God ;
cf. also Ps. 102 (103)²¹. " We can trace in Hellenistic
Judaism," says Dodd (*The Bible and the Greeks*, pp. 17 ff.
1935]), a tendency to rationalize the angels of popular mythology in terms of δυνάμεις, as divine agencies " ; and he
refers to the Test. xii. Patr., Judah 25², where " the powers
(αἱ δυνάμεις) of glory " are mentioned in a list along with
the Angel of the Presence, heaven and earth, the sun, the
moon, and the stars. " It certainly seems more natural here

to understand the δυνάμεις as individual divine agencies. It is surely as such that they appear in lists of the angelic orders, along with ἀρχαί, ἐξουσίαι, κυριότητες (Col. 1¹⁶). Thus we recognize a tendency in Judaism parallel with the monotheistic tendency which we have noted in paganism, to represent subordinate supernatural beings (the 'gods' of paganism, the 'angels' of Judaism) as 'powers' or 'agencies' of the one God, and in this sense δυνάμεις." In this connexion we recall Mark 13²⁵, " the powers (αἱ δυνάμεις) that are in the heavens shall be shaken," where the powers are "the discarnate intelligences supposed to inhabit and control the astral universe, among the Jews identified with orders of angels " (Dodd, *The Parables of the Kingdom*, p. 83 [1935]).

In its origin the identification of the angels with the stars is Babylonian (see Zimmern, *Keilinschriften und Alte Testament*, pp. 456 ff. [1903]). The passage quoted above from Job implies that the angels existed before the Creation ; in later Judaism, however, it was held that God created the angels on the first day of Creation, otherwise—so it was thought— since the angels were not included among created beings, it might be suggested that they assisted the Almighty in the work of creation ; in Jub. 2¹, it is therefore said : " On the first day He created the heavens which are above . . . and all the spirits which serve before Him, the angels of the presence . . ." and then a long list is given of the various orders of angels (see also 2 Enoch 29¹·³). Still later it was taught that they were created on the second day (Midrash *Bereshith Rabba* on Gen. 1⁵, *Pirke de R. Eliezer*, iii.). It is well known how often earlier thought is reflected in the Rabbinical literature.

As to the *nature* of the angels, there appear the echoes of very ancient conceptions in their being represented as elemental spirits ; this is illustrated in the passage from *Jubilees* just quoted, where mention is made of the angels of the spirit of the winds, of the spirit of the clouds, of darkness, snow, hail, hoar-frost, etc. (cf. 1 Enoch 60¹¹⁻²¹ and elsewhere). Their nature, "like that of fire," is spoken of in 2 Enoch 29¹⁻³ ; see also Syr. Apoc. of Baruch 59¹¹ ; cf. the Seraphim. Similar ideas occur in the New Testament ; in Rev. 7¹ mention is made of the " four angels standing at the four corners of the earth, holding the four winds of the earth, that no wind should blow on the earth, or on the sea, or upon any tree " (see also 14¹⁸, fire ; 16⁵, waters ; 19¹⁷ " an angel standing in the sun ") ; and it would seem that St. Paul was thinking of this when referring to " the elements of the world " in Col. 2⁸·²⁰. The

spiritual nature of the angels appears in a different form in
1 Enoch 15⁴⁻⁷, where it is said that the angels are immortal
and dwell in heaven, and that therefore they do not marry :
" And therefore I have not appointed wives for you ; for as
for the spiritual ones of the heaven, in heaven is their dwelling."
This recalls the words of our Lord in Matt. 22³⁰ : " For in the
resurrection they neither marry, nor are given in marriage, but
are as angels in heaven."

Significant in the developed belief in angels during the
Greek period is that they received names, thus emphasizing
their personality. The earliest instance of this in Jewish
literature, so far as is known, occurs in the Book of Tobit,
where the angel Raphael plays a leading part, and is often
mentioned (3¹⁷, etc.). He is introduced in a way which suggests that his name was familiar ; this applies, too, to 1 Enoch
9¹, where the names of four angels are mentioned as though
well known ; indeed, to judge from 1 Enoch 20¹ff·, belonging
to a slightly earlier portion of the book, the names of a number
of angels were already quite familiar early in the second
century B.C., probably before. The artificiality of the names
given may be gathered from 1 Enoch 8³. In almost every
case the names of angels are compounded with -el, indicating
that they were subordinate to God. Of the names which occur
in post-Biblical, but pre-Christian, literature, two only appear
in the New Testament : Gabriel, in Luke 1¹⁹· ²⁶, and Michael
in Jude 9, Rev. 12⁷.

Apart from names, there are various *designations* applied
to the angels which demand notice. The earliest of these, as
we have seen from Old Testament usage, is " messengers " ;
whether this term was used in early post-Biblical Jewish
literature it is impossible to say, as scarcely any of the books
belonging to it have been preserved in Hebrew ; but it occurs
in Midrashic literature, *e.g. Bereshith Rabba*, on Gen. 32²⁶, where
mention is made of the heavenly choir of angels (*kat mal'akim*) ;
elsewhere also in this literature the term is used. The designation " host, or hosts, of heaven " (see above what is said
about δυνάμεις), based on such passages as Gen. 32²⁶, Josh. 5¹⁴,
Ps. 33⁶, 2 Chron. 18⁸ ; cf. also Dan. 8¹⁰, is frequent in post-
biblical literature (*e.g.* 1 Enoch 61¹⁰, Prayer of Man. 15 and
often elsewhere) ; and in Luke 2¹³ we read of a " multitude of
the heavenly host praising God." The designation " sons of
God " (*běnē Elohim*), also based on Old Testament usage
(*e.g.* Gen. 6²·⁴, Job 1⁶ ; cf. Ps. 89⁷), is frequent in the later
literature (1 Enoch 6², 13⁸, 14³, 101¹, and elsewhere).

The same is to be said of the term " the holy ones "

(*Qedôshim*, Ps. 89⁶, Job 5¹ etc.), which occurs very often, too, in the later literature (Ecclus. 42¹⁷, Tob. 11¹⁴, 12¹⁵, 1 Enoch 1⁹, 12². ³, Jub. 31¹⁴, Wis. 5⁵, 10¹⁰). Finally, the designation "Watchers" (*'Irîn*), which in the Old Testament occurs only in Dan. 4¹⁴⁽¹⁷⁾, and in the singular in vv. ¹⁰. ²⁰ (¹³. ²³), is frequent in 1 Enoch, *e.g.* 12². ³, 20¹, 61¹², etc.

Most striking, as illustrating a developed angelology, are the *Orders* into which the angels are divided. Highest in rank are the seven archangels, mentioned first in Tob. 12¹⁵ : " I am Raphael, one of the seven holy angels " ; in 1 Enoch 20¹⁻⁸ their names are given : Uriel, Raphael, Raguel, Michael, Saraqael, Gabriel, Remiel. The thought of the seven archangels, as they came to be regarded, was derived from Ezek. 9²⁻¹¹ : " And behold, six men came from the way of the upper gate, which lieth toward the north . . . and one man in the midst of them, clothed with linen, with a writer's ink-horn by his side . . ." But the prototype of these seven were the seven planets, all of them Babylonian deities ; the man with the ink-horn by his side clearly represents the god Nabu, who was the writer of the book of fate. The idea of these seven holy angels is adapted for the purpose of glorifying the Levitical priesthood, in Test. xii. Patr., Lev. 8¹ᶠᶠ· ; and in Rev. 1⁴ there is a further adaptation, mention being made of " the seven spirits which are before his throne " (see also 1²⁰, 3¹, 4⁵, 5⁶, 8². ⁶). The Babylonian origin of the names, as well as the personalities, of the angels is witnessed to by the celebrated third century Rabbi, Simeon ben Lakish, who says that " the names of the angels, such as Michael, Raphael, and Gabriel, they (*i.e.* the Israelites) brought from Babylon " (*Bereshith Rabba* on Gen. 18¹). Among these seven archangels Michael stands pre-eminent as the " prince " or guardian angel of Israel (Dan. 10²¹, 12¹) ; in 1 Enoch 20⁵ he is spoken of as " he that is set over the best part of mankind and over Chaos "(=Tiamat, see also 24⁶, 40⁹) ; similarly in later Judaism Michael is described as the head of all the angels, and next to him comes Gabriel ; it has already been pointed out that these are the only two angels mentioned by name in the New Testament. Other orders are enumerated in 1 Enoch 61¹⁰ : Cherubin, Seraphin, Ophannin, the angels of power, the angels of principalities, and the other powers on the earth, and over the water, cf. 2 Enoch 20¹.

There are various passages in which the *outward appearance* of angels is described. Here we naturally think first of the six-winged Seraphim in Isa. 6²ᶠᶠ·, and of the winged Cherubim so often referred to in the Old Testament ; but these, though included among the angelic hosts in 1 Enoch, do not, strictly speaking, belong to the angelology with which we are dealing ; this applies also to Ezek. 1¹³, though the descriptiom there given no doubt influenced later thought : " As for the likeness of the living creatures, their appearance was like burning coals of fire ; like the appearance of torches. . . ." Closely connected with this is the description of the angel in Dan. 10⁵· ⁶ : ". . . a man clothed in linen, whose loins were girded with pure gold of Uphaz ; his body was like the beryl, and his face as the appearance of lightning, and his eyes as lamps of fire and his arms and feet like in colour to burnished brass, and the voice of his words like the voice of a multitude." From this it is evident that the angel was pictured as of human form ; there is no mention here of wings. That the angels were thought of as wearing garments is to be gathered from Ascension of Isaiah (8¹⁴· ¹⁵). In the fragment from a Noah Apocalypse (preserved in 1 Enoch 106, 107) the angel—though of human birth—is thus described : " . . . his nature is not like man's nature, and the colour of his body is whiter than snow and redder than the bloom of a rose, and the hair of his head is whiter than white wool, and his eyes are like the rays of the sun " (1 Enoch 106¹⁰, cf. vv. ¹· ²). A striking description occurs in 2 Enoch 1⁴· ⁵, and here there is mention of wings : " And there appeared to me two men very tall, such as I have never seen on earth. And their faces shone like the sun, and their eyes were like burning lamps, and fire came forth from their lips. Their dress had the appearance of feathers ; their feet were purple ; their wings were brighter than gold ; their hands whiter than snow," cf. also 19¹. In various passages we get a somewhat similar picture of angels in the New Testament, e.g. " dazzling apparel " (Luke 24⁴, cf. Matt. 17², Acts 6¹⁵), " angels in white " (John 20¹²), " angel of light " (2 Cor. 11¹⁴), their " might and power " (2 Peter 2¹¹) ; and especially in Revelation where they are spoken of as being arrayed in a " golden girdle," as having " eyes as a flame of fire," " and feet like burnished brass " ; further, it is said that " his voice is as the voice of many waters," that " his countenance is as the sun shineth in his strength," and " his hair is as white wool, white as snow " (1¹³ᶠᶠ·), see also 19¹², and elsewhere.

Regarding the *functions* of the angels, there is, first and foremost, that of praising God ; thus, in 1 Enoch 39¹²· ¹³ it is said : " Those who sleep not (*i.e.* the Watchers) bless Thee ; they stand before Thy glory, and bless, praise and extol, saying, ' Holy, holy, holy is the Lord of Spirits.' . . . ' Blessed be thou, and blessed be the name of the Lord for ever and ever.'" This occurs, of course, very often ; similarly in the New Testament : " . . . multitude of the heavenly host praising God, and saying . . ." (Luke 2[13. 14]; cf. Rev. 5[8ff.] and often). One of their duties is to bring the prayers of the righteous before the throne of God ; thus in Tob. 12[12], the angel says : " And now, when thou didst pray, and Sarah thy daughter-in-law, I did bring the memorial of your prayer before the Holy One "; and in v. [15] it is said of the seven holy angels that they " present the prayers of the saints, and go in before the glory of the Holy One." With this cf. Rev. 8[3. 4], where it is said of one of the angels that " there was given unto him much incense, that he should add it unto the prayers of all the saints upon the golden altar which was before the throne . . . "; see also Acts 10[3. 4].

Another function of the angels is that of bearing the messages of God to men, and of carrying out His will on earth ; illustrations of this occur in well-known passages in the Old Testament ; in the post-Biblical literature this angelic action is so often mentioned that quotations are unnecessary ; it will suffice to recall the episode of the angel and Habakkuk (Bel and the Dragon, 33 ff.), and the angel-riders described in 2 Macc. 5[1-3] (cf. 2 Kings 2[11], 6[17] ; Zech. 1[8ff.], 6[1-8] ; Rev. 19[11]) In the New Testament there are the well-known instances of the angel of the Lord appearing to Joseph (Matt. 1[20-21], 2[13.19]) and to Zacharias (Luke 1[11ff.]), and of the message of Gabriel to Mary (Luke 1[26ff.]) ; an angelic message is given to Philip (Acts 8[26]), and to Cornelius (Acts 10[3ff.]; cf. 11[13] ; Rev. 22[6. 16]). Closely connected with this is angelic ministration ; Raphael, in the Book of Tobit, has already been mentioned, cf. Ep. of Jer. 7, and elsewhere ; in the New Testament a number of cases of ministering angels are recorded (Matt. 4[11], 28[2. 5-7] ; Luke 1[11ff.], 22[43] ; John 5[7] ; Acts 5[19]).

This leads us to the subject of guardian angels ; here we have, first, the idea of an angel being the special protector of the Jewish nation ; thus, in Dan. 10[21], Michael appears as the " prince," *i.e.* guardian angel of Israel, and in 10[13] the " prince of the kingdom of Persia " is mentioned. In Ecclus. 17[17] it is said that " for every nation He appointed a ruler, but Israel is the Lord's portion," which suggests a Sadducæan *trait* ; on the other hand, it is said in the *Targum of pseudo-Jonathan* on Gen. 11[7.8], that every nation has its own guardian angel who pleads the cause of the nation under his protection before God. Michael, as the guardian angel of Israel, is also mentioned in Jub. 35[27]. As the guardians of individual men angels appear often, *e.g.* prominently in Tobit ; and according to Test. xii. Patr., Jos. 6[6], it is by means of an angel that the wickedness of Potiphar's wife is revealed to Joseph, and he is kept from temptation ; in 2 Macc. 11[6ff.] it is told of how a " good angel " came to the help of Judas Maccabæus, and rode at the head of his army. For instances of the mention of guardian angels in the New Testament see Matt. 18[10], 26[53], Acts 12[7ff.], 28[23], Rev. 1[20].

Prominent is the function of the angels as *intercessors* on behalf of men before the Almighty ; of the many instances of this, Tob. 12[12] may be quoted : " I did bring the memorial of your prayers before the Holy One " ; see also Test. xii. Patr., Dan. 6[2], Asher 1[6], Lev. 5[6] ; in 1 Enoch 39[5] it is said of the angels that " they petitioned and interceded, and prayed for the children of men " ; and so often. In the New Testament it is not the angels, but our Lord, Who does this (Rom. 8[34] ; Heb. 7[25]).

Very noticeable is the mention of the angels in connexion with the eschatological drama ; this is so obvious in the apocalyptic literature that quotations are not needed ; not less striking is it in many passages in the Gospels (Matt. 13[39ff.], 16[27], 24[31], 25[31] ; Mark 8[38], 13[27] ; Luke 9[26]). Finally, there is the angel of death who is frequently referred to in post-Biblical Jewish literature (*e.g.* Syr. Apoc. of Bar. 21[23], Test. xii. Patr. Asher 6[4]) ; in this connexion we recall Luke 16[22], where the angels carry Lazarus into Abraham's bosom, Michael contending for the body of Moses (Jude 9), and he who sat on a pale horse whose " name was Death " (Rev. 6[8]).

The fallen angels form the link between Angelology and Demonology, to which we come next.

II

The belief in demons, like the belief in angels, was an outcome of animistic conceptions ; but this, naturally enough, was in course of time lost sight of, perhaps never fully realized ; hence, with the growth of monotheistic tendencies, and especially with the definite monotheistic belief of the Jews in post-exilic times, there arose the necessity of accounting for the existence of evil spirits ; for with the growth of the sense of sin, those who from time immemorial had been merely harmful spirits, became spirits who were morally bad. To account, therefore, for the existence of evil spirits—demons as now generally understood—a theory was framed ; with this theory we must first concern ourselves.

The myth, a fragment of which is preserved in Gen. 6[2ff.]

that " the sons of God saw the daughters of men that they
were fair ; and they took them wives of all that they chose,"
is utilized in 1 Enoch 6, 7, 8 and elsewhere, to account for the
origin of evil spirits, or demons ; the details given, however,
suggest that the Genesis passage is not the basis of what is
said in 1 Enoch, but that more than one ancient tradition has
been placed under contribution. According to 1 Enoch 15[8],
" the giants (=the Nephilim of Gen. 6[4], Num. 13[33]), who are
produced from the spirits and flesh, shall be called evil spirits
upon the earth, and on the earth shall be their dwelling. Evil
spirits have proceeded from their bodies ; because they are
born from men, and from the holy watchers is their beginning
and primal origin ; they shall be evil spirits on earth, and evil
spirits shall they be called." Much is said of the evil they
brought on earth, and of the harm they do among men. That
this theory of the origin of the demons, that they are the
offspring of the fallen angels, was widespread is evident ; it is
referred to in Jub. 5[2], 2 Enoch 18[3-5], and elsewhere in this
literature, and in later times a similar belief is expressed ; see
2 Peter 2[4], Jude 6 ; Justin Martyr, too, speaks of the angels
who " transgressed the divine ordering, and by sinful intercourse with women produced offspring who are demons "
(in the second *Apologia*, § 5). In the Rabbinical literature,
also, this is referred to (*e.g.* in the *Yalkut Shimeoni, Bereshith,*
xliv.) ; but more frequent in this literature is the mention of
the offspring of Satan and Eve (*e.g.* Midrash, *Bereshith Rabba*
on Gen. 5[1]), which is probably a modification of the original
myth.

But further, the countless offspring of the fallen angels
have as their head a " prince," to whom a variety of names is
given ; in the Book of Jubilees he is called Mastema (identified
in 10[11] with Satan), the " enemy " ; and his activity, as
described in this book, corresponds with that of Satan in the
Old Testament (Job 1[6ff.], 2[2ff.] ; Ps. 109[6] ; 1 Chron. 21[1] ;
Zech. 3[1]), as the accuser, adversary, and the tempter of men
(cf. Matt. 4[1, 10] ; Mark 4[15] ; Luke 13[16], 22[13] ; 1 Cor. 7[5] ;
Rev. 12[9]). Both Satan and Mastema are the names of the
head of demons as given in various other apocalyptic writings ;
the latter name occurs also in the Damascus Fragments of a
Zadokite Work 20[2]. Another name is Sammael, though this is
rare (Greek Apoc. of Baruch 4[9] ; Martyrd. of Isa. 2[1]) ; in the
Rabbinical literature he appears as the " angel of death "
(Jerusalem Targum on Gen. 3[6]) ; but otherwise his activities
are identical with those of Satan. Sometimes the prince of
the demons is called Azazel (cf. Lev. 16[7-28]) ; at other times

Azazel is subordinate to Satan.   And, finally, there is the name
Beliar or Belial ; as a proper name this occurs first in Ps. 18[5]
(E.V. 4 mg.) ; in 2 Sam. 22[5], " The waves of death compassed me
and the floods of Belial made me afraid " suggests that Belial
was originally thought of as the " angel " of death, like
Sammael ; the name'occurs often in the Zadokite Fragments,
and also in the Martyrd. of Isa. 2[4] and elsewhere ; in the
Test. xii. Patr., in the form Beliar, he is very frequently
mentioned, and clearly represents the author of all evil; see,
e.g., Simeon 5[3]: " . . . separating from God, and bringing
near to Beliar " ; in this passage the warning is against fornication, which recalls 2 Cor. 6[14, 15] : " Be not unequally yoked
together with unbelievers ; for what fellowship have righteousness and iniquity ? or what communion hath light with darkness ? And what concord hath Christ with Beliar ? "

All these, then, are various names applied to the being
who is represented as the " prince " of the countless offspring
of the fallen angels.   According to the theory mentioned,
therefore, the demons, or evil spirits, with their " prince,"
form an element of evil in the world, opposed to the " Lord of
Spirits," regarded as the head of the angels, or good spirits,
so frequently mentioned in 1 Enoch.   We are thus confronted
with a dualism which is strongly reminiscent of the religious
system of Mazdaeism ; this centred in the perennial warfare
between the two opposing powers of good and evil, Ahura
Mazda and Angra Mainyu, with their respective innumerable
retinues in the spiritual world.   That the Jews were strongly
influenced by ancient Iranian belief in the domains of both
angelology and demonology does not admit of doubt ; but
orthodox Judaism, with its unassailable monotheism, was
always able to withstand such dualism.   In the present case
it was countered by the doctrine that evil, as well as good, was
from God ; this belief, as pointed out above, appears already
in the Old Testament, where, e.g., in 1 Sam. 16[14-16] it is said
that " an evil spirit from Yahweh " troubled Saul (cf. Job 1[12]
and elsewhere) ; in Ecclus. 33[14, 15] there is similar teaching,
and it occurs again and again in the Rabbinical literature.

To come now to some details regarding the nature and
activity of demons.   They are spoken of as spirits, e.g. in
1 Enoch 15[9], and therefore they have not flesh and blood like
human beings ; similarly in Eph. 6[12] : " Our wrestling is not
against flesh and blood, but against the principalities, against
the powers, against the world-rulers of this darkness . . ."
(see also 1 Enoch 16[1]).   On the other hand, they have human
passions (Tob. 3[8], 8[3]), they hunger and thirst (1 Enoch 15[11]) ;

there are both male and female demons, and they beget children.

In the Rabbinical literature, which reflects traditional beliefs, the male demons are called *Shedim* (Deut. 32[17]; Ps. 106[37]), the female being known as *Lilin* (cf. Isa. 34[14]). According to 1 Enoch 19[1], they assume many different forms ; with this agree the words in 2 Cor. 11[14], " even Satan fashioneth himself into an angel of light." Like the angels they have wings, and fly from one end of the earth to the other (Bab. Talm. *Chagiga* 16a). Their countless numbers are often spoken of ; according to ancient Arab belief the whole world is full of them ; the same was held by the Rabbis ; their number is given by one Rabbi as seven and a half millions ; in the Midrash on the Psalms (91[7]) it is said : " If a thousand evil spirits assemble at thy left hand, they fall . . . and if ten thousand assemble at thy right, they fall " ; this being due to the protection of angels. Their presence is often unperceived since they are able to make themselves invisible.

An echo of what were originally animistic conceptions is the harmful and destructive activity of demons ; it is said of them in Jub. 10[5] that they are " malignant and created in order to destroy " ; hence one of the general terms for them used in Rabbinical literature is *Mazzikin*, " harmful ones," in the sense of physical harm. Though always harmful, there are certain times at which they are especially dangerous ; thus, in Psalm 91[5], we read : " Thou shalt not be afraid because of the night-terror " (*pachod layelah*), on which the comment in the Midrash on the Psalms runs : " There is a harmful spirit that flies like a bird and shoots about like an arrow " ; by this is doubtless meant the demon *Lilith*, the head of the female demons, the *Lilin* mentioned above ; her name appears in Isa. 34[14] ; in Rabbinical literature she is known as the Night-hag, and it is said that she got her name from *Layelah*, " night " ; the etymology was false, nevertheless *Lilith* was the night-demon *par excellence*. We have here an instance of Babylonian influence ; among the many Babylonian demons there appears the triad *Lilu, Lilitu,* and *Ardat Lili* ; the male, the female, and the handmaid ; the Biblical *Lilith* would correspond to the second of these ; all three are said to rush about at nights ; *Ardat Lili* is spoken of as " flitting in through a window " after a man. In Jewish belief *Lilith* is the particular enemy of children. The activity of evil spirits during the hours of darkness is perhaps implied in Luke 22[53] : " But this is your hour, and the power of darkness," spoken to those who came to take our Lord (cf. Col.

1¹³) ; more direct are the words in Acts 26¹⁸, " that they may turn from darkness to light, and from the power of Satan to God."

At midday, again, demons are especially harmful ; in Ps. 91⁶ mention is made of " Keteb and the midday demon " ; the Septuagint renders Keteb as " demon " ; and in other passages where the name occurs there are reasons for believing that in each case a demon is referred to (Deut. 32²⁴ ; Isa. 28² ; Hosea 13¹⁴). In the Midrash on the Psalms it is said in reference to Keteb that it is a demon (Shed), and it is added : " The poisonous Keteb is covered with scales and with hair, he sees only out of one eye, the other is in the middle of his heart."

But it is not only physical harm that the demons perpetrate ; the originally animistic conceptions regarding them developed in a moral direction, and they became also the instigators of sin in men. This side of demoniacal activity is greatly emphasized. It appears often, for example, in the Test. xii. Patr. ; a striking passage occurs in Reuben 3, where reference is made to seven evil spirits who originate the following vices in men : lust, greed, pugnacity, chicanery, pride, deceit, and injustice (see also Simeon 3¹⁻³, Judah 16¹⁻⁵, Issachar 7⁷, Dan. 5⁵, 6¹, Benj. 3³). In the Book of Jub. 7²⁷ it is said : " For I see, and behold, the demons have begun their seductions against you and against your children . . ." (cf. 10¹ᶠᶠ·, 15³¹) ; instructive is what is said in 11⁴·⁵ : " Malignant spirits assisted and seduced them into committing transgression and uncleanness. And the prince Mastema exerted himself to do all this, and sent forth other spirits, those which were put under his hand, to do all manner of wrong and sin, and all manner of transgression, to corrupt and destroy, and to shed blood upon the earth." The " evil spirits of Belial " are spoken of in the Zadokite Fragments 14⁵ (cf. Jub. 1²⁰, 10³). That evil thoughts are prompted by demons is expressed in Jub. 12²⁰ : " Deliver me from the hands of evil spirits who have dominion over the thoughts of men's hearts, and let them not lead me astray from thee, my God." The belief that wickedness is inspired by demons was far from being confined to Judasim. In Babylonian demonology such things as impure love, hate, and envy in men were ascribed to the power of demons. In Brahmanism and Buddhism it is precisely the same. But nowhere is this belief more strongly in evidence than in Iranian demonology, to which much that we meet with in Judaism must be ascribed. Here vices are personified as demons ; from Ahriman himself proceed seven evil spirits, each of which is a sin personified, namely, lust, passion, envy,

hate, uncleanness, lying and violence. A striking illustration
of this belief occurs in Ps. 78[49], where fierce anger, wrath,
indignation, and tribulation are spoken of as a "band
(lit. sending) of evil angels." In the Rabbinical literature the
same idea occurs, e.g. in Bereshith Rabba on Gen. 38[15], lust
is personified as an evil angel ; and a similar personification of
demons is found in the Gospels : "Then goeth he, and taketh
with himself seven other spirits more evil than himself . . ."
(Matt. 12[45], cf. also the "seven demons" who had gone out of
Mary Magdalene, Luke 8[2]).

These beliefs in the harmfulness of demons both in the
physical and moral spheres must be supplemented by a reference to that of their being the cause of sickness, etc., for it is
particularly here that the connexion between sin and suffering
appears. That illness and disease is due to demons is a very
widespread belief ; but we are thinking more especially of
the Semitic area, though a few cases of ancient Iranian beliefs
will also be mentioned, owing to their influence on Jewish
demonology. By the Babylonians many diseases were thought
of as personified, just as vices were ; thus Namtaru was the
plague demon, Ashakku was the demon of consumption ;
headache, lunacy, and every other ailment were directly
ascribed to demonic activity ; similarly among the ancient
Arabs, all illness was ascribed to demons. In the Old Testament this is usually ascribed to Yahweh (e.g. Deut. 28[21, 22, 27-29]);
but that had its special reasons ; originally this was due to
demons, though in some cases demons were gods. The
Persians believed that all diseases were sent by Angra Mainyu,
either directly from him or else by one of his innumerable
retinue. In early post-Biblical Jewish literature the same
belief appears, the demons "afflict, oppress, destroy, attack,
do battle, and work destruction on the earth, and cause
trouble" (1 Enoch 15[11], and often elsewhere ; so, too, in
the Rabbinical literature). The same belief is found also
in the New Testament, e.g. in Luke 4[39], where it is said that
Christ "rebuked the fever" ; see also Luke 9[42], and in 13[16]
we read of the woman with a spirit of infirmity, "whom
Satan hath bound" ; other examples occur in Matt. 17[18],
Mark 9[25], and elsewhere. It is interesting to note that,
contrary to the popular belief, Christ does not regard disease
or infirmity as due to sin, with which demons were so closely
connected ; in reply to the question ; "Rabbi, who did sin,
this man, or his parents, that he should be born blind ?" the
answer is : "Neither did this man sin, nor his parents ; but
that the works of God should be made manifest in him"

(John 9². ³). That blindness was popularly believed to be caused by demonic activity is clear from Matt. 12²².

A few words must be said, next, as to the means employed to counteract the evil machinations of the demons. One of the most effective means of driving away demons was to recite a magic formula ; the immense number of Babylonian texts of this kind which exist shows how efficacious this method was believed to be ; these are for the most part lengthy ; but that short formulæ were also in use can be seen from Zech. 3², " Yahweh rebuke thee,. Satan." It was the same among the Persians ; one such short formula, given in the Bundahesh 28³⁶, is : " In the name of God " ; that overpowers a demon. This is also found in Rabbinical literature ; for example, according to the Midrash *Sifre* 12a, the utterance of the Aaronic blessing (Num. 6²⁴⁻²⁶) is fatal to demons. According to Matt. 12²⁷, the Pharisees held that Christ cast out demons by the utterance of the name of Beelzebub ; instructive here is Acts 19¹³ : " But certain also of the strolling Jews, exorcists, took upon them to name over them which had the evil spirits the name of the Lord Jesus, saying, I adjure you by Jesus whom Paul preacheth." From Acts 19¹⁹ it would appear that magicians had whole collections in books of recipes against the onslaughts of demons ; these would, no doubt, have included various magical performances in addition to formulæ ; reference to a book of this kind occurs in Jub. 10¹². ¹³, where it is said that Noah, having received instruction on the subject, " wrote down all things in a book as we instructed him concerning every kind of medicine. Thus the evil spirits were precluded from hurting the sons of Noah." Again, Josephus, in lauding the wisdom of Solomon, says, among other things : " God also enabled him to learn that skill which expels demons ; it is a science useful and healthful to men. He composed such incantations also by which distempers are alleviated. And he left behind him the manner of using exorcisms, by which they drive away demons, so that they never return " (*Antiq.* viii. 45) ; clearly a book is here referred to. Other means, in addition to exorcisms and the like, were used ; an interesting example occurs in Tob. 8²⁻⁴, where the heart and liver of a fish are placed on the ashes of incense ; the demon, on smelling the smoke, flees. Prophylactic measures of this kind were also employed against witches ; according to ancient Arab and Babylonian belief, there was a close relationship between witches and demons. The Arabs believed that witches were the incarnations of demons ; the Babylonians held both of them to be equally dangerous since they were in league with one another, and played into each other's hands ; both, magicians and witches, had the power of impressing demons into their service.

The belief was also widespread in the relationship between demons and certain animals, whose form they assumed ; thus the ancient Persians held that lizards, toads, frogs, mice, snakes, and ants, were all demon-animals ; it may well be due to a similar belief that such animals were regarded as unclean among the Hebrews. The Arabs, too, regarded serpents as the incarnations of demons (cf. Isa. 34[15]). According to later Rabbinical teaching, all the demons were originally serpents (Bab. Talm. *Baba Kamma* 16a). In Luke 10[19] the disciples are given authority " to tread upon serpents and scorpions, and over all the power of the enemy " ; the context speaks of demons being subject to the disciples in the name of Christ ; clearly the serpents are here identified with demons. In Rev. 12[9], " the old serpent " is identified with " the Devil and Satan " (cf. 20[2]). A great deal more could be said on the subject did space permit.

Finally, a few remarks may be offered on the subject of the places of abode of demons. In various Old Testament passages it is said that the demons inhabit desert places (Isa. 13[21]), and ruins (Isa. 34[14]) ; in Baruch 4[35] it is said that Babylon shall be burned, and that " she shall be inhabited by demons for a great time " ; and in Rev. 18[2] it is said that Babylon which is fallen " is become a habitation for demons . . . " ; and so frequently elsewhere. In Rabbinical literature a similar belief is expressed, *e.g.* in the Bab. Talm. *Berachoth* 3a, it is said that they abide in the desert, and that their howling can be heard there, cf. Deut. 32[10], " the waste, howling wilderness." In Matt. 12[43] we read of the unclean spirit passing through " waterless places." The belief was also held that the demons hovered about tombs ; as " unclean " spots they would be especially favoured by demons. This belief was held by the Babylonians, ancient Arabs, Persians, and other peoples ; so, too, in the Rabbinical literature, *e.g.* Bab. Talm. *Berachoth* 18b, and elsewhere ; it is also reflected in the Gospels, where we read of the man with an unclean spirit " who had his dwelling in the tombs " (Mark 5[2, 3]).

For the further study of the subject recourse must be had to many volumes ; there is no one work that covers the whole ground.

XIII. BIBLICAL ETHICS

FOR most people, Biblical Ethics are comprehended in the two great commands of love to God and love to one's neighbour. Actually, they are the two commands in which Jesus summed up, or accepted as summing up, the law of Moses, *i.e.* the Old Testament (Luke 10[27]). Can they be taken as summing up New Testament ethics also ? Certainly, it may be said, the Christian law is also the law of love ; but to say that is to give little guidance to conduct, and even to do little justice to the New Testament itself. For what sort of conduct is meant when I am told to love my neighbour, or my enemy (Matt. 5[44]), or all men ? What is to be understood by love in such a context ? And the question is even more perplexing when I am told also to love God. For if there is some one emotion that I can feel and show alike to friendly and hostile individuals around me, can it be possible to identify this with any feeling or attitude that I may show to One who is so far above me and unlike me as the infinite and eternal God ?

Moreover, a good deal more is said in the Bible about righteousness and sin than about love. The test and the goal of good conduct indeed may be said to be righteousness ; and its opposite is sin. But what is the relation of righteousness to love ? Sometimes it is regarded as distinct, and even opposed. The law of righteousness is represented as obedience to a code of rules, as love is represented as an attitude. Righteousness will be rewarded, sin will be punished. But it may at least be observed that righteousness, like love, is regarded as something which exists in God, and must be manifested in man ; and that it can be manifested by man because it has been revealed first by God. That codes of rules and even conventional customs have their place in the Biblical account, or accounts of conduct is undeniable ; but no system of ethics can be built up on an enumeration of them, still less on a selection from them, since many of them are quite independent of the rest, and to be satisfied with this would neglect what is at least as much stressed throughout the Bible, certain personal relations between man and man, and between man and God.

A single authoritative code of morals clearly does not exist in the Bible. In the New Testament we have a number of *obiter dicta* of Jesus, and more or less scattered references to points of conduct in the apostolic letters. In the Old Testament we have mostly pictures of various states of society, and the ideas of right and wrong obeyed or disobeyed therein, often with the reflections of the sacred writers upon them. Both in the acts and ideas described, and in the criticisms on them, there is often a good deal that is crude, while the judgements in some sections of the Old Testament often clash with those in other sections (Ex. 20⁵ ; Ezek. 18⁴ ; Ps. 106²³, 103⁸). Historians, prophets, and psalmists will disagree with one another, and even among themselves. There is no system, and indeed only a derived interest. In fact, though we may find ethics in the Bible, we cannot call the Biblical writers ethical. Their main interest is not with men, but with God ; His will, His purposes, His commands, His pleasure and displeasure. Men are important to the sacred writers only as they obey or disobey those commands, and are punished or forgiven by His almighty power and wisdom. And even if we too turn from men to God, and base our account of the ethics of the Bible on what is told us of the commands and purpose of God, we shall find that the writers' conception of these changes from century to century and almost from book to book.

Is, then, the task beyond our powers ? Yes, if we are searching for a system, co-ordinated and logical like that of Aristotle or Kant, or even Hobbes. But not if we are content to turn to the documents themselves, to ask what they thought about that part of life which we designate by the term conduct —there is no real equivalent for the word either in Hebrew or in the Greek of the New Testament ; and to find out why ethics, as we understand the term, was something so alien from them. We shall have to search, not for formulæ or rules, but for ideas.

We must begin with the Old Testament ; for the New, in whatever sense it may be said to fulfil the Old, certainly grew out of it (Luke 24²⁷). And the Old Testament can only be safely studied with its history in view. That is to say, we must begin with the pre-prophetic portions, the sections containing or (to speak cautiously) based on writings earlier than the middle of the eighth century ; next, the earlier writing prophets ; then, the great law-book of Deuteronomy ; this will be followed by the later prophets, the Psalms, and the later stages of the Law. This is a plain distinction, and can be worked on independently of critical uncertainties as to details.

Within all these divisions, there are definite differences of moral and religious outlook. But everywhere we meet, in the centre of the Hebrews' thought, with Jehovah, the God of Israel ; however their ideals of conduct may differ, conduct is important because *He* cares about it. The Decalogue itself begins with " God spake these words and said " (Ex. 20¹). The rules that follow are not so much rules between man and man, which is what we mean by ethics, but between man and God (cf. Ex. 20¹¹· ¹²). It is this which makes the Old Testament writings unique in the literature, historical, moral, or religious, of the world. And Jehovah differs from other gods, not simply because He cares about man's conduct to man, but still more because He launched Israel on its career by a signal mercy ; He brought the nation out of Egypt, and placed it in its own land of Palestine in order that, once there, it might be the recipient of His continued goodness, and might offer to Him the obedience which He chooses or requires of it.

In the Old Testament phrase, He has made a covenant or compact with them; He binds Himself down to act in a certain way to them, on the understanding that they will act in a certain way to Him. He is their God ; they are His people. In the pre-prophetic writings, not much is actually said about the Covenant. Little more is said about the distinctly religious practice of the cult of the sanctuary or the altar. These are rather taken for granted than enjoined. But what is stressed, alike in the narratives and the one short code of law that has come down to us, significantly known as the Book of the Covenant, Ex. 21–23¹⁹ (cf. Ex. 24⁷), a kind of primitive digest of customs and decisions, is the importance of brotherly and, as we might almost say, family principles of conduct between the members of the community. What is enjoined upon these simple peasants and farmers, not nearly so advanced as the Babylonians for whom the Code of Hammurabi had been drawn up a thousand years before, is that they must treat one another with scrupulous fairness and justice, as being members of one and the same community which owes its allegiance, in all its conduct, to Jehovah. The stern *lex talionis* has its place here (Ex. 21²⁴), but the code is specially thoughtful for the needs of widows and orphans (Ex. 22²²ᶠᶠ·), and is more anxious to avoid perpetrating " what is not done in Israel " (2 Sam. 13¹²) than to refine on old customs. Law passes easily into equity ; the great sin is oppression and harshness.

By the middle of the eighth century a social revolution had come about. Wealth had found its way into the simple communities of Southern and Central Palestine, giving a new strength to temptations that before were comparatively mild. Rich and poor were now distinct ; and in their crude selfishness the rich could exploit the poor, lending money to them at exorbitant rates of interest, selling them up, reducing them to serfdom, and living in luxury and debauchery while their neglected countrymen were starving. The writings of the eighth century prophets are one long protest against disloyalty to the traditions of Jehovah's people (Amos 3^{10}, $4^{1, 4}$, $5^{11ff.}$; Isa. 1^{15}, 5^8) ; their zeal in the service of the sanctuary is only held to aggravate their revolt against their God. " What doth Jehovah require of thee but to do justly, and love mercy, and walk humbly with thy God ? " (Micah 6^8). Justice is nothing but honesty ; and mercy really stands for loyalty to personal relations, whether between members of the same family or of the same community (Jer. 2^2 " kindness," E.V.) ; and its frequent reference to Jehovah shows that the principle of the conduct of Jehovah Himself to His people was this same loyalty to the relation which He had established with His people. Righteousness itself means rather being " in the right " than showing obedience to a code ; it is a personal rather than a legal term ; and sin (which can be committed against man as well as against God) is the opposite, being " in the wrong," breaking the personal bond (1 Sam. 24^{17}, 26^{23}).

When we turn to Deuteronomy, the law-book of 621 B.C., we are more distinctly in the region of a code ; but it must be remembered that the very word law (*torah*) in Hebrew means instruction ; the *torah* is the instruction which God has graciously given to men, to inform them how to keep " in the right " with Him. Unlike the " Book of the Covenant," Deuteronomy gives a large space to the practice of the shrine and the altar ; it forbids all worship save at one centre (Deut. $12^{2ff.}$) ; but still more space is given to conduct ; and here it moves entirely on prophetic lines ; honesty, fairness, care for the distressed classes, widows, foreigners, orphans, and landless priests or Levites (Deut. 14^{29}, $24^{17, 21}$, 22^8, $14^{27ff.}$). It even provides for railings on house roofs, exemption from military service for the newly married, and against undue violence in wartime (Deut. $20^{5ff, 19}$; but also *vv.* $^{16ff.}$). And all this follows from the primal command to love Jehovah with one's whole soul and strength ; the love which is owed because (as the Deuteronomist is never tired of insisting)

Jehovah had founded His Covenant in delivering His people from the Egyptian bondage (Deut. 6⁵· ¹⁰).

By the beginning of the sixth century B.C. all seemed to be in vain. First Israel and then Judah was driven into exile. The Covenant had been hopelessly broken. But no. In exile, so to speak, Jehovah laid a new task upon Himself. The Covenant, broken by the disloyalty of the people, had now to be restored. Jehovah's mercy, or loyalty to the bond, consisted not only in doing good to His people while they were obedient, but in restoring them from their disobedience. As the prophet of the Exile expressed it, when he foretold their deliverance, Jehovah was revealing His righteousness; that is, He was showing Himself to be " in the right " with them ; and they were to be restored to their land, to His land, and to their righteousness—to their "being in the right," in the old personal relations, with Him (Isa. 45⁸, cf. 51⁵).

When we turn to the Psalms, composed for the most part in the age that followed this return, we find the same insistence on the two elementary but cardinal good qualities of honesty and truthfulness, and of kindness or loyalty. The good man will swear to his own hurt and keep his word, and he will be kind, like Jehovah Himself, to the widow and fatherless, and to the unthankful and the evil (Ps. 15, 62¹⁰). But, as the old Hebrew outlook passes into what must be known now as Judaism, three new notes emerge. First, the identification between wealth and greed has become closer, so that rich and bad, poor and good, are almost synonymous (Ps. 10²· ⁹, 35, 37), though the stress is always on the moral rather than on the economic characteristics of the two classes. Second, the provisions of the law take up a much larger space in the attention of the Jew than before the Exile—naturally, since when politics are impossible, religion takes their place as the bond of racial union (cf. Ps. 119; also Ps. 51¹⁶ᶠᶠ.). Further, the ritual aspect of the law was vigorously developed after the Exile ; but this, so far from leading the pious Jew to pit the ritual against the moral, bound up his conception of covenant loyalty to Jehovah with obedience to all that He had commanded, whether in the Temple or in the street or in the home. Thirdly, we meet a new emphasis on both individualism and nationalism. It is often said that individualism was introduced into Hebrew thought by Jeremiah and Ezekiel. This is misleading. To the Hebrew, Jehovah's Covenant was with the nation as a whole ; the nation was bound together by the almost physical tie of blood ; it stood in Jehovah's favour or fell from it as one man. Within the nation was the family ;

and the guilt of an individual and the liability to punishment would attach to his relations and his descendants (Jos. 7²⁴, Amos 1–3). But this still left the individual as the subject of moral judgements ; the innovation of Jeremiah and Ezekiel was to deny that the children were punished for their fathers; it was their own sins that brought ruin on men (Jer. 31²⁹, Ezek. 18⁴). But the Hebrews shared with most other ancient peoples (though in a stronger degree) the conviction that it was to their own community that the duties of honesty and loyalty were paramount, as it was to their own nation that the Covenant had been given (cf. Ex. 21²). They seldom looked outside. After the Exile, this national consciousness grew stronger. The foreigners, to whom neither the Covenant nor the law had been given, could neither please Jehovah or even know Him. Dislike and condemnation of the Gentiles went together—an attitude that was quickly reciprocated ; and the vicious circle was drawn more and more firmly, until loyalty to Jehovah was felt to involve hatred to all His creatures who did not share descent from His covenant-friend Abraham (Ezr. 9¹ff). The attitude is seen at its most unlovely in the Book of Esther (however intelligible it there becomes) ; but against it were the traditions of the part played in Israel by resident aliens (e.g. Ittai the Gittite and Uriah the Hittite (2 Sam. 15¹⁹, 11⁶)), the demands made in the law for their kindly treatment, and the actual protests in Jonah and Malachi.

On the other hand, the results of the Exile, which drove the Jews in Palestine into themselves, drove them also out of themselves in the various countries of the dispersion where, after the Exile, they came in increasing numbers to find their homes. In what is known as the Wisdom literature, which was indeed Palestinian as well as extra-Palestinian in origin, morality ceases to be thought of in terms of the Covenant. The same type of goodness is emphasized, honesty, fairness, truthfulness, refusal to press or to take advantage, care for poor relations and dependants (Job 31). For all this the individual is responsible ; but the obligations are such as to rest on all men as such. Thus individualism and universalism emerge together ; and while the authors of the Wisdom literature undoubtedly think first of their own Jewish community, they are expressing, perhaps in spite of themselves, an ethics that has become universalistic.

A further word must here be said on the subject of sex-morality among the Hebrews. The covenant was made with the nation as a whole ; but within the nation, the importance of the family was taken for granted ; the nation-wide loyalty which Jehovah demanded included loyalty to the family bonds of husband and wife, parents and children, and kinsfolk one with another. No poor-law was needed when convention bade an individual in distress look confidently for assistance to his kinsmen and his community. Blood was stronger in the family than in the race as a whole. Blood that was shed in violence was the blood of the family rather than of the individual. Hence the duty of the next-of-kin, both to avenge the shedding of blood and to maintain, by the Levirate marriage, the family continuity (Num. 35[6] ; Deut. 25[5]). The régime of the family was strongly patriarchal. Crimes against women in the early codes are regarded, as with most Semitic peoples, as crimes against more or less valuable property (Ex. 22[16]). As human beings, women are dependants, like children and slaves, and must receive the consideration and kindliness which Hebrew feeling demanded towards the weak. Monogamy was not thought of as a duty ; it was prescribed in none of the codes; and it had the examples of Jacob, of David, and Solomon against it, although in practice it was naturally the usual rule. The concubine and the slave had a regularized place in the Hebrew family (Gen. 30[4], Ex. 21[7]). But all irregular connexions, that is, all sexual relations outside what traditional custom was understood to smile on, were strongly condemned (2 Sam. 13 ; Amos 2[7] ; Hosea 2). And there is plenty of evidence to show that throughout the history women could hold a high place in general esteem and wield a considerable influence (Judg. 5 ; 1 Sam 25[14] ; 2 Sam. 14[2] ; 2 Kings 4[8]). When, in the Wisdom literature, attention is turned more explicitly to the place of women in society, almost equal emphasis is laid on the benefits a good woman can secure for her husband and her family, and the dreadful temptations exercised by the profligate and the mercenary (Prov. 7[10], 31[10]). Of chivalry and romantic love in our modern Western sense the Hebrew knew nothing. The woman was there to satisfy his physical needs, to produce and nurse his children, and to supervise his household. But the *hetaira* was never to be tolerated. We can understand why in later times divorce could be carried out for the most frivolous reasons, why the man thanked God, in the worship of the synagogue, that he was not a woman, and yet why the Jewish family life maintained a level far beyond anything in the reach of the Greek world. Loyalty between man and wife was as much a part of Jehovah's will as the loyalty of the nation to Himself. National disobedience could not be more scathingly condemned than by calling it national adultery (Ezek. 16).

Looking back now for a moment, we can see both the strength and the limitation of the Jewish ideas on ethics. The two key-words, covenant and law, both of them religious rather than ethical, because both of them intelligible only in terms of Jehovah's will, can best be understood, with their implications, when we remember that law is simply Jehovah's instruction as to the way in which the Hebrews were to keep their part of the compact between Him and them. Their ideas on the details of this instruction naturally and inevitably varied from time to time. Life was one thing in the simple farming villages of the highlands of Palestine, when the tramp of the Assyrian legions was as yet unheard and even the Canaanite pedlar was a rare visitor, and quite another in the crowded streets of Tarsus or Alexandria. What makes it possible to speak about the continuity of Hebrew ethics is the persistence of its spirit and the importance, never forgotten, of the attitude as opposed to the act. Six centuries after the appearance of Deuteronomy, the Jewish doctors had lost themselves in decisions as to the tithing of mint and cummin, and ridiculous discussions as to how many ounces a man might carry on the Sabbath (Matt. 23[23]; John 5[10]), giving a freer rein to casuistry than it has ever enjoyed, before or since, even with the Jesuits. Yet the best of them never lost sight of the end of the law, the confidence that not even involuntarily were they departing from the path of Jehovah, but that they were walking with Him, not in the hope of some future bliss, but in the actual enjoyment of His presence and grace.

To the student of Greek or modern ethics, all this will seem thin and jejune. He will miss the discussion of many important virtues, such as bravery and self-control, and of great ethical principles or of familiar distinctions, between reason and intuition, duty and happiness, or even the self and the community. Yet he will perhaps find himself comparing Plato, at least in the central doctrine of the Republic, with the Mosaic tradition. Both are dealing with righteousness ; both look at the individual in relation to the community, and both see virtue " writ large " in the state.

The difference is that the Hebrew looks on the community (which includes Jehovah as well as His people) as one great family, and to be interpreted in terms of the family and its life and needs, while to Plato the family and the family ideals, in so far as they are thought of at all, are subordinated entirely to the community. The result is, for Plato, as artificial as for the Hebrew it is, in the best sense of the word, natural. It may be that in history the family did not actually precede the humblest forms of society or tribal life. But society itself is based on the recognition of personal relations within a group. These relations are based on the existence of mutual rights and duties. The rights and duties differ between different individuals ; the father and the child, the husband and the wife, the chief and the serf, the priest and the worshipper, the patron and the client, and so on. And they will be formulated differently at different times and in different places. The important thing is the personal relations on which they rest. These are ultimate. The Greek was not far from this truth. He knew that each individual had his station with its duties and its rights. This is as clear in Aristotle and Epictetus as in Plato. But to him the ultimate was the State, or humanity as a whole. This inevitably carried his thoughts away from persons to laws. To the Hebrew, laws are only the application of law, and law is the embodiment of an attitude of personal loyalty and fellow-feeling. The members of his community are bound each to each " in natural piety." They can act rightly to one another because they are the people of God ; they are " in the right " to one another when they are " in the right " to Him. " He hath showed thee, O man, what is good."

It is now time to turn to the New Testament, and to Jesus. Jesus has been regarded as the greatest and gentlest of the Pharisees ; the rival (and not always the successful rival) of Socrates, Buddha, Confucius, and the rest ; the founder of the world's greatest ethical system ; or a teacher whose enthusiasm led him to lose himself in the clouds, to leave us a set of beautiful impossibilities ; the formulator of a set of precepts which run counter to all that is noble in human nature ; or a fanatic who, with his eyes set on the coming cataclysm, bluntly refused to give men any serious moral guidance. All these are inadequate, for one clear reason : Jesus cannot be simply looked on as an ethical teacher. Indeed, His ethics cannot be regarded apart from His religious consciousness and His mission. He left no writings, and He left no system. Taken by themselves, His remarks on conduct are so many *obiter dicta*, as perplexing, in their inconsistency with themselves and with the demands of ordinary human life, as were, viewed from the outside, His actions and His character. Himself confident and meek, dominating and gentle, passionate and calm, cautious and daring, simple in

His teaching yet extraordinarily obscure, reverent to the past yet a fearless innovator, His actual words on the subject of conduct were as little an end in themselves as were His acts of healing. They were an expression of Himself. They can only be understood in the light of His conception of the Father in heaven, the Kingdom, and the Cross. He came to lay down His life. " Fear not, little flock ; it is your Father's good pleasure to give you the kingdom " (Luke 12^{32}). If we knew nothing of the life of Butler or Bentham we should still be able to understand the teaching of the three famous *Dissertations* and the *Principles of Morals and Legislation*. If we knew nothing of the life of Jesus, His ethics would be a hopeless riddle.

" To give you the Kingdom." This is the sign-post. To follow its guidance will lead us to the heart of the other two conceptions of Jesus. But to understand it is not altogether easy. It is generally agreed that the term kingdom on the lips of Jesus is an abstract rather than a concrete term; kingship rather than kingdom ; sovereignty ; supremacy. This sovereignty exists in heaven rather than on earth. It is ideal rather than actual, much as Plato felt the pattern of his own Republic to be. But it implies a community in which it is exercised and fulfilled. Men are bidden to act as if it was really there, and as if they were its subjects. And its head is a father. It is noteworthy that Jesus, though constantly speaking of the Kingdom, hardly ever uses the term king when He is speaking of God. Father is indeed more frequent on His lips than the term God itself. Thus, if the sovereignty of God is real and essential, and is on its way to become actual, the community to which it points is one wherein men know themselves to be members of a family, acting towards its head as if he were a father, and to each other as if they were brothers.

It is the personal attitude once more. And this family attitude, which looks to its head as the Father in heaven, is expressed in a wealth of parabolic teaching which emphasizes its value and preciousness, its ability to answer every human need, its gradual growth, its stern demands—" enter or be cast out " (Matt. 8^{12}, 22^{13}, 25^{30})—its presence in the bewildering variety of human life, and the certainty of its final supremacy. To live and act as if you were bound to one another as brothers because you are bound to God as His sons, and can therefore count on Him for all that a father would do to his children—this is to live the ideal and the rapturous life, and the only life that can be worth calling life at all. To refuse it is to condemn

24

yourself to darkness and to death. You cannot escape the choice, whether you will live in such an attitude or not ; and yet you cannot make it. You may snatch at it with violence ; but you must receive it as a gift from Him who waits to be known and reverenced as your Father (Matt. 11²⁰ ; Luke 12³²).

So far the Synoptists will take us, challenging but perplexing. But if we may look for the teaching of Jesus also in the Fourth Gospel, we find there that this relation of sonship and brotherhood is seen at its highest in Jesus Himself, and that its supreme manifestation was the great act of obedience in which He laid down His life (John 15¹³), in which He showed His utter devotion to God and to those who, through Him, were to become like Him the sons of the Father in heaven.

It is when we grasp this that the ethical teaching of the Synoptists, as we call it, becomes intelligible. Jesus is not thinking of the average man at all, *l'homme moyen sensuel*, and what can be expected of him ; nor is He thinking of the citizen of a well-ordered State. He is thinking of such men as He saw around Him, who were placed on the simpler levels of social and economic life in Palestine, but who had found their way into this new attitude, and were living as if in a new community ; who, in the language of the Fourth Gospel, had been born from above (John 3³ R.V. marg.). It was to such men that Jesus applied what may be called the attitude of the family. In the family one does not think of " the lore of nicely calculated less or more." One does not ask " how much ? " One does not even think of justice as it is understood outside. There are no limits to what the father will wish to do for wife or child, or what brothers will do for one another. One does not stand on one's own rights ; they are safe, or they ought to be, in the keeping of the rest. Hence, to give or to lend on request, to do what is asked of one and more, to refuse to criticize, to hope for the best, to give up what one has the strength or the position to claim, to forgive as often as there is anything to be forgiven, are only natural (Matt. 5⁴⁰. ⁴², 7¹, 18²²).

But this attitude of devotion to the members of the great family involves even more. It becomes an eager passion for service and the meeting of all human needs ; the enthusiasm of humanity, as Seeley called it in a happy phrase. This is best seen in the fashion in which, regarding it evidently as the most natural thing to do, Jesus answered every call for help by which He was met, breaking off every other occupation in His instant concentration (Mark 5²². ²⁴). And this mark of the good life receives quite extraordinary endorsement when, in His last recorded public discourse, carrying further the truth that lay in the parable of the Good Samaritan, He practically identifies fitness to receive eternal blessedness with readiness to feed the hungry and clothe the naked and visit the prisons, as if no other morals and no other convictions were necessary (Matt. 25[34ff.]). "This do, and thou shalt live" (Luke 10[28]). Yet even this is not all. Those who should be brothers, and who are to be treated as if they were, may themselves show an entirely opposite disposition; ungrateful, injurious, hostile. Indeed, it is only with these that the member of the kingdom will show his true character; any one can be kind to the appreciative and friendly. And it is the very mark of God Himself to be good to those who scorn Him (Matt. 5[45f.]). This doctrine of love to enemies, coupled with the principle of non-resistance to evil (Matt. 5[39]), has often been interpreted as a call to passivity in the face of aggression or wrong-doing, and as the condemnation of war under any circumstances. Jesus, whose immediate horizon was always bounded by His day and generation, did not contemplate war as history knows it; nor can direct guidance on that subject be found in His actual words. The enemies He thinks of are personal rather than political; the evil which is not to be resisted is wrong or injury or insult done to oneself. It is clear that He Himself had no notion of using force to set up His kingdom (John 18[36]); how could He, His kingdom being what it was? The incident of the scourge of cords is hardly a case in point (John 2[15]). His positive principle He expresses as self-denial; not in our tepid sense of the word, but treating oneself as if one had no existence and did not matter (Matt. 16[24], 10[33]). Sooner than assert yourself, suffer mutilation! (Matt. 5[29]). But evil is to be overcome with good; the foe is to be won over by unfaltering and courageous service (Matt. 18[15]); and if any one thinks that the Beatitudes suggest a meek passivity, let him try to put them into practice.

All this will explain the attitude of Jesus to the Pharisees and to the party which is called in the Fourth Gospel "the Jews." It has often been pointed out that the Pharisees were the best type to be found in Palestine in our Lord's day; and that most of His own words can be found in the later Pharisaic writings. But it was not with this type of Pharisee that Jesus was concerned. The men He had in mind were men who went about to establish their own righteousness, and to gain their own reward—the attitude with which St. Paul accuses himself before his conversion (Matt. 6[2]; Rom. 10[3]). On this attitude Jesus had no mercy. It defied everything for which He had come. It could only meet, from Him who forbade His followers to resist evil, with scorn and pitiless denunciation. It is true that much that He said can be paralleled from Jewish writings. What cannot be paralleled is His independence; His refusal to appeal to any authority but His own (Matt. 7^{24}); the inwardness by which He insisted on turning from the act which a judge might deal with, to the motive, which lies outside the range of law (Matt. 5^{28}); and the defiance of convention which made Him, who came to seek and save the lost (what Pharisee ever thought of doing that ?), the friend of publicans and sinners and loose women (Luke 19^{10}; Matt. 11^{19}).

What has been said makes clear what we can expect and what we cannot expect to find by way of direct guidance in the moral teaching of Jesus. What are we to conclude as to His attitude or the attitudes of His followers to the State? Here, too, we must remember the concrete interests of Jesus. Of philosophical principles, political or social, we have and can have no hint in His words. The State to Him was the actual Government of Galilee or Judæa, Herod or Cæsar. And He took no interest in either beyond keeping out of their way till the Jews caught Him and hurled Him at Pilate (Luke 13^{32}; John 7^{1}). That He had no idea of initiating legislation, for His own time or the future, is evident from the character of His precepts; these could, most of them, never be embodied in laws. His own plan was to keep on good terms with the authorities as long as He could; His followers were to do the same. Taxes must be paid (Matt. 17^{24}). And when His enemies tried to force from Him some political pronouncement, He was content with the enigmatic but unanswerable reply "Render unto Cæsar . . ." (Matt. 22^{21}). On the other hand, He calmly laid the axe at the root of the tree of the old Jewish particularistic nationalism. He said little on the subject; He did not travel outside Palestine unless He was forced. But His first public address showed His hearers where He stood (Luke 4^{26}); He mixed with Samaritans or foreigners as easily as with Jews (John 4); and He left His disciples with the conviction that after His death their mission was world-wide. He did not challenge the position of the Old Testament explicitly; He undermined it. The fatherhood of God as He taught it made nationalism impossible.

Another question on which the words of Jesus have been eagerly canvassed is that of sex. And it has been confidently asserted that even if Jesus refused to legislate or even arbitrate on other subjects, He left clear directions for the

Statute-book in the matter of divorce. If he did so, it is unfortunate that His words as they are recorded are ambiguous (Matt. 5³², 19⁹; Mark 10²ᶠᶠ·). Did He intend to forbid divorce altogether or to allow it after adultery or fornication ? But a study of the relevant passages will show that He was not thinking of marriage as a civil institution, universal in human society in some shape ; but of marriage as it was intended to be in God's purpose, and in the heart of those who enter into it with that purpose in mind. He uses the solemn words "one flesh," though He does not explain them. Here, He seems to say, divorce will be unthinkable. On the other subjects that have teased succeeding ages He is equally reticent. Naturally, He has nothing to say on homosexuality, on birth control or pre-marital incontinence. But could anything go further than his identification of the licentious glance with the licentious act ? (Matt. 5²⁸). And indirectly, how much we can learn. His beautiful courtesy to all the women with whom He came in contact, from His own mother to the Samaritan or the woman of the streets, involved, primarily, a condemnation of the Jewish view of women, which even His own disciples appear to have shared (Matt. 19¹⁴) ; indirectly it raised all women to a level where it was impossible to regard them either as playthings or the instruments of the needs of men. We have no need of laws. We have but to ask what is consistent with what we have heard from Him. Yet he was no prude. Inchastity appeared to fill Him with a burning sense of shame (John 8⁶) ; yet He never inveighed against it as He inveighed against the Pharisaic hypocrisy. He gave His friendship to the unchaste ; and by His friendship He redeemed them. Such is the teaching that He has left to His followers. Women are the children of God even as men. And all that has been done to lift the position of women in twenty centuries is the result of what Jesus said and did, and refused to do.

We may now consider the relation of the ethics of Jesus, if the term may be allowed, to the ethics of the Old Testament. That there is a close similarity is clear. It does not lie so much in actual words, precepts or laws, nor in a certain type of virtue enjoined—honesty, kindliness, or the readiness to help and serve. It lies rather in the fact that both systems rest on a definite set of personal relations, on which they base their authority, and from which they develop their implications. In each, the conduct of men to one another depends on their recognition of One who demands obedience, but who pledges Himself to supply all their need. In the Old Testament, this is a heavenly King, who has bound Himself by a covenant ; in the New, a heavenly Father, who is bound by His own fatherly nature, which He cannot deny. In the Old, men are instructed in the conduct to one another which that covenant requires, by their own social traditions, and the laws in which those customs have been transmitted and elaborated ; in the New, by a Teacher who has come to embody all that God has to say to men about their relation to Him, or to one another, in His own peerless life. To rest content with the first is to run the risk of letting loyalty to the Covenant and its personal source fall back into the sphere of law ; righteousness, from being right with a person, slips back into satisfaction with the performance of the required act. But to hold to the second lifts us right out of the sphere of law. For there are no prescribed acts apart from the expression of the inevitable and passionate attitude. And this expression can never be adequate. We can never do enough. Morality has bade farewell to law altogether. All imperatives are left behind in the intercourse of the Father's house.

On the other hand, there can equally be no question of reward. Utilitarianism in every form is also left behind. For when once the son and the brother has lost himself in the new family community, when he has come to treat himself, regarded as an isolated self, as if he had no existence, it is obvious that what would appeal to him as an individual can have no interest for him. His one delight will be in the activity that belongs to the actual spirit of the community of which he is a member. The end cannot be obedience to a law, for its own sake, or for the satisfaction of obeying it ; nor can it be anything to be obtained or received. It can only be what moralists call the approach to perfection, and what the Christian would call growth in grace ; coming nearer and nearer to the full union with the other members of the family, in Him through whom the family is founded. But this approach will always be asymptotic. It will never reach finality. An action may be repeated till it is perfect. A personal attitude has endless possibilities of growth (Phil. 3^{12}).

Such, then, is Jesus' doctrine of love. As we have seen, the word was hardly ever used by Him in His public teaching ; He preferred other more concrete and less easily discounted terms. And when, if we may follow the Fourth Gospel, He used the word in His more private conversations with His disciples (and this indeed hardly till His last evening with them) He meant by it that profound intimacy of thought and purpose

and feeling by which He knew Himself to be joined to the
Father, and by which He and the Father were one. When
applied to the disciples, it meant the same kind of paternal
and filial communion between God and them, which, as Jesus
taught them, was attainable through Him. If, however, we
use the term with a freedom from which Jesus appears to have
shrunk, we must beware of allowing it to bear a merely philanthropic or a semi-erotic significance. The very difficulty
that we noticed previously, of giving to the one word a meaning that should fit our love to God, and to men, and God's love
to us, is really its own explanation. We must start from
God's love to us, His purpose that we should enter into the
intimacy of fatherhood and sonship; such will be our love
to Him ; and our love to men will take its shape from His love
to them. They too, through us as it may be given to us,
must enter into the same relation, the only relation that
gives conduct its value ; because the only conduct that has
value to God is conduct animated by the adoring obedience of
children to their father (John 13^{34}, 14^{23}, 15^{9}, 17^{26}).

An admirable and striking commentary on all this is
supplied by the Epistle of James. At first sight this Epistle
seems open to the adverse criticism of Luther ; having no
mention of saving or Pauline faith, it hardly appears worthy
of the name of a Christian writing. Luther might have added
that beyond the first verse there is hardly a direct reference to
Jesus Himself. It is when we turn to the actual words of
the Epistle that we see how it is saturated with echoes of the
teaching of the Synoptic Gospels. Humility, endurance,
carefulness of speech, reverence for the poor rather than for
the rich, embodiment of belief in action, prayer—on all these
we see the Old Testament illuminated by recollection of the
actual words of Jesus ; and the well-known definition of " pure
religion " (that is, the sincere practice of religion) recalls at
once the great passage in Matt. 25 (James 1$^{9. 12. 23}$, 2$^{2. 16}$, 3$^{13ff.}$,
4^{11}, 5^{8}; 1^{27}). What is even more striking is that most of the
topics to which the Epistle refers have to do with the filial
attitude to God, or the brotherly attitude to men ; the attitudes against which warnings are given are not so much what
would be called positive sins, but the marks of the man who,
like the Pharisee, would grasp his own righteousness for his
own ends (James 1^{19}, 3^{16}, 4$^{1. 13}$).

With Paul the matter is more complex and subtle. Paul
had been brought up a Pharisee ; he had never known Jesus ;
on the contrary, he had been filled, after the crucifixion, with a
deep and passionate hatred of all that concerned Him. After

his conversion, it would seem that he was dependent on whatever the disciples could tell him about his new master (Gal. 1[18]). Moreover, he spent the larger part of his active life in the Græco-Roman world, in a society which Jesus had never entered, and to which He made no allusion ; a society, moreover, where the moral problems and temptations were very different from those familiar to the simple Galilean circles where Jesus was most at home. Further, Paul's nature was very different from that of Jesus ; what likeness could there be between the calm aphorisms of Jesus and the dark rushing periods of Paul ? Yet, when we turn to the later portions of his letters, in which he deals with conduct, we find likeness as marked as difference. He does not attempt to give systematic outlines of conduct to his converts. He appears to treat of subjects as they occur to him. To three subjects indeed he constantly refers ; quarrelsomeness, sexual licence, and greed. It would seem that he felt his ex-heathens were specially in need of such warnings (Eph. 4[2. 26], 5[2. 5] ; Col. 3[5. 8. 12]). But when we read more carefully, we find allusions to the words of Jesus as clear as in the Epistle of James (Gal. 4[14] ; Rom. 13[8] ; Col. 3[14] ; Rom. 3[31] ; 2 Cor. 3[3.6]) ; a stress on Christian conduct as a matter of personal and even family relations, for parents and children, masters and slaves ; the recognition that these must be discharged " in the Lord," i.e., in Christ, who is thus not simply the teacher of morals, but its inspiration ; and all this against the background of what has already become familiar to us in the Gospels, that Jesus has brought us into a new relation to God the Father, and that right conduct is conduct that is fitting to that relation and flows from it. Paul is, as we know, writing for members of his churches ; and some of those members had reached only a very elementary stage of morality (Eph. 4[28]—" stole " should be in the present tense ; 1 Cor. 5[9ff.]). But, to judge from the kind of conduct that he mentions, every church is looked on as a family ; forbearance, hospitality, liberality, readiness to aim at another's interest rather than one's own, speaking the truth *in love* (Eph. 4[15]), and all that is said about love in the famous chapter in 1 Corinthians—all these will flourish on the soil that we have already learnt to know. Others, which would more naturally grow in the city state of the Greek writers on ethics, are passed over ; and even the maxims of the Stoic treatises, with which Paul may have had some acquaintance, are baptized into the Christian community.

The Stoic had learnt, in Paul's day, that if one would live for oneself one must live for another ; and that the whole

world, like some " dear city of Zeus," was bound together like
a great organism, where every man was a member or a limb
of every other.   Such language was not unwelcome to Paul
(Rom. 12⁴ ; 1 Cor. 12¹²) ; but it would never have satisfied him.
The world was one, with no difference at all even between Jew
and Gentile (Gal. 3²⁸ ; Col. 3¹¹), because Christ had died for
all, and revealed to men the common Father of all ; and he
had come to live, not merely to find his own happiness in
serving the happiness of another (a somewhat refined form of
selfishness) ; but to find a new joy in flinging himself into the
life of the new community—to spend and to be spent for it
(2 Cor. 12¹⁵)—which Christ had redeemed in His own blood.

Such are the main outlines of Biblical ethics, if Biblical
ethics there can be ; sketches, very imperfectly systematic,
of types of conduct appropriate to certain ancient states of
society, or certain communities, very unlike our own, founded
on certain religious conceptions of the relation of God to
men which are foreign to the majority of people to-day.
How then can we hope to receive guidance from such precepts
for our complicated modern life ?   The answer is, first, that
such guidance as is here probably meant can be received from
no system of ethics whatever.

What answer will be given by Kant's Categorical Imperative, or the Greatest Happiness Principle, or Butler's
identification of conscience with reasonable self-love, or
Aristotle's reliance on the Mean ?   In every case we have to
take a very general rule and work it out for ourselves, conscious
that different persons would work it out very differently.
But, further, when we take the principles arrived at above,
and regard the questions as to be worked out on the basis of
personal relations which have their source in the Will of God,
and are seen by us in the light of One in whom that will is
known as mercy and love, we can then work them out with a
new confidence and precision, and carry them into spheres
never contemplated by those who first set them before the
world.   And this is what has actually happened.   No one
can say that the great ethical systems of the past, important
and fascinating as they may have been, have ever meant a
definite ethical advance on a large scale in the world.   But
the great conception that underlies the whole of the Old
Testament lifted the Jews, in spite of all their short-sighted-
ness, to a level which the ancient world could admire but could
imitate with only very partial success ; while Christian thought,
applying at first its similar yet far profounder view of the
relations between God and man in the simple ways of honesty

and cleanness, kindliness and forbearance and brotherly sympathy, has given to the world a moral heritage which it will not easily surrender, and in which lies its only hope of survival and peace.

BIBLIOGRAPHY

(Books on the general subject of Christian Ethics are not here referred to.)

O. Cone, *Rich and Poor in the N.T.* 1902.
W. E. Chadwick, *Social Relationships in the Light of Christianity.* 1910.
A. B. D. Alexander, *Ethics of St Paul.* 1910.
A. B. D. Alexander, *Christianity and Ethics.* 1914.
W. Manson, *Christ's View of the Kingdom of God.*
C. Ryder Smith, *The Bible Doctrine of Society.* 1920.
J. M. P. Smith, *The Moral Life of the Hebrews.* 1923.
E. F. Scott, *The Ethical Teaching of Jesus.* 1924.
J. Pedersen, *Israel : Its Life and Culture.* 1926.
A. B. Scott, *Christ, the Wisdom of God.* 1928.
F. A. M. Spencer, *The Theory of Christ's Ethics.* 1929.
C. A. Anderson Scott, *New Testament Ethics.* 1930.

XIV. THE LIFE AND TEACHING OF JESUS CHRIST

1. Sources of Information

FROM sources outside the New Testament there is little to be learned of Jesus. Early in the second century Pliny, governor of Bithynia, having occasion to investigate charges against Christians in his province, discovered that they " sang hymns to Christ as to a god " (*Epistles* x. 96). About the same time his friend Tacitus, being engaged on a history of the early Roman Empire, came to the persecution of Christians under Nero, and learned that " the originator of that name, Christ, was put to death in the reign of Tiberius by the procurator Pontius Pilate " (*Annales*, xv. 44). Thus the Roman world became aware of Christ as at once an object of worship and the historical founder of a religious community. The same twofold character belongs to Him all through the New Testament.

Jewish sources are somewhat more informing. The passage, indeed, referring to Jesus in Josephus's *Antiquities* (xviii. 3, §§ 63-64) is probably an interpolation, though his allusion to James " the brother of Jesus called Christ " (xx. 9, § 200) may be accepted as genuine. But among the references in the Talmud, which are mostly legendary, there are some passages which can be traced to early tradition, from which we learn that Jesus was remembered in Jewish circles as a Rabbi of the period before the fall of the Temple, who gathered disciples, some of whose names are given (though only two of them occur in the Gospels), who was condemned for " practising sorcery and leading Israel astray," and hanged on the Eve of Passover. There is here just enough to anchor the figure of the Founder of Christianity to its setting in history, and to assure us that the Gospels are not mere myth.

From the New Testament outside the Gospels we learn less than might have been expected about the life of Jesus, but a number of important facts can be collected from Paul and the Epistle to the Hebrews, and these have weight as evidence, because Paul, as a personal acquaintance of Peter and others of the original Christians, was in a position to know the facts ;

while the author to the Hebrews says that he had learned the Gospel from hearers of the Lord. In the Acts of the Apostles we have certain passages which seem to rest upon the early apostolic preaching, and one of these, Peter's speech before Cornelius (10^{34-43}), is of especial importance (especially if, as is probable, it is taken from an early Aramaic tradition), because it contains a brief account of the ministry and passion of Jesus which may well represent the kind of outline which served as framework for the Gospel narratives.

The Gospels themselves, however, remain our principal sources. These four brief writings are the survivors of a larger body of literature, and we may take it that the fittest survived. But both Mark and the later Gospels which used Mark as a source rest upon oral tradition which goes back to an early period, and it is the measure of their fidelity to tradition which gives them their historical value. There is good reason to believe that the first three evangelists did little more than give literary shape to the tradition as it reached them. The Fourth Evangelist has dealt with it more freely. This tradition, however, was not shaped by purely historical or biographical interests, in the first place. It was developed in the course of the Church's efforts to present the Gospel to outsiders, and to apply the remembered teaching of Jesus to its own problems. It appears from the speeches of the apostles in Acts, as well as from Paul's references to the tradition which he received (1 Cor. 11^{23}, 15^{1-7}), that from early days the preaching of the Church dwelt in some detail upon the facts of the death and resurrection of Jesus, and included some account of His ministry, but it does not appear that anything more than a very brief summary of its course was given (see Acts 10^{37-42}, 13^{23-31}). Thus it is unlikely that our earliest Gospel rests upon any detailed information of the historical succession of events. The order of the narrative differs considerably in the other Gospels, and the Fourth Gospel notably gives an order difficult to reconcile with that of the Synoptics. Recent criticism inclines to the view that none of the evangelists gives anything like a strictly chronological account of the ministry.

The type of Gospel narrative common to them all consists of a comparatively full and continuous account of the sufferings and death of Jesus, preceded by a selection of episodes from His ministry, often arranged according to topics rather than chronologically. Two of the Gospels, those of Matthew and Luke, prefix stories of His birth and childhood. These stories are so different in detail that it is difficult to harmonize them, and they clearly contain legendary elements.

Of His antecedents and early life there are few facts that may be affirmed with confidence: He was brought up at Nazareth as the son of Joseph, a carpenter, and Mary his wife ; He had, besides sisters, four brothers whose names are recorded, and who, with their descendants, were later important as " Founder's kin " in the Church of Jerusalem ; the family claimed descent from the royal line of David, though their actual position in society was that of *petits bourgeois* ; Jesus Himself seems to have worked as a carpenter. But any account of His private life must rest upon imaginative reconstruction. It is idle to attempt to write anything like a biography of Jesus from our Gospel sources. The materials for it do not exist.

2. THE COURSE OF EVENTS

It does, however, seem possible to obtain a broad impression of the course of His public ministry, which has good claim to be historical, so far as it goes. If we start, as it is best to do, with Mark, we observe that in the first six chapters we have a series of episodes staged in Galilee or about the shores of the Lake, while from chap. 10 onwards the scene changes to Judæa. The division of the ministry between Galilee and Judæa is present in the summaries given in Acts 10 and 13, and reappears in Matthew and Luke. In the Fourth Gospel the ministry appears to alternate between the two districts. But in John 7^{1-14} we have a clearly marked transition from Galilee to Jerusalem, and after this point there is no further visit to Galilee. The Fourth Gospel therefore seems after all to represent a tradition according to which Galilee was at least the chief scene of the earlier ministry.

The Judæan period is in Mark (followed by Matthew), separated from the Galilæan by a period of travels in the mainly Gentile regions to the north and north-west. These travels are obscured in Luke, and they have disappeared from the Johannine narrative. But there is no good reason to reject the statement of our earliest Gospel that at some time before the final transference of His activity from Galilee to the south Jesus did travel outside the Holy Land.

The two Gospels which ignore Mark's story of travels abroad have compensated by introducing other stories which cannot readily be fitted into Mark's framework. Luke represents Jesus as making a somewhat leisurely progress through the central districts of Palestine towards Jerusalem. While the section of the Gospel covering this journey (9^{51}–18^{14}) seems to be somewhat artificially composed, it does appear to preserve traditions of contacts with Samaria which Mark has ignored, but which have left their traces also in the Fourth Gospel. John again represents Jesus as spending, after the final abandonment of Galilee, more time than we should suppose from Mark's account, in Judæa and Trans-Jordan, as well as in Jerusalem itself. In view of the fragmentary nature of Mark's Gospel, and its lack of detailed chronology, we may not dismiss out of hand these suggestions of movements not represented in it, though any attempt to place them in chronological relations with the Marcan record must be precarious.

Without resorting too much to conjecture, we may suggest a general scheme of the ministry, on the following lines.

The story opens (in all its forms) with the appearance of John the Baptist. He was a prophetic figure who, like the prophets of an older time, called the nation to repentance and amendment of life, and foretold an approaching divine judgement. His baptism seems to have been intended as an anticipatory initiation into the Messianic community which should be brought into being at the Judgement. His proclamation of a Coming One, mightier than he, who should come after him, was regarded by Christians as a prophecy fulfilled in the coming of Christ. In any case it is clear that his work prepared the way. Jesus Himself was baptized by John. The Fourth Gospel may be right in representing Him as working for a short time in Judæa alongside of the Baptist, though independently ($3^{22\text{-}23}$, 4^1).

But His real work began after John had been thrown into prison by Herod Antipas, tetrarch of Galilee and Trans-Jordan. He then moved into Galilee, where He was at home. His chief centres seem to have been the towns near the Lake, Capernaum, Bethsaida, and Chorazin. He preached in synagogues, taught in the open, performed miracles of healing and exorcism, and collected a band of disciples. These He sent out to carry on the same kind of work as He was doing Himself. His ministry attracted much popular attention and even enthusiasm. Opposition, however, developed between Him and the religious leaders. The principal grounds of such opposition were His attitude to the Jewish Law and traditions, in such points as Sabbath observance, fasting, and ritual purity; His association with " publicans and sinners; " and the forgiveness of sin. Herod, already disturbed by his experience with the Baptist, became suspicious, and the

" Herodians," we are told, made common cause with the Pharisees in seeking to compass His death.

Jesus now left Galilee, the territory of Antipas, and wandered in the north. No clear itinerary can be traced, but we find Him in the territory of Tyre, in the Decapolis, and near Caesarea in the tetrarchy of Philip. He is said to have revisited Galilee, but this time incognito.

Ultimately He abandoned Galilee, and set out on a journey, Mark says, " to the borders of Judæa and Trans-Jordan " (10^1). There is no further note of place or time until Jericho is reached, and we then find that Jesus enters Jerusalem shortly before Passover, and within a few days is done to death. There are, however, indications even in the Synoptics which suggest that Jesus had in fact been in Jerusalem before the last week of His life. There are episodes recorded in Luke which are difficult to fit in either to the Marcan Galilæan period or to the hurried journey to Jerusalem which Mark seems to imply. John again records a comparatively lengthy ministry in the south. We may perhaps indulge in a little chronological speculation. Mark says that Jesus fed multitudes in the season when the grass was green (6^{39}). The grass dries up early in Galilee. A date shortly before Easter would fit very well, and this is the date given in the Fourth Gospel, for what it is worth. A much later date would be impossible. We have therefore the greater part, or the whole, of a year to account for before the Passover of the Crucifixion. The Feeding of the Multitude evidently represents a crisis in the ministry, and it was closely followed by the retirement from Galilee. If this was about Easter, it would leave the best part of the year for travel in the hilly regions of the north, which are inclement in winter. If now we follow the Fourth Gospel, Jesus finally transferred His work from Galilee to the south in time for the Feast of Tabernacles in September or October. The circumstantial account of an attempt to arrest Him during this festival in John 7^{32-52}, if it is historical, would prepare us for the situation revealed in the Marcan account of the final visit to Jerusalem. Moreover, John asserts that after the Feast of the Dedication in December, Jesus retired to Trans-Jordan. We recall that Mark says that He left Galilee for " Judæa and Trans-Jordan," without relating any actual sojourn in this latter region. It may therefore be that we should at this point supplement the Marcan narrative by saying that after a summer spent in the north Jesus went to Jerusalem in September, and met with severe opposition there, and that at some time between then and the following Easter, instead of returning to Galilee, He worked in Judæa and Trans-Jordan. We should then have to regard Mark's account of the last journey to Jerusalem as " telescoped."

It is at any rate clear that when Jesus entered Jerusalem shortly before Passover, the opposition between Him and the authorities was irreconcilable, and His actions are those of one who felt that the time had come to bring the conflict to a head. His entry into Jerusalem took the form of a popular demonstration, whether planned as such by Him or not, and His act in expelling the traders from the Temple (which we should date here, with Mark, and not with John, at the beginning of the ministry) was a direct challenge to the authorities. They responded by suborning one of His disciples to betray Him. He was arrested at dead of night, brought hastily before the Procurator next morning, and condemned on the charge of claiming to be " King of the Jews." He was immediately put to death by the Roman method of crucifixion. In the account of the closing scenes the four Gospels differ only in detail.

So much of the story seems to be fairly secure. It provides a framework into which the various episodes recorded in the Gospels may be fitted. But however we fit them in, we feel the need of some guiding conception which will make the story intelligible, as a whole. It is because different conceptions are assumed as a basis by various writers that we have such a bewildering variety of " Lives of Jesus." In recent times the story has been widely conceived as that of a moral and religious reformer who went a step too far and fell a victim to the forces of the established order. It is possible to tell the story in that sense without more reading between the lines than might appear legitimate. But as such, it is a story all too common in history to arrest more than passing attention. It does not account for the significance which the life and death of Jesus possess, not only for the faith of Christians, but in the history of religion. It is not, in fact, in this sense that the evangelists tell the story. They tell it as the story of God's Messiah, designated as such by a divine voice at His baptism, confessed as such by His disciples, put to death as such, and raised as such for the salvation of men.

As the Gospels were admittedly composed by believing Christians, it is open to any one to say that this Messianic significance was read into the story from the faith of the Early Church. But in that case we are driven to speculation to account for this faith, and the story itself still hangs in the air. It cannot reasonably be doubted that Jesus was condemned

and executed as " King of the Jews," and as there is no reason
to suppose that He was in the ordinary sense a pretender to the
throne of David, we can only conclude that the expression is
a paraphrase, for Roman ears, of the Jewish title " Messiah,"
as the Gospels themselves suggest.

3. THE MESSIAH AND THE KINGDOM OF GOD

The meaning, however, of Messiahship as attributed to
Jesus can be understood only from the Gospels themselves,
for the term " Messiah " was vague and variable in Jewish
usage.

We shall do best to start from the expression " the Kingdom
of God," as used in the Gospels. In itself it expresses the idea,
familiar in the Old Testament, that " the Lord is King "—
King of Israel, and sovereign Ruler of the whole world. But
during the bad times through which the Jewish people passed,
the idea took hold of them that the world was temporarily
under the rule of the powers of darkness ; and the assurance
that in the future God would effectually assert His sovereignty,
or " set up His Kingdom," became a resting-point for faith.
Thus the coming of the Kingdom of God, as judgement upon
evil and the redemption of God's people, was an element in
the eschatological hope by which the Jewish people sustained
their spirits under suffering and oppression.

Jesus came into Galilee proclaiming, " The time is fulfilled and the Kingdom of God is at hand : repent and believe
the Gospel " (Mark 1^{14-15}). Challenged by His opponents,
He declared, " If I by the finger of God cast out demons, then
the Kingdom of God is come upon you " (Luke 11^{20} ; Matt.
12^{28}). The prophets until John had lived in anticipation : His
own disciples, He said, had the privilege of seeing that which
prophets and kings had desired in vain to see (Luke 10^{24},
Matt. 13^{17}), the inauguration of the Kingdom of God on earth.
This truth is illustrated by His parables, and the stories of
His miracles are related as signs that the powers of the
Kingdom of God were abroad.

The Messianic idea is closely related to those conceptions
of coming judgement and redemption which were included in
the hope of the Kingdom of God. The proclamation that the
Kingdom has come carries with it the implication that the
Messiah has come. The title which Jesus Himself seems to
have preferred is " The Son of Man " (which is an Aramaic
idiom for " The Man "). There is no evidence that this title
had wide currency among the Jews, or that it was popularly
understood in any precise sense. In the Book of Daniel,

which was most influential in forming the eschatological beliefs of the time, the Son of Man is a figure symbolic of the triumphant people of God of the future, to whom the Kingdom is to be given (Dan. 7^{9-27}). In Psalm 80^{17} the term is applied either to Israel or to a Messianic figure representative of Israel, who by divine help emerges out of humiliation into triumph. In the Book of Enoch it is applied to a supernatural being who exercises judgement at the last as God's vice-regent (69^{26-29}, etc.). Without tying down the Gospel usage closely to any particular antecedents, it is clear that the title "The Son of Man" was appropriate to describe Jesus in His Messianic character as the One in and through whom the Kingdom of God came upon men. But He appears to have added to its meaning ideas expressed in those passages of the Second Isaiah which speak of the Servant of the Lord. The Servant again is a figure of which it is difficult to say whether it is individual or representative of the community. But the distinctive thing about the Servant is that He suffers according to the will of God for the salvation of others, and triumphs through his suffering (Isa. 53).

In using therefore the mysterious title "Son of Man," Jesus appears to have been suggesting a rich complex of symbolism through which He disclosed, to those who could hear, the "mystery of the Kingdom of God," the truth that in His own life of service and conflict, in His suffering and death, God was at work bringing in His Kingdom, and that beyond suffering and death lay eternal glory in which He should reign as Lord of a redeemed humanity. The forecasts of death and resurrection which the Gospels contain thus appear, not as additions to the narrative for apologetic purposes, but as arising out of the fundamental conception of the coming of the Kingdom of God which stood at the centre of the teaching of Jesus.

The various predictions of that which is to come to pass after the death of Jesus are among the most difficult parts of the Gospels. The language and the imagery employed are taken from the traditional eschatology of Judaism. There is no reason why Jesus Himself should not have used such imagery, though there is also no reason why He should not have had His own interpretation of it. But a critical analysis of the Gospels suggests that during the formation of the tradition it was just the eschatological elements in it that suffered most expansion and development. If we compare various eschatological passages, we shall find that they cannot without violence be reduced to a consistent scheme. (For example, the coming of the Son of Man is in Mark 13 heralded by a long series of portents, ending with the darkening of the sun and moon and the collapse of the starry system. In Luke 17[26-27. 34-35]; Matt. 24[37-41], it is to supervene unexpectedly upon the ordinary life of men, engaged in eating and drinking, marrying, working in the fields, grinding corn, or asleep in their beds.) It seems that predictions belonging to different planes of thought have been confused. Some of them refer to the peril of war and social upheaval overshadowing Judæa, and may have been particularized in the tradition as that peril visibly drew nearer in the years preceding the great rebellion of A.D. 66. Others refer to troubles and persecution awaiting the disciples, and these may well have been made more explicit in the light of subsequent experience.

We are left with a few more or less direct allusions to the coming of the Son of Man, in terms evidently borrowed from the mythology of Jewish apocalyptic. These again, as we follow the tradition backward from Matthew to Mark and " Q," and further still (more precariously but not wholly speculatively) to the oral tradition, are seen to be less explicit, as well as less prominent, in the earlier stages of tradition than in the later. We are justified in concluding that the developing eschatological thought of the early Church has had its effects.

What Jesus actually said on the subject it is difficult to say. But where there is smoke there is fire. It would be impossible to account for the tradition if He had not spoken, no doubt in mysterious language, not only of " the sufferings of the Messiah," but of " the glory to follow " (cf. 1 Peter 1[11]). Perhaps the most explicit of the best attested sayings is that which Mark records as addressed to the high-priest : " You will see the Son of Man seated on the right hand of the Power, and coming with the clouds of heaven " (Mark 14[62]). This is a clear reference to Daniel 7[13-14], " There came with the clouds of heaven one like unto a son of man, and he came even to the Ancient of Days, and they brought him near before Him. And there was given him dominion and glory and a kingdom." This is a symbolic utterance, which the writer interprets (7[18. 22. 27]) : the Son of Man stands for " the people of the saints of the Most High," and His coming with the clouds of heaven means the triumph of that people over the pagan empire. We may suppose it was equally symbolic in the mouth of Jesus. That He meant by it, in the spirit of Daniel, a victory of the Jews over Rome, is not to be supposed.

We may recall that while He declared that the Kingdom of

God was already inaugurated on earth, He also spoke of its consummation, not on earth, but in another world, where men live as angels, and feast with the blessed dead (Mark 12[25]; Matt. 8[11]); the world in which, as He said at His last supper, He would drink the wine of the new creation (Mark 14[25]). We may infer that when He spoke of the triumph of the Son of Man He was referring, not to an event like other events in history, but, in some sense, to a reality transcending history.

The early Church understood Him to mean that this world of time would shortly come to an end, and the eternal world be revealed. If this is what He really intended, we must regard it as a case of the prophetic " foreshortening " of historical perspective. In the prophets we observe that the spiritual conviction that God will *certainly* work judgement and redemption dramatizes itself, as it were, in the prediction that judgement and redemption will come *speedily*. The processes of history are less simple. But though the hope of speedy redemption was deferred, the spiritual certainty of redemption was not discredited. The view, however, that Jesus did literally expect that history would come to an end very shortly is unlikely in face of His ethical teaching, which implies that human life will go on, under much the same outward conditions, with the same temptations and moral problems, and the same need of forgiveness and grace, as well as of " daily bread " (see further C. H. Dodd, *The Parables of the Kingdom*, chaps. ii.–iii.).

Whatever we are to make of the eschatological predictions of the Gospels, it is clear that the proclamation, " The Kingdom of God has come upon you " broke up the eschatological scheme of Jewish apocalypse. For that which had been altogether an object of hope was declared to be, in part at least, an object of experience. All through the New Testament there is a clear consciousness that the really decisive crisis in God's dealings with man has already happened. The early disciples expected that history would soon come to an end, but meanwhile they were aware that history was a new thing, because " the powers of the Age to Come " (Heb. 6[5]) were at work in it. This was the central purport of the Gospel as preached by the Church (see pp. 402–404), and this was the central purport of the preaching of Jesus.

It is important to realize how strikingly this broke with current Jewish ideas. It was commonly held that God would reveal His Kingdom (or send the Messiah) in response to repentance and strict obedience to the Law. But the preaching of Jesus implies that God has not waited for repentance. His Kingdom has come upon men without any merit of theirs. It is an act of pure grace (cf. Luke 12^{32}). The call to repentance is based upon this fact. This corresponds to the character attributed to God as Father. He is kind to the unthankful and the evil. He seeks the sinner as a shepherd seeks a lost sheep until he finds it. He forgives as royally as a magnanimous king remits a debt to a man who cannot pay it. He receives sinful men as a father receives a scapegrace son— and as Jesus Himself received the " publicans and sinners."

The proper attitude of men to such a fatherly God is one of trust or faith, a faith which may be described as " receiving the Kingdom of God as a little child " (Mark 10^{15}). He who has such faith enters into the Kingdom of God, that is to say, into a sphere where the power of evil is in principle overcome, and the merciful power of God is available for succour.

To receive the Kingdom of God is also to acknowledge God's unlimited claim upon man. No man can serve two masters. If God is his King, he cannot divide his allegiance. To this the devout Jew of the time would have most heartily assented. " To take upon oneself the Kingdom of God " was an expression used to describe precisely that undivided allegiance. It was, however, commonly understood in the sense of meticulous obedience to the Law. That Jesus intended something different is clear.

His teaching about the Law is at first sight somewhat perplexing. He sometimes appeals to its authority against the oral tradition of Pharisaic Judaism. At other times He freely reinterprets, amends, or supersedes it. His own conduct, and that which He permitted to His disciples, seemed to the champions of the Law to defy its plain precepts. His opponents rightly divined that His teaching did not stop with criticism of this or that detail of the Law or the tradition, but involved a claim to authority which they could not accept without acknowledging that Jesus was greater than Moses and the prophets. This they could not acknowledge. They therefore branded Him as a false prophet. It is as a false prophet who supported his claims with sorcery that Jesus appears in the Talmud; and the accusation recorded in the Gospels, that He was possessed by Beelzebul and cast out devils by the Prince of devils (that is, that He used black art) has the same implication.

It appears that Jesus recognized the Law, rightly understood, as an authentic revelation of the will of God, for " this age," but held that with the breaking in of the " age to come "

it was superseded by a more immediate revelation of God as
Father.   In so far as its contents could be summarized in the
two great commandments of love to God and neighbour—
provided that " neighbour " was rightly understood—it had
eternal validity.   In so far as its minor precepts did not
interfere with the full exercise of such love, they should not
be left undone.   In so far as they obscured the " weightier
matters " of justice, mercy, and the love of God, they must
be disobeyed (Luke 11^{42} ; Matt. 23^{23}).   This means that the
absolute validity of the Law is in any case rejected, for it is
being tested by an overruling conception of God, His will,
and His relation to man.   In principle, to live within the
Kingdom of God is to live in relations with God which go
beyond mere legality.   It is to have God for Father, and to
live as His sons.

4. Ethical Teaching of Jesus

Jesus did not replace the Law by a new code.   His ethical
teaching cannot be reduced to a comprehensive body of precepts literally and directly applicable to human conduct
from day to day.   It has indeed been held that it was intended
as " interim ethics," that is to say, as precepts for the regula-
tion of the disciples' conduct during the very short interval
expected to elapse before the second advent, when this whole
order of time and space would pass away, and with it the
sphere for ethics in the ordinary sense.   As we have seen,
it is by no means clear that in speaking of His resurrection
and coming in glory, Jesus intended to imply that within a
short time history would come to an end.   And if we consider
the actual teaching recorded, it becomes difficult, not to say
impossible, to understand that it was intended as nothing
more than provisional regulations for a very short interval.
There is nowhere in it any appeal to motives determined by
the shortness of the time (as there is, for example, in 1 Cor. 7$^{29ff.}$,
a good example of genuine " interim ethics ").   On the contrary, it is given in absolute terms and grounded in fundamental and timeless religious principles.

On the other hand, there is nothing abstract or vaguely
general about the teaching of Jesus.   Nor is it related to some
ideal state of society.   It is to be applied in a world where
one may be injured or insulted by a fellow-man, or wrongfully sued at law, or conscripted for labour by an oppressive
government ; a world where the temptations of fear, anger,
lust, and greed still have force.   There is no suggestion that
the disciples may expect soon, or at any time (save at death),

to be freed from the problems and difficulties of such a world. To be " in the Kingdom of God," therefore, is not to be out of the work-a-day world. It is to have such a relation to God and to the world that the evil in the world and in oneself is overcome by His goodness. The ethical teaching of Jesus may best be described as an ideal for those who have received the Kingdom of God as a little child, and who live in this world in the reality and the power of that kingdom.

The situation contemplated in Christian ethics is one in which the values of the spiritual order, experienced as realities, are at each moment confronting the brute facts of evil, as in the ministry of Jesus they confronted the evil things which drove Him to death. The Kingdom of God is offered as a gift of grace, but the gift is also a challenge, for the Kingdom of God, as manifested in Jesus, is not sheer victory, but victory through conflict and loss. The ethical life lies within that conflict. But now we reverse the proposition. It is not sheer conflict, but victorious conflict, as the issue of Christ's conflict was not death, but resurrection from the dead. Hence, in a real sense, in Christian ethical action, a man denies both this world and himself, in affirming the Kingdom of God ; but in denying the world and himself he recovers the world as the sphere of God's Kingdom, and " finds himself " as God's child.

If now we attempt to express this in the eschatological language native to the Gospels, we must say, not that the ethical teaching of Jesus is " interim ethics " for those who expect that the world will shortly come to an end, but that it is absolute ethics for those who have experienced in themselves the end of the world and the coming of the Kingdom. Ethical conduct is not dictated by the interests or utility either of the individual or of any social organization (such as nation, state, or class). It springs at each moment, as it were, afresh from its roots in the very constitution of the Kingdom of God, as determined by the nature and character of God Himself, the living God and our Father.

The one universal ethical principle is that which is revealed in God's free grace to undeserving men in offering them the blessings of His Kingdom. The unqualified benevolence and beneficence of the heavenly Father towards all His creatures is to be imitated by His sons. They will always be before-hand with loving actions towards a " neighbour," that is to say; to any one in a position to need such beneficence, whether he be a brother, a stranger, or even an enemy. They will not be concerned to judge his conduct, knowing that they

themselves deserve the judgement of God, but that His mercy
saves them from it. Still less will they wish to requite wrong
with wrong, since to forgive and to be forgiven by God are
two sides of the same experience. Since God their Father
attaches a mysterious and immeasurable value to each individual creature of His (even to a sparrow, much more to a
man), His sons will similarly regard every " little one " ; and
Jesus emphasized this by saying that to receive a child was to
receive Him, and in receiving Him to receive God (Mark 9^{37}).

An ethical ideal such as this could not in the nature of
things be reduced to precise rules of conduct. It is a matter
of personal attitudes. At the same time Jesus left no excuse for
supposing that a vague unpractical benevolence is all that is
required. He appealed to the imagination by concrete
examples of the kind of conduct to which a right attitude would
lead. Thus : " Whoever strikes you on the right cheek, turn
the other to him " ; " Whoever impresses you for one mile, go
with him two miles " ; " Give to every one who asks, and if
any one takes what is yours, do not demand it back " (Matt.
$5^{39. \ 41. \ 42}$; Luke $6^{29. \ 30}$). These are not legal regulations.
If they were, it would be relevant to point out that to turn
the other cheek may be in some circumstances a most pro-
vocative act, that to help a robber or a murderer on his way
is not philanthropic conduct, and that indiscriminate charity
may have disastrous effects. They are an aid to the imagination in making concrete the kind of action called for by the
principle, " Be merciful as your Father is merciful " (Luke
6^{36}). It is an even more powerful aid to the imagination to
consider how Jesus Himself acted (" leaving you an example,
that you should follow His steps "(1 Peter 2^{21})), though here
again it is impossible to make the " imitation of Christ " a
mechanical rule of conduct.

It is to be observed that the ethics of Jesus are not ethics
of self-culture for the attainment of " virtue." They are
concerned with relations between persons, as they are based
upon our personal relations with God our Father. Thus
Christian ethics are social ethics. Not that the Kingdom of
God is to be thought of as an ideal society, like Plato's
Republic or More's *Utopia.* But inasmuch as the reality of the
Kingdom of God is revealed in social attitudes, there is a
Christian standard from which social practices and institutions
may be criticised.

Thus Jesus condemned that form of society in which " the
kings of the Gentiles lord it over them," and commended a
form of society in which the greatest is he who serves. And

He did so with direct reference to the fundamental principle of His own life, in which the grace of God was directly manifested—" the Son of Man came not to be served but to serve, and to give His life a ransom for many " (Mark 10$^{42-45}$, Luke 22$^{25-27}$). Similarly, a society in which the acquisitive motive is dominant is condemned by the principle that " You cannot serve God and Mammon " (Matt. 6^{24}, Luke 16^{13}).

The social institution of which He spoke with most positive approval was the family, naturally enough, since He conceived the true relation of men as that of brothers in the family of God. Thus He condemned an abuse of the Law by which the natural duty of children to their parents was evaded (Mark 7$^{9-13}$). He declared marriage to be a part of God's aboriginal purpose for man, and to be by His will indissoluble (Mark 10$^{2-12}$, Matt. 5^{32}, Luke 16^{18}). The Law had permitted divorce, because of human " hard-heartedness," but now that the Kingdom of God is come, His purpose in its fullness comes into play in this as in all human relations. Nevertheless, while the family is thus an institution falling within the purpose of God and His Kingdom, it is not ultimate. Circumstances may arise in which for the sake of higher ends within the Kingdom of God, a man should leave father and mother, wife and child (Mark 10^{29}).

Nothing human is ultimate, not even the most sacred human institutions, not even the preservation of human life : a man may be called upon to " hate " father and mother, in the same sense as he must " hate " his own life (Luke 14$^{26-27}$). Such renunciation was in actual fact demanded of those who in the immediate crisis followed Jesus when He went to death. In principle the same renunciation is demanded of all His followers. All good things of this life are enjoyed within the Kingdom of God, on condition that we are willing to renounce them all for the supreme and universal Good, which is the Kingdom itself. To possess the Kingdom, even though everything else is lost, is perfect blessedness : " Blessed are ye poor, for yours is the Kingdom of God. . . . Blessed are the persecuted, for theirs is the Kingdom of Heaven " (Luke 6^{20}, Matt. 5^{10}).

5. THE LIFE OF JESUS IN THE LIGHT OF HIS TEACHING

We may now turn back to the consideration of the life of Jesus, and enquire how far the bald outline of historical events can be filled out with meaning drawn from His teaching.

In the first place, it is clear that if we are to understand His career, it must be upon the basis of His fundamental declaration that the Kingdom of God came in His ministry, death and resurrection, with its implication that He came as Messiah. If we follow our earliest source, Jesus was designated as Messiah from the outset, though in a way private to Himself ; but Messiahship plays scarcely any part in the story explicitly until, after Peter's confession, His Messianic passion and death become its leading motive.. So far as the general public is concerned there is no avowal of His Messiahship until the last moment, when it leads at once to His death. To the people at large, and to their leaders, He is rabbi, perhaps prophet, perhaps false prophet, but not, until nearly the end, Messiah, or a claimant to Messiahship. Not only so, but according to Mark, Jesus was at pains to nip in the bud any possible suggestion that He should be acclaimed as Messiah.

One school of critics explains this situation by the hypothesis that Jesus in fact never claimed to be Messiah, and was not recognized as such until after His death. The evangelist, believing that He came as Messiah, had to account for the absence of explicit Messianic elements in the story and did so, by the theory of a " Messianic secret." This hypothesis seems to raise more difficulties than it solves, and if the view of the teaching of Jesus given above is anywhere near the truth, it is untenable. Yet there is this measure of truth in it : if we may trust our earliest sources, Jesus never did put forward explicitly a *claim* to be Messiah. When Peter first, and the high-priest afterwards, confronted Him with the Messianic idea, He replied in both cases in terms which substituted the title " Son of Man " for " Messiah." We may say, not that He claimed to be Messiah, but that He did not disavow Messiahship when it was put to Him, while He did describe Himself as " Son of Man." This meant for Him, as we might put it, Messiah *plus*. But the *plus* was such that it completely transformed any idea of Messiahship which had previously been held, since it included a call to suffering and death.

The term " Messiah " in Jewish usage had no clear and constant significance (" Jewish Messianic doctrine " as it is found in the text-books often makes large use of Rabbinical material later than the New Testament), but it is safe to say that in the popular mind it was associated with political leadership and with the political independence and sovereignty of Israel in the world. If therefore Jesus had said, " I am Messiah," He would inevitably have aroused hopes of political deliverance which were completely at variance with His intentions. That. this is so is clear from what actually happened. According to Mark, the " Messianic secret " was out when the beggar Bartimæus hailed Jesus as " Son of David,' and the crowd accompanied Him to Jerusalem with hurrahs for " the coming kingdom of our father David " ; and the immediate sequel was that He was crucified as a political pretender. We may indeed suspect that Mark has possibly exaggerated the extent to which the Messiahship did remain a complete secret. According to John, after the feeding of the multitude there was an attempt " to take Him by force and make Him king." (John 6¹⁴⁻¹⁵). If something of the kind happened, we could better understand the withdrawal from Galilee so soon after this episode.

In any case, there was good reason why Jesus, conscious of a more-than-Messianic destiny, should not have put Himself forward as the expected Messiah. Instead, He started with the proclamation of the Kingdom of God, endeavouring to persuade people of the true nature of that Kingdom in the light of the Fatherhood of God, and to bring them to accept it as a present reality. This is the main burden of His teaching in Galilee. Those who took it with any seriousness would soon be led on to ask what was the relation of Jesus Himself to the Kingdom. It is entirely credible that many took Him for a prophet, some for Elijah, sent a second time as the herald of the Kingdom, and some for John the Baptist miraculously raised from the dead to continue his work. If any of them approached the idea of His Messiahship from a consideration of His teaching about the Kingdom of God, they would in some measure be prepared to have that idea reinterpreted.

It is probable that the withdrawal from Galilee was due not simply to the menace of death from Herod and the Pharisees, but even more to the fact that the Galilæan populace responded in the wrong way to the proclamation of the Kingdom of God. They surrounded Jesus with a mistaken enthusiasm, but did not " repent." If He was to remain in Galilee, the only alternative to falling a victim to the plots of His enemies was to throw Himself upon an excited and morally worthless popular movement, which would rapidly become a revolt. Meanwhile, however, Jesus had attracted to Himself a small body of followers who, even though they may in some measure have shared the mistaken hopes of the populace, had at least understood something of what the Kingdom of God meant as a spiritual and moral reality, and had " repented " in the sense which Jesus intended. With these He retired beyond the reach alike of Herod and of His would-be adherents.

Here Peter, in answer to a question, spoke the fateful

words, "Thou art the Messiah." The first concern of Jesus was to make sure that the dangerous word should not be uttered outside the select circle ; His second, to explain to Peter what He understood by Messiahship : " The Son of Man must suffer and be killed and rise again." That it was only now that Jesus Himself had formed this conception of His mission and destiny is unlikely. The story of the Temptation suggests that before His ministry began He had faced alternative forms of the Messianic idea, and had rejected them ; and His whole conception of the Kingdom of God was such that its coming must involve the most intense conflict with evil, and the utmost renunciation, even unto death, for Him who was its bearer. But also it must involve victory in conflict and life through death. Jesus invited His followers to share with Him in the conflict and the triumph—to drink of the cup of which He drank, and to be baptized with the baptism with which He was baptized. As things turned out, they proved themselves unequal to the demand. Only after He had died and risen for them did they know the fellowship of His sufferings and the power of His resurrection (cf. Phil. 3^{10}).

To return to Galilee was not in Jesus' plan. Indeed, we may suspect that Galilee was never more than a starting-point. His message and His appeal must be delivered at Jerusalem, the centre of the life and religion of Israel, and there, where the blood of the prophets was shed, the Messiah must die (Luke 13^{33}). It is probable, as we have seen, that Jesus was active in Jerusalem and the south for some time before things came to a final crisis. But of the nature of this activity we have no satisfactory information. That it provoked not less, but even more, bitter hostility than in Galilee seems clear. At last He made up His mind (in the words of the Fourth Gospel) that His time was come. He chose the moment when Jerusalem would be full of pilgrims from all the world, the moment of the Feast that commemorated the redemption of Israel from Egyptian bondage by the grace and power of God.

His actions from this time forward can best be understood on the analogy of the symbolic actions of the Old Testament prophets (see H. W. Robinson, " Prophetic Symbolism," in *Old Testament Essays*, edited by D. C. Simpson). A good example is the story of Jeremiah making and wearing a yoke as a symbol of the coming subjugation to Babylon (Jer. 27$^{2-11}$, 28$^{12-14}$). The act in itself accomplishes nothing, but it is conceived as in some sort identical with that which it symbolizes, so that in wearing the yoke Jeremiah is taking his part in the actual working out of the divine purpose. It is not merely an

illustration but an effectual sign. We may recognize a similar
character in three significant actions of Jesus during His last
days.

The first is the Triumphal Entry into Jerusalem. Here
Jesus for the first time lends Himself to popular enthusiasm.
But He so contrives it that the people shall greet Him in the
guise of the Messiah as described by Zechariah—" meek and
riding upon an ass " (Zech. 9⁹). There is irony in the situation.
Jesus knew now, as well as He knew in Galilee, that the
enthusiasm of the people was mistaken and hollow. Yet He
allowed them to hail the coming kingdom of David, because,
unknown to themselves, they were confessing that in Him, as
He went to His death, the Kingdom of God came.

The second symbolic act is the Cleansing of the Temple.
The Temple was conceived as the place where God dwelt on
earth, the throne and centre of His Kingdom. Since His
Kingdom was universal, the Temple should have been " a
house of prayer for all nations." The Jewish priesthood had
made it a place of profit for themselves, a house of Mammon.
Jesus swept the traders out of its courts. The action can
hardly be regarded as the *coup d'état* of a religious reformer,
for according to Mark, Jesus, having gained His advantage,
left the Temple and went outside the city, to find on the morrow
the priesthood firmly entrenched in their old position. The
Cleansing was a symbol of the coming of God in His Kingdom,
sweeping away the old order of religion with its corruptions.
So the prophet Malachi, foretelling the Day of the Lord, had
said, " The Lord whom ye seek shall suddenly come to His
temple, but who may abide the day of His appearing ? " (Mal.
3¹⁻²). As an attempt at religious reformation the act accom-
plished nothing. In its true intention as an act of prophetic
symbolism it was an aspect of the coming of the Kingdom of
God in the person of the Messiah. Jesus now proclaimed that
the Temple itself and the unrepentant Jewish nation had no
further place in God's purpose (Mark 12¹⁻¹², 13² ; Matt. 23³⁸ ;
Luke 13³⁵, etc.).

The effect of the Cleansing of the Temple was to precipitate
the attack upon Jesus which had long been contemplated. It
appears that the dangerous popular enthusiasm which had
surrounded Him in Galilee, and had found expression at the
Triumphal Entry, made the authorities hesitate to arrest Him
openly, " lest there be a tumult of the people." (Had their
experience of a previous abortive attempt to arrest Him
during a festival, as recorded in John 7, been a warning ?)
But now an opportunity offered itself to make the arrest in

secret. The motives which led Judas to agree to betray his Master must always remain obscure. All we know is that he did so. This must be regarded as a firm historical fact. No community ever invented a story so derogatory to itself as the treachery of one of its members to its leader.

It appears to have been the evening of the day before that on which the paschal lambs were slaughtered in preparation for the celebration of Passover, when Jesus and His disciples met for supper in a room at Jerusalem lent for the purpose. (So John has it, confirmed by Jewish tradition. The less clear narrative of Mark suggests twenty-four hours later.) It was probably not the Paschal supper, unless Jesus deliberately gave it that character, knowing that He would be dead before the Passover proper. Some authorities hold that it was a preparatory meal, called by the Jews " Kiddush." At this meal He performed the third and most significant of His acts of prophetic symbolism. He took bread, broke it, and gave to His disciples, with the words, " This is my body." He gave them a cup, saying, " This cup is the new covenant in my blood " (or words to that effect : the wording differs slightly in our various sources).

In order to approach an understanding of the words and actions, we should remember (i) that the glories of the Age to Come (the Kingdom of God) were commonly pictured as a feast, and that Jesus had Himself used this symbolism in parables, and, probably, in the act of feeding the multitude ; (ii) that Passover commemorated the divine act of redemption by which Israel was marked out as the people of God ; (iii) that Jesus had declared that the Jewish nation, having rejected the offer of the Kingdom of God, was no longer His people ; (iv) that He had said that He would give His life as a means of redemption for many, and had spoken of His approaching fate as His " cup." It appears, therefore, that in solemnly setting apart the bread and the cup He was making them the pledge of life in the Kingdom of God. In speaking of the broken bread as His body, and associating the cup with His blood, He was effecting in a symbol that sacrifice of Himself which He was about to accomplish in fact. In giving to His disciples the bread to eat and the cup to drink, He was associating them with Him in that sacrifice and its consequences, and that in spite of (or in view of) the fact that He no longer expected them to die with Him. To this we must add that in accordance with the nature of prophetic symbolism the significant act was not a mere illustration, but an " efficacious sign "—in other words, a sacrament. The disciples rose from table as men redeemed by the death of their Lord, as the people of the new covenant to whom the Kingdom of God was given. And yet they were so far from being righteous or virtuous men that, before the night was out, one of them was to deny their Master and all were to forsake Him. It was His final and most convincing declaration of the truth that the gifts of God are given to the undeserving.

After supper Jesus and His disciples left for their usual nightly bivouac on the Mount of Olives. On the way Jesus lingered to pray in a garden known as Gethsemane. Here He was found by a posse sent by the high-priest, under the guidance of Judas the traitor. Jesus was arrested; the disciples scattered.

The account of the trial that followed is not without difficulties, historical and legal. It is well to bear in mind that the business was being rushed through in view of the beginning of the festival, and it may be that rules of procedure were not too minutely observed. It appears that Jesus was first brought before the Sanhedrin for an examination which the Jews regarded as a legal trial, but which was under Roman Law no more than " Grand Jury proceedings," to determine the charge which should be preferred in the Procurator's court. An attempt was made to formulate a charge on the basis of reported words of Jesus against the Temple. Ultimately He was convicted, on His own admission, of claiming to be Messiah, and this charge, in the form of a treasonable claim to be King of the Jews, was brought before Pilate.

In court, Jesus neither admitted nor denied that He was King of the Jews. He made no attempt at a defence. Pilate's view seems to have been that if He did not disavow His alleged claim, He was technically guilty, but that He was nevertheless politically harmless, and might well be released as a concession to the people. The Procurator therefore must have supposed that Jesus was still the people's favourite. It surprised him, as it still surprises us, to find that they had turned against Him. Why they did so we could only speculate. Since the people did not wish Him to be released, and the priests pressed for a conviction, Pilate let the law take its course, and Jesus was condemned.

In reading the story of the trial, we cannot but be struck by the strange passivity of Jesus throughout the proceedings. His followers were also struck by it (cf. 1 Peter 2[23]). If we have understood the Gospels aright, the whole affair was to Him of no moment at all. He had already devoted His life. What the Sanhedrin or the Procurator could do was only the appointed way by which this self-devotion was to be carried into effect. The only moment of concern to Jesus was that at which the high-priest asked : " Art thou the Messiah, the Son of the Blessed ? " Then, perhaps for the first and only time in His life, He made the avowal, " I am," passing however at once to language which expressed His meaning more adequately. By doing so, He affirmed the true significance of the death to which He was going. It was no mere miscarriage of justice, and no mere martyrdom. It was the fulfilment of His calling as Messiah to die, and it lay within the coming of the Kingdom of God.

If it is a " life of Jesus " with which we are concerned, the story ends with the Crucifixion, for a man's life ends with his death. But as we have seen, the Gospel story can be understood only as the story of the Messiah in whom the Kingdom of God came, as the story therefore of a victorious conflict and of life through death. We must therefore add that before many days had passed, the followers of Jesus had proof which convinced them that He was alive. Our earliest evidence for this is that of Paul, who in 1 Cor. 15³⁻⁷ formally cites the tradition which he had received, " that Christ died for our sins according to the Scriptures, that He was buried, and that He rose again the third day according to the Scriptures, and appeared to Cephas, then to the Twelve," —and subsequently to many others, most of whom were still alive when Paul wrote. To this Mark (followed by Matthew and Luke) and John (perhaps independently) add that the tomb of Jesus was found to be empty.

Some critics hold that the story of the Empty Tomb, which is not mentioned explicitly by Paul or in the summaries contained in the apostolic preaching in Acts, is a later addition ; but there seems no good reason for separating it from the whole Passion narrative, which probably existed in tradition substantially complete before Mark wrote. We are here in a region where direct historical evidence is not available, and, if it were, would not be applicable. For even supposing that the evidence were irrefragable that the tomb of Jesus was found empty, it would not necessarily prove that He was alive. Still less would it prove, what the Church believed, that He had risen in glory and was " on the right hand of God."

Whatever was the origin of this belief, it is clear that it brought the Church into being. It is impossible to disprove formally the view that the Church is founded on a delusion. If it was a delusion, then it is not only the story of the Empty

Tomb that goes by the board. The central purport of the teaching of Jesus is involved, and the only clue we have to the understanding of the story of His life. The teaching and the story cohere, and are full of meaning, if He is believed to be the Saviour who died and is alive for evermore.

BIBLIOGRAPHY

B. W. Bacon, *The Story of Jesus.*
F. C. Burkitt, *Jesus Christ : an Historical Outline.*
C. H. Dodd, *The Parables of the Kingdom.*
T. W. Manson, *The Teaching of Jesus.*
R. Otto, *The Kingdom of God and the Son of Man.*
A. Schweitzer, *The Quest of the Historical Jesus.*

XV. THE HISTORY AND DOCTRINE OF THE APOSTOLIC AGE

A. The First Century of Church History

I. THE PRIMITIVE CHURCH AT JERUSALEM

THE author of the Acts of the Apostles has composed in chap. 2 an impressive frontispiece to the history of the Christian Church. The presence of supernatural power is shown in its universal symbols of wind and fire. Its consequences are witnessed by "Parthians, Medes, and Elamites..." and all those nations whose names roll so sonorously in the catalogue of the multitude at the Feast of Pentecost. We are made aware that a world-wide religion is emerging in history. That all these nations heard the proclamation in their own languages is another symbolic trait. Pentecost is among the Jews the festival of the giving of the Law, and Rabbinical tradition held that the Law was proclaimed on Sinai in the seventy languages of mankind, though only Israel hearkened and obeyed. So the new Law is proclaimed to all mankind in words which they can understand.

Actually, "speaking with tongues" is a phenomenon sufficiently well known from the New Testament itself and from other passages in the history of religion. It is not a miraculous power to speak foreign languages, but the utterance, under stress of intense emotion, of religious experience so deep and mysterious that it breaks the bounds of ordered speech. Such utterance therefore is often simply unintelligible to the ordinary hearer, who may suppose the speaker to be drunk (Acts 2[13]) or mad (1 Cor. 14[23]). It needs interpretation (1 Cor. 12[30], 14[27ff.]). So at Pentecost the multitude divined that the apostles were speaking of "the mighty works of God" (Acts 2[11]), but were left bewildered until Peter interpreted.

"Speaking with tongues" therefore belongs, as Paul saw (1 Cor. 12[28]), to the whole series of praeter-normal phenomena which accompanied the emergence of the Church— visions, prophecy, spiritual healing, and so forth. That such phenomena did in fact occur we know from Paul's first-hand testimony (see also Rom. 15[18-19], Gal. 3[5], and cf. Heb. 2$^{3-4}$). They signify in the first place the enhancement of " psychical " powers which accompanies conditions of religious " revival." Their value depends on the nature of the religious experience, and the content of the religious insight, which underlies the outward phenomena. What this was we can best learn from observation of what actually happened.

The immediate effects of Pentecost are noted by the historian in the new confidence, courage, and spiritual energy which possessed the followers of Jesus, and in the emergence of a corporate life distinguished by a joyful and peculiarly intimate fellowship, and by self-sacrificing devotion to the common good (Acts 2$^{42-47}$, 4$^{13. 19-20. 31-33}$). These are clearly the signs of some inward spiritual change, associated with the vivid apprehension of new ideas. What these new ideas were we may learn from the speeches put into the mouth of the apostles, which may fairly be taken to represent in broad lines the preaching of the primitive Church, especially as their main points can be corroborated from what Paul tells us of the tradition he received.

Briefly, the followers of Jesus now realized the meaning of His death and resurrection in the light of His teaching about the Kingdom of God. That meaning they expressed in terms of eschatology. The new dispensation foretold by prophets and apocalyptists had been inaugurated by Jesus, who by His resurrection had been exalted " at the right hand of God " as Messiah and Lord of a New Age. He would shortly be manifested in glory to consummate the dispensation thus inaugurated. This Second Advent is conceived as the impending corroboration before all eyes of a truth already known by faith. The stress is laid on what has already come to pass. God has visited and redeemed His people (Luke 1^{68}). To belong to the company of believers in Christ is to be within the true " Israel of God," the people of the New Covenant, to whom is granted, as Jeremiah had foretold, forgiveness of sins and knowledge of God. It is this sense of living in a new age, as the direct objects of God's mercy, under the direct guidance of His Spirit, that most clearly distinguishes the outlook of the early Church, and gives power and reality both to its communal life and to its religious appeal to the Jewish people at large.

Leadership in the community naturally fell to the body of apostles whom Jesus Himself had commissioned. They were both its teachers, the centre of its fellowship, and the mouthpiece of its message to the people. Their preaching resulted in gathering many converts to the new faith. These were initiated into the fellowship by Baptism. The rite had been taken over from John the Baptist, and was administered as the effectual sign of the forgiveness of sins and the gift of the Spirit. It was apparently normally accompanied by laying on of hands, a Jewish rite adapted to new intentions.

The fellowship of the Church was expressed in a common meal, "the breaking of bread," accompanied by prayers. Direct evidence of the significance attached to this rite in the earliest period is lacking, but on the basis of slightly later evidence we may reasonably infer that it included (a) the commemoration of Jesus ; (b) testimony to His continuing presence with His people, and (c) the anticipation of His second coming—all these included in the unity of a present experience of corporate life in the new order which He had inaugurated, the bread (and wine) becoming an effectual sign of the "spiritual food and drink" of the Age to Come.

The inward cohesion of the Christian community was expressed in what has been called an "experiment in communism." Communism in the strict sense it was not, for private control of property was not abrogated (Acts 5⁴). But under the impulse of that love for one another which Jesus had inculcated, holders of real property sold it and voluntarily handed over the proceeds to the apostles, who out of it formed a common fund from which the poorer members of the community were assisted (Acts 2⁴⁵, 4³⁴). The practice was an impressive demonstration of the reality of Christian fellowship. But it lent itself to abuse (cf. Acts 5¹⁻⁵, 6¹), and the wastage of capital left the Church at Jerusalem without resources when bad times came (see p. 400). It is noteworthy that Paul, while accepting and emphasizing the principle of mutual economic responsibility among Christians (Rom. 12¹³, 15²⁷; Gal. 6²), enjoined that the common fund should be supplied out of earned income (Eph. 4²⁸; cf. 2 Thess. 3¹⁰). The obligation to provide support for the poor by the sharing of resources became a permanent principle in the Church, though the precise methods adopted at Jerusalem were modified through experience.

The Church appears at first as a closely knit religious group within the Jewish community. Its members were, so far as we know, all either born Jews or proselytes to Judaism (cf. Acts 2¹¹). While in its own estimation it was the nucleus of the true Israel of God, the people of the New Covenant, outwardly it hardly differed from the numerous separate synagogues which existed in Jerusalem (cf. Acts 6⁹). Like members of other synagogues, its members took part in the regular worship of the Temple, observed the Jewish festivals, and in general kept the Mosaic Law. According to the early chapters of Acts they were favourably regarded by the populace of Jerusalem, and the converts they won included both priests and adherents of the sect of the Pharisees (Acts 2^{47}, 4^4, 5^{14}, 6^7, 15^5). It is not suggested that such priests ceased to be liable to their sacerdotal duties in the Temple, or that Pharisaic converts ceased to observe their strict traditions. When the apostles were made the objects of disciplinary action by the Sanhedrin, it does not appear that they were charged with disloyalty to the Temple or the Law. The authorities feared that their proclamation of Jesus as Messiah, accompanied by miracles which they attributed to His power, might lead to undesirable excitement, in the course of which the people might be moved to avenge the death of Jesus upon those responsible for it (Acts 4^{15-18}, 5^{28}). That the great priestly families, in whose hands lay political power under the Romans, were nervous about a possible popular uprising, is natural enough. According to Acts it was a leader of the Pharisaic party, the great Gamaliel, whose intercession secured a cautious toleration for the new sect (Acts 5^{34-40}).

2. THE RISE OF HELLENISTIC CHRISTIANITY

Presently a change took place. Its occasion was the emergence into prominence of a new group of Christian leaders, of whom the best known are Stephen and Philip. Their emergence was due to dissensions within the Church itself between two parties denominated " Hebrews " and " Hellenists." The term " Hellenist " might be used of any one whose language, outlook, or way of life was Greek, whether he was a born Greek or not. Here it probably means Christian Jews (or proselytes) whose habitual use of the Greek language implied a certain detachment from the narrowly nationalist outlook and the severe legalism of the typical Palestinian Jew. They may have been mainly persons whose native connexions were with the Judaism of the Dispersion rather than with Jerusalem. At any rate, among the companions or adherents of Stephen we find a proselyte of Antioch and men of Cyprus and Cyrene (Acts 6^5, 11^{20}).

These Hellenists conceived themselves to be treated with insufficient consideration by the " Hebrew " section of the Church, particularly in that their widows were not given their share in the dole distributed to poorer members of the

Church (Acts 6[1]). We may fairly suppose that this was only one symptom of an attitude of superiority on the part of the " Hebrews." At the instance of the Apostles a board of seven was appointed to look after their interests. The Seven all bear Greek names. While this does not necessarily imply either Greek origin or connexions with the Dispersion (names of two out of the original Twelve are Greek—Andrew and Philip), yet it is hardly a coincidence that the whole seven have Greek names. It would appear that what we have is not simply an administrative expedient for the better distribution of the dole, but an attempt to give the " Hellenist " party a definite status in the community.

Stephen certainly does not appear to have regarded himself as confined to " serving tables," for he took a leading part in proclaiming and defending the new faith. It is significant that he was especially in touch with the synagogues of the Dispersion in Jerusalem (Acts 6[9]). The effect of his preaching was to arouse intense opposition. Charges were brought against him which apparently had not been brought against the Church hitherto, though they are very like those which were brought against Jesus Himself. He was accused of saying that Jesus of Nazareth would destroy the Temple and abolish the Law (Acts 6[14]). The author of Acts says the charges were false, but there is reason to believe that in substance they were true. The speech attributed to Stephen, which may well represent the general trend of his teaching, treats the building of the Temple as an act of apostasy (Acts 7[47-51]), and it lays stress upon the fact that the revelations and providential acts of God had taken place, not in the Holy City but in Mesopotamia, Egypt, Midian, and Sinai (Acts 7[2. 9-10. 29-32. 36. 38]). It mentions Moses and the Law with all respect, but declares that Moses had predicted Christ as his successor. In killing Him, the rulers of the Jews had proved themselves heirs of the murderers of the prophets (Acts 7[51-52], cf. Matt. 23[29-35]; Luke 11[50-51]; Mark 12[1-9]) and apostates from the Law (Acts 7[53]; cf. Matt. 23[2 4]). The general implication of all this is clear. Stephen stands for a Christianity which is emancipated from Jewish national limitations, and while claiming to be itself the true Israel, disowns contemporary Judaism as apostate. There is much in the teaching of Jesus as recorded in the Gospels which has a similar purport, and Stephen may be regarded as one who brought into prominence the revolutionary aspect of the Gospel, which was concealed under the conformity of the Apostles and the " Hebrews " in the Church.

The result was an outbreak of persecution. Stephen was the first victim, and the Church was broken and dispersed. According to Acts 8¹ all the Christians were scattered except the Apostles. It is difficult to believe that in literal fact only twelve Christians were left in Jerusalem, and those twelve the leaders who, if the persecution was general, would be expected to suffer its worst attacks. We may reasonably conjecture that while those who were tarred with Stephen's brush had to flee, the more moderate party which followed the Twelve still enjoyed, though precariously, the toleration that Gamaliel had secured for them.

The refugees of the Hellenistic party went afield, preaching their version of the faith. Philip went to Samaria, a district in which a by-form of Judaism lived alongside various pagan cults. The narrative of Acts, which is somewhat obscure, and may have legendary elements, brings him into touch with Simon Magus, who is well known as an important figure in the development of religious syncretism. The work known as "The Great Assertion," attributed to him, sets forth a curious medley of Jewish and Oriental pagan beliefs, superficially hellenized, which is the precursor of much Gnostic speculation of later times. According to Acts 8⁹⁻¹³ Simon and many of his followers were baptized as Christians. The apostles in Jerusalem, however, taking cognizance of Philip's work, sent Peter and John to supervise it. They confirmed many of his converts, but expelled the most distinguished of them, Simon himself, and Philip retired from the scene. Whatever may have been the actual facts, this curious story is symbolic of the destiny of Hellenistic Christianity in its contact with the wider world. Until the end of the second century the Church was occupied with the Gnostic controversy, which was at bottom the question, how far a Christianity divorced from Judaism could come to terms with other religious movements in the Hellenistic world. It may be that the episode of Simon Magus foreshadowed this controversy, though the author of Acts has missed its full significance. In any case the Samaritan converts, after Peter's purge, were recognized as members of the Church whose seat was at Jerusalem, and Philip worked in the neighbouring districts, ultimately settling down at Cæsarea (Acts 8²⁶⁻⁴⁰, 21⁸).

Others of the refugees preached in Cyprus and Phœnicia, until some of them—natives of Cyrene and Cyprus—reached Antioch, and there preached (for the first time, it would appear) to pure pagans. The foundation of the Antiochene Church is a landmark in the history of early Christianity.

It was here, in fact, that the use of the term "Christian" marked the recognition (by the outside public, obviously) of a new religion, standing on its own feet, and now no longer a peculiar form of Judaism (Acts 11$^{19-21.\ 26}$).

The chronology of the narrative of Acts at this point is not quite clear, but after the account of the foundation of the church at Antioch we hear of renewed persecution at Jerusalem ; and this time it is the apostles themselves who are its objects. Herod put to death James, the son of Zebedee, and seeing that this gratified the Jews, he imprisoned Peter, with the intention of making him a second victim (Acts 12$^{1-4}$). Previously persecution had been directed against the Hellenistic party in the Church, and the apostles had been spared. What caused the change of policy ? We may reasonably connect it with Peter's reception of the Gentile Cornelius into full fellowship with the Church (Acts 10$^{44-48}$). This action was unpopular with many Christians (Acts 11$^{1-3}$), and would certainly be counted against the Church by those Jews who watched it narrowly for signs of disloyalty to the Law. After his escape from prison, Peter left Jerusalem.

Leadership in the Church of Jerusalem seems now to have fallen to James, the Lord's brother (Acts 12^{17}, 15^{13}, 21^{18}). Everything we know of him suggests that he always remained a strict Jew, and was in good odour with the Jews of Jerusalem. Under his leadership the Jerusalem Church, which had already lost its Hellenistic left wing, became the headquarters of a strictly Jewish Christianity, critical of the forward missionary policy which the friends of Stephen had initiated. This Jewish Christianity had no future. It maintained itself for a long time, but after the fall of Jerusalem it was out of touch with the bulk of Christendom, as from the beginning of the second century it was finally disowned by the Synagogue. In isolation it dwindled and disappeared.

3. PAUL AND THE GENTILE MISSION

Interest now passes from Jerusalem to the Gentile-Christian Church. Its headquarters at first was Antioch on the Orontes. The Church there had been founded, as we have seen, by followers of Stephen from Cyprus and Cyrene. When we next hear of it (Acts 13^1) its ministry included Barnabas of Cyprus and Lucius of Cyrene, as well as another Jewish Christian of the Dispersion, whose name now begins to dominate the story—Saul of Tarsus, better known as Paul.

Born in Cilicia of a Jewish family which possessed the

Roman citizenship, Paul was by training and conviction a Pharisee. He studied for the Rabbinate at Jerusalem. It is not too hazardous a conjecture that he was among those Cilician Jews with whom Stephen disputed, and he was certainly a consenting party to his death. It is important to observe that it was the " left-wing " Christianity of the Hellenists with which Paul was brought into contact. He must have seen from the first that the new faith was incompatible with the religious nationalism of the Pharisaic system, must have seen it more clearly than did James and his party. It was for this reason that he now took a leading part in the persecution that followed the death of Stephen. On his way to Damascus to root out Christianity in the synagogues there he was converted. It is significant that it did not occur to him to report himself to the apostles at Jerusalem (Gal. 1^{17}). He went off alone to Arabia, and only after three years visited Jerusalem, where he was Peter's guest for a fortnight. At this time he saw James, but no other apostle (Gal. 1^{18-19}), though he seems to have had friendly relations with the Cypriot Barnabas, who according to Acts 9^{27} sponsored him when the Jerusalem Church was, not unnaturally, doubtful of his credentials. He then returned home to Tarsus, and worked for about fourteen years as an independent missionary in Cilicia and Syria, eventually settling, with Barnabas, at Antioch (Gal. 1^{21-23} ; Acts 9^{30}, 11^{26}).

They had, however, not been long together there when the Antiochene Church decided on a forward movement, and designated the two friends as missionaries to the wider world. They were accompanied by Mark, who belonged to a group in Jerusalem closely in touch with Peter (Acts 12^{12}). They went to Barnabas's native island of Cyprus, and then crossed to the Anatolian mainland and preached in the cities of Pisidian Antioch, Iconium, Derbe, and Lystra, which belonged to the Roman Province of Galatia. They met with some success among the Jewish synagogues, but apparently with much greater success among the Gentile population, which aroused intense Jewish opposition.

On their return to Antioch, emissaries from the Jerusalem Church, anxious that the Gentile mission should be put at once on a satisfactory basis, raised the question of the relation of converts from paganism to the Jewish Law. Christian Pharisees put forward the view that since the Christian Church was the direct heir of ancient Israel, converts from paganism should in the ordinary way become Jews by submitting to the rite of circumcision and accepting the obligations of the

Law (Acts 15¹). Antioch took a different view. Paul and Barnabas went up to Jerusalem, and the matter was discussed. Paul's account of the conference (Gal. 2¹⁻¹⁰) is somewhat different from that given in Acts 15²⁻²⁹, which perhaps represents the Jerusalem account of the matter. In Paul's view, he was given a perfectly free hand. According to to Acts 15 certain minimum restrictions on Gentile converts were laid down. But in any case the issue was in substance a victory for the more liberal party. The demand that converts from paganism should be circumcised and subject themselves to the Mosaic Law was set aside.

Paul evidently took this to imply that henceforward Gentile Christians stood on exactly the same footing as Jews, enjoying full rights of intercourse with Jewish Christians. But the case was not really so simple. Not even Paul claimed (cf. 1 Cor. 9²⁰⁻²¹) that Christian Jews should cease to observe the Law. But if they still observed its regulations as interpreted by the Pharisees, there might be difficulties about the free association of Jews and Gentiles in the common meals in which Christian fellowship found its centre. Antioch seems to have practised "open communion." After the conference (Gal. 2¹¹⁻¹³) Peter, who had supported Paul and Barnabas at Jerusalem, visited Antioch, and conformed with local usage in eating at the same table with Gentile Christians. But other visitors from Jerusalem, claiming the authority of James, pointed out the difficulty that this made for strict Jewish Christians. Peter thought their objection reasonable and withdrew from table-fellowship with Gentiles. Barnabas joined him. Paul felt that this was to nullify the liberty that had been conceded by the Jerusalem conference. For him there was no half-way house. Either Gentiles were to be admitted unconditionally to full Christian fellowship, or the Church was still essentially a Jewish institution, and this was to him a misunderstanding of the Gospel. In his indignation he charged Peter and Barnabas with cowardice and hypocrisy. We may more charitably give them credit for an attempt to meet a situation of real difficulty by a fair compromise. But Paul was more far-sighted. It was a vital principle that was at stake.

Paul now parted company with Barnabas, and set out with a fresh companion, Silas, or, to give him the Roman name which Paul uses, Silvanus. The account of their journey in Acts 16 gives the impression that Paul now felt himself to be free as he had never been before, with all the world before him. After revisiting his churches in South Galatia he does not seem to have had any very definite plans. Providentially, as he believed, he was led to cross over into Europe. He was now probably between forty and forty-five years of age, just about the middle of his career as a Christian. Much experience lay behind him, and his powers were ripe. The years which followed were his most fruitful, and resulted in the foundation of strong, predominantly Gentile-Christian churches in the provinces of Macedonia and Achaia on the west of the Ægean, and in the province of Asia on the east.

Here he was in the ancient home of Greek civilization, and he was clearly stimulated by the vigorous intellectual life of his environment. It was not altogether strange to a citizen of Tarsus, which was itself a centre of Greek culture, though with a distinct Oriental colouring. While he still started work by preference among the adherents of the synagogue, he readily found opportunities in the open forum, like any wandering Stoic or Cynic philosopher, or hired a room for daily lectures (Acts 17^{17}, 19^9).

His theology as we have it in his epistles was worked out in the stress of missionary work in this stimulating environment. In part it was called forth by the necessity of defining Christianity as a way of thought and life over against popular religious movements in the pagan world, in part by the exigencies of his long controversy with Jews and judaizing Christians. The Thessalonian and Corinthian correspondence best reveals his mind at work upon the problems of a pagan environment, the Epistle to the Galatians his masterful advocacy of the liberty of the Christian man against Jewish legalism, while the Epistle to the Romans is a carefully reasoned exposition and defence of the whole Christian faith as he understood and preached it.

This, his greatest epistle, seems to have been called forth by a project which he formed to extend his missionary activities from the eastern to the western part of the Roman Empire. He proposed to start work in Spain, and to this end he sought a base of operations in Rome, where there was already a Christian community in whose foundation he had had no part (Rom. $15^{14\text{-}24}$). One aim at least of the epistle was to enlist sympathy for his project in a church which had been reared on a different type of Christian preaching. The name of Peter has always been connected in tradition with the Roman Church, and if we take that name as standing for a type of Christianity no less liberal than Paul's in its recognition of the universality of the Gospel, but less radical in its revolt from Judaism, then Rome may fairly be described as Petrine rather than Pauline. There are some possible hints in the New Testament that Paul found some lack of sympathy among Christians at Rome (Phil. 1^{15-17}, 2^{20-21}; 2 Tim. 4^{16}, if the reference in those places is to Rome).

Before starting for the West, Paul had one task to accomplish in the East. In spite of his controversy with the Judaistic Christians he always retained a profound respect for the Mother Church of Christendom at Jerusalem, and cared greatly for unity between the Gentile and Jewish wings of the Church. The Christians of Judæa were an impoverished community. The blame for their poverty may perhaps be divided between famine, persecution, and the unwise conduct of the " experiment in communism." Paul saw in it a golden opportunity for impressing upon his Gentile converts the practical implications of the maxim that " we are members one of another." He raised over several years a relief fund to which all his churches in Galatia, Macedonia, Achaia and Asia contributed (1 Cor. 16^{1-4}; 2 Cor. 8^{1-15}, 9^{1-15}; Rom. 15^{25-27}). When the fund was complete, delegates from these churches met and accompanied him to Jerusalem (Acts 20^{3-6}). Paul was well aware that by going there he was putting his head in the lion's mouth, for Jewish hostility to him had reached the point of frenzy, but he determined none the less to appear as an ambassador of Christian fellowship.

Arrived at Jerusalem, he was met by a demand from James that he should give public demonstration of his continued loyalty to the Law by associating himself with a group of men who were about to perform the ritual of a vow in the Temple. Paul agreed ; but his appearance in the Temple was the signal for an uproar instigated by Jews from Asia, who knew him all too well. He was almost lynched, and rescued in the nick of time by the Roman troops on guard. He was now a prisoner of the Roman commandant, who sent him under custody to Cæsarea. He stood his trial before the Procurator, but no verdict was given, and Paul remained in prison for two years. Then, faced by a proposal to try him at Jerusalem, which he rightly judged would mean certain death, he appealed to the emperor. In consequence he attained his ambition of going to Rome—as a prisoner. There he was placed in a kind of free custody for two years. Whether after that time he had another spell of liberty we do not know, but there is a credible tradition that he was ultimately condemned to death under Nero, and was beheaded, as a Roman citizen, on the Ostian Way. It is probable that the Epistles to the Colossians, to Philemon, to the Ephesians and to the Philippians were written from Rome, and that they contain his ripest thoughts.

Paul was not the only missionary to the Gentiles, but his energy, his capacity for missionary strategy and for organization, his understanding of the Hellenistic world, and his intellectual mastery of the situation, added to those indefinable factors which we can only sum up as " personality," made him the outstanding leader in the remarkable advance of Christianity in the middle decades of the first century. It was due to him more than to any other one person that Christianity became aware of itself as a world-religion, equipped with a theology and a cultus of its own, and with a strong and flexible corporate discipline. No doubt also it was partly due to Paul's instinctive tact, as one who understood and appreciated the best side of Roman order and Greek culture, that the Christian movement in Greece and Anatolia avoided on the whole collisions with the imperial authorities during his lifetime. He encountered sporadic opposition from popular paganism, but most of his difficulties came from the Jews, and in such difficulties he found protection in Roman justice.

4. PERSECUTION AND CONSOLIDATION

With the end of the Acts of the Apostles and the cessation of Paul's literary activity, we are in a much less favourable position for following the history of the Church. It appears that the persecution under Nero, though it was immediately directed against the Church of Rome, meant a change in imperial policy which affected the whole position of Christians in the empire. It is no accident that writings which must be attributed to the period between A.D. 64 and the end of the first century are marked by an insistence on the fact of persecution and the necessity for steadfastness under it. This note is prominent in 1 Peter, Hebrews, and the Revelation. The Gospel according to Mark, by the emphasis it lays on the exhortations to Christians to " bear the cross," and its forecasts of persecution, betrays the same atmosphere. The Revelation of John indicates the bitter resentment which persecution aroused in some sections of the Church. 1 Peter, on the other hand, maintains, under greater difficulties, the Pauline attitude of respect for the imperial power, and enjoins patience and forbearance. The Lucan work, consisting of the Third Gospel and the Acts, was evidently written partly with a view to clearing up misunderstanding and commending the new religion to the Græco-Roman public and the authorities as worthy of toleration.

It was in part, no doubt, the impact of persecution that led the Church to consolidate its discipline. It was also in part the appearance of eccentric doctrines, which were due to the attempt to assimilate Christianity to other popular religious movements. From both these causes we find in writings of the period round about the turn of the first and second centuries an increased emphasis on Church order and on the definition of the faith. Already in the Gospel according to Matthew we observe an " ecclesiastical " note which is absent from Mark, and the Lucan work betrays a definite interest in the origin and development of Christian institutions. But it is naturally in the later epistles that the tendency is most clearly displayed. The Epistles to Timothy and Titus, which go under the name of Paul, are probably in their present form the product of the early second century —though this is not to deny that they may contain genuine work of the Apostle. They are very largely concerned with ecclesiastical discipline. Similarly the Epistles of John, which belong to about the same period, deal with dissensions in the Church and with heresy. At the same time the Fourth Gospel is evidence of a determination to find an authentic re-interpretation of Christianity in terms congenial to the thought of the time, and so to cut the ground from under the insidious growth of heresy.

To complete our view of this later period, we should properly take into consideration non-canonical writings which are almost contemporary, such as the Epistle of Clement which deals with disorders in the Church at Corinth, the earliest part at least of the Teaching of the Twelve Apostles, a manual of Church order, and the Epistles of Ignatius, which are mainly concerned with the unity of the Church under the episcopate and with rebutting heresy. We see the Church from the end of the first century, consolidating itself into an imposing organization, well-equipped for the astonishing advance which it made during the following centuries. But precise and detailed information is lacking.

B. Christian Thought in the First Century

I. THE PRIMITIVE GOSPEL

We have seen that the Church started with a Gospel which proclaimed that in the coming of Christ, His life, death, and resurrection, a new age had been inaugurated, in which the prophetic expectations of the Kingdom of God were fulfilled.

The sign and proof of this was given in the presence of the Holy Spirit in the Church, itself a fulfilment of prophecy.

The New Testament in almost all its parts bears witness to the diligence with which early Christian teachers " searched the Scriptures " for anticipations of Christ and the Christian era.   It is probable that the earliest work of Christian theological research (if it may be called so) was the collection of " testimonies " or proof passages from the Old Testament, and that some such collection lay before some of the New Testament writers.   The proof from prophecy is often to our minds artificial and unconvincing.   But it bears witness at once to the Church's sense of a divine purpose in history, and to the consciousness of a unique fulfilment of that purpose in the coming of Christ.   The fact that Christian theology from the first developed with constant reference to the Old Testament was of the greatest value in preserving continuity with the religious tradition of Judaism, and in placing limits to the tendency to meet Hellenistic thought half-way.   That tendency was in itself inevitable and even beneficial, but there was always a certain danger in it.

The proclamation that the new age had begun with Christ was accompanied with the assurance that it would be consummated by His second coming to judgement.   This, it was believed, was immediately impending.   So long as this belief maintained itself in its full force, the coming of the Kingdom of God could be felt as one single divine event, though realized in two stages.   But as months and years passed, and the second advent receded into the future, a problem arose.   It was this disappointment of expectations that provided the most powerful stimulus to the development of Christian theology.

On the one side, the eschatological expectations of apocalyptic Judaism revived.   Impatient spirits sighed for the coming of the Lord, echoing the ancient cry, " O Lord, how long ? "   Attempts were made to discover signs from which the approach of the end might be inferred, and its character was depicted in vivid, even lurid, colours.   The chief monument, in the New Testament, of this mode of thought is the Revelation of John, but it may be illustrated also from 2 Thessalonians and other writings and it has affected the tradition of the teaching of Jesus especially in the Gospel according to Matthew.

This concentration upon the future might easily lead to a sense that the historical coming of Christ was only preliminary, or even provisional.   But this was not the central

mind of the Church. Whatever else might be in prospect,
the life, death, and resurrection of Jesus Christ constituted
an act of God unique and decisive in its character and effects.
The Gospels, as we have seen, are inspired by this conviction,
and it is worked out in masterly fashion by the first Christian
theologians.

2. PAUL

Paul shows himself in his earliest letters much preoccupied
with the expectation of an early second coming of the Lord.
But 1 Corinthians is the latest of his letters in which that
expectation is acute, and already it is being overshadowed by
other ideas. After that point the advent hope is in the background rather than the foreground of his thought.

The philosophy of history which is developed in the
Epistles to the Romans and the Galatians shows a firm grasp
of the belief that the coming of Christ is the fulfilment of a
purpose which ran through all the history of Israel from the
call of Abraham onwards. God's purpose was to bring into
active existence a people whose relation to Him was that of
a son to his father, a relation of unclouded faith, obedience,
and love. In the call and the faith of Abraham, the promise
of such a people was already given and fulfilled in principle.
But among the descendants of Abraham not all were chosen,
in the inscrutable Providence of God, as bearers of His purpose.
Ishmael and Esau fell out of the running ; Isaac and Jacob
were called. Among the posterity of Jacob, " not all who are
of Israel are Israel " (that is, the people of God) (Rom. 9⁷⁻¹³).
Indeed, in the presence of general apostasy, only a faithful
remnant carried forward the promise and the hope of God's
calling (Rom. 9²⁷⁻²⁹). At last the strange situation arose
that one Man only stood out from an apostate people as the
embodiment of the true Israel (Gal. 3¹⁶). This was Jesus,
who (as the Gospels record), when the Jews rejected Him and
His disciples forsook Him, bore alone the burden of His
Messianic destiny as representative of the people of God.
He alone realized in Himself that ideal of a Son of God, in
perfect faith, obedience, and love. He was the true " seed
of Abraham," but He was more ; He was the Son of God
sent from heaven in human form (Rom. 8³ ; Gal. 4⁴). He
was the second Adam, representative not only of Israel, but
of humanity in the image of God (1 Cor. 15⁴⁵⁻⁴⁷· ²¹ ; Rom. 5¹⁴⁻¹⁷).
In Him Israel, or the true humanity, died to this world, and
rose again in the glory of the Age to Come. Henceforward
the new Israel of God grows by incorporation into " the Body

of Christ." The purpose of God no longer advances by exclusion, as in the strange history of Israel's past, but by the inclusion of men of every race, for in Christ " there is neither Jew nor Greek, barbarian, Scythian, bondman, freeman " (Col. 3¹¹; Gal. 3²⁸). This Body of Christ, this Israel of God, is the Church, which lives on the farther side of that supreme crisis in which the death of Christ ended the old age and His resurrection ushered in the new.

What God did for men at this supreme crisis Paul expresses in various ways, and chiefly in three terms which are the keywords of his theology.

(i) Redemption. The nearest true equivalent of this word in our current speech is " emancipation." It was commonly used of the process by which a slave became a free man. But in the Old Testament it is specifically used of the divine act of deliverance by which a horde of serfs in Egypt became the people of God (e.g. Deut. 7⁸), and, by analogy, of that later act of deliverance by which the exiles in Babylon were given liberty to return to their own country (e.g. Isa. 44²³). A cognate word had been used by Jesus, when He spoke of giving His life as " a ransom for many " (Mark 10⁴⁵). Its associations made it a fitting word to express Paul's conviction that through the death and resurrection of Christ the people of God had emerged out of bondage to sin into " the liberty of the glory of the children of God " (Rom. 8²¹; see Gal. 3²³–4⁵).

(ii) Justification. Paul's use of this term is derived from the teaching of the prophets, and in particular of the Second Isaiah, according to which the " righteousness of God " is manifested in the vindication or deliverance of His people (Isa. 46¹³, 51⁵, etc.). The verb " justify," therefore, which in Hebrew and Greek is etymologically cognate with the words " righteous " and " righteousness," can be used as a virtual synonym for " deliver " (e.g. Isa. 45²⁵). But the Hebrew verb has also a forensic sense, to " acquit." The Greek word is also capable of a similar sense, and in this sense Paul opposes it to the word " condemn." This fluctuation of meaning cannot be reproduced in English. It enables Paul, whose turn of mind and whose training were legal, to represent the deliverance of God's people under the figure of a process of law. Man, the prisoner at the bar, is guilty. God, the Judge, of His free grace, acquits him—" justifies the ungodly " (Rom. 4⁵). It is a forcible way of putting the truth which runs all through the teaching of Jesus, that God gives His Kingdom to undeserving men.

It is, however, to be observed that justification becomes

effective for men only as they respond by faith to the divine offer (as they " receive the Kingdom of God as a little child "). But faith is the right attitude of man to God (and is His gift, Eph. 2[8]) ; and since in the teaching of Jesus the whole of ethics turns upon personal attitudes, it follows that the justified sinner is already in principle " righteous." Justification, therefore, is not merely a legal fiction. Paul was perfectly aware what a paradox it was to say that God, the righteous Judge of all the world, acquits the guilty, but if legal terms are to be used, one can say nothing else. The true conclusion is that legal terms are inappropriate to describe the ultimate relations of God and man. " Christ is the end of the Law to every one who has faith " (Rom. 10[4]). This is the logical outcome of that attitude to the Law which we observed in the teaching of Jesus.

(iii) Reconciliation, or Atonement. Here Paul is no longer using mere illustrations, but giving a direct description of experience. By reason of sin man is at enmity with God. This is common experience wherever ethical religion is a reality. If the supreme object of worship is the moral ideal personified, then the more sincerely a man tries to worship, the more bitterly does he feel that in his moral imperfection he is estranged from the God in whom alone his spiritual nature can find satisfaction. Hence it is that a gloomy sense of sin haunts the devout mind, when it is not only devout but also morally in earnest.

Such was Paul's state as a devout Pharisee. Nor could he find any way of overcoming the estrangement in self-discipline regulated by the Law. For the more deeply he pondered the Law, the more lofty did his conception of the holiness of God become, and the more impotent did he find himself to fulfil the high ideals set before him. He even found, as others have found, that the prohibitions of the Law (which are so much more numerous than positive precepts, whether in statutory law or in the law of conscience), provoked the desire for the prohibited thing. Thus Paul's experience was that his very religion was increasing his sense of alienation from God. Then he learned from Jesus that this alienation was on his side and not on God's. He was God's enemy ; God was not his. On the contrary, " God displays His love for us, in that while we were yet sinners, Christ died for us " (Rom. 5[8]). In other words, " God was in Christ reconciling the world to Himself " (2 Cor. 5[19]— not, be it observed " Christ was reconciling God to us ").

To these three leading conceptions, redemption, justification, and reconciliation, we must add a fourth, which is not prominent in Paul, but has been given undue importance by his expositors, the conception of expiation through sacrifice. It is a common assumption of antique religion, and of ancient Judaism among others, that when sin has been committed, a kind of taint is contracted which makes a man incapable of approaching God, and that by the offering of the appropriate sacrifices the taint may be removed. This is what is called expiation. It may be defined as an act annulling the taint of sin. The higher thought of Judaism seems already to have divined that the only ultimate means of annulling the taint was forgiveness granted by God Himself, but this belief was obscured by the elaborate system of sacrificial expiation.

Now if God in Christ has redeemed, justified, and reconciled sinful humanity, then the same truth may be expressed in terms of sacrifice, if we say that God Himself provided a sacrifice by which the sin of man was annulled. And this is what Paul says : " We are justified freely by His grace, through the redemption in Christ Jesus, whom God set forth as a means of expiation, through faith, by virtue of His blood " (*i.e.* His sacrificial death). (Rom. 3^{24-25}. The translation " propitiation," which would suggest that the sacrifice of Christ pacified the anger of God, is not only theologically inappropriate, but probably incorrect philologically.)

Paul has thus defined precisely what was involved in the passage from the old order to the new which was effected by the representative death and resurrection of Christ. It was essentially a new relation to God. When he now turns to consider the experience through which this new relation is realized, he speaks of it, as the primitive Church did, as life in the Spirit. His understanding of it, however, is more profound. The præter-normal phenomena, such as miracles of healing and " speaking with tongues," upon which the first Christians laid so much stress, appear to him to have only subordinate value, though he recognizes them as " gifts of the Spirit." The power of the Spirit is more fundamentally revealed in moral and intellectual qualities—in spiritual insight (" knowledge " and " wisdom "), and above all in love or charity, which is " the love of God shed abroad in our hearts through the Holy Spirit given to us " (Rom. 5^5). Christian ethics spring organically out of charity in its various applications. And it is love that " builds up " the Body of Christ (1 Cor. 8^1 ; Eph. 4^{16}), and holds it together in unity (Col. 3^{14}). Since, therefore, love is the supreme and all-inclusive " gift of the Spirit," Paul describes the quality of the fellowship created by it as " the communion of the Holy Spirit " (2 Cor. 13[13]; Phil. 2[1]), finding so a new and significant expression for a fact which had existed from the beginning, an expression which appropriately recognizes the supernatural or eschatological character of the Church as the new Israel of God.

In view of Paul's doctrine of the Church as at once the Body of Christ and the communion of the Spirit, the sacraments take on a special significance. Baptism was from the beginning closely connected in the primitive Church with the gift of the Spirit, which marks a man as a member of the new Israel. For Paul it is initiation into the Body of Christ, and as such it is the re-enactment for the individual convert of the death and resurrection through which the people of God passed in the representative person of the Messiah. Having " died " to sin, the law, the " flesh," and the world, the Christian is " alive unto God," in the life of the Spirit, " in Christ " (Rom. 6[1-11]). Again, the Lord's Supper, in which the Church both commemorated the death of Christ and partook sacramentally of His " Body " as offered for the salvation of men, has special significance when the Church itself is thought of as His " Body," which died and rose again. Indeed, it may well be that the thought of the Church as the mystical Body of Christ was suggested to Paul's mind by the symbolism of the sacrament.

Once again, if the conception of the Church as the Body of Christ is put together with the conception of it as the communion of the Spirit, it follows that the Spirit is the mode of Christ's own indwelling in the Church. Indeed, Paul can go so far as to say, " The Lord is the Spirit " (2 Cor. 3[17]). This character belongs to Christ as the " second Adam," or heavenly Man. The first man (Paul quotes from Genesis) " became a living soul " (*psyché*, the organic principle of natural life), but the second Man, he proceeds, is " life-giving Spirit " (1 Cor. 15[45]). In Christ, that is to say, in His Body, Spirit becomes the principle of a life higher than the natural (Rom. 8[6-11]). It is the life of sons of God, for it is in the Spirit that we call God, Father (Rom. 8[15]; Gal. 4[6]).

This profound theological intuition has great influence in the formation of Paul's doctrine of the Person of Christ. The Church started, as we have seen, with the conviction that Christ was the Lord of the new age, " at the right hand of God." As Messiah, He was Son of God. We seem able to discern various attempts made to define more precisely the implications of this. Thus we have traces of the view that He was Messiah and Son of God, because the plenitude of the Spirit

of God rested upon Him at His Baptism, or because He was
" appointed " as such by God at His resurrection.   According
to the prologues to the First and Third Gospels, He was Son
of God because He was miraculously born, with no human
father, through the descent of the Spirit upon His mother.

It seems probable also, though the proof is not complete,
that some teachers, independently of Paul, had associated
His authority as the revealer of God with the Old Testament
idea of the divine Wisdom, which in Hellenistic Judaism represents some of the functions of the Holy Spirit.   Paul, in
1 Cor. 1^{24}, says that Christ is " the Power of God and the
Wisdom of God."   In Col. 1$^{15-19}$, without mentioning the
word " wisdom," he uses language which can be traced in
every point (except the one word " fulness ") to Jewish
Wisdom theology.   According to this, Christ (as " life-giving
Spirit ") is, so to speak, the thought of God projected from
Him, to be the principle by which the world is both created
and sustained, and finally brought to the perfection and unity
designed by the Creator.   The redemption of mankind, and
its unification in the Body of Christ, is thus seen as an aspect
of the redemption of the whole universe, the reconciliation of
man to God as a pledge of the final reconciliation of all powers
in heaven and earth (Col. 1^{20}).   For as man is created in the
image of God, which is Christ, so the world is created in holy
Wisdom, which is Christ, and both man and the world find
their destined perfection only as " summed up " in Him
(Eph. 1^{10}).

This " Wisdom-Christology " made it possible for Paul to
give a more adequate account of what was meant by calling
Christ the Son of God.   He did not begin to be such at His
resurrection, or at His baptism, or at His birth.   He is a
revelation in time of the eternal Wisdom, or thought of God,
proceeding from Him, yet eternally one with Him.   Being
from all eternity in the form of God, He took the fashion of
man.   As such He died, and being risen from the dead, He
is revealed in His divine character as " Lord " (Phil. 2$^{5-11}$).
That title for Christ is primitive (the prayer, " Our Lord,
come ! " is preserved from the most primitive period in its
Aramaic form, " Marana tha ! ", 1 Cor. 16^{22}).   In Paul it
acquires a fuller significance.

In the Old Testament (both Hebrew and Greek), the title
" Lord " is regularly used as a substitute for the divine name.
Paul seems to have taken it as the title of God in His relation
to men, and particularly to Israel, the people of the covenant.
To his Gentile converts the title " Lord " would convey a not

dissimilar meaning, for it was frequently applied to gods who stood to their worshippers in a relation analogous to the " covenant " relation between Israel and Jehovah. Now Paul cites passages from the Old Testament which speak of " the Lord," meaning the God of Israel, and applies them directly to Christ. He could do so, because Christ, as the Wisdom of God, is He in whom " dwells all the fulness of the Godhead corporately." That is to say, while he does not call Christ God (Rom. 9^5 is probably to be otherwise translated), he does believe that all the divine attributes and functions are present and active in Him. What God is to men, that Christ is, and the relation of Father and Son is as close as that between a man and his thought. In this definition of the relation of Christ to the Spirit on the one hand and to the Father on the other, Paul has already provided the data for the theology of the Creeds.

3. THE EPISTLE TO THE HEBREWS

Among post-Pauline writings in the New Testament we may select the Epistle to the Hebrews as being of especial importance in the development of Christian theology.

The writer, whoever he was, is in spirit and outlook closely akin to Hellenistic Jewish teachers of whom Philo is the best known. He is profoundly influenced by Greek thought of a Platonic type. According to the Platonic philosophy, there are two orders of being, the eternal and the temporal. The eternal is alone fully real, the temporal a " shadow " or symbol of the eternal. The author to the Hebrews translates the Jewish and primitive Christian distinction between " this age " and " the age to come," into the Platonic distinction between the two orders of being. Where the primitive Gospel declared that with Christ the former age passed away and a new age began, he declares that through Him man is enabled to pass from the realm of shadows into the realm of reality.

He works out this conception with especial reference to the religious system of Judaism. In the Old Testament it is said that Moses was instructed to make the Tabernacle and its furniture according to the pattern shown to him upon Mount Sinai. For a Platonist it was easy to see here a reference to the eternal " archetypes " of phenomena, " laid up," as Plato had said, " in heaven." Philo had, in fact, taken this step. It follows that the whole system of sacrifice and priesthood known to the Old Testament lies within the realm of shadows (Heb. 8^5). It *is* not what it *means*. Thus sacrifice *means* cleansing from sin, but it does

not really effect such cleansing (Heb. 9^{9-10}).   Priesthood *means*
a permanent mediation between God and man, but it is
actually occasional, temporary, and evanescent (Heb. 7^{23}, 9^{6-8}).
The reality of priesthood and sacrifice lies in the eternal
Tabernacle, which is the world of perfect reality, which is the
presence of God.   But at one point of time and space the
eternal reality of priesthood and sacrifice was perfectly revealed, namely, in the willing death of Christ in perfect obedience to the Father's will (Heb. 9^{11-14}, 10^{1-14}).   The death of
Christ, therefore, is both an event in the temporal order, and
the eternal reality which all priesthood and sacrifice symbolize.
By it He passed into the eternal Tabernacle, as our forerunner
(Heb. 6^{19-20}), and through Him we, too, " are come unto
Mount Sion, and to an innumerable company of angels, and
to God the Judge of all " (Heb. 12^{22-23})—in other words, we
pass out of shadows and images into the real.

This conception of Christ as the great High-Priest was
peculiarly well adapted to the Wisdom Christology which the
author shares with Paul (though he does not use the word) ;
for divine Wisdom is the mediating principle between the
transcendent God and the world.   Philo, similarly, who uses
the term " Logos " in part as an equivalent for the Biblical
" Wisdom," represents the Logos, the Word or projected
Thought of God, as an interceding priest.   But while for Philo
the conception is purely abstract, for the author of Hebrews
the Priest, while He is "the effulgence of His glory and the
express image of His substance, upholding all things by the
word of His power " (Heb. 1^3), is also a real historical Person,
made like unto His brethren, perfected through suffering, and,
in that He has suffered being tempted, able to succour them
that are tempted ;   the author of our faith and an example
for our imitation (Heb. $2^{10, 17-18}$, 4^{15}, 12^{2-3}).

4. THE FOURTH GOSPEL

In the Epistle to the Hebrews we have recognized an essay
in the reinterpretation of Christianity in terms of Hellenistic
thought.   But the most thoroughgoing attempt at such reinterpretation within the New Testament is to be found in
the Fourth Gospel.   It is a singularly successful attempt.
The writer shows himself, on the one hand, to be deeply versed
in Judaism—the native Judaism of Palestine, within which
Christianity arose, and from which it took its earliest forms
of expression—and on the other hand, he has a sympathetic
understanding of the mystical thought of the Hellenistic
world, whether he was acquainted with it directly, or, as is

more likely, through the medium of Hellenistic Judaism.
His mind moves with equal freedom in the Jewish and in the
Hellenistic ways of thought, not as though he had learned
either the one or the other from the outside, but as though
both were native to him, so that they are deeply fused into a
philosophy which is neither Jewish nor Greek, but intelligible
from both sides. He had behind him the faith and experience
of the primitive Church, and the work of pioneer thinkers
like Paul. The result is that in the Fourth Gospel we have a
restatement of Christianity which, while firmly based upon
the fundamental apostolic tradition, is addressed to the wider
world in an idiom which was likely to find a sympathetic
hearing for it among all thoughtful religious people. From
the second century onwards the Johannine idiom became in
large measure that of Greek-speaking Christian theology in
general.

The Gospel, as we have seen, was first expressed in terms
of eschatology, and in particular, it announced the " eschatological " fulfilment of the divine purpose in the life, death,
and resurrection of Christ, and in the emergence of the Church
as the fellowship of the Holy Spirit. Along with this announcement, the early Church also proclaimed that before long the
whole meaning of what had happened would be revealed in
the second coming of Christ. The hope of an early second
advent was in Paul gradually relegated to the background of
thought, while he elaborated in his theology the significance
of that which is already a matter of history and experience
—the historical redemption wrought by Christ, and life " in
Christ." In John the mood of expectancy has almost entirely
yielded to the sense of realization. Eternal life here and
now is the main burden of his Gospel. And the experience
of eternal life realized through Christ is projected backward
upon the past, so that His whole ministry, as well as His death
and resurrection, is clearly seen as the coming of the life of
eternity into time.

As in the Epistle to the Hebrews, so in the Fourth Gospel,
but more completely, the idea of the two orders of being has
replaced that of the two " ages." There is a world of perfect
reality, or " truth," which is the world of Spirit, the world
of light and life. There is a lower world, the world of
" flesh," which partakes of reality so far, and only so far, as
it reflects or shadows forth the higher world, but is deeply
involved in darkness, death, error, and unreality. God is
transcendent, and dwells in the world of light, for " God is
Spirit " (John 4²⁴). Human existence lies within the lower

order, for man is "born of flesh." How then—this is the
whole problem—can man rise out of darkness and death into
the realm of light and life ? Only by knowledge of God,
says the evangelist, with many thinkers of his time. Eternal
life *is* to know God, the only Real (John 17³). But like is
known by like, and man is unlike God. "That which is
born of the flesh is flesh, and that which is born of the Spirit
is Spirit " (John 3⁶). Consequently, " except a man be born
again, he cannot see the Kingdom of God " (3³), which is the
realm of life and light.

In Jewish apocalyptic it was taught that at the final consummation mankind should be transfigured into the nature
of angels. This transfiguration is occasionally referred to as
" regeneration " (Matt. 19²⁸). If now the eschatological hope
is fulfilled in the redemption wrought by Christ, then this
" regeneration " is a fact of experience—not indeed in the
mythological sense intended by apocalyptic, but in the sense
of a real change in the inward man, which makes him able
to know God. It is that passage from the domain of the
" flesh " to that of the " Spirit " of which Paul had already
spoken. In describing it as birth " from water and the
Spirit " (3⁵), John shows that he is speaking of the change
involved in becoming a member of the Church by Baptism,
from earliest days the effectual sign of the gift of the Spirit.

It is clear that a man cannot be born again by his own
power and will, any more than his own power and will brought
him into this world. The new life, which belongs to the trans-
scendent sphere, must be mediated to him from above.
Hellenistic thought was well acquainted with the doctrine
of mediating powers. One of the terms sometimes used in
this connexion was " Logos." In ordinary Greek usage this
term has a wide range. It may denote " reason," or " rational
principle." It may denote the " meaning " which a man
has in his mind when he thinks or wills. It may denote the
" word " in which this meaning is uttered. It was used in
the Stoic philosophy for the rational principle discovered by
man's reason in the universe, the " meaning " of the world,
as we might put it. Philo the Jew, playing upon the double
sense of the word, identified this meaning or rational
principle of the universe with the " word of the Lord " by
which, according to the Old Testament, heaven and earth
were made, and which came to the prophets as revelation.
Thus the Logos mediates God to the world both as the source
of its being and as the source of knowledge in man—as life
and as light.

The weakness of all Hellenistic doctrines of mediation, including that of Philo, was that they never really bridged the gap between the rational or spiritual order and the material world in which man lives. They offered release from the dominance of the material by contemplation of the rational order, but left the whole material basis of man's life (which includes, for example, his sexual life, work, and the economic order) unredeemed and unredeemable. It is here that John, reinterpreting the fundamental Christian Gospel, takes an unprecedented step. " The Logos became flesh " (1¹⁴). The creative thought of God, which is both the power by which the world was made and the meaning immanent in it, both life and the light of men, identified itself with human existence in this material order. This actual world, therefore, the world of things and events, became, in the life of Christ the incarnate Word, the vehicle of Deity. There is, therefore, in the Johannine philosophy of religion, as in no other contemporary system, *real* mediation, and the possibility is opened for man to enter into the life of God.

Another conception of mediation which meets us in contemporary Hellenistic thought is that of the heavenly or archetypal man. Mankind as we know it is partly of the earth earthy, and partly spiritual or rational. The spiritual or rational part of man is thought of as an aspect of the eternal Idea of Man (in the Platonic phrase). Some taught that this eternal Man in men was of divine essence. He had in some sense " fallen " into the world of matter. By enlightenment He might be liberated from matter, and ascend to His Father again. Now John seems to have been acquainted with this conception of the heavenly Man (as he might well be, for it had entered into Hellenistic Judaism, as we know from Philo). Jesus had spoken of Himself as " the Son of Man," which John (who can be shown to be familiar with Aramaic idiom) knew to mean " the Man." With this clue, he has represented Christ as the " heavenly Man " who descended into the world of matter, not however by a " fall," but according to the will of God (3¹³· ³¹). The humanity of Christ, therefore, is " real " humanity in the Platonic sense, that is to say, spiritual, eternal, divine humanity ; but also " real " humanity in our ordinary sense. He spoke and acted as a man. He suffered weariness, thirst, grief, and pain. He died and was buried. By His life and death He united men with Himself, and in ascending to His Father again, He " draws " all men with Him into the unity of the divine life (12³²).

It follows that for John the life of Jesus has at every

point a double character. His words and deeds are those of a man (" Jesus of Nazareth, the son of Joseph," 1^{45}), but they are also the words and deeds of God ($5^{19\text{-}20}$, 14^{10}) mediated by His Word, who is also the Man from heaven. They are a part of history, having historical antecedents and consequences, but they are also " signs " of eternal realities. What He did, He did once for all ; but also, what He did He does always, for all men everywhere. He was an active and influential figure in the past (long past already for John, as for us), but He is also the eternal Contemporary.

It is in this sense that the story of Jesus is told in the Fourth Gospel. He gives sight to the blind ; that is to say, the eternal Word enlightens the soul of man. He feeds the multitudes ; that is to say, the divine life is sustained in man by participation in the eternal Word. He raises the dead to life ; that is to say, the eternal Word brings man into that union with God which is life eternal. He dies on the Cross ; that is to say, God goes to the utmost lengths of self-giving that men may share His life. But all the same, it is historically true that Jesus did thus minister to the needs of men, and above all that He did truly " lay down His life for His friends " (15^{13}). History has become symbolic of the suprahistorical, without ceasing to be history.

If then eternal life is knowledge of God, and if God (whom " no man has seen at any time," 1^{18}) is known only through the mediation of His Logos (as John's readers in the Hellenistic world would readily agree), then it is through Christ in His historical life and death that He is known. There is no true vision of God, such as the mystics promised, through sheer contemplation of the *concept* of God. It is God in His word made flesh whom we see. " He that has seen Me has seen the Father " (14^9).

What then is it that we know of God through Christ ? John answers, with the whole early Church; it is the love of God. In His life, and above all in His death, Christ was moved by sheer love for men, and this love was the love of God, by which the Incarnation itself was willed. " God so loved the world, that He gave His only Son, that whosoever believes in Him should not perish but have everlasting life " (3^{16}).

Then how does man appropriate the eternal life offered in the love of God ? The answer is given in the great series of discourses, ending with a prayer, in chaps. 13–17. The scene is laid in the upper room, where, as recorded in the other Gospels, Jesus ate His last meal with His disciples.

At this meal an episode took place in which John sees a fitting prelude to the whole conversation that follows. Jesus, " knowing " (says the evangelist) " that the Father had given everything into His hands, and that He came from God and was going to God " (in full consciousness, that is to say, that His action expressed His divine origin, mission, and destiny), washed His disciples' feet. It is a striking illustration of His words recorded in Mark 10⁴⁵, " The Son of Man came not to be served but to serve, and to give His life a ransom for many."

This episode introduces a long conversation between Jesus and His disciples—His " friends," as He emphatically calls them (15¹⁵). It ranges over many topics, but its keynote may be found in the words, " As my Father loved me, I loved you. Abide in my love. If you keep my commandments, you will abide in my love, as I have kept my Father's commandments and abide in His love " (15⁹⁻¹⁰). Trust, obedience, love, are the appropriate response on the part of men to the love of God revealed in Christ. And this is what it is to know God, and to be one with God. The discourse ends with a prayer offered by Christ for His " friends "—" That they may all be one, as thou, Father, art in me and I in thee, that they also may be one in us . . . that they may be one as we are one : I in them and thou in me, that they may be perfected into one " (17²¹⁻²³).

That mystical union of the soul with God is the goal of all our striving, has been taught by many religious thinkers in many lands and centuries. But it is important to realize the difference between the Johannine mysticism (if we are to call it so) and some other types. Union with God is not, for this evangelist, a " flight of the alone to the alone," in which the human self is at last absorbed in the divine essence as a drop of water in the ocean. It is life in a community of friends of Jesus, in which we know ourselves the objects of divine love, shown in His dying for us ; in which, so far as we are able, we return that love in trust and obedience, and love our brethren as ourselves. And this is life eternal.

If now we look back over the whole New Testament, we are disposed to conclude that the Fourth Evangelist, who of all its major writers stands farthest in time from the life and teaching of Jesus, has understood more clearly, and expressed more powerfully than any of them, the central purport of His teaching and the meaning of His life and death. His presentation of the Gospel has the profundity of a great philosophical thinker, the universality of one who has passed beyond the distinction of Jew and Greek, and in the end the simplicity appropriate to that Wisdom of God which is " revealed to babes."

BIBLIOGRAPHY

W. M. Ramsay, *St. Paul the Traveller and the Roman Citizen.*
A. D. Nock, *St. Paul.*
A. H. M'Neile, *St. Paul, his Life, Letters, and Christian Doctrine.*
B. W. Bacon, *Jesus and Paul.*
C. H. Dodd, *The Apostolic Preaching and its Developments.*
C. H. Dodd, *The Meaning of Paul for To-Day.*
C. A. Scott, *Christianity according to St. Paul.*
A. Schweitzer, *The Mysticism of Paul the Apostle.*
A. Nairne, *The Epistle of Priesthood.*
E. F. Scott, *The Fourth Gospel : its Purpose and Theology.*
J. E. Carpenter, *The Johannine Writings.*
W. F. Howard, *The Fourth Gospel in Recent Criticism and Interpretation.*

XVI. THE PRIESTHOOD AND THE TEMPLE

1. THE PRIESTLY CASTE

AT first sight the history of the development of the Hebrew priesthood is simple 'and straightforward. There were no priests before the time of the sojourn at Sinai. There Moses acted as priest for seven days (Ex. 29^{35-37} ; Lev. 8), in order that, with all due solemnity, he might institute his brother Aaron to the priesthood " by a perpetual statute " (Ex. 29^9). Aaron the Levite was, therefore, the first true priest, and from him all subsequent priests were descended. His brethren, the Levites, were given to Aaron and his sons to perform various minor Temple duties, but only Aaron and his sons were full sacrificing priests (Num. 3^{6-10}). The priestly caste was therefore completely and exclusively Aaronic from the beginning. This is the dominant theory of Jewish tradition. It is the theory of the writers of the Priestly Code, and represents substantially the attitude of the Chronicler. Actually it portrays the state of affairs which obtained during the last three hundred years or so of the pre-Christian era, continuing until the last and final destruction of the Temple in A.D. 70. The modern study of the Old Testament has shown clearly, however, that the Priestly Writers were assuming the conditions which obtained in their day to have existed from the time when the Hebrews first began to be a people. Similarly, the Chronicler has clothed the events of other days with the garments of his own time (cf. 1 Chron. 15^1–16^{43} with its throng of Levites and singers and the simple picture of 2 Sam. 6) There are many passages in the Old Testament which show that the Aaronic priestly caste of later days was a development from a very different state of affairs. Once all Levites were priests, and not the sons of Aaron only. Earlier still it was not even necessary to be a Levite in order to be a priest. Any man could be a priest, provided that he had been properly consecrated.

The position in the time of the judges is illustrated by the story of Micah's Levite (Judg. 17, 18). Micah, of the hill country of Ephraim, possessed a " house of gods," *bet 'elohim* a private sanctuary in which were housed an ephod (an image used in divination, not to be confused with the linen ephod, a garment worn by priests), and teraphim (household gods). These images needed a guardian, and Micah therefore consecrated one of his sons as priest. This happened in the old days, before ever there was a king in Israel, when " every man did that which was right in his own eyes " (17⁶). Whilst, however, it was perfectly legitimate for Micah's son to be a priest, it was nevertheless desirable, if possible, to have a Levite. And so, when a wandering Levite appears, Micah rejoices, and forthwith displaces his son in favour of the newcomer, confident that, because of the Levite, greater blessings will accrue from Jehovah. The migrating Danites are apparently of the same opinion, with the result that Micah loses both priest and image, and the Mosaic priesthood of Dan is established (Judg. 18³⁰). The incident raises problems which pierce right to the roots of this matter of the priesthood. How comes it that this Levite is said to be of the family of Judah ? Is the word Levite here used to denote some kind of cult official, as almost certainly it is used in Ex. 4¹⁴ (J) ? If Levite is a tribal name, how can a man belong to two tribes ?

These questions cannot be answered fully in our present state of knowledge. Undoubtedly the word " levite " came ultimately to denote a cult official, since almost certainly in later times even non-Jews were reckoned as Levites (see p. 425) ; but equally clearly Levi was once a tribe in precisely the same way as any other of the sons of Jacob. This latter is essential to the story of the untoward fate of Shechem (Gen. 34), nor can any other point of view be urged without doing violence to the plain sense of the narrative. How then did Levi, once a secular tribe, become a priestly caste ?

It may be inferred from Gen. 49⁵⁻⁷ that the reprisals feared by Jacob as a result of the treacherous raid on Shechem actually took place, and that Simeon and Levi were indeed " divided in Jacob," and " scattered in Israel." We know definitely that Simeon ultimately became absorbed into Judah, as did various semi-Arab and Edomite clans. Not only is there the evidence of Josh. 19¹ and Judg. 1³, but cities which in Josh. 19²⁻⁷ are allocated to Simeon are in Josh. 15²⁶⁻³². ⁴² assigned to Judah. Simeon ceased at a comparatively early date to be counted as a separate tribe, for it is not found in the list of Deut. 33 (ninth century B.C., but Sellin, in the time of the judges). Did Levi suffer a similar fate ? In Deut. 33⁸⁻¹¹ Levi is no longer a secular tribe with territory, but exclusively a priestly caste, giving oracles, teaching, and sacrificing. If, as seems probable, Simeon and Levi were so reduced in numbers as to be forced to ally themselves with Judah, or to wander, as in the case of one Levite at least, from tribe to tribe in search of work and food, then the "levite from Bethlehem-Judah of the family of Judah," appearing in a state of destitution among the hills of Ephraim, receives a ready explanation.

Further knowledge, however, has rendered the answer less certain. In 1883 Julius Euting found, and in 1889 D. H. Mueller published, a number of Minæan inscriptions from El-'öla, approximately four hundred miles from Jerusalem and eight hundred miles from Sana, in South Arabia, the true home of the Minæans. In three of these inscriptions there are references to a *lawi'a*. It is extremely probable, though not wholly certain, that this word is from the same root as the Hebrew *lewi* (Levi), and it definitely denotes some kind of cult official. If we could be certain of the date of these inscriptions, the whole matter would be clear, but unfortunately there is considerable disagreement on this point. Hommel advocated a date *c.* 1500 B.C. ; Mueller, *c.* 700 B.C. ; Meyer, as late as the sixth or fifth century. G. B. Gray (*Sacrifice in the Old Testament*, pp. 242–247, where the whole matter is carefully and fully discussed) estimated them as not later than the time of the kingdoms. If Hommel is right, then "levite" signified "cult-official" among the Hebrews certainly from before the entrance into Canaan, especially since El-'öla cannot be far from the Midianite country, where Moses first met Jehovah of the Bush, and was later instructed by his father-in-law, the priest of Midian. The word, in this case, will be a loan-word in Hebrew from Minæan. If, however, the inscriptions date from the time of the kingdoms, then the word may be a loan-word in Minæan from Hebrew, and have been borrowed when already among the Hebrews it had come to mean a cult official. Meyer pointed out that Kadesh, for some time the Hebrew headquarters, is centrally situated both to Palestine and El-'öla. The incident at Shechem must have been prior to the going down into Egypt, so that Levi, already disorganized, may have wandered from Kadesh, mostly with Judah but not wholly, finding priestly occupations with desert tribes, because chiefly of its association with Moses, and its pre-eminence as champion of the true worship of Jehovah (Ex. 32[26]). In spite of the Priestly Code, Moses was a priest (Ps. 99[6]), and he undoubtedly performed priestly functions (see p. 418) all the time he was leader of the tribes.

Further, lest the similarity of the two words, Minæan and Hebrew, should lead to an immediate decision in favour of " levite " as being always a cult term (as it may be if Hommel is right), we have the fact that in the Tell el-Amarna letters (Knudtzon, Nos. 246, 254, 287, 289) there occurs the name Labaya. He, with his sons, is associated with Shechem of all places, and, though he protests his loyalty to Egypt, he is alleged to have gone over to the Habiru. The identification of the two words " Labaya " and " Levi " is not certain (see Jastrow, *Dictionary of Targumim*, p. 689 ; cf. Lebbæus in Matt. 10³ A.V.), but there may be here confirmation of an early association of a secular Levi with Shechem.

We therefore reconstruct the story of the development of the priestly caste on the following lines.

At first any man can be a priest. By the time of the judges it was preferable to employ a Levite, but if none was available, men managed without one. When the Ark was returned from the land of the Philistines, the men of Kirjath-jearim " brought it into the house of Abinadab in Gibeah, and sanctified his son Eleazar to guard the ark of Jehovah " (1 Sam. 7¹). This, as we have seen, is precisely what Micah did, though he soon changed to a Levite when the opportunity offered. Presumably, in their search for a living, the Levites tended to gather at the local shrines, until what was at first desirable came ultimately to be regarded as a necessity. The tendency would then develop to interpret the word " levite " as if from the root *lawah* (" attach," Num. 18². ⁴ ; Isa. 56⁶), since in the course of time no one would have any experience of a Levite as a member of a tribe, but only as one who was " attached " to the service of a sanctuary. If Samuel was a Levite, then it was in this way that he came to be reckoned as such (1 Chron. 6²⁸), since the early evidence is that he was an Ephraimite by birth (1 Sam. 1¹). The same must be true of Obed-edom (1 Chron. 16⁴ᶠ·), for according to 2 Sam. 6¹⁰ᶠ· he was a Gittite, and therefore no Hebrew at all.

Towards the end of the time of the judges, we find the House of Eli established at Shiloh as priestly guardians of the Ark. The tradition is that they were chosen in Egypt (1 Sam. 2²⁷ᶠ·), and their priesthood is regarded as being fully legitimate. When the Ark was captured by the Philistines, it is probable that Shiloh was destroyed, and that the priests migrated to Nob, carrying with them the ephod. These priests were massacred at the command of Saul, Abiathar being the sole survivor. He joined David, and shared with

him as his priest all his varying fortunes. At Jerusalem we
find associated with him another priest named Zadok, whose
descent is not stated, though later (1 Chron. 6⁸· ⁵⁰⁻⁵³) he is
regarded as being descended from Eleazar, son of Aaron,
through Phinehas. Both Abiathar and Zadok are faithful
to David during the abortive rebellion of Absalom, but later
Abiathar supports Adonijah and Zadok adheres to Solomon.
Zadok therefore becomes Solomon's priest at Jerusalem, and
the sons of Zadok continue as priests so long as any Temple
stands. It is often pointed out that there were other priests
in the time of David, apart from Abiathar and Zadok. This
is true, for David's sons are named as priests in the earlier
list of David's officials (2 Sam. 8¹⁸ R.V., but not A.V., which
follows the "corrected" 1 Chron. 18¹⁷), and their place is
taken in the second list by Ira, a Manassite of the clan of
Jair (2 Sam. 20²⁶). Again, even after the Temple has been
built, a son of Nathan is described as priest (1 Kings 4⁵).
It has not always been noticed that these other names appear
always separately from the names of Abiathar and Zadok,
though in the same lists. The inference is that the priesthood
of these others is in some way different from that of Abiathar
and Zadok. The priesthood is settling into families, and
heredity is becoming the deciding factor. Solomon established Zadok in the new Temple at Jerusalem and there the
sons of Zadok remain, though there is no early evidence that
Zadok was a Levite. Similarly, Jeroboam appointed non-
Levitical priests in the North, so the writers of the Books of
the Kings alleged (1 Kings 12³¹), counting it to him for wickedness. There is no evidence that, even if he did, he was doing
anything improper according to the ideas of the time. Certainly in the early legislation there was no such restriction
(Ex. 20³³–23¹⁹, 34¹⁰⁻²⁸), and even if it be simply an omission
in these passages, neither Amos nor Hosea have anything
to say against the legitimacy of the Northern priests, however much they may say against them on other grounds.
Apart from the Zadokites, the Southern priests seem to have
been Levites. The claim that the Northern priests were
non-Levitical receives some colour from the fact that, according to one tradition, the Levites were called to the priesthood
as champions against the worship of the golden calf (Ex. 32).
That there is an association between the golden calf and the
bull images of Bethel and Dan is seen by the common cry,
"These be thy gods, O Israel, which brought thee up out
of the land of Egypt" (Ex. 32⁴ ; 1 Kings 12²⁸). The position
of Aaron is most curious. He is the priest of the golden calf

(Ex. 32^5), and in E is never represented as coming near the Tent of Meeting except to be condemned (Num. 12$^{4ff.}$). His name nowhere seems to be original in J. How, then, did the post-exilic priests come to be called the sons of Aaron? Aaron's record in the earliest traditions does not entitle him to any high eminence in the service of Jehovah. The problem is unsolved. It is probable that in the time of the two kingdoms the Levites were at the Southern shrines, non-Levites at the Northern shrines, the sons of Zadok at Jerusalem, and the sons of Moses at Dan. This is supported, so far as the high-places generally are concerned, by 2 Kings 23$^{20.}$ ^{8}, where Josiah is said to have slain all the Northern priests, but to have intended to bring the faithful Southern priests up to Jerusalem. Were the sons of Aaron at Bethel, as Kennett and Driver suggested?

Ultimately all Levites are priests, and all priests are Levites. This is the position in the Book of Deuteronomy, where the reiterated phrase is " the priests, the Levites." When, however, Josiah sought to establish the country Levites on equal terms with the city Zadokites, he failed (Deut. 18$^{6-8}$; 2 Kings 23^9). As we might expect, the innovation was not welcomed by the priests in possession. The Zadokites were willing enough to support the new reforms in so far as Jerusalem was to be the One Sanctuary, but their enthusiasm did not extend to sharing the new benefits thus accruing with the newcomers from the country. The legislation failed, therefore, in so far as it had reference to the provision to be made for the Levites, and this problem of the now unemployed Levite had not been solved when Temple and priests alike were swept away by the Babylonians. It is probable that the country Levites were against the reforms from the start. Such a situation would account for the attitude of Jeremiah's relations, and their enmity against him (Jer. 11$^{18-23}$), if, as some believe and as indeed seems most probable, he at first supported the Deuteronomic reforms (Jer. 11$^{1-10}$), only to find out later what exactly was the attitude of the Jerusalem priests (Jer. 8^8). Jeremiah was " of the priests that were in Anathoth " (Jer. 1^1), and it has been suggested, on the basis of his references to Shiloh (7, 26) and his lamentation over the Ephraimite hill country (31$^{15-20}$), that this family was descended from the ancient House of Eli, dispossessed by the Zadokites (1 Kings 2$^{26f.}$).

The next step in the development of the priestly caste is the attempt in the Book of Ezekiel (44) to solve the Levite problem. Here the writer (almost certainly not the Ezekiel

of the major portion of the book) seeks to justify the position
as it was before 586 B.C. He throws the whole blame for
the idolatrous high-places on the Levites, and allocates to
them by way of punishment certain menial duties in the
proposed new Temple. Here, incidentally, is clear testimony
that it was an innovation for the Levites to be anything less
than fully qualified priests. The solution has the additional
advantage of removing what the writer has always considered
an abomination, for hitherto these duties had been discharged by non-Jews (44⁴⁻¹⁴). He confirms the Zadokites
as the only legitimate priests (44¹⁵ff·). Admirable as this
suggestion was from the Zadokite point of view, it can scarcely
have materialized, for we find no distinction in Malachi
between priest and Levite (2⁴, 3³). The distinction is not
shown in Lev. 17–26 (H), nor is it clear even in Ezek. 40 to
end, for the priests of 40⁴⁵ seem to be the Levites of 44¹¹· ¹⁴.
It becomes clear only in the Priestly Code itself, where Levites
are definitely forbidden to be priests (Num. 18²⁻⁷), and only
Aaron and his sons are fully consecrated (Lev. 8). This
is the situation during the last centuries of the Second
Temple.

The strange thing, however, in the Priestly Code is that
the priesthood is reckoned as Aaronite and not Zadokite, as
we would expect, especially since actually it is predominantly
Zadokite. In this final organization of the priesthood, there
were twenty-four courses, of whom sixteen were Zadokite,
their descent being reckoned from Eleazar, father of Phinehas,
and eight descended from Ithamar, *i.e.* Aaronic. The prior
claims of the Zadokites seem to be established by the story
of Num. 25¹⁰⁻¹⁵, but that makes it all the more strange that
in the Priestly Code the phrase should be " the priests, the
sons of Aaron." Kennett's suggestion (*Cambridge Essays*,
p. 102) is the most plausible. When the Zadokite priests
were carried into exile, other priests migrated to Jerusalem
(still a shrine, Jer. 41⁵). These were chiefly from the royal
sanctuary of Bethel, and possibly were Aaronites. When,
therefore, the Zadokites returned, they had to come to terms
with the priests in possession. That, at any rate, would be
a just retribution for what had happened in Josiah's time,
and it is in the highest degree probable that some non-
Zadokites, who would be true Levites, would take advantage
of the misfortunes of the Jerusalem priesthood. It is very
unlikely that the Levite problem was settled without difficulty, and the Zadokites may very well have been forced to
make this concession. The suggestion has been made that

Zech. 3 is the story of an attempt to oust Joshua from the high-priesthood during the troublous early post-exilic days.

The Levites were now definitely excluded from the priest-hood, which was confined to Aaronites and Zadokites. In the last days of the Temple, in the time of Herod Agrippa II (A.D. 50), such Levites as were singers regained a semblance of their former glory when they were permitted to wear the white robes of the priesthood (Jos. *Ant*. xx. 9, 6).

There were still, however, some changes to be made among the Levites. In Ezra 2⁴¹ the Temple-singers are distinguished from the Levites, and this is true generally of the older parts of Ezra-Nehemiah (end of the fifth century). In the fourth century, however, in the time of the Chronicler, we find that the temple-singers are reckoned as Levites, and their descent is traced from Asaph, Heman, and Ethan, contemporaries of David, who is said to have instituted the whole system of Levitical choirs exactly as it existed in the Chronicler's day (1 Chron. 16⁴⁻⁷). Actually these temple-singers had originally been temple prophets (cf. 2 Kings 23² and 2 Chron. 34³⁰; *Expository Times*, April 1936, p. 317, in a very important article by A. R. Johnson under the title " The Prophet in Israelite Worship "). Finally the term Levite came to include even non-Jews. We have seen that the Philistine Obed-edom becomes a Levite in the end (p. 421). So also did the temple slaves, whose existence had been an offence to the writer of Ezek. 44. There were originally two classes of these slaves, the Nethinim and the Children of the Servants of Solomon. The Nethinim were originally captives in war (Num. 31²⁸⁻³⁰), " given " to the Levites as tribute from the men of war. The custom may have begun with the Gibeonites, " hewers of wood and drawers of water " (Josh. 9²³·²⁷). In Neh. 10²⁸, these slaves are reckoned as Israelites, though still separate from the Levites, as also still were the porters and singers. Both here and in Ezra 2⁵⁸, Neh. 7⁶⁰, the Children of Solomon's Servants are reckoned with the Nethinim, though not in Neh. 11³. According to the Mishnah (*Yeb*. ii. 4; *Kidd*. iv. 1), the Nethinim are classed as foreigners, and inter-marriage with them is forbidden, but this is flatly contra-dictory to Neh. 10²⁹ᶠᶠ·, where the Nethinim are among those Israelites who are forbidden to intermarry with the heathen. It is probable that ultimately all Temple servants of what-ever grade became classed as Levites, so that the word came at last to be the cult-term used to decribe all the inferior members of the priestly hierarchy.

After the Exile, when there had ceased to be a king in

Israel, we find the priests, especially the high-priest, assuming
greater and still greater power. In the days of the kingdoms
the king had been supreme. Ahaz (2 Kings 16¹⁰) saw a new
style of altar at Damascus, and commanded his priest at
Jerusalem to build a copy of it against his return. Josiah
set the pace even in the case of Hilkiah the king-maker
(2 Kings 22³ᶠᶠ·). In the late sixth century, Haggai appealed
to both prince and priest (1¹· ¹⁴, 2²), there being then no
king, but only a governor appointed by his Persian overlord.
The prince has the first place, but the two olive trees stand
one each side of the golden candlestick (Zech 4²ᶠ·). In the
end the priest obtains the crown. In Hag. 1¹, for the first
time we find the phrase high-priest (*hakkohen haggadol*),
though there must always have been a chief of the priests,
as we find in 2 Kings 12⁸· ¹⁰ (EVV, 12⁷· ⁹), and in the commanding position held by Hilkiah, Jehoiada, and many
another. There was a second priest also (2 Kings 25¹⁸), and
already also " elders of the priests " (2 Kings 19²). Here,
or possibly in Jer. 29¹ and Ezek. 8¹, we have the seed of the
later growth which developed into the Sanhedrin and the
tradition of the Great Synagogue. The days of the Second
Temple mark the time of the ever-increasing power of the
high-priest, until he becomes virtually, and in some cases
officially also, civic as well as religious leader. In H he
has special sanctity, though still he is one with his brethren
(Lev. 21¹⁰⁻¹⁵), but in P he is separate in sanctity and dignity
(Lev. 4³, etc.). It is in the highest degree probable that
the chief reason for Nehemiah's failure to establish his policy
of exclusiveness was because Eliashib the priest was associated, through his son-in-law, with the opposition, and certainly
the friendship of Jehohanan, the high-priest who in 401 B.C.
had murdered his brother in the Temple, was a major factor
in Ezra's success. (We take Nehemiah's first governorship
to have commenced in *c.* 445 B.C., and Ezra's arrival to have
been 397 B.C.) For the succeeding years direct evidence
is most meagre, but when the scene once more becomes clear
we find a sorry story of intrigue and treachery. The high-
priesthood, now a position of great power and profit, has
become the aim of worldly and unscrupulous men. Jesus,
or Jason as he called himself in the Greek style, buys the
office for a four hundred talent increase in the tribute. Young
priests become expert in throwing the discus and in all the
games of Greece ; circumcision is held to be unseemly, and,
to crown all, Jason sends three hundred silver drachmæ for
the sacrifices of Herakles-Melkart of Tyre. Menelaus, in

171 B.C., outbids Jason, but the latter seizes the Temple on rumours of the death of Antiochus IV (Epiphanes) in Egypt. This is the last straw, and Antiochus, very much alive, determines once and for all to have done with this religion of continual ferment. This leads to the rise of the Maccabees, and in their time the high-priesthood regains its former glory, though always the high-priest is both religious leader and civic head. The greatest of all the post-exilic princely priests was the Simon son of Onias of whom Ben Sirach (50 [1-21]) writes in most fulsome praise. This is probably Simon II (c. 225–200 B.C.; see Oesterley, *Introduction to the Books of the Apocrypha*, pp. 225 f.). In this chapter concerning Simon the Just the double office, civic and religious, is most clearly shown. John Hyrcanus (135–106 B.C.), son of the last of the five Maccabæan brothers, rivalled Onias in splendour, but he was politician first and priest second.

Intrigue or no intrigue, worldly or other-worldly, the devotion to the Temple of the priests in these latter days knew no bounds. They may have been " blinded—by professional prejudices—by homage to tradition, and by the curiously close and rigorous logic of their scribes " (G. A. Smith, *Jerusalem*, ii. 578), but they stand out as zealous, devoted, and brave. They fought for the Temple to the very last, resisting all change which might damage the Law, forming themselves into the most desperate of soldiery, and at the end stood calmly in their places, priests and Levites alike, continuing the Service of the Altar, until they were cut down by the inrushing victorious heathen hordes.

2. PRIESTHOOD AND TORAH

According to Num. 18[3] (P) the function of the priest was the care of the vessels of the Sanctuary and the Service of the Altar. This is the impression left from a general reading of the Old Testament. Once more, as in the constitution of the priestly caste, we have a development from a very different state of affairs. In P a clear distinction is made between the duties of priest and Levite (Num. 18[2-7]), but in D, as we would expect, all levitical functions are priestly functions also, and no differences are laid down (Deut. 10[8], 21[5]). In Deut. 10[8] the priestly duties are defined as "to bear the ark of the covenant of Jehovah, to stand before Jehovah to minister to him, and to bless in his name." The first passed with the loss of the Ark, and its place was taken by the service of the vessels of the Sanctuary. The last two are the definitely priestly functions, the one as representative of the people before God, and the other as representing God before the people. For the former, as the Chronicler puts it, " it appertaineth not unto thee, Uzziah, to burn incense unto Jehovah, but to the priests the sons of Aaron who are consecrated to burn incense " (2 Chron. 26¹⁸) ; and for the latter, the priestly blessing is that with which the sons of Aaron are commanded to bless the people (Num. 6²⁴⁻²⁷, P).

The priest, therefore, is representative in a double capacity, God before the people, and the people before God. Januslike, he faces two ways. The essential fact is that he is associated with a shrine. In pre-Deuteronomic days, when there were high-places and shrines throughout the country, no priest was required for a simple altar, nor even for a high-place. Wellhausen (*Prolegomena to History of Israel*, E.T., p. 134) makes a distinction between a high-place (*bamah*) and a "house of a high-place " (*bet bamah*) 1 Kings 12³¹. It was for the service of the latter that Jeroboam son of Nebat " made priests from among the people." A high-place was a hill where there was a simple altar, the sort of altar presumably raised by both parties on Mount Carmel, 1 Kings 18²⁶⁻³². On the other hand, a bamah-house was a shrine containing an image, and here a priest was necessary as the guardian of sacred things. He would be there partly as protector, since the tradition of the Tent of Meeting (Ex. 33⁷) doubtless reflects the idea that a holy place ought to be in an outside, open, separated place, but certainly there in order to ensure that the god was approached in the proper way, according to the god's own particular "manner" (*mishpaṭ*). This function of the priest is clear from 2 Kings 17²⁴⁻²⁸. The settlers imported by the Assyrians are slain by lions, because, it is explained, " they know not the mishpaṭ of the God of the land." One of the priests is therefore brought back in order to teach (*moreh*) them how they should worship God. Knowing, then, the proper way in which men should approach God, it is through the priest that men will enquire of Him. The priest, therefore, is the interpreter of God to men. Through him God speaks to those who enquire of Him. God certainly speaks through the prophets also, the difference being, in the first place, that the priest is definitely tied to the shrine, whilst the prophet is not necessarily so limited, and in the second place, that the priest receives his message through the oracle and the prophet in an ecstasy. Since the priest was necessarily associated with the shrine, the tendency naturally developed that, whilst the priest and the prophet were by no means

always at enmity as has in time past been supposed, the priest,
and with him the cult-prophet, would become the conserver
of established tradition, and the prophet the free-lance and
general innovator.

The priest is the mouth of the God who is worshipped at
the shrine.   This is seen very clearly, and all the more
certainly because the inference is obviously unpremeditated,
in Ex. 4[15f.] (J).   Moses once more protests that he is too slow
of speech to speak for God to the people.   Whereupon
Jehovah answers, " I will teach (*wehoreti*) you . . . and he
shall be to thee a mouth, and thou shalt be to him as God."
Aaron, that is, is to act as priest to Moses, in that he is to
speak to the people the words which Moses puts into his
mouth.   This is a primary function of the priest.   When
Moses had pitched the Tent of Meeting without the camp,
the visits made to it were always for the purpose of receiving
an oracle.   God spake through Moses particularly, though
Joshua was always there (Ex. 33[7-11]).

Inasmuch as the priest teaches (*yarah*) the ways of God
to men, the words he speaks are teachings (*toroth*).   Each
oracle is a teaching (*torah*).   Since the priest knew the Torah
of Jehovah, the people came to him.   One of the complaints
of Hosea (5[5f.]) against the priests of his day, and the cult
prophets with them, was that, stumbling by day and by
night, they had forgotten the Torah of their God, so that
His people were destroyed for lack of knowledge.   If the
priest had forgotten, how could the people ever learn ?
According to Micah also, the great function of the priests is
to teach.   The heads in Jerusalem may judge, the prophets
divine, but the priests are the teachers (3[11]).   His charge is
that they teach for hire, and give no true oracle from Jehovah.
According to Deut. 33[10] the Levitical (*i.e.* priestly) function
is "they shall teach Jacob thy judgements (*mishpatim*) and
Israel thy law (*torah*)."   The teaching function of the priest
therefore falls into two divisions, Torah and Mishpat.   The
Torah is the revealed and declared will of Jehovah.   Mishpat
is the precedent for all cases similar to that for which the
will of Jehovah was first revealed.   Mishpat refers more
particularly to that which custom and experience decree that
men must do.   It is a rule of action in general, and so can be
used for the right practice of religion, Isa. 42[1] (judgement),
much in the same way as the Arabic *din*.   In this way the
priest is also judge (*shophet*, from the same root as *mishpat*),
for he can give judgement according to mishpat (righteousness, judgement, precedent).

Originally the priest found out the will of the God by a process indistinguishable from divination, by rods (Hos. 4¹²), or by arrows (Ezek. 21²¹), in whatever way they were manipulated. The chief method was the Urim and Thummim, the furniture of the sacred lot (Deut. 33⁸), the care and use of which was the distinction and privilege of the priest in every age (Ezra 2⁶³; Neh. 7⁶⁵). According to Jerome, Urim signified Guilt, and Thummim Acquittal, the words being derived from 'arar (curse) and tamam (perfect). Evidently the will of Jehovah was determined by a series of questions so framed as to involve by way of answer the plain alternative of Yes or No. Sometimes it was a lengthy process, and once Saul (1 Sam. 14¹⁹) had to dispense with it because of the immediacy of the battle. The casting of the sacred lot is probably to be identified with the custom of divination by use of the ephod. This image could not have been heavy, since when Abiathar barely escaped with his life, sole survivor from the massacre at Nob, he managed to carry the ephod with him (1 Sam. 23⁶), and again and again David commanded him to " bring hither the ephod," when he needed divine guidance. Later, Urim and Thummim were two stones which fitted into pockets of the high-priest's breast-plate (Ex. 28³⁰; Lev. 8⁸; P).

But the priest also represented the people before God. They came to the shrine with their offerings. The priest's duty was to see that all was done decently and in order (1 Sam. 1⁹⁻¹³), and that the God was approached in the proper way. He had a specified portion of the offering as his portion. At Shiloh, for instance, there was a well-known mishpaṭ (custom), and we read of great indignation when the sons of Eli attempted to vary it to their own advantage (1 Sam. 2¹²⁻¹⁷). But the priest was never the actual slaughterer of the animals offered for sacrifice. The worshipper did his own slaughtering (1 Sam. 1⁴); the title of the captain of the royal guard is rab ṭabaḥim, chief of slaughterers, and at Sinai the " young men of the children of Israel " (Ex. 24⁵) killed the animals. In the days of the Second Temple, every worshipper killed his own offering (Lev. 1⁵·¹¹, 2²·¹³, etc.), the only time when the priest killed the animal being when he himself was making the offering on his own behalf, Lev. 4²⁹, etc. His part is the actual ceremony, dedicating the gift, or burning the incense, ensuring that men do the right things. All this is in his capacity of representative of the people before God. At the same time, because he knows how things should be done, he can interpret the will of God to man. This he does through the oracle, and here is the difference between the priest of the shrine and the prophet at the shrine. Both speak the Torah of God, the priest through the oracle, and the cult-prophet through an ecstasy. In this respect the Hebrew counterpart to the Arabic *kahin* (soothsayer) is not so much the priest (*kohen*) as the cult-prophet.

We have seen that the giving of a Torah by word of mouth was the function of the priest equally with the ordering of the sacrifices (Deut. 33^{10}). Gradually things changed. It was not that the priest ceased to give Toroth, or that others ordered the sacrifices. Rather it was a matter of emphasis. At one time it was legitimate for a king (David, 2 Sam. 6^{17}; Solomon, 1 Kings 3^4) or for a prophet (Elijah, 1 Kings 18) to offer sacrifice. Later, these duties belong to the priests alone, and not even the king may infringe the priest's prerogative (2 Chron. 26^{18}). Gradually, also, the cultus assumes a greater importance, and there are many tirades of the prophets against sacrifice as a substitute for religion. This involves the prophets from the eighth century onwards in attacks on the whole sacrificial system. Because of these attacks, the general idea is that the prophets were against sacrifice as such, and that there was a great gap between prophets and priest. The gulf is more imaginary than real (see A. C. Welch, *Prophet and Priest in Old Israel*), and the confusion arises from the failure to realize that the priest is not primarily a sacrificing official, but the giver of Torah and the guardian of Mishpaṭ. The complaint of the prophets was against a change of emphasis. Perhaps the shrines had retained or adopted idolatrous Canaanite cults, but the prophets were certain that instruction (Torah) in the will of God, and the doing of it, is of far more account than tens of thousands of rivers of oil (Mic. 6$^{6-8}$). Amos (5^{25}) and Jeremiah (7^{22}), therefore, do not deprecate sacrifice as sacrifice, but only as a substitute for true religion. The priest should first fulfil his original and true function, and then the people would not perish ignorantly. The priests are the teachers, Isa, 30$^{20f.}$, the men who say "this is the way, walk ye in it." It is not true to say there was no sacrifice in the desert, for in those days every slaughter was a sacrifice. Jeremiah wants the priests to get back to the old ways, with the sacrifices viewed in their proper perspective. Possibly this is why he first supported the Deuteronomic reforms, but withdrew the moment he found that the priests were thinking more of the sacrificial system and its dues than of their ancient privilege of teaching the Torah of Jehovah. With the restoration of worship after the Exile, the priests obtain greater and still greater power. They become the sole repositories of the ancient traditions. At the same time the sacrificial system develops amazingly. Already in the time of Ezra, we have the beginning of what in later days was an outstanding feature of Jewish life. When Ezra reads the Law to the people, they do not understand, so that the Levites have to act as interpreters of the Law, Neh. 8[7]. From this time onwards the priests more and more are sacrificing officials, and the teaching is done by others. Here we have the beginning of the Targums and of the office of the scribe.

The divorce of the priests from their original function of teaching and handling the Torah (Jer. 2[8], 18[18] ; Ezek. 7[26]) comes with the rise of written tradition. So long as tradition was mainly oral, and every decision came from the very mouth of the priest, the old ways prevailed, and the priests declared the Law just as Moses himself had declared it beyond Jordan. In the time of Haggai (2[10-19]) the priests are still asked for a *torah*, that is for a direction from God on a point where no previous *torah* applied. It was over a matter of cleanness and uncleanness, whether both are contagious. L. E. Browne (*Early Judaism*, pp. 109–112) holds that the priests here gave a deliberately false *torah* in order to exclude the Samaritans, and that it conflicts with Lev. 6[20f.] (EVV, 6[27f.]). That sometimes the priest did give a false *torah* is seen in Zeph. 3[4]. As soon as the Torah was written down, specialists in the study of the sacred Word must necessarily have arisen. The beginning came with the writing down of the ancient traditions in J and E. The origin of these traditions was almost certainly the ancient shrines. They contain stories of the experiences of the patriarchs at Shechem, Gilgal, Hebron, Bethel, and the rest, and doubtless were the actual stories which the priests told to the worshippers who visited the shrine. Parts of the earliest codes probably go back to Moses (Ex. 20[23]–23[19], the Book of the Covenant ; the Ten Words in Ex. 34, J ; and the Ten Commandments in Ex. 20, E), but it is difficult to say how much as they now stand. Later we find the codification as developed in Deuteronomy, in connexion with which the phrase " the Book of the Law " first appears (2 Kings 22[8]), and so, through the proposals of Ezek. 40–48 and the Code of Holiness (Lev. 17–26, mostly), to the. finally developed Priestly Code. From those days the Jews became the people of a Book, and that book the written Torah, that is, the Pentateuch. This written Torah marks the difference between the old Israel of pre-exilic days and the Judaism of post-exilic days. Torah now, generally speaking, no longer meant oral instruction from the priest. It referred to the written and authoritative word, which first the priest, then the Levite, and ultimately the scribe alone was qualified to interpret. There still remained a certain amount of tradition outside the written Torah, and there seems to have been a reluctance to codify this until the time of the Mishnah and later. In the last days, the interpretation of the Torah by the scribes, the enforcement by the priests of the rules of clean and unclean, made the Torah the guide of daily life ; and the priest became the master, with the increase of all the demands and penalties this engendered and all the innumerable regulations which careful custom and pious devotion evolved.

There was, however, a survival of the use of the word *torah* with the meaning of " instruction." This was due to the wise men of Israel with their insistence on " instruction " (*torah*) and " understanding " (*binah*). It comprised the wisdom of the wise, Prov. 3^{1-10}. It stands for that general ethical and moral instruction which was the product, to a large extent, of independent thinking. It marks the beginning of Hebrew philosophizing. This is something quite apart from what any priest could give as priest, and has little to do with the Torah of Moses, except in so far as every honest searcher after knowledge must necessarily proceed along lines that are not contrary, and must be nearing the one ultimate goal.

There remains one further effect of the change of emphasis in the function of the priest. Ceasing, to some extent at least, to be mediator between God and man, he became increasingly mediator between man and God, particularly when in Hebrew thought the idea of the transcendence of Jehovah became increasingly emphasized. With the growth of that Church-state which was Judaism, the high-priest more and more stands before God on behalf of the people. This is typified supremely on the Day of Atonement, when he made atonement for himself and for the whole people, himself slaughtering the goat of the sin-offering (Lev. $16^{11. 15}$), and later himself alone entering the Holy Place (Lev. 16^{17}), there to speak the Ineffable Name, bearing on his breastplate the names of the sons of Israel, " for a memorial before Jehovah continually " (Ex. 28^{29}). This means, for the development of Christian theology, that the roots of vicarious sacrifice are in the ritual of the Second Temple as well as in such passages as Isa. 52^{13}–53^{12}.

3. The Temple and its Ritual

The earliest stage discernible in the history of Hebrew worship belongs to the time when the Hebrews, in religious ideas, natural characteristics, and general culture were indistinguishable from other Semite peoples. Their religion was animistic, and we find in the records numerous traces of these beliefs ·of far-off days. The patriarchs receive oracles at sacred trees (*e.g.* Gen. 12[6ff.], 21[33], 35[8]). Presumably in. yet more ancient times, the inquirer sought the dæmon who lived in the tree, and back of that is the belief that the tree had power and will of its own. Not only was there the sacred tree, but also the sacred stone (*maṣṣebah*), unhewn (Ex. 20[25]), because originally it was regarded as the home of the spirit, and the sacred well (Beersheba, Gen. 21[22ff.]) or spring (En-mishpaṭ, which is Ḳadesh, Gen. 14[7]).

There was sacrifice in the earliest times, called *zebaḥ* (lit. slaughter). The blood was poured out at the base of, or over the sacred stone, and the worshipper ate the flesh. In this way the offering was shared by god and worshipper. It was a common meal, a "communion." Robertson Smith (*Religion of the Semites*) held that this was the primary idea of sacrifice, and that the idea of a gift was later, a development from this first idea. Gray (*Sacrifice in the Old Testament*, pp. 1 ff.) points out that, equally from early times, there are traces of a gift-sacrifice (*minḥah*). Cain and Abel bring their firstlings and first-fruits to Jehovah, each as a *minḥah* (Gen. 4[2-4]). The word means "present," "tribute," and is used in a general way for presents to men and tribute to kings, as well as in this particular sense of an offering to Jehovah.

With the advent of Moses we pass from a religion of many sacred places and (probably) many dæmons (Elim) to that of the Ark, the one abode of Jehovah, Himself the one God of the Hebrews. The Ark moved from place to place, and Jehovah with it, at first with the Hebrews in all their Wanderings or sheltered in a tent at Ḳadesh during their long sojourn there, and at last housed in a shrine at Shiloh. When the Philistines captured the Ark, then the Glory (*i.e.* the Presence of Jehovah) had departed from Israel (1 Sam. 4[22]). There seem to have been images of Jehovah in use (ephods in the time of the judges at Ophrah and at Shiloh). There were various cult objects, the Brazen-serpent, Neḥushtan, which Moses had lifted up in the Wilderness, the rod of Moses, which, it has been suggested, some identified with Jehovah, and the

tables of stone, but these gradually disappeared for one reason
or another, until at last quite definitely the worship was
imageless.

When the Hebrews entered Canaan they found there a
form of Nature worship, that of the Baals and the Astartes,
these being the generic names for the local deities, male and
female. Each deity had also a personal name, Baal-hermon,
Baal-peor, or Astarte-karnaim (Astarte of the two horns, of
whom figurines have been found during excavations). The
Hebrews found sanctuaries " upon the hills and under every
green tree," altars, sacred stones, sacred wooden poles, groves
(Deut. 12$^{2, 3}$), all the objects and institutions of a cult in
which sacred prostitution played an important part. Some
of these sanctuaries were taken over by the Hebrews, such
as Gilgal, Shechem, and Hebron. Doubtless at Shiloh a
tolerably pure form of Jehovah worship was observed, with
sacrifices, feasts, and the elements of a developing ritual.
Other shrines remained Canaanite, with all those observances
against which the prophets ceaselessly thundered. At some
shrines undoubtedly Jehovah was identified with the local
Baal, and was worshipped in association with the Astarte.
The Ras Shamra tablets (found recently in North Syria, and
dating from c. 1400 B.C.) give a picture of Canaanite worship
before the Settlement of the Hebrew tribes in Canaan. Here
we have a complete polytheism, and it is probable that something of the same type of religion existed in Palestine during
the time of the kingdoms. Such a situation is suggested by
the warfare of Elijah and his successors against the House
of Omri. Elijah not only fought against the worship of the
Baal of Tyre in conjunction with Jehovah, but also against
any recognition of Baal-zebub, god of Ekron, as the giver
of life. This name is known from the Ras Shamra tablets
to be Baal-zebul, and is the name of the high god Aleyn as
god of the underworld whence come the life-giving streams.
This means that not only was there syncretism in the worship,
but also polytheism in the religion.

It was a great step forward when Solomon built the Temple,
for this shrine, being the royal shrine, increased in splendour
and importance with the passing of the years. It contained
many characteristics of heathen Temples, and in the days of
such idolatrous kings as Ahaz and Manasseh was the scene
of many abominations. With the collapse of the Northern
Kingdom, Jerusalem remained without a rival, especially
when after the Exile the centralizing reforms were at last
carried out. The Second Temple became the One Sanctuary

of which the Deuteronomists had dreamed (if, as most scholars still maintain, the centralization was part of the original Deuteronomic programme). The Samaritans objected, but for the Jew the statement of John 4[20] held good.

We have seen that the earliest sacrifices consisted of the *zebah* and the *minhah*. The first was any slaughter, the flesh of the animal being eaten by the worshipper and priest, and the blood being offered to the Deity, poured out at the sacred stone, or on any stone in case of need (1 Sam. 14[32-35]), which forthwith became an altar (*mizbeah*, lit. " place of slaughter "). The second was a gift to the Deity. With the entrance into Palestine, the Hebrews were introduced to a new life, agricultural instead of pastoral. This meant a difference in the material of sacrifice. *Minhah* now comes to signify an offering of cereals as distinct from animals (note that in Gen. 4[4] the Jehovist is careful not to say that Abel brought a *minhah*, as he says of Cain, though in *v*.[5] he slips back into t   old meaning of the term), and finally the word *korban* takes its place as a general description of sacrifices which are wholly gifts to Jehovah. As the years pass by the ritual becomes more stereotyped, and in Ahaz's time there is a morning *'olah* (EVV, burnt-offering) and an evening *minhah* (EVV, meal-offering), 2 Kings 16[15] (cf. also 1 Kings 18[29]). Certainly at this peri   *'olah* meant an animal wholly offered on the altar, and possibly *minhah* meant a cereal gift, wholly offered. There were atoning sacrifices before the Exile (1 Sam. 3[14]), but these by no means occupied the outstanding place of later times. In Deut. 21[1-9], we have the survival of a primitive purification rite with a substituted victim, but this particular rite has nothing to do with worship proper at a shrine. There is evidence, however, that human victims once formed the material for sacrifice, sporadically through all the years down to the Exile, Ex. 13[13]; Gen. 22[13]; Judg. 11[39]; 1 Sam. 14[45] (?); 2 Kings 16[3], 21[2. 6]; and the frequent tirades of the prophets, chiefly Mic. 6[7].

In the fully developed ritual of the Priestly Code, that is, in the full glory of the Second Temple, the term *'olah* (EVV, burnt-offering) signified an animal sacrifice, the whole of which was burnt on the altar. An equivalent term was *kalil* (EVV, whole burnt-offering), expressing more clearly the exact meaning of *'olah*. When part of the animal only was burnt on the altar, the term was *zebah* (EVV, sacrifice) as before the Exile. We have seen that *korban* was the post-exilic equivalent of the pre-exilic *minhah*. An equivalent term for those gifts, part of which only were consumed on the altar, was *shelamim* (EVV, peace-offerings, or, in the margin, thank-offerings). *Shelamim* was a general term, and was subdivided into three classes, *todah* (EVV, thank-offering), *neder* (EVV, vow), and *nedabah* (EVV, freewill-offering), these being mainly private and voluntary as against public and obligatory. *Kodashim* is a comprehensive term, denoting not any particular form of sacrifice, but sacred gifts and offerings in general. These never reached the altar, but were the perquisite of the priests. The term *'ishsheh* (R.V. an offering made by fire) corresponds most closely to the English word " sacrifice." It refers properly only to that part of the victim which is burned on the altar. According to some authorities, the word meant originally " fellowship-offering," but certainly later ideas bore no relation to this possible early significance of the term.

We have said that *korban* replaced *minḥah* as the term for gifts, but *korban* became ultimately a wider term, and was applied to any property destined, at the time or at some future date, to the service of God. The word is not earlier than Ezekiel, is very frequent in the Priestly Code, and is found in the New Testament, where (Mark 7¹¹) it has its proper significance in that what once has been vowed to Jehovah cannot be alienated from Him, not even under the most pressing demands of family loyalty. The difference between *korbanim* and *kodashim* is seen in the examples given in Num. 18⁸⁻³² and Lev. 1–7; Num. 7, 31. *Korbanim* includes all sorts of offerings, but *kodashim* refers primarily to those parts of offering which are reserved for the use of the priests. They include first-born and first-fruits. The first-fruits included *re'shith* (the first-portion) and *bikkurim* (first-fruits). According to the Mishnah, the *bikkurim* were limited to the first-fruits of wheat, barley, vines, fig-trees, pomegranate, oil, and honey. Other *kodashim* were the *ma'aseroth* (tithes), the *terumoth* (heave-offerings), and the *tenuphoth* (wave-offerings). All these went to the priests. It is difficult to make any distinction between *terumoth* and *tenuphoth*, both refer to the portion of the priest from such offerings as were not wholly consumed on the altar, *terumoth* referring to the fact that it was the part " lifted up," and *tenuphoth* to the ritual " waving " to and fro of the portion. Counted also among the *kodashim* was the offering of bread, the " shew-bread," an ancient custom already established at Nob, and always observed at Jerusalem and probably wherever there was a shrine. The primitive idea was that of setting food and drink before the Deity. With every *minhah*,

29

and with voluntary sacrifices generally, a *nesek* (drink-offering)
was poured out, and frankincense (*lebonah*) was a necessary
accompaniment of every offering except that of a pauper.
Apart from this, at the morning and evening offerings the
ketoreth tamid (perpetual incense) was burned on the altar
of incense.   All these terms are post-exilic terms, so far as
the Old Testament is concerned.   Further knowledge may
prove them to have been known in pre-exilic Israel also, since
many of them are found in the Ras Shamra tablets.   As yet,
however, there is no Israelite pre-exilic evidence.

The most noteworthy development of the post-exilic
period was the ever-increasing importance attached to expiatory
offerings.   There were four terms in frequent use, *ḥaṭṭath*
(sin-offering), *'asham* (trespass-offering), *reaḥ niḥoaḥ* (sweet
savour), and *kippurim* (atonement).   Both *ḥaṭṭath* and *'asham*
referred to payments made for ritual offences.   The latter is
found in the Ras Shamra tablets and also at El-ʻöla with
the general significance of " compensation," this also being
the pre-exilic meaning of the word among the Israelites.
Later, after the Exile, both words become technical terms
for offerings.   Both are means of removal of sin, sometimes
accompanied by a payment in cash, but neither are necessarily
consumed on the altar.   Usually they are burned " without
the camp " (Num. 19³).   *Reaḥ niḥoaḥ* is applied to expiatory
offerings, as that which makes a sweet savour to rise up and
is pleasing to God.   Originally the idea was that the anger
of God was appeased when He smelt the sweet savour (cf.
the sacrifice offered by Uta-napishtim in the Babylonian flood
story), but the later " refined " idea, in Septuagint and Targum,
was that the term referred to the pleasure of Jehovah at the
proper discharge of His service.   The climax of the atoning
sacrifices, and the keystone of the whole sacrificial system,
was the Day of Atonement (*Yom Kippur*), when the high-
priest made atonement for himself and for all the people.
On this day Israel sought of old, and modern Jewry still seeks,
with passionate contrition and abject abasement, to atone
for the sins of the year, and to obtain the pardon and good
favour of the God of their fathers and of all their succeeding
race.

The word *kippurim* is the comprehensive Hebrew term
for atonement.   The verb *kipper* came ultimately to describe
the whole object of Jewish sacrifices, though the expiatory
intent was felt more in some sacrifices than in others.
Primarily the word occurs in connexion with sin-offerings
and guilt-offerings, but it is extended to the burnt-offering,

some peace-offerings, and to many other elements of Jewish ritual. The whole matter is discussed fully in Gray's *Sacrifice in the Old Testament*, pp. 67–81. The reader is referred to that book for fuller details concerning the various types of sacrifice and all matters connected therewith.

We now turn to the matter of the times of sacrifice, and of appointed times and seasons generally.

Every day the "continual daily sacrifice" (*tamid*) was offered, "in the morning and between the two evenings" (Heb. *ben ha'arbaim*), Ex. 29$^{39-41}$; Num. 28^4. At the beginning of the Christian era these times were the third hour (9 a.m.) and the ninth hour (3 p.m.), but there has been endless discussion as to precise limits specified by the phrase "between the two evenings." It was of prime importance because it occurs in the Passover regulations. Each offering consisted of an *'olah* (burnt-offering), accompanied by a *minhah* (meal-offering), and a *nesek* (drink-offering). Meanwhile the incense was burned on the Altar of Incense. There had been libations of water in Old Israel (1 Sam. 7^6; 2 Sam. 23^{16}), but the libation of the Second Temple was of wine, the water-pouring being reserved for the Feast of Tabernacles. The transitional Ezek. 46$^{13-15}$ speaks of an *'olah* and a *minhah*, but both in the morning alone. On the Sabbath there was an additional *'olah*, with its *minhah* and *nesek* (Num. 28$^{9f.}$). There were special sacrifices on the new-month day, and at the feasts (Num. 28$^{11-40}$). The voluntary sacrifices and personal atonement offerings were naturally brought as occasion demanded.

There were in the Jewish Calendar a number of special occasions, "appointed times." The first is the Sabbath. This is of ancient and uncertain origin. Associations have been sought in Babylonian ritual, and there is certainly a close connexion. Among the Hebrews it was associated always with the first day of the month (Isa. 1^{13}). Beyond question it was in origin a lunar festival. In post-exilic days the rules concerning Sabbath observance became more and more rigid. From early times, both new-month days and Sabbaths were days on which particularly individuals went to consult with holy men (2 Kings 4^{23}). Before the Hebrews entered Canaan, they had one great festival in the year, that of Pesah (Passover). It goes back to pre-Mosaic times, but received new meaning with the exodus. To this day the Jew eats the Passover lamb, simulating that same haste with which his fathers hurried from the land of bondage.

When the Hebrews entered Canaan, they adopted the three great Canaanite agricultural feasts, *Massoth* (Unleavened

Bread), *Ḳaṣir* (Wheat Harvest), and *'Asiph* (Ingathering). These were all *haggim* (pilgrimages), when every male had to appear before Jehovah (Ex. 34²³). Passover (at the full moon of Abib) was now immediately followed by Maṣṣoth. This lasted for seven days, and was the festival of the beginning of the barley harvest, when the sickle was put to the standing corn (Deut. 16⁹). Seven weeks were counted from this day to the Feast of Ḳaṣir (wheat-harvest or Weeks), a time of rejoicing and freewill offerings. The greatest of the pre-exilic feasts was 'Asiph (Ingathering), celebrated at the turn of the year, Ex. 23¹⁶ (E), 34²² (J). It was the vintage feast, when all the produce of every kind had been gathered in, and the Hebrew settled down hilariously to enjoy the good gifts which Jehovah had given him. At the same time, there was from the first an element of penitence, as there must always be, among primitive peoples, and indeed cultured peoples also, in any festival which looks both back into the year that has gone and forward on to the year that lies ahead. At times when the harvest had failed, or in the days when the Hebrews nationally met with increasing misfortune, the element of penitent concern would dominate. One of the features of the feast, which we may be sure goes back to earliest days, was the water-pouring. Probably Isa. 12³ is a reference to this. In any case, the "House of Water-pouring" of the last days of the Second Temple, as described in the Mishnah (*Sukkah* iv. 9; see Edersheim, *The Temple and its Services*, pp. 232-249), must be a survival of a primitive sympathetic magic rite to ensure the falling of the rain necessary for the crops of the coming year. The "former rain" was due to fall immediately after the summer drought, so that the importance of good rains would be immediate to the minds of all. Similarly, the great night feast of Tabernacles must have a long history behind it from the very earliest times. Of these Canaanite feasts, two were reinterpreted by the Hebrews. Maṣṣoth was now a memorial of the unleavened cakes which the Hebrews brought with them when they left Egypt, having had no time to add the leaven, and the booths of the vintage feast were no longer the leafy shelters used in the vineyards, but the shelters which the Hebrews had used during the Wanderings.

With the Exile came a change of calendar, and the Hebrews adopted the Babylonian system (originally the calendar of Nippur) in which the year began with the new moon of Nisan (March to April). This was of small account so far as Passover and Massoth were concerned. Passover remained a

full-moon feast and followed the full moon of Abib, which
now fell on the 14th to 15th of Nisan. Ḳaṣir (now Weeks,
and later Pentecost) was reckoned from Maṣṣoth, so no
difficulty arose there. The keeping of the old New Year
feast of 'Asiph was thrown into complete confusion, since
that feast still tended to go with the full-moon. (We hold
that in pre-exilic days the month began with the full-moon.)
This now was the 15th of Tishri. The celebration of the
New Year could not continue to be in the middle of the
seventh month, and after an attempt to make a special
observance of the 1st of Nisan (Ezek. 45[18]), the pre-exilic
end-of-the-year feast was divided into three feasts, Rosh
hashShanah (New Year's Day) on the 1st of Tishri, the Day
of Atonement on the 10th, and the Feast of Tabernacles
(Sukkoth) on the 15th, this being an eight days' feast.
Tishri 1 was a Memorial of Trumpet-blowing. It marked the
opening of the Ten Penitential Days of the year, when every
Jew afflicted himself in tears and sorrow, ending in a climax
of Repentance on the Day of Atonement. The later tradition
was that on Tishri 1, three books were opened in Heaven,
one for Life for the good, one for Death for the wicked, and
one for those who were neither wholly good nor wholly wicked.
Every man's name was written in one of these books, but
on the Day of Atonement those in the third book were transferred to the book for Life or to the book for Death, and
every man's fate for the ensuing year was sealed. This fixing
of the fate for the coming year was an idea always associated
by the Hebrews with the autumnal feast. In this way they
were like all peoples the whole world over. A number of
scholars have seen in this fixing of the fate, and in other
features of these three post-exilic feasts of Tishri, indications
of close associations with the Babylonian festal calendar and
ritual. Mowinckel, following on earlier work by Gressmann
and Volz, has propounded the theory that at the Feast of
Asiph in pre-exilic times, and on New Year's Day in post-
exilic times, Jehovah was installed as King each year with
dramatic representation in the cultus, just as Marduk was
installed in the Babylonian ceremonies. He has allocated a
number of Psalms as the liturgy of this Coronation Feast,
chief among them Pss. 93–99. His views have been received
with considerable favour, especially with the development
of the idea that there was a general myth pattern throughout
the near East (see *Myth and Ritual*, ed. S. H. Hooke). The
weakness of the theory is that there is no direct evidence
that there ever was such a ceremony either before or after the

Exile, and there is still less evidence that any of the Coronation psalms (93–99) were specially connected with any of the Tishri feasts. These psalms, in Jewish liturgy, are Sabbath psalms.

In later times many other festivals were introduced. The Feast of Purim, celebrated on the 14th and 15th of Adar (beginning of March), the deliverance of the Jews as recorded in the Book of Esther (the " roll " which was read at this feast). The Feast of Wood-offering was on the 15th of Ab (August), but the greatest of the post-Mosaic festivals (as these later festivals are called) was the Feast of *Hanukkah* (Dedication of the Temple), or the Feast of Lights, instituted by Judas the Maccabee to commemorate the re-dedication of the Temple after his triumph in 164 B.C. It lasted for eight days from the 25th of Kislew (December), and was in many respects similar to the Feast of Tabernacles. Other Maccabæan feasts were the Day of Nicanor on the 13th of Adar, and the Feast of the Captured Fortress (Akra in Jerusalem, captured by Simon in 142 B.C.) on the 23rd of Iyyar, but this feast, like that of the Reading of the Law and the Feast of Baskets, was of little importance. Numerous fasts were observed in the last days of Jerusalem, but none approached the importance of the Day of Atonement, and the only one worthy of mention was the 9th of Ab, in sorrowful commemoration of the Destruction of the Temple by the Babylonians.

The services of the Temple did not consist only of sacrifices of animals, cereals, wine, and incense. Ben Sirach gives a glowing account (50^{11-21}) of the majesty of the high-priest in his glorious apparel performing the concluding acts of the service. Oesterley (*Jewish Background of the Christian Liturgy*) has shown that much of the Christian liturgy goes back to the days of the Second Temple. Many of the modern Jewish prayers go back to this time, especially portions of the famous Eighteen Benedictions. We know from the Mishnah, confirmed by the Septuagint in every case but two, that certain psalms were allocated to the days of the week, 24 for the first day, 47, 82, 94, 81, 93 for the succeeding days, and 92 for the Sabbath. The psalms were sung in three sections, in the intervals of which two priests blew with their trumpets, after the sacrifice had been offered, when the drink-offering was being poured. As the Rabbis said, " There is no song except over wine." On the Sabbath, at the close of the additional Sabbath sacrifice, the Deuteronomic Song of Moses (32^{1-43}) was sung, divided into six sections for six successive Sabbaths. After the evening Sabbath sacrifice, the Exodus

Song of Moses was sung (15^{1-18}), divided into two portions, with the Song of Israel (Num. $21^{17f.}$) for a third (see the Talmud, b.*R.H.* 31*a*, and j.*Meg.* iii.).

The custom of reading from the Law can be traced back to the days of the Second Temple, soon to be followed by a reading from the Prophets, but these customs belong to the Synagogue rather than to the Temple. Various attempts have been made to establish the fact of a similar Triennial Cycle for the Psalter, by which every psalm was recited in its turn during the Sabbath services. The extraordinary feature is the extreme paucity of the information which the Rabbis have handed down concerning the singing of the psalms in the ritual. The Psalter must have been extensively used, and it is probable that, as we have it now, it was formed expressly for Temple use. It was certainly formed from earlier collections, the two Davidic collections and the two Levitical collections, Asaph and the Sons of Korah, with cross references to the music-master's collection. The latter half of the Psalter, 90–150, is composed of a series of liturgical groups of psalms for the most part. We know that some of these groups were used on special occasions, but the only information we have refers to Sabbaths, Festivals, and the ordinary daily psalms. In what particular way the remainder of the psalms was used remains to be definitely established. The probability is that in the matter of chanting psalms the Christian churches are following the pattern of the Second Temple, as we know them to have done in the matter of many prayers and liturgies.

Whenever they were sung, the psalms were accompanied by instrumental music. There are continual references to the harp and psaltery (lyre), and to the wind instruments, particularly the *shofar* (ram's horn) and the trumpets. An emumeration of the Temple instruments is given in Ps. 150^{3-5}, and tradition has it that there was a pipe-organ (*magrephah*) in Herod's Temple, but details vary as to its size and efficiency.

BIBLIOGRAPHY

Gray, G. B., *Sacrifice in the Old Testament* (1925).
Edersheim, A., *The Temple, its Ministry and Services* (1874).
Oesterley, W. O. E., *The Psalms in the Jewish Church* (1910).
Oesterley, W. O. E., *The Jewish Background of the Christian Liturgy* (1925).
Oesterley, W. O. E., *Sacrifices in Ancient Israel* (1937).
Welch, A. C., *Prophet and Priest in Old Israel* (1936).
Smith, W. Robertson, *Religion of the Semites* (3rd edition, 1927).

XVII. THE SCRIBES AND THE LAW

THE advent of Ezra from Babylon to Palestine in the year 458 B.C. [or 398 (see above, p. 259)], marks a turning point of the highest significance in the religious history of Israel, since it was due to his activity that the Torah became the rule of life and the guide of conduct for future generations. Ezra is called " a ready scribe in the Law of Moses " (Ezra 7[6]), and it is almost certain that the name of *soferim* or scribes applied to the expounders and interpreters of the Law during the period between Ezra and the Mishnah, when the Oral Law was codified and its development to a certain extent arrested, means neither more nor less than " the spiritual successors of ' the Sofer ' *par excellence*," that is Ezra, and that they were regarded as carrying on his epoch-making work. It means more than a writer of sacred books, and even the Talmudic explanation of the term, that they were so-called " because they counted (*sofrim*) all the letters of the Torah " (*Kiddushin*, 30a) is merely an indication of one aspect of their activity, the meticulous care which they took in preserving Holy Writ, and in certain cases amending the text (*Tikkune Soferim*, the emendations of the Scribes) to avoid anthropomorphisms or other doubtful expressions.

It ought to be made clear at the outset that there is a slight distinction between the use of the word in the New Testament and its Hebrew equivalent in the Talmud. The latter ascribes the name to the exponents of the law of a bygone age which preceded that of the Tannaim, although " the words of the Scribes " is used to denote the Oral Law as a whole (cf. Mishnah, *Sanhedrin*, xi. 3), while the New Testament uses it as applicable to the doctors of the Law of its own period, and it is this latter which is treated of here.

It is, in fact, in the activity of Ezra that we see the germ of the idea which it was the life-work of the Scribes to bring to fruition. That activity is summed up in two verses (1) that " Ezra had set his heart to expound the law of the Lord, and to do it, and to teach in Israel statutes and judgements " (Ezra 7[10]), and (2) " So they read in the book in the law of

God distinctly, and gave the sense, and caused them to understand the reading " (Neh. 8⁸).

In other words, there were two fundamental tasks to be
undertaken if the Torah was to retain its place for ever in the
hearts of Israel, and if it was to be prevented from rapidly
becoming an archaic and obsolete record of the past, becoming
more and more out of touch with the demands of life. The
first was that it had to become the possession of all Israel,
not of one section, whether priests or teachers, and it is in
this sense that the maxim of the immediate successors of
Ezra, the Men of the Great Synagogue, " Set up many disciples "
(*Aboth*, i. 1), is to be understood. It is not without interest
in this connexion to observe that even Malachi, the last of
the prophets, still envisages the priest as the repository of the
Torah, the duty of the people being but the passive one of
" seeking the law at his mouth " (Mal. 2¹⁻⁷), and the trans-
formation which took place in the succeeding centuries, which
alone explains the valiant resistance of the people in the
Maccabæan revolt, is to be attributed to the Scribes.

But the second task was of even greater importance, and
that was to establish the true meaning of Holy Writ in order
that the Will of God might be clearly known without question
or doubt. There was naturally at the beginning no divergence
of opinion such as characterized the opposing sects of Pharisees
and Sadducees later. All agreed on the sanctity of the
Divine Word and all agreed on the necessity of establishing
its meaning. It is this which is meant by the word *Darash*,
" to expound," in the above-quoted sentence, which gave
rise to the word Midrash found as early as 2 Chron. 24²⁷.
An interesting example of this necessity is seen in Neh. 8¹⁵.
In the first flush of their enthusiastic reception of the
Torah the people proceeded to celebrate the Festival of Tabernacles. But it is obvious that they understood Lev. 23⁴⁰ to
refer to the components of which the Tabernacle was to be
erected, and not, as later exegesis established, to quite a
separate commandment. It is to this period that we have
to attribute such Mishnahs as *Sotah*, viii. 1–6, *Negaim*, xii. 5–7,
and *Maaser Sheni*, v. 10–13, which differ from the other Mishnahs
in that they are a running commentary on the Scriptural
text and their sole purpose is explanatory and elucidatory.

Had the Torah been an academic study only, the function
of the Scribes would have ended there, but it was more. It
was not enough that life had to be in accordance with the
Torah, the Torah had to legislate for every problem of life.
To the Jew the Torah was the be-all and end-all of his existence.

It was co-extensive with life as a whole, it was given not for one age or for one time, but for all time. It was inconceivable that any problem could arise for which the Torah if not explicitly, at least implicitly, had not a ready answer, and it is expressed succinctly in the statement of a disciple of Hillel, " Turn it and turn it over again, for everything is in it " (*Aboth*, v. 22), the metaphor being of the spade which uncovers hidden treasures. The infinite variety of life continually raises new problems. Circumstances of life arise which the Torah did not contemplate, but for which it must provide an answer if it is not to become a dead letter, and it was this idea of the Scriptures which the Scribes developed. The Torah was to be not a dead letter, but a letter ever living, a text whose meaning was plastic because it was subject to fresh interpretations in every age, all of which were implicit in the text. As a later maxim expressed it, " Whatever a clever scholar is destined in the future to reveal in the Torah was already stated to Moses on Mount Sinai."

This idea expressed itself in two ways. In the first place, it raised the study of Torah for its own sake to a duty of paramount importance, since by uncovering the spiritual treasures hidden beneath the surface, it led to a greater and ever fuller unfolding of the Divine will in human affairs. But this in itself is but one of the two foundation stones upon which the structure of the Oral Law was erected. The other grew from the needs of life itself, and from the determined attempt to bring *everything* within the compass of the Law. It was this view which dominated the whole conception of the Law and which made it an ever-flowing well of living waters for future generations. Customs arose which became accepted by the people as law, ordinances were enacted from time to time to deal with specific problems which arose and for which the Torah did not legislate, and yet the sole claim of such an ordinance to authority, whether it was a *Takkanah* (an enactment) or a *Gezerah* (a prohibitive decree) was its justification in the Torah. Originally it would appear that it was frankly admitted that these enactments and decrees were not to be found in the Torah, and their relationship to the Torah and their claim to authority rested upon the conception that they constituted a " fence round the Torah " (*Aboth*, i. 1), a protective barrier round it to protect it against encroachment from without and dissipation from within. To this class belong such *Takkanoth* as those ascribed by the Talmud to Ezra (*B.K.*, 82*a*), the most important of which were his institution of the reading of the Law on Mondays and Thursdays and the sessions of the Court on the same days, both due to the fact that they were the market days when the inhabitants of the villages came to town, as well as the earliest recorded *Gezerah*, that of Jose b. Joezer and Jose b. Johanan (*c.* 200 B.C.) decreeing that the land of the Gentiles was unclean (*Shabb.* 14*b*), in order to prevent Jews from leaving the Holy Land, so continuing the work of Ezra in raising a barrier between the Jews and the surrounding heathens, for the protection of the Jew in living the life ordained by God. There is no attempt to justify them on Scriptural grounds; the beautiful Midrash justifying Ezra's institution of reading the Law on Mondays and Thursdays on the basis of Ex. 15^{22} that "one should not go for three days without the waters of the Torah" is centuries later; they were accepted because they were a "fence round the Torah."

As long as the conception of the extra-Scriptural Laws remained at this stage, there was no breach or open rupture between the more conservative element, which developed into the Sadducees, and the progressive element which was the origin of the Pharisees. All agreed on the sanctity of the Torah, all agreed on the need of enactments, and there were Sadducæan tradition and enactments which go beyond the Torah as there were Pharisaic. It was when this extra-Scriptural tradition was raised to the level of an Oral Law, of equal validity and of equal age to the Written Law, that the breach took place. This is the writer's own view which he hopes to develop on a future occasion. Certainly this zealous partisanship of the unwritten Law was the distinguishing characteristic of the Pharisees and the fundamental issue in their controversy with the Sadducees. In opposition to the Pharisees who maintained the obligation of the traditional laws and observances for which there was no Biblical authority, the Sadducees maintained that the written Law alone was valid, although they also had non-Biblical ordinances. The first rupture between the two sects took place in the reign of John Hyrcanus 135–104 B.C. (Josephus, *Antiquities*, xiii. 10, 5–6), and by the first century the idea of the Oral Law was firmly established, the earliest reference to it in the Talmud being in a controversy between Hillel and Shammai (*Shabb.* 31*a*) about the beginning of the Christian era, when it received its first systematic, though oral, codification, and we can, therefore, date its growth as an independent idea to the second and first pre-Christian centuries.

It is this Oral Law which is referred to in the New Testament (Mark 7³⁻⁵) as the " tradition of the elders " (παράδοσις τῶν πρεσβυτέρων) and by Josephus as "the tradition of the fathers " (παράδοσις τῶν πατέρων), although neither term is found in Rabbinical literature and Josephus (B.J. ii. 629) refers to the " ten thousand other precepts which relate to unwritten custom."

Once this idea was firmly established and universally held, the way was clear for its development, and during the first two Christian centuries the Oral Law was successively interpreted, discussed and codified until it received its final authoritative codification in the Mishnah of Rabbi Judah Hannasi (c. 200) which, owing to the veneration in which he was held and his undisputed authority, was accepted as the authoritative code for all time, and with it, to a very large extent, the development of the Oral Law was arrested, future exponents of Judaism being permitted only to elucidate the meaning, but not to dispute the authority, of the Mishnah.

A brief historical review of the Scribes must be given. The first and most important body, of whom we know very little, and who are either identical with, or closely connected with, the Soferim, are the Men of the Great Synagogue (Aboth, i. 1). Tradition ascribes their formation to Ezra, and they continued their activity until the time of Simeon the Just (Aboth, i. 2), probably about 270 B.C. Except for his name, they are an anonymous body. We know of their decisions, but not who they were, and it is probable that this was done deliberately, in order that no precepts should be perpetuated as resting on their authority, but only on the authority of the Torah. It is to them that the formation of the Shemoneh Esreh (see Chap. XVIII) is ascribed, as well as the emendations of the Scriptural text called the Tikkune Soferim (Tanhuma Beshallah), where they are identified with the Soferim.

The change in the political status in Palestine, owing to the end of the Persian rule and the rise of the Seleucid and Ptolemaic Empires, brought about a change in the ordering of the religious life of the Jews, and it is to this that the end of the Men of the Great Synagogue is to be ascribed. Their place was taken by the Gerousia or senate, which was either identical with, or developed into, the Sanhedrin of later days. In their case, although decisions were still given by the body as a whole, the veil of anonymity is slightly lifted, and in Aboth, i. 4–12, we are given the list of names and maxims of the " Pairs " who, according to Jewish tradition, were the

President (Nasi) and Vice-President (Ab Beth Din) of the Sanhedrin. This they were certainly not, since the high-priest always presided over the Sanhedrin, unless there were two, but they did act as the leaders of some body, and as the Sanhedrin always contained some " Opposition Party," such as Hellenists in the third and second centuries and Sadducæans later, it is probable that they were the leaders of that group which regarded itself as the successors of the Soferim. These " Pairs " extend their activity from Jose b. Joezer and Jose b. Johanan about 200 B.C. (There is an unaccountable gap in the chain of tradition from Antigonus of Socho the disciple of Simeon the Just to these two, a period of some sixty years) to Hillel and Shammai, who were older contemporaries of Jesus, and it was during this period, as has been mentioned, that the rise took place of the two opposing parties, the Pharisees and the Sadducees, consequent upon the develop-ment of the Oral Law to a status of binding authority. The word Pharisees (Heb. Perushim) means " those who are separated " and refers to their higher standard of ritual purity, whereby they separated themselves from the ritual contamination of the Ame-Haarez, the common people. The number of actual Pharisees was comparatively small, only some thousands, but there is sufficient evidence to show that they had the complete and unqualified support of the mass of the people (cf. Jos. *Ant.* xiii. 10. 6). The Sadducees (Heb. Saddukim, Zadokites) were recruited from the aristocratic caste in Israel, who alone used to intermarry with the high-priestly and distinguished priestly families, descendants of Zadok the high-priest, from whom they took their name. Tradition ascribes their origin to Zadok, a disciple of Antigonus, and although it was probably in his time that they first took their rise, there is no other historical basis for it.

The reign of Salome Alexandra, 76–67 B.C., was the halcyon time for the Pharisees. Energetically supported by the queen, headed by her brother Simeon b. Shetah, they purged the Sanhedrin of Sadducæan elements, reintroduced the Pharisaic Code and enforced their own ideas on the service and ritual of the Temple, which up till then had been a strong-hold of the Sadducees. The two leaders of the Pharisees during the reign of Herod, Shemaiah and Abtalion (the Sameas and Pollio of Josephus, *Ant.* xv. 10. 4) were shown favour by Herod, not an account of any leaning which he had towards the Pharisees, but because of the fact that they exerted their influence on the leaders in Jerusalem to open the gates to him in 37 B.C.

With Hillel, the disciple of Shemaiah and Abtalion, a new epoch opens in the history of Jewish tradition and the Oral Law. In the first place, the seven hermeneutical laws which he formulated for the interpretation of Scriptures (later developed into the thirteen rules of R. Ishmael. See Singer, *Daily P. B.*, p. 13) gave a new impetus to the study of the Scriptures, and secondly, the end of the Hasmonean rule made it possible for the Pharisees to pursue their work without interference from the ruling power. With him commences the era of the Tannaim (lit. teachers) who pursued their activity for two centuries until the redaction of the Mishnah, both he and his contemporary Shammai founding schools, the Beth Hillel and the Beth Shammai, the period of whose activity covers and extends beyond the time of Jesus. For the first time the corporate nature of the decisions of the Pharisaic party disappears. On nearly every question the two schools found themselves in direct disagreement, and the Talmud rightly complains that " when the disputes increased between the school of Shammai and the school of Hillel, the Torah became like two Torahs." With the destruction of the Temple in A.D. 70, and the establishment of the school at Jabne (Jamnia) by Johanan b. Zaccai, a disciple of Hillel, this tendency became aggravated. Every teacher gave his own independent decisions, and many compiled their own Mishnahs, with the result that by the end of the second century there were innumerable conflicting decisions, and the task of R. Judah Hannasi was not only to codify the huge mass of oral tradition, but to decide between conflicting views, the result being the Mishnah. After the destruction of the Temple, the Patriarchate, which was now the leadership of the Sanhedrin, became hereditary in Hillel's family at the request of Johanan b. Zaccai to Vespasian. Three members of the family deserve special mention, Gamaliel I, his grandson, the teacher of Paul (Acts 22[3]), who gave prudent advice in the Sanhedrin regarding the treatment of the apostles (*ibid.* 5[34ff.]), and who lived before the destruction of the Temple ; his grandson, Gamaliel II, who effected the final breach between the Judæo-Christians and the Jews by his adoption of the imprecation against Nazarenes in the Shemoneh Esreh (see Chap. XVIII), and Judah Hannasi the redactor of the Mishnah.

That the insistence upon external observance by the Pharisees opened the door to hypocrisy cannot be denied, nor that there were hypocrites among them. The outward act can be performed and all men see it, the inward intention may or may not be there, and it therefore exposes its adherents to the charge of formalism and hypocrisy. The Talmud itself quotes an ancient Baraita enumerating seven classes of Pharisees, of whom five are either fools or hypocrites : " the shoulder Pharisee " who ostentatiously parades his virtues, the " wait-a-little " Pharisee, who is always parading the fact that he has a religious duty to perform, the " bruised Pharisee " who in his virtuous haste to flee from looking at a woman bruises himself against the wall, the " pestle Pharisee " who shows a Uriah Heep-like humility and walks with head down as a pestle in a mortar, and the " Pharisee who says what is my duty that I may perform it," while it enumerates only two virtuous ones, the God-fearing Pharisee and the God-loving (*Sotah*, 22b), and in the same context it preserves the advice given by Alexander Jannai to his wife, the Queen Salome Alexandra, " Fear neither the Pharisees nor those who are not Pharisees (the Sadducees), but fear the double-dyed hypocrites who perform the actions of Zimri and expect the reward of Phinehas." Again, a passage in the Midrash (*Pes. R.*, xxii.), censuring those who wear phylacteries and fringes but harbour evil intention in their heart, is an exact parallel to Matt. 23[5].

But to call Pharisaism a doctrine based upon hypocrisy is a perversion of the truth, and the fact that it is the Pharisees themselves who preserve the above quoted statements, to which many parallels could be given, is in itself sufficient refutation of the charge. One has but to study the life of the noble Hillel to realize the piety, humility, and subservience to the Will of God which characterized the true Pharisee and Scribe ; one has but to read the ethical maxims of *Aboth* to realize that ethical teaching was by no means neglected in favour of insistence upon ritual and external observance ; and the fact that the Talmud ascribes the rise of the Sadducees to the inability of their founder to rise to the ethical heights of the maxim of his teacher Antigonus " Be not like servants who minister to their master upon the condition of receiving a reward, but be like servants who minister to their master without the condition of receiving a reward, and let the fear of heaven be upon you," shows that this was regarded as the principle of the Pharisaic life.

A system of life under which its devotees have continued to live for over two thousand years, cannot be founded upon a basis of hypocrisy. It was a consistent system which held that specified actions must be performed in a specified way, since thereby the Will of God was being done as He enjoined it to be done, but that result could not be attained unless together with the outward act there was the inward purpose, for without it, it was worthless both in a moral and a religious sense, and the Pharisees continually insisted upon the paramount necessity of this inward intention.

BIBLIOGRAPHY

R. Travers Herford, *The Pharisees*, London, 1924.
Jewish Encyclopedia, art. " Pharisees," vol. ix., pp. 661–6.
Smith, *Dictionary of the Bible*, art. " Scribes."
Lauterbach in *Kohler Festschrift*, 1913, pp. 177–198.
G. F. Moore, *Judaism*, Harvard, 1927. Part I., chap. iii.
E. Schürer, *History of the Jewish People in the time of Jesus Christ.* English edition, Div. II., vol. ii., pp. 4–44.
L. Finkelstein, *The Pharisees*, 1938.

XVIII. THE SYNAGOGUE AND ITS WORSHIP

THERE is probably no subject concerning whose origin and early history there is a more complete lack of historical reference, and at the same time such a universal consensus of opinion, as the subject of the origin and development of the Synagogue.

The birth of this institution, so fateful for the future of organized religion, took place unheralded and unnoticed. It grew to maturity and underwent its most important development during that period of Jewish history between the close of the Bible and the Maccabæan revolt (444–170 B.C.) which is called the " Dark Age " of Jewish history, dark only in so far as little light is thrown on it by history, but full of the light of the spirit ; and it first emerges to history at the beginning of the Christian era as a virile, fully grown and firmly established institution, exercising a profound influence upon the development of Judaism and the birth of Christianity. Although the references to it in the Talmud in Temple times are almost non-existent, and the first coherent accounts of its services are to be found in the New Testament (Luke 4 ; Acts 13), the stage of development at which it is found there is such that a history must be assumed for it.

It is to the Babylonian Exile, which marks a turning point of the highest significance in Jewish history, that we must look for its primal origin, since this period presents the conditions under which its birth can be most naturally explained. Deprived of the Temple, and in a strange land, feeling sorely the need for consolation and comfort in their distress, the exiles would meet from time to time, probably on Sabbaths, to encourage one another and to find comfort in their affliction. It is probable that in the repeated mention of the assembly of the elders before Ezekiel (Ezek. 8⁶, 14¹, 20¹, 33¹) we have the actual beginning of this momentous institution, and it is a true instinct which makes the Talmud (*T.B. Meg.* 29*b*) refer the "little sanctuary" of Ezek. 11¹⁶ to the Synagogue. The Jews who had remained in Palestine taunted the exiles with the fact that they were far from the Temple, and the prophet retorts that God is with them as much in their " little sanctuary " as He had been in the Temple.

There is no mention of Synagogues in the history of the
Return, or of Ezra and Nehemiah, but the whole history of
the former presupposes the habit of periodic assemblies of
the people (Ezra 8¹⁵ ; Neh. 8² ; Zech. 7⁵).

Again, the influence of the Synagogue as a factor in the
religious life of the people in the time of Ben Sira was much
more deeply felt than the scarcity of references to it in his
book would lead us to believe, and it is to its influence that
we must ascribe the fact that during the Maccabæan revolt
the bulk of the people, far from being affected by the apostasy
of their political leaders, arrayed themselves in organized
resistance. Since these political leaders came from the
priestly aristocracy, we must assume that there were spiritual
forces at work other than the Temple which prepared the
people for the coming crisis. Such a force was the Synagogue.

As a matter of fact, the Book of Maccabees is strangely
silent about any attacks on the Synagogue, but this is easily
explained. The main interest in that history is Jerusalem
and the Temple, and the only reference which might bear
upon the Synagogue is an incidental one to the gathering of
the Jews at Mizpeh, " a place where they prayed aforetime in
Israel " (1 Macc. 3⁴⁶). The fact that it is called " a place of
prayer " (τόπος προσευχῆς) and not an altar or shrine implies
that the reference is not to its ancient glory, but to a more
recent custom, or, if to the former, it shows the reading into
ancient history of the prevalent custom, a common device of
the Rabbis of old, applying to the shrines of old the function
of the contemporaneous Synagogue. We also see in this
book that the people were in possession of scrolls of the Law
from which they read publicly (1 Macc. 1⁵⁷, 3⁴⁸), and that
they sang hymns to the refrain of " His mercy is good and
endureth for ever " (4²⁴), on which we find a whole hymn in
Ecclesiasticus (51).

These meagre details are all we know of the Synagogue
before the account of it in the New Testament, but in them
we have an inkling of its function and purpose.

" The Synagogue was a local assembly for the promotion
of religion through the two main functions of worship and
instruction. This twofold purpose has been characteristic
of the Synagogue in all ages of its known history " (Travers
Herford, *The Pharisees*, p. 92). It will be convenient to treat
of it under these two headings.

The constant parts of the Synagogue service consisted of
an invitation to prayer, the prayer proper, the reading of a
portion of the Pentateuch and of a selection from the Prophets

in their original, accompanied by a translation in the vernacular and, if a competent person were present, a homily based on the Scriptural lesson, concluding with the Priestly Benediction, and we know from Philo's account of the Greek Synagogue that all these features were present there also.

The invitation to prayer consisted of the proclamation by the Reader of the words, " Bless ye the Lord who is to be blessed," to which the congregation responded, " Blessed be the Lord who is to be blessed for ever and ever." This was followed by what is properly the Confession of Faith, called by its first word the " Shema," originally consisting probably only of Deut. 6^{4-9}, to which the other two paragraphs, Deut. 11^{13-21} and Num. 15^{37-41}, were later and successively added, the whole introduced by two blessings and concluded with a blessing. Then came the prayer proper.

This prayer proper is called Tephillah (Prayer), Amidah (Standing (sc. Prayer)), Shemoneh Esreh (Eighteen (sc. Benedictions)), and in the oldest form which has come down to us consists of eighteen benedictions. Tradition ascribes their composition to the Men of the Great Synagogue (*Ber.* 33*a*), whose period of activity is roughly from the fifth to the third centuries before Christ, although they were finally fixed in the time of Rabban Gamaliel, *c.* A.D. 100, by one of his disciples, Simeon the flax-dealer, who arranged them before his master in the sequence in which they have been handed down to us, while another disciple, Samuel the Little, composed the blessing, or rather the imprecation, against heretics (*Ber.* 28*b*, 29*a*), now the twelfth in the order, which brings the number of blessings to the nineteen in vogue to-day. It was this blessing, whose original form was " against Nazarenes and heretics," which finally drove the Judæo-Christians from the Synagogue and completed the rift between Judaism and the nascent Church. This arrangement of Simeon was but the systematic arrangement of existing forms of prayer dating back to previous centuries, and there is a striking similarity between some of the blessings of the Amidah and the hymn of Ben Sira alluded to above. But even then it was only the actual blessing itself whose terminology was established, the actual wording of the preceding paragraph, of which the blessing forms the conclusion, being extempore' (cf. Luke 2^1), prayers under no circumstances being committed to writing until the seventh century.

The custom of reading Scripture during service on Sabbath is coeval with the Synagogue; and the Talmud, Josephus (*Cont. Ap.*, ii. 17) and the New Testament (Acts 15^{21})

emphasize its hoary antiquity by ascribing its institution to
Moses, the Talmud differentiating between the custom of
reading it on Sabbaths, Festivals, and New Moons, which it
ascribes to Moses, and on Mondays, Thursdays, and Sabbath
afternoons, which it ascribes to Ezra. Whether, as is commonly
assumed, the narrative of Nehemiah (8) served as the model
of the Synagogue or whether it was the example of the
Synagogue which formed the model of the narrative, we have
in this chapter the reading of the Law in the fourth pre-
Christian century as it appears in the Synagogue.

Originally the appropriate Scriptural passages were read
on the respective festivals, and expounded. The next stage
was almost certainly the institution of the special readings
for the four special Sabbaths, Shekalim (Ex. 30^{11-16}) to
remind the people of the approaching collection of the half-
shekel ; Zakor (Deut. 25^{17-19}) before Purim, with its command to exterminate Amalek of whom Haman was regarded
as a descendant ; Parah (Num. 19^{1-22}) some weeks before
Passover, emphasizing the purifications necessary for Passover ; and Ha-Hodesh (Ex. 12^{1-20}) nearer to the Festival
containing the actual laws of Passover. The last stage
was the consecutive reading of the whole Pentateuch on
successive Sabbaths in a triennial cycle, although the exact
division of the pericopes which is reflected in the Midrash
may be as late as the third century.

The prophetical reading which followed that of the
Pentateuch is of much later origin, and this is reflected in
the fact that the Talmud does not ascribe to it the hoary
antiquity which it does to the latter ; in fact, even tradition is completely silent as to the period and circumstances
in which it took its rise and the assumption, first made
by Abudraham in the fourteenth century, that it had its
origin during the troublous period of the Maccabæan revolt
when, the reading of Scriptures being interdicted, the people
substituted for it the reading of passages of similar content
from the prophetical books, has been more universally accepted
than its lack of basis in fact would warrant. The only
evidence in favour of it is that the only limitation to the
selection of the passage was that its contents had to be similar
to those of the Pentateuchal passage, and this is easily
explained on the assumption that the reason for its institution was in order to emphasize, reinforce, and interpret the
Pentateuchal lesson. It had the added advantage that it acquainted the people with the prophetical books and emphasized
the fact that the whole of canonical Scripture represents a

unity. It is for this reason also that the Midrash, almost without exception, opens its exposition with that of a verse from the Hagiographa, the exposition finally leading up to a homiletical connexion with the scriptural section, although it is impossible to decide when the custom first arose.

As suggested, a much more free selection was permitted in the case of the prophetical reading than with the Pentateuchal. The two instances in the New Testament of these readings (Luke 4[17]; Acts 13[15]), even in the differences between them, represent normal practice. In the former case, the scroll of Isaiah is handed to Jesus ; He opens it and finds the passage Isaiah (61[1f.]) which He reads, after which He rolls it up, hands it to the attendant (see later) and proceeds to the exposition. Unfortunately, the language does not make it clear whether the passage had been prepared beforehand or not, but the point is immaterial, since a certain freedom was permitted. In the latter case Paul does not appear to have read the lesson, but only to have delivered the homily, and there is other evidence of this interesting difference of practice, although generally the reader of the prophetical passage was one who was able to preach.

Before passing to a discussion of the homily, a word must be said about the translation into the vernacular (Aramaic). The interpreter stood at the side of the person reading from the Law, and more or less freely paraphrased the reading, sometimes erring on the side of a too great literalness, sometimes on the side of too great freedom. When the custom arose cannot be decided with certainty, although the traditional interpretation of Nehemiah 8[8], which has much to commend it, is that the reading of the Law was accompanied by a full translation into the vernacular. The sacred language was no longer familiar to the people, and it was essential for this translation to take place if the reading were not to fail of its purpose. In Mishnaic times the rule was laid down that every verse was translated singly and separately by the Meturgeman (Translator), in the case of the Prophets every three verses. There is no evidence whether the interpreter was a permanent official or whether any competent member of the congregation could act.

The word Haftarah used for the prophetical reading corresponds with the Latin word *demissio*, and with it in Temple times the service concluded, in the absence of a competent person to deliver a homily, except for the priestly benediction. The additional service which occurs in the modern Synagogue service after the sermon was introduced after the destruction of the Temple as a vicarious form of the sacrificial system, its main contents being a prayer for the restoration of the Temple service with its sacrificial system and the appropriate scriptural passage from Num. 28 and 29 for the Sabbath, New Moon, or Festival respectively.

The homily was delivered immediately after the prophetical reading, and the two instances cited in the New Testament represent the normal practice, not, as Schürer suggests, exceptions. In view of the meaning of the word Haftarah, he assumes that normally the homily followed the Penta teuchal reading, the service always concluding with the Haftarah. But from the Talmud (*Bezah*, 15*b*) it is clear that the homily was the end of the service, and in any case, as Elbogen suggests, the word may indicate the conclusion not of the service, but of the scriptural readings. Competence was the sole criterion for the privilege of delivering the homily, and this is clearly shown from the New Testament narrative. In the one case, Jesus is known and proceeds to deliver the homily without being formally invited, His selection as the reader of the prophetical portion being the proof of His competence ; in the other, Paul and his company visit Antioch, and after the prophetical reading the rulers of the Synagogue (see later) ask them whether they have any exhortation to make, whereupon Paul proceeds to deliver the homily. These homilies delivered first in the Synagogue and later, as they grew in length, in the school, form the basis of the extant Midrashim, some of them (the Pesiktas) still retaining the concluding formula " Whence do we know this ? From what has just been read in the Prophet (or in the Pentateuch)."

The preacher used to sit during his exposition, but the fact that he sat on an elevated place made him visible to the congregation.

The service finally closed with the benediction pronounced by the priests, and in order to make a distinction between its utterance in the Temple and in Synagogue, various differences were introduced, the most important being that the congregation responded Amen after every verse. Where there was no priestly member of the congregation present, the blessing was probably not uttered, the custom of transforming it into a prayer being a much later one.

The above is a description of the main Synagogue service of the week, that of Sabbath morning, during the first century. Prayers, however, took place thrice daily (Acts 3^1, 10$^{3-9}$ and

cf. Ps. 55[17]; Dan. 6[10]), the service on Sabbath afternoons
and Monday and Thursday mornings being characterized by
a short reading from the Pentateuch. Originally it appears
that the consecutive reading of the Pentateuch was extended
to this portion, but later the custom was established, and
has persisted, of reading the first portion of the section of the
following Sabbath morning.

The service on festivals was substantially the same as
that on Sabbath mornings, the main differences being the
selection of the appropriate section and the reading of the
Hallel (Ps. 113–118) after the Amidah.

Every community had its own Synagogue, the larger towns
having more than one (cf. Acts 24[12]), and it would appear
that every assembly of Jews from the provinces in the capital
had their own Synagogue ("The Synagogue of the Alex-
andrines," *Tos. Meg.* iii.), although the statement of the
Talmud that before the destruction of the Temple there were
four hundred and eighty synagogues in Jerusalem is to be
regarded as an exaggeration. The presence of a Synagogue
within the precincts of the Temple itself (*Yoma*, vii. 1;
Sotah, vii. 7) is striking evidence of the lack of antagonism
between the two institutions and of the widespread manner
in which the Synagogue had spread its influence.

There was no fixed size or shape for the Synagogue, as
there was for the Tabernacle and Temple, the only desiderata
being that it should be erected on the highest possible point
of the town or village and that the Ark (see later) should be
placed facing Jerusalem, and it was here that the "chief
seats" (Matt. 23[6]) were placed where sat the notables and
leaders of the community (cf. Jas. 2[3]).

The furnishings of the Synagogue were of the simplest,
consisting of the Ark or chest already mentioned, in which
the scrolls of the Scriptures were kept, wrapped in a linen
covering and placed in a case. This Ark was separated from
the body of the Synagogue by a curtain, and when, as on
the occasion of fasts, prayers were held in the market-place, it
was transported there (*Taan*, ii. 1). In the centre of the
Synagogue was a raised dais or platform upon which there
was a reading-desk whereon the scroll of the Scriptures was
laid for the reading of the lesson, and where the preacher
used to sit when delivering his homily, and apart from the
benches this was the sum total of the furnishings, unless
lamps, trumpets (see later), and other requisites of worship
are included.

Officers. The lay-officers of the Synagogue consisted of a body of elders over whom, and probably chosen from whom, was the " ruler of the Synagogue," the archisynagogus. Their function, and the function of the archisynagogus, was confined to the general supervision of the actual conduct of the service and of the building, and they do not appear necessarily to have had supervision of the affairs of the community as a whole. It was the archisynagogus who invited members to lead the congregation in prayer and to read the Scriptures, and according to the Mishna (*Yoma*, vii. 1, repeated in *Sotah*, vii. 7), the scroll of the Law was handed to him by the attendant, and he handed it to the reader, and it was he who invited strangers to deliver the homily (Acts 13). This office, like all offices according to the Pharisees, was hereditary, and the name " archisynagogus " found on the tombstones of women does not mean that they held the office, but that they belonged to a family in which the office was hereditary.

The religious officiants were the Meturgeman already referred to and the *Shaliah* or delegate of the congregation who led them in prayer. Both these offices were honorary ones, any competent adult member of the congregation being invited to read the service. In fact the only paid officer was the *hazzan*, or "minister" (Luke 4[20]), who was in every sense the servant of the congregation. This word is in modern times employed as a synonym of *Shaliah*, denoting the cantor or reader, but in Talmudic times it refers to the salaried attendant of the Synagogue who only on exceptional occasions read the service, in which case his duties were taken over by another. These duties were various and manifold. He had to look after the building and its furniture, especially the scrolls of the Law, to give the signal by a blast of the trumpet from the roof of the Synagogue (the origin of the muezzin) of the incidence of the Sabbath and the consequent cessation from work, as well as of the close of the holy day. It was he who brought out the scroll from the Ark and who handed it to the reader, either directly or through the medium of the archisynagogus (see above), and from him to the one appointed to deliver the homily if he were another, and on the conclusion of the reading to roll it up and return it to the Ark. But many other duties not directly connected with the Synagogue devolved upon him, especially that of acting as schoolmaster and of carrying out the sentence of scourging inflicted by the Synagogue authorities.

It was the Synagogue which more than the Temple represented and determined the religious life of the people during the period of the second Temple, and its influence upon the future both of Judaism and of Christianity cannot be overestimated. It is from the Synagogue that the use of fixed prayer came ; it was the Synagogue which introduced the idea of a united act of worship which despite the apparent rejection of it by Jesus (Matt. 6[5]) became as characteristic and essential an aspect of Christianity as it did of Islam and Judaism, and in this respect only it can be claimed for it that it was the most momentous institution for the history of religion which the world has known. " Their (the Jews') genius for the organization of public religion appears in the fact that the form of communal worship devised by them was adapted by Christianity and Islam, and in its general outline still exists in the Christian and Moslem worlds " (C. Toy, *Introduction to the History of Religions*, 1913, p. 546), and " Judaism gave to the world not only the fundamental ideas of these great monotheistic religions, but the institutional forms in which they have perpetuated and propagated themselves " (G. F. Moore, *Judaism*, i. p. 285).

BIBLIOGRAPHY

G. F. Moore, *Judaism*. Harvard, 1927. Part I., chap. v.

E. Schürer, *A History of the Jewish People in the time of Jesus Christ*. English edition, 1901. Div. II., vol. ii., pp. 52–83.

I. Abrahams, *Studies in Pharisaism and the Gospels*. First series. Cambridge, 1917, pp. 1–17.

Hastings, *Dictionary of the Bible*, art. " Synagogue."

S. Krauss, *Synagogale Altertümer*, 1922.

H. St J. Thackeray, *The Septuagint and Jewish Worship*.

S. Singer, *The Authorised Daily Prayer Book*.

I. Abrahams, *Companion to the Daily Prayer Book*.

I. Elbogen, *Der jüdische Gottesdienst*. 3rd edition. Frankfurt, 1931.

XIX. THE ORGANIZATION AND WORSHIP OF THE PRIMITIVE CHURCH

1. THE SOCIETY AND ITS ORGANIZATION

The Church. Ecclesia, the word used for Church in the New Testament, denotes a gathering or assembly of people (and so Acts 19$^{32.\ 39.\ 41}$). In St. Paul's Epistles it is used of an assembly of Christians gathered together for worship (1 Cor. 11^{18}, 14$^{19.\ 34.\ 35}$). The word was adopted by the Greek translators of the Old Testament as their usual rendering of the Hebrew word, *qāhāl*. Both words, the Hebrew and the Greek, were used with two shades of meaning : either (1) a gathering of the congregation (or people) of Israel or (2) the congregation (or people) itself.

Corresponding with the second shade of meaning we find ecclesia used in St. Paul's Epistles to denote the company of Christians : either the company in any particular place (the Church of the Thessalonians (1 Thess. 1^1) ; the Churches of God which are in Judæa (1 Thess. 2^{14}) ; all the churches of the Christ (Rom. 16^{16}) ; the church that is in their house, *i.e.* the house of Aquila and Prisca (1 Cor. 16^{19})) ; or the whole company of Christians ("I persecuted the Church of God " (Gal. 1^{13} ; cf. Phil. 3^6, 1 Cor. 12^{28})). The use of "the ecclesia" to denote the whole Church is specially characteristic of the Epistles to the Colossians and the Ephesians. There the whole is spoken of as a building—a great building in the course of erection (Eph. 2$^{19\text{-}22}$) ; or, more frequently, as a body, a living and growing organic unity of members with various functions, the body of which Christ is the head (Eph. 4$^{15.\ 16}$; Col. 2^{19}). The idea occurs in St. Paul's Epistles as early as 1 Corinthians—" ye are the body of Christ, and severally members thereof " (12^{27}). And in Eph. 1$^{22.\ 23}$ the language used suggests that the Church and the Christ are so one that " the Christ in a true sense still waited for completion, and would find that completion only in the Church " (Armitage Robinson)—" Him hath He given to be head over all things to the Church, which is His body, the fullness of Him who all in all is being fulfilled " (cf. Col. 1^{24}).

It is interesting to observe that in the only two passages in the Synoptic Gospels in which ecclesia occurs, in one the word denotes the local church (Matt. 18[17]), and in the other it denotes the church universal (Matt. 16[18]).

It is remarkable that the word does not occur in the Fourth Gospel. In the Epistle to the Hebrews it is found only twice, once in a quotation from Ps. 22[22] (2[12]) and then in the beautiful but difficult phrase (12[23]) "Church of the first-born who are enrolled in heaven," which may refer to the angels (Peake), or the patriarchs (Nairne), or the elect people of God here in earth (Moffatt).

In the speech of Stephen reported in Acts 7 a reference to Moses includes the sentence "This is he that was in the church (*i.e.* ecclesia—R.V. margin, congregation) in the wilderness. . . ." Although this is, in fact, an echo of the LXX phrase "the day of the ecclesia" *i.e.* the day of the assembly to receive the law, yet the phrase "the ecclesia in the wilderness" does suggest a parallel to the new ecclesia, the new people of God (cf. Matt. 21[43]), the Christian Church, which has in a sense taken the place of the old people of God, the nation of Israel.

Some of the parables in St. Matthew's Gospel are clearly interpreted by the evangelist in the light of the new ecclesia as he knew it. That is really in mind sometimes when the phrase "the Kingdom of Heaven" is used. So, for example, the parables of the Wheat and the Tares and the Drag-net are interpreted to mean that even in "the beloved community" an admixture of good and bad will have to be tolerated until "the end of the age."

In the Pastoral Epistles the word ecclesia occurs only three times, all in I Timothy. In the last of these passages (I Tim. 3[15]) a church of the living God, *i.e.* a local Christian community (Hort) is said to be a pillar and stay of the truth. Space forbids reference to the other passages of the New Testament where the word ecclesia occurs ; but they will be found to exemplify the usages already described.

The New Testament conception of the ecclesia is that of a growing community of men and women who have been new-created in Christ Jesus, knit together in love and mutual service, with a real sense of corporate responsibility and of a corporate witness to give to the world : a body, Christ's body : not yet free from spot and blemish, but still chosen, destined, for that high purpose and end. Geography separates that great ecclesia into the local ecclesiæ at Rome, Corinth, Ephesus, Jerusalem, and so on. Each individual member of the Church wherever he may be feels himself united with all other members all over the world, in spite of all differences of nationality and social status, in a common loyalty to Jesus. As other religious associations were formed for the worship of some Kurios, *i.e.* Lord, so the Christians everywhere confessed Jesus as their Kurios (1 Cor. 12³). His law was that they should bear one another's burdens (Gal. 6²)—which they were eager to do.

The highest standard of practical morality was upheld unwaveringly by the Christian leaders (1 Thess. 5¹⁴⁻²² ; Rom. 12⁹⁻¹⁴, etc.). This, and nothing less, is the norm for those who, in becoming Christians, have died to their old life and risen to a new. St. Paul often speaks as though any falling short of that standard is unthinkable for a Christian man. At all events he uses all his efforts to make his readers regard it as unthinkable. " Ye died, and your life is hid with Christ in God " . . . logically it should not have been necessary to go on . . . " Mortify therefore your members " . . . (Col. 3³⁻⁵). But so it was. The theoretical problem was never worked out by St. Paul, though from the psychological point of view his procedure has much to commend it.

Actually the results attained, in the face of suspicion, hostility, and every kind of temptation, were a striking proof of the power of the Spirit of Jesus which animated the whole Christian society. It was by their lives even more than by their words that the Christians co-operated in the furtherance of the Gospel, the good news, of Christ (Phil. 1⁷· ¹²). The kindly messages and little greetings which are found at the end of the Epistles (especially 1 Cor. 16 ; Rom. 16 ; Col. 4) are eloquent and touching evidence of thoughtfulness and good-will and real affection.

Organization. At first when numbers were small very little organization would have been needed. The Christians adopted no political or social programme. They had simply " turned from idols, to serve a living and true God and to wait for His Son from heaven " (1 Thess. 1⁹· ¹⁰). Yet in this very epistle (if not the earliest, one of the earliest of St. Paul's) we find a reference to some in authority : " We beseech you, brethren, to know them which labour among you, and are over you in the Lord, and admonish you ; and to esteem them very highly in love for their work's sake. And be at peace among yourselves " (5¹²· ¹³). These persons are to preside, to superintend—and they are to do it with diligence (Rom. 12⁸, where the same word is used). They are also to admonish—the word is repeated just below (5¹⁴) to admonish the disorderly, to put them in mind of their duty.

These superintendents are to receive recognition, and to be esteemed exceedingly highly in love on account of their work. The discipline is discipline within a family. St. Paul himself, sorely troubled by what was happening to his Galatian converts, claims the position and authority of a parent towards them—" My little children, of whom I am again in travail until Christ be formed in you " (Gal. 4^{19}).

In this Epistle to the Galatians (which competes with I Thessalonians for the position of being the earliest of the Pauline Corpus) the only reference to local officials occurs in 6^6, where we gather that it is the duty of the taught to support their teachers. Teachers are mentioned in the next of St. Paul's Epistles—I Cor. 12^{28}, " And God hath set some in the Church, first apostles, secondarily prophets, thirdly teachers, after that miracles, then gifts of healing, helps, governments, diversities of tongues." As Dr. Findlay points out, helps and governments correspond with the *diaconoi* and the *episcopoi* of Phil. 1^1 (some years later—see below). In I Cor. 16^{15}, the household of Stephanas is mentioned as having arrayed or appointed themselves for ministering, and St. Paul enjoins voluntary submission to the direction of such persons.

The whole impression, so far, is of a rather fluid organization in charge of leaders whose functions are by no means precisely defined. The apostle, who has a very high conception of apostolic authority, is very anxious to avoid anything like domineering—" Not that we have lordship over your faith, but are helpers of your joy " (2 Cor. 1^{24}). What was aimed at was unanimity (Phil. 2^2, etc.) and a corporate consciousness of the Spirit's guidance (Acts 13^2, 15^{28}). That was taken to be the normal state of things, and where it prevailed the governing needed would be just presiding—a comparatively easy matter. Hence the function of government is ranked below that of apostles, prophets, teachers, " powers," " gifts of healing," and even " helps " in I Cor. 12^{28} (already quoted and cf. Rom. 12$^{6.\ 7.\ 8}$).

At the same time there was no escaping from the fact that disorderliness of one sort or another did occur. That involved the president in the more difficult duty of administering discipline. But that disciplinary action normally took the form of admonishing (I Thess. 5$^{12.\ 14}$). Anything so drastic as expulsion was rarely attempted. St. Paul has to recommend it in very exceptional circumstances (I Cor. 5$^{5.\ 13}$, cf. I Tim 1^{20}). But a policy of unfailing patience and long-suffering could claim the authority of the Lord Himself in more than one of His parables (Matt. 13²⁹· ⁴⁷). See further below.

Actually the earliest mention of *episcopoi* (bishops) and *diaconoi* occurs in Phil. 1¹, and the fact that St. Paul singles them out in his greeting must mean that they have a position of importance. It seems clear that in the New Testament the words elder (*presbuteros*—never found in the ten letters of St. Paul which have greatest claim to be considered authentic) and bishop (*episcopos*) were used of one and the same official (Acts 20¹⁷· ²⁸; Tit. 1⁵· ⁷, etc.), the latter referring to his function of oversight (*episcopos*—overseer or inspector).

In the Epistle to the Ephesians we have another list similar to that in 1 Cor. 12 (Eph. 4¹¹) : " And he gave some, apostles ; and some, prophets ; and some, evangelists ; and some, pastors and teachers." Pastors (bracketed with teachers), are evidently equivalent to *episcopoi* (cf. Acts 20²⁸). Deacons are not mentioned. Evangelists are distinguished from teachers. This distinction corresponds with the distinction between *kerugma* (proclaiming the " good tidings ") and *didache* (moral instruction), on which see C. H. Dodd, *The Apostolic Preaching*, p. 5 f.

The general impression with which this brief survey leaves us is that while in the Pauline churches regard is had to order in ministry as in worship (1 Cor. 14⁴⁰ and see below), in neither case are the details yet stereotyped. The offices of presbyter-bishops and deacons, however, have become a regular element in church organization. The presbyters are not, of course, any-where described as sacrificing priests. In the only passages in the New Testament where the word *hiereus* is used of Christians (Rev. 1⁶, 5¹⁰, 20⁶) it is applied to the whole body of Christians. The New Testament knows nothing of a priestly caste within the Church.

Presbyters. The office of the presbyters must correspond to that of the elders of a synagogue. According to Acts 14²³ Paul and Barnabas appointed the converts whom they thought best fitted to be presbyters of the Churches which had been established on the first missionary journey ; and the same account shows that in each place their practice had been to begin their work in the synagogue. When they were driven out and had to establish a group of their own, it would be natural to form it on, at least in some respects, similar lines.

Deacons. As to deacons—while the word itself merely suggests ministering in general, it seems that the special duty of the deacon was the administration of relief. The corresponding verb (*diakoneo*) occurs in Acts 6 in the description of the appointment of the Seven to " serve tables."

The procedure on this occasion is significant : the proposal of the Twelve was accepted by all the congregation, and they chose Stephen . . . " whom they set before the apostles : and when they had prayed, they laid their hands on them." This laying on of hands " is not only a well-known Jewish custom, but frequent in all ages and in all countries " (New, in *The Beginnings of Christianity* ; add. note xi). Jewish Rabbis were ordained in this way (the *Semikha*). Paul and Barnabas were thus set apart for missionary work (Acts 13³) and this is regarded as the outcome of the guidance of the Holy Spirit given to the whole community and as the act of the whole community.

Harnack (*The Constitution and Law of the Church in the First Two Centuries*, E.T., 1910), distinguishes two distinct kinds of ministry : first, a " universal " ministry comprising apostles, prophets, and teachers the scope of whose activity was general and not limited to any particular area ; and secondly, a local ministry of presbyters and deacons whose authority was confined to the local church to which they were appointed. The distinction is suggestive though it must not be pressed too far. As Streeter points out, the fact that some prophets led the wandering life referred to in the Didache is no evidence that all did so ; and no doubt both prophet and teacher were important figures in the normal ministry of a local church (*The Primitive Church*, p. 77—on prophets see further below).

Apostles. There is insufficient evidence to support Harnack's suggestion that the word " apostle " was borrowed from Jewish sources. More likely " it was the Greek-speaking church of Antioch which hit on the idea of using the rare but natural word " (K. Lake, *Beginnings of Christianity*, v. 50), meaning by its derivation " envoy." In St. Paul's Epistles the word is used " in the sense of a Christian missionary who has been commissioned to the service of the Gospel," and it is not confined to the Twelve (Gal. 1¹⁹ ; 1 Cor. 9⁵ᶠ· ; Rom. 16⁷, and cf. the Didache). In the Acts the apostles are those who are commissioned by Christ to be " his witnesses " throughout the world. It is also their function to govern and administer the Church. They are primarily the Twelve but also include Barnabas (Acts 14⁴· ¹⁴).

Professor C. H. Turner (*J.Th.S.*, xxviii (1927), p. 27, observes that in Mark from 8²⁷ onwards the phrases " the disciples " and " the Twelve " are practically synonyms (note 14¹²⁻¹⁷). " Q " contains the saying " ye also shall sit upon twelve thrones, judging the twelve tribes of Israel" (Matt. 19[28] ; Luke 22[30]). Thus it is clear that the Twelve were regarded as standing in a specially close relation to Christ ; and they, and to some extent all who like St. Paul shared with them the title Apostle, held a position of unique influence and authority throughout the Church.

Strictly speaking, the apostles themselves, so far as we know, had no successors. But, as Clement of Rome, writing to the Corinthians about A.D. 96, says, " they provided a continuance ; that if these (*i.e.* the presbyter-bishops appointed by the apostles) should fall asleep, other approved men should succeed to their ministration. Those therefore who were appointed by them, or afterwards by other men of repute with the consent of the whole Church, and have ministered unblameably to the flock of Christ in lowliness of mind, peacefully and with all modesty, and for long time have borne a good report with all— these men we consider to be unjustly thrust out from their ministration" (*Ad Cor.* 44).

" Other men of repute, with the consent of the whole Church " (*i.e.* the context suggests, the whole local church) —whom has Clement in mind ? The phrase would cover both the " approved men " mentioned before who succeeded to the ministration of the presbyter-bishops appointed by the apostles, and also any delegates of the apostles like Timothy and Titus, who survived their masters. The supply of the latter would have soon died out. Then the continuance would be preserved by the former; that is, it would be a collegiate, as opposed to an individual, succession (Streeter, *Primitive Church*, p. 216).

Though Timothy at Ephesus and Titus in Crete may well be regarded as examples of apostolic delegates, the Epistles which bear their names are now considered by many scholars to be, in the form in which we have them, the result of a process of editing about the end of the first century. By this time in Asia, where this editing took place, the monarchical episcopate already existed ; and Streeter is very likely right in finding in these Epistles portrayals of " the ideal Bishop " —in the one case of a large city (Timothy), in the other of a country district (Titus).

In some country districts development must have been comparatively slow. The Didache is addressed " to backward and out-of-the-way churches " (about A.D. 90 Streeter, *op. cit.*, p. 145). In some of these churches there appear to have been prophets and teachers, but as yet no presbyter-bishops or deacons. " The Didache marks the stage when the system in which prophets and teachers were the natural leaders of the churches is breaking down, and gradually being replaced by a ' regular ' ministry of bishops and deacons " (*ibid.*, p. 138 ; cf. J. M. Creed in *J.T.S.*, 1938, pp. 370 ff.).

As to the monarchical episcopate itself, Lightfoot's thesis still stands firm that it " was formed not out of the apostolic order by localization but out of the presbyteral by elevation : and the title, which originally was common to all, came at length to be appropriated to the chief among them " (*The Christian Ministry* in Com. on Phil., p. 196). It is, after all, only natural for a " college of officials " to have a head. Every synagogue had, similarly, its " ruler," the *archisynagogos*. Lightfoot regards the position held by James, the Lord's brother, at Jerusalem as the type of the early stage of the true episcopate ; " he was, in fact, the head or president of the college " of presbyters in the Mother Church. He owed his position partly to his personal character and partly to the fact that he was the eldest male of the Messianic House (Streeter, *op. cit.*, p. 73).

In his brilliant study of the Primitive Church to which reference has already been made, Streeter argues with much force that " the evolution of Church order in the New Testament culminates in the Johannine writings," and that John " the Elder " was Bishop of Ephesus, the Mother Church of Asian Christianity.

Diotrephes must have held the office of Bishop (in the monarchical sense) for he claimed, apparently on his own sole authority, the power of excommunication ; but " the elder " assumes " an almost apostolic authority " over him.

It is noteworthy that the passages in the New Testament which refer to the Christian congregation as a flock, and to the ministers as pastors (*i.e.* shepherds), Christ being the Chief Shepherd (Acts 20^{28} ; Eph. 4^{11} ; 1 Pet. 5$^{1-4}$; John 10, 21$^{15-17}$), have all some connexion with Asia Minor. It looks as though the standing of the ministry rose more rapidly here than in any other part of the empire. Perhaps the people of Asia Minor were more amenable to authority in matters of religion. It must not be forgotten that Pergamum and Nicomedia (in Bithynia) were the first places to build temples to Cæsar (not yet Augustus) in 29 B.C., and the presidents of the provincial diets, the Asiarch in Asia, the Bithyniarch in Bithynia, conducted the celebration of the public festivals in connexion with the cult of the emperor.

At the beginning of the second century it appears that mon-episcopacy did not yet exist at Rome or Corinth (Clement) or at Philippi (Polycarp). Streeter maintains that it was about the time of Ignatius and partly due to his impassioned advocacy that mon-episcopacy became established at Rome.

At all events, by A.D. 180 the usual, indeed, the almost universal, practice was for the local communities each to be governed by a bishop assisted by presbyters and deacons.

When mon-episcopacy became general at a later stage, the practice was that all the bishops of the province should be summoned to assist at the consecration of a new bishop. The date when this practice began is unknown. In the third century Cyprian refers to it (*Ep.* lxviii.). One of the canons of the Council of Nicæa laid it down that the minimum number of bishops to take part in a consecration should be three. There is, however, evidence that right into the third century the Bishop of Alexandria was elected by the twelve presbyters of the churches in the city and consecrated by them (Streeter, *op. cit.*, 254).

It will be noted that the idea of succession which has so far emerged is that of authority delegated from stage to stage. Actually the process would seem to have been : Apostle (*e.g.* St. Paul)—presbyter-bishops (*e.g.* at Antioch in Pisidia)—their president who gradually became the mon-episcopos, the sole bishop of that particular community. Further, when mon-episcopacy had become practically universal (as it had by A.D. 180) the apostolic succession on which Irenæus (and after him Augustine, etc.) laid such stress is succession in the chair of a particular see, *i.e.* " from holder to holder, not from consecrator to consecrated " (C. H. Turner, in *The Early History of the Church and the Ministry* (2nd ed. 1921), p. 193).

Ordination. The appointment and ordination of the Seven (Acts 6) have already been referred to. As being men " full of the Spirit and of wisdom," they were elected by " the whole multitude," presented to the apostles, and ordained by the laying on of hands with prayer. It is highly probable that by the date when Acts was written, this had become the normal procedure. Associated with ordination, according to the evidence of the Pastoral Epistles (and so of a somewhat later date), was a divine gift, " Neglect not the gift that is in thee, which was given thee by prophecy, with the laying on of the hands of the presbytery " (1 Tim. 4^{14}) ; " stir up the gift of God, which is in thee through the laying on of my hands " (2 Tim. 1^6).

Government and Discipline. It is necessary to add a little more under this heading. The actual condition of Church life in the period A.D. 80–120 is to some extent reflected in the Gospels.

On the one hand, there were warnings current in the name of Christ Himself against domineering on the part of Christian ministers, even the highest of them (Mark 9³³⁻³⁵, 10⁴²⁻⁴⁵, and parallels). "The kings of the Gentiles exercise authority. Their great ones have dominion over them. No such position is intended for the Christian minister. He is appointed to serve and not to rule" (A. C. Headlam, *The Doctrine of the Church and Reunion*, p. 194). On the other hand, there are a few passages which declare that a certain power of binding and loosing, of remitting and retaining, has been committed to "the disciples." The most striking are Matt. 16¹⁸·¹⁹, 18¹⁵⁻²⁰; John 20²²·²³.

In the first of these St. Peter is singled out: "And I also say unto thee, that thou art Peter, and upon this rock I will build my church; and the gates of Hades shall not prevail against it. I will give unto thee the keys of the kingdom of heaven; and whatsoever thou shalt bind on earth shall be bound in heaven: and whatsoever thou shalt loose on earth shall be loosed in heaven." St. Peter had in his "great confession" just given proof that he was the leader of the others in understanding and insight and loyalty, and so he "was to be the one through whom in a particular way the new community was to be built up; and also that he, in the first place, as others with him, was to possess authority, discipline, and the right of teaching." (A. C. Headlam, *The Doctrine of the Church and Christian Reunion*, p. 35; for further suggestions see Oman, *Vision and Authority*, pp. 119 ff.) This authority to "bind" and "loose" means power to give an authoritative decision as to what Christians may do and may not do (Dalman, *Words*, pp. 214, 216); and this authority is committed to the disciples in general in Matt. 18¹⁸ and in John 20²³, which represents an application of the same authority with the rite of baptism in view: "whose soever sins ye forgive, they are forgiven unto them; whose soever sins ye retain, they are retained." Baptism (see below) in the primitive church was "baptism unto the remission of sins," and the disciples are here given the right to decide as to who should be admitted to baptism and who should be refused. It is important to observe that on the occasion described in John 20¹⁹⁻²³ others were present beside the Twelve, *e.g.* Cleopas and his unnamed friend (Luke 24³³⁻³⁶: with the use of the word "disciples" in John 20¹⁹; cf. its use in John 4¹·², etc.).

Expansion. According to the tradition preserved in Matt. 15²⁴ (cf. Mark 7²⁷), 10⁵, Jesus felt that His mission was specially to the lost sheep of the house of Israel. The Twelve were presumably all Jews, though two of them, Andrew and Philip, are known by names of Greek origin. But in the teaching which Jesus gave there was nothing nationalist in the narrow sense. On the contrary, it is obviously addressed to men and women as such and is plainly of universal application. In the parable of the Good Samaritan, and the special commendation of the centurion, " I have not found so great faith, no, not in Israel " (Q—Matt. 8¹⁰ ; Luke 7⁹), we have striking illustrations of Christ's appreciation of the good qualities of individuals belonging to nations against which the Jews themselves were specially prejudiced.

It is not surprising then to find the earliest Church historian in Acts tracing the spread of the Gospel from Jerusalem and its environs to Samaria, Antioch, Asia Minor, Macedonia and Greece, and to Rome itself. Proselytes as well as Jews by birth were converted on the day of Pentecost and Cornelius the uncircumcised centurion was discovered and baptized under the direct guidance of God. The narrative of Acts is plainly incomplete. Many of the adventures of Paul, the leading character in the second part of the book, are omitted (2 Cor. 11²⁴⁻²⁶). We are not told what became of the Twelve : we are not told how the Gospel first reached Rome : the great city of Alexandria, soon to become one of the leading centres of Christianity, is hardly mentioned at all.

The historian (who may with confidence be regarded as Luke, a travelling companion of St. Paul's and author of the third Gospel) places in the very centre of his volume an account (to some extent idealized ?) of a conference at Jerusalem at which it was decided that Gentiles need not be required to submit to circumcision in order to join the Church.

What St. Luke evidently feels his narrative shows is (i) that the natural course for the Jews, the course God intended them to take, was to accept Jesus as the Christ (the Messiah) and become Christians. Most of them actually took the unnatural course of not becoming Christians ; but that did not alter the fact that the Christians are now the true and direct heirs and successors to God's ancient people, Israel ; (ii) that such protection as Roman law gave Judaism was now naturally and rightly being given to Christianity (Acts 18¹⁴· ¹⁵) ; and so his book closes with the picture of the chief Christian missionary preaching and teaching in the capital city of the empire itself, " none forbidding him."

The third Gospel and Acts together are an attempt to present Christianity to the educated Roman world. Possibly Theophilus, as Streeter suggests (*The Four Gospels*, p. 539), was Flavius Clemens, first cousin of the Emperor Domitian, put to death in A.D. 96. Domitilla, the wife of Clemens, was secretly an adherent of the Church, and Clemens himself would seem to have been at least an inquirer (*ibid.* p. 535).

Enemies without. In Acts disturbances generally owe their origin to Jewish hostility, occasionally to mob violence. Rome is represented as the protector, upholding law and order. Liability to the death-penalty merely for being a Christian could not have come into existence earlier than Nero. It had come into existence by the time I Peter was written (4$^{15. 16}$). Streeter is probably right in dating this document about A.D. 90 at Symrna, when persecution was threatening ; and the Apocalypse gives evidence of an outbreak of persecution in Asia near the end of Domitian's reign (A.D. 90–95). The Epistle to the Hebrews, addressed most likely to Christians in Rome, also alludes to persecution in language which may be reminiscent of the persecution under Nero (10$^{32. 33}$, 13^{7}).

Enemies within. The Conference at Jerusalem (Acts 15) decided against the Judaizers, who thought that Gentiles, in order to be Christians, should be circumcised and keep the Jewish Law. They had been bitter opponents of St. Paul's, as the Epistle to the Galatians shows. To some extent they continued to dog his footsteps still (Phil. 3$^{2. 3}$; Col. 2^{16}). He had other enemies on the opposite wing of Libertinism (Gal. 5^{13}— see J. H. Ropes, *The Singular Problem of the Epistle to the Galatians* (cf. J. M. Creed in *J.T.S.*, 1930, pp. 421 ff.). —Rom. 6^{15}, cf. I Pet. 2^{16}). There were teachers too who exalted worldly wisdom at the expense of the simple proclamation of the Gospel (I Cor. 1, 2), and some who claimed to impart esoteric lore (Col. 2$^{8. 18}$). And the Church included numbers of weaker brethren who must not be made to stumble (I Cor. 8^{13}) in face of the many problems of conscience that must of necessity arise for Christians sharing the life of pagan cities (of which the problem of meat offered to idols is a good example). Moreover, before long, unworthy presbyters made their appearance (Acts 20^{29} ; I Pet. 5$^{1-3}$) ; and, of course, the party spirit (I Cor. 1^{12}) and the failure to live up to the Christian standard (Gal. 5^{16} ; Phil. 3$^{18. 19}$; Col. 3$^{5-10}$), which have marred the life of the Church all down the ages.

Missionary Zeal. One of the strong bonds which kept the various types of Christians from falling apart was missionary zeal. " There was nowhere any break, because all were united in something that transcended any difference : that is to say in their loyalty to Jesus Christ and their desire to spread His Kingdom " (C. H. Turner, *Catholic and Apostolic*, p. 242). Thus without any serious split or division Christianity gradually took " a form which could neither be understood in, nor directed from, a centre wholly alien to the culture of the great world " like Jerusalem (Streeter, *Camb. Anc. Hist.*, xi. p. 272).

Conditions in Jerusalem had, indeed, been peculiar from the first. Christians continued to worship in the Temple (Acts 2[46]) up to the great rebellion of A.D. 66–70 which resulted in its destruction. Moreover, the Church in Jerusalem had an unusual number of poor to look after, and, for a time at least, attempted a kind of communal life (Acts 4[32-35]). St. Paul took special pains to collect money for them (1 Cor. 16[1-4] ; 2 Cor. 8, 9). He evidently had an affectionate regard for the Jerusalem Church as the Mother Church. The destruction of the city was naturally a great interruption in the life of its Church, but even in the latter part of the second century there were still Christians who looked to Jerusalem as the centre of Christendom (*Clementine Homilies*).

2. RITES AND WORSHIP

Baptism. The rite of admission to membership of the Church was Baptism, the earliest references to which in the New Testament occur of course in St. Paul's epistles. St. Paul has in view the admission of adult instructed believers (cf. Acts 19[4. 5]). For them to be baptized means to be made to drink of the one Spirit : " by one Spirit, be we Jews or Greeks, slaves or free men, we have in baptism all been merged in one body and all imbibed one Spirit " (1 Cor. 12[13] —W. G. Rutherford).

The plunge beneath the water suggests death—death to the old pre-Christian manner of living. " Can it be that you are ignorant that all of us, who in baptism have been united with Christ, have in baptism partaken in His death ? In our baptism we were indeed laid in the grave with Him, partaking in His death, that, as Christ was raised from the dead by a manifestation of His Father's glory, so we also may regulate our conduct by a new principle, life. If we have come to share in one nature with Him by participation in the manner of His death, it cannot but be that we shall share therein by participation in the manner of His resurrection ; knowing, as we do know, that our former self was for this end

crucified with Him that our sinful self should be so reduced
to impotence that we should no longer be in subjection to
our sin. A man who has died to his sin is delivered from
his sin and made righteous. If we have died with Christ,
we believe that we shall also live with Him, being assured
that Christ raised from the dead never dies again, that death
never again has authority over Him. The death which He
died, He died for sin once for all ; the life which He lives, He
lives to God. So also must you conclude yourselves to be
dead but alive to God with Christ Jesus " (Rom. 6$^{3-11}$—
W. G. Rutherford).

Those who are baptized into the name of Jesus (1 Cor. 1^{15})
belong to Him. Baptism is baptism into Christ, *i.e.* into
union with Him, and so marks the beginning of a new life—
" in Him."   In Christ the Christian is a new creature
(2 Cor. 5^{17}) and his former sins no longer count against him.
1 Cor. 6^{11}—" but ye were washed, but ye were sanctified, but
ye were justified in the name of the Lord Jesus Christ, and
in the Spirit of our God "—must refer to baptism and the gift
of the Spirit associated with it. Perhaps " in the name of
the Lord Jesus Christ " is the baptismal formula.

Very similar ideas appear in Acts, *e.g.* Acts 2^{38}, " Repent
ye, and be baptized every one of you in the name of Jesus
Christ unto the remission of your sins ; and ye shall receive
the gift of the Holy Spirit."

The fact that the Holy Spirit had been received was
expected to manifest itself in some unmistakeable way, *e.g.*
by ecstatic utterance (Acts 10^{46}, 19^6). It is not surprising
that such manifestations did not always follow the rite of
baptism, *e.g.* at Samaria (Acts 8^{16}). Here the laying on of
hands with prayer is used by Peter and John to supplement
the other rite, and " they received the Holy Ghost."

We gather, indeed, that by the date when Acts was
written it had become customary for baptism into the name
with water to be followed by the laying on of hands with
prayer, almost as two parts of one initiatory rite (Acts 19$^{5. 6}$).
The writer, however, clearly recognizes that the gift of the
Holy Ghost is not tied to any rite. In 10$^{44ff.}$, for instance,
Cornelius and his friends receive the Spirit while Peter is
speaking and then are baptized—" Can any man forbid
water, that these should not be baptized, which have received
the Holy Spirit as well as we ? "   It must be added that in
Justin Martyr's account of baptism (*Apol.* i. 61, 65) there is
no mention of the laying on of hands, nor is it mentioned in
the short account in the Didache.

In 1 Cor. 1[14-18] St. Paul speaks of baptizing in such a way as to imply that he did not attach any great importance to the outward act : " Christ sent me not to baptize, but to preach the gospel . . . the word of the Cross . . . unto us which are being saved . . . is the power of God." Similarly, in 1 Pet. 3[21] the emphasis is removed from the mere lustration of the body to " the answer of a good conscience toward God."

As to the origin of baptism we have no precise information. According to later tradition Jesus Himself did not baptize, though His disciples did (John 4[2]). Very likely in this they were following the example of John the Baptist. " Baptism of converts as a ceremonial preliminary was a Jewish custom and was not regarded as having a sacramental efficacy " (New, *op. cit.* p. 135).

Matt. 28[19]—" Go ye therefore, and teach all nations, baptizing them into the name of the Father and of the Son and of the Holy Ghost "—belongs, of course, to the latest strata of that Gospel. The same baptismal formula appears in the Didache (7), and in Justin Martyr (*Apol.* i. 61), and no doubt it won its way fast.

The New Testament contains no clear instance of infant baptism. When the Philippian gaoler was baptized " with all his household " the household would mean dependents and slaves rather than babes. It is arguable that St. Paul (1 Cor. 7[14]) thought that the children of Christian parents did not need to be baptized. Still, the practice of infant baptism probably dates back to the apostolic age. Polycarp must have been baptized in infancy, and Justin Martyr refers to men who " had been made disciples from childhood." Infant baptism, however, did not become universal until much later. Tertullian objects to the practice. Even in the fourth century as pious a mother as Monnica did not feel bound to baptize her children in infancy (see Gwatkin, *Early Church History*, i. p. 250).

Worship. Starting again with St. Paul's epistles, we find Christians being exhorted to " pray without ceasing and in everything give thanks " (1 Thess. 5[17. 18]). Also they are not to despise prophesyings (*ibid.* 20) : and this letter is to be read to all the brethren at Thessalonica (*ibid.* 27). Christians must further study the Old Testament Scriptures (Rom. 15[4]). Groups of Christians used to meet in the house of one of their number. The church in the house of Prisca and Aquila and perhaps two other house-churches are referred to in Rom. 16. In 1 Cor. 14 we have a short description of the gathering of a local church.   Every one (*v.* 26) can take part in the meeting : one may have a psalm to sing, another a teaching to impart ; another may offer an ecstatic utterance, another the interpretation of such an utterance, another may wish to communicate a revelation.   It is evident that at that time (about A.D. 55) at Corinth such meetings were marked by great exuberance and women wished to speak as well as men.   The whole congregation felt itself swept away by a spiritual influence which they took to be the influence of the Spirit of Jesus.   Some were recognized as being more deeply and constantly inspired than the rest. These were spoken of as prophets ; and there were numbers of prophets in the congregation at Corinth.   The claims of such men were unchallenged.   " We received, not the spirit of the world, but the spirit which is of God ; that we might know the things that are freely given to us by God. Which things also we speak, not in words which man's wisdom teacheth, but which the Spirit teacheth ; comparing spiritual things with spiritual.   Now the natural man receiveth not the things of the Spirit of God : for they are foolishness unto him ; and he cannot know them, because they are spiritually judged.   But he that is spiritual judgeth all things, and he himself is judged of no man " (1 Cor. 2^{12-15}).

By the time St. Paul wrote, the situation, indeed, was getting out of hand, and St. Paul made a great effort to reduce the proceedings to order : " God is not a God of confusion, but of peace ; as in all the churches of the saints. . . . Let all things be done decently and in order " ($14^{33, 40}$).   The women are to keep silence in the churches (v.^{34})—though St. Paul's actual argument on this point is no longer convincing.

Reduced to order, such a meeting as that described in this passage, with the inclusion of readings from the Old Testament and occasionally of a letter from some leader like St. Paul himself (Col. 4^{16}), would be, generally speaking, on the lines of a service in a Jewish synagogue, with the congregation responding Amen to the prayers and thanksgivings (1 Cor. 14^{16}). The chief difference would be that the atmosphere would be freer and that more speakers would take part.   Moreover, the services were marked by overflowing joyfulness, finding expression in psalms and hymns and spiritual songs (Eph. 5^{19}), both old and new.   They were also permeated by a deep sense of fellowship of men and women with one another " in Christ."   It must be remembered that at first the Sacred Scriptures of the Church were simply the Old

Testament, and as few Christians would be rich enough to possess a copy even of a part of the Old Testament, their only opportunity of studying it was when they heard it read and expounded in Christian assemblies.

During the earliest period the persons of most importance in these Christian gatherings would be the prophet and the teacher (Acts 13¹), particularly the former. The passage quoted above (1 Cor. 2¹⁵) almost places the prophet above criticism. Soon the Church was driven to a more critical view: " Beloved, believe not every spirit, but prove the spirits whether they are of God : because many false prophets are gone out into the world "(1 John 4¹, cf. Didache, 11). Gradually prophet and teacher were eclipsed by presbyter-bishop and deacon. The Didache, as has already been mentioned, marks the transition : " Appoint for yourselves, therefore, bishops and deacons . . . despise them not, for they are your honourable men along with prophets and teachers "(Didache, 15). Gradually the services took a more settled form, even the seats being arranged in recognized order, not without regard for precedence (Jas. 2². ³).

In addition to such services at regular intervals, there were special gatherings on special occasions or for special purposes. Thus, for instance, at Antioch when it was decided that Barnabas and Saul should be sent out on missionary work "when they had fasted and prayed and laid their hands on them, they sent them away " (Acts 13³). Or, again, St. Paul directs that the Church at Corinth should assemble for the excommunication of a man living in flagrant immorality (1 Cor. 5⁴. ⁵).

Acts, especially, emphasizes what Streeter calls (*Camb. Anc. Hist.*, xi. p. 266) " communal spirit-possession " experienced in meetings for prayer (Acts 4³¹, 13²; cf. 15²⁸, 16⁶), and " the habitual submission of all problems, individual and communal, to the direction of the Holy Spirit."

The Lord's Supper. Besides services of the type we have been considering, the Christians from the first gave a prominent place to a common meal of a religious character. Here again it is St. Paul who gives us our earliest evidence. St. Paul refers to it as " the Lord's Supper," *i.e.* a meal in honour of Jesus. At Corinth it was a real meal, as the word *deipnon*, " supper," suggests, where people ate heartily and might drink even too much. Such abuse had indeed actually occurred, and that was why St. Paul referred to the subject. In his view it should not be a hunger-satisfying meal (1 Cor. 11²². ³⁴), but a religious meal. He had delivered to

them, he said, that which he had received (cf. 15³) of the
Lord (*apo*, not *para*, suggests " through others, ultimately
from the Lord "), " how that the Lord Jesus in the night
in which he was betrayed took bread : and when he had
given thanks, he brake it, and said, This is my body which
is for you : this do in remembrance of me.   In like manner
also the cup, after supper, saying, This cup is the new covenant
in my blood : this do, as oft as ye drink it, in remembrance
of me.   As often as you eat of this bread and drink of this
cup, you rehearse the Lord's death—until he come."

From this passage we certainly gather that when St. Paul
presided at the Lord's supper at Corinth, his first aim was to
fulfil the Lord's injunction, " Do this in remembrance of
me."   Do what ?   " Take a loaf of bread, give thanks,
break it, and eat it as representing my body, given for you "—
is that what St. Paul did ?   Did he simply take a loaf, give
thanks, break it, and distribute portions to those present,
telling them that the loaf represented Christ's body given
for them and they were to eat it in remembrance of Him ?
And similarly with the Cup ?   In what words did he give
thanks ?   Did they at all resemble those provided in the
Didache (9) : " But with regard to the Giving-of-thanks,
give thanks after this manner.   First, with regard to the
Cup, ' We give thanks to Thee, our Father, for the holy
vine of Thy child David, which Thou hast made known to us
through Thy child Jesus ; to Thee be glory for ever.'   But
with regard to the broken bread, ' We give thanks
to Thee, our Father, for the life and knowledge which Thou
hast made known to us through Thy child Jesus ; to Thee
be glory for ever.   As this broken bread was scattered upon
the mountains and gathered together became one, so let
Thy Church be gathered together from the ends of the earth
into Thy kingdom, for Thine is the glory and the power
through Jesus Christ for ever.' "

Did St. Paul use words in any way resembling these ?
If so, did he distribute the portions of bread and administer
the cup without saying anything further : especially if as in
the Didache (10) there was a further thanksgiving said after
all had partaken ?   " But, after being filled, give thanks
thus : We give thanks to Thee, Holy Father, for Thy holy
Name, which Thou hast caused to dwell in our hearts, and
for the knowledge and faith and immortality which Thou
hast made known to us by Jesus Thy Child ; to Thee be glory
for ever.   Thou, O Almighty Ruler, didst create all things
for Thy Name's sake ; Thou gavest men food and drink for

enjoyment that they might give thanks to Thee, but us Thou blessedst with spiritual food, drink, and eternal life through Thy Child. Before all things we give thanks to Thee that Thou art mighty ; to Thee be glory for ever. Remember, O Lord, Thy Church to deliver her from all evil and to perfect her in Thy love, and gather her together from the four winds, her the sanctified, into Thy kingdom which Thou preparedst for her ; for Thine is the power and the glory for ever. Let grace come, and let this world pass away. Hosanna to the God of David. If any one be holy let him come, if any one be not holy let him repent. Maranatha. Amen."

This seems hardly sufficient as a rehearsing of the Lord's death. Did St. Paul make sure of a proper rehearsal by briefly telling, on each occasion, the story of the Last Supper as he does here ?—suiting his actions to the words ?

To such questions we can give no certain answers, but we may be sure that somehow St. Paul made it clear that the whole point of the Lord's Supper was the rehearsal of the Lord's death and the remembrance of Him. He regards it as a most solemn memorial, and any lack of seriousness or reverence will bring swift judgement upon the offender.

" Wherefore every one who shall eat of the bread, or drink of the cup of the Lord as if to do so were an act not differing from any other, shall be held responsible in respect of the body and the blood of the Lord. Let a man scrutinize his own motives, and then, not before, let him eat his portion of the loaf and drink from the cup. For he who eats and drinks, eats and drinks judgement against himself, if the body he discern not. This is the reason why many among you are ill and infirm, and why quite a number have died."

Some commentators press this passage to mean that St. Paul identified the actual particles of bread with the literal body of Christ. But if there was anything of the Jew left in St. Paul this is a most unlikely interpretation. Moreover, his mystical and darting thought had certainly discovered another association of ideas. Later on in this same epistle he says to the Corinthians (12^{27}), " Ye are the body of Christ "; and earlier ($10^{16, 17}$) he had already brought that conception into connexion with the Lord's Supper. " The cup of blessing which we bless, is it not that whereby we have communion with each other in the blood of Christ ? The loaf which we break, is it not that whereby we have communion with each other in the body of Christ ? Seeing that we who are many, are one loaf, one body : for we all partake of the one loaf." (See F. C. Burkitt, *Eucharist and Sacrifice*.)

But how is the Lord's Supper of 1 Corinthians related to "the breaking of the bread" in the Lucan writings (Luke 24[35]; Acts 2[42, 46], 20[7])? From the last of these passages we infer that it was the custom to gather on the first day of the week "to break bread." This particular gathering was held in the evening, and Paul's discourse was so long that it was not until after midnight that he actually broke the bread. We may be sure that he made it the occasion of a rehearsal of the Lord's death. But was there this special reference to the Lord's death on every occasion when, according to Acts, the bread was broken? In particular the language of Acts 2[46]—"Day by day, continuing steadfastly with one accord in the temple, and breaking bread at home, they did take their food with gladness and singleness of heart, praising God and having favour with all the people"—does not naturally point to such a conclusion. There is, moreover, a great deal to be said for the view advocated by Blass, Wellhausen, E. Meyer, and other scholars, that the original text of Luke 22 did not include verses 19 and 20 as printed in our English version—that is to say, did not include any account of the institution of the Lord's Supper. In that case it becomes still easier to regard "the breaking of bread" as a fellowship-meal, and to suppose that such fellowship-meals were a regular feature of Christ's intercourse with His disciples (Luke 9[16]—cf. the common meal among the Essenes) and were continued in the early Church. On this theory it would only be on some occasions and not on all that there would be a rehearsal of the Lord's death. Even without that there might be a vivid sense of the Lord's presence (Matt. 18[20]). But very soon, or even from the first, this rehearsal may have been included in "the breaking of the bread" on the first day of the week.

Another question arises: Did the Christians always have wine at their common meal? It may not be altogether fanciful to see in the exact wording of the phrase "Do this, as often as ye drink it, in remembrance of me" an indication that wine was not provided at every common meal. Jewish custom might suggest the provision of wine at least on the first day of the week; and it may be that it was on the first day of the week when wine was provided that "the breaking of the bread" regularly found its climax in the rehearsal of the Lord's death.

A further question cannot be evaded: can the words "this do in remembrance of me . . . this do, as oft as ye drink it, in remembrance of me" be regarded as *ipsissima verba* of Jesus ? They are not in the original text of any of the gospels. If they were not actually uttered by Jesus Himself, how came they to be attributed to Him ? Have we here an instance of words spoken " in the spirit " by some Christian prophet in the name of the Lord ? In moments of inspiration Christian prophets seem to have had complete assurance—" we have the mind of Christ " (1 Cor. 2¹⁶). The Odes of Solomon contain remarkable examples of the utterances of a Christian prophet-poet who in moments of ecstasy seems to feel that he is simply opening his mouth for Christ to speak through him.

What then did Jesus actually do and say " in the night in which he was betrayed " ? There would seem to be two main streams of tradition, one that of Mark and Paul, and the other that of the " Western " text of Luke which receives some support from the Didache and from 1 Cor. 10¹⁶.

St. Mark's narrative is as follows, " And as they were eating, he took bread, and when he had blessed, he brake it, and gave to them, and said, Take ye : this is my body. And he took a cup, and when he had given thanks, he gave to them : and they all drank of it. And he said unto them, This is my blood of the covenant, which is shed for many. Verily I say unto you, I will no more drink of the fruit of the vine, until that day when I drink it new in the kingdom of God."

The Western text of St. Luke reads thus : " And he said unto them, With desire I have desired to eat this passover with you before I suffer : for I say unto you, I will not eat it, until it be fulfilled in the Kingdom of God. And he received a cup, and when he had given thanks, he said, Take this, and divide it among yourselves : for I say unto you, I will not drink from henceforth of the fruit of the vine until the Kingdom of God shall come. And he took bread and when he had given thanks, he brake it, and gave it to them, saying, This is my body. But behold, the hand of him that betrayeth me . . ."

The evidence at our disposal being so fragmentary, it is natural to ask which is the simplest reconstruction of the narrative which will give the account both most probable in itself and also most likely to have given rise to the other accounts. It will be noted that according to the Western text of St. Luke the cup is a preliminary and is not connected with the idea of blood. The " rehearsal of death " is thus confined to the bread broken and the words " This is my body." Thus the difficulty to which Klausner refers would be removed—" The drinking of blood, even if it was meant symbolically, could only have aroused horror in the minds of such simple Galilæan Jews" (*Jesus of Nazareth*, E.T., p. 329). If the idea of the wine as representing blood was introduced at a later stage, the thought being of "the blood of the covenant," the difficulty at that stage would not have been so acute.

Further, in St. Paul's account, the words "after supper" may suggest the deliberate correction of another account in which a different use of an earlier cup was described.

This is not the place to discuss the arguments in detail, but there is much to be said for the view that the Western text of Luke gives us the story which takes us nearest to the actual events and the story which most easily would have given rise by natural modification to the others. It must be admitted, however, that the evidence is inconclusive.

By far the best attested Words of Institution are the four : "This is my body." Although the Last Supper was not the actual passover meal, passover associations lay behind it. Must not Jesus have been thinking of the bodies of the lambs which would the next day be left lifeless in the Temple as He broke the loaf and said " (This is what is to be done to me)—this is my body." If so, whatever modification of detail may have been introduced by his time or by him into the remembrancing, St. Paul has preserved the heart of the matter when he writes " Our passover lamb has been sacrificed, namely, Christ " (I Cor. 5^7).

A further question must now be considered. Do the Christian rites as described in the New Testament show any sign of the influence of the so-called Mystery Religions ? Judging from St. Paul's attitude to paganism in general (I Cor. $8^{4. 5}$, $10^{20. 21}$), we should expect him to regard the Mysteries as mere "trickery and buffoonery," just as his older contemporary Philo of Alexandria did (*De Spec. Leg.* I (12), 319). "Christianity is in its main features a continuation of Judaism. There is no real parallel to be traced between the vague and fleeting forms of pagan myth and the historic story of the Christian redemption. . . . There is no adequate evidence for the notion that there was in the pagan Mysteries anything at all parallel to the Christian Eucharist " (Percy Gardner, "The Pagan Mysteries," *Modern Churchman*, Oct. 1926, pp. 318, 322). When St. Paul is speaking of " the table of demons " (I Cor. 10^{21}), he is not referring to pagan Mystery cults, but to feasts in honour of the deities, or demons as he calls them, who were worshipped at Corinth, that is, the deities of the public cult, of which Christians might be invited to partake

(Percy Gardner, *ibid.*; cf. "the table of the Lord Serapis," *Ox. Pap.* 110, 523).

At the same time there is evidence that the influence of the Mysteries was hovering on the fringes of the Church. Thus in Col. 2¹⁸ St. Paul, in warning his readers against a certain type of teacher, quotes the phrase " walking on things which he has seen." This seems to be a phrase from a Mystery Religion, for Ramsay discovered two tablets in a Greek temple in Asia Minor containing the sentences " I have seen : I have walked " *i.e.* " I have looked upon the sacred drama : I have entered upon the mystic way of life " (*Athenæum*, 25th Jan. 1913). In another passage St. Paul himself makes an allegorical use of the Old Testament to warn the Corinthians that the eating of " spiritual meat " and the drinking of " spiritual drink " do not necessarily give spiritual life (1 Cor. 10¹⁻¹²). Before the middle of the next century the Mystery cults had made a distinct mark upon the Church. Thus Ignatius speaks of " breaking one bread, which is the medicine of immortality and the antidote that we should not die but live for ever in Jesus Christ " (Eph. 20).

Developments, however, came very slowly, and it is not at all a far cry from the services as described by St. Paul to the Sunday morning service at Rome about A.D. 150 as described by Justin Martyr (*Apol.* i. 65–67). With Justin's account this chapter may now conclude. After describing a baptism he goes on : " But after having thus washed him that is persuaded and has given his assent, we bring him to where the brethren as they are called are gathered together, to make earnest prayers in common for ourselves and for the newly enlightened, and for all others everywhere, that we may be counted worthy after we have learned the truth, by our works also to be found right livers and keepers of the commandments, that we may be saved with the eternal salvation. We salute each other with a kiss when our prayers are ended. Afterwards is brought to the president of the brethren bread and a cup of water and wine, and he takes it and offers up praise and glory to the Father of the universe through the name of the Son and the Holy Spirit, and gives thanks at length, that we have received these favours from Him ; and at the end of his prayers and thanksgiving the whole people present responds, saying Amen. Now the word Amen in the Hebrew language signifies So be it. Then after the president has given thanks and all the people have responded, the deacons as we call them allow every one of those present to partake of the bread and wine and water for which thanks have been given ; and for those absent they take away a portion.

"And this food is called by us Eucharist, and it is not lawful for any man to partake of it unless he believes our teaching to be true, and has been washed with the washing which is for the forgiveness of sins and unto a new birth, and is so living as Christ commanded. For not as common bread and common drink do we receive these ; but as Jesus Christ our Saviour, being made flesh through the word of God, took both flesh and blood for our salvation, so also were we taught that the food for which thanks are given by the word of prayer that comes from Him—food by which blood and flesh by assimilation are nourished—is both flesh and blood of that Jesus who was made flesh. For the apostles in the memoirs which they composed, which are called Gospels, declared that Jesus commanded them to do as follows : He took bread and gave thanks and said, This do in remembrance of me, this is my body ; and in like manner He took the cup, and after He had given thanks said, This is my blood, and gave of it only to them. Which the evil demons imitated, commanding it to be done also in the mysteries of Mithras ; for that bread and a cup of water are set forth with certain formulæ in the ceremonial of initiation, you either know or can learn.

"But we afterwards henceforward continually put each other in mind of these things, and those of us who are wealthy help all that are in want, and we always remain together. And for all things that we eat we bless the Maker of all through His Son Jesus Christ, and through the Holy Spirit. And on the so-called day of the Sun there is a meeting of all of us who live in cities or in the country, and the memoirs of the Apostles or the writings of the prophets are read, as long as time allows. Then when the reader has ceased, the president gives by word of mouth his admonition and exhortation to follow these excellent things. Afterwards we all rise at once and offer prayers ; and as I said, when we have ceased to pray, bread is brought and wine and water, and the president likewise offers up prayers and thanksgivings to the best of his power, and the people responds with its Amen. Then follows the distribution to each and the partaking of that for which thanks were given ; and to them that are absent a portion is sent by the hand of the deacons. Of those that are well-to-do and willing, every one gives what he will according to his own purpose, and the collection is deposited with the president, and he it is that succours orphans and widows, and those that are in want through sickness or any other cause, and those that are in bonds, and the strangers that are sojourning, and in short he has the care of all that are in need."

BIBLIOGRAPHY

B. H. Streeter, *The Primitive Church*, with the review by Bishop Headlam in the *Church Quarterly Review*, April 1930, pp. 89–119.
"The Rise of Christianity" in *The Cambridge Ancient History*, XI. (pp. 253–293).
S. Cave, *The Gospel of St. Paul* (1929).
A. C. Headlam, *The Doctrine of the Church and Christian Reunion* (1920), with the review by C. H. Turner, *Catholic and Apostolic* (1931), pp. 273–294.
H. B. Swete and C. H. Turner, *Essays on the Early History of the Church and the Ministry* (2nd ed. 1921).
H. Lietzmann, *Messe und Herrenmahl* (1926).
F. C. Burkitt, *Eucharist and Sacrifice* (2nd ed. 1927).

APPENDIX

THE CALENDAR

FOR the purpose of measuring time we may use natural divisions (day, lunar month, year) or artificial (minute, hour, week, calendar month). The difficulties of time-measurement arise from the incommensurability of the natural periods. The lunar month is not a whole number of days, but rather more than $29\frac{1}{2}$; the year is not a whole number of days, but rather less than $365\frac{1}{4}$; the number of lunar months in a year is rather less than 12.37.

The natural unit is the day. In the earliest parts of the Bible this usually means the period from sunrise to sunset, the period of daylight, as distinguished from night. The day is roughly divided into periods : daybreak, midday, afternoon, evening ; but there is no exact division into hours. The night is divided into three watches (Lam. 2^{19} ; Judg. 7^{19} ; Ex. 11^4, 14^{24} ; 1 Sam. 11^{11}). In the post-exilic period the Jews adopted the Babylonian system of reckoning the civil day from sunset to sunset. In the New Testament and Talmud we find the division of the day into temporal hours. In this system, probably borrowed from the Babylonian, the period from sunrise to sunset is divided into twelve equal parts ; and the "hour" may vary from 49 to 71 minutes according to the time of the year. A similar division is in use for the night (Acts 23^{23}). In the New Testament the Roman division of the night into four watches is found (Mark 6^{48}, 13^{35}), though the older Jewish three-watch system seems to survive in Luke 12^{38} (Q).

For the marking of longer periods recourse was had at first to the recurrent phenomena of the agricultural year. The so-called Calendar-inscription of Gezer (Driver, *Notes on Samuel*, pp. vii f.) begins with "the month of ingathering" and ends with "the month of summer-fruits " ; and the oldest month-names in the Old Testament (Ābīb, Zīw, Ēthānīm, and Būl) are probably to be explained agriculturally. In the exilic period the Jews became acquainted with the Babylonian calendar of twelve months, whose beginnings were fixed by observation of the lunar crescent. Now 12 lunar months = 354 days, so that the year of 12 lunar months is short of the solar year by $11\frac{1}{4}$ days. This was met by repeating a month from time to time, and so the months were kept in the same season of the year. The Babylonian calendar was already in use in the Jewish Colony at Elephantine in the fifth century B.C. The names of the months are.: Nīsān (=Ābīb=March-April), Iyyār (=Zīw=April-May), Sīwān (=May-June), Tammūz (=June-July), Āb (=July-Aug.), Elūl (=Aug.-Sept.), Tishrī (=Ēthānīm=Sept.-Oct.), Marcheshwān (=Būl=Oct.-Nov.), Kislew (=Nov.-Dec.), Ṭēbēth (=Dec.-Jan.), Shebāṭ (=Jan.-Feb.), Adār (=Feb.-March). When an extra month was required, Adār was repeated.

In this calendar the year begins in the spring, whereas the old Hebrew calendar put the New Year in the autumn. It seems that the division of the year into two parts, with new beginnings at 1 Nīsān and 1 Tishrī goes back to the Sumerian origins of the system. At the beginning of the Christian era the Jews observed both days, 1 Nīsān as the beginning of the ecclesiastical year and 1 Tishrī as the beginning of the civil year (Josephus, *Ant.* I. iii. 3, § 81 ; cf. Mishnah, *Rosh Hashanah*, i. 1). The later Jewish calendar, still in use, reckons from 1 Tishrī.

The week is an artificial unit of time whose origin still presents problems. The nearest analogy is the Assyrian system promulgated by Ashurbanipal in the seventh century B.C., ordaining as days of rest the 7th, 14th, 19th, 21st and 28th of each month. The 19th was a kind of *dies nefastus*. If it be put on one side we have the seven-day week. But the weeks do not go on continuously. There is a break of one or two days at the end of the fourth week, so that the beginning of next month may coincide with the first day of a new week. In the Biblical system this rule is no longer observed ; the weeks continue in a regular cycle without regard to the new moon, and the first day of the month may fall on any day of the week. Equally the seventh day of the week, the day of rest, may fall on any day of the month.

This rest-day, the Sabbath, is, along with circumcision, a fundamental observance in Judaism. Its origin presents difficult problems. In Babylonian the 15th of the month is called *shapattu* or *shabattu* ; but it is not a day of rest. In Babylonia there is the interdiction of work on the seventh day, but the seventh day is not called Sabbath. In the Old Testament the two things have somehow been combined, and the name *shabattu* transferred to the weekly day of rest. How this happened is a mystery. It is to be noted that the Sabbath is a whole day running from sunset on Friday to sunset on Saturday.

The year is marked by the recurrence of the annual festivals. The festal calendar in Lev. 23 gives the following, in addition to the Sabbath :

> Passover on Nīsān 14.
> Maṣṣōth (unleavened bread), Nīsān 15 (–21).
> Firstfruits (Pentecost or Feast of Weeks), 50 days after the Sabbath in Nīsān 15–21, *i.e.* on a day in the first week of Sīwān.
> Day of Remembrance (New Year's Day), Tishrī 1.
> Day of Atonement, Tishrī 10.
> Feast of Booths (Tabernacles), Tishrī 15–21 and 22 (Eighth Day).

At a later date other feasts and fasts are added, so that we get the following calendar (Thackeray, *The Septuagint and Jewish Worship*, p. 137):

Nīsān 1 . .	Ecclesiastical New Year.
,, 14–21. .	Feast of Passover and unleavened bread (Maṣṣōth).
Sīwān *c.* 6 .	Feast of Weeks (Pentecost).
Tammūz 17 .	Fast. (Babylonian capture of Jerusalem.)
Āb 9 . . .	Fast. (Burning of the Temple.)
Elūl 1 . .	New Year for tithes.
Tishrī 1 . .	Civil New Year (Rosh ha-Shanah.)
,, 3 . .	Fast of Gedaliah.
,, 10 . .	Day of Atonement (Yom Kippur.)
,, 15–22 .	Feast of Tabernacles (Sukkoth) and Eighth Day.
Kislew 25 to ⎱ Tēbēth 2 ⎰	Feast of Dedication (Ḥanukkah.)
Tēbēth 10 . .	Fast. (Beginning of Babylonian siege of Jerusalem.)
Ādār 14–15 .	Feast of Purim.

In addition to the fasts in the calendar additional public fasts could be decreed by the authorities in any time of national distress or danger ; and among the Pharisees there grew up the practice of regular private fasts twice a week (on Mondays and Thursdays). Cf. Luke 18[12].

The sabbatical year, in which no agricultural work was permitted and the land lay fallow, was observed every seventh year in the post-exilic period (see Lev. 25[1-7] ; 1 Macc. 6[49, 53] ; Jos. *Ant.* XIV. xvi. 2 and cf. Lev. 26[34ff.] ; Ex. 21[2ff.], 23[10ff.] ; Deut. 15[12ff.]). The sabbatical year ran from autumn (1 Tishrī) to autumn. There is evidence that it was observed in 164–3 B.C. 38–37 B.C., and A.D. 68–69. From these fixed points it is easy to calculate the intervening sabbatical years. The year of jubilee (Lev. 25[8-55], 27[17-25] ; Num. 36[4]) should be observed after every seventh sabbatical year, *i.e.* every fiftieth year. It appears to have been calculated but not observed.

CHRONOLOGY

The simplest method of dating an event is by placing it before or after another : the prophetic ministry of Amos is dated " two years before the earthquake," and doubtless the earthquake was a well-remembered event when the note of time was written. More convenient points of reference are provided by the regnal years of kings. The chronology of the Kings of Israel and Judah is set out in this way. Jehoram became King of Israel in the eighteenth year of Jehoshaphat of Judah, and he reigned twelve years (2 Kings 3[1]) ; in Jehoram's eleventh year Ahaziah became King of Judah (2 Kings 9[29]), and so on. From such data as these a relative chronology can be constructed, showing the order of events in the period and the intervals between them. An absolute chronology is obtained when we are able to measure the interval between the present time and these dated events in the past. For this purpose a fixed point of reference is required from which there may be continuous reckoning by years. The oldest system of this kind is the Seleucid era, whose epoch is 1st October 312 B.C. (in Babylonia probably 1 Nīsān 311 B.C. to fit the Babylonian New Year). Given a date in the Seleucid era it is a simple matter to reduce it to a date B.C. or A.D. For the earlier times fixed points can be obtained where astronomical events have been recorded, e.g. the eclipse of the sun in the reign of Ashurdan III. of Assyria, which is calculated as having happened on 15th June 763 B.C. With the help of such data it is possible to construct a chronological table, in which some dates may be regarded as fairly certain, others as probably correct within a few years, others as still uncertain. It is, for example, still a matter of debate whether the Israelite entry into Palestine is to be dated c. 1400 B.C. or c. 1185 B.C., or divided between the two dates. (For a survey of recent discussion see H. H. Rowley's article in the *Bulletin of the John Rylands Library*, xxii. (1938), 243–290.) In the following table only the more important dates are given ; for more detailed tables and synchronisms reference may be made to the *Cambridge Ancient History*, or to Oesterley and Robinson's *History of Israel*.

B.C.
c. 1200. Philistine entry into Palestine.
Period of the Judges.
c. 1025. Saul.
c. 1010. David.

B.C.

c. 974.   Solomon.

c. 937.   Break-up of Solomon's kingdom.

[The Old Testament fixes the relative chronology
of the subsequent period by giving the length of each
king's reign, and the year of his accession in terms
of the regnal years of his neighbour.   Here length
of reign is given in brackets after the name and
accession year in roman numerals.]

	JUDAH	ISRAEL
	Rehoboam (17).	Jeroboam I (22).
	Abijam (3).	XVIII
	Asa (41).	XX
	II	Nadab (2).
	III	Baasha (24).
	XXVI	Elah (2).
	XXVII	Zimri, Tibni.
c. 887–6.	XXXI	Omri (12).
c. 876.	XXXVIII	Ahab (22).
	Jehoshaphat (25).	IV

Prophetic ministries of
Elijah and Micaiah ben
Imlah.

853.   Battle of Karkar.

	XVII	Ahaziah (1).
	XVIII (2 Kings 3¹).	Jehoram (12).

c. 850.   Composition of J.   Revolt of Mesha of Moab.

	Jehoram (8).	V
	Ahaziah (1).	XII
	Prophetic ministry of Elisha.	
841.	Athaliah (6).	Jehu (by revolution).

Jehu pays tribute to Assyria
(841).

	Jehoash (40)	VII
	XXIII	Jehoahaz (17).

805.   Damascus subdued by Adad-Nirari III. of Assyria.

	XXXVII	Jehoash (16).

c. 800–750.   Composition of E.

	Amaziah (29).	II
c. 785.	Azariah (Uzziah) (52).	Jeroboam II (41).
c. 760.		Prophetic ministry of Amos
	(Jotham co-regent from *c.* 755).	
	XXXVIII	Zechariah (½).
	XXXIX	Shallum (1 month) Menahem (10).
	Jotham (alone).	

c. 740–722.   Prophetic ministry of Hosea.

738.   Menahem pays tribute to
Assyria.

	L	Pekahiah (2).

Prophetic ministries of Isaiah
and Micah.

c. 735.   Ahaz,   Pekah (by revolution).

B.C.	JUDAH	ISRAEL
735–4.	Syro-Ephraimite attack on Judah. Assyrian defeat of Damascus and Samaria. Ahaz, vassal of Assyria, *c.* 734–3.	
732.	XII	Hoshea
732.	Fall of Damascus Hezekiah (29)	III
724.		Assyrian invasion of Israel and siege of Samaria.
722–1.	VI	Fall of Samaria. End of Northern Kingdom.
711.	Rebellion in Philistia, Assyrians capture Ashdod.	
701.	Sennacherib's campaign in Palestine.	
c. 692–6.	Manasseh, King of Judah (55).	
c. 675.	Manasseh, vassal of Assyria.	
c. 638–41.	Amon.	
c. 637–9.	Josiah.	
626.	Prophetic ministry of Zephaniah and (626–*c.* 586) of Jeremiah.	
c. 621.	Josiah's reforms.	
614.	Ashur sacked by the Medes.	
612 (Aug.).	Fall of Nineveh. Prophecy of Nahum.	
610.	Fall of Harran.	
608.	Battle of Megiddo ; death of Josiah. Jehoahaz, King of Judah (three months). Jehoiakim, King of Judah.	
605.	Battle of Carchemish.	
598–7.	Jehoiakim's revolt. Jehoiachin (597).	
597.	Jerusalem captured. First deportation. Zedekiah, King of Judah.	
c. 596–586.	Prophetic activity of Ezekiel (Ezek. 1–32).	
586.	Zedekiah's revolt. Fall of Jerusalem. Second deportation.	
c. 584–572.	Ezekiel 33–39. Ezekiel 40–48 after 572.	
581.	Third deportation.	
c. 550.	Deutero-Isaiah.	
539. (Oct.-Nov.)	Capture of Babylon by Cyrus.	
538–7.	Return of Jewish exiles.	
520–516.	Building of second Temple. Prophetic activity of Haggai (520) and Zechariah (520–518).	
c. 460.	Composition of Malachi.	
c. 445.	Nehemiah's return.	
[444.	Ezra's promulgation of the Law, if not to be dated in 397.]	
c. 432.	Nehemiah's second visit to Jerusalem.	
c. 400.	Composition of Job.	
398.	Return of exiles under Ezra.	
397.	Ezra's promulgation of the Law [or 444].	
335.	Samaritan schism.	
334–330.	Alexander's campaigns against Persia.	
332.	Alexander's conquest of Judæa.	
330.	Death of Darius.	
323. (June 13)	Death of Alexander.	

B.C.

c. 319.	Palestine under Egyptian rule (Ptolemy).
312.	Seleucus establishes himself at Babylon.
301.	Battle of Ipsus.
300.	Foundation of Antioch.
	Composition of Chronicles, Ezra, Nehemiah (after 300) ; Ecclesiastes (*c.* 250).
223–187.	Antiochus III, the Great.
217. (June 22)	Battle of Raphia.
c. 200.	Palestine passes to Seleucid Empire.
176–5. (winter)	Accession of Antiochus IV, Epiphanes.
168 or 167. (Dec.)	Profanation of the Temple.
c. 166.	Composition of Daniel.
165 or 164. (Dec.)	Rededication of Temple.
160. (spring)	Death of Judas Maccabæus.
152. (autumn)	Jonathan appointed High Priest.
c. 150.	Composition of Esther.
143 (end).	Death of Jonathan.
142. (spring)	Jewish autonomy under Simon, High Priest and Ethnarch.
135–4.	Death of Simon : accession of John Hyrcanus.
104.	Death of John Hyrcanus: accession of Aristobulus I. (104–103).
103–76.	Alexander Jannæus (High Priest and King).
76–67.	Alexandra Salome, Queen of Judæa
67–63.	Civil War between Hyrcanus II. and Aristobulus II.
63.	Surrender of Jerusalem to Pompey. Judæa under Roman control.
63–40.	Hyrcanus II.
40–37.	Antigonus Mattathias.
37.	Herod captures Jerusalem.
27–A.D. 14.	AUGUSTUS.
20–19.	Building of Herod's Temple begun.
4.	Death of Herod. His kingdom divided between :
	Herod Antipas, Tetrarch of Galilee and Peræa, 4 B.C.– A.D. 39.
	Herod Philip II., Tetrarch of Batanæa, Trachonitis, etc., 4 B.C.–A.D. 34.
A.D.	Herod Archelaus, Ethnarch of Judæa, Idumæa, and Samaria, 4 B.C.–A.D. 6.
14–37.	TIBERIUS.
26.	Pontius Pilate becomes Procurator of Judæa.
28–29.	Beginning of John the Baptist's ministry.
	[The date of the Crucifixion presents an unsolved, probably insoluble, problem. The dates chiefly favoured are Passover of 29 (see C. H. Turner, art. " Chronology " in Hastings' *Dictionary of the Bible*) and 33 (April 3) (see Fotheringham in *Journal of Theological Studies*, xxxv. (1934), 146–162).]

A.D.

37–41.	GAIUS (Caligula).
37.	Herod Agrippa I. ruler of Ituræa and Trachonitis.
40.	Herod Agrippa I., ruler of Galilee.
41.	Herod Agrippa I., ruler of Judæa and Samaria. (Died, 44.)
41–54.	CLAUDIUS.
c. 46.	Famine in Judæa (Acts 11).
49–50.	Paul's arrival in Corinth.
50–100.	Agrippa II.
51–52.	Gallio Proconsul of Achæa.
52–60(?)	Antonius Felix, Procurator of Judæa.
54–68.	NERO.
58.	Paul's last visit to Jerusalem.
60(?)–62.	Porcius Festus, Procurator of Judæa.
64.	Great Fire at Rome. Persecution of Christians by Nero.
66.	Outbreak of Jewish War.
68–69.	Civil wars following death of Nero.
69–79.	VESPASIAN.
70.	Fall of Jerusalem.
79–81.	TITUS.
81–96.	DOMITIAN.
c. 96.	Persecutions of Christians. Letter from Roman Church to Corinthian (1 Clem.).
96–98.	NERVA.
98–117.	TRAJAN.
c. 107.	Martyrdom of Symeon of Jerusalem.
112.	Persecution of Bithynian Christians by Pliny.
c. 115.	Martyrdom of Ignatius.
115–117.	Jewish revolt in Cyrene, Cyprus, and Mesopotamia.
117–138.	HADRIAN.
132–135.	Jewish revolt under Bar Cocheba.
135.	Jerusalem destroyed and rebuilt as *Aelia Capitolina*.

WEIGHTS, MEASURES, AND MONEY

Length :

4 Fingerbreadths (*'esba'*) = 1 Handbreadth (*tōphach* (Ex.
  (Jer. 52²¹)   25²⁵).
3 Handbreadths   = 1 Span (*zereth*) (Ex. 28¹⁶).
2 Spans   = 1 Cubit (*'ammah*) (*passim*).
6 Cubits   = 1 Reed (*ḳāneh*) (Ezek. 40⁵).
2000 Cubits   = 1 Sabbath day's journey.

The cubit is a variable unit. In Babylonia, Egypt, and
Israel there are two standards, the common cubit and the
" royal " or " holy," which is ⅙ greater than the common.
The Babylonian common cubit is reckoned at 49·5 cm. (*c.* 19·5
in.), Egyptian, 45 cm. (*c.* 17·7 in.); Babylonian " royal,"
55 cm. (*c.* 21·6 in.), Egyptian, 52·5 cm. (*c.* 20·7 in.).

The " furlong " (Luke 24¹³) is also variable : the shorter
" furlong " 202 to 209 yds., the longer about 228 yds. The
mile (Roman) (Matt. 5⁴¹) is reckoned at 1478 metres, or about
1617 yds.

Capacity :

(Dry)   1 Cab   = 2·024 litres (*c.* 3·55 pints).
         6 Cabs   = 1 Seah (*c.* 2·66 gals.).
         3 Seahs   = 1 Ephah (*c.* 7·98 gals.).
        10 Ephahs = 1 Homer or Cor (*c.* 79·8 gals.).
(Liquid) 1 Log   = 0·5 litre (*c.* 0·88 pint).
        12 Logs   = 1 Hin (*c.* 10·56 pints).
         6 Hins   = 1 Bath (= 1 Ephah = *c.* 7·98 gals.).

Measures mentioned in the New Testament are the ξέστης
(Mark 7⁴, R.V. " pots ") = *sextarius* = *c.* 0·96 pint ; the χοῖνιξ
(Rev. 6⁶, R.V. " measure ") = *c.* 1·92 pints ; the μόδιος (Matt.
5¹⁵, R.V. " bushel ") = 1·92 gals. ; the σάτον (seah) (Matt. 13³³ ;
Luke 13²¹, R.V. " measure ") = *c.* 2·66 gals. ; the κόρος (Luke
16⁷, R.V. " measure ") = cor = 79·8 gals. ; the βάτος (Luke 16⁶,
R.V. " measure ") = bath = *c.* 7·98 gals. ; the μετρητής (John
2⁶, R.V. " firkin ") = *c.* 8·66 gals. ; the λίτρα = Lat. *libra*
(John 12³, 19³⁹, R.V. " pound ") = *c.* 11½ oz.

Weights. The Israelite system in its earliest form is closely allied to the Babylonian. It is sexagesimal :

> 60 Shekels = 1 Mina.
> 60 Minas = 1 Talent.

At a later time 50 shekels went to the mina. By the Babylonian standard the shekel is estimated at 16·37 grammes = 0·577 oz. avoirdupois or 252·59 grains. The Phœnician shekel of 14·55 grammes or 224·5 grains was used for silver.

The shekel was divided into half-shekels (*beḳa'*, Gen. 24^{22}), quarter-shekels (1 Sam. 9^8), and twentieths (*gērā*, Ex. 30^{13}).

Money. The oldest Palestinian coins are Persian darics (1 Chron. 29^7), which circulated all over the East in the Persian period. The daric was a gold coin of 8·36 grammes or 129 grains. There was silver coin = $\frac{1}{20}$ daric (Neh. 5^{15}, " shekel of silver," 86·4 grains). It now appears that Judah, in the Persian period, also had a provincial silver coinage of its own. To this coinage is assigned the British Museum specimen (*Catalogue*, Plate XIX. No. 29), on which the inscription is now read as YHD (Judah) instead of YHW (Yahu). Coins of Alexander the Great, the Ptolemies, and the Seleucids also circulated in Palestine, as did the coins of Tyre and Sidon. In 139–8 B.C. Simon Maccabæus obtained the right to mint his own coinage. It is uncertain whether a series of silver shekels and half-shekels should be assigned to him or to the period of the Jewish War of A.D. 66–70 (weight of shekel 14·27 grammes or 220·18 grains). A second series of silver shekels and quarter-shekels was struck during the Bar Cocheba revolt (A.D. 132–135). For the rest the native coinage was in bronze only.

For the payment of the Temple tax of half a shekel the money had to be of the Phœnician heavy standard (shekel = 224·4 grains). For ordinary purposes much foreign money was in circulation. The standard Roman coin was the *denarius* (δηνάριον, A.V. and R.V., " penny ") a silver coin of 60 grains (rather more than $\frac{2}{3}$ of the weight of a shilling). It was a day's wage for an agricultural labourer ; the Roman legionary got $\frac{5}{6}$ denarius per day. The ἀσσάριον (Matt. 10^{29} ; Luke 12^6, R.V. " farthing ") is probably to be reckoned as $\frac{1}{24}$ denarius ; the λεπτόν (Mark 12^{42} ; Luke 12^{59}, 21^2, R.V. " mite ") is $\frac{1}{96}$ denarius. The κοδράντης (Matt. 5^{26} ; Mark 12^{42}, R.V. " farthing ") is the Roman *quadrans* = $\frac{1}{64}$ denarius. It does not seem to have been in circulation in Palestine in New Testament times.

BIBLIOGRAPHY

Calendar and Chronology :

Relevant articles in Encyclopædias and Bible Dictionaries.
S. Langdon, *Babylonian Menologies and the Semitic Calendars.*
S. Krauss, *Talmudische Archäologie,* ii. 416–423.
J. K. Fotheringham, The Calendar in *Nautical Almanac,* 1935, 754–770.
H. Lietzmann, *Zeitrechnung.*
E. Bickermann, *Chronologie.*
Chronological Tables in the *Cambridge Ancient History.*

Weights, Measures, and Money :

Articles in Encyclopædias and Bible Dictionaries.
S. Krauss, *op. cit.* ii. 382–416.
P. Volz, *Die Biblischen Altertümer,* 399–407.
F. W. Madden, *Coins of the Jews.*
G. F. Hill, *Catalogue of the Greek Coins of Palestine* (British Museum).

INDEXES

I. SCRIPTURE REFERENCES

(Including Apocrypha and Pseudepigrapha)

GENESIS :

1^{26}	. .	37
$4^{23, 24}$	. .	288
4^{26}	. .	289
6^{2}ff.	. .	340
11^{3}	. .	192
14^{4}	. .	176
14^{7}	. .	289
49^{5-7}	. .	419

EXODUS :

1^{11}	. .	221
3^{6}	. .	289
3^{7}	. .	289
3^{14}	. .	288
4^{14}	. .	419
$4^{15, 16}$	. .	429
6^{3}	. .	289
15^{1-18}	. .	288
15^{21}	. .	288
18	. .	288
20^{1-17}	. .	214
20^{2}	. .	290
20^{22}ff.	. .	197
$21-23$	. .	214
21^{23-25}	. .	288
24	. .	213
29^{38-42}	. .	304
32	.	292, 422, 423

LEVITICUS :

16^{8}ff.	. .	288
23	. .	491

NUMBERS :

5^{11-31}	. .	288
10^{35}	. .	289
$10^{35, 36}$	. .	291
13^{29}	. .	153
14^{45}	. .	217
19	. .	288
21^{3}	. .	217
$21^{14, 15, 27-30}$	.	216
$21^{17, 18}$	. .	288
21^{21-35}	. .	216
25^{10-15}	. .	424
$32^{1, 4}$	. .	205

DEUTERONOMY :

1^{28}	. .	179
17^{16}	. 233, 234,	235
17^{20}	. .	235
21^{1-9}	. .	436
33^{8-11}	. 419,	420
33^{10}	. .	429

JOSHUA :

3	. .	217
$15^{26-32, 42}$	. .	419
19^{1}	. .	419
19^{2-7}	. .	419

JUDGES :

1^{3}	. .	419
1^{3-21}	. .	217
1^{16}	. .	217
2	. .	215
4	. 220,	222
5	. 222,	294
9	. .	222
11	. .	216
$17, 18$	. 418,	419

1 SAMUEL :

4	. .	224
7^{1}	. .	421
10^{17-27}	. .	225
10^{27}	. .	227
13^{2}	. .	226
14^{21}	. .	225
14^{52}	. .	226
17^{18}	. .	227
18^{13}	. .	227
20^{29}	. .	287

2 SAMUEL :

8^{18}	. .	422
$9-20$	. .	232
22^{5}	. .	342
24^{1}	. .	35
24^{24}	. .	35

1 KINGS :

15^{14}	. .	35
22^{43}	. .	35

2 KINGS :

$4^{1, 2}$	. .	244
17^{4-6}	. .	247
17^{24-28}	. .	428
19^{2}	. .	426
23^{8}	. .	423
23^{9}	. .	41
23^{20}	. .	423
23^{29}	. .	251
24^{14}	. .	202

1 CHRONICLES :

21^{1}	. .	35
21^{25}	. .	35
29^{5}	. .	202

2 CHRONICLES :

14^{5}	. .	34
17^{6}	. .	34
33^{11-16}	. .	249
35^{20-24}	. .	251

EZRA :

7^{6}	. .	304
7^{7}	. .	303
7^{10}	. 444,	445

NEHEMIAH :

$8-10$	. .	304
8	. .	456
8^{1}	. .	304
8^{7}	. .	432
8^{8}	. 445,	457
8^{15}	. .	445

JOB :

38^{7}	. .	334

PSALMS :

35^{10}	. .	16
37	. .	19
80^{17}	. .	374
110	. .	310
119	. .	19
148^{1-3} (LXX)	.	334

33

PROVERBS :
8¹³ . . . 16
31¹⁰⁻³¹ . . 19

ISAIAH :
26¹⁹ . . . 309
53¹⁰ . . . 324
63¹⁵ . . . 16

JEREMIAH :
7 . . . 423
7²² . . . 295
8⁸ . . 298, 423
11¹⁻¹⁰ . . . 423
11¹⁸⁻²³ . . 423
12¹ . . . 323
18³· ⁴ . . 202
22¹³ . . . 235
22¹⁵ . . . 252
24 . . . 253
24¹ . . . 202
26 . . . 423
31¹⁵⁻²⁰ . . 423
52²⁸⁻³⁰ . . 253

LAMENTATIONS :
1 . . 19, 255
3 . . . 255

EZEKIEL :
1¹³ . . . 338
8⁶ . . . 453
9²⁻¹¹ . . . 337
11¹⁶ . . . 453
14¹ . . . 453
16³ . . . 176
16⁴⁵ . . . 176
18 . . . 301
20¹ . . . 453
33¹ . . . 453
36²⁴⁻²⁸ . . 301
36³¹ . . . 301
37 . . . 301
40³· ⁴ . . 333
40⁴⁵ . . . 424
44 . . 423, 424
44² . . . 333

DANIEL :
7⁹⁻²⁷ . . 374
7¹³ . . . 310
7¹³· ¹⁴ . . 375
7²² . . . 375
7²⁷ . . . 375
10⁵· ⁶ . . 338
12² . . . 309

HOSEA :
11⁸ . . . 322

AMOS :
5²⁵ . . . 295
6¹⁻⁶ . . . 243

ZEPHANIAH :
3⁴ . . . 432

HAGGAI :
2¹⁰⁻¹⁹ . . 432

ZECHARIAH :
1–8 . . . 333
3 . . . 425

APOCRYPHA AND
PSEUDEPIGRAPHA
1 MACCABEES :
3⁴⁶ . . . 454
9²² . . . 87
14⁴⁻¹⁵ . . 263
16²⁴ . . . 87

TOBIT :
3¹⁷ . . . 336
11¹⁴ . . . 334
12¹⁵ . . . 337

SIRACH :
50¹⁻²¹ . . 427
50¹⁴ff. . . 325

EPISTLE OF JEREMY :
v. 3 . . . 80

JUBILEES :
2¹ . . . 335
7²⁷ . . . 344
10¹²· ¹³ . . 346
11⁴· ⁵ . . 344
12²⁰ . . . 344

ASCENSION OF ISAIAH :
7²¹ . . . 334

1 ENOCH :
8³ . . . 336
15⁴⁻⁷ . . 336
15⁸ . . . 341
20¹ff. . . 336
39¹² . . . 334
69²⁶⁻²⁹ . . 374

TESTAMENTS OF THE XII
PATRIARCHS :
Simeon 5³ . . 342
Judah 25² . . 334

NEW TESTAMENT
MATTHEW :
5¹⁸ . . . 19
6¹· ² . . . 26
8¹⁰ . . . 472
10³ . . . 421
15²⁴ . . . 472
16¹⁸· ¹⁹ . . 471
18¹⁸ . . . 471
19²⁸ . . . 468
22³⁰ . . . 336
23²⁶ . . . 24
24³⁷⁻⁴¹ . . 375
28¹⁹ . . . 476

MARK :
6⁴⁸ . . . 489
10¹ . . . 371
13 . . . 375
13²⁵ . . . 335
14¹²⁻¹⁷ . . 467
14⁶² . . . 375
16⁸ . . . 115

LUKE :
4¹⁷ . . . 457
9⁵¹⁻18¹⁴ . 369, 370
10¹⁹ . . . 347
11⁴¹ . . . 24
12³⁸ . . . 489
17²⁶· ²⁷ . . 375
17³⁴· ³⁵ . . 375
18¹² . . . 491
22¹⁹· ²⁰ . . 481
22³⁰ . . . 468
22⁵³ . . . 343
24³³⁻³⁶ . . 471

JOHN :
1¹⁴ . . . 414
3⁵ . . . 413
3¹³· ³¹ . . 414
7¹⁻¹⁴ . . . 369
7³²⁻⁵² . . 371
9²· ³ . . . 346
13²³ . . . 122
15⁹· ¹⁰ . . 416
19²⁶ . . . 122
20²ff. . . 122
20¹⁹⁻²³ . . 471
20²³ . . . 471
21⁷ . . . 122
21²⁰ . . . 122

ACTS :
2 . . . 390
2⁴⁶ . . . 481
6 . . 467, 470
7 . . . 394

ACTS—(continued)
8^1 . . . 395
8$^{9-13}$ . . . 395
10$^{44ff.}$ . . . 475
13^{15} . . . 457
14^{23} . . . 466
18^{24} . . . 28
19$^{5. 6}$ . . . 475
19^{19} . . . 346
20^7 . . . 481
20$^{17. 28}$ . . . 466
20^{28} . . . 466

ROMANS :
3$^{24. 25}$ . . . 407
3^{25} . . . 26
6$^{1-11}$ . . . 408
6$^{3-11}$ . . 474, 475
9^5 . . . 410

1 CORINTHIANS :
1$^{14-18}$ . . . 476
1^{24} . . . 409
6^{11} . . . 475
7^{14} . . . 476
10$^{1-12}$ . . . 484
10^{11} . . . 27
10^{21} . . . 483
11 . . 479–483
12^{13} . . . 474
12^{28} . . . 465
15$^{3-7}$ . . . 388
16^{22} . . . 409

2 CORINTHIANS :
1^{22} . . . 27
3^{17} . . . 408
6$^{14. 15}$ . . . 342

GALATIANS :
5^1 . . . 29
5^{13} . . . 29

EPHESIANS :
1^{10} . . . 409
4^{11} . . . 466
6^{12} . . . 342

PHILIPPIANS :
1^1 . . 465, 466
2$^{5-11}$ . . . 409
2$^{9-11}$ . . . 25
4^8 . . . 27
4^{15} . . . 27
4$^{17. 18}$ . . . 27

COLOSSIANS :
1$^{15-19}$ . . . 409
1^{20} . . . 409
2^8 . . . 335
2^{18} . . 29, 484
2^{20} . . . 335

1 THESSALONIANS :
5$^{12. 13}$ . . . 464
5^{14} . . . 464

1 TIMOTHY
2^5 . . . 328

TITUS :
1$^{5. 7}$ . . . 466

HEBREWS :
10^{32} . . . 473
11^1 . . . 27
13^7 . . . 473

JAMES :
1–5 . . . 363
1^1 . . . 118
1^3 . . . 28

1 PETER
1^7 . . . 28
2^2 . . . 28
4$^{15. 16}$ . . . 473

1 JOHN :
4^1 . . . 478

2 JOHN :
v. 1 . . . 124

JUDE :
v. 1 . . . 119

REVELATION :
5^1 . . . 23
7^1 . . . 335

II. AUTHORS

ABBOT-SMITH, 29.
Abel, 30, 156.
Abelson, 333.
Abrahams, 461.
Albright, 156, 203.
Alexander, 366.
Anderson Scott, 26, 366, 417.
André, 96.
Athanasius, 11.
Augustine, 308.

Bacon, 92, 389, 417.
Ball, 96.
Balla, 63.
Barton, 203.
Baudissin, 281.
Bauer, 30.
Baumgartner, 74.
Baynes, 267.
Benzinger, 21, 203.
Bernard, 123.
Bevan, E. R., 267, 328.
Bewer, 77.
Bickermann, 499.
Blass, 30.
Brooke, 121.
Brown, Driver, and Briggs, 21.
Browne, 432.
Budde, 47, 60, 66, 68.
Burkitt, 119, 125, 326, 389, 480.
Burney, 330.

Caiger, 203.
Calder, 171.
Carpenter, 417.
Cave, 486.
Chadwick, 366.
Charles, 25, 89, 93, 96, 121, 125.
Cheyne, 66.
Clement of Rome, 450.
Clogg, 129.
Cone, 366.
Cook, S. A., 77, 283, 286.
Cornill, 47, 66, 71.
Creed, 469.
Cyprian, 470.

Dalman, 74, 156, 471.
Davidson, 21.

Debrunner, 30.
Deissmann, 27, 29.
Delitzsch, 68, 71.
Demosthenes, 23.
Dionysius of Alexandria, 120.
Dodd, 12, 26, 121, 124, 334, 376, 389, 417, 466.
Doughty, 288.
Driver, G. R., 21.
Driver, S. R., 77, 489.
Duhm, 59, 62.
Duncan, 129.

Edersheim, 440, 443.
Eissfeldt, 43, 45, 47, 72.
Elbogen, 312, 461.
Emmet, 91.
Erman, 293.
Eusebius, 99.
Ewald, 68.

Fotheringham, 499.
Friedländer, 71.

Galling, 71, 320.
Gardner, 483.
Garstang, 156, 177.
Georgius Hamartolus, 121.
Glahn, 53.
Graham, 281, 286.
Gray, 33, 66, 77, 92, 325, 331, 420, 434, 439, 443.
Grotius, 101.
Gunkel, 63.

Haller, 74.
Harford, 56.
Harnack, 113, 117, 467.
Harrison, 120, 127, 129.
Headlam, 471, 486.
Hempel, 43.
Herntrich, 55.
Herodotus, 179.
Hill, 499.
Hölscher, 44, 55, 74.
Hooke, 286, 441.
Hoonacker, 66.
Howard, 120, 123, 417.

Huddilston, 30.
Humbert, 59.
Hylander, 48.

Irenæus, 121.

Jack, 203, 282.
James, E. O., 286.
James, M. R., 129.
Jastrow, 421.
Jerome, 28, 79, 430.
Johnson, 425.
Jones, 267.
Josephus, 116, 117, 267, 346, 367, 490.
Joüon, 68.
Justin Martyr, 475, 476, 485.

Kautzsch, 21, 96.
Keil, 171.
Kennedy, 47.
Kennett, 44, 64, 424.
Kent, 74.
King, 21.
Klausner, 482.
Kleinert, 318.
König, 21.
Kraetzschmar, 55.
Krauss, 461, 499.
Lagarde, 72.
Lake, 129, 467.
Lake and Jackson, 117, 309.
Langdon, 71, 173, 499.
Lauterbach, 452.
Leszynsky, 90, 93.
Lietzmann, 486, 499.
Lightfoot, 108, 114, 469.
Lods, 48, 267.
Loewe, 314.
Luther, 113.

McNeile, 71, 129, 417.
Madden, 499.
Mallon, 175.
Manson, T. W., 389.
Manson, W., 366.
May, 281, 286.
Meek, 69.
Meinhold, 74.
Moffatt, 129.
Montgomery, 74.
Moore, 314, 331, 452, 461.
Mowinckel, 63, 64, 441.

Nairne, 417.
Nock, 129, 417.
Nunn, 30.

Oesterley, 65, 427, 443.
Oesterley and Robinson, 33, 43, 48, 50, 52, 53, 54, 56, 61, 71, 77, 267, 331.
Oestreicher, 43.
Origen, 78, 122.
Otto, 366.

Papias, 99, 116, 118.
Peake, 12, 66.
Pederson, 366.
Petrie, 181.
Philip of Side, 121.
Philo, 483.
Phythian-Adams, 156.
Pliny, 367.
Polybius, 23.
Pouget and Guitton, 68.

Rad, G. von, 43, 77.
Ramsay, 171, 417.
Ranston, 77.
Ricciotto, 68.
Robertson Smith, 285 f., 434, 443.
Robinson, H. W., 34, 53, 77, 267, 315, 33', 384.
Robinson, T. H., 331.
Ropes, 473.
Rowley, 492.
Rudolf, 44, 58.
Ryder Smith, 366.
Ryle, 12.

Schürer, 452, 461.
Schweitzer, 366, 417.
Scott, E. F., 129, 366, 417.
Sellin, 40, 44, 48, 58, 59, 65, 71, 74, 77.
Simpson, 77.
Singer, 450, 461.
Skinner, 331.
Smith, G. A., 156, 427.
Smith, James, 55.
Smith, J. M. P., 366.
Souter, 11, 29.
Stevenson, 21.
Strabo, 165, 168.
Strack, 21.
Streeter, 119, 125, 129, 467 f., 470, 473 f., 478, 486.
Swete, 486.

Tacitus, 266, 367.
Taylor, 129.
Tertullian, 113, 122.
Thackeray, 461.
Thomsen, 156.
Thumb, 29.
Torrey, 24, 53, 55, 74, 77.

Toy, 461.
Travers Herford, 328, 452, 454.
Turner, 467, 470, 474, 486.

Volkmar, 96.
Volz, 44.

Wace, 96.
Weber, 333.

Welch, 43, 74, 77, 431, 443.
Wellhausen, 428.
Wetzstein, 68.
Wittekindt, 69.
Woolley, 173.

Zahn, 12.
Zimmern, 73.

III. GENERAL

AARON, 418 f., 423, 429.
Aaronic priesthood, 418, 424.
Abana, R. (Barada), 151.
Abda, 155.
Abel-beth-Maacah (Abl), 145.
Abel Meholah, 240.
Abiathar, 422.
Abijam, 493.
Abimelech, 35, 319.
Abner, 45.
Abraham, 35, 113, 135, 148, 152, 174, 319, 404.
Abtalion, 449.
Accadian, 13, 21.
Achæa, 102, 400.
Achzeb (Zib), 141.
Acre, 137, 139, 141.
Acts, Book of, 114, 116.
Adam, ford of (Danieh), 150.
Adonis, cult of, 69.
Agabus, 110.
Agriculture, Israelite, 201.
Agur, 65.
Ahab, 42, 180, 237 f., 493.
Ahasuerus, 72.
Ahaz, 51, 247, 494.
Ahaziah, 493.
Ahikar, Wisdom of, 82.
Ahiram, Tomb of, 184.
Ahura Mazda, 342.
Ai, 178.
Akabah, Gulf of, 154 f.
Akhenaten, 185.
Akiba, 314.
Akkadians, the, 192.
Alexander, 23, 259.
Alexandria, 259.
Alexandretta, Gulf of, 137.
Alphabetic Writing, 184, 188.
Amanus, 134, 137.
Amaziah, 155, 493.
Amen-em-Ope, Wisdom of, 65.
Amidah, 455.
Amman, 154.
Amorites, 134.
Amos, 51, 57, 152, 242, 245, 294 f., 431, 492.
Amraphel, 175.
Ancyra, 100.
Angels, 332 f., 335, 337 f., 340 f.

Angra Mainyu, 342.
Antioch, Phrygian, 161.
Antioch, Pisidian, 397, 470.
Antioch, Syrian, 99, 102, 396 ff.
Antiochus Epiphanes, 22, 73, 261 f.
Aphek (Baka), 145
Apocalypse of Abraham, 95
Apocalypse of John, 22, 125, 307, 309, 401, 403.
Apocalypse, little, 99.
Apocalyptic, in Religion, 308.
Apocrypha, 78 f.
Apollos, 102, 113, 114.
Apostles, the, 391 f., 467.
Apostolic Succession, 470.
Aquila, 32, 328.
Arabah, the, 154.
Arabia, 13.
Aramaic, 13, 20, 31, 72 f., 122, 457.
Aram Naharaim, 134 f.
Aristion, 117.
Aristobulus, 92.
Ark, the, 47
Ark of the Covenant, 291, 459.
Arnon (Wadi mojib), 150.
Arpachshad (Kirkuk), 135.
Arrapha, 135.
Artaxerxes, 258, 303.
Arumah (el Ormeh), 149.
Arvad, 138.
Asa, 35, 493.
Ascalon, 138, 146.
Ascent of Akrabbim (Umm el Akareb), 155.
Ashdod (Esdud), 52, 145.
Asherah, 292.
Asherim, 40.
Ashur (Qal'ah Sharqât), 185.
Ashurbanipal, 249, 490.
Asia Minor, 157, 165 f., 169 f., 469.
Asia, Province of, 159.
Assyria, 238, 246, 250.
Assyrian Inscriptions, 181.
Assyrian Libraries, 184.
Astarte, 435.
Athens, 101 f.
Atonement, day of, 433, 438.
Auja, 155.
Azazel, 279, 288, 341 f.

507

Baalism, 292.
Baal-zebul, 435.
Baasha, 493.
Bab el Wad, 152.
Babylon, 52, 54, 248, 253, 299.
Babylonia (Akkad), 134.
Balaam, 42.
Baptism, in the primitive Church, 474 f.
Baptism, infant, 476.
Barak, 222.
Bar cocheba, 308, 314.
Barnabas, 99, 113, 396 ff.
Barnabas, Epistle of, 128.
Baruch, 51, 54.
Baruch, Book of, 88.
Baruch, Greek Apocalypse of, 96.
Baruch, Syriac Apocalypse of, 94.
Bashan, 145.
Beeroth (Tell el Nasbeh), 151.
Beer-sheba (Tell es-Seba), 35, 39, 151, 153, 434.
Behemoth, 66.
Beit Jibrin, 153.
Bel and the Dragon, 86.
Beliar, 342.
Belshazzar, 73.
Ben-Hadad, 238 f.
Ben Sirach, 442.
Berœa, 101 f.
Bethany, 152.
Beth Din, 314.
Bethel (Beitin), 35, 38 f., 149.
Bethlehem, 152.
Bethoron (Beit Ur), 151.
Bethpelet (Tell el Fara), 181, 196.
Bethshan (Beisan), 144, 146, 148.
Bethshemesh (Ain Shems), 147, 184.
Bethuliah (Meseliah), 148.
Biruta (Beirout), 138.
Bithynia, Province of, 160.
Body of Christ, 462, 464, 480.
Bozra (el Buseira), 154.
Buddhism, 5 ff.

Cæsarea, 102, 107, 141, 147.
Caleb (ites), 37, 41, 219.
Calendar, Jewish, 439 ff., 489 ff.
Canaan (ites), 13, 135, 292 f.
Canaanite Religion, 278 ff.
Canon of Scripture, 11, 33, 112, 311.
Cappadocia, province of, 161.
Cappadocian Tablets, 185.
Carchemish, 251, 494.
Carmel, 133, 140, 293, 428.
Centralization of Sacrifice, 251, 423, 436.
Chaldæans, 250 ff.
Chepirah (Kefirah), 152.
Christ (see also Messiah), 407, 411, 462, 464, 480.

Christianity and Gnosticism, 395.
Chronicles, Books of, 75, 418.
Church, Christian, 391 ff., 408, 462 ff.
Cilicia, province of, 160.
Cimmerians, 250.
Circumcision, 284, 291, 399, 490.
Civilization, antiquity of, 182.
Claudius, 266.
Clement, Epistle of, 126.
Colossæ, 110, 159.
Colossians, Letter to the, 110.
Commerce, Antiquity of, 183.
Communications, 157, 205.
Communism in Christian Church, 392, 400.
Conquest of Palestine, 215 ff.
Corinth, 101 f., 103, 108.
Corinthian, Letters to the, 102 f., 399.
Cornelius, 368, 396, 475.
Corporate Personality, 321 f., 353, 408.
Covenant, Book of, 350.
Covenant of Sinai, 211 ff., 319, 350 ff.
Council of Jerusalem, 105 f., 398, 472.
Cuneiform, 21, 183.
Cyrus, 52, 73, 75, 256.

Dagan, 134.
Damascus, 148, 236 ff., 241 f., 246, 397.
Dan (Tell el Kadi), 145, 220, 224.
Daniel, Book of, 11, 22, 72, 307.
Darius Hystaspis, 60, 75.
Darius the Mede, 73.
David, 48, 155, 228 ff., 421 f., 492.
Day, divisions of the, 489.
Day of Yahweh, 57, 290, 310.
Deacons, 394, 466.
Dead Sea, 153.
Debir (Tell Beit Mirsim), 153.
Deborah, Song of, 45, 222, 294.
Decalogue, 214.
Demons, 341 ff.
Derbe, 397.
Deutero-Isaiah, 53, 255, 300 f.
Deuteronomic Source (D), 39 f., 351.
Deuteronomy, Book of, 37 f., 251, 298, 351, 423.
Diaspora, 63.
Didache, 127, 467 f., 475 f., 478 f.
Diognetus, Epistle to, 129.
Discrepant Laws, 37.
Discrepant Narratives, 36.
Displacements, 67, 123.
Divination, 419, 430.
Divorce, 354, 361.
Documentary Hypothesis, 38 ff.
Documents, Earliest Christian, 99.
Domitian, 89, 473.

Dor, 146.
Dothan, Plain of, 143.
Doublets, 35 f.
Dress, Israelite, 201.

Ebal (Jebel Eslamiyeh), 148.
Ecclesia, Christian, 462 f.
Ecclesiastes, 70, 306.
Ecclesiasticus, 13, 82 f., 306.
Eden, Garden of, 36.
Edom, 58, 155, 255.
Egypt, 13, 23, 211, 246, 251.
Ekron, 146.
Elah, Vale of (Wadi es Sunt), 147.
El Amarna Letters. (See Tell el Amarna.)
El Arish, 145.
Elath, 155.
El Burak, 152.
Election, Doctrine of, 320, 327.
Elephantine, 299, 490.
Elephantine papyri, 73, 76, 305.
El Harbej, 142.
Eliashib, 76.
Elihu, 66.
Elijah, 40, 50, 239, 294, 434.
Elisha, 50, 240.
El Nahas, 154.
Elohim, 39, 62.
Elohistic source, 39, 48.
El Shaddai, 36.
Elusa (Khalasa), 155.
Endor, 144.
Engedi, 153.
Enoch, Book of, 89.
Enoch, Secrets of, 93.
Enthronement Festival, 63, 441.
Epaphroditus, 107 f.
Ephesians, Letter to the, 111.
Ephesus, 102, 107, 123, 158 f.
Ephod, 419, 430.
Ephraim, 150.
Epictetus, 23.
Esarhaddon, 249.
Esbeita, 155.
Eschatology, 307 ff., 374 ff., 391, 412.
Esdraelon, Plain of, 137 f., 142.
Esdras, Books of, 81, 89.
Eshcol, 41.
Esther, 71, 85, 442.
Ethical Teaching of Jesus, 356 ff., 361 f., 378 ff.
Ethics, basis of Biblical, 348 f., 355 f.
Ethics, Hebrew, 321, 349 f.
Euphrates, 134.
Exile, 13, 19, 254 f.
Exodus, 177, 211.
Exorcism, 346.
Ezekiel, 41, 51, 255, 300 f., 333, 423.
Ezekiel, Book of, 155, 423.

Ezion-geber (El-Meniyyeh), 155, 180.
Ezra, 42, 70, 73, 75, 81, 258, 303, 426, 444.

Fallen Angels, 340 f.
Family, Religious importance of, 355 ff., 379.
Farwardigan, 72.
Feasts, Agricultural, 439 f., 489.
Feasts, Annual, 491.
Fertile Crescent, 205 f., 273.
Festus, 102.
Flavius Clemens, 473.
Flood, 36 f., 173.
Formgeschichte, 43.
Fortifications, Canaanite, 179.
Fourth Gospel, 411–417.

Gabriel, 336.
Gadara (Um Keis), 150.
Galatia, Province of, 160, 397.
Galatians, Letter to the, 100, 105, 399.
Galilee, 140, 371.
Galilee, Sea of, 140.
Gamaliel I, 395, 451.
Gamaliel II, 450, 455.
Gath, 146.
Gaulanitis (Jaulan), 151.
Gaza, 145 f., 181.
Geba, 151.
Gebal (Gubla, Byblos), 138.
Gedaliah, 151, 253 f.
Gentile Converts, 398, 473.
Gentile Mission, 396 ff.
Gerar (Tell Jemmeh), 153, 181.
Gerasa, 150.
Gerizim (Jebel et Tor), 148.
Geshur, 145.
Gezer, 21, 147, 179, 184.
Gibeon (El Jib), 151.
Gilboa (Jebel Fukua), 140, 143.
Gilead, 43, 150.
Gilgal (Juleijil), 149, 435.
God. (See Yahweh.)
God, Rabbinic Doctrine of, 314.
Gomer, 56.
Gospels, Synoptic, 93, 98, 114, 358, 368.
Gospel, the Primitive, 403.
Greek Language, 23 ff.
Greek Philosophy, 71.

Habakkuk, 59.
Habiru, 135.
Hagar, 35.
Haggadah, 313.
Haggai, 60, 302, 432.
Haifa, 140 f.
Halakhah, 313.

Haman, 72.
Hamath, 138, 238.
Hammurabi, 175, 187, 197, 350.
Hanukkah, 88, 442.
Harod, Spring of (Ain Jalud), 143.
Harran, 134 f.
Hauran (Darb el Hawarneh), 139 f.
Hazael, 240.
Hazezon Tamar, 153.
Hazor (Tell el Kedah), 144, 179, 196.
Hebrew Alphabet, 20 f., 189.
Hebrew Bible, Divisions of, 33.
Hebrew Language, 13 ff., 31, 188.
Hebrew Verse, 19, 70.
Hebrews, Letter to the, 11, 25, 113, 410.
Hebrews, the, 174.
Hebron (Kiriath Arba), 37, 39, 41, 152.
Hellenist Party, 393, 397.
Hellenization of Judah, 260 ff.
Herem, or Ban, 218.
Heresy, Colossian, 111, 114.
Hermon, 139 f.
Herod the Great, 264.
Herod Agrippa, 266.
Hexateuch, 44.
Hezekiah, 40, 51, 248.
Hierapolis, 159.
High Places, 292, 428.
Higher Criticism, 31, 33 f.
Hillel, 447, 450.
History, Lesson of Hebrew, 204, 290, 316, 318.
Hittite Tablets, 186.
Hittites, 193.
Hivites, 134, 194.
Holiness Code (H), 43, 300.
Homs (Abzu ?), 138.
Horeb, 154.
Horites, 134, 194.
Hosea, 51, 56, 245, 295.
Huleh, Lake of, 141, 220.
Humman, 72.
Hurrians (Haru), 134, 175, 186, 194.
Hyksos, 135, 195.
Hymn of Ikhnaton, 64.

Ibleam (Tell Belameh), 143.
Iconium, 397.
Ignatius, 127, 470, 484.
Incarnation, Doctrine of the, 414.
Individualism in Religion, 298, 300, 306, 352.
Irkata, 138.
Isaac, 35.
Isaiah, 13, 50, 51 f., 242, 245, 295 307.
Isaiah, Ascension of, 95.
Ishmael, 35.

Ishtar, 72.
Israel, 198 f., 207, 242 ff.

Jabbok (ez-Zerka), 150.
Jabin, 220, 222.
Jacob, 35, 148.
Jaddua, 75.
Jaffa, 146.
James, General Epistle of, 118, 363.
James, son of Zebedee, 396.
James, the Lord's brother, 396 f., 469.
Jamnia, 314.
Jarmuth (Khurbet el Yarmuk), 147.
Jehoahaz, 241, 493.
Jehoash, 241, 493.
Jehoiachin, 53.
Jehoiakim, 251 f.
Jehoram, 493.
Jehoshaphat, 35, 493.
Jehu, 240, 493.
Jenin, 142 f.
Jerash (Gerasa), 150.
Jeremiah, 50 f., 53, 70, 189, 252 f., 295, 298, 317, 320, 323, 423, 431.
Jeremiah, Book of, 54.
Jeremy, Epistle of, 80.
Jericho (Tell-es-Sultan), 134, 149, 177, 182, 218.
Jeroboam, 234, 493.
Jeroboam II, 43, 242, 493.
Jerusalem, 52 ff., 102, 151, 176, 189, 221, 247 f., 249, 252, 255, 371, 385, 396.
Jesus of Nazareth, 9, 11, 22 ff., 115, 122, 356 ff., 369 ff., 375 f., 377 f., 387 f., 409, 411, 482.
Jezebel, 239.
Jezreel (Zerin), 143.
Jezreel, Vale of (Nahr Jalud), 143.
Joash, 56.
Job, Babylonian, 68.
Job, Book of, 65, 306, 323.
Joel, Book of, 56.
Johanan, 76.
Johanan ben Zakkai, 314, 450.
John, General Epistles of, 22, 124.
John, Gospel of, 11, 120 f., 358, 411 ff.
John Hyrcanus, 87, 155, 263 f.
John, son of Zebedee, 120.
John the Elder, 122 f.
Jokneam (Keinum), 142.
Jonah, Book of, 58, 302.
Jordan Valley, 139.
Jose b. Joezer, 449.
Jose b. Johanan, 449.
Joseph, 36, 42, 148.
Joshua, Book of, 44, 177 ff., 215 ff.
Josiah, 40 f., 250, 252, 423.
Jubilees, Book of, 90.

Judah, 56, 242, 248, 251, 256 ff.,
259 ff., 264 ff.
Judah the Patriarch (Hannasi), 314,
450.
Judas Maccabæus, 155, 262.
Jude, General Epistle of, 119.
Judges, Book of, 45, 215 ff.
Judith, Book of, 84.
Justification, 405 f.
Juttah, 153.

Kadesh Barnea, 153 f.
Kadesh (Tell Nebi Mindu), 138, 145,
420.
Kanes (Kara Eyuk), 185.
Karkar, Battle of, 238, 493.
Karkor (Keraker), 150.
Kasdim, 59.
Khons, Tractate of, 82.
Kiddush, 386.
Kingdom of God, 308 f., 357 f., 373,
391.
Kings, Book of, 48 f., 233 ff., 248 f.
Kingship, The, 234 f., 273 ff., 431,
441.
Kir (Kerak), 154.
Kiriath Jearim (Kuryet el Enab),
147, 152.
Kish, 173, 182.
Kishon (Nahr el Mukutta), 142.
Kittim, 59.
Koheleth, 71.
Koine, the, 23 ff.
Korban, 436.
Kornub, 154.
Kulonieh, 152.
Kurn Hattin, 145.
Kurnub, 155.

Lachish (Tell el Duweir), 146, 184,
189, 196.
Ladder of Tyre (Ras en Nakura), 137.
Lagash, 182.
Laish, 139.
Lamech's Song, 288.
Lamentations, Book of, 70.
Laodicea, 159.
Last Supper, 386, 482 f.
Law (see Torah), 259, 313 ff., 351,
400, 406, 427 f., 444 ff.
Law Codes, Ancient, 187.
Latron, 152.
Lay Source (L), 116.
Lebanon, 133, 137.
Lemuel, 65.
Leviathan, 66.
Levites, 37, 418 ff., 424, 425.
Life after Death, 307, 308 f., 315,
388.
Lilith, 343.

Litani R. (Nahr el Kasimiyeh), 137 f.
Little Hermon (Jebl Duby), 141.
Liturgies, 59 f., 63, 68 f., 442 f., 454 f.,
479 ff., 484 f.
Logos, 413.
Lower Criticism, 31 ff.
Lucius of Cyrene, 396.
Luke, Gospel of, 24, 114, 116, 401,
482.
Luz, 35.
Lycia, 161.
Lycus, R., 110.
Lydda, 145 f.
Lystra, 397.

Maccabæan Age, 262 ff.
Maccabæan Priest-Kings, 262 f.
Maccabæus, Judas, 155, 262.
1 Maccabees, 86.
2 Maccabees, 87.
3 Maccabees, 91.
4 Maccabees, 92.
Macedonia, 100, 400.
Maeander, R., 158.
Makhneh Plain, 148.
Malachi, Book of, 61, 257.
Man, Rabbinical Doctrine of, 315.
Manasseh, 40, 55, 249 f.
Manasses, Prayer of, 85.
Marcion, 7, 110 ff.
Marduk, 72.
Mareshah, 153.
Mari (Tell Hariri), 182, 187.
Mark, Gospel of, 24, 114, 401, 482.
Mark, John, 397.
Mark, Lost ending of, 115.
Marriage, Levirate, 70.
Marriage Songs, 68.
Martyrologies, 121.
Mashti, 72.
Massoretes, 21, 31.
Mastema, 341, 344.
Matthew, Gospel of, 24, 99, 114, 463.
Mazzeboth, 40, 293, 434.
Mediation, forms of, 324 ff., 411, 414,
430.
Megiddo (Tell el Mutasselim), 142 f.,
179 f., 247.
Meir, Rabbi, 314.
Melchizedek, 113, 275.
Menahem, 246.
Messiah, 97 f., 308 ff., 373 f., 382 f.
Micah, 245, 295.
Micah, Book of, 58.
Micah of Ephraim, 418 f.
Micaiah, 50.
Michael, 336.
Michmash (Mukhmas), 151.
Midrash, 446.
Minæans, 420.

Minhah, 436.
Miriam's Song, 288.
Mishnah, 313 f., 328, 445, 448.
Mishpat, 428 ff.
Missionary character of Primitive Church, 472, 474.
Mizpah, 151, 179, 189.
Moabite Stone, 13.
Modin (Medieh), 147.
Mohammed, 6, 8.
Monarchy, Hebrew, 228 ff., 239.
Monotheism, 301, 305, 464.
Months, Hebrew, 489 f.
Morality and Religion, 306, 321, 350 ff., 358 f., 464.
Mordecai, 71 f.
Moses, 35 f., 53, 210, 211 f., 418, 429.
Moses, Apocalypse of, 90, 95.
Moses, Assumption of, 92.
Mother Goddess Cult, 169, 435.
Musnus Pass (Wadi Arab), 142.
Myra, 161.
Mystery Religions and Lord's Supper, 483 ff.

Nabonidus, 73.
Nabopolassar, 250, 252.
Naboth, 239.
Nahor, 187.
Nahum, Book of, 59.
Nazareth, 145, 369.
Nazirites, 240.
Nebuchadrezzar, 73, 252 ff.
Necho, 250 f.
Negeb, 140, 153.
Nehemiah, 53, 61, 75, 81, 257 f., 303, 426.
Nehushtan, 434.
Nephilim, 341.
Nero, 118, 400 f., 473.
Nethinim, 425.
Netophah (Lifta), 152.
New Year Festival, 72, 441.
Nicanor, 88.
Nicomedia, 469
Nile, R., 22.
Nineveh, 58 f., 250.
Nippur (Nuffar), 187.
Noah, 36 f., 319.
Nob, 421.
Northern Kingdom, 235, 237 ff., 248.

Obadiah, Book of, 57.
Olives, Mount of, 152, 387.
Omri, 148, 180, 237 f.
Onesimus, 111 f.
Ophir, 155.
Oral Law, 447 f.
Ordination in the Primitive Church, 470.

Orontes, 138.
Osiris, 274.

Palestine, 138, 205, 215 ff., 221.
Papyrus, 21 ff.
Pasebkhanu, 182.
Passion Narrative, 98, 373, 386 f.
Passover, Feast of the, 40, 438.
Pastoral Epistles, 120, 463.
Patriarchal Conditions, 174, 208.
Patriarchal Narratives, 207 f.
Paul of Tarsus, 23, 25, 97, 99, 100, 107, 117, 363 f., 396 f., 399 ff., 404 f., 407 ff., 462, 465 f., 474, 476 f., 479 f.
Pekah, 247.
Pella (Khurbet Fahil), 150.
Penuel, 148.
Peræa (Belka), 150, 371 f.
Pergamum, 159, 469.
Perizzites, 134.
Persecution of Christians, 395, 401 f., 473.
Persia, 256.
Personal Relations in Religion, 298, 356, 357 f., 365, 462 f.
Pessinus, 100.
Peter, Simon, 368, 396, 398, 399, 471.
1 Peter, 117, 401.
2 Peter, 117.
Petra, 154.
Pharisees, 83, 85 f., 90, 94, 313, 447, 449 f.
Phasaelis (Khurbet Fusail), 149.
Philadelphia (Amman), 150.
Philadelphia (Asian), 159.
Philemon, Letter to, 22, 110, 111.
Philippians, Letter to the, 107.
Philistines, 46, 135 ff., 196, 223, 224.
Phœnicia, 135.
Polycarp, Martyrdom of, 127, 470.
Preaching, the Apostolic, 97, 403, 466.
Presbyters, 466.
Priest as Mediator, 324, 411, 430.
Priesthood, the, 418 ff., 423 f., 426 f., 466.
Priestly Code (P), 38, 42, 300, 424.
Priscilla, 113, 476.
Proof-Texts, 403.
Prophetic Revolution, 240.
Prophets, the, 44 ff., 50 ff., 456 f.
Prophets, Religion of, 294 ff., 351.
Propitiation, 407.
Proverbs, 306.
Psalms, Book of, 62, 305, 352, 442 f.
Psalms, Babylonian and Egyptian, 64.
Ptah-hotep, Teaching of, 65.
Ptolemais, 141.

Punon (Fenan), 154.
Purim, Feast of, 72.

Q Source, 98 f., 115.

Rabbinic Doctrines, 314 ff.
Ramah (er Ram), 151 f.
Raphael, 336.
Raphia (Rafah), 145.
Ras Shamra Tablets, 135, 184, 188, 277, 282, 435.
Rechabites, 240, 294.
Rehob, 37, 41, 144.
Rehoboam, 235.
Relief Fund, Jerusalem, 104, 107, 400, 474.
Religion, 278 ff., 287 f., 299 f., 305 f., 311 ff., 316 f., 320 f., 326 ff., 355. (See also Jesus and Paul.)
Rephaim, Plain of, 152.
Retribution, Doctrine of, 306.
Reuben, 39.
Revelation, 5, 8 f.
Revelation, Book of, 11, 22, 25, 125 f., 307, 309, 401, 403.
Rezon, 247.
Roman Government of Judæa, 265 f.
Romans, Letter to the, 109, 399.
Rome, 22, 23, 101, 107, 399 f.
Ruth, Book of, 69.

Sabbath, 439, 456, 490.
Sabbatical Year, 491.
Sacred Stones, 292, 434.
Sacrifice, 304, 325, 407, 430, 433, 436 ff.
Sacrifice, Early forms of, 291, 434.
Sadducees, 90, 313, 447.
Safed, 140.
Sa-Gaz, 185 f.
Sakaia, Festival of, 72.
Salome Alexandra, 449, 451.
Samaria (Sebustieh), 56, 148, 180, 241, 247, 395.
Samaritan Pentateuch, 32.
Sammael, 341.
Samuel, 46, 152, 421.
Samuel, Book of, 46 f.
Samuel the Little, 455.
Sanballat, 76, 258.
Sarai, 35.
Sardis, 159.
Sargon of Akkad, 175, 183, 185.
Sargon (II) of Assyria, 248.
Satan, 66, 67, 341.
Saul, 46, 155, 225 ff., 493.
Saul of Tarsus, 396. (See Paul.)
Scapegoat, 279.
Scribes, the, 444 ff.
Scythians, 60, 250.

Seir, Mt. (Jebel el Shera), 134, 154.
Sela, 155.
Semitic languages, 14 ff.
Sennacherib, 51, 248.
Serâbit el-Khâdim, 184.
Servant Songs, 53, 300.
Shalmaneser III, 238, 247.
Shalmaneser V, 247.
Shammai, 447, 450.
Sharon, 140, 145.
Sharuhen (Tell el Sheria), 153.
Shechem (Baleta), 39, 148, 179, 196, 419 f., 435.
Shema, 455.
Shemaiah, the Pharisee, 449.
Shemaiah, the Prophet, 235.
Sheol, 307, 309.
Shephelah, 146, 151.
Shepherd of Hermas, 128.
Sheshonk, 234 f.
Shew-bread, 437.
Shiloh (Seilun), 148, 421 f., 430, 435.
Shishak, 181.
Shupiluliu, 186, 193.
Sibylline Oracles, 90.
Sidon, 138.
Siloam Inscription, 13.
Silvanus (Silas), 100, 102, 113, 117, 398.
Simeon ben Lakish, 337.
Simeon b. Shetaḥ, 449.
Simeon the flax-dealer, 455.
Simeon the Just, 448.
Simon Magus, 395.
Sin, Ancient meaning of, 276, 407.
Sin-offerings, 438 f.
Sinai, site of Mt., 212.
Sisera, 220, 222.
Smyrna, 159, 473.
Soferim, the, 444.
Solomon, 68, 233 ff., 422, 493.
Solomon, Psalms of, 91.
Solomon's Stables, 179, 233.
Son of Man, 373 f., 382 ff.
Song of Songs, 68.
Song of the Three Holy Children, 83.
Sorek, Vale of (Wadi Surar), 147, 152, 224.
Soter, 127.
Soul, O.T. Doctrine of the, 315.
Sources used by O.T. writers, 34.
Sources used by the Chronicler, 76.
Spirit, the, 407 ff., 413, 475.
Stephen, 393 f., 463.
Subbililiuma, 135.
Suffering, Problem of, 67, 323, 329.
Sumerians, 183, 192.
Susanna, History of, 86.
Sycamonium (Tell es Semak), 142.
Sychar (Askar), 148.

Symbolism, prophetic, 384 f.
Synagogue, 300, 304, 312, 453 ff., 459 f., 461.
Synoptic Gospels, 93, 98, 114, 358, 368.
Syracuse, 71.

Taanach (Tell Taanuk), 143, 179.
Tabernacle, the, 36, 410 f.
Tabernacles, Feast of, 37, 441.
Tabor (Jebel et Tor), 142.
Talmud, 20, 328.
Tammuz, Myth of, 274.
Targum, 13, 20, 32.
Tavium, 100.
Tekoa, 152.
Teleilat Ghassul, 175.
Tell Abu Shushah, 142.
Tell Arad, 153.
Tell el Ajjul, 153.
Tell el Amarna Tablets, 13, 136, 176, 185, 221, 421.
Temple at Elephantine, 305.
Temple, the, 302 f., 434 ff., 442.
Terah, 174.
Teraphim, 419.
Testaments of the Twelve Patriarchs, 90.
Textual Corruption, causes of, 31, 32.
Theodotion, 32.
Theophilus, 116, 473.
Thermaic Gulf, 101.
Thessalonians, Letters to the, 101, 108, 399.
Thessalonica, 100.
Thyatira, 159.
Tiglath Pileser III., 246, 247.
Timothy, 100, 102, 468.
Tirzah (Tell Farah), 148.
Titus, 468.
Tobit, Book of, 81, 82, 336.
Tongues, speaking with, 390.
Torah, the, 311 f., 326, 351, 427 ff., 432, 433, 456. (See Law.)
Trachonitis (El Leja), 151.
Trees, Sacred, 434.
Trito-Isaiah, 53, 257.
Troas, 159.
Tyre, 138.

Ugarit (Ras Shamra), 135, 138, 188, 277.

Ur (al-Mugayyar), 173, 182.
Urartu, Kingdom of, 246.
Urim and Thummim, 290, 430.

Vashti, 72.
Vatican Council, 11.
Vespasian, 267.
Vulgate, 28, 32.

Wadi el Afranj, 153.
Wadi el Arish, 137.
Wadi el Hasa, 154.
Way of the Sea, 140.
Weapons, Israelite, 202.
Wedding Customs, 68.
Week, Jewish, 490.
Weights and Measures, Biblical, 497.
Wells, Sacred, 434.
Wisdom Literature, 307, 353.
Wisdom, Personification of, 307, 409.
Women, Status of Hebrew, 354.
Worship, in primitive Church, 476 ff.
Writing, Antiquity of, 190.
Writing Materials, 21, 22.
Writings, the, 62 ff.

Xerxes, 72.

Yahweh, 34, 36, 39, 62, 63, 210, 215, 234, 273, 284, 288 f., 289 f., 290, 316 f., 318 f., 322.
Yahweh, Day of, 57, 290, 310.
Yahweh, Servant of, 53, 63, 301.
Yahwism, 287 f., 292 f.
Yahwistic Source (J), 39, 45.
Yarmuk, R., 150.
Yashar, Book of, 42, 44.
Year, Sabbatical, 491.
Yebnah (Jamnia), 145.
Yenoam (Abeidiyeh), 144.

Zadok, 422.
Zechariah, Book of, 60, 302.
Zedekiah, 253.
Zephaniah, Book of, 60.
Zerubbabel, 53, 61, 75, 81, 256, 310.
Zimri, 148.
Ziph, Wilderness of, 153.
Zoan, 153.
Zophar, 67.
Zoroaster, 5, 8.

ἄδολος, 28.
ἀπάτη, 28.
ἀπέχω, 28.
ἀρραβών, 27.
ἀρχαί, 335.

διαθήκη, 27.
δικαιοσύνη, 26.
δοκίμιος, 28.
δυνάμεις, 334 f.

ἐλεημοσύνη, 26.
ἐμβατεύω, 29.

ἐπ᾽ ἐλευθερίᾳ, 29.
ἐξουσίαι, 335.

ἡλικία, 28.

ἱλάσκομαι, 26.
ἱλαστήριον, 26.

κύριος, 25, 98.
κυριότητες, 335.

λογεία, 28.

λογικός, 28.
λόγιος, 28.

οἱ ἔξω 79.

συκοφαντέω, 29.

ὑπόστασις. 27

φιλοτιμέομαι, 28.

ψυχή, 408.

PRINTED BY
MORRISON AND GIBB LTD.
LONDON AND EDINBURGH

PHYSICAL MAP
OF PALESTINE

Land over 3000 feet
1200 to 3000 "
600 — 1200 "
0 — 600 "
below sea level

miles

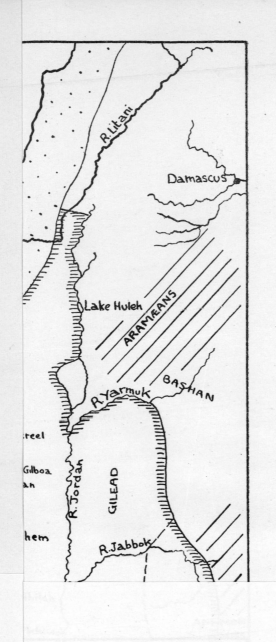

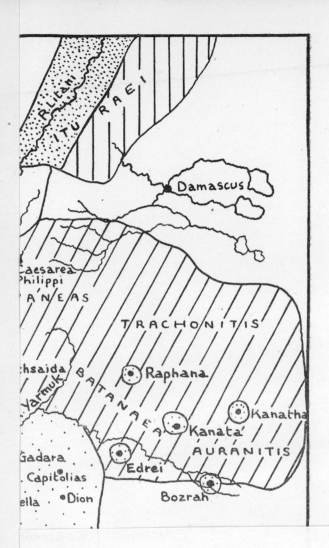

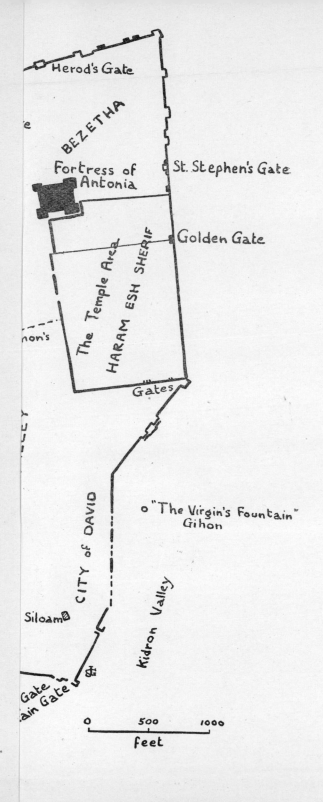

Herod's Gate

BEZETHA

Fortress of Antonia

St. Stephen's Gate

Golden Gate

The Temple Area

HARAM ESH SHERIF

non's

Gates

"The Virgin's Fountain"
Gihon

CITY of DAVID

Siloam

Kidron Valley

Gate
ain Gate

0   500   1000
feet

On the Mount of Olives

New Gate

Church of the
Holy Sepulchre

Pool of Hezekiah
Reservoir

Jaffa Gate

Probable line of the
North Wall

Valley Gate

Valley of the son of Hinnom

JERUSALEM